Introduction to

Child Welfare

Introduction to

Child Welfare

Building a Culturally Responsive, Multisystemic, Evidence-Based Approach

Michele D. Hanna, Rowena Fong, Nancy Rolock, and Ruth McRoy

Bassim Hamadeh, CEO and Publisher
Amy Smith, Senior Project Editor
Celeste Paed, Associate Production Editor
Emely Villavicencio, Senior Graphic Designer
Stephanie Kohl, Licensing Associate
Natalie Piccotti, Director of Marketing
Kassie Graves, Vice President of Editorial
Jamie Giganti, Director of Academic Publishing

Printed in the United States of America.

Brief Contents

Detailed Contents

ACTIVE LEARNING

This book has interactive activities available to complement your reading.

Your instructor may have customized the selection of activities available for your unique course. Please check with your professor to verify whether your class will access this content through the Cognella Active Learning portal (http://active.cognella.com) or through your home learning management system.

Preface

Designed as a core textbook for child welfare courses, the *Introduction to Child Welfare: Building a Culturally Responsive, Multisystemic, Evidence-Based Approach* text uses an evidence-based practice approach and provides a comprehensive review of child welfare services through a culturally responsive and multisystemic lens. The goals of this textbook are to have readers:

1. Become familiar with evidence-based practices in child welfare;
2. Gain knowledge about the diverse populations and the often complex needs of populations served by child welfare agencies;
3. Understand child welfare in the context of multiple systems; and
4. Be prepared to work in child welfare from a culturally responsive, multidisciplinary, and multisystem approach.

The text is divided into two parts, with Part One providing: 1) a comprehensive overview of the U.S. child welfare system, policies, and practices; 2) a review of evidence-based child welfare practices, with a focus on the impact of trauma on children, youth, and families; and 3) innovative practices for engaging families in child welfare services.

Part Two of the text focuses on the diverse populations served in child welfare, including children and families disproportionately represented in the child welfare system (African American, Native American, Latino, Asian American/Pacific Islander), immigrant and refugee children and families, victims of human trafficking (domestic and international), LGBTQ youth and families, emancipating/emancipated youth, kinship families, post-adoption/guardianship families (including families and children impacted by rehoming), children with mental health needs, and crossover youth. For each of these diverse populations, disproportionality and disparities, evidence-based practices, and relevant policies will be discussed.

In each chapter the experiences of youth and families served by the child welfare system are incorporated through case illustrations and scenarios which can be used as teaching tools. Using a multisystemic approach, the interaction between services provided to children, youth, and families through child welfare, education, mental health, and juvenile justice systems is discussed. A culturally responsive, multisystem approach is used in the textbook by examining how diverse clients in public child welfare systems interact with educational, health, mental health, and juvenile justice systems, as well as issues of disproportionality and disparities.

A total of 31 child welfare scholars brought their expertise and experiences to contribute to this volume. Some of the authors have decades of child welfare practice experience and a long history of child welfare education; others have more recently transitioned from child welfare practitioner to scholar. One theme that runs through all of the scholars is the importance of their engaged work, as practitioners and as scholars. The editors of this book want to thank each of the authors for their valuable contributions. Their expertise brings this work to life and adds to our understanding of the current child welfare system.

With 31 contributing scholars, readers may find some variation, which may be viewed as inconsistency across text in terminology as well as some minor redundancy related to child welfare history, policies, and practices. For example, different contributing authors may use different variants of initialisms such as LGBT, LGBTQIA, and LGBTQ. Similarly, descriptive terms related to racial groups may vary from chapter to chapter, such as Hispanic or Latinx, African American or Black, Native American or American Indian. History, policies, and practices within each chapter will be specific to the chapter topic or population; however, as you will discover, while the relevance of the history, policies, and procedures may be unique to different populations, most, if not all, impact every child and family who comes into contact with child welfare holistically. While the editorial team has made every effort to limit the repetition from chapter to chapter, there may still seem to be inconsistent language across chapters. However, the editorial team opted for a diverse set of terms across the chapters, rather than one common voice, to represent both the diversity of the populations, the multiple perspectives of the authors, and the complex dimensions of the work that we do.

The text concludes with a list of key terms discussed throughout the text as well as a list of additional resources available on the internet. It is our hope that this text will continue to serve as a resource for students after graduation, as they prepare to enter into one of the most challenging—and yet rewarding—fields of social work practice.

As the editorial team, our desire is to train, work alongside, and empower the next generation of social workers to use the power of science to engage in creating and sustaining evidence-supported interventions that work for a diverse set of families. It is our hope that this book will help provide the basis for students to become staff who work to serve and empower families engaged with child welfare systems and to recognize the multidisciplinary nature of our work and the need to join across disciplines to best serve families who come into contact with the child welfare system. We hope that you enjoy the book as much as we enjoyed putting it together.

Michele, Rowena, Nancy, and Ruth

CHAPTER • 1

Overview of Child Welfare History, Policies, and Practices

Michele D. Hanna, Rowena Fong, Nancy Rolock, and Ruth McRoy

What Is Child Welfare?

According to the U.S. Children's Bureau, child welfare is a "continuum of services designed to ensure that children are safe and that families have the necessary support to care for their children successfully" (Child Welfare Information Gateway, 2018, p. 1). The primary responsibility of child welfare service delivery rests with state and local public child welfare agencies; however, collaboration with public and private community-based agencies creates a systemic response to the federal mandates, policies, and funding requirements authorized by federal legislation that guides and impacts child welfare policy. This chapter provides a brief overview of the history of child welfare in the United States; a short description of the relationship between federal, state, and local child welfare policies; and a chronological summary of the major federal legislation that guides child welfare practice today.

History of Child Welfare in the United States

The beginning of child welfare in the United States is often attributed to the case of Mary Ellen Wilson, who was removed from her guardian in 1874 in New York by charity worker Etta Angell Wheeler. According to this story, Etta Wheeler found Mary Ellen severely physically abused and because there were no laws at that time protecting children from abuse, she sought help from the New York Society for the Prevention of the Cruelty to Animals (NYSPCA) and had the child removed under the authority of laws that protected animals from abuse (Jalongo, 2006; Watkins, 1990). In reality, there were laws in place in New York that provided for the removal of abused or neglected children by special authorities (i.e., the mayor, aldermen, special justices) as early as 1825; however, these laws were not consistently enforced (Watkins, 1990). As was the case with Mary Ellen, authorities were often reluctant to "interfere" in the relationship between parent/guardian and child. While visiting Hell's Kitchen in December 1873, several neighbors informed Etta Wheeler of concerns about Mary Ellen, stating that she was being beaten, left alone for long periods of time, and locked in a room inside the house (Watkins, 1990). Ms. Wheeler first went to the police, who would not remove the child without witnesses to the assault and then to the charity organizations that did not have the authority to remove the child (Jalongo, 2006). Wheeler was not able to remove Mary Ellen from the home until April of 1874, after appealing several times to Mr. Henry Bergh, president of the New York Society for the Prevention of the Cruelty to Animals (NYSPCA). At first, Bergh was also reluctant to "interfere"; however, after sending out an NYSPCA investigator and a census worker to the home to gather more information, he and his attorney, Elbridge T. Gerry, reached out to the courts, and Mary Ellen was forcibly removed from the home (Watkins, 1990). Bergh also contacted the *New York Times*, which covered the case. The notoriety of Mary Ellen Wilson's case led to the creation of the New York Society for the Prevention of Cruelty to Children (NYSPCC) in 1874.

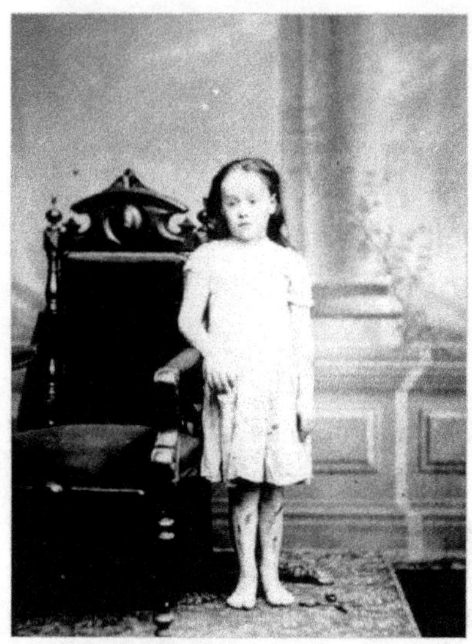

FIGURE 1.1. Mary Ellen Wilson

The Connollys made no appearance in court, and on her examination the child made a statement as follows:

My father and mother are both dead. I don't know how old I am. I have no recollection of a time when I did not live with the Connollys. I call Mrs. Connolly mamma. I have never had but one pair of shoes, but I cannot recollect when that was. I have had no shoes or stockings on this Winter. I have never been allowed to go out of the room where the Connollys were, except in the night time, and then only in the yard. I have never had on a particle of flannel. My bed at night has been only a piece of carpet stretched on the floor underneath a window, and I sleep in my little under-garments, with a quilt over me. I am never allowed to play with any children, or to have any company whatever. Mamma (Mrs. Connolly) has been in the habit of whipping and beating me almost every day. She used to whip me with a twisted whip—a rawhide. The whip always left a black and blue mark on my body. I have now the black and blue marks on my head which were made by mamma, and also a cut on the left side of my forehead which was made by a pair of scissors. [Scissors produced in court.] She struck me with the scissors and cut me: I have no recollection of ever having been kissed by any one—have never been kissed by mamma. I have never been

The New York Times, Mary Ellen Testimony, April 10, 1874, from "The Case of 'Little Mary Ellen'," *New York Times*, The New York Times Company, 1874.

taken on my mamma's lap and caressed or petted. I never dared to speak to anybody, because if I did I would get whipped. I have never had, to my recollection, any more clothing than I have at present—a calico dress and skirt. I have seen stockings and other clothes in our room, but was not allowed to put them on. Whenever mamma went out I was locked up in the bedroom. I do not know for what I was whipped—mamma never said anything to me when she whipped me. I do not want to go back to live with mamma, because she beats me so. I have no recollections of ever being on the street in my life.

Source: Watkins, 1990, p. 502

While this was a significant event that brought public attention to the need for a more organized response to the plight of abused and neglected children, early criminal cases related to child abuse and neglect were recorded as early as 1655, most often involving the abuse or murder of young apprentices at the hands of their masters (Bremmer, 1970). The early colonists patterned their laws and practices related to poor and dependent children after the Elizabethan Poor Laws, "binding out" poor children as labor. Seen as a "means of social control," binding out was "a way of finding foster homes for orphans and illegitimate children; and it was used by magistrates to secure new family situations for children of parents who were deemed incompetent to provide suitable homes or who allowed children to grow up in idleness and ignorance" (Bremmer, p. 64). This was most often done at the expense of the city or town.

This practice of providing for dependent children through the indenture or apprentice system was afforded only to White children, as Black children were predominantly part of the slave trade. It was very rare for criminal charges to be brought against parents as children were often seen as property or possessions of the parents, and parents were presumed to have primary control over their children and to know what was best for them (Rodham, 1973). In the early 1800s, New York was possibly one of the only states to recognize that it was the "right and duty of the public authorities to take action in cases of parental cruelty and gross neglect and, if necessary, to remove the child from the home" (Watkins, 1990, p. 500).

Children's Aid Society and the Orphan Trains

Often seen as the early beginnings of foster care, Charles Loring Brace founded the Children's Aid Society (CAS) in New York in 1853 to locate homes for children determined to be neglected, dependent, or abandoned (Cook, 1995). Initially, CAS placed children individually; however, it was determined that it would be more efficient, given the large number of children and youth needing homes, to move them out in groups. Between the years of 1854 and 1930, Charles Loring Brace and the CAS relocated approximately 150,000 children from New York to the Midwest on what is commonly referred to as the "Orphan Trains" (Cook, 1995).

Although referred to as "orphans," the majority of the children relocated were not orphans but rather poor urban children whose families were in crisis and unable to care for them (Bates, 2016). Most were male, immigrant children of German, English, and Irish-Protestant descent, with less than 1% being Irish Catholic or Jewish children. CAS agents would visit different towns in the Midwest and promote the arrival of the Orphan Trains, approving potential families for the children prior to the train's arrival. Upon arrival, children who did not already have families identified would be viewed by potential families and hopefully chosen. Smaller, younger children would be put up on boxes so that they could be seen, often thought to be the origins of the term "put up for adoption." By the late 1800s, social workers began promoting the placement of children, and states began passing laws regulating interstate placements, eventually leading to the end of the Orphan Train era.

FIGURE 1.2. Orphan Train

Children who were considered "incorrigible," sickly, or mentally handicapped were excluded from the Orphan Trains, as families in the Midwest most often were looking for children who could help work the land. Charles Loring Brace also excluded children of color, believing that European children would be more acceptable to Midwestern

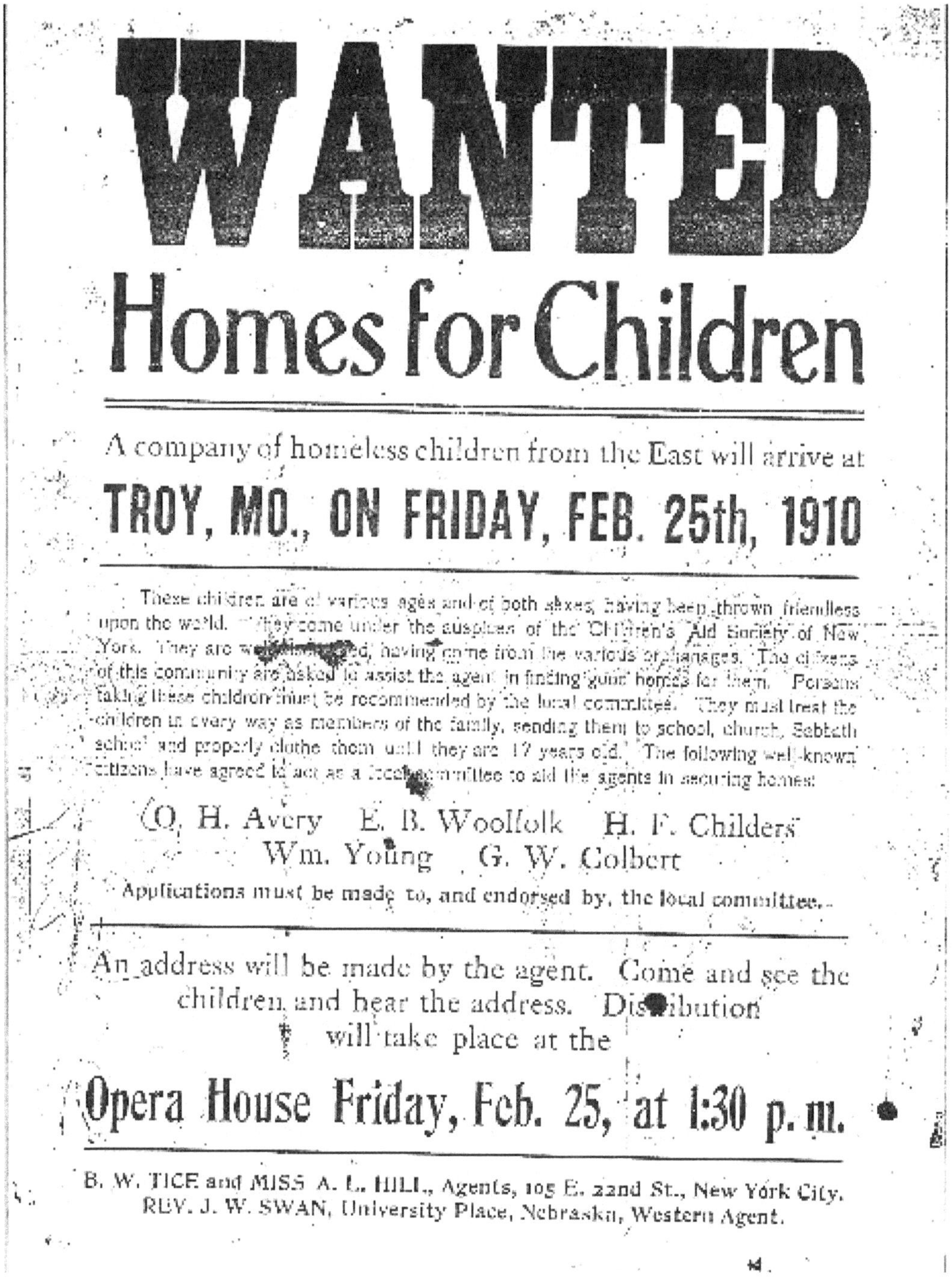

WANTED

Homes for Children

A company of homeless children from the East will arrive at

TROY, MO., ON FRIDAY, FEB. 25th, 1910

These children are of various ages and of both sexes, having been thrown friendless upon the world. They come under the auspices of the Children's Aid Society of New York. They are [illegible], having come from the various orphanages. The citizens of this community are asked to assist the agent in finding good homes for them. Persons taking these children must be recommended by the local committee. They must treat the children in every way as members of the family, sending them to school, church, Sabbath school and properly clothe them until they are 17 years old. The following well-known citizens have agreed to act as a local committee to aid the agents in securing homes:

O. H. Avery E. B. Woolfolk H. F. Childers
Wm. Young G. W. Colbert

Applications must be made to, and endorsed by, the local committee.

An address will be made by the agent. Come and see the children and hear the address. Distribution will take place at the

Opera House Friday, Feb. 25, at 1:30 p.m.

B. W. TICE and MISS A. L. HILL, Agents, 105 E. 22nd St., New York City.
REV. J. W. SWAN, University Place, Nebraska, Western Agent.

FIGURE 1.3. Wanted: Homes for Children

families (Bates, 2016). Prior to the Civil War, African American children were often sold into slavery or cared for in local almshouses—not private orphanages. Separate facilities were founded for "colored children" in Philadelphia such as the Philadelphia Association for the Care of Colored Children and later, in New York, the Colored Orphan Asylum (Billingsley & Giovannoni, 1972). The passage of the Indian Civilization Fund Act in 1819 marked the beginning of forced assimilation of American Indian/Alaska Native children funded and sanctioned by the federal government through the Indian Boarding Schools. Initially, these schools were located on the reservation and were a combination of day and boarding schools. In 1879, the first off-reservation school, Carlisle, was founded (Stout, 2012). Thousands of children were forcibly removed from their homes and reservations between 1879 and 1930 and forced to attend boarding schools around the country. Once there, they were not allowed to speak their native languages, practice their religion, or follow any of their native practices. They were given Christian names and forced to convert to Christianity. They were not allowed to return home until they were adults, being involuntarily sent to White homes in the summer to work (Stout, 2012).

Establishment of the Children's Bureau

In 1909, President Theodore Roosevelt called the first White House Conference on Children, bringing together approximately 200 experts from social work, education, and research from across the nation. President Roosevelt is quoted as having called for the conference, stating, "Surely, nothing ought to interest our people more than the care of the children who are destitute and neglected but not delinquent" (Mink & Solinger, 2003, p. 22). Social workers and humanitarians Jane Addams and Lillian Wald helped to organize the conference, whose goal was to set the agenda for the soon-to-be-formed Children's Bureau, the federal government's first attempt to address issues related to the welfare of children (Beck, 1973; Zigler, 1993; U.S. Children's Bureau, 2012).

FIGURE 1.4. White House Conference on Children 1909

Three years later, the establishment of the Children's Bureau by President William Howard Taft was significant as it was the first time a federal agency was established to oversee activities previously considered under the purview of the states and was seen by many as an intrusion on states' rights (Beck, 1973). As a federal agency, the Children's

Bureau was charged with the responsibility for the welfare of all the nation's children, not just the poor or neglected. There was much debate regarding the level of funding appropriated relative to other economic expenditures at the time. Reportedly, Congress only appropriated $25,000 to the work of the Children's Bureau in comparison to the $375,000 appropriated to the study of the cotton boll weevil and the $600,000 appropriated to hog cholera (Beck, 1973). Under the leadership of the first chief of the Children's Bureau, Julia Lathrop, public support for the Children's Bureau spread, and its annual budget expanded, eventually leading to the passing of the Sheppard-Towner Act of 1921 (McGowan, 2005). Under this act, the concept of the federal government administering and providing federal payment to states for direct services to children and families was first established.

The Social Security Act of 1935

Shortly after the creation of the Children's Bureau, the Social Security Act of 1935 was passed. The Social Security Act created Title IV, Grants to States for the Aid to Dependent Children—the federal aid program that provided assistance to fatherless families. These grants provided funding to the states under the condition that the state establish or designate a single state agency to administer or supervise administration of a state plan to aid dependent children (Social Security, n.d.(a)). Grants mandated coverage in each state yet allowed autonomy in setting eligibility standards. Title V, Part 3 of the Social Security Act of 1935 also created provision for Child Welfare Services defined as public welfare services "for the protection and care of homeless, dependent, and neglected children, and children in danger of becoming delinquent" (Social Security, n.d.(b)). Prior to the passage of the Social Security Act of 1935, protection of dependent children varied greatly from state to state with only 14 states having any statewide provisions for child welfare services (Getz, 1940).

The Relationship Between Federal Legislation, State Statutes, and Child Welfare Policy

Every state has a public child welfare agency responsible for the delivery of child welfare services. Dependent on the administrative structure of the state (state, county, or hybrid), (Child Welfare Information Gateway, 2018), agency workers follow policies and procedures detailed in state or county manuals based on state statutes enacted in response to federal legislative mandates, policies, and/or funding. As the federal agency responsible for oversight of child welfare services, the Children's Bureau provides guidance to states in response to all federal legislative mandates that result from federal legislation signed by the president that creates or amends federally funded child welfare services (Child Welfare Information Gateway, 2015b). This guidance comes in several formats including the Child

Welfare Policy Manual (CWPM) based on federal law and/or program regulations available through the Children's Bureau website (see Additional Resources at the end of the text).

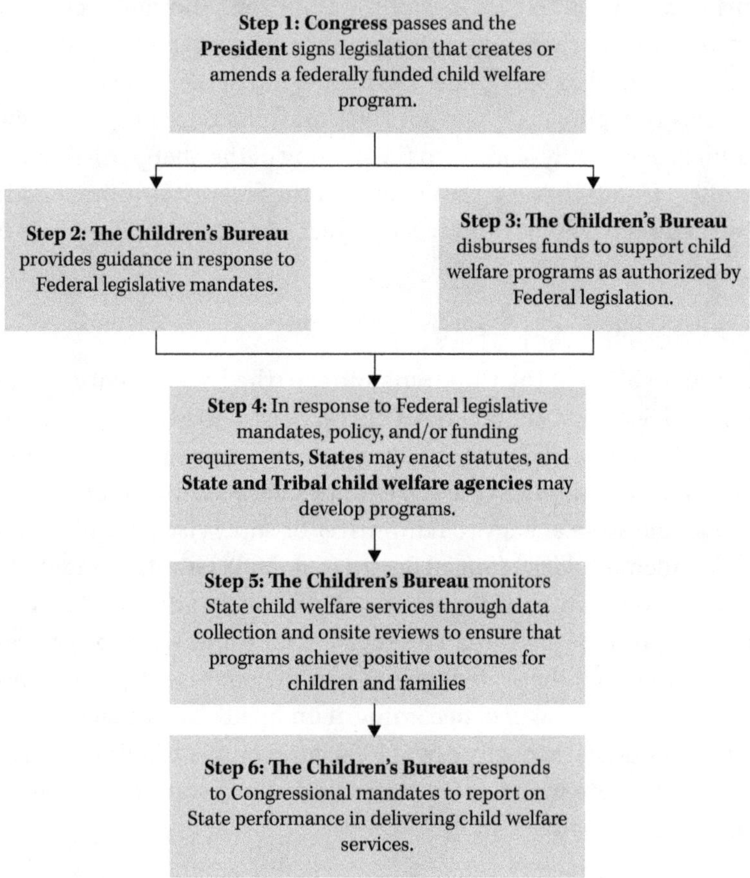

FIGURE 1.5. How Federal Legislation Impacts Child Welfare Service Delivery

The Children's Bureau is also authorized to distribute federal funds in accordance with federal legislation to support child welfare programming. These funds are distributed through mandatory formula and discretionary grants (Child Welfare Information Gateway, 2015b). Depending on the criteria, grants are awarded to states, tribes, and territories, as well as local agencies, universities, and faith-based, community-based, nonprofit, and for-profit organizations.

As stated above, states enact statutes in response to federal legislation. The Children's Bureau provides guidance to states regarding which portions of the federal legislation are mandated and which portions may be optional. It also provides regulations regarding funding requirements. State, county, and local agencies develop programs, policies, and procedures in compliance with these statutes that guide the day-to-day practice of child welfare workers. Understanding the societal context and historical evolution of the significant federal legislation that impacts child welfare practice is essential to the effectiveness of child welfare service delivery.

Significant Federal Legislation Impacting Child Welfare

The Social Security Act of 1935 provided federal aid to children in three areas: maternal and child health; services for "crippled" children; and child welfare. Prior to 1935, because of the Depression and depletion in resources, local child welfare services were limited to urban centers and basically nonexistent in rural communities (Getz, 1940). Therefore, federal funds available to states for child welfare service delivery were focused primarily on rural communities. According to Oettinger (1960), initially the primary use of these funds was for graduate training in social work for child welfare personnel, as the Children's Bureau felt the best way to serve children and families was to have competent staff. The children and families served varied across jurisdictions, including children who were in care for both dependency (abuse/neglect) and delinquency (commission of criminal acts). Eventually, services to delinquent children diverged from services to dependent and neglected children. In 1950, Congress authorized states' access to funds to broaden child welfare service delivery to voluntary agencies within local communities as the number of children in need of child welfare intervention and foster care increased. In 1958, Title V, Part 3 was amended to expand the use of federal funds beyond rural areas, allowing states to allot funds throughout the state as they saw fit; 1960 marked the first time that states were required to match federal funds received (Oettinger, 1960).

Image 1.1

Foster Care and Aid to Families with Dependent Children (AFDC)

In 1960, the public became outraged after learning that 23,000 children were expelled from the welfare rolls of the state of Louisiana because their homes were deemed "unsuitable." Their homes were deemed "unsuitable" because the child(ren) were born outside of marriage (Lawrence-Webb, 1997). During the 1950s it had become a common practice, particularly in the South, to close the welfare aid cases of families found "unsuitable" without investigation or intervention. The reason for closing was usually listed as "neglect" based on inadequate income to provide for the needs of their children or, as in the case of the Louisiana families, the children were born "out of wedlock." Over 90% of the families impacted by these policies were African American. The Flemming Rule, named after Dr. Arthur Flemming, the secretary of the Department of Health, Education, and Welfare, 1) provided due process protections for families that a state deemed unsuitable; and 2) required a state to provide intervention and services to families as opposed to simply expelling them from the AFDC rolls if deemed "unsuitable" (Lawrence-Webb, 1997, p. 12). This was a significant first step in the development of child welfare practice as it is known today.

According to Oettinger (1960), "the number of children receiving foster family care under public agency auspices increased from 49,000 in 1933 to 123,000 in 1955, or 151%" (p. 46), and by 1960 the number of children receiving services was 364,300, with approximately 43% of them in foster homes and another 17% in other out of home placements (p. 48). Up to this point, only a small percentage of federal child welfare funds was being used to support the needs of these children in foster care. In 1961, P.L. 87-31 amended Title IV of the Social Security Act, allowing federal funds to be used to pay for foster care for any dependent child who was removed from a family who, at the time of removal, met the criteria for receipt of AFDC (Rollin, Vandervort, & Haralambie, 2005).

The impact of the implementation of the Flemming Rule and the passage of P.L. 87-31 was significant for children of color. The first nationwide study of children receiving child welfare services, published by the Children's Bureau in 1963, showed an increase in the proportion of non-White children receiving services from both public and voluntary child welfare agencies between 1959 and 1961 (Jeter, 1963). The majority of the non-White children were African American (24%), followed by American Indian/Alaska Natives (2%), then "other" (1%) (Jeter, 1963). Interestingly, the proportion varied by state and region of the country and demonstrated early signs of racial disproportionality. For example, in 1961, American Indian/Alaska Native children were 39% of the children served by public child welfare in South Dakota and 28% in Nevada (Jeter, 1963). African American children were 49% of the children receiving services in Mississippi and 46% in Illinois (Jeter, 1963). Concerns about the negative cultural ramifications of the Flemming Law appear to be supported as well. Jeter reported that in comparison to White children, larger

Image 1.2

proportions of African American children served by public and voluntary agencies had unmarried parents or were living with their mother only. For many, this time period and these two policies combined mark the beginning of decades of disproportionality and disparities for African American children in the U.S. foster care system (Bass, 1997).

The Child Abuse Prevention and Treatment Act (CAPTA) (P.L. 93-247)

CAPTA, originally enacted in 1974, provides ongoing guidance for public child welfare practice: specifically, identification, prevention, and treatment of child abuse and neglect. Most significantly, the original legislation provided the first federal definition of child abuse and neglect. CAPTA created funding mechanisms for financial assistance to states as they developed programming for the prevention and treatment of child abuse and neglect including training and research. Among other criteria, CAPTA required states to develop mandatory reporting statutes to receive funding grants (Brown & Gallagher, 2014). Amended by the Child Abuse Prevention and Treatment and Adoption Reform Act of 1978, CAPTA established the Adoptions Opportunities Program to help facilitate adoptive placements of children with special needs and establish a national adoption information exchange system.

Indian Child Welfare Act of 1978 (ICWA)

After years of forced removal and placement in boarding schools, between 1958 and 1967 the Bureau of Indian Affairs, under the auspices of the Child Welfare League of America, placed 395 American Indian/Alaska Native children for adoption in White families, as part of the Indian Adoption Project. By 1976, American Indian/Alaska Native children were reported to be removed from their homes at disproportionate rates, moved more frequently in placement, and remained in foster care longer than White children (Barsh, 1980). The Indian Child Welfare Act (ICWA) was passed in response to concerns from American Indian/Alaska Native tribes across the nation that their culture was systematically being erased through the removal of their children. Political battles and congressional testimony resulted in federal policy that provides clear criteria related to the removal of American Indian/Alaska Native children (Matheson, 1996). It also governs the placement of American Indian/Alaska Native children in foster or adoptive homes. ICWA only applies to children who are members of, or are eligible for membership in, a federally recognized tribe. Chapter 7 provides more detailed information related to American Indian/Alaska Natives and child welfare service delivery and the implementation of ICWA.

The Adoption Assistance and Child Welfare Act of 1980 (AACWA)

While CAPTA helped to establish federal guidelines and best practices related to the identification, prevention, and treatment of child abuse and neglect, AACWA focused primarily on the services provided to children and families in foster care and children discharged from care through reunification and adoption (Sheldon, 1997; Townsend, Hignight, & Rubovits, 2008). AACWA created the federal adoption assistance program, requiring states to provide adoption assistance payments to parents who adopted children with special needs, as defined by the act, if the child adopted was eligible for AFDC at the time of removal.

Under AACWA, states were mandated to provide services to children and families as conditions of receiving federal foster care matching funds. For example, AACWA required courts or agencies to review the status of any child in temporary placement every 6 months. States were required to make *reasonable efforts* first, to do all they could to prevent the removal of the child, and second, to return the child as soon as possible. AACWA also required states to place children in the *least restrictive* placement, the placement that would be the most home-like or closest to that of their parents (Edwards, 1994). Lastly, AACWA was the first federal law to establish a timeframe for making a decision for permanency (Edwards, 1994). Under AACWA, the decision to reunify, pursue adoption, or continue a child in foster care was to be made within 18 months after the initial placement into foster care. The policies under AACWA remained in place until the passing of the Adoption and Safe Families Act of 1997 (Townsend, Hignight, & Rubovits, 2008).

Multiethnic Placement Act of 1994 as Amended by the Interethnic Adoption Provisions of 1996 (MEPA-IEP)

African American children have been disproportionately represented in the child welfare system since the 1960s (Jeter, 1963). As the foster care population increased over time, the number of children in foster care waiting to be adopted also increased. In 1994, 43% of the 500,000 children waiting to be adopted were African American (Hollinger & the ABA Center on Children and the Law National Resource Center on Legal and Court Issues, 1998), whereas only 16% of the children in the United States under 18 were African American at that time (Child Trends, 2018). At the time MEPA was originally passed, it was stated that the primary purpose was to eliminate barriers to adoption for the many African American children waiting to be adopted; however, the high profile death of an African American child who was killed by African American adoptive parents, in tandem with a negative portrayal on the negative effects of race matching African Americans in need of adoptive placement that aired on the television news show *60 Minutes*, spurred Senator Howard Metzenbaum to introduce the bill (McRoy, Mica, Freundlich, & Kroll, 2007). Testimony centered around the concerns that race-matching policies and practices were hindering White families' ability to adopt African American children and asserted that policies promoting same-race placements were not serving African American children's best interest. Proponents of the bill and the media appeared to ignore the universal practice of only placing White children with White families, or the fact that at that time, up to 50% of African American infants and two thirds of Latinx infants were being placed transracially (McRoy, et al., 2007).

After much negotiation the final version passed with language that allowed race to be considered as one factor, but not the determining factor. In addition, the law required states to diligently recruit foster and adoptive families who reflected the racial and ethnic background of the children in care. Shortly after the passing of the original bill, complaints were lodged stating that race was still being used as a decision-making factor in placements (McRoy et al., 2007). As a result, Senator Metzenbaum drafted the Interethnic Adoption Provisions (IEP), which was inserted into the Small Business Protection Act and became law in 1996 without any hearings or statements on record. The IEP amendments to MEPA explicitly stated that race couldn't be used as a means to delay a child's placement (Hollinger & the ABA Center on Children and the Law National Resource Center on Legal and Court Issues, 1998). Although both MEPA-IEP and ICWA address the placement of children of color in foster care and adoption, MEPA-IEP states that the two laws are mutually exclusive. If a child meets the criteria for ICWA, MEPA-IEP does not apply. However, MEPA-IEP does apply to all other children, including White children (Hollinger et al., 1998).

Safety, Permanency, and Well-Being

Federal legislation regarding the three pillars of child welfare—safety, permanency, and well-being—are summarized below. This summary focuses on significant pieces of federal legislation covering the period from 1997 to 2008. Key features of these pieces of legislation are highlighted; additional and more specific information is available to the reader in a summary document prepared and updated regularly by the Child Welfare Information Gateway entitled *Major Federal Legislation Concerned with Child Protection, Child Welfare, and Adoption* (Child Welfare Information Gateway, 2019). In addition to the federal legislation, practitioners should become familiar with state, county, and tribal legislation that may also guide the delivery of child welfare services and supports where they are working. Local policies often provide important policies or mandates that impact how services are delivered.

Image 1.3

Adoption and Safe Families Act (ASFA) of 1997—P.L. 105–89

The Adoption and Safe Families Act (ASFA) was passed in 1997, with a goal of promoting the adoption of children who were in foster care, with a specific focus on timely placements for children and youth in foster care (Child Welfare Information Gateway, 2015a).

In the late 1990s there were more children in foster care in the United States than there had ever been. In 1996, for the first time, the number of children in foster care was over 500,000. This increase in the number of children in foster care resulted in efforts to move children safely out of foster care and into permanent homes. One of these efforts was ASFA. The promotion of adoptions was made explicit through provisions that rewarded states with additional funds (called adoption incentive funds) if they increased the number of children who were adopted through the foster care system. Prior to adoption, ASFA requires child welfare systems to make "reasonable efforts" to maintain children in their homes, to prevent removal or placing children into state custody (foster care) if at all possible; and if removed, to make reasonable efforts to reunite the child with the family as a means of family preservation. ASFA refocused the concept "reasonable efforts," clarifying that the primary goal for children placed in foster care should be permanency—which may or may not mean reunification with the family from whom they were removed. This clarification included the requirement that states specify situations where services to prevent a child from entering foster care were made explicit and situations where reunification with birth parent(s) was not required. These changes were intended to speed up the process of adoption for children for whom reunification was not possible. ASFA also mandated shorter time periods surrounding key decision points for a child. These included a requirement that permanency hearings occur within 12 months after a child entered foster care.[1]

ASFA also required that states initiate the termination of parental rights (TPR) after the child had been in foster care for 15 of the prior 22 months, unless 1) the child was in the long-term care of a relative or kin family; 2) it was determined it was in the best interest of the child not to terminate parental rights; or 3) it was determined the state had not appropriately provided services to the family to address the issues that brought the child into care. In addition, ASFA provided adoption incentive payments to states that were able to increase adoptions of children from foster care over time.

Initially, many states won accolades for the number of children they moved from foster care to adoption. The majority of these early adoptions were children who were residing in long-term foster care placements, but because of the previous interpretation of the concept of "reasonable efforts," these children were legally languishing in foster care. ASFA provided an expedited avenue for termination of parental rights, and these long-term relationships were made legally permanent. However, once this backlog of adoptions was consummated, concern was voiced that children were moving too quickly to adoption, and as a result a revolving door where children would reenter foster care after adoption was being created (Hanna, Tokarski, Matera, & Fong, 2011). In short, there was fear that the adoptive placements that were intended to endure through adulthood

1 This is "either the date of the first judicial finding that the child has been subject to abuse or neglect (date of the adjudication hearing) or 60 days from the date that the child was placed into foster care, whichever is earlier" (Child and Family Service Reviews Information Portal, 2007–2019).

may end prematurely. These issues will be discussed in Chapter 15 on Post-Adoption and Post-Guardianship.

Foster Care Independence Act of 1999—P.L. 106-169

During the late 1990s research related to the outcomes of children who entered foster care, but did not achieve **legal permanence**, was conducted. These are children for whom permanency (either reunification with a family member, adoption, and guardianship) did not occur. When children reach the age of majority (18) and do not have an identified permanency resource, they transition to living independently. For youth who make this transition (referred to as "aging out of foster care" or "emancipation"), they often have difficulty making this transition without the support of families. This may include housing insecurity, difficulty finding or keeping jobs, limited or no access to mental health services, and incarceration (Courtney et al., 2011; Kerman, Wildfire, & Barth, 2002; Tweddle, 2007).

The Foster Care Independence Act of 1999 was passed to address these issues. It provided states with additional funding to support the transition from foster care to self-sufficiency for these youth. The act provided greater flexibility in the design and implementation of programs to prepare youth to live independently. These programs included services (e.g., employment services or financial planning), education, and financial support. The act allowed funds to be used to pay for room and board for former foster youth ages 18 to 21. It also required that prospective parents be prepared to provide for the needs of the child. Finally, it increased funding for adoption incentive payments.

Fostering Connections to Success and Increasing Adoptions Act of 2008—P.L. 110–351

Whereas prior federal legislation brought focus to the need for permanence and adoption, there was not a strong focus on working with and supporting families of origin (Alpert & Britner, 2005). This changed eight years later when Congress passed the Fostering Connections to Success and Increasing Adoptions Act of 2008 (Fostering Connections). Among other things, Fostering Connections permitted states and tribes to provide kinship guardianship assistance programs (GAP). This legislation expanded the permanency options available to children and youth in foster care by including guardianship as an additional option. Expanding permanency options for children cared for by kin has strong research support. Research shows that children do well when cared for by relatives (Koh & Testa, 2011; Winokur, Holtan, & Batchelder, 2014; Wu, White, & Coleman, 2015) and that guardianship can provide children with an alternative to spending a long time in foster care (Rolock & White, 2017). GAP allows federal funds to be used to support state subsidies for children cared for by relatives for whom reunification and adoption are not appropriate permanency options.

This Fostering Connections legislation is a good example of how work being conducted in states can have a strong influence on federal legislation (Testa, 2010). As discussed in Chapter 15, several states were involved in research that tested the idea of guardianship as an additional permanency option for children who could not return home (for whom reunification had been ruled out). Due to strong research findings showing that guardianship provided an alternative pathway out of foster care for children living with kin, the idea that was tested in states became federal legislation. With Fostering Connections, states were able to apply for federal funds to support the permanent placement of children living with kin. States and tribes vary in the specifics associated with their guardianship programs. Additional state-level information is available through the Child Welfare Information Gateway (Child Welfare Information Gateway, 2015c). A by-product of the changes included in the Fostering Connections legislation was the reinforced notion of permanency as a bond that endures during and beyond child welfare supervision (Cushing & Kerman, 2009).

Fostering Connections also reauthorized the Adoption Incentives payment program, originally started in 1997 with ASFA. This reauthorization expanded federal support to include children adopted at the age of 9 or older. These changes recognize the specific and unique needs of older children in foster care. The act also expanded the scope of the Foster Care Independence Program to include services and supports to youth who leave foster care for kinship guardianship or adoption after age 16. It also permitted states to offer assistance to youth in foster care after the age of 18 and who are in school, employed, or engaged in activities related to removing barriers to employment. The act was comprehensive in its attempt to address pressing issues for children and youth involved in the child welfare system, including provisions to promote educational stability and the need for a coordinated health care coordination. This legislation lays the groundwork for the idea that support and service needs do not end once a child has achieved legal permanence or has reached the age of majority.

Family First Prevention Services Act

Signed by the President in February 2018, the Family First Prevention Services Act (FFPSA) dramatically changed the way states, tribes, and territories use **Title IV-E** funds. The act provides funding for prevention services designed to maintain children (candidates for foster care) safely in their own home for up to 12 months in efforts to prevent removal and placement in out of home or foster care (National Conference of State Legislatures [NCSL], 2018). Eligible services include in-home skill-based programming as well as mental health and substance use services. All services provided are to be trauma-informed and evidence-based meeting one of the following thresholds:[2]

2 See Chapter 3 for more about evidence-based practice in child welfare and Chapter 4 for more information on the impact of trauma on children, youth, and families.

- **Promising Practice**: Created from an independently reviewed study that uses a control group and shows statistically significant results.
- **Supported Practice**: Uses a random-controlled trial or rigorous quasi-experimental design. Must have sustained success for at least six months after the end of treatment.
- **Well-Supported Treatment**: Shows success beyond a year after treatment. (NCSL, 2018)

FFPSA provided a one-time, $8 million competitive grant available through 2022 to support the recruitment and retention of high-quality foster families. It provided national model licensing standards for foster homes, including limiting the number of children in a foster home to no more than six children except under special circumstances. States are required to ensure that licensing standards for kinship family foster homes are aligned with the national model. In response to concerns about the misuse and overuse of congregate or residential care for children with mental health needs in foster care, this act provides strict criteria and guidelines to states regarding the placement of children in out of home placements that are not foster homes or relative/kinship foster homes (National Conference of State Legislatures [NCSL], 2018).

Under this new legislation, congregate care providers must be designated as a Qualified Residential Treatment Program (QRTP) to be eligible for federally funded reimbursement of services. To be designated as a QRTP, agencies must be accredited, use a trauma-informed treatment model that includes clinical services, have licensed or registered nursing staff, be inclusive of family members in the treatment of the children, and offer at least 6 months of follow up services upon discharge (Alliance for Strong Families and Communities, 2018). Given the pivotal role that judges and juvenile court staff play in the placement of children, the act requires judges and court staff to be trained on the funding limitations to placing a child in out of home care; that is, not family foster care (Alliance for Strong Families and Communities, 2018).

Additional provisions of the act include the continuation of adoption incentives to states to promote adoption and guardianship. The act gradually extends the exemption from an income test for federal adoption assistance, ending the requirement altogether in October 2024. Lastly, the act requires states to clearly describe what they are doing to address the developmental needs of all vulnerable children under 5 years of age receiving benefits or services under either title IV–B programs or the title IV–E foster care and permanency program (not just children in foster care). States must also create a plan and fully document how they will track and take steps to prevent child maltreatment deaths (Alliance for Strong Families and Communities, 2018).

Child Welfare Practice Today

Today, all states, the District of Columbia, and all U.S. territories have public child welfare programs to address child abuse and neglect by persons responsible for the care of minors under the age of 18 who are not emancipated minors (U.S. Department of Health & Human Services [USDHHS], 2018). Children and families become known to the child welfare system when a mandatory reporter or a concerned citizen report concern that a child has been abused or neglected to the local child protection service (CPS) agency. During the Federal Fiscal Year (FFY) 2016,[3] approximately 4.1 million referrals were received nationwide (USDHHS, 2018). Education personnel were the largest source of referrals (18.9%) followed closely by legal/law enforcement (18.4%). Agencies screen these referrals based on the state's definition of child abuse and neglect and determine how CPS will respond. While every state defines child abuse and neglect differently, the minimal definition as defined by CAPTA in 1974 and amended by the CAPTA Reauthorization Act of 2010 remains the same:

- Any recent act or failure to act on the part of a parent or caretaker which results in death, serious physical or emotional harm, sexual abuse or exploitation; or
- An act or failure to act which presents an imminent risk of serious harm.

Reportedly, 58% of referrals were screened in, which is approximately 31.3 children per 1000 in the national population (USDHHS, 2018). Once screened in, child welfare caseworkers are responsible for completing an initial assessment or investigation into the allegations. Several factors determine exactly what this initial assessment or investigation looks like, including, but not limited to, whether or not the child(ren) are at imminent risk of harm, the severity of the allegations, and access to the alleged perpetrator. In cases where risk and safety concerns are high or significant, CPS will most often respond immediately, attempting to contact the family and see the child(ren) within 24 hours. Often law enforcement will work in tandem with the CPS caseworker on the investigation. The caseworker (often referred to as the "intake" or "investigative" worker) will assess the safety of the child and determine whether there is a need for emergency removal. Completed investigations end with a disposition of either 1) substantiated or indicated (allegations of abuse or neglect are supported or founded); 2) unsubstantiated (a lack of sufficient evidence to support a finding that abuse or neglect has occurred), or unfounded (determined to be false, no alleged maltreatment) (USDHHS, 2018). Dependent on the severity of the abuse or neglect, services may be provided to the family with the child(ren) in the home, possibly under court supervision; or the child(ren) are removed and placed in out of home care, usually with a foster or kinship family, while the parents work to correct the conditions that led to the removal. For cases in which the safety risks are moderate or low, several states offer an alternative response, also known as differential

3 FFY 2016 = October 1 through September 30, 2016.

response, in lieu of an investigation. Differential response is an alternative, less adversarial response to the referral that often results in the family receiving preventive services in an effort to prevent removal (USDHHS, 2016).

For FFY 2016, of the screened-in referrals, 56% were unsubstantiated, 17.2% of the children were found to be victims of abuse or neglect, and 13.9% received alternative response services (USDHHS, 2018). While many children are victims of multiple forms of maltreatment (physical abuse, sexual abuse, psychological maltreatment, or neglect), the majority of the substantiated cases of maltreatment involve neglect (74.8%) followed by physical abuse (18.2%) and sexual abuse (8.5%). The mother, acting alone or with the father/non-parent, was the perpetrator for approximately 70% of the children. The largest percentage of perpetrators were White (49.8%), followed by African American (20%) and Hispanic (18.8%) (USDHHS, 2018). The racial/ethnic distribution of the victims during this same time period was 44.9% White, 22% Hispanic, and 20.7% African American, an underrepresentation of White and Hispanic children and an overrepresentation of African American children. The rate of victimization for American Indian/Alaska Native children was the highest at 14.2 per 1000 children, followed by African American children at 13.9 per 1000 children (USDHHS, 2018). An estimated 1,750 children died nationally as a result of child abuse or neglect in 2016, with approximately 78% of those involving at least one parent (USDHHS, 2018). The rate of child fatalities for African American children was 2.2 times greater than that of White children and 3 times greater than that of Hispanic children.

The Adoption and Foster Care Analysis and Reporting System (AFCARS) gathers national case-level data for children in foster care or placed for adoption. All the data presented here is from the most recent AFCARS data available at the time. AFCARS data is updated biannually and has been publicly available since 1998 on the Children's Bureau website. Nationally, the average number of children in foster care annually is 477,650, with the greatest number of children reported being 567,000 in 1999. The percent of males versus females has remained stable over time, with the average percent of males being 52% and females 47%. Since 1998, the average age children enter care has decreased from 8.6 years to 7.1 years. Similarly, the percentage breakdown of placement types has been relatively stable, with most being placed in non-relative foster family care (46.5% annual average), relative foster family care (26.4%), and group home/institution (16.3%).

The percentage of children with a **case plan** goal of reunification has gradually increased, with 39% having this goal in 1998 and 56% having this goal in 2017 (annual average 49.2%). Adoption as a case plan goal has also increased, with 20% having this goal in 1998 and 27% in 2017 (average 23%). Case plan goals of living with a relative or guardianship as well as emancipation have vacillated over time, averaging 7.2% for relative/guardianship and 5.4% emancipation. By comparison, an average of 5.4% of children annually have exited care through reunification, 19.3% adoption, 14.7% living with a relative/guardianship, and 8.9% emancipation. The average age at exit from care has decreased over time, with 10.3 years average in 1998 and 8.7 years in 2017. The average length of time children spend in foster care before exiting has also decreased over time, with 22.3 months average in 1998 and 19.2 months in 2017.

The number of children waiting to be adopted has varied over time with a recent pattern of increase. In 1998, the reported number of children waiting to be adopted was 125,000. In 2007, the number reached an all-time high of 132,000 decreasing steadily to 100,000 in 2012. Since 2012, the number has gradually increased, with an estimate of 123,000 being reported in 2017. On average, waiting children have spent 38.5 months in continuous foster care (decreasing gradually from 45.1 months in 1998 to 30.9 months in 2017), while the average age of the waiting child has ranged from 7.6 years to 8.7 years, with the average age of adoption ranging from 6.2 years to 7 years. The majority of children adopted from foster care were adopted by their foster parents (annual average 57.1%, decreasing over time from 64% in 1998 to 51% in 2017), followed by non-relative adoption (annual average 15.4%, decreasing over time from 21% in 1998 to 14% in 2017). The percent of children adopted by relatives has doubled since 1998, with 16% in 1998 and 35% in 2017. The percent of families receiving adoption subsidy to assist with meeting the needs of their adopted child has also increased over time, with only 87% being reported in 2003 (the earliest year data available) to 93% in 2017.

The Child Welfare Workforce

Child welfare caseworkers are responsible for providing services and making key decisions across the child welfare continuum—from referral to case closure (see Figure 1.6, Overview of Child Protection Process). In most urban settings, child welfare workers are grouped in *specialized* units that perform different functions across the child welfare continuum—screening, investigation, differential response, reunification/permanency, and foster/adoptive parent recruitment and retention (DePanfilis, 2018; Hanna, 2009). A child welfare unit most often consists of a supervisor and 5–6 caseworkers. In many rural settings, workers are *generic*, meaning that one worker performs all of the functions across the child welfare continuum, usually because there are not enough workers to staff specialized units. In some areas, the workers may specialize in one area yet be a part of a generic unit that is cross-functional (a unit made up of workers who specialize in one of the functional areas) (Hanna, 2009).

Public child welfare and the social work profession have been intertwined since the creation of the Children's Bureau (Perry & Ellett, 2008). In the 1960s, child welfare was a primary employer of master's level social workers (MSW), and social work embraced the field wholeheartedly. In the 1970s, the Council on Accreditation (COA) for Children and Family Services began accrediting both public and private child welfare agencies (GAO-03-357, 2003). In 2014, COA reported that 54 public state and county agencies were accredited (COA, 2014). COA standards continue to recommend that child welfare

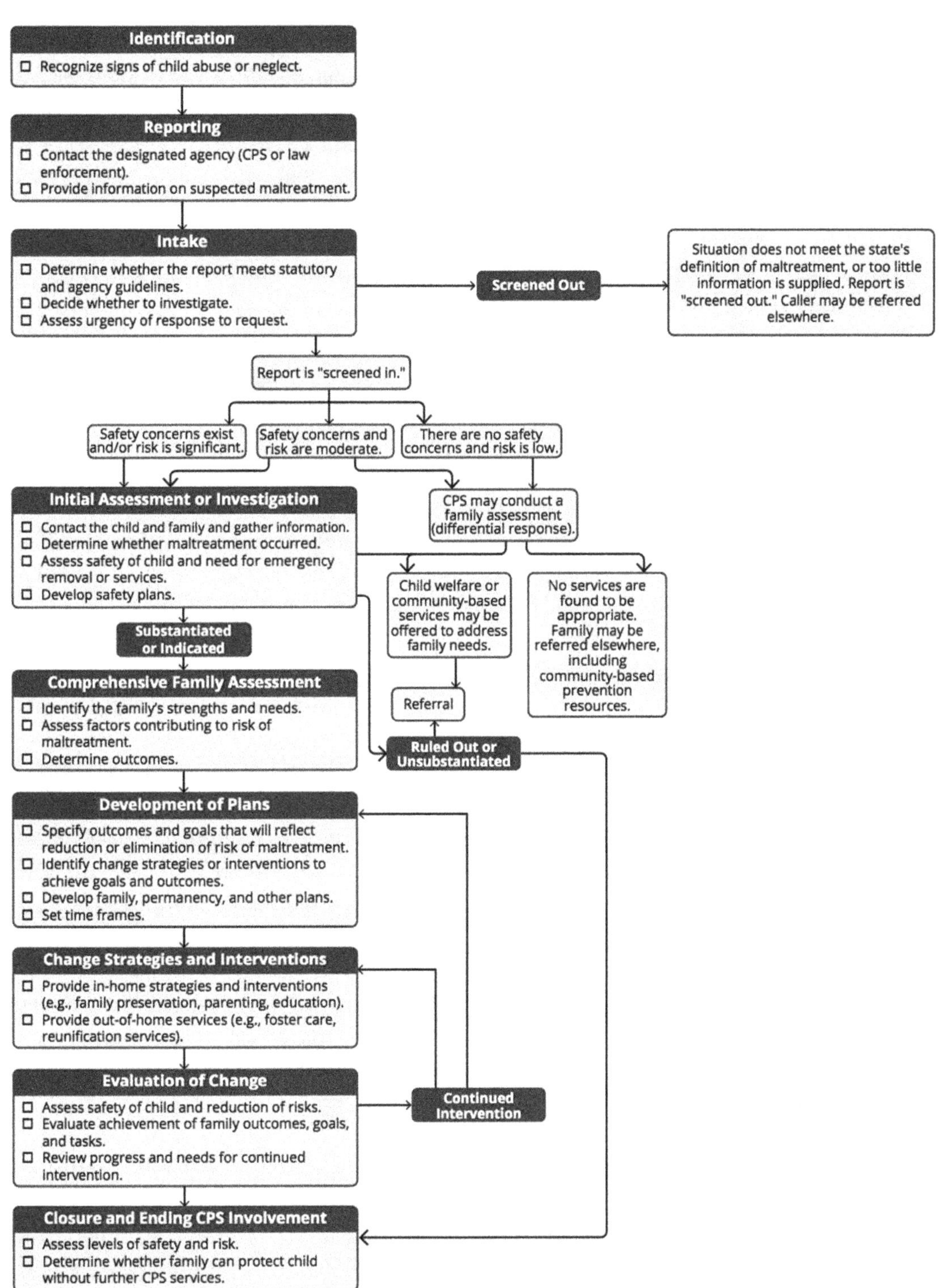

FIGURE 1.6. Overview of Child Protection Process

workers have either "an advanced degree in social work or a comparable human service field" or "bachelor's degree in social work or a comparable human service field with two years of related experience" (COA, 2018).

However, as the social work profession broadened, fewer and fewer social work students chose to pursue child welfare as a focus of study. By the 1990s, studies showed that less than 15% of child welfare agencies required social work degrees for child welfare workers, and less than 40% of the child welfare workers held a social work degree (Whitaker, 2012). Barth, Lloyd, Christ, Chapman, and Dickinson (2008) found that while less than half of child welfare workers either had a BSW or MSW, workers with either degree reported higher job satisfaction and more self-confidence. The majority of the workers responding were White females under the age of 40 years and had, on average, 5 years of experience. Public employees reported earning more than private child welfare employees, and those working in rural settings reported greater job satisfaction (National Child Welfare Workforce Institute [NCWWI], 2012).

Caseload management continues to be key to worker retention (NCWWI, 2011). High caseloads and workloads have been found to have a negative impact on both child welfare practice and child welfare outcomes (e.g., CWIG, 2010; Children's Research Center, 2009; Social Work Policy Institute, 2010). Delayed response and completion of CPS investigations, decreased worker contact with families and children, delay in case plan completion or updates, and delay in service provision have all been linked to high caseloads (NCWWI, 2011). Additionally, research has shown a relationship between high caseloads and the increase in foster placements, longer length of time in foster care, and higher rates of recidivism or recurring maltreatment.

Image 1.4

Emerging Populations and Contemporary Issues in Child Welfare

Problems related to **child abuse** and neglect have typically dominated the public **child welfare** systems (Fong, McRoy, & Hendricks, 2006; Mallon & Hess, 2014). There are, however, newer or emerging populations with additional complex problems, which may be changing the historical issues of child abuse and neglect and formulating contemporary issues prevalent in the public child welfare system, demanding a review and reform of services (Dettlaff & Fong, 2016; Zayas, 2015).

Victims of Human Trafficking

Sex abuse has been a concern in public child welfare systems as well as physical and emotional abuse (Faller, 2014). But sex abuse has become more focused and associated with a contemporary issue such as domestic minor sex trafficking (DMST) (Fong & Berger-Cardoso, 2010). Victims of human trafficking, particularly sex trafficking, have federal legislations that have been updated since the problem came to the public attention in 2000 with the first federal Trafficking Victims Protection Act (TVPA) in 2000 (see Chapter 9). This legislation was concerned with international victims, but the focus has shifted more about domestic victims, especially minors and children in the foster care system. Recent federal legislations, Prevent Sex Trafficking Strengthening Families Act of 2014 and Justice for Victims of Trafficking Act of 2015, are relatively recent policies addressing the contemporary issues faced by victims of human trafficking, specifically sex trafficking.

Preventing Sex Trafficking and Strengthening Families Act

Signed in 2014 by President Barack Obama, the Preventing Sex Trafficking and Strengthening Families Act amended the Social Security Act to "prevent and address sex trafficking of children in foster care, to extend adoption incentives, and to improve international child support recovery" (Preventing Sex Trafficking and Strengthening Families Act, P.L. 113-183, 2014). Among other major provisions, this legislation established a National Advisory Committee on the Sex Trafficking of Children and Youth to advise the federal government on a national response to the issue. Most significantly, the act required state and tribal agencies receiving Title IV-E funds to create (or modify) their child welfare program to include policies and procedures for identifying and reporting child victims of sex trafficking, to track and report children and youth at risk or becoming victims, and to provide services to child victims including appropriate placements and activities (Child Welfare Information Gateway, 2017).

The legislation also expanded on state requirements toward older children in care, explicitly giving children age 14 or older the authority to participate in the development of their case plans, limiting the option of a "planned permanent living arrangement" as a permanency plan to children age 16 or older, requiring that children leaving care be given copies of important legal documents such as their social security card and birth certificate, and requiring states report on efforts to ensure that children and youth in care maintain long-lasting connections to an adult in spite of changes in placement or caseworker.

Justice for Victims of Trafficking Act

Enacted in 2015, the Justice for Victims of Trafficking Act extended the federal definition of child abuse to include human trafficking and the production of pornography (Child Welfare Information Gateway, 2017). The bill provides grants to states to provide justice to trafficking victims through investigation and prosecution, additional services, and deterrence programs for domestic child trafficking. Funding was also provided for specialized training of caseworkers, law enforcement, first responders, health officials, prosecutors, and judges to identity victims, acts of child human trafficking, and facilitate rescue.

Political Status Populations

Historically, the public child welfare system in the United States primarily served U.S.-born children and families; however, immigrant and refugee populations also come to the attention of the system due to child abuse and neglect. Some of these children and families have political status and/or legal attributes, such as unaccompanied minor, special immigrant juvenile, or undocumented family (Zayas, 2015), that also warrant child welfare services. These political or legal attributes often create additional challenges for the children and families to receive services from the public child welfare system due to ongoing political battles over immigration. Children and youth who are Unaccompanied Refugee Minors (URM), or youth with Special Immigrant Juvenile Status (SIJS), and/or families involved in Deferred Action for Childhood Arrivals (DACA) may be affected by agency policies and federal legislations, impacting the timeframes and the nature of services available to them (see Chapter 8).

The intersection of child welfare law and immigration law is complex in terms of the implications for children and youth who experience abuse and neglect and live in the United States without legal authorization. The Immigration Act of 1990 created the Special Immigrant Juvenile Status (SIJS) for children and youth who are not residents of the United States but have been found to be abused or neglected by one or both parents (Wasem, 2014). In fact, SIJS may be extended to any minor under the age of 21 who: 1) was born in another country; 2) remains in the United States as an unauthorized resident; 3) suffered abuse, neglect, or abandonment by one or both parents; and 4) meets certain other eligibility criteria. SIJS creates a legal pathway for this population to permanently remain in the United States. Over the course of the 21st century, there have been increasing numbers of immigrant children and youth applying for and receiving SIJS status, with many ultimately achieving legal permanent resident status.

LGBTQIA Population

Just as children, adults, and families with political and legal status attributes encounter challenges in the public child welfare system, so do **lesbian**, **gay**, bisexual, transgender, queer or questioning, intersex, and asexual youth, their families, and other adults involved with the system. Historically, LGBTQ children and youth experienced compounding trauma in the system that mirrored the trauma and oppression of those in the general population. Myths and misinformation, a lack of understanding, and ongoing "heterocentrism" (Mallon, 1999; Mallon, 2018) continue to plague this population not only within the public child welfare system but also within collaborative systems responsible for providing services to these children, youth, and their families. Within child welfare these concerns extend to LGBTQ persons desiring to foster or adopt children in care. All continue to struggle at some point with micro-aggressive encounters, stereotypical discrimination, and biased judgments because of their sexual orientation, gender, and gender expression (see Chapter 10).

Culturally Responsive Practice

Children and families in the public child welfare system are as diverse as the general population, requiring child welfare practice to be culturally responsive. Cultural competence training has been part of the child welfare repertoire since the 1980s (McPhatter, 1999) in response to the growing awareness of the increasing disproportionality of children of color, particularly African Americans, in foster care. Recently, Ortega and Faller (2011) called for "training child welfare workers from an intersectional cultural humility perspective" (p. 27), promoting cultural humility as a "complement to cultural competence."

An intersectional approach with cultural humility recognizes the intersectionality and diversity of the children, youth, and family served, empowering workers to engage with the whole person, taking into account their multiple identities and cultural experience (Ortega & Faller, 2011). This approach is vital in helping caseworkers understand the trauma and migration journeys that some immigrant and refugee children and families may have endured leaving their trauma-filled home environments and coming to the United States (Fong, 2004; Dettlaff & Fong, 2016). It is just as vital in helping caseworkers understand the impact of historical trauma and mistrust on their ability to effectively engage domestic racial and ethnic minority families due to issues of power and privilege. This approach of using cultural humility, which messages the importance of learning about the client's values and beliefs in assessing and treating the client, is important in its application to all clients—White, Black, Latinx, Asian/Pacific Islander, American Indian/Alaska Native, LGBTQ, trafficked—in the public child welfare system.

Chapter Summary and Overview of Text

This chapter has provided an overview of the history of the child welfare and the foster care system in the United States. A historical chronology of the major federal legislation that governs child welfare practice showed the evolution from a passive, reactive system that privileged the rights of parents/guardians to treat their children as they deemed appropriate, to a much more complex and somewhat proactive system charged with the protection of children through prevention and intervention. This same legislative history provided insight into the underlying systemic issues that lead to and perpetuate racial and ethnic disproportionality and disparities within the child welfare system.

Chapter 2 expands on these topics by providing a more in-depth description of the complex multisystemic approach to child welfare practice, including both the public and private sector. The relationship between child welfare and collaborative systems including the courts, health care, and education is discussed, as well as innovative approaches to child welfare intervention. Chapter 3 discusses the history and current status of evidence-based child welfare practice giving examples of both successes and challenges. Given that an estimated 90% of children in foster care experience some form of trauma (Fratto, 2016), Chapter 4 discusses the impact of trauma on children, youth, and families. Chapter 5 concludes the first half of the text with an in-depth discussion on multidimensional engagement in child welfare. The second half of the text (beginning with Chapter 6) highlights the variety of populations involved in child welfare. This includes domestic children of color, native peoples, immigrant children and families, victims of human trafficking, LGBTQIA youth, emancipating youth, kinship families, foster and adoptive families, post-adoption and guardianship families, children with mental health needs, and crossover youth. Each chapter provides an overview of the history of child welfare intervention and culturally responsive practice with these populations, as well as the relevant policies and practices.

DISCUSSION QUESTIONS

1. Discuss the key historical events and policies that, in hindsight, may have laid the foundation for the disproportionality and disparities impacting children and families of color involved in child welfare today.
2. Define the three key areas of focus for child welfare practice: **safety**, **permanency**, and **well-being**. Discuss how federal legislation has addressed these priorities over time and the impact of current legislation on states and public child welfare agencies' capacity to address these priorities in practice. What, if any, recommendations would you have to improve current policy or legislation to better address these priorities?

References

Alliance for Strong Families and Communities. (2018). Overview of provisions in the Family First Prevention Service Act. https://www.alliance1.org/web/news/2018/feb/overview-provisions-family-first-prevention-services-act.aspx

Alpert, L. T., & Britner, P. A. (2005). Social workers' attitudes toward parents of children in child protective services: Evaluation of a family-focused casework training program. *Journal of Family Social Work, 9*(1), 33–64.

Barsh, R. L. (1980). The Indian Child Welfare Act of 1978: A critical analysis. *Hastings Law Journal, 31*(3), 1287–1336.

Barth, R. P., Lloyd, E. C., Christ, S. L., Chapman, M. V., & Dickinson, N. (2008). Child welfare worker characteristics and job satisfaction: A national study. *Social Work, 53*(3), 199–209.

Bass, S. F. (1997). The public foster care system and the transracial placement of African-American children: Exploring the history and the issue. *Hybrid: The University of Pennsylvania Journal of Law and Social Change* 4, 73–90.

Bates, J. (2016). The role of race in legitimizing institutionalization: A comparative analysis of early child welfare intiatives in the United States. *Journal of the History of Childhood and Youth, 9*(1), 15–28. doi: https: // doi.org/ 10.1353 /hcy.2016.0014

Beck, R. (1973). The White House conferences on children: An historical perspective. *Harvard Educational Review, 43*(4), 653–668.

Billingsley, A., & Giovannoni, J. (1972). *Children of the Storm: Black Children and American Child Welfare.* New York: Harcourt Brace Jovanovich.

Bremmer, R. H. (ed.) (1970). *Children and Youth in America: A Documentary History* (Vol. 1: 1600–1865). Cambridge, MA: Harvard University Press.

Brown III, L. G., & Gallagher, K. (2014). Mandatory reporting of abuse: A historical perspective on the evolution of states' current mandatory reporting laws with a review of the laws in the Commonwealth of Pennsylvania, *Villanova Law Review: Tolle Lege, 59*(6), 37–44. http://digital-commons.law.villanova.edu/vlr/vol59/iss6/5

Child and Family Service Reviews Information Portal (2007–2019) *Permanency Hearing*. JBS International, Inc. https://training.cfsrportal.acf.hhs.gov/section-2-understanding-child-welfare-system/3025

Child Trends. (2018). Racial and ethnic composition of the child population. https://www.childtrends.org/indicators/racial-and-ethnic-composition-of-the-child-population

Child Welfare Information Gateway. (2019). *Major federal legislation concerned with child protection, child welfare, and adoption.* Washington, DC: U.S. Department of Health and Human Services, Children's Bureau.

Child Welfare Information Gateway. (2018). *State vs. county administration of child welfare services.* Washington, DC: U.S. Department of Health and Human Services, Children's Bureau.

Child Welfare Information Gateway. (2018). *What Is Child Welfare? A Guide for Educators.* Washington, DC: U.S. Department of Health and Human Services, Children's Bureau.

Child Welfare Information Gateway. (2017). *Human Trafficking and Child Welfare: A Guide for Child Welfare Agencies.* Washington, DC: U.S. Department of Health and Human Services, Children's Bureau.

Child Welfare Information Gateway. (2016). *Racial disproportionality and disparity in child welfare.* Washington, DC: U.S. Department of Health and Human Services, Children's Bureau.

Child Welfare Information Gateway. (2015a). *Major federal legislation concerned with child protection, child welfare, and adoption.* Washington, DC: U.S. Department of Health and Human Services, Children's Bureau.

Child Welfare Information Gateway. (2015b). *How federal legislation impacts child welfare service delivery.* Washington, DC: U.S. Department of Health and Human Services, Children's Bureau.

Child Welfare Information Gateway. (2015c). *Kinship guardianship as a permanency option.* Washington, DC: U.S. Department of Health and Human Services, Children's Bureau.

Child Welfare Information Gateway. (2010). *Caseload and workload management. State Managers Series—Issue Brief,* April 2010.

Children's Research Center. (2009). Agency workforce estimation: Simple steps for improving child safety and permanency. FOCUS: News from the Children's Research Center, April 2009.

Council on Accreditation (COA). (2018). *Standards for public agencies.* http://coanet.org/standard/pa-cps/14/

Council on Accreditation (COA). (2014). *A look back: 2014 annual report.* New York: Author.

Cook, J. F. (1995). A history of placing-out: The orphan trains. *Child Welfare, 74*(1), 181–197.

Courtney, M. E., Dworsky, A., Brown, A., Cary, C., Love, K., Vorhies, V., & Hall, C. (2011). *Midwest Evaluation of the Adult Functioning of Former Foster Youth: Outcomes at age 26.* Chicago: University of Chicago, Chapin Hall Center for Children.

Cushing, G., & Kerman, B. (2009). Permanence is a state of security and attachment. In B. Kerman, M. Freundlich, & A. Maluccio (Eds.), *Achieving Permanence for Older Children and Youth in Foster Care* (pp. 109–122). New York: Columbia University Press.

DePanfilis, D. (2018). Child protective services: A guide for caseworkers. Washington, DC: U.S. Department of Health and Human Services Administration for Children and Families, Administration on Children, Youth and Families, Children's Bureau, Office on Child Abuse and Neglect.

Dettlaff, A. J., & Fong, R. (Eds.). (2016). *Immigrant and refugee children and families: Culturally responsive practice.* New York: Columbia University Press.

Edwards, L. P. (1994). Improving implementation of the federal Adoption Assistance and Child Welfare Act of 1980. *Juvenile & Family Court Journal, 45(*3), 139–168.

Faller, K.C. (2014). Sexual Abuse Issues. In G.P Mallon, & P. M. Hess (Eds.), *Child welfare in the twenty-first century: A handbook of practices, policies, and programs.* (2nd ed., pp. 288–298). New York: Columbia University Press.

Fratto, C. M. (2016). Trauma-informed care for youth in foster care. *Archives of Psychiatric Nursing, 30*(3), 439–446.

Fong, R. (Ed.). (2004). *Culturally competent practice with immigrant and refugee children and families.* New York: Guilford Press.

Fong, R., & Berger Cardoso, J. (2010). Child human trafficking victims: Challenges for the child welfare system. *Journal of Evaluation and Program Planning, 33*(3), 311–316. PMID: 19716601. doi:10.1016/j.evalprogplan.2009.06.018

Fong, R., McRoy, R., & Hendricks, C. (Eds.). (2006). *Intersecting child welfare, substance abuse, and family violence: Culturally competent approaches.* Alexandria, VA: Council on Social Work Education.

Getz, C. (1940). *Child Welfare Services under the Social Security Act.* New York: Child Welfare League of America, Inc.

Government Accountability Office. (2003). Child welfare: HHS could play a greater role in helping child welfare agencies recruit and retain staff [GAO-03-357]. Washington, DC: Author.

Hanna, M., Tokarski, K., Matera, D., & Fong, R. (2011). Happily ever after? The journey from foster care to adoption. *Adoption Quarterly, 14*(2), 107–131.

Hanna, M. D. (2009). The Child Welfare Unit. In C. Potter & C. Brittain (Eds.), *Child Welfare Supervision: A Practical Guide for Supervisors, Managers, and Administrators* (pp. 83–118). New York: Oxford University Press.

Hollinger, J. H., & the ABA Center on Children and the Law National Resource Center on Legal and Court Issues. (1998). *A Guide to the Multiethnic Placement Act of 1994 as Amended by the Interethnic Provisions of 1996.* Washington, DC: American Bar Association. https://www.americanbar.org/content/dam/aba/administrative/child_law/GuidetoMultiethnicPlacementAct.pdf

Jalongo, M. R. (2006). The story of Mary Ellen Wilson: Tracing the origins of child protection in America. *Early Education Journal, 34*(1), 1–4. doi: 10.1007/s10643-006-0121-z

Jeter, H. R. (1963). *Children Problems and Services in Child Welfare Programs* (No. 403). Washington, DC: U.S. Department of Health, Education, and Welfare, Welfare Administration, Children's Bureau.

Kerman, B., Wildfire, J., & Barth, R. P. (2002). Outcomes for young adults who experienced foster care. *Children and Youth Services Review, 24*(5), 319–344.

Koh, E., & Testa, M. (2011). Children discharged from kin and non-kin foster homes: Do the risks of foster care re-entry differ? *Children and Youth Services Review 33,* 1497–1505.

Lawrence-Webb, C. (1997). African American children in the modern child welfare system: A legacy of the Flemming rule. *Child Welfare, 76*(1), 9–30.

Mallon, G. P. (1999). A call for organizational trans-formation. *Journal of Gay & Lesbian Social Services, 10*(3/4), 131–142.

Mallon, G.P. (2018). A practice guide for working with LGBTQ Youth in the child welfare system. Baton Rouge, LA: Louisiana Department of Children and Family Services.

Matheson, L. (1996). The politics of the Indian Child Welfare Act. *Social Work, 41*(2), 232–235.

McGowan, B. G. (2005). Historical evolution of child welfare services. In G. P. Mallon & P. M. Hess (Eds.), *Child Welfare for the Twenty-first Century: A Handbook of Practices, Policies, & Programs* (11–44). New York: Columbia University Press.

McPhatter, A. R. (1999). Cultural competence in child welfare: What is it? How do we achieve it? What happens without it. *Serving African American Children: Child Welfare Perspectives.* Piscataway, NJ: Transaction Publishers.

McRoy, R., Mica, M., Freundlich, M., & Kroll, J. (2007). Making MEPA-IEP work: Tools for professionals. *Child Welfare, 86*(2), 49.

Mink, G., & Solinger, R. (Eds.). (2003). *Welfare: A Documentary History of U.S. Policy and Politics.* New York: New York University Press.

National Child Welfare Workforce Institute (NCWWI). (2012). Workforce demographics & job satisfaction. *Workforce Resource One-Page Summary*, December.

National Child Welfare Workforce Institute (NCWWI). (2011). Caseload/workload. *Workforce Resource One-Page Summary*, February.

National Conference of State Legislatures (NCSL). (2018). *Family First Prevention Services Act (FFPSA): Overview*. http://www.ncsl.org/research/human-services/family-first-prevention-services-act-ffpsa.aspx

Oettinger, K. B. (1960). Title V of the Social Security Act: What it has meant to children. *Social Security Bulletin*, 23, 39–50.

Ortega, R. M., & Faller, K. C. (2011). Training child welfare workers from an intersectional cultural humility perspective: A paradigm shift. *Child Welfare, 90*(5), 27–49.

Perry, R. E., & Ellett, A. J. (2008). Child welfare: Historical trends, professionalization, and workforce issues. In B. White (Volume Editor) and K. M. Sowers & C. Dulmus (Editors in Chief), *The Comprehensive Handbook of Social Work and Social Welfare, Volume 1: The Profession of Social Work*. Hoboken, NJ: John Wiley & Sons.

Rodham, H. (1973). Children under the law. *Harvard Educational Review, 43*(4), 487–514.

Rollin, M., Vandervort, F., & Haralambie, A. M. (2005). Federal child welfare law and policy: Understanding the federal law and funding process. In M. R. Ventrell & D. N. Duquette (Eds.), *Child Welfare Law and Practice: Representing Children, Parents, and State Agencies in Abuse, Neglect, and Dependency Cases* (143–183). Wheatridge, CO: Bradford Publishing.

Rolock, N., & White, K. R. (2017). Continuity for children after guardianship versus adoption with kin: Approximating the right counterfactual. *Child Abuse & Neglect, 72*, 32–44.

Sheldon, S. (1997). 50,000 Children are waiting: Permanency, planning, and termination of parental rights under the adoption assistance and child welfare act of 1980, 17 B.C. Third World L.J. *Domestic Social Justice Edition*, 17(1), 73–100.

Social Security (n.d.(a)). *Legislative history: Social security act of 1935: Title IV-grants to states for aid to dependent children*. https://www.ssa.gov/history/35activ.html

Social Security (n.d.(b)). *Legislative history: Social security act of 1935: Title V-grants to states for maternal and child welfare*. https://www.ssa.gov/history/35actv.html#Part3

Social Work Policy Institute. (2010). *Child welfare: Professional social workers in child welfare work: Research addressing the recruitment and retention dilemma*. http://www.socialworkpolicy.org/research/child-welfare-2.html

Stout, M. A. (2012). *American Indian/Alaska Native Boarding Schools*. Santa Barbara, CA: Greenwood.

Testa, M. F. (2010). Evaluation of child welfare interventions. In M. F. Testa & J. Poertner (Eds.), *Fostering Accountability: Using Evidence to Guide and Improve Child Welfare Policy* (pp. 195–230). New York: Oxford.

Townsend, S., Hignight, A., & Rubovits, D. (2008). Factors affecting permanency outcomes for foster children before and after passage of the adoption and safe families act of 1997. *Illinois Child Welfare, 4*(1), 59–73.

Tweddle, A. (2007). Youth leaving care: How do they fare? *New Directions for Youth Development* (113), 15–31, 9–10. https://search-proquest-com.du.idm.oclc.org/docview/70543939?accountid=14608

U.S. Children's Bureau. (2012). *The story of the children's bureau.* Washington, DC: Author.

U.S. Department of Health & Human Services (USDHHS), Administration for Children and Families, Administration on Children, Youth and Families, Children's Bureau. (2018). *Child maltreatment 2016.* https://www.acf.hhs.gov/cb/research-data-technology/statistics-research/child-maltreatment

U.S. Department of Health & Human Services (USDHHS), Office of the Assistant Secretary for Planning and Evaluation. (2016). *Differential Response and the Safety of Children Reported to Child Protective Services: A Tale of Six States.*

Wasem RE (2014) Special immigrant juveniles: In Brief (No. R43703). Washington D.C.:Congressional Research Service.

Watkins, S. A. (1990). The Mary Ellen myth: Correcting child welfare history. *Social Work, 35*(6), 500–503.

Whitaker, T. (2012). Social workers and workplace bullying: Perceptions, responses and implications. *Work, 42*(1), 115–123.

Winokur, M., Holtan, A., & Batchelder, K. (2014). Kinship care for the safety, permanency and wellbeing of children removed from the home for maltreatment. *Cochrane Database Systematic Review, 1,* Art. No.: CD006546. doi: 10.1002/14651858.CD006546.pub3

Wu, Q., White, K., & Coleman, K. (2015). Effects of kinship care on behavioral problems by child age: A propensity score analysis. *Children and Youth Services Review, 57,* 1–8.

Zayas, L. H. (2015). *Forgotten citizens: Deportation, children, and the making of American exiles and orphans.* New York: Oxford University Press.

Zigler, E. (1993). Reinstituting the White House conference on children. *American Journal of Orthopsychiatry, 73*(3), 334–336.

Figure Credits

Fig. 1.1: Source: https://commons.wikimedia.org/wiki/File:McCormack-MaryEllen_001a.jpg.

Fig. 1.2: Source: https://www.tpr.org/post/riders-orphan-train-preserves-unforgettable-stories-unwanted-children.

Fig. 1.3: Source: https://commons.wikimedia.org/wiki/File:Orphan_train_flyer.jpg.

Fig 1.4: Source: https://www.archives.gov/publications/prologue/2010/summer/youth.html.

Fig. 1.5: Source: How Federal Legislation Impacts Child Welfare Service Delivery.

Img. 1.1: Copyright © 2011 Depositphotos/ivelin.

Img. 1.2: Copyright © 2016 Depositphotos/zdenkam.

Img. 1.3: Copyright © 2019 Depositphotos/fizkes.

Fig. 1.6: Source: Child protective services: A guide for caseworkers.

Img. 1.4: Copyright © 2010 Depositphotos/.shock.

CHAPTER • 2

Multisystems Approach to Child Welfare Services

Krista Thomas, Nancy Rolock, Rowena Fong, and Ruth McRoy

Introduction

Children and families who become involved with a public child welfare system face complex issues. Children who are victims of abuse and neglect may have needs that go beyond what a child welfare system can provide. For instance, there may be food security issues or mental health issues in the family, in addition to the maltreatment that may have brought the child to the attention of the child welfare system. It is, therefore, important for persons working with these children and families, including child welfare caseworkers, school counselors, and public health nurses, to know how to approach and address the needs of these families from a multisystems approach. This chapter emphasizes the importance to include multiple systems in servicing children and families in need. As an example of how this occurs, the child welfare system is described from the perspective of a fictitious family (see Box 2.1). Collaborative systems such as courts, health, and schools will also be discussed. This will be followed by an overview of the child welfare system, inclusive of both the public system and private agencies. Finally, a discussion and examples of federally funded interventions addressing the concerns and needs of child welfare–involved children and families will be provided. A case example is offered highlighting the complexities and the importance of working across multiple systems.

BOX 2.1. Multisystem Approach: A Case Example

The problems and trauma facing children and families in the public child welfare system are complex. To provide an example of the complex needs that may face families who come in contact with the child welfare system, the child welfare system is described from the perspective of a fictitious young girl, Fatima, and her family. Fatima is a Mexican American 9-year-old girl whose family is involved with the child welfare system. Her family is receiving court-ordered, in-home family preservation services by the county child welfare agency because of a substantiated report of child maltreatment, specifically neglect due to inadequate supervision.

Fatima lives with her father, Manuel, and her 6-year-old brother Antony in public housing, a high-rise apartment building comprised primarily of low-income families with children. The building is in disrepair, with frequent citations for cockroach infestations and visible mold within many of the housing units. Fatima is in the third grade and Antony is in the first grade at their neighborhood public school. Fatima has dyslexia, which causes her difficulty with reading and comprehension in school. Antony suffers from severe asthma, which is challenging to control. The family receives their health insurance through Medicaid.

Manuel works as a line cook in a neighborhood restaurant during the dinner shift, which requires him to be at work when the children come home from school through the evening hours. Previously, he relied on a neighborhood teenager, Ana, to care for Fatima and Antony in the afternoons and evenings. However, Ana's family recently moved away, and Manuel was left without anyone to provide child care. Because Manuel is at risk of losing his job if he does not report for work, he had been leaving the children home alone, assigning 9-year-old Fatima the responsibility for caring for her younger brother.

One evening while Manuel was at work, Antony experienced an asthma attack and was in severe distress. Fatima could not locate his inhaler and was unable to reach her father on his cell phone while he was at work. She knew to call 911 in an emergency, so she did. The paramedics arrived, stabilized Antony, and took both children to the hospital where her brother could receive follow-up care. In the emergency room, the nurse called the county Department of Child and Family Services (DCFS), since the children did not have a parent or other adult with them at the hospital.

DCFS investigated the case and substantiated Manuel for neglect due to inadequate supervision. Christopher, the family preservation caseworker assigned to their case, was responsible for working together with Manuel to assess the family's needs and identify the right set of services and supports to help Manuel safely care for his children and hopefully avoid the need for foster care. Another part of Christopher's job involves going to court and testifying in front of the judge about the family's progress and whether Fatima and Antony are safe at home with Manuel.

Through Christopher's assessment of Manuel and his children, he uncovered several issues. First, he learned that the primary challenge Manuel was facing was a lack of child care. Therefore, Christopher's big priority is identifying an affordable, public child care program in the community where Fatima and Antony can go after school. Second, Christopher learned that Fatima's poor performance in school is due to her dyslexia, but she does not have an individualized education program (IEP) to help address her needs. Therefore, another priority is connecting with Fatima's school social worker to help develop and implement an IEP for Fatima.

Next, there is the problem of Antony's asthma. After connecting with his pediatrician, Christopher learned that asthma is worsened by exposure to cockroaches and mold, which are both present in the family's home. Another priority is finding the family a different place to live that is safer for Antony.

Although this is a child welfare case, Christopher and Manuel must work within several different systems to make sure the children's safety is protected and that their needs are met. These systems include the judicial, education, child care, health care system, and the public housing system. Child welfare caseworkers must learn to be successful navigating these multiple, interconnected systems, which all play a major role in providing key services to vulnerable children and families.

Multisystem Approach: An Overview of Systems

The following sections will focus on a few of the critical systems that substantially intersect with the child welfare system. This begins with the court system, a system that is critical to the understanding of how child welfare systems work. This is followed by a discussion of child welfare and health care, followed by child welfare and education. Each of these systems impacts the lives of children in general but can sometimes work at odds for child welfare–involved families. Understanding how these systems interact, as indicated in the case example of Fatima presented in Box 2.1, is a primary focus of this chapter.

Child Welfare and the Courts

The juvenile and family court systems play a principal role in child welfare cases. Child protective services cases are heard in civil court, not criminal court, and juvenile and family court judges are accountable for ensuring the safety, permanency, and well-being of all children and youth that enter their courtrooms (Gatowski, Miller, Rubin, Escher, & Maze, 2016). As a result, judges are responsible for making a number of critical decisions. At the beginning of a child welfare case, judges are responsible for determining whether children and youth, alleged to be victims of maltreatment, are able to remain safely in their homes or whether they need to be removed and placed in foster care. Judges are then also responsible for deciding whether there is sufficient evidence to determine whether or not child maltreatment occurred. This decision is often referred to as the **adjudication**.

Image 2.1

For children and youth found to be victims of child maltreatment, but still allowed to remain at home, the judge may decide that the family must remain under court-ordered supervision from the child welfare agency. This means that the judge may want to make sure that parents are participating in services identified as necessary to address whatever needs or problems that contributed to child maltreatment and ensure that the children and youth remain safe from harm. For children and youth who are removed, judges must determine whether **reasonable efforts** were put forward by the child welfare agency to prevent removal (Child Welfare Information Gateway, 2016b, 2020). This means the judge must decide whether the child welfare agency did everything it could to provide support and services to help the family remain safely together. Following the removal and placement into foster care, the judge must make regular determinations whether the child welfare agency is making "reasonable efforts" to reunify the children and youth with their caregivers. In cases where caregivers are unable to make progress on their case plans and children and youth are deemed unlikely to be able to return home, the judge must make the difficult decision to terminate the parental rights of biological caregivers (Child Welfare Information Gateway, 2016c). Relatedly, juvenile and family court judges are responsible for finalizing alternative permanency plans for children and youth placed in foster care, such as guardianship with relatives or adoption.

In addition to judges, there are a number of additional legal and judicial personnel that play important roles in the child welfare case process. Parents' attorneys are important partners and advocates in the process for ensuring that parents' rights are protected and they receive the support they need to increase their capacity to safely care for their children. While national guidance and best practice dictate that all parents be appointed competent legal counsel due to the complexities of the legal proceedings in child welfare cases, there is still much opportunity to improve their access to quality legal representation (Children's Bureau, 2017).

Child welfare agencies also have attorneys that represent them in court. There are two primary approaches for agency representation that may vary by state or other jurisdiction (American Bar Association, 2004; "CASAs and GALs," n.d.). In one approach, the child welfare agency is the client and the attorney is the legal entity that represents agency interests in court. In an alternate approach, often called a prosecutorial model, the attorney is appointed or elected and represents the interest of the state or county. The difference in these models is that in the second one, the attorney may present a position that overrides or contradicts the agency's position. In either model, transparent communication and collaboration between the child welfare agency and the attorney are critical for ensuring the child welfare case process proceeds smoothly and in the best interests of the children involved.

Lastly, children and youth involved in child welfare cases also have a right to legal representation (Malempati, 2013). There are three different legal entities that can be involved in this process. First, children and youth are assigned an attorney to represent them in court; this attorney functions as their legal advocate and presents their positions. There may also be **guardians ad litem (GALs)** who are appointed by the court to represent the best interests of the child. A GAL can be a lawyer, social worker, psychologist, or trained community volunteer called a **court-appointed special advocate (CASA)**, depending on the specific requirements of the jurisdiction. GALs are charged with representing the best interests of their client, regardless of whether that position aligns with the wishes of the child or youth involved. For example, it is possible to imagine the difficult scenario where a GAL may declare that it is in the best interest of a child to be adopted, even though the child is still maintaining the hope that a safe reunification with his or her parents is still possible. In addition to the number of legal and judicial personnel involved, there is also a significant number of court proceedings necessary to govern a child welfare case from start to finish. Child welfare caseworkers often spend a significant amount of time preparing for or attending court hearings, and interacting with the legal and judicial system is an essential component of their professional responsibilities.

Child Welfare and Physical Health, Mental Health, and Substance Use Treatment

Child welfare agencies are responsible for promoting positive physical and mental health outcomes for the children and youth in their care and supporting child and family well-being. This involves investing considerable efforts to ensure that children and youth receive the right assessments, medications, and services to meet their needs (Children's Bureau, 2014). Research shows that many children and youth involved in the child welfare system experience physical health problems, and many have chronic conditions (Allen, Pires, & Mahadeven, 2012). A high percentage of children show symptoms of significant emotional and behavioral health conditions, and rates of psychotropic drug use among children and youth in care are significantly higher among this group than the general U.S. child population (Children's Bureau, 2012a). Furthermore, there is evidence that children and youth from minority racial and ethnic backgrounds fare even worse in their health outcomes (Child Welfare Information Gateway, 2016a). This may be due to factors unrelated to the health condition, per se. For instance, the availability and accessibility of services may differ based upon where a particular family lives.

A study from Texas found that one-quarter of predominantly minority communities (African American and Latinx) did not have child-welfare services, such as parent education and transportation, within the community (Dorch et al., 2010). This is a significant finding, given that services are often key features of case plans that allow children to remain at home (and not enter foster care) and plans for children in care to successfully reunite with their parents or family of origin. In another study, Osterling, Lee, and Hines (2012) examined the use of court-mandated family reunification services. They found that, despite being more likely to be referred for substance abuse treatment, and that substance abuse treatment was associated with higher reunification rates, African American parents were less likely to have access to these services. Issues around transportation to services and problems related to work conflicts were noted as barriers by social workers involved in the study. The availability of culturally competent, community-based services is critical for child welfare–involved families.

When a parent is mandated to attend services, they may be ordered to attend a large number of services all at once. This can interfere with employment, transportation may be unreliable or unavailable, and language or other barriers may occur (Hines et al., 2003; Osterling et al., 2012). To adequately address these issues requires child welfare agencies to collaborate effectively with their partners in the health care system to address the needs of the children in their care. Medicaid is the primary insurer for children and youth involved with the child welfare system. State child welfare agencies are required to work together with their state Medicaid agency to develop a plan for the ongoing oversight and coordination of health care for children and youth in foster care (Children's Bureau, 2012b).

Recent legislation, the Family First Prevention Services Act passed in 2018, stipulates that states should use evidence-based interventions in their work with child welfare–involved families (Children's Defense Fund, 2018). This is an example of efforts underway nationally to increase the use of evidence-based clinical interventions to address the trauma and mental health needs of child welfare–involved children and youth and to reduce the inappropriate use of **psychotropic medications** for this population. Relatedly, this means that caseworkers must also invest their time in facilitating assessments and treatment and overseeing the physical and mental health care needs of the children, youth, and families on their caseloads. Knowing about resources on evidence-based and informed programs and policies is an important part of a caseworker's role (see Box 2.2). For more resources, see Chapter 3 on evidence-based practice in child welfare.

BOX 2.2. Resources on Evidence-Based/Evidence-Informed Programs and Practices

Social workers and others working with child welfare–involved families can look for evidence-based interventions at the following websites:

- California Evidence-Based Clearinghouse for Child Welfare
- Coalition for Evidence-Based Policy—Top Tier Evidence
- Office of Juvenile Justice and Delinquency Prevention—Model Programs Guide
- Promising Practices Network on Children, Families, and Communities
- Institute of Education Science What Works Clearinghouse
- National Registry of Evidence-Based Programs and Practices
- Evidence-Based Program Directories—Youth.gov
- The Office of Justice Programs—CrimeSolutions.gov

Child Welfare and Education

In addition to meeting the physical and mental health needs of children and youth involved in the child welfare system, child welfare agencies are equally responsible for meeting their educational needs and promoting positive educational outcomes for children and youth of all ages. As such, there is a wide range of educational issues and concerns relevant to the developmental, academic, and job readiness needs of child welfare–involved children and youth.

In 2017, 184,000 young children (5 years old or younger) entered foster care, comprising 68% of all children entering care during the year (Children's Bureau, 2018). Young children who experience maltreatment, particularly neglect, are at increased risk for experiencing developmental delays than their counterparts who have not been maltreated (Ward, Yoon, Atkins, Morris, Oldham, & Wathan, 2009). Identifying and facilitating quality early care and educational services for this young population, such as evidence-based home visiting, quality child care, and Head Start and Early Head Start, are important considerations for child welfare agencies.

Image 2.2

Another significant educational issue in child welfare is promoting school stability for children who have been placed in foster care. Children in foster care lag behind their counterparts in achieving positive educational outcomes, with studies demonstrating lower test scores and graduation rates for this vulnerable population (U.S. Department of Education & the U.S. Department of Health and Human Services, 2016). Relatedly, children and youth in foster care experience much higher degrees of school instability, as placement changes often require accompanying changes in school assignment. This instability may impact students' academic progress and contribute to an achievement gap between children and youth in foster care and their peers (National Working Group on Foster Care and Education, 2014). Federal legislative provisions and guidance require state agencies to preserve foster care children and youth in their schools of origin whenever possible. This requires thoughtful collaboration between child welfare agencies and school system partners to devise effective strategies such as sharing responsibility for transportation costs and facilitating the associated logistics, such as scheduling extracurricular and community activities for students placed further away from their schools of origin (American Bar Association, 2011).

Older youth and young adults transitioning out of foster care are also impacted by a range of educational challenges and priorities. Caseworkers and other child welfare professionals who work specifically with older youth invest time and effort focusing on education-related issues like strategies to promote youths' graduation from high school, college attendance, or enrollment in job training or vocational programs. There is a specific federal program called the John H. Chafee Foster Care Independence Program (the Chafee program) that is designed to support this type of programming for youth transitioning out of care into independence (Children's Bureau, 2017). The Chafee program includes education and training vouchers to provide additional financial support for these much-needed services (Children's Bureau, 2017). In order to promote successful outcomes for the older foster youth population, caseworkers and independent living workers must develop and maintain strong collaborations with partners in higher education, job training, and employment programs in their states and communities. In summary, the child welfare system does not stand alone, but instead requires intentional collaboration and coordination across a wide range of public and community programs to promote positive safety, permanency, and well-being outcomes for vulnerable children and families.

The Child Welfare System

To fully understand child welfare services today, it is essential to consider some key factors that have influenced the provision of services to children served by public and private child-serving agencies. As a nation over the last two centuries, the child welfare system has evolved from a system focused on trying to "find a solution to the problems of children and youth whose parents are unable to provide adequate care" to a system that considers a broader array of issues, including the safety, permanency and well-being of children and their families (McGowan, 2014, p. 11). With these shifts have come challenges in trying to balance such issues as parents' rights versus children's needs, or child protection versus family preservation (McGowan, 2014).

An example of this tension can be seen in the scenario around an infant who was born substance exposed and a decision has been made to bring the child into state custody. From a parent's perspective, it could be argued that every effort should be made to help the parent obtain the services and supports she or he needs to address their substance abuse issues. However, a parent can be involved with substance abuse treatment for several years. On the other hand, from a child's perspective, is it in their best interest to continue to live in temporary foster care while their parent(s) receive treatment? Some might argue that what is best for the child is to move as quickly as possible to a family where a permanent and loving home can be established. For an infant of 6 months, waiting another 6 months, or possibly years, for services to be provided, may not be in the child's best interest. While there is no one answer, and the response to an individual family situation needs to be specific to the family, it is easy to see how conflicting points of view can develop in terms of the best course of action in a case like this. These situations require that workers take a holistic view of the family, including the supports and services available to them, and consider how multiple service providers can work together to address family needs.

For years, concerns have been raised about the number of children entering foster care, and legislation has been passed in efforts to prevent foster care entry when possible. This includes, for instance, the Adoption Assistance and Child Welfare Act of 1980, which required states to make "reasonable efforts" to prevent children from entering care. Furthermore, due to the growing concern about the length of time children spent in foster care, the Adoption and Safe Families Act of 1997 (ASFA) had provisions aimed at moving children quickly out of foster care and into adoptive homes in a timely manner (Blackstone, Buck, & Hakim, 2004).

An additional shift occurred when the public systems began engaging the private sector more in the provision of services to child welfare–involved families. The private sector began providing supplemental support to the public system (Steen & Duran, 2013). Privatization was thought to be superior to public agency service delivery, as the agencies would not be burdened with challenging bureaucratic structures, and could be more flexible in service delivery. It was also thought that private agencies would be embedded in the community and that competition and performance-based contracting could help an agency become much more responsive to family and community needs (Blackstone et al., 2004; Steen & Duran, 2013).

In response to these aforementioned concerns, some states have privatized all elements of their foster care systems (Steen & Smith, 2011). For example, after a 1996 American Civil Liberties suit against the state of Kansas over children remaining in foster care for long periods of time and limited numbers of adoptions, Kansas began privatizing foster and adoption services in order to improve the system. "It became the first state in the nation to fully privatize its adoption, foster-care and family preservation services" (Eggers, 1997, p. 43). Contractors were selected for a 4-year period, and standards included "no more than three placement moves and 65% of children were to achieve permanency within 12 months of referral, 70% of children would be placed within 180 days of referral and that 90% of adoption shall be intact for 18 months from finalization" (Blackstone et al., 2004, p. 1038).

As a result of Kansas's privatization, better data collection occurred to track cost and performance, and findings revealed a significant reduction in unsuccessful adoptions, an increase in children being placed in foster homes instead of group homes or institutions, and a significant decrease in unsuccessful adoptions (Blackstone et al., 2004, p. 1039). Privatization of these services led public social workers to have more time to focus on investigations, which led to an increase in the identification of abused children (Blackstone et al., 2004; Snell, 2000). Additional states that have implemented large scale privatization efforts are Florida, Illinois, and Nebraska.

However, despite the assumption that privatization would improve service delivery, some states have found that there has been an increase in multiple placements after privatization. As Barillas (2011) noted, "privatization requires government to have the necessary fiscal and institutional resources, or *state capacity*, to properly select and monitor private contracts" (p. 112). This suggests that "private sector responsibilities built on a lack of public sector capacity, diminish the potential of each sector to work toward realizing innovative policy solutions" (Barillas, 2011, p. 123).

By 2006, 9 of the 29 states that had implemented some form of privatization reported that they were reducing or terminating efforts due to inadequate outcomes from the private sector (Collins-Camargo et al., 2006). Steen and Smith (2012) found that a variety of factors influence outcomes by organizational type (public versus private) and that "successful agencies exist in both public and private sectors and that success is not inherently connected to any organizational type" (p. 857). These authors suggested that research is needed to explore factors such as public–private outcomes in terms of placement stability within out of home care, differences in privatization models across geographical areas, workforce characteristics (experience levels, salaries), work conditions, and outcomes (Steen & Smith, 2012).

Children's Bureau Resources

Created in 1912, the United States Children's Bureau is a federal agency under the U.S. Department of Health and Human Services, Administration for Children and Families, which is charged with administering federal child welfare programming. The Children's Bureau (CB) works with state and tribal agencies to improve the well-being of children and families in the United States, with a primary focus on children and families who come to the attention of child welfare systems. The CB works to prevent child abuse and neglect when possible, to protect children who have experienced abuse or neglect, and they strive to ensure that all children have a permanent family. The CB works with state and tribal agencies to improve outcomes related to safety, permanence and well-being. To accomplish this work, the CB provides federal funding to states, tribes, and local jurisdictions through a variety of mandatory and discretionary grant opportunities designed to support the provision and monitoring of child welfare services across the continuum of care. In addition, the CB monitors state performance on key child welfare outcomes and critical dimensions of child welfare system functioning through the Child and Family Services Review process, requiring Program Improvement Plans to address areas that are not found to be in substantial conformity with federal requirements. The CB also sets federal policy, issues guidance, and provides capacity building services to states, courts, and tribes in an effort to promote high-quality service provision and attainment of positive outcomes for children and families. In recent years the CB has developed an array of projects, innovative engagement strategies, grants, and research projects aimed at building evidence for best practice in child welfare. Some of these more recent innovations are described below. Readers interested in more details are encouraged to visit the Children's Bureau web page (acf.hhs.gov). Furthermore, April 9, 2012, marked the 100th anniversary of the Children's Bureau. In honor of its 100th year, the CB put together a series of materials documenting their history for interested students on the CB website.

Image 2.3

A key feature of this work by the CB is the development of materials to be used by practitioners, policy makers, researchers, and others interested in the development and dissemination of knowledge on how to best serve children and families impacted by the child welfare systems in the United States. The CB established a workgroup in 2012 comprised of researchers, federal, tribal, and state-level policy makers, practitioners, and key stakeholders. The workgroup developed the *Framework to Design, Test, Spread, and Sustain Effective Practice in Child Welfare* (Framework Workgroup, 2014), which is considered critical to those interested in providing high-quality services.

Too often, interventions in child welfare are piloted with limited evaluation, and untested interventions are hastily adopted and spread in response to politics, poor agency performance, or public pressure. Changes in service delivery have the potential to improve outcomes for children and families, but child welfare agencies and systems often miss opportunities to build the knowledge base and to answer questions about whether these new practices work, for whom they are most and least effective, and how consistently they are implemented (Framework Workgroup, 2014, p. 23).

The framework provides stages that are critical to the development of evidence-based practice. This begins with guidance on identifying and understanding a problem. It then describes important considerations for researching solutions. A checklist of considerations for selecting, and then testing, interventions is also provided.

In the absence of a systematic and deliberate approach to building, sharing, and using knowledge, those responsible for making decisions and for performing evaluations can be left without answers. These missed opportunities leave decision-makers, program evaluators, funders, and their many partners in the field of child welfare without the necessary information to understand and explain why the outcomes changed (or did not change) the child welfare system, and whether the new practice made a difference (Framework Workgroup, 2014, p. 23).

Below are some examples of how the CB is working to improve services and supports available to families involved with the child welfare system.

Video Series on Data-Driven Decision Making (DDDM)

In three parts, the series provides an overview of DDDM. The videos feature examples of how service providers can understand data that needs to be collected, what can be done with it once collected, and how to disseminate findings. With a goal of improving organizational services or understanding when polices may need to be changed, DDDM aims to inform practice and policy changes that improve an organization's operations and outcomes. The videos are available on the CB website by searching for Data-Driven Decision Making (James Bell Associates, 2018). Available at: https://www.jbassoc.com/resource/guide-data-driven-decision-making-using-data-inform-practice-policy-decisions-child-welfare-organizations/

Child Welfare Information Gateway

The Child Welfare Information Gateway provides free access to up-to-date information for professionals and families. Launched in 2006, this information covers a wide array of topics, including child abuse prevention, family preservation, foster care, domestic and intercountry adoption, and search and reunion. It also includes links to tools and resources aimed at improving practices related to child welfare and is a source for recent research findings. This includes information on federal legislation and policies, training resources, data, and research on key topics related to child welfare. The Gateway has produced a series of podcasts from a variety of perspectives. These include recordings from communities served by child welfare agencies and the experiences and lessons learned from professionals who have implemented innovative services. The Child Welfare Information Gateway hosts a website that can be accessed for additional information.

AdoptUSKids

In an effort to increase adoptions for children in the U.S. foster care system, the CB, in conjunction with nonprofit and corporate partners, including the National Adoption Center, funded AdoptUSKids in 2002. The AdoptUSKids website posts photographs and biographies of children in the foster care system who are available for adoption. Through this website, families are able to read about children who are available for adoption and make contact with the appropriate professionals if they are interested in pursuing adoption. Over 33,000 children photolisted on AdoptUSKids now live with permanent families (AdoptUSKids.org, 2020). AdoptUSKids conducts public service announcements and uses social media to bring attention to the need for foster and adoptive parents and to assist U.S. states, territories, and tribes in recruiting, engaging, and supporting families who become foster or adoptive parents.

Quality Improvement Centers

In 2001, the CB launched a set of Quality Improvement Centers (QICs). Each QIC focused on a specific topic of interest to the CB, an area that the Bureau wanted to learn more about. The goal of the QICs is to generate and disseminate research, with a goal to disseminate findings to child welfare agencies, staff, and other professionals. Early QICs focused on topics such as culturally appropriate interventions for families of color involved with child protective services (CPS) due to **neglect**, and families struggling with **child maltreatment** and substance abuse, and effective supervision (James Bell Associates, 2008). Examples of more recent topics include QICs for Differential Response, Non-Resident Fathers, Early Childhood, Legal Representation, Infant-Toddler Court Teams, Adoption and Guardian Support and Preservation, and the Tailored Services, Placement Stability, and Permanency for Lesbian, Gay, Bisexual, Transgender, and Questioning (LGBTQ) Children and Youth in Foster Care.

Federal Data Collection

The CB collects data to capture information from states, tribes, and territories about the experiences of children in foster care. Data are collected at the individual level for all children who are involved in the public child welfare system. States and tribal agencies are required to submit data to the federal government every 6 months. These data are collected and sent to the CB for data analysis and review. These data become part of the Adoption and Foster Care Analysis and Reporting System (AFCARS). One of the benefits of collecting the AFCARS data is that there is a national record that provides basic information on children in foster care. Additional information on AFCARS can be found in Chapter 6 on Domestic Children of Color in Child Welfare and on the Children's Bureau website.

Minority Professional Leadership Development (MPLD)

Funded by AdoptUSKIDS, the **Minority Professional Leadership Development (MPLD)** program is a 12-month fellowship program designed for emerging minority leaders working in direct services in child welfare. It provides participants with mentoring opportunities and exposure to national experts. There is no fee to participate, and the work occurs online and in the workplace, with periodic visits to the Washington, DC, area. MPLD was developed to increase the leadership capacities of potential emerging minority leaders. It is designed to inform practice and promotes new perspectives for increasing permanency options for children and families in the child welfare system. Additional information can be found on the following website: https://adoptuskids.org/forprofessionals/mpld.

Title IV-E Waiver Demonstration Grants

In 1994, Congress authorized the use of Title IV-E waiver demonstration programs. This authorization allowed states to forgo ("waive") certain restrictions to what types of costs were federally reimbursable. By waiving restrictions to paying for certain items, Congress provided states the opportunity to test new ideas. In other words, Congress provided states with the opportunity to evaluate new approaches to the delivery of child welfare services. The Child and Family Services and Innovation Act of 2011 revived the federal government's authority to grant Title IV-E waivers (U.S. Department of Health and Human Services, n.d.). The waivers allowed states to spend money normally restricted for only foster care programs on interventions designed for children and families involved at any point of the child welfare spectrum. Through this waiver demonstration authority, in 2017 there were 30 active **Child Welfare Waiver Demonstrations**. Additional information on the waiver programs is available at the CB website; a search for child welfare waivers should take interested readers to relevant information.

Case Application

A case of an American Indian minor involved in sex trafficking is presented below. Additional information on sex trafficking is in Chapter 9.

Case Vignette

Mira, a 16-year-old American Indian youth, was arrested for prostitution in Los Angeles, California. Tipped by an anonymous caller, the Los Angeles Police Department (LAPD) conducted a raid in a motel near Los Angeles Airport (LAX) and discovered multiple young women in several motel rooms engaged in sex acts with older men. All the men and women discovered in the raid were arrested and taken down to the local precinct. Mira, a minor, was processed and quickly transferred to a juvenile detention center when they learned her age. She was subjected to a toxicology test where she tested positive for heroin.

During her initial interrogation with Karen, the juvenile corrections officer, Mira stated that she was a member of the Blackfeet Nation of the Blackfeet Indian Reservation in Montana. However, she had been living in Los Angeles at that motel for the previous 9 months. The officer asked Mira about her family. She indicated that her father had died in a car accident when she was a toddler. She and her older brother Frank were raised by her mother, Paulette, though Mira shared that her mother had struggled for many years with a substance use disorder. Her mother and her acquaintances frequently used alcohol and heroin in her home, and Frank had also begun to struggle with addiction in recent years. In fact, when the officer probed more deeply, the connection to her brother's emerging addiction issues became more pronounced. As Frank's drug use increased, his work attendance decreased, and he lost his job. He became unable to pay for the drugs he needed and so when his dealer Trey asked him what else he might have that is valuable, he introduced him to his sister Mira.

Mira said that Trey promised her an escape from her challenging home life and a brighter future in Los Angeles. Trey indicated that she would be able to make new friends and finish high school in Los Angeles—the only condition was that she had to work a little for his friends in order to earn her room and board. Mira, depressed and despondent about her home life, agreed to leave the Blackfeet Indian Reservation and go with Trey to Los Angeles.

When Mira arrived in Los Angeles, Trey immediately took her to the motel and locked her in a room alone for several days without food and without her belongings. What little money she had was taken away. Trey told her that her job was to provide sex services for the men who would come to the motel. Mira said at first she refused, but then Trey hit her repeatedly in her face and stomach. She lay bloodied and locked up in the motel room for several more days with access only to water. When Trey returned the second time, she was more resigned to her new fate. Within the week Mira started seeing "customers" in her motel room. In lieu of wages, Trey and his associates provided food and drugs to the young woman held captive in the motel. Mira learned that the heroin made the "work" that was required of her easier to perform, and soon she also developed an addiction. Within a few days of entering the juvenile detention center, she began to demonstrate withdrawal symptoms.

Karen soon realized that Mira was likely the victim of sex trafficking. Given the information shared about Mira's mother and brother, Karen also realized that Mira may also be a child in need of protective services. At her initial hearing, Karen provided the judge with the information she learned regarding the circumstances that led to Mira being arrested in the motel. With the agreement of the state's attorney, the judge ordered Mira's juvenile justice case be closed and a child welfare case opened. The judge ordered that Mira be placed immediately in treatment foster care, while a more suitable long-term placement was identified and a case plan developed. Mira was then sent to a residential treatment facility for adolescents with substance use disorders and assigned to a child welfare caseworker in Los Angeles named David. David now assumed the challenging task of working with Mira and beginning to think through what permanency goal and case plan would be in Mira's best interest.

DISCUSSION QUESTIONS

1. How should David approach the identification of an appropriate foster care placement for Mira? What considerations apply, and what steps should the caseworker take?
2. What identified needs or concerns will likely need to be addressed in Mira's case plan? What types of services or supports might be appropriate for Mira?
3. What are the different human service systems that will need to be engaged in order to meet Mira's needs?
4. Who are the legal partners that might become involved in Mira's case? What roles and responsibilities might they have, and how would they differ?
5. As you consider the examples provided of projects undertaken by the Children's Bureau to address changes in child welfare practice, can you think of why the lessons learned might be important to consider when implementing a new project, specifically designed to improve outcomes for American Indian children?

References

Allen, K., Pires, S., & Mahadeven, R. (2012). *Improving outcomes for children in child welfare: A Medicaid managed care toolkit.* Center for Health Care Strategies. https://www.chcs.org/media/Child_Welfare_Quality_Improvement_Collaborative_Toolkit.pdf

American Bar Association. (2011). *Making it work: Child welfare and education agencies collaborating to ensure school stability for children in foster care.* https://www.americanbar.org/content/dam/aba/publications/center_on_children_and_the_law/education/making_it_work_final.authcheckdam.pdf

American Bar Association. (2004). *Standards of practice for lawyers representing child welfare agencies.* https://www.americanbar.org/content/dam/aba/administrative/child_law/agency-standards.authcheckdam.pdf

Barillas, K. H. (2011). State capacity: The missing piece in child welfare privatization. *Child Welfare, 90*(3), 111–127.

Blackstone, E. A., Buck, A. J., & Hakim, S. (2004). Privatizing adoption and foster care: Applying auction and market solutions. *Children and Youth Services Review, 26*, 1033–1049.

CASAs and GALs (n.d.) Retrieved from: https://www.childwelfare.gov/topics/systemwide/courts/specialissues/casa-gal/)

Child Welfare Information Gateway. (2020). *Reasonable efforts to preserve or reunify families and achieve permanency for children.* Washington, DC: U.S. Department of Health and Human Services, Administration for Children and Families, Children's Bureau.

Child Welfare Information Gateway. (2016a). *Racial disproportionality and disparity in child welfare.* Washington, DC: U.S. Department of Health and Human Services, Children's Bureau.

Child Welfare Information Gateway. (2016b). *Reasonable efforts to preserve or reunify families and achieve permanency for children.* Washington, DC: U.S. Department of Health and Human Services, Children's Bureau.

Child Welfare Information Gateway. (2016c). *Understanding child welfare and the courts.* Washington, DC: U.S. Department of Health and Human Services, Children's Bureau.

Children's Bureau. (2018). AFCARS Report #25. Washington, DC. https://www.acf.hhs.gov/cb/resource/afcars-report-25

Children's Bureau. (2017). *ACYF-CB-IM-17-02: High Quality Legal Representation for All Parties in Child Welfare Proceedings.* Washington, DC. https://www.acf.hhs.gov/sites/default/files/cb/im1702.pdf

Children's Bureau. (2017). *John H. Chafee Foster Care Independence Program.* https://www.acf.hhs.gov/cb/resource/chafee-foster-care-program

Children's Bureau. (2014). *Child and family services reviews fact sheet for mental health professionals.* https://www.acf.hhs.gov/cb/resource/cfsr-fact-sheet-mental-health-professionals

Children's Bureau. (2012a). *ACYF-CB-IM-12-03: Promoting the safe, appropriate, and effective use of psychotropic medication for children in foster care.* Washington, DC. http://www.acf.hhs.gov/sites/default/files/cb/im1203.pdf

Children's Bureau. (2012b). *ACYF-CB-IM-12-04: Promoting social and emotional well-being for children and youth receiving child welfare services.* Washington, DC. http://www.acf.hhs.gov/sites/default/files/cb/im1204.pdf

Children's Defense Fund. (2018*). The Family First Prevention Services Act historic reforms to the child welfare system will improve outcomes for vulnerable children.* http://www.childrensdefense.org/library/data/ffpsa-short-summary.pdf

Collins-Camargo, C., Leavey, J., Metzenthin, J., & Torres, E. (2006). *Preparing for Privatization: What Experience Has Taught Us. Transforming Systems of Care: Best Practices for Children and Families.* Marlborough, MA.

Dorch, E. A., Bathman, J., Foster, D., Ingels, L., Lee, C., Miramontes, C., & Youngblood, J. (2010). Social service availability & proximity and the over-representation of minority children in child welfare. *Journal of Health and Human Services Administration*, 33, 277–320.

Eggers, W. D. (1997). "There's no place like home—privatization of Kansas child-welfare." *Policy Review*, May-June.

Framework Workgroup. (2014). A framework to design, test, spread, and sustain effective practice in child welfare. *Children's Bureau, Administration for Children and Families, U.S. Department of Health and Human Services.*

Gatowski, S., Miller, N., Rubin, S., Escher, P., & Maze, C. (2016). *Enhanced Resource Guidelines: Improving Court Practice in Child Abuse and Neglect.* Reno, NV: National Council of Juvenile and Family Court Judges.

Hines, A. M., Lee, P. A., Drabble, L., Lemon, K., Chow, J., Perez, A., & Snowden, L. R. (2003). *An evaluation of factors related to the disproportionate representation of children of color in the child welfare system: Final report.* San Jose, CA: San Jose State University.

James Bell Associates. (2018). Guide to Data-Driven Decision Making: Using Data to Inform Practice and Policy Decisions in Child Welfare Organizations. Washington, DC: Children's Bureau, Administration for Children and Families, U.S. Department of Health and Human Services.

James Bell Associates. (2008). *The Children's Bureau Quality Improvement Centers, 2001–2007.* Washington, DC: James Bell Associates.

Malempati, S. (2013). Beyond paternalism: The role of counsel for children in abuse and neglect proceedings. *UNH Law Review, 11*, 97–128.

McGowan, B. (2014). Historical evolution of child welfare services. In G. P. Mallon & P. M. Hess (Eds.), *Child Welfare for the Twenty-First Century: A Handbook of Practices, Policies and Programs* (pp. 11–43). New York: Columbia University Press.

National Working Group on Foster Care and Education. (2014.) *Fostering success in education: National factsheet on the educational outcomes of children in foster care.* http://www.fostercare-andeducation.org/OurWork/NationalWorkingGroup.aspx

Osterling, K. L., Lee, P. A., & Hines, A. H. (2012). The influence of family reunification services on racial/ethnic disparities in permanency outcomes for children in the child welfare system. *Journal of Public Child Welfare, 6*, 330–354.

Snell, L. (2000). Child welfare reform and the role of privatization. Policy Study No. 271, Reason Public Policy Institute.

Steen, J., & Duran, L. (2013). The impact of foster care privatization on multiple placements. *Children and Youth Services Review* (35), 1503–1509.

Steen, J., & Smith, K. (2011). Foster parent perspectives of privatization policy and the privatized system. *Children and Youth Services Review* (33), 1483–1488.

United States Department of Health and Human Services, Administration for Children and Families, Administration on Children, Youth, and Families, Children's Bureau. (n.d.). *General findings from the Federal Child and Family Services Review.* Washington, DC: http://www.acf.hhs.gov/sites/default/files/cb/summary_of_the_results_of_the_2001_2004_cfsr.pdf

U.S. Department of Education & the U.S. Department of Health and Human Services. (2016). *Non-regulatory guidance: Ensuring educational stability for children in foster care.* https://www2.ed.gov/policy/elsec/leg/essa/edhhsfostercarenonregulatorguide.pdf

Ward, H., Yoon, S., Atkins, J., Morris, P., Oldham, E., & Wathan, K. (2009). *Children at risk in the child welfare system: Collaborations to promote school readiness.* Edward S. Muskie School of Public Service, Catherine E. Cutler Institute for Public Policy, University of Southern Maine.

Figure Credits

Img. 2.1: Copyright © 2018 Depositphotos/AeriealMike.
Img. 2.2: Copyright © 2014 Depositphotos/monkeybusiness.
Img. 2.3: Copyright © 2019 Depositphotos/Valerii_Honcharuk.

CHAPTER • 3

Evidence-Based Practice in Child Welfare

Nathanael J. Okpych and Megan Feely

Introduction

This chapter provides an overview of evidence-based practice in child welfare. The first part of the chapter describes what evidence-based practice is, outlines its historical development, and introduces the two versions of evidence-based practice in use today. The second part of the chapter provides examples of evidence-based programs used in different stages of a family's involvement in the child welfare system. The third part of the chapter discusses challenges, obstacles, and critiques of evidence-based practice in child welfare. The third part also covers the basic aspects of implementation science, which includes tailoring interventions to specific practice settings and populations.

An early emphasis of child welfare services was on intervening with children and families after it was deemed that the child became orphaned, was in danger, or that caregivers were unable to care for a child. Over the years, child welfare has broadened its focus. It is now charged with providing services that prevent child maltreatment from occurring in the first place and improving the well-being of children and families who are, or were previously, involved in the system. Additionally, more attention has been paid to the unique needs of subpopulations of children involved with the child welfare system, such as older youth who will age out of foster care, LGBTQ children, and children in Native tribes, to name a few.

Throughout most of child welfare's history, the practices and interventions used by professionals in the field have been based largely on convention, but it was not known if the customary practice techniques were effective. For example, child welfare investigators in the 1920s were trained to scan the home environment and character of the parent using Mary Richmond's (1917) *Social Diagnosis* method, which was essentially a compendium of practice experience (Myers, 2004). This is in stark contrast to today's investigative process, which is informed by **data-driven decision-making** tools that assist in making a determination about the level of risk for maltreatment. The tide began changing in the 1970s and 1980s as federal laws mandated systematic data collection on child welfare outcomes, and more explicitly in the 2000s with the rise of the evidence-based practice movement (Okpych & Yu, 2014).

Image 3.1

In today's child welfare system, there is a push to incorporate evidence into everyday practice on many levels. Critically reflecting on the effectiveness of practices is important because child welfare departments and workers have an ethical responsibility to the children and families to provide them with the best services possible. With the increasing awareness of the diversity of families served by child welfare, approaching the work from a stance of cultural humility is important for child welfare practice (Ortega & Coulborn Faller, 2011). This approach strives to offset some of the power imbalance between professional and client, positions the worker as learner, and incorporates clients' preferences and cultural values into intervention decisions. Ultimately, embracing a cultural humility approach in "micro" practice strives to counteract larger systems of oppression and privilege. Thus, searching for and using evidence in child welfare practice must be accompanied by a keen attention to culture.

The increasing use of evidence in child welfare practice is visible in recent federal legislation. As discussed in Chapter 1, the Family First Prevention Services Act was signed into law in February 2018 (Campaign for Children, 2018). Beginning in October 2019, states have the option to use Title IV-E funds to pay for **prevention services** and programs for children who are at risk of being placed into foster care, for the child's parents or caregivers, and for youth in foster care who are pregnant or parenting. Mental health, substance use treatment, and in-home parenting training can be provided to families for up to 12 months. However, in order for states to get reimbursed by the federal government, the prevention programs and services that are used must be trauma-informed and must meet a certain level of research evidence (i.e., they must be "promising," "supported," or "well-supported"). This evidence-based requirement reflects an emphasis on providing services that have a certain level of effectiveness and responsible spending of public dollars.

This desire to infuse child welfare work with research-informed practice is codified by the National Association of Social Workers (NASW) Code of Ethics. For individual social workers who work in child welfare, keeping abreast of research evidence, using evidence in practice, and evaluating practice are part of the NASW Code of Ethics (NASW, 2017, p. 27). EBP, or evidence-based practice, is an approach to practice that social work uses to ensure that research is incorporated in decisions about which interventions to use and to evaluate whether the interventions are effective (Barth, 2008). This chapter provides a view of the landscape of what evidence-based practice is, how it evolved, how it is currently being integrated into child welfare services, and some of the practical dilemmas around putting EBP into practice in child welfare.

Part 1: Evidence-Based Practice: What Is It? Where Did It Come From? Why Is It Important?

What Is Evidence-Based Practice?

Over the past 2 decades, **evidence-based practice** (EBP) has become a familiar term among medical and human service providers. Ask any child welfare professional about EBP and one would be hard-pressed to find someone who has not heard of the term. However, if they were asked a slightly different question—what is EBP?—they would likely provide a wide range of answers. The most common description of EBP would probably involve favoring interventions that have been shown to work in research studies over interventions that have not. As will become evident later in the chapter, this is one of the two main ways EBP is conceptualized—preferentially using treatments and practices with strong research support (Rubin & Parrish, 2007). However, there is a second version of EBP that goes beyond simply using research-supported interventions. This version of EBP describes a multistep *process* that social work practitioners utilize to critically investigate research studies, identify interventions that are strongly supported, make a decision with their clients about which interventions to use, and evaluate their interventions as they are implementing them (Rubin & Parrish, 2007). Below is a description of the evolution of the rise of EBP in social work. Having an understanding of the profession's past helps to understand why EBP has come to be such a force in the social work profession today.

History of EBP in Social Work

The EBP movement in social work began in earnest in the early 2000s, but there was a strong push to make social work practice more research-informed much earlier in the profession. For most of social work's history, direct service practitioners have used interventions that were designed from practice experiences and promoted by experts. These were techniques that were taught in schools of social work, used widely in the field, and accepted as good practice (Okpych & Yu, 2014). The problem is that it was not truly known whether the practice techniques that were routinely used were in fact effective for the majority of clients. Did the interventions actually meet their intended goals? Did client outcomes improve as a result of the intervention? Like many medical and human service professions, rigorous evaluation of practice was not common in the early days of social work (Okpych & Yu, 2014).

1960s–1970s

The 1960s and 1970s were a time of change in child welfare. The confluence of a few important events caused social work to take a hard look at assumptions that were made about its standard practices and interventions. Research studies that reviewed the main interventions used in social work revealed that many of the interventions were not effective, and some actually had negative impacts on clients (Briar, 1967; Fischer, 1973, 1976, 1978). For example, Fischer (1973) reviewed several studies of various social casework techniques (e.g., child guidance therapy) used with children and adolescents. All of the studies had a comparison group that received no treatment, and Fischer reported that none of the interventions resulted in positive outcomes favoring the casework group. The news was a jarring discovery for the profession. This occurred during a time when the federal government increased demands for efficiency and accountability. More pressure was put on social work to demonstrate that it was using federal funds responsibly to fund services that were effective. Around this time, there were important advances in computer technology and research methods that made it much more feasible for researchers and practitioners to evaluate their practice, both on a large scale (compiling findings across multiple studies) and on a small scale (individual social workers evaluating their practice with clients).

1970s–1990s

In response to these converging factors, some scholars in the field of social work responded by initiating the empirical clinical practice (ECP) movement in the 1970s (Reid, 1994). ECP is called a "movement" because it had the goal of making some fundamental changes to social work practice, including child welfare practice (Witkin, 1991). There were three main principles. First, the collective knowledge base of the profession would greatly increase by more and more rigorous empirical research, carried out by both researchers and specially trained practitioners. Second, social work practitioners would use empirical research studies to inform which interventions they would choose to use with their clients. Finally, practitioners would evaluate their own work with clients, which would give them ongoing feedback about how effective their interventions were (Okpych & Yu, 2014).

The ECP movement was a watershed moment in the history of social work because it represented an attempt to shift from being a profession that was based on practice wisdom and customs, to a profession that would be fundamentally grounded in evidence (Okpych & Yu, 2014). However, despite its ambitious agenda, the ECP movement floundered in the 1980s and 1990s. Not all schools of social work embraced ECP, and students trained in degree programs that offered ECP rarely used what they learned when they entered the professional world. Moreover, the ECP movement was largely concentrated in universities and colleges, and the social services practice world was largely unfazed and unaltered by the ECP movement (Okpych & Yu, 2014).

1990s–2000s

However, around the time the ECP movement was declining in the 1990s, a distinct movement was gaining attention and support in the medical profession. Like the ECP movement, evidence-based medicine (EBM) grew out of concerns that doctors were too heavily relying on passed-down practice wisdom and underutilizing research evidence to inform decisions about how to treat their patients (Guyatt, 1991; Evidence-Based Medicine Working Group, 1992). Very rapidly, by the early 2000s EBM was translated and adopted by professions such as nursing, education, and criminal justice, as well as social work (Mullen & Streiner, 2004).

2000s–Present

Using EBM as a model, several social work scholars in the late 1990s and early 2000s developed a version of EBM for the profession, which was called EBP (Gambrill 1999; Rosen, Proctor, & Staudt, 1999). When looking at EBP in the historical arch of the profession, this was the second major attempt to convert social work from a profession based on practice wisdom and custom to one that was based on using evidence to inform practice (Okpych & Yu, 2014). Many practical challenges that faced ECP are still at play with EBP, although there is broader support for adopting the use of evidence in guiding practice. Today, the profession stands at the crossroads of using customary interventions and the push to make practice more scientifically grounded in empirical research. As discussed later in the chapter, child welfare has unevenly incorporated and implemented EBP.

Description of the Two Versions of EBP

At its core, the EBP movement espouses the three objectives of the earlier ECP movement: to increase the volume and quality of research evidence; to train social workers to routinely use research evidence to guide their treatment decisions; and to train workers to routinely evaluate their practice with clients (Okpych & Yu, 2014). With these overarching aims in mind, two dominant versions of EBP have come to rise in social work today (Barth, 2008): (1) preferentially using empirically supported interventions; and (2) engaging in the evidence-based process. The main difference between the two versions rests in the extent to which individual social workers are responsible for searching for, selecting, and evaluating interventions versus simply using interventions that have been found to be effective. These two versions of EBP are discussed below.

TABLE 3.1. Clarifying the Two Versions of Evidence-Based Practice

Term	Explanation
Evidence-based practice (EBP)	A broad definition of EBP is engaging in social work practice that is based on the best available scientific evidence (McNeece & Thyer, 2004). However, there are two common versions of EBP that are used in social work: using empirically supported interventions and engaging in the evidence-based process.
Empirically supported intervention (ESI)	One common version of EBP involves preferring to use ESIs over other interventions. ESIs are interventions that have been rigorously evaluated in research studies and have been shown to effectively impact desired outcomes.
Evidence-based process	A second common version of EBP involves engaging in a five-step process when working with clients. The five steps guide social workers through a process of deciding which intervention to use with the client and evaluating the impact that the intervention had on the client.

Using Empirically Supported Interventions

The first version of EBP entails the practice of preferentially using more **empirically supported interventions** (ESIs) over interventions with weaker or nonexistent empirical support. Often, ESI is used interchangeably with EBP (an evidence-based practice), but in this chapter *ESIs* is used to accentuate the distinction between the two versions of EBP. To be classified as empirically supported (aka evidence-based), an intervention must have undergone one or more rigorous evaluations where the intervention was found to have a statistically significant impact on its intended outcome(s). In a research study, a "statistically significant" finding means that the effect was large enough to give confidence that it was unlikely to be a chance finding.[1]

There is a reason for encouraging practitioners to use interventions supported by research instead of interventions with less support or that are untested: using well-supported interventions increases the probability of attaining desired outcomes. While it is impossible to predict whether an intervention will be successful with a specific client, using well-supported interventions with clients will increase success rates overall. For example, if intervention A has a 60% success rate and intervention B has a 45% success

1 A standard threshold for statistical significance is $p<.05$, which means that, if the intervention truly had no impact on the outcome, findings in the study that were this large or larger would occur less than 5 times out of 100. This is quite rare, so when an impact is observed that passes this threshold, one can be reasonably confident that the intervention impacted the outcomes rather than it being a chance finding.

rate, then all things being equal, a child welfare department that uses intervention A is expected to have higher rates of positive outcomes than if they had chosen to use intervention B. To be clear, it does *not* mean that if a social worker uses intervention A with a client, there is a 60% chance of getting a positive outcome. Since the "success rate" is based on outcomes averaged across a *group* of clients, the expected benefit applies to what we expect to see over a *group* of clients (not an individual client).

How do interventions get labeled as "evidence-based," and how much research support must an intervention have before it can be called "evidence-based?" There are different **clearinghouses** that undertake the process of identifying evidence-based interventions. Each clearinghouse has its own set of criteria that are used to rate interventions. Table 3.1 presents the process that one widely used clearinghouse uses to identify ESIs. As its name implies, the California Evidence-Based Clearinghouse for Child Welfare (CEBC) is a repository of interventions that are specifically used with child welfare populations, including some interventions that treat mental health and substance use.

Table 3.2 gives an overview of the steps that the CEBC uses to determine the evidence status of an intervention. The first step involves compiling a list of interventions that could potentially be evaluated. The second step involves **screening** out interventions from the list that do not meet certain criteria. One important criterion is that an intervention must have been evaluated in one or more research studies, and the results of the studies must have been published in a **peer-reviewed journal**. While the peer-review process does not automatically guarantee that a study is of high quality, it does mean that the study was deemed acceptable for publication by multiple experts who reviewed the study. In Step 3, CEBC staff gather all of the peer-reviewed articles that have been published on each intervention. Step 4 involves expert researchers critically evaluating published articles (i.e., the evidence for and against the intervention). Each reviewer rates the intervention based on several criteria, such as how rigorously the intervention was evaluated, whether the intervention was administered as intended, and how large of an impact the intervention had on targeted outcomes. Step 5 involves assigning the intervention a score. Interventions with higher scores have consistently shown to have a positive impact on client outcomes and have been evaluated rigorously (usually by multiple studies with different clients). In evaluating research, *rigorous* means that a strong study design is used, the study was carefully carried out, appropriate statistical methods were used to analyze the data, and the conclusions are supported by the findings. Interventions with scores in the middle range have some support for their effectiveness, but either the studies were not sufficiently rigorous, the impact was small, or there were mixed findings. Interventions in the lowest categories do not have empirical evidence that suggests that they are effective.

TABLE 3.2. Process for Identifying Empirically Supported Interventions Used by the CEBC

Step	Description
1. Identify potential interventions for review	Three ways that interventions are considered for review by CEBC include: CEBC topic experts generate a list of potential programs CEBC staff search for promising interventions Intervention developers or representatives nominate their intervention during an open submission period each year
2. Screen out inadequate interventions	After a list of interventions has been compiled, each intervention is screened. Interventions must have a treatment manual, clear outcomes, and a contact person who can provide detailed information about the intervention. Interventions not meeting these criteria are screened out.
3. Search for results from research studies	For the remaining interventions, CEBC staff conduct a literature review to identify all peer-reviewed published studies that evaluated the intervention.
4. Evaluate the quality of evidence	Once all peer-reviewed published studies have been identified, the quality of the evidence and the support for the intervention's effectiveness are evaluated. Using a standard rating system, the topic expert and two CEBC staff independently review and evaluate the quality of evidence on areas such as: (a) rigor of the research design and analysis; (b) absence of case data of harm suggesting that the risk of harm to clients was severe or frequent; (c) absence of legal or empirical basis to suggest that the intervention constitutes a risk of harm; and (d) the intervention has a practice manual or other kind of writing that describes the intervention components and how to administer them.
5. Rate the intervention's status	Finally, based on the evidence, each intervention is assigned a score: Well-Supported by Research Evidence Supported by Research Evidence Promising Research Evidence Evidence Fails to Demonstrate Effect Concerning Practice NR Not able to be rated

Clearinghouses are very useful resources for identifying promising interventions. In addition to the CEBC, the Pew Charitable Trusts has developed the Results First

Clearinghouse Database. This excellent resource brings together the results of nine social policy clearinghouses. The Results First webpage[2] allows users to browse interventions and see side-by-side scores of how each of the clearinghouses rated the intervention.

Although clearinghouses are useful for identifying ESIs, two caveats are in order. First, research knowledge is constantly evolving; and new studies evaluating interventions are being conducted every year. This means that the status of an intervention can change over time, as more evidence is gathered. One intervention that was previously deemed as effective may be downgraded if new studies find that it is not effective, while other interventions may be upgraded if new evidence emerges supporting their effectiveness. The reality is that what is known about the effectiveness of interventions changes as more and better information accrues, and child welfare professionals need to stay up-to-date. This will help to ensure that clients are receiving the best services based on the best, current knowledge.

A second caveat is that just because an intervention has been found to be successful in a research study does not automatically mean that it will be successful in other contexts. In research studies, the interventions are usually tested on a carefully selected group of clients by professionals who were trained to deliver the intervention as intended. Real-life practice is not always as controlled. Characteristics of clients and the agency may differ from those of the study. Interventions may not be able to be delivered exactly by the book and may be modified. These and other differences mean that the results of the study may not carry over into the practice setting. In research, the issue of whether outcomes in intervention studies hold in real-world practice settings is called **external validity**.

The populations that an intervention was tested with is an especially important aspect of external validity for child welfare professionals to consider. Too often, research studies have been carried out with populations that do not adequately represent the families served by child welfare, particularly in terms of race and ethnicity. Ideally, an intervention would have been tested with people who are similar to the population of clients served by the agency. The difficulty comes when an intervention has not been tested on a similar population. The lack of evidence does *not* mean it will be ineffective. Rather, it means that we just do not yet have clear evidence of effectiveness. The issue of whether an intervention is suitable for a specific client and practice setting leads to the second version of EBP: evidence-based process.

Evidence-Based Process

Compared to the first version of EBP (i.e., preferentially using ESIs), the second version of EBP involves social work practitioners playing a much more hands-on role in searching for evidence, assessing evidence, selecting an intervention, and evaluating the impact of the chosen intervention on clients (Gibbs, 2003; Rubin & Babbie, 2013; Shlonsky & Gibbs, 2004). This is what is called the **evidence-based process** version of EBP (Barth, 2008).

---

2 The Results First webpage is: https://www.pewtrusts.org/en/research-and-analysis/data-visualizations/2015/results-first-clearinghouse-database

The social worker follows a step-by-step process to select and evaluate an intervention that meets a client problem at hand (see Figure 3.1).

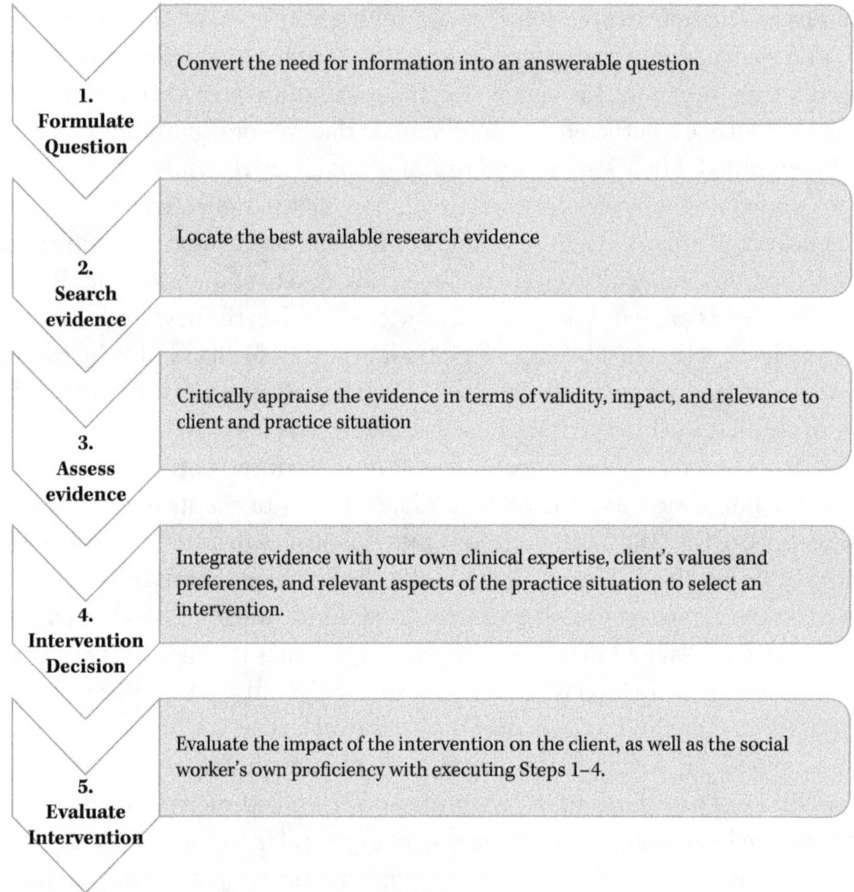

FIGURE 3.1. Five Steps of Evidence-Based Process

The evidence-based process has five steps. Step 1 involves converting a practice need into an answerable question. The question needs to be specific enough to so that the existing research literature can be effectively searched.[3] An example of a specific, searchable question might be, "What are effective interventions that promote family stabilization for school-age children at risk of being placed into foster care?" Identifying which issues become intervention targets should involve both the child welfare worker's judgment as well as the clients' perceptions of problem areas. Empowering the family to take part in identifying the problem (and later the intervention) can reduce some of the power

3 Gambrill (2005) identified seven categories that EBP questions typically fall into: effectiveness, prevention, assessment, description, prediction, harm, and cost-benefit.

imbalance that constitutes the professional-client relationship. It also aligns with a cultural humility approach (Ortega & Coulborn Faller, 2011), whereby workers listen and learn from the family from their cultural frame.

With a clear, specific question, Step 2 entails conducting a search to find relevant research studies on effective interventions. The use of a clearinghouse such as the CEBC are excellent places to start because they gather and synthesize available research. However, clearinghouse reviews of an intervention may be dated. Thus, social workers will likely have to conduct a search of research studies. Box 3.1 at the end of this chapter has useful tips for how to conduct a search.

Once the relevant research studies have been collected, the social worker then assesses the state of the research evidence for an intervention or interventions (Step 3). Similar to above, what is being assessed is whether the intervention had a positive impact on client outcomes, how rigorous the study design was that was used to evaluate the intervention, and the extent to which the intervention, clients, and treatment context in the study are similar to the contexts in which one works. The research study design plays an important part in how strong the evidence is for an intervention. Research studies that used a rigorous design (e.g., an experimental design) provide a more accurate estimate of the impact of the intervention on client outcomes. Different research study designs are often classified in the evidence hierarchy, which is presented in Figure 3.2. The study designs become more rigorous as one moves up the triangle. Table 3.3 has a brief description of each level. It is beyond the scope of this chapter to cover research study designs in depth, so Figure 3.2 and Table 3.3 give students an overview of different study designs. One thing worth

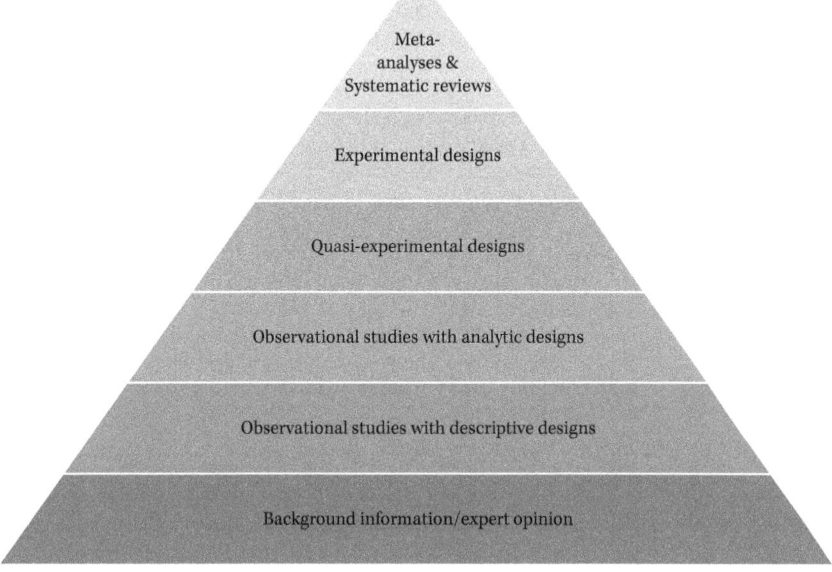

FIGURE 3.2. Hierarchy of Research Evidence

drawing attention to is the top of the pyramid. Systematic reviews and meta-analyses are actually summary studies. When several research studies have been conducted on an intervention, systematic reviews and meta-analyses pull the results together of the studies to reach an overall conclusion about the effectiveness of an intervention. The main difference between the two is that systematic reviews simply summarize the results as a narrative, while meta-analyses mathematically compute an overall effect of the intervention.

TABLE 3.3. Brief Descriptions of Each Level of the Hierarchy of Evidence

Systematic review and meta-analyses	These types of studies combine results from existing evaluation studies of an intervention. Meta-analyses combine results across studies to provide a quantified score of the impact that an intervention has on outcomes, while systematic reviews provide a narrative summary of the results across studies.
Experimental designs	Experiments are rigorous study designs for evaluating the effectiveness of an intervention. These types of studies randomly assign participants to the intervention or a comparison condition (e.g., wait list, treatment as usual).
Quasi-experimental designs	Quasi-experiments are similar to experiments except there is no random assignment. Since participants are not randomly assigned to the intervention or comparison conditions, the groups may be different in ways that affect the outcomes, and differences in the outcome may be mistakenly attributed to the treatment.
Observational studies with analytic designs	Observational studies with analytic designs do not compare an intervention group to a comparison group. Rather, these studies compare changes in the outcomes in a single population over time, before the intervention was received and after the intervention was received (cohort studies). Alternatively, some studies distinguish participants by differences in outcomes and retrospectively determine whether they received the intervention (case-control studies).
Observational studies with descriptive designs	Observational studies with descriptive designs involve collecting data on participants at just one point in time (cross-sectional) or that track individuals who received an intervention over time (case studies). These studies are not appropriate for evaluating the impact of interventions because there is no valid comparison group.
Background information/ expert opinion	Relying on background information or opinions of experts are considered less reliable than other forms of evidence in this hierarchy because the data are anecdotal and were not collected and evaluated systematically.

After the social worker has reviewed the available evidence for viable interventions, intervention options are then brought to the client in **Step 4**. Together, the social worker and the client make a decision about which intervention to use based on what the evidence suggests are the best options, the worker's own clinical judgment about the situation, and the client's preferences and values. Clients may prefer some treatments and be opposed to others. Their opinion is very important both because it aligns with social work's professional value of self-determination (NASW, 2017), and because buy-in from the client will affect their engagement with treatment and likely their outcomes. Ideally, one wants to find an intervention that has a good track record of effectiveness, that adheres to one's clinical judgment and the practice context, and to which the client is amenable. Engaging clients in the dialogue to select an intervention involves skills and knowledge that must be cultivated. In the practice of cultural humility, initially the worker's role is to learn about the relevant experiences and perspectives from each family they work with (Ortega & Coulborn Faller, 2011). Critically, the role of power in the helping process is acknowledged and attempts are made to shift the power dynamic away from a "powerful expert worker" and a "powerless client" to a more balanced relationship. Cultural humility is an important guiding practice principle throughout a worker's engagement with families. In the evidence-based process steps, it is especially salient as a way to understand the initial problem clients are experiencing and converting this to a question (Step 1), to work with the client to select an appropriate treatment (Step 4), and to receive feedback from the client about the intervention and make necessary modifications (Step 5).

The final step in the evidence-based process is evaluation of the intervention once it is implemented (Step 5). One part of this involves evaluating the impact of the intervention on the client in an ongoing manner. This can be done using single-system designs (SSDs), which are research designs used to evaluate interventions with individual clients or client systems. SSDs are commonly taught in social work research classes. Ongoing evaluation is important both to determine if an intervention is not effective and should be modified, and if the intervention has worked at the end of treatment. In some instances, interventions may need to be culturally adapted to better fit clients' language preferences, cultural beliefs, and explanatory models (Cabassa & Baumann, 2013). This may involve adapting the concepts, content, goals, methods, and other aspects of the intervention to improve its relevance, acceptability, and sustainability (Baumann et al., 2015). Some ESIs have adapted versions, but far more work is needed in the area of cultural adaptation (Baumann et al., 2015). Some EBP process proponents also recommend that social workers evaluate their skill and adeptness at conducting the five previous steps. This is important because becoming skilled at executing the five steps takes time and practice.

BOX 3.1: Tips for Conducting a Literature Review

As a first step, see if the intervention of interest has been reviewed by a clearinghouse (e.g., NREPP or CEBC). If it has, examine the conclusions of the review. Be sure to search for studies that were published ***after*** the clearinghouse review was conducted.

Identify keywords that are pertinent to the research question (e.g., trauma-focused CBT). Ask a scholar or a professional familiar with the topic for advice on keywords.

Put keywords in quotation marks when searching for articles. This will yield only studies that use that exact phrase. Doing this will help weed out irrelevant studies.

Begin by searching for studies published in the current year, and work backward from year to year. Use the bibliographies in recently published studies to identify relevant studies that were published earlier.

When a study is found that may be relevant, read the abstract first to determine if it is relevant.

Keep track of the relevant studies that are found. This is particularly important when conducting the literature review at different times and if multiple search tools are used (e.g., Google Scholar, PsychInfo). A references manager program such as RefWorks is very helpful in storing a record of relevant studies.

Part 2: Evidence-Based Programs in Child Welfare Services

This section reviews different types of evidence-based interventions that are found in child welfare. There are many different types of intervention and services that fall under the broad umbrella of "child welfare services." One way to categorize services is to map them on to the stage in which a family is involved in the child welfare system. A simple diagram illustrating the different degrees of involvement is presented in Figure 3.3. The unshaded arrows represent situations in which a child is still at home with family, whereas the shaded arrows represent involvement in which the

Image 3.2

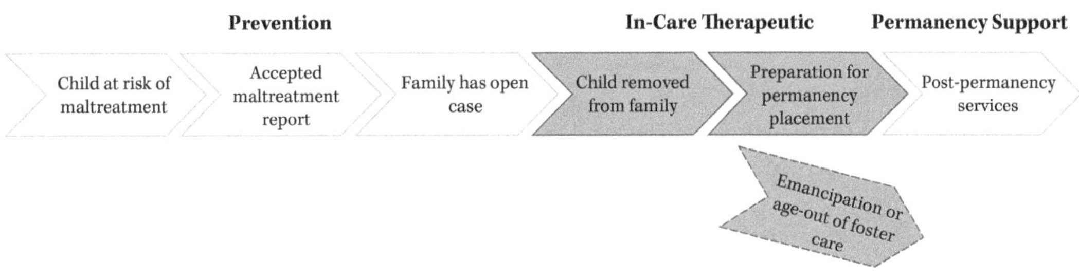

FIGURE 3.3. Stages of Involvement with Child Welfare System

child has been removed from the family and is in foster care. The first three arrows on the left under "Prevention" denote children in families: (1) in which there may be a risk of maltreatment; (2) that have had an accepted maltreatment report; and (3) with an open case but where the child remains in the home. Services provided at these three stages of involvement tend to be preventative and the focus is on addressing issues to reduce the risk of a child being maltreated.

The fourth and fifth arrows fall under "In-care Therapeutic." During this phase, a child has been removed from their home of origin and is in foster care (including kinship care and congregate care). Child welfare services at this stage tend to focus on therapeutic services for children and services for the child's family to help reduce the maltreatment risks so the child can return home (e.g., mental health services, substance use services, housing, and employment support). Services, such as parent training, may be provided to birth and adoptive parents and guardians to prepare for the child.

The arrow to the far right is under "Permanency Support" and denotes a case in which a child has entered a permanent placement and is no longer in foster care. Often, child welfare agencies will provide post-placement services. These services are supportive and offered to increase the likelihood that the placement will endure, preventing reentry into foster care after adoption, guardianship, or reunification. Note the titled arrow with dashed lines at the bottom of the diagram. This denotes exits from foster care for adolescents and young adults who have not been placed in a permanent placement and exit foster care through emancipation or by reaching the state's foster care age limit (typically 18 or 21). A collection of child welfare services exists to equip older foster youth with skills and resources to help with the transition to adult independence.

This broad description of different degrees of child welfare involvement helps to lay out the landscape of services provided to children and families at different points of contact with the child welfare system. Instead of attempting to cover all of the service areas, the remainder of this section focuses on services that are relatively conducive to the process of becoming an ESI, as described in the previous section. These services tend to be mental health or behavioral services, rather than services that help with material needs like housing. The purpose of this section is to give a brief introduction to a few examples of ESIs available for different points of child welfare involvement. In particular, three common points of involvement with the child welfare system will be focused on: (1) prevention services; (2) therapeutic services for children who have been removed from their homes; and (3) services provided to parents in preparation for reunification. For each, the main goals of services are described, followed by an example of an ESI.

Maltreatment Prevention and Family Stabilization Programs

Maltreatment prevention programs are usually directed at families with young children who are at high risk of maltreatment. The primary goal of many of the programs is to prevent maltreatment by improving parenting skills and knowledge. Secondary goals usually include child health and development outcomes. Prevention programs provide a range of types of services including, but not limited to, child development information, non-corporal discipline techniques, positive parent-child interactions, problem-solving skills, and basic household safety. These programs have expanded their reach in recent years, at least partially because specific evidence-based home visiting programs that include a maltreatment prevention outcome can receive federal funding from the Health Resources and Services Administration, Maternal and Child Health Bureau through the Maternal, Infant, and Early Childhood Home Visiting (MIECHV) program. There is likely to be additional funding for prevention services following the passage of the Family First law mentioned at the beginning of the chapter.

BOX 3.2. Example ESI for Maltreatment Prevention: SafeCare

SafeCare, which has the second-highest level of evidence according to the CEBC, is an example of a home-visiting, maltreatment prevention program. It has been used extensively in child welfare settings to prevent initial and recurrent maltreatment (Chaffin, Hecht, Bard, Silovsky, & Beasley, 2012). The program includes parenting skills assessment and training, home safety assessment and training, and basic child health training, such as when to take a child to the doctor. The visits typically last 60–90 minutes, and the full course of sessions is usually 18–20 weeks. SafeCare is one of the few programs that targets neglect in addition to abuse.

Family stabilization programs are more intensive maltreatment prevention programs for families who have already had at least one incident of maltreatment. Many different terms are used for these programs, including intensive in-home, family preservation, and family support (CEBC, 2018). The overarching goals of these programs are to prevent abuse, neglect, and placement into foster care. Family stabilization programs generally combine usual assessment and case planning with intensive case management and other services, such as parent training/support, general knowledge about child development, and mental health services. In some programs, the child welfare worker is the primary service provider (e.g., Ingram, Cash, Oats, Simpson, & Thompson, 2015). The programs aim to reduce conflict within the family, improve child behavior problems, increase the family's capacity to solve problems, improve the physical condition of the home so it is safer, and work with parents to increase positive engagement with their children.

BOX 3.3. Example ESI for Family Stabilization: Homebuilders

Homebuilders has the highest rating for research evidence on the CEBC for a family preservation program. The program has been found to reduce out of home placement rates and increase reunification rates (Fraser, Walton, Lewis, Pecora, & Walton, 1996). The program is intensive, tailored to the individual needs of each family; it focuses on increasing family capacity and working with their strengths, and, depending on the family's needs, may include a wide array of services. Typically, Homebuilders' therapists work with a family three to five times per week for about 2 hours for each visit. There is telephone contact in between visits, and the program usually lasts for 4 to 6 weeks. Because of the intensive nature of the program, therapists usually work with just one or two families at a time (Schweitzer, Pecora, Nelson, Walters, & Blythe, 2015).

Children's Therapeutic Services

Many children who have experienced the trauma associated with maltreatment may also exhibit mental health or behavioral issues (Burns et al., 2004). These issues may include problems like externalizing behavior problems such as oppositional defiant disorder, internalizing problems such as depression, or complex-trauma responses (Cook et al., 2005). Therapeutic services focus on reducing problematic behaviors and symptoms and improving functioning.

BOX 3.4. Example ESI for Children's Therapeutic Services: Treatment Foster Care Oregon–Adolescents

Treatment Foster Care Oregon–Adolescents (TFCO-A), formerly Multidimensional Treatment Foster Care (MTFC), is a comprehensive program for youth with severe emotional or behavioral disorders. It has the highest rating for evidence according to the CEBC. The goals of the program are to reduce and manage youth behavior problems, prevent higher-level placements (e.g., inpatient psychiatric facilities), and to prepare parents or other caretakers with the skills to deal with challenging behaviors.

The programs combine structure and expectations with clear and consistent consequences, mentoring of positive behaviors and life skills, and support and assistance in establishing positive peer relationships. Therapists work directly with youth and foster parents to create and reinforce structured, supportive home environments. There are also TFCO-Children and TFCO-Preschool versions for younger children.

Family Reunification Services

Reunification services tend to be parent-training programs. These programs are some of the most common child welfare services (Barth et al., 2005), and completing a parenting program is often a requirement of a court-ordered reunification plan. In addition to improving parenting, many programs achieve a secondary outcome, such as reducing children's disruptive behavior problems (Horwitz, Chamberlain, Landsverk, & Mullican, 2010). Behavioral parent-training programs have demonstrated stronger results than traditional didactic programs, many of which were ineffective (Barth et al., 2005). Behavioral parent-training programs include a practice element to help parents develop new skills and parenting behaviors. The skills may focus on problem solving common parenting challenges, effective alternatives to corporal punishment, or techniques to engage with children in a positive manner.

In addition to parent training, many parents may have individual issues that need to be addressed, such as their own mental health problems like depression, substance abuse problems, and intimate partner violence. An additional type of service unique to child welfare that may promote reunification is supported or supervised visitation; however, none of the programs reviewed by the CEBC have sufficient scientific evidence to be rated.

BOX 3.5. Example ESI for Family Reunification Services: Triple P

Positive Parenting Program, or Triple P, is a suite of parent training programs to address a range of parenting challenges and is appropriate for children ages 0–16 years old (Sanders, Kirby, Tellegen, & Day, 2014). The CEBC rates the evidence in the second or third level, depending on the specific program. The goals of Triple P are to increase positive parent-child interactions, reduce coercive and punitive discipline, increase parents' knowledge about child development and common behavior problems, and reduce parenting stress. Strengthening parents' ability to identify problems, develop solutions, and set goals for change for themselves and their children are the focuses of Triple P. The program has a practice component, and trained practitioners work with parents to develop more positive patterns of interaction. Triple P can be delivered one-on-one as a home-visiting program or in groups.

The examples provided in this section give a brief overview of some interventions used with child welfare–involved families. To learn more, visit the CEBC website mentioned earlier in the chapter. The extent to which a given child welfare department uses ESIs will vary from state to state, and in some cases, local jurisdiction to local jurisdiction. Next, the barriers that prevent ESIs from being adopted in child welfare are discussed.

Part 3: Challenges and Obstacles to EBP in Child Welfare

Although there has been enthusiasm about how EBP could shape child welfare practice (Barth, 2008), because of philosophical objections and organizational barriers, the uptake of EBP in child welfare has been slow (McCue Horwitz et al., 2014; Wells, Merritt, & Briggs, 2009).

Image 3.3

Several studies have gathered feedback from practitioners, administrators, and other stakeholders in human service agencies about their perceptions of EBP and identified practical barriers to putting EBP into practice (Gray, Joy, Plath, & Webb, 2011). These barriers pertain to the EBP process (i.e., the five-step version). Here are some of the main practical barriers to using the EBP process:

- **Not enough time.** Child welfare workers are usually stretched to capacity and simply do not have time during the workday to search for and assess research studies.
- **Inadequate access to published studies.** Most peer-reviewed journal articles are behind paywalls, limiting child welfare workers from conducting a comprehensive search.
- **Underprepared to assess complex studies.** Some research studies use highly sophisticated research methods that require advanced statistical training to assess. Critically evaluating the validity, reliability, and generalizability of research study findings is also very challenging and requires advanced training, which BSW-level and MSW-level social workers may not have been exposed to.
- **Lack of training and supervision to effectively deliver interventions.** If a child welfare worker identifies an intervention with good research support and that the client is amenable to, training and supervision may not be available for the social worker to effectively deliver the intervention.

These four obstacles noted above most closely pertain to the five-step evidence-based process that is carried out by individual practitioners. However, as described above, in child welfare it is more common to see implementation of the second type of EBP: using ESIs. This involves child welfare departments adopting a service model, program, or practice that meets a certain evidence-based rating (McCue Horwitz et al., 2014; Mildon & Shlonsky, 2011). If the department uses external providers to deliver services, this involves establishing contracts with agencies to provide the services. Social work scholars have found that practical barriers exist with adopting ESIs. Here are a few barriers to implementing ESIs:

- **Inadequate research evidence.** Often, promising practices and interventions have not undergone rigorous evaluation (Barth, 2008). This results in knowledge gaps of which interventions work. Moreover, most research studies use a clinical sample for their study population rather than child welfare–involved children and families. For example, Trauma-Focused Cognitive-Behavioral Therapy (TF-CBT) has a rating of "1–Well-Supported by Research Evidence" on the CEBC's scale and is identified as "High" relevance for child welfare. However, the published studies used to establish this rating used clinical populations of sexually abused children and youth. Some of the children were involved in the child welfare system, but none of the studies focused on the population specifically (e.g., Cohen & Mannarino, 1996; Deblinger, Lippmann, & Steer, 1996). Despite the lack of rigorous testing in a child welfare–involved population, TF-CBT has been used extensively in child welfare settings (Bartlett et al., 2018). There may be overlapping characteristics between individuals in efficacy studies and clients involved with the child welfare system, but a fundamental question about generalizability arises—will positive impacts found in studies of (mostly) children and families who were not involved in child welfare hold for child welfare–involved children and families?
- **Systems-level and organizational-level difficulties with adopting new practices.** When an agency is accustomed to a model of delivering services, it is difficult to shift to adopt a new intervention. This requires close collaboration between researchers and child welfare personnel (administrators, managers, and front-line staff), who often speak different professional jargon and require translation (Palinkas, Saldana, Chou, & Chamberlain, 2017). Implementing a new intervention often means that many aspects of the service delivery system must be altered, which can affect referral processes, reporting requirements, training and supervision, and data collection (Mildon & Shlonsky, 2011). There may be resistance by staff to the changes, especially if the adoption is experienced as something that is imposed on them from the outside (Cunningham & Duffee, 2009).
- **Funding.** Funding for training and sustaining the program is a consistent challenge for agencies, particularly when the child welfare agency is administering the ESI itself (rather than contracting with another agency to deliver services).

ESI trainings are often expensive, and if staff are being pulled off other duties to provide the ESI, then additional staff are needed to cover their original workload.

- **Staff turnover.** Additionally, because of high rates of staff turnover in child welfare agencies, frequent trainings may be needed to ensure that staff can competently deliver the ESI. In addition to costs, sometimes the service delivery and dosing (i.e., how much services are provided) requirements or components of the ESI do not align with the agency. In these cases, it is necessary to carefully modify an ESI so that it better fits with the resource constraints and capacity of the agency and particular needs of the client populations that the agency serves.
- **Many activities done by child welfare workers do not involve delivering interventions.** Many activities, such as assessing risk, making placement recommendations, engaging families, and making appropriate referrals have not been systematized into a specific intervention. The relevance of EBP are less clear for these activities (Barth, 2008). The most common type of child welfare service is case management, but few case management ESIs have been rigorously evaluated. Currently, EBP has more direct application to areas of child welfare practice that involve preventative services and interventions with families and children, some of which were reviewed earlier in this chapter.

Even though adopting evidence-supported services and interventions is more common in child welfare than is individual practitioners engaging in the EBP process, adoption of ESIs still occurs infrequently. For example, McCue Horwitz and colleagues (2014) surveyed 83 public child welfare directors across the United States about their adoption of new interventions. The researchers found that while most had initiated a new program or intervention in the past 5 years (93.9%), only about one in four (24.8%) of the programs could be considered evidence-based.

EBP Critiques from Critical Race Theory

Critical race theory (CRT) has also been used to draw attention to concerns about EBP (Abrams & Moio, 2009). A key tenet relevant to this chapter is that racism is endemic and structural; most research is presumed to be color- and race-blind, with the result being that it is race- or color-ignoring; and the perspectives of people of color are routinely excluded.

One implication of these tenets is that because ESIs are primarily micro-level programs that focus on individual change, they do not address—or even acknowledge—"systemic and institutionalized oppressions" (Abrams & Moio, 2009, p. 247) or move clients to collective action for systems change. Social workers' focus on individual change detracts from systems change and replicates oppressive practices. This tension between focusing on individual and societal change permeates the field of social work (e.g., Abrams & Moio, 2009). When applied to social work practice, CRT calls for an explicit focus on societal change as the solution for the oppressive structural issues of racial inequality, racialization, and racism. Focusing on individual behavior limits the types of changes that can be addressed through ESIs and the type of work that social workers are able to do.

Much of the research used to establish the evidence base for ESIs has not explicitly addressed race. Studies typically do not systematically explore differential impacts by race and ethnicity or address the impact that race and racism has on individuals. This omission may lead to privileging dominant cultural norms and values. One way this can happen is through the outcomes that are chosen and/or the behaviors that are taught and encouraged. To address this deficit, the voices and the perspectives of people of color who are targeted by systemic racism should be explicitly included in all parts of the development and testing of ESIs.

While ESIs may be far from addressing the first issue of prioritizing individual over society change, at least in small ways, future research can address some of the other limitations. First, traditional research studies could take small steps to systematically explore the effects participants' race may have on their experience and outcomes. For example, conducting studies in areas where the population is sufficiently diverse to provide a representative sample of people of color is important. Second, the results of interventions could be compared across race/ethnicities to analyze potential differential effects by race across outcomes. Additionally, mixed methods analyses of client's satisfaction with the intervention could more directly include questions about the participant's race and their perceptions about the appropriateness or fit of the intervention.

A more thorough way to address the lack of race-conscious research is through community-engaged research and community-based participatory research (CBPR). In community-engaged research, the researcher identifies the questions but works with the community to develop the research plan and outcomes. Designing the research methods may include defining new outcomes and ways to measure those outcomes. By moving away from the position of power and expertise that the evaluator often holds, a more egalitarian and collaborative approach to research is facilitated that may include community members' experiences of structural oppression. Additionally, the outcomes in community engagement research are identified by the community, making them more relevant than outcomes prescribed by the research community. In CBPR the community defines the problem, the solution, and the research. A CBPR process could result in the implementation of a structural anti-oppressive change, for instance, to systemic practices of child welfare departments. If that intervention-driven change could be replicated in other areas, it would begin to meet the standards for becoming an ESI.

In summary, CRT offers trenchant critiques of ESIs as they are currently implemented, but some issues can be addressed through more thoughtful research and implementation. The next section turns to implementation science, which is a field of study that identifies effective strategies of incorporating ESIs into usual care while at the same time addressing real-world obstacles.

Implementation Science and ESIs

One may wonder, what are some of the differences in how an ESI could be implemented that affects whether or not it gets adopted? This is precisely the focus of **implementation science**, which is "the use of strategies to introduce or change evidence-based health interventions within specific settings" (NIH, cited in Proctor et al., 2011). It is a systematic approach to changing individual and organizational behavior so that new interventions are adopted the way they were designed. Before getting into specifics, there are a few general principles to keep in mind. Integrating an ESI into the usual services is an ongoing process, not a one-time activity. Programs that are successfully adopted tend to be those that staff see as appropriate for their clients, and sufficient resources exist to support and train staff. Additionally, some level of flexibility with the intervention is often needed to accommodate the complex situations encountered in child welfare settings. Second, learning a new, highly detailed intervention is difficult and takes time. Staff need time for training, learning, and ongoing supervision to learn and grow comfortable with the new ESI. Although this is not always feasible, when ESIs show an immediate impact on client outcomes (even if it is modest), staff tend to be more motivated to put in the effort to accurately implement the ESI.

Implementation science develops systematic approaches to translate an ESI from a manual into a dynamic operating system of care. These techniques apply to staff and administrators at many levels within an organization. The process of implementation begins with the selection of the ESI and continues through maintaining a sustainable intervention. Here are some specific concepts that are central to implementation of ESIs in child welfare settings.

Feasibility: *Can an agency realistically adopt a particular ESI, given the funding, staffing, training levels, and service-delivery models of the agency? This is of particular concern in state agencies that may have limited training budgets and little flexibility to change job requirements.*

Acceptability: *Is the ESI considered satisfactory to stakeholders, such as the families receiving the intervention and the staff delivering it? For example, whether clients feel like an ESI fits with their cultural beliefs and practices is an aspect of acceptability. Reception of the ESI will be better when practitioners and clients feel that their perspectives are valued and heard.*

Appropriateness: *Is the ESI relevant to, and will fit into, a particular setting and population? An intervention may be acceptable to staff and families, but not appropriate to the funding or staffing setting, or to the way services are typically delivered. For example, in child welfare settings, the caseworker may need an ESI that is a discrete and time-limited type of intervention. Longer, more therapeutic interventions may not be appropriate for that agency. An important part of appropriateness involves considerations of families' preferred language and cultural beliefs and practices. For* *example, whenever feasible, it is appropriate to conduct meetings with parents in the language they feel most comfortable with. Some ESI components, such as mixed-gender parent training groups, may be at odds with the cultural norms of some families, and accommodations need to be made so families can be involved in services in a way where their preferences are respected.*

Fidelity: *To what degree is the ESI delivered as it was intended to be delivered? Fidelity is a multidimensional concept that includes caseloads, dose, training, supervision, and in-session adherence to the intervention (Feely, Seay, Lanier, Auslander, & Kohl, 2018). Adherence to the prescribed intervention and dose are the most commonly measured and discussed dimensions. While these are important, the other aspects are often ignored in the adoption process, and they may have a critical impact on the effectiveness of the intervention.*

Dose, training, and supervision are all subcomponents of fidelity. Dose is how much of the intervention has been received by the clients. Completion rates tend to be low in child welfare services (Barth, 2008), which means that families may not receive the full benefit of programs that they started. Training and supervision are also critical aspects of fidelity. High rates of turnover in child welfare agencies may make it difficult to maintain a fully trained staff. ESIs often have mandatory and structured supervision that focuses on the delivery of the intervention. This helps maintain a high quality of delivery but requires additional supervision time from a supervisor.

Outcomes: *Which outcomes will be assessed, how will they be measured, and how often will they be tracked? A key aspect of evidence-based practice is evaluating client change, both with individual families and at the aggregate level across the agency. This often involves additional assessments and record keeping. Building in the time and training to appropriately administer assessments and use the record-keeping system is critical. If families or youth are not achieving the expected or desired outcomes, then the agency needs to be aware of this so that they can adjust the implementation of the ESI.*

Flexibility: *How should the ESI be adapted to the particular characteristics of the clients, service setting, and resource constraints? Many ESIs allow for some flexibility in the delivery, but this flexibility should be identified in collaboration with the model developer. This is particularly important for child welfare–involved families. Agencies need to identify areas where their clients may require some flexibility to be able to benefit from the intervention, such as how family crises are addressed. Cultural adaptations may need to be made to the process and content of the ESIs, for example, by slowing the pace of interventions, building in time to discuss the political context of parenting, reframing the goals of the intervention to match culturally valued goals (Baumann et al., 2015).*

Staff at all levels play an important role in supporting the success of ESIs in child welfare agencies, and a few specific strategies are listed in Table 3.4 for staff in different positions. For a more complete discussion of strategies, readers can see the article written by Powell and colleagues (2015).

TABLE 3.4. Implementation Strategies for Child Welfare Professionals (adapted from concepts in Powell et al., 2015)

Position	Strategies
Administrator	Assess for readiness and identify barriers and facilitators to implementation of the ESI. Include providers and other stakeholders in the selection of an ESI to hear their perspective on the needs of the population and the appropriateness of the intervention.
Manager	Identify champions who are interested in promoting the new ESI. Incentivize the adoption of the ESI. Conduct educational meetings with staff and outside stakeholders who may refer to or in other ways support the ESI.
Frontline—case manager	Work with clients to encourage them and help them problem-solve how to complete the ESI. Be attentive to cultural norms, practical barriers, and language preferences that can interfere with families participating in the ESI. Attend trainings, booster trainings, and other educational meetings to be informed on the available ESIs.
Frontline—service provider	Organize clinician implementation meetings to discuss and problem-solve implementation issues, particularly around the complex issues faced by child welfare–involved families. Become a champion or early adopter to better understand the program and proactively suggest adjustments to better serve children and families.

Training and Maintaining a Workforce in an ESI

ESIs have specific training and support requirements to maintain the quality of the delivery of the intervention, including traveling to a multi-day training, a post-training accreditation process, and/or ongoing supervision. Fortunately, there are more efficient models of training and maintaining a workforce than training staff one by one. One common method is train-the-trainer (TOT), where the developer creates one training for practitioners providing the intervention and an additional training to teach a more experienced practitioner how to deliver the training. This model allows the agency to have local staff to train new staff in the intervention. A more comprehensive model to disseminate and implement an ESI across a number of sites is called the Breakthrough Series Collaborative (BSC). It has been used in wide-scale implementation of ESIs, including in child welfare (Lang, Franks, Epstein, Stover, & Oliver, 2015). The BSC combines several different strategies, including TOT, and usually takes between 6 and 15 months to fully implement. In addition to the training for the in-person interaction with the client, the BSC focuses on organizational change, leadership, and sustainability. The BSC can be a thorough model of implementing a new ESI, but it is time consuming and costly.

Chapter Summary

This chapter focused on a variety of issues, including a brief history of EBP, an introduction to two primary versions of EBP, and a review of how interventions make their way to the short list of being classified as an ESI. Example ESIs for different child welfare service areas were described. In the last two sections, readers were encouraged to think critically about some of the practical barriers of EBP, as well as strategies from implementation science that promote the adoption of ESIs. Since populations served by child welfare is increasingly diverse, the authors encourage readers to take a cultural humility approach to practice, being cognizant of important gaps in the evidence base, and recognizing that ESIs may need adaptation to meaningfully fit with clients' worldview and customs.

We encourage readers to approach ESIs and the EBP process with a mixture of optimism and skepticism. While imperfect, using evidence to inform practice to promote positive outcomes for clients is an important component of practice. Throughout one's career as a social worker, the field will continue to develop new evidence, new interventions, and will gradually improve the services offered to families.

DISCUSSION QUESTIONS

1. Thinking about the history of social work practice, what are the two movements that attempted to make social work more grounded in evidence? What were two common goals of the movements?
2. What is the role of evidence-based clearinghouses? How might you use the clearinghouses in your everyday practice as a child welfare worker?
3. What do you think is the most significant obstacle to using the evidence-based process? If you have worked in social services or if you are currently in a field placement internship, draw on your practice experience.
4. Think about the implementation science concepts that were introduced in this chapter. If you were talking to a child welfare director who was considering adopting an ESI, what are two issues the director should pay attention to? What strategies might the director use to address these issues?

References

Abrams, L. S., & Moio, J. A. (2009). Critical race theory and the cultural competence dilemma in social work education. *Journal of Social Work Education 45*(2), 245–261.

Barth, R. P. (2008). The move to evidence-based practice: How well does it fit child welfare services? *Journal of Public Child Welfare, 2*(2), 145–171.

Barth, R. P., Landsverk, J., Chamberlain, P., Reid, J. B., Rolls, J. A., Hurlburt, M. S., ... Kohl, P. L. (2005). Parent-training programs in child welfare services: Planning for a more evidence-based approach to serving biological parents. *Research on Social Work Practice, 15*(5), 353–371.

Bartlett, J. D., Griffin, J. L., Spinazzola, J., Fraser, J. G., Noroña, C. R., Bodian, R., ... Barto, B. (2018). The impact of a statewide trauma-informed care initiative in child welfare on the well-being of children and youth with complex trauma. *Children and Youth Services Review, 84*, 110–117.

Baumann, A. A., Powell, B. J., Kohl, P. L., Tabak, R. G., Penalba, V., Proctor, E. K., Domenech-Rodriguez, M. M., & Cabassa, L. J. (2015). Cultural adaptation and implementation of evidence-based parent training: A systematic review and critique of guiding evidence. *Children and Youth Services Review 52*, 113–120.

Briar, S. (1967). The current crisis in social casework. In A. M. Pins & the Editorial Committee of the National Conference on Social Welfare (Eds.), *Social Work Practice* (pp.19–33). New York: Columbia University Press.

Burns, B. J., Phillips, S. D., Wagner, H. R., Barth, R. P., Kolko, D. J., Campbell, Y., & Landsverk, J. (2004). Mental health needs and access to mental health services by youths involved with child welfare: A national survey. *Journal of the American Academy of Child and Adolescent Psychiatry, 43*, 960–970.

California Evidence-Based Clearinghouse. (2018). *Family stabilization programs.* http://www.cebc4cw.org/topic/family-stabilization/

Campaign for Children. (2018). *Fact sheet: Family First Prevention Services Act.* https://campaignforchildren.org/resources/fact-sheet/fact-sheet-family-first-prevention-services-act/

Cabassa, L. J., & Baumann, A. A. (2013). A two-way street: Bridging implementation science and cultural adaptations of mental health treatments. *Implementation Science, 8*(1), 90.

Chaffin, M., Hecht, D., Bard, D., Silovsky, J. F., & Beasley, W. H. (2012). A statewide trial of the SafeCare home-based services model with parents in Child Protective Services. *Pediatrics, 129*(3), 509–515.

Cohen, J. A., & Mannarino, A. P. (1996). A treatment outcome study for sexually abused preschool children: Initial findings. *Journal of the American Academy of Child & Adolescent Psychiatry, 35*(1), 42–50.

Cook, A., Spinazzola, J., Ford, J., Lanktree, C., Blaustein, M., Cloitre, M., ... Van der Kolk, B. (2005). Complex trauma in children and adolescents. *Psychiatric Annals 35*(5), 390–398.

Cunningham, S., & Duffee, D. E. (2009). Styles of evidence-based practice in the child welfare system. *Journal of Evidence-Based Social Work, 6*(2), 176–197

Deblinger, E. Lippmann, J., & Steer, R. (1996). Sexually abused children suffering posttraumatic stress symptoms: Initial treatment outcome findings. *Child Maltreatment, 1*(4), 310–321.

Evidence-Based Medicine Working Group. (1992). Evidence-based medicine: A new approach to teaching the practice of medicine. *Journal of the American Medical Association, 268*(17), 2420–2425.

Fischer, J. (1978). Does anything work? *Journal of Social Service Research, 1*(3), 215–243.

Fischer, J. (1976). *Effectiveness of Social Casework.* Springfield, IL: Charles C. Thomas.

Fischer, J. (1973). Is casework effective? A review. *Social Work 18*(1), 5–20.

Feely, M., Seay, K. D., Lanier, P., Auslander, W., & Kohl, P. L. (2018). Measuring fidelity in research studies: A field guide to developing a comprehensive fidelity measurement system. *Child and Adolescent Social Work Journal, 35*(2), 139–152.

Flinders University. (2019). Evidence-based medicine. http://flinders.libguides.com/c.php?g=203799&p=1719021

Fraser, M. W., Walton, E., Lewis, R. E., Pecora, P. J., & Walton, W. K. (1996). An experiment in family reunification: Correlates of outcomes at one-year follow-up. *Children and Youth Services Review, 18*(4/5), 335–361.

Gambrill, E. (2005). *Critical Thinking in Clinical Practice* (2nd ed). Hoboken, NJ: John Wiley & Sons.

Gambrill, E. D. (1999). Evidence-based practice: An alternative to authority-based practice. *Families in Society, 80*(4), 341–350.

Gibbs, L. (2003). *Evidence-Based Practice for the Helping Professions: A Practical Guide with Integrated Multimedia.* Belmont, CA: Brooks/Cole.

Gray, M., Joy, E., Plath, D., & Webb, S. A. (2011). Implementing evidence-based practice: A review of the empirical literature. *Research on Social Work Practice, 23*(2), 157–166.

Guyatt, G. H. (1991). Evidence-based medicine. *American College of Physicians Journal Club, 114*(2), A16.

Horwitz, S. M., Chamberlain, P., Landsverk, J., & Mullican, C. (2010). Improving the mental health of children in child welfare through the implementation of evidence-based parenting interventions. *Administration and Policy in Mental Health and Mental Health Services Research, 37*(1–2), 27–39.

Ingram, S. D., Cash, S. J., Oats, R. G., Simpson, A., & Thompson, R. W. (2015). Development of an evidence-informed in-home family services model for families and children at risk of abuse and neglect. *Child & Family Social Work, 20*(2), 139–148.

Lang, J. M., Franks, R. P., Epstein, C., Stover, C., & Oliver, J. A. (2015). Statewide dissemination of an evidence-based practice using Breakthrough Series Collaboratives. *Children and Youth Services Review, 55*, 201–209.

McCue Horwitz, S., Hurlburt, M. S., Goldhaber-Fiebert, J. D., Palinkas, L. A., Rolls-Reutz, J., Zhang, J., Fisher, E., & Landsverk, J. (2014). Exploration and adoption of evidence-based practice by US child welfare agencies. *Children and Youth Services Review, 39*, 147–152.

McNeece, A., & Thyer, B. A. (2004). Evidence-based practice and social work. *Journal of Evidence-Based Social Work, 1*(1), 7–25.

Mildon, R., & Shlonsky, A. (2011). Bridge over troubled water: Using implementation science to facilitate effective services in child welfare. *Child Abuse & Neglect, 35,* 753–756.

Mullen, E. J., & Streiner, D. L. (2004). The evidence for and against evidence-based practice. *Brief Treatment and Crisis Intervention, 4*(2), 111–121.

Myers, J. B. (2004). *A History of Child Protection in America.* Bloomington, IN: Xlibris.

National Association of Social Workers. (2017). *Code of Ethics.* https://www.socialworkers.org/About/Ethics/Code-of-Ethics/

Okpych, N. J., & Yu, J. L-H. (2014). A historical analysis of evidence-based practice in social work: The unfinished journey toward an empirically grounded profession. *Social Service Review, 88*(1), 3–58.

Ortega, R. M., & Coulborn Faller, K. (2011). Training child welfare workers from an intersectional cultural humility perspective: A paradigm shift. *Child Welfare, 90*(5), 27–49.

Palinkas, L. A., Saldana, L., Chou, C.-P., & Chamberlain, P. (2017). Use of research evidence and implementation of evidence-based practices in youth-serving systems. *Children and Youth Services Review, 83,* 242–247.

Powell, B. J., Waltz, T. J., Chinman, M. J., Damschroder, L. J., Smith, J. L., Matthieu, M. M., Proctor, E. K. & Kirchner, J. E. (2015). A refined compilation of implementation strategies: Results from the Expert Recommendations for Implementing Change (ERIC) project. *Implementation Science, 10*(1), 21.

Proctor, E., Silmere, H., Raghavan, R., Hovmand, P., Aarons, G., Bunger, A., Griffey, R., & Hensley, M. (2011). Outcomes for implementation research: Conceptual distinctions, measurement challenges, and research agenda. *Administration and Policy in Mental Health and Mental Health Service Research, 38*(2), 65–76.

Reid, W. J. (1994). The empirical practice movement. *Social Service Review, 68*(2), 165–184.

Rosen, A., Proctor, E. K., & Staudt, M. S. (1999). Social work research and the quest for effective practice. *Social Work Research, 23*(1), 4–14.

Rubin, A., & Babbie, E. (2013). *Research Methods for Social Work* (8th ed.). Belmont, CA: Brooks/Cole.

Rubin, A., & Parrish, D. (2007). Problematic phrases in the conclusions of published outcome studies: Implications for evidence-based practice. *Research on Social Work Practice 17* (3), 334–347.

Sanders, M. R., Kirby, J. N., Tellegen, C. L., & Day, J. J. (2014). The Triple P-Positive Parenting Program: A systematic review and meta-analysis of a multi-level system of parenting support. *Clinical Psychology Review, 34*(4), 337–357.

Schweitzer, D. D., Pecora, P. J., Nelson, K., Walters, B., & Blythe, B. J. (2015). Building the evidence base for intensive family preservation services. *Journal of Public Child Welfare, 9*(5), 423–443.

Shlonsky, A. & Gibbs, L. (2004). Will the real evidence-based practice please stand up? Teaching the process of evidence-based practice to the helping professions. *Brief Treatment and Crisis Intervention, 4*(2), 137–153.

Wells, S. J., Merritt, L. M., & Briggs, H. E. (2009). Bias, racism, and evidence-based practice: The case for more focused development of the child welfare evidence base. *Children and Youth Services Review 31*(11), 1160–1171.
Witkin, S. (1991). Empirical clinical practice: A critical analysis. *Social Work 36*(2), 158–163.

Figure Credits

CHAPTER • 4

The Child Welfare System and Trauma-Informed Care

Integration of Emerging Traumatology into Child Protection

Annette Jackson and Bruce D. Perry

Introduction

There is no public system more impacted by the consequences of developmental trauma than child welfare. Children, youth, and adults served by the child welfare system experience remarkably high rates of chaos, threat, loss, cultural disconnection, food and housing insecurity, and interpersonal traumatic violence (e.g., domestic violence). Children's entry into the child welfare system is often characterized by their experiences of sexual abuse, physical abuse, emotional abuse, neglect, and attachment disruptions. Transgenerational and historical trauma contribute to the challenges many of these children and families face (Belsky, 1993; Child Welfare Information Gateway, 2015). All of this has been true since the origins of the child welfare system; yet systemic focus on, and understanding of, the impact of trauma has only entered the "collective consciousness" of child welfare in the last decade or so. Reflection on the history of child welfare systems and the emergence of "traumatology" as a fully articulated discipline can help clarify the irony that most child welfare systems are just now becoming committed to "trauma-informed" practices, programs, and policies.

The concept of a child welfare system was created in many countries in response to child-related needs not being met through ordinary means by families or communities. The focus of child welfare has varied over the generations and across different countries depending on which needs each society prioritized at the time. For example, the focus of child welfare policy and systems has at times been on protecting society and the public order from "street urchins" and "youth delinquents"; at other times, it has been on preventing children from being raised by unmarried mothers or from growing up in their Indigenous culture (Human Rights and Equal Opportunity Commission, 1997;

Jaggs, 1986; Kucherenko, 2012; Standing Senate Committee on Social Affairs, Science and Technology, 2018). In other words, the history of child welfare is replete with misdirection and institutionalized racism usually reflecting the dominant culture and values of the time and place.

In contemporary times, it is more commonly recognized that most children have their essential needs met within their family circle, which also buffers pressures and stressors from the outside, however big or small the circle may be. Child welfare, as a part of a broader family welfare construct, recognizes that some families require more support, education, and resources in order to meet their children's needs. Historical and current pressures can impinge on the family's resources and capacity in a time-limited, chaotic, or ongoing way. Nonetheless, child welfare policy and practice continue to be characterized by systemic oppressions such as of race, gender, sexual identity, and disability as it continues to reflect the dominant culture of the times (Ortega & Coulborn Faller, 2011). This is most acutely seen in public child welfare when the degree of family difficulty or other issues are so significant that the government or delegated authority intervenes. Public child welfare seeks to intervene through child protection services to respond and ensure the family receives assistance, so they can keep the child safe or to remove the child from the family and provide short- or long-term care alternatives. This is where concepts of child abuse, child neglect, child protection, out of home care, trauma, and deprivation have specific relevance.

Today, in many Western countries, including the United States, Canada, the United Kingdom, and Australia, responding to children at risk of child abuse and neglect is a multibillion-dollar endeavor (Australian Institute of Health and Welfare, 2019; Fang, Brown, Florence, & Mercy, 2012). Society spends enormous amounts of money aimed to protect children from their own families at the same time as aiming to support and strengthen families.

Even as the focus of child welfare has changed over decades and centuries, the recognition and definition of **trauma** and its common aftermath has undergone a separate fluctuating path. It is relatively recent that child welfare and trauma theory have directly intersected. This chapter explores this intersection with a focus on potential benefits as well as limitations. While trauma theory and its implementation through **trauma-informed** practice has much to offer child welfare, it does not, and cannot, alone make sense of the enormous complexities facing child welfare practitioners and policy makers. What it does offer are important insights into key policy and practice challenges that, alongside other frames of reference, can contribute meaningfully to improved outcomes for children and families and to help protect children from further trauma.

History of Integrating Child Welfare, Child Maltreatment, and Trauma Perspectives

Thirty years ago, it was not uncommon to read about child welfare and out of home care yet see little discussion about the "trauma" related to physical, sexual, and emotional abuse and/or neglect; indeed, these experiences were often simply not mentioned. Similarly, it was not uncommon to read texts or academic papers on child mental health or maltreatment and see minimal acknowledgement that many of these children had been removed from their families and were living in out of home care. Even less was written that such abuse and neglect were likely to be traumatic, as were some of the out of home care experiences. This is, in part, due to the complexities of developmental trauma and a general under-recognition of the impact of trauma across all academic disciplines. Even today, 2020, the history and timing of exposure to developmental trauma are rarely measured or acknowledged in research studies in medicine or mental or social health, despite clear evidence that these factors are major contributors to physical, emotional, social, and cognitive health.

A Brief History of the Concept of Trauma

The history of understanding and explicitly recognizing "trauma" is fraught with ambivalence and confusion. The effects of emotional loss, exposure to violence, and other traumatic experiences have been prominent in literature for thousands of years (see Perry, 2017). Medical science usually only turned its attention to the impact of psychological trauma when faced with the obvious emotional and physical effects of combat. Trauma-related syndromes similar to post-traumatic stress disorder (PTSD) were described as "irritable heart" following the U.S. Civil War (DaCosta, 1871) and "shell shock" following combat in World War I (Myers, 1915).

Despite this relative ambivalence, the origins of modern psychiatry had roots in the study of trauma. Charcot, Freud, Janet, and Cover-Jones all had classic clinical cases involving the effects of trauma (Ellenberger, 1970). This waxing and waning of attention to trauma as a factor in mental health formulation continues. Trauma-specific diagnoses did not enter the *Diagnostic and Statistical Manual of Mental Disorders* (DSM) until 1980. The current DSM (DSM-V) does not adequately capture or describe **complex trauma**- or neglect-related developmental problems such as those often seen with severely maltreated children. These children "accumulate" DSM labels and, when viewed primarily through the conventional medical model lens, will often be given four or five different diagnoses (Gaskill & Perry, 2014). The prognosis using this approach is poor; the effects are often overmedication and fragmented clinical care. The developmental nature of maltreatment confounds the "non-developmental" perspective that dominates modern psychiatry.

Aside from combat exposure, sexual assault has been an area where trauma has historically been intermittently acknowledged. Understanding the trauma of sexual assault for "hysterical" women was very contentious in the 1800s and 1900s. By the 1970s, the Women's Movement gave voice to the impact of rape and domestic violence on women; some, but not much, was mentioned about the impact of sexual abuse or exposure to domestic violence on children (Herman, 1997; Van der Kolk, Weisaeth, & Van der Hart, 1996).

Society has had long-standing difficulties in acknowledging the existence of child sexual abuse. There were some who, while recognizing its existence, argued that sexual abuse was not harmful and could even be beneficial to the child. Sloane and Karpinski (1942) argued that although there were some negative consequences of sexual abuse, the child's unconscious desires for sexual activity led them to become a more or less willing partner, and therefore the experience was less traumatic (Salter, 1995). Rascovsky and Rascovsky (1950) argued that consummation of incestuous fantasies could prevent psychosis for the adult. Bender and Blau (1937), in a review of 16 cases of children aged 6 to 12 years, stated there was little evidence of trauma effects following sexual activity with adults, of which they were often the initiator or at least an active participant. They argued against seeing this as a form of abuse by the adults: "This study seems to indicate that these children undoubtedly do not deserve completely the cloak of innocence with which they have been endowed by moralists, social reformers and legislators" (p. 514). At a child abuse conference in 1979, a social work professor in the United States announced that incest "may be either a positive, healthy experience or, at worst, neutral and dull" (DeMott, 1980 as cited by Salter 1995, p. 165). Fortunately, the field matured. In contrast to this denial of the prevalence or harms of sexual abuse, there have recently been large-scale public inquiries into the existence and harms associated with child sexual abuse, such as in Australia and the United Kingdom (Wright, Swain, & McPhillips, 2017; Murphy, 2013). High-profile court cases and the emergence of the #MeToo movement (Zawada, 2018) are bringing to light the broader reality of sexual assault in the United States and other countries, although with less attention to the heightened powerlessness and silence of children at this time.

Trauma theory has also shed light on aspects of the historical and current experiences facing people from different cultural and religious backgrounds and identities, and the application of trauma theory in this context has contributed to the theory's evolution. The ramifications of invasion, colonization, slavery, massacres, war, genocide, and famine can partially be understood through a

Image 4.1

trauma lens. Even seeking refuge and safety has been traumatic for many (Eyerman, 2001; Jackson, Frederico, Cox, & Black, 2018; Newman, 2016).

Culture applies to everyone. "Human beings construct elaborate and sophisticated cultures, which they teach to children in ways that are marvelous to behold" (Garbarino & Kostelny, 1996, p. 45). Definitions of culture incorporate notions of shared ideas, rules, meanings, and interpretations. Culture shapes how people understand and express pain, hardship, and seek solace, comfort, and recovery. Culture provides the context in which children are born, grow, live, and participate (DeVries, 1996; Gough & Lynch, 2002; Lewis & Ghosh Ippen, 2004). "[Culture] is the backdrop against which all circumstances and events affecting children occur" (Gough & Lynch, 2002, p. 341). It makes sense that to understand trauma, understanding the cultural context is important to not only understand the experience but to also understand healing.

Some cultural groups have undoubtedly experienced a disproportionate amount of historical as well as current exposure to traumatic events, and culture has shaped how these have been experienced and expressed. For example, being disenfranchised and oppressed due to race can form part of an individual and collective identity (Eyerman, 2001). A hallmark of many child welfare service systems is the disproportionate representation of different cultural groups in these systems, such as the comparative over-representation of Hispanic and African American children in the U.S. child welfare system (Detlaff & Fong, 2011). Such disproportionate representation of children from certain cultural backgrounds in child welfare also reflects their disproportionate exposure to trauma.

Child welfare is itself a social and cultural construct that is alien and fear-evoking to many cultures and may induce associations with the oppressive role of government, loss of children, loss of identity, and powerlessness (Victorian Foundation for Survivors of Torture Inc., 1998). Many historical child welfare practices applied to Indigenous communities, such as in the United States, Canada, and Australia, where children were removed from families and communities as a matter of public policy, are now widely recognized as traumatizing and continue to cast a shadow on the current health and well-being of these communities (Bamblett, Blackstock, Black, & Salamone, 2018; Brave Heart, Chase, Elkins, & Altschul, 2011).

Dr. Lenore Terr (1990) was one of the first to bring an overt child developmental focus to trauma. Early in her research, she studied a group of children who had been kidnapped at gunpoint in a school bus in Chowchilla, California. Terr's discussion of trauma relating to children and how this presented in their play and language was groundbreaking. Similar to other aspects of the history of trauma theory, there was an initial lack of acceptance and even derision of her findings (Benedek, 1985). She continued her work and subsequently wrote regarding children who had been traumatized in other ways, such as following abuse.

It was becoming clear that horrible life experiences could scar the minds of children. Many youngsters were living for years with unrecognized traumatic effects." (Terr, 1990, p. 25)

Further confusion regarding trauma-related problems arises from the complex effects of trauma on attachment early in life *and* the traumatic impact of impaired bonding (which provides, for the infant, external stress regulation). This, despite the long-standing and pioneering work of Winnicott, Bowlby, Anna Freud, and others using an attachment "lens" to describe aspects of relational trauma for children. The interplay between neglect and trauma during development can create diverse and heterogeneous emotional, behavioral, social, and cognitive problems. This complexity further challenges the current diagnostic (DSM) and treatment approach of the medical model.

The Neuroscience of Developmental Adversity and "Trauma"

In parallel with this evolution of trauma-related formulations in clinical disciplines was a similar growth in understanding the neuroscience of stress, "traumatic" stress, and

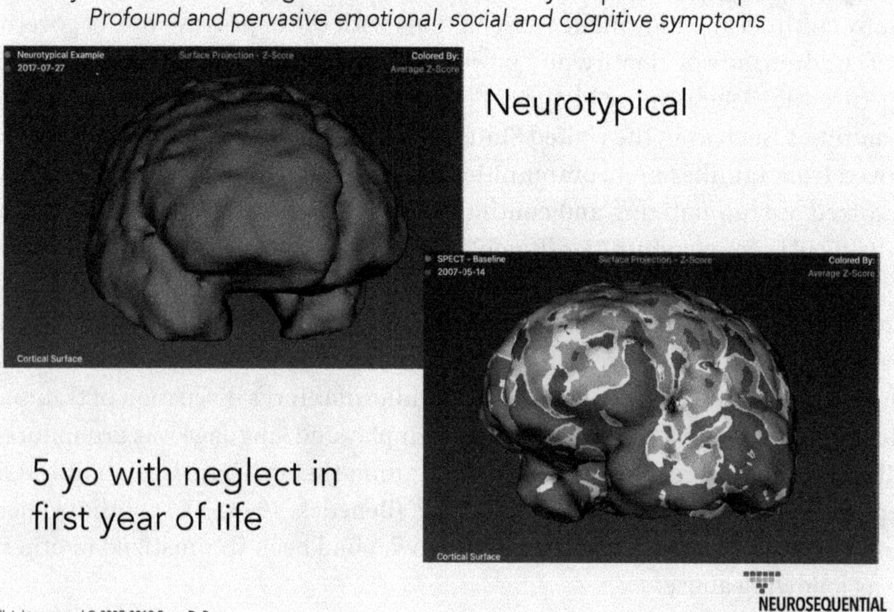

FIGURE 4.1

adversity (for review, see Perry, 2017). In animal models, the complexities of the stress-response systems in the brain and the rest of the body had been studied since Cannon's landmark work (Cannon, 1914). Selye was the first person to borrow the language of engineering and use the term "stress" to describe "the nonspecific response of the body to any demand" (Selye, 1936). By the 1980s, recognition of stress-related neuropsychiatric conditions was advanced by the integration of neuroscience with preclinical psychiatry (Krystal et al., 1989). Similar integration of clinical child psychiatry and the developmental neurosciences led to an awareness of the impact of trauma on brain development and related functioning (Perry, 1994). The **developmental perspective**, informed by neuroscience, has led to child welfare practice and programs that would be considered trauma-informed (e.g., Jackson et al., 2018; Perry, 2019).

Methodological and technical innovations in the neurosciences have allowed more direct examination of the impact of developmental stress, adversity, and trauma on the development and functioning of the human brain. For decades, indirect study of brain-related neurochemicals (such as cortisol, epinephrine, norepinephrine, serotonin, dopamine, and oxytocin) through analysis of saliva, plasma, and urine gave clues about possible trauma-related pathophysiology. Direct examination of the brain using a range of methods including, but not limited to, the electroencephalogram (EEG), Magnetic Resonance Imaging (MRI), and Positron Emission Tomography (PET) scans (Teicher & Samson, 2016) has started to provide more information.

Collectively, these studies demonstrate "psychological" trauma has physiological impacts on key systems in the brain and body, which in turn influence psychological, social, emotional, and behavioral functioning of the individual. A growing number of studies, such as those summarized by Anda and colleagues (2006), Garfinkel and Critchley, 2014, Hull (2002), Teicher and Samson (2016), Twardosz and Lutzker (2010), and Van der Kolk (1996), suggest that stressors and "trauma" are mediated through and can have an effect on multiple neural networks and areas of the brain, including the following:

- Prefrontal cortex (involving the mediation of executive functioning);
- Broca's area (involving the capacity to put words to emotions);
- Amygdala (involving processing emotional content, including fear);
- Hippocampus (involving memory consolidation);
- Hypothalamic-pituitary-adrenal (HPA) axis (involving the regulation of cortisol release and related peripheral responses to stressors);
- Vagus nerve (involving the regulation of multiple organs, including the heart)
- Corpus callosum (involving integration of the two neural hemispheres);
- Cerebellum (involving some motor control, balance, and regulation of both cognitive and emotional input); and
- Locus coeruleus (involving the primary origin of norepinephrine-containing neuronal networks in the brain, which are central elements of the brain's core regulatory networks).

When stress and threat are chronic or unpredictable and overwhelming, it is not surprising that there is often a biological, psychological, and social cost. Considering the multiple areas of the brain enlisted to respond to threat, the range of problems resulting from unrelenting or chaotic threat and stress are equally numerous and can include:

- Hyperarousal and difficulty in controlling or regulating arousal (figh-or-flight response);
- Dissociation;
- Problems with information processing and working memory;
- Problems with attention and concentration;
- Fear response to trauma-related stimuli or that reminds someone of trauma-related stimuli (through senses of sight, smell, sound, taste, touch, body movement, balance);
- Increased startle response;
- Impulsivity;
- Hypervigilance;
- Problems with sleep and appetite;
- High or low (atypical) resting heart rate;
- Problems with relationships with others; and
- Intrusive memories, flashbacks, nightmares. (e.g., Anda et al., 2006; Garfinkel & Critchley, 2014; Teicher & Samson (2016); Twardosz & Lutzker (2010); Perry, 2000; Perry, 2006; Van der Kolk, 1996)

These and other threat-related responses and behaviors help explain what is "underneath" the challenging emotional, social, and cognitive issues seen in many children and youth in the child welfare system. If a 6-year-old child is having a threat response to the violence in the home that is similar to a soldier in combat, then being hypervigilant, having sleep problems, not playing well with others, not paying attention at school, and having behaviors that "come out of nowhere" makes more sense. Further, because these core regulatory networks play a key role in development, these threat-based neurobiological responses can alter their ongoing brain development.

Threat activates the brain's stress-response neurobiology. This activation, in turn, can affect the development of the brain by altering neurogenesis, migration, synaptogenesis, and neurochemical differentiation (Lauder, 1988; McAllister et al., 1999). Indeed, the developing brain is exquisitely sensitive to stress. (Perry, 2001)

Neuroscience has much to teach—as well as much still to learn—about how the human brain develops throughout life—beginning in utero—and the optimal or disastrous environmental contexts that can impact development in childhood. As human development is largely influenced by a combination of genetics and environment and the interaction between these, environment matters (Perry, 2002). The most significant influencers in a child's environment are the people around them. The most significant person for the child in utero is the mother and those adults who impact on the mother's safety, health and well-being. Following birth, the most significant influencers are those who have the roles of nurture, physical care and safety, and skin-to-skin contact. With this in mind, neuroscience offers several principles that inform practice in working with children impacted by abuse and neglect.

The brain changes in a use-dependent way: A child who is regularly exposed to predictable, age-appropriate stimulation and nurturing experiences will develop neurobiological capabilities that anticipate and adapt to grow in that environment. Conversely, a child who is regularly exposed to chaos, absence, or overstimulation, lack of nurture, and/or abusive experiences will develop neurobiological capabilities that anticipate and adapt to survive in that environment. Just because the child is then moved from a threatening or neglecting environment to a caring and safe one does not mean their brain will quickly adjust, especially if their previous experiences were long-standing and began at a young age (Perry, 2006).

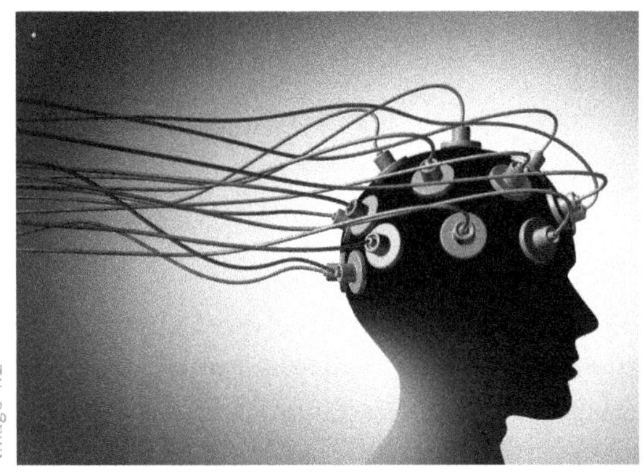
Image 4.2

The brain develops sequentially. Starting with the lowest areas in the brain, the brain develops in utero and later in childhood through to adulthood. These lower areas, such as the brain stem and diencephalon, are largely responsible for regulation of the body, such as heart rate, blood pressure, respiration, sensory processing, and sleep and motor skills. The newborn must be able to breathe on his or her own, and so the part of the brain responsible for mediating that function is usually almost fully developed at birth. This is in contrast to the higher parts of the brain, such as the limbic system and the neocortex, which are largely responsible for emotional and cognitive functions. It is quite a while before a child needs to learn to read and write (mediated by the neocortex), but the building blocks of literacy are language (mediated by the limbic system) and the building blocks for language include sensory processing of information (mediated by the brain stem and diencephalon). This sequential nature of development has implications for recovery from developmental insults such as trauma and neglect. For example, if an infant is subjected to abuse and neglect while the lower parts of their brain are actively developing, these areas are likely to be dysregulated. If the lower parts of the brain are dysregulated, it not only impacts on functions mediated by these areas, but also impacts on the regulation of higher areas of the brain (Perry, 2006).

The brain develops most rapidly early in life: The young child's brain is eminently suited to grow and develop in the early years by being more plastic and experience-dependent. Think about the amazing changes from the embryonic cells to the typical newborn, who can breathe on his or her own and sense touch, sound, light, movement, and smell among many other abilities. Witnessing the changes from the newborn to the toddler are also dramatic and possibly due to the malleability of the brain and its ability to learn from experience. The brain continues to be able to change later in life but nothing like the pace and amount of change possible in this earlier stage of development. This principle highlights not only the vulnerability of the young child when exposed to trauma and neglect, but also the potential power of early-in-life intervention to make a substantive shift in their current well-being and developmental pathway. It also suggests that when working with older children and adolescents, higher doses of intervention may be required (Perry, 2006).

Historical Understanding of Child Maltreatment and Child Welfare

The history of our systems recognizing and acknowledging maltreatment has a similar episodic trajectory. In 1868 and 1878, Tardieu documented evidence of childhood physical and sexual abuse, whereas others, such as Fournier, discounted its existence (Van der Kolk et al., 1996). In many Western countries, the late 1800s and early 1900s saw the building of children's homes and the passing of legislation to remove children from families when there were concerns of neglect and abuse. These concepts remained relatively vague until the invention of the X-ray, which was used to show the extent of damage to a child as a result of physical abuse. In 1944, Caffey (a pediatric radiologist) published findings of subdural hematomas and fractured bones inconsistent with accidental injury. Kempe and colleagues later went on to popularize the phrase "battered child syndrome" to describe the clinical condition of physical abuse, which he attributed to being first coined by Tardieu from a century earlier (Kempe, Silverman, Steele, Droegemueller, & Silver, 1962; Van der Kolk et al., 1996).

Neglect is another story. "Feral" children, who were abandoned to fend for themselves in the wild, and other neglect-related conditions have been described for hundreds of years, yet neglect remains a poorly understood and minimally researched area of maltreatment. In the 19th century, neglect was a major concern in many cities. Legal and social systems were established to protect the neglected child from the slums and to protect society from the neglected child. There was minimal distinction between neglect and poverty and little understanding of the implications for children, other than that they may pose a risk to the public order due to their delinquency (Jaggs, 1986).

In the 20th century, animal research (e.g., Harlow & Harlow, 1966), research on the impact of institutional care (e.g., O'Connor et al., 2000), and research and practice papers on attachment (Winnicott, Winnicott, & Shepherd, 2012; Bowlby, 1951) spoke to the detrimental impact on the child of lengthy exposure to neglect. In the latter part of the 20th century, with its emphasis on supporting families and nonjudgmental practice, neglect has often been relegated to something that should be treated through family support alone. Although there is growing evidence of the range of physical, emotional, and developmental harms associated with neglect for children (e.g., Hildeyard & Wolfe, 2002), there is little written about how to help children recover from such harms. "Child neglect is the most prevalent, but least empirically studied, form of child maltreatment" (De Bellis, 2005, p. 150).

The Rise of "Trauma-Informed" Systems

An interesting aspect from a historical perspective is the almost total absence over many decades of the connection between trauma theory—primarily within the purview of mental health and neurobiology fields and child maltreatment—primarily within the child welfare, legal, and pediatric fields. Although trauma theory's origins focused on adult responses to overwhelming threat, it has more recently provided a means of exploring the potential effects on children of abuse and neglect (Van der Kolk et al., 1996). It has become clear that children can have a profound and enduring neurobiological and socioemotional response to traumatic events, even though the outward signs often present differently to adults, depending upon the nature, timing, and pattern of trauma as well as the current age of the child or youth. Dr. Arthur Green (1967) was one of the first to overtly link the emotional impact of maltreatment with trauma (Putnam, 1997). These observations, however, were focused on understanding individuals. Systemic awareness continued to lag.

Beginning in the 1980s, awareness of the impact of stress, distress, trauma, and various patterns of neglect on development began to percolate into public systems. As the field of traumatology grew, so did efforts to "translate" these findings into improvements in practice, programs, and policy. Changes in therapeutic approach preceded integration of "trauma-aware" practices into systems. One of the first explicit "trauma-informed" efforts focusing on organizations and systems came from Dr. Sandra Bloom and was ultimately framed as the Sanctuary Model (Bloom, 2005). Development of trauma-aware, trauma-informed, trauma-specific, and trauma-responsive practices and programs continues; the field is young but maturing.

Many factors have contributed to the integration of trauma concepts into child welfare; key among them are the creation of the National Center for Child Traumatic Stress (NCCTS), founded in 2001, and a more recent public engagement effort in the last ten years (largely nonprofessional) promoting awareness of the Adverse Childhood Experience (ACE) epidemiological studies originally conducted in the late 1990s (Felitti et al.,

1998). Both of these efforts—NCCTS well funded by the US government and targeting clinicians and clinical systems, and the ACE movement largely a public-engagement and advocacy focus driven by a combination of advocates and professionals—have begun to demonstrably inform the child welfare systems in the last decade (Centers for Disease Control [CDC], n.d.).

With mounting awareness of the prevalence of trauma and its burden on individuals, families, and communities has come the realization that "business as usual" approaches are often insufficient or even in some circumstances contraindicated. There has been a corresponding debate about definition, scope, possible mechanisms of harm, and potential treatment or interventions in response to trauma over many years (Eagle, 2014; Herman, 1997; Van der Kolk, et al., 1996). Among the challenges of creating trauma-aware programs and practice is defining *trauma*. A practical and useful way to "define" trauma was crafted by Substance Abuse and Mental Health Services Administration (SAMHSA) after a multiyear process and is described as the "3 Es":

> *Individual trauma results from an* **event**, *series of events, or set of circumstances that is* **experienced** *by an individual as physically or emotionally harmful or life threatening and that has lasting adverse* **effects** *on the individual's functioning and mental, physical, social, emotional or spiritual well-being. (SAMHSA, 2014, p. 6)*

Even with this clarity, many will refer to the event (e.g., the school shooting) as the trauma; others will refer to the overwhelming emotional response of the individual (experience) witnessing the event as the trauma; while others will refer to the long-term effects (e.g., increased startle response, evocative cues) as the trauma. This lack of clarity and conflation of trauma concepts across the neurosciences, clinical approaches, and systems frameworks continue, as do efforts to define and clarify these concepts.

Trauma-informed frameworks have been developed over the last decade or so to operationalize some of the key elements of understanding trauma for organizations as well as for individual practice. Many trauma-informed frameworks share similar principles following the seminal work by Fallot and Harris (2006). Table 4.1 (updated from Perry & Jackson, 2018) summarizes guiding principles for trauma-informed practice informed by the following frameworks: Adults Surviving Child Abuse (2012); Atkinson (2013); Bloom (2005); Bouverie Centre (2013); Chadwick Trauma-Informed Systems Project (2013); Fallot & Harris (2009); Guarino et al. (2009); Hummer, Dollard, Robst, & Armstrong (2010); Jackson & Waters (2015); Mental Health Coordinating Council (2013); SAMHSA (2014); and Sweeney et al. (2016).

TABLE 4.1. Trauma-Informed Principles

Trauma lens	Trauma is not everywhere, but it can be anywhere. Understanding prevalence, signs, and impacts of trauma, not just focused on at-risk behaviors.
View of person's uniqueness and strength	Acknowledging the person who has experienced trauma is more than a victim. Each is unique in abilities and vulnerabilities, personality, history, and potential.
Safety for all	An emphasis on safety for all, including physical, emotional, social, moral, and cultural safety. This is true for clients, workers, carers, volunteers, and community.
Re-traumatization	Proactive attention to reducing or avoiding re-traumatization. People exposed to trauma are at increased risk of re-exposure. This can be influenced by their adaptations to the initial trauma, placing them in more high-risk situations. However, it can also be due to the way systems respond after a trauma. Overt and covert operational practices and power differentials can exacerbate already precarious client-worker relationships. Sometimes we cannot avoid a potentially re-traumatizing experience such as a medical examination or inpatient treatment. We can work to minimize or eliminate the negative implications of these and other experiences.
Recovery is possible	Acknowledging that recovery is possible and that it looks different from one person to another. Recovery does not equate to the trauma never having occurred or the person not being changed by the experience. We are not born resilient. Resilience is developed in the context of individual growth and relationships. It can be strengthened through exposure to adversity, but only when the person is not isolated in the face of overwhelming threat. Therapy is not the only path to recovery, although it can be vital for some. Recovery signals the importance of hope, fun, joy, and support.
Access to trauma-specific services	Ensuring accessible pathways to trauma-specific services delivered by appropriately trained professionals. Trauma-specific services directly provide therapeutic interventions to help people recover from the impact of trauma.
Attention to culture and community	Being culturally respectful and ensuring we are culturally informed are cornerstones of best practice, with particular resonance when acknowledging community- and cultural-specific trauma. Recognizing cultural ways of healing is pivotal to trauma-informed practice.

Gender respect	Whether or not the service is gender-specific, the service must be gender-appropriate and gender-respectful. This includes acknowledging structural and historical power issues and different ways trauma and healing can be expressed.
Attention to workers	Workers and carers need to be safe and feel safe. This acknowledges the potential for vicarious trauma as well as more direct exposure to trauma and emphasizes the need for self-care and organizational care.
Trustworthiness	Ensuring decisions are transparent and inclusive, with the aim of building trust. This includes not promising the impossible and following through on commitments; and being honest when we don't know something or don't know what to do next.
Relationships	Healing occurs through relationships. Ensuring respect and facilitating connections are key to safe and genuine relationships. This is not just between the worker and client but also involves supporting safe and strong relationships for the person with his or her family and friendships.
Empowerment, choice, and voice	Supporting the person's control, choice, and voice to have or work toward genuine autonomy, self-determination, participation, and respect for human rights. This includes sharing power in a genuinely inclusive way. Even when the client or staff member does not have the final say over an issue, their voice must be heard.
Processes and systems	Building and reviewing transparent and trauma-informed policies, processes, and systems within each organization for clients and staff.
Trauma-informed leadership	A trauma-informed organization needs trauma-informed leadership. This involves ensuring a healthy and transparent organizational culture and processes and a positive, strong, and collaborative leadership approach.

(Perry & Jackson, 2018)

In a similar fashion, the National Child Traumatic Stress Network lists the following elements for a *trauma-informed* organization on their website:

A service system with a trauma-informed perspective is one in which agencies, programs, and service providers:

1. Routinely screen for trauma exposure and related symptoms.
2. Use evidence-based, culturally responsive assessment and treatment for traumatic stress and associated mental health symptoms.

3. Make resources available to children, families, and providers on trauma exposure, its impact, and treatment.
4. Engage in efforts to strengthen the resilience and protective factors of children and families impacted by and vulnerable to trauma.
5. Address parent and caregiver trauma and its impact on the family system.
6. Emphasize continuity of care and collaboration across child-service systems.
7. Maintain an environment of care for staff that addresses, minimizes, and treats secondary traumatic stress, and that increases staff wellness.

These activities are rooted in an understanding that trauma-informed agencies, programs, and service providers:

1. Build meaningful partnerships that create mutuality among children, families, caregivers, and professionals at an individual and organizational level.
2. Address the intersections of trauma with culture, history, race, gender, location, and language, acknowledge the compounding impact of structural inequity, and are responsive to the unique needs of diverse communities. (NCTSN, n.d.)

These are laudable goals for any organization. As anyone embedded in the child welfare system knows, they remain aspirations. And with all the potential benefits of meeting these "trauma-informed" elements, these alone will *not* address fully the complex challenges facing a child welfare system, or the complex needs of the children, youth, and families served by these systems. Arguably, these elements are necessary but insufficient for optimal functioning of a child welfare system. For example, trauma-informed practice and the underlying trauma theory work best when understood in the context of other intersecting theories and perspectives relevant to the child welfare field, several of which are portrayed in Table 4.2.

TABLE 4.2. Cross-Cutting Theories and Perspectives in Child Welfare

Theory/ Perspective	Children in Child Welfare	Examples of Implications for Practice	References
Trauma theory	Many entered this system due to exposure to traumatic events (e.g., physical abuse, sexual abuse, family violence). They often present with time-limited or longstanding biopsychosocial effects. Additional traumatic events may be experienced throughout child welfare involvement.	• Assessment of children and effects of trauma. • Risk assessment to prevent or reduce exposure to trauma. • Recognizing that many of the parents have also been affected by trauma. • Referral for therapy. • (see later in chapter for trauma-informed care)	Chadwick Trauma-Informed Systems, 2013; SAMHSA, 2014

Continues on next page

Theory/ Perspective	Children in Child Welfare	Examples of Implications for Practice	References
Attachment theory	May have insecure attachment reflecting inconsistent, chaotic, or insufficient nurturing care received. At the most severe, they may have a disorganized attachment style due to potential source of comfort being the source of danger and trauma. Abuse and neglect are forms of relational trauma that can disrupt attachment. Those placed in care have had disrupted attachment and need to learn anew what to expect from those entrusted with their care. Children's attachment experience is likely to impact on their capacity to self-regulate.	• Assessment of children, parent-child relationship, and/or caregiver-child relationship. • Risk assessment to prevent or reduce attachment disruption. • Recognizing many of the parents have unresolved attachment style due to their childhood experience and need assistance to meet their children's needs. • Planning how to support sustainable reunification. • Planning for other permanent care options.	Cassidy, 2008; Baim & Morrison, 2011; Main, Kaplan, & Cassidy, 1985; Dozier et al., 2001
Ecological systems perspective	The children are interacting daily with micro-systems such as their family, their placement, and their school. These micro-systems interact and are also influenced by the broader macro-system. This perspective looks at the multidirectional transactions between these environments and systems. This perspective not only focuses on problems but also on potential and actual resources, skills, positive adaptations, and strengths	• Continuous exploration of multiple explanations for abuse and neglect. • Always see children in context of their many relationships. • Hold a strength focus, including what can protect the children and assist recovery as well as risks and harms. • Emphasizes family in the small and large sense whether or not the child is living with them. • Considers past, present, and future. • Is an active agent of change of individual, family, and community systems.	Belsky, 1993; MacKenzie, Kotch, & Li-Ching, 2011; Sidebotham, 2001
Loss and grief	Grief and mourning are healthy normal responses to significant loss and are culturally embedded. Children dealing with separation from family and friends are likely to experience this as loss and associated grief. Unresolved and disenfranchised griefs are risks for children and families in child welfare and may also have intergenerational and community legacies. Loss and trauma can compound each other, and an aspect of loss can be loss of a hoped-for future.	• Recognizing the experience and expression of loss and grief for children and family. • Ensure children have space to mourn and resolve losses. • Avoiding unnecessary placement changes and other potentially avoidable losses. • Recognizing the multiple possible losses and reactions from a cultural and community perspective as well as for individual and family.	Bloom, 2000; Brave Heart et al., 2011; Fearon & Mansell, 2001; Victorian Foundation for Survivors of Torture Inc., 1998.

Continues on next page

Theory/ Perspective	Children in Child Welfare	Examples of Implications for Practice	References
Child Development	Children are not small adults and need to be understood in terms of what is happening for them distinctive to their age and developmental stage. There are several domains, including emotional, cognitive, language, social, moral, and physical development, and these are not always in sync with the child's age, especially when dealing with trauma and deprivation. Each developmental stage represents certain needs of the child and tasks for the child to achieve and requires a supportive ecological and relational context to do so.	• Recognizing that neglect is when the child's essential developmental needs are not met and can have destructive implications. • Assessment and plans based on the child's developmental stage. • Respond in age respectful, but developmentally informed, ways acknowledging not the same. • Consider what the child has missed developmentally and find ways for these gaps to be filled.	Dubowitz, 2009; Perry, 2014; Shonkoff & Phillips, 2000
Human Rights	The United Nations' (UN) *Universal Declaration of Human Rights* (1948) states that children are "entitled to special care and assistance." The UN *Convention on the Rights of the Child* (1989) incorporates the full range of human rights—civil, cultural, economic, political, and social rights. The UN *Guidelines for the Alternative Care of Children* is directly about children involved with child protection and out of home care. Human rights are not just the purview of the UN but are a template for child welfare and trauma-informed practice.	• Children and parents have rights and needs, but the best interests of the child are paramount. • Children's rights include safety, development, love, happiness, spirituality, contact with family, and for timely assessment for reunification and other permanent options for the future. • Paying attention to gender, age, culture, sexual preference, faith, and the myriad of other aspects of identity, belonging, and human rights.	Sweeney et al., 2016; UN, 1948; Office of the UN, 1989; UN, 2009
Cultural Perspective	Culture influences everyone's perspectives, assumptions, and how they understand and express pain, trauma, and seek healing. Child welfare has a bleak history with many Indigenous communities and other cultural minority groups, which continue to be felt and seen in the overrepresentation of children from these groups in current child welfare systems. Child welfare systems and processes are predicated on cultural biases and assumptions.	• The legacy of child welfare with different cultural groups requires a commensurate duty of care to not only cease explicit and implicit racist practices but to work with communities to work toward cultural competence. • There remain power differentials and institutionalized racism that must be recognized in day-to-day practice as well as laws and policies. • To not make assumptions about others' culture and to recognize no one can be an expert in someone else's culture.	Bamblett et al., 2018; Brave Heart et al., 2011; Detlaff & Fong, 2011; DeVries, 1996; Garbarino & Kostelny, 1996; Gough & Lynch, 2002; Lewis & Ghosh Ippen, 2004

Continues on next page

Theory/ Perspective	Children in Child Welfare	Examples of Implications for Practice	References
Complexity Theory	Complex systems are open, multilayered, dynamic and can include emergent, chaotic, and inexplicable as well as simple and predictable behaviors. Children are complex systems, as are families, as is the child welfare and associated systems.	• There can be a tendency to become overwhelmed by complexity or to avoid it through oversimplification. • To not rely on simple linear explanations. • To hold multiple theories, ideas, and be open for new challenging perspectives.	Kurtz & Snowden, 2003; Perry, Jackson, & Waters, 2018

Limitations of Trauma-Informed Practice

With mounting efforts over recent years to incorporate more understanding of the prevalence and impacts of trauma, the value of trauma-informed practice has been recognized in a range of fields, including health, mental health, child protection, out of home care, youth justice, substance abuse, homelessness, disability, education, cultural services, and family violence. In contrast to years of ignorance, avoidance, and denial of trauma and its consequences, trauma-informed practice offers a way of encapsulating key messages for policy and practice. However, as with many new paradigms, it can be exaggerated in importance, misunderstood and misapplied, or reduced to a catchphrase.

If trauma theory is overstated as the only useful construct to make sense of children's development, behaviors, and emotional state in the face of adversity, it is doomed to be ineffective and likely to be rejected. Clearly, childhood, development, and adversity are too complex to be restricted to any one theory or paradigm. To treat trauma-informed practice as the answer to every problem is to relegate it to become the "emperor's new clothes"—reducing it to a fad doomed to failure and derision. For example, for children and families at risk, in addition to and integrated with trauma theory, an ecological perspective along with being developmentally informed, attachment-informed, ensuring human rights, and culturally respectful and a critical race perspective are other important lenses, to name a few.

A trauma perspective does not and cannot describe all adversity. Further, for enthusiastic advocates of "trauma-informed" perspectives to co-opt and insist that all issues be viewed and addressed through a "trauma" lens is oversimplifying and minimizing complex and multidimensional problems (e.g., misogyny, racism, poverty, transgenerational cultural genocide). For example, neglect can have lasting detrimental consequences on a child's developing brain and body and their development, and certainly in many cases include traumatic stress, but this alone cannot address the multidimensional problems related to neglect (e.g., attachment disruption; see Hambrick et al., 2019). A child who has never had someone sit and play with her will probably not present with a traumatic reaction to this absence of experience. However, her development and emotional well-being will be significantly affected by this deprivation of an essential experience. A neurodevelopmental perspective provides a more comprehensive picture beyond trauma theory. Whether or not the adversity is traumatic, trauma-informed principles are of assistance as long as not every experience is reduced to a single phenomenon (Chadwick Trauma-Informed Systems Project, 2013; Perry & Jackson, 2018).

Examples from the authors' practice of the misconstruction and misapplication of trauma-informed practice include: indiscriminate screening of ACEs without adequate training or available therapeutic resources, workers describing trauma-informed to mean "young people do not need limits, routines or boundaries"; staff, caregivers, and the community's physical safety being considered inconsequential compared to the young person's need for support and understanding; if staff and caregivers are encouraged to ask their clients about the details of their trauma experiences; or clients being labeled as traumatized (with a diagnosis of post-traumatic stress disorder) in order to receive a service. Indeed, these are each contrary to genuine trauma-informed practice. Referring back to the principles outlined in Table 4.1 provides a useful means of clarifying whether a particular approach is trauma-informed, keeping in mind that being trauma-informed alone will forever be insufficient to affect meaningful change.

Trauma and Child Welfare in Practice

The picture of a child growing up in a close nurturing relationship with parents connected with their own families and the child's school is less common for children involved in the child welfare system. From an ecological perspective, too many children are torn between multiple and disconnected micro-systems such as parents, stepparents, foster families, and schools, which may frequently change and have few positive transactions with each other. For some children, a peer group or the neighborhood may also act as a micro-system that directly shapes the child's day-to-day experience and exposure to relational health or adversity. These micro-systems are often fragmented and rarely interact with each other in a positive way. As such, the child falls through the cracks.

There are numerous complex policy and practice challenges in child welfare where trauma-informed practice has much to offer, such as:

- Ensuring children's physical and psychological safety when they and their family are primed for danger and risk;
- Protecting children from harm when their own behavior may place them in danger;
- Strengthening children's attachment to a parent who has previously been a source of danger;
- Redressing and reversing the overrepresentation of particular cultural groups in child welfare, shining a light on implicit and explicit racism, and building on culture as a source of resilience;

- Decision-making about potentially competing choices, such as frequency and duration of parent-child contact, placement prevention or removal from parents, reunification or permanent alternatives, whether or not to place the child with siblings, and whether to remove a child from a "good enough" but not optimal placement or prioritize stability;
- Facilitating parent-child contact that does not retraumatize the child or repeat the experience of loss and separation;
- Helping parent/s who have experienced a litany of betrayals and failures to trust workers and succeed in making necessary changes to retain the care or reunite with their children;
- Reducing secondary traumas that may be experienced through court cases, medical assessments, contact visits, placement changes, and other common experiences for children involved in the child protection system;
- Supporting the child dealing with loss and grief following separation from parent/s, caregivers, or both;
- Supporting parents and caregivers dealing with loss and grief following separation from the child;
- Helping a child settle in a new home that is filled with strange and inexplicable sights, sounds, tastes, smells, and touches, where the caregiver does not know about the big or little things in the child's life;
- Supporting children, parents, and caregivers in their interactions with services and the legal system that can feel blaming, impenetrable, and nonresponsive;
- Building a child's history from discontinuous case records, especially if the child has had multiple moves with family and/or in out of home care;
- Empowering children, family, caregivers, and workers with a sense of efficacy in a system where each person may feel disempowered;
- Presenting coherent evidence in court, including being able to explain complex child and adult behaviors;
- Conceptualizing and articulating the mechanisms by which physical, sexual, and emotional abuse and neglect can lead to emotional and behavioral harms for the child; and
- Implementing strategies to reduce the likelihood of further violence from family members, the child or young person, and others.

Image 4.3

Applying a trauma perspective, while not sufficient on its own, can significantly contribute to responding to these and other practice challenges. An informative trauma-informed framework applicable to child welfare was developed as part of the Chadwick Trauma-Informed Systems Project (2013). Following are some more detailed examples of how a trauma-informed perspective can influence practice in a child welfare context.

Clinical Practice and Casework

The bedrock of practice for children in the child welfare system is to ensure their safety. This begins with relationships. If the child does not have access to positive, safe relationships, then other interventions are likely to fail. Whether it is in their parents' care or foster care, kinship care or other forms of care, trauma-informed practice requires vigilance and clarity about privileging safety. However, removing a child from an unsafe situation is not sufficient to ensure future safety.

A common role in child welfare is working with children in out of home care and their families and caregivers. Helping traumatized and confused children settle into a new placement, whether it is the first or the twenty-first placement, is a major challenge and an example where a trauma lens, along with attachment, developmental, and cultural lens, provide an invaluable perspective. What food does she like, what is his favorite TV show, how does she like her hair brushed, what makes her skin crawl, is he a morning or evening person, why is she sitting so close to the TV, why did he jump when the doorbell rang, what helps her go to sleep. The caregivers will often be left to guess these and other questions while quickly trying to learn "who this child is."

Even when the child is old enough to express his or her needs or desires in words, it may not make sense, be consistent from one day to the next, or be possible to fulfill. Often, the child may tell workers outright or give clues along the way. Some answers may be found by talking to parents, grandparents, or older brothers and sisters as well as previous caregivers. Often, it is more important to patiently watch, listen, and learn.

Thinking about what helps a child feel calm and comforted in an unfamiliar and even scary setting guides workers to ask questions from each sense (i.e., sounds, sights, smells, touch, tastes, movement). Limiting the newness and unfamiliarity as much as possible is another important element. This can include finding out what the child is used to, such as shampoo (smell), food (taste, smell, and touch), bedding (touch and weight), books, social media, and television (sights and sounds). Finding out as much as possible about the child's routine before coming to live with new caregivers is of course important, but this is often elusive information if not asked at the time.

When children are first welcomed into a new placement, regardless of what the caregivers say, they may not take much in. This is not about their hearing or cognitive ability but their heightened alert state that will influence them to prioritize information about potential threat. They will watch actions more than listen to the words.

Caregivers will often need to repeat themselves, such as where the bathroom is, leaving on extra lights, and not giving the child too much information too soon. Where possible, it can be helpful to limit what is happening in the first few days, especially as there are some events, such as contact visits with family, and court or medical appointments that may be unavoidable.

Reducing surprises as much as possible is another important consideration. Letting a child know before a transition in incremental steps, such as 15 minutes before bedtime, then 10 minutes, then 5 minutes, talking and doing little things that helps the child adjust to the idea that it's bedtime. Similarly, before going out—even to something they are looking forward to—letting them adjust to the idea of change. Trauma and developmentally informed practice can mean guiding and supporting caregivers in these and related principles.

Many children who come into care feel threatened by closeness as well as fearful of being abandoned. This "relational sensitization" has its roots in inconsistent or even abusive early caregiving (see Perry, Hambrick, & Perry, 2016). This negative or ambivalent relational "template" makes it difficult to know how to respond to the child. Side-by-side activities with them, rather than always being face to face, can help the child become familiar with the caregiver and give him or her control as to when to face them. It's the same principle that often helps children talk more in the car or while an adult is walking beside them, than when they are looking face to face and eye to eye. Adults can play board games, do the dishes, watch television, sit at the dinner table, sit beside their bed, etc.—all side by side. Children usually let people know when they are comfortable with more face-to-face contact.

Assessment

A major implication of a trauma-informed child welfare approach is the need to create and utilize a better assessment process. What is important to measure? How can the assessment help workers understand the child, family, and cultural context in order to provide optimal educational, therapeutic, and enrichment opportunities—for both child and parent? A trauma-aware approach dictates that the nature, timing, pattern of adversity (to the extent possible), and the presence of relational supports in family, community, and culture are documented. These will help identify the strengths and needs of the child coming into care, as well as potential opportunities for "connectedness" that can help the child buffer present stressors and heal from past trauma (Hambrick, Brawner & Perry, 2018).

A common element of child welfare practice is assessing parenting capacity. Many approaches to this make little reference to the implications of trauma and other adversity on parents and parenting, despite most parents of children in or at risk of being in care having experienced trauma. An example of how this could inform parenting capacity assessment is to incorporate understanding the state-dependent nature of functioning. In other words, if a parent is feeling under threat or distress, this is likely to impact on their functioning, and the assessment process would benefit from recognizing this (Jackson

& McConachy, 2014). Many of the parents involved in the child welfare system will have experienced a lifetime of trauma, loss, and grief and feel threatened themselves. Placement prevention and reunification imply hope in the face of threat, loss, and trauma, as such concepts of resilience, attachment, and trauma can directly inform our practice.

Training and Development of Child Welfare Workers

A shift to trauma-informed child welfare practice also dictates the integration of more trauma-aware content and trauma-specific experience during undergraduate and post-graduate education and professional development and training. Many schools of social work and child welfare systems are beginning to provide training in core concepts related to attachment, trauma, and neglect. The quality and depth of these offerings vary tremendously, but it is a start.

Integrating trauma theory along with other core theories discussed in this chapter, such as ecological perspective, cultural perspective, attachment theory, child development, and neurodevelopment provides a bedrock of knowledge and research, as well as being fields where new research, knowledge, and practice will emerge.

As reflected in the trauma-informed principles, the focus of an education and training strategy should not just be on the frontline workforce, nor should it be one-off. It is crucial that foster parents, residential treatment staff, early childhood staff, case management staff, clinical staff, child protection, family support workers, youth justice workers, education, police, health, and allied health are all able to access ongoing training, coaching, supervision, and support. It is an absolute that training, coaching, and support are also in place for leaders of teams and organizations. Leaders need to lead and enable a safe and trauma-informed workplace, recognizing vulnerability and strengths, power and powerlessness. Leaders also need to be aware that they are not immune to pressure, stress, and the impacts of trauma.

> *The importance of self-care for the trauma-informed leader—and her team—becomes obvious. A regulated leader can create a positive, healing and productive organisational climate—a dysregulated leader can literally make people develop stress-related emotional and physical health problems. (Perry & Jackson, 2018, p. 134)*

Leaders in child welfare will often be confronted with events and situations requiring them to advocate, inspire, and show courage through leadership in multiple ways. Trauma-informed leadership also recognizes they need the courage to be vulnerable.

The coevolution of child welfare and traumatology continues. The hope is that with better integration of concepts and continuing evidence-generating practice, both fields will grow and create improved practice, programs and policy—and that will benefit children, families, and our communities.

Case Application

This vignette tells the story of a young woman with a history of trauma and neglect who is now a young mother.

Case Vignette

Senya is a 16-year-old young woman who knows little of her family or her family history. She has been moved from one foster care placement to another and sometimes stayed in shelters. At last count she had lived in over 45 homes since she was 3 years old. Even as young as 4 years of age, she was moved due to being described as difficult and unruly. Sometimes the placement changes were due to caregivers being ill, but mostly they identified they could not warm to Senya and she was untrustworthy. When Senya was 8 years old, she disclosed to a police officer that her foster father had touched her where he shouldn't, but she had kicked him and run away. The foster parents said she was attention seeking and denied any of the allegations. No further action was taken other than moving Senya to a new placement.

Senya last saw her mother when she was 5 years of age and no longer knows where she lives. Her mother's parental rights were terminated around that time, and there was no information about her extended family. Senya has no information about her father except she thinks she was named after his mother. She thinks he is African American or African but does not know for certain. Senya is not sure what culture or race her mother was but believes she was a princess. She remembers her mother's boyfriend as an angry man who yelled and hurt her mother.

The records show that when Senya first came into care at the age of 3, she was barely walking, had little language, and could not swallow or chew food without assistance. She would flinch when the caregivers tried to cuddle her and sometimes lashed out in tantrums that seemed to last for hours. Senya has had almost as many schools as placements and struggled to keep up with the academic work. She was, however, described as canny and cleverer than she looks. She last went to school when she was 13 years old.

For the last 2 years, Senya has spent a lot of time on the streets and has been reported to use methamphetamine, cocaine, and alcohol at times. She has evaded welfare workers and police although occasionally caught shoplifting. She has been couch-surfing with acquaintances and episodically using homeless shelters.

Senya gave birth to a baby son 1 month ago. He was born 6 weeks premature and was placed in intensive care due to withdrawing from substances at birth. It is not known who his father is, although it is believed Senya knows. Senya had not attended any antenatal care. She went into labor at a shopping center and was taken to hospital by ambulance.

Senya says she is determined to keep her son and presents as angry and frightened that the "welfare" will remove him and that he will have a life like hers. She initially refused to name him, in case it made it easier for the authorities to do the legal paperwork to place him in care. She eventually called him Jay after her favorite singer. Senya has moved to live in a transitional housing program with specialized services for substance abuse and dependence. She has said she will do anything to give Jay a better life than hers.

DISCUSSION QUESTIONS

1. When reflecting on the case scenario: What are some of the implications when considering how to best work with her and her son with a trauma-informed developmental perspective?
2. What do the trauma-informed principles look like in practice, and what does it look like when practice or organizations are not trauma-informed?
3. Discuss trauma theory and its cross-cutting with one or more other theories and how this intersection can inform some of the practice dilemmas.
4. What is different now in the child welfare field due to trauma-informed practice? What could be next?
5. What are some of the implications if practice, program, and policy developments are limited to the "trauma lens" alone?
6. Are there differences in the application of trauma-informed practice when working with infants, elementary school-age children, and adolescents? Why is this an important consideration?

References

Adults Surviving Child Abuse [ASCA]. (2012). *Practice guidelines for treatment of complex trauma and trauma informed care and service delivery.* Kirribilli, NSW: Author. http://www.recovery-onpurpose.com/upload/ASCA_Practice%20Guidelines%20for%20the%20Treatment%20of%20Complex%20Trauma.pdf

Anda, R. F., Felitti, V. J., Bremner, J. D., Walker, J. D., Whitfield, C., Perry, B. D., Dube, S. R., & Giles, W. H. (2006). The enduring effects of abuse and related adverse experiences in childhood: A convergence of evidence from neurobiology and epidemiology. *Eur Arch Psychiatry Clin Neurosci, 256*, 174–186.

Atkinson, J. (2013). *Trauma-informed services and trauma-specific care for Indigenous Australian children.* [Resource sheet no. 21 produced for the Closing the Gap Clearinghouse] 18/10/2013; http://www.aihw.gov.au/uploadedFiles/ClosingTheGap/Content/Publications/2013/ctg-rs21.pdf.

Australian Institute of Health and Welfare. (2019). *Child Protection Australia 2017–2018.* Child Welfare Series, Number 70. Canberra: Author. https://www.aihw.gov.au/getmedia/e551a2bc-9149-4625-83c0-7bf1523c3793/aihw-cws-65.pdf.aspx?inline=true

Baim, C., & Morrison, T. (2011). *Attachment-Based Practice with Adults: Understanding Strategies and Promoting Positive Change—A New Practice Model and Interactive Resource for Assessment, Intervention and Supervision.* Brighton: Pavilion Publishing Ltd.

Bamblett, M., Blackstock, C., Black, C., & Salamone, C. (2018). Culturally respectful leadership: Indigenous staff and clients. In M. Frederico, M. Long, & N. Cameron (Eds.), *Child and Family Practice* (pp. 83–99). London: Routledge.

Belsky, J. (1993). Etiology of child maltreatment: A developmental-ecological analysis. *Psychological Bulletin, 114*(3), 413–434.

Bender, L., & Blau, A. (1937). The reaction of children to sexual relations with adults. *American Journal of Orthopsychiatry, 7*(4), 500–518.

Benedek, E. P. (1985). Children and psychic trauma: A brief review of contemporary thinking. In S. Eth & R. S. Pynoos (Eds.), *Post-Traumatic Stress Disorder in Children* (pp. 1–16). Washington, DC: American Psychiatric Press.

Bloom, S. L. (2005). *The Sanctuary Model of organizational change for children's residential treatment.* http://www.sanctuaryweb.com/PDFs_new/Bloom%20TC%20Sanctuary%20Model%20Organization%20Development.pdf

Bloom, S. L. (2000). Creating Sanctuary: Healing from systemic abuses of power. *Therapeutic Communities: The International Journal for Therapeutic and Supportive Organizations, 21*(2), 67–101.

The Bouverie Centre. (2013). *Guidelines for Trauma-Informed Family Sensitive Practice in Adult Health Services.* Brunswick, Victoria: La Trobe University.

Bowlby, J. (1951). *Maternal care and mental health: A report prepared on behalf of the World Health Organization as a contribution to the United Nations programme for the welfare of homeless children.* Geneva: WHO.

Brave Heart, M. Y. H., Chase, J., Elkins, J., & Altschul, D. B. (2011). Historical trauma among Indigenous peoples of the Americas: Concepts, research, and clinical considerations. *Journal of Psychoactive Drugs, 43*(4), 282–290.

Cannon, W. B. (1914). The emergency function of the adrenal medulla in pain and the major emotions. *American Journal of Physiology, 3*, 356–372.

Cassidy, J. (2008). The nature of the child's ties. In J. Cassidy & P. R. Shaver (Eds.), *Handbook of Attachment: Theory, Research, and Clinical Applications* (pp. 2–22). New York: Guilford Press.

Chadwick Trauma-Informed Systems Project. (2013). *Guidelines for Applying a Trauma Lens to a Child Welfare Practice Model.* San Diego, CA: Chadwick Center for Children and Families.

Centers for Disease Control and Prevention. (n.d.). https://www.cdc.gov/violenceprevention/childabuseandneglect/acestudy/

Child Welfare Information Gateway. (2015). Developing a trauma-informed child welfare system. Washington, DC: U.S. Department of Health and Human Services, Children's Bureau.

DaCosta, J. M. (1871). On irritable heart: A clinical study of a form of functional cardiac disorder and its consequences. *American Journal of Medical Science, 61*, 17–52.

De Bellis, M. D. (2005). The psychobiology of neglect. *Child Maltreatment, 10*, 15–172.

Detlaff, A. J., & Fong, R. (2011). Conducting culturally competent evaluations of child welfare programs and practices. *Child Welfare, 90*(2), 49–68.

DeVries, M. W. (1996). Trauma in cultural perspective. In B. A. van der Kolk, A. C. McFarlane, & L. Weisaeth (Eds.), *Traumatic Stress* (pp. 398–413). New York: Guilford Press.

Dozier, M., Stovall, K. C., Albus, K. E., & Bates, B. (2001). Attachment for infants in foster care. The role of caregiver state of mind. *Child Development, 72*, 1467–1477.

Dubowitz, H. (2009). Tackling child neglect: A role for pediatricians. *Pediatric Clinics of North America, 56*, 363–378.

Eagle, G. (2014). From evolution to discourse: Key conceptual debates in the history and study of traumatic stress. *Psychology in Society, 47*, 1–20.

Ellenberger, H. (1970). *The discovery of the unconscious: The history and evolution of dynamic psychiatry.* New York: Basic Books.

Eyerman, R. (2001). *Cultural Trauma: Slavery and the Formation of African American Identity.* Cambridge: Cambridge University Press.

Fallot, R. D., & Harris, M. (2009). *Creating Cultures of Trauma-Informed Care (CCTIC): A Self-Assessment and Planning Protocol.* Washington, DC: Community Connections.

Fallot, R. D., & Harris, M. (2006). *Trauma-Informed Services: A Self-Assessment and Planning Protocol.* Washington, DC: Community Connections.

Fang, X., Brown, D. S., Florence, C. S., & Mercy, J. A. (2012). The economic burden of child maltreatment in the United States and implications for prevention. *Child Abuse & Neglect, 36*, 156–165. doi: 10.1016/j.chiabu.2011.10.006

Fearon, P. R. M., & Mansell, W. (2001). Cognitive perspectives on unresolved loss: Insights from the study of PTSD. *Bulletin of the Menninger Clinic, 65*(3), Summer, 380–396.

Felitti, V. J., Anda, R. F., Nordenberg, D., Williamson, D. F., Spitz, A. M., Edwards, V., ... Marks, J. S. (1998). Relationship of childhood abuse and household dysfunction to many of the leading causes of death in adults: The adverse childhood experiences (ACE) study. *American Journal of Preventive Medicine, 14*, 245–258.

Garbarino, J., & Kostelny, K. (1996). What do we need to know to understand children in war and community violence? In R. Apfel & B. Simons (Eds.), *Minefields in Their Hearts* (pp. 33–51). New Haven, CT: Yale University Press.

Garfinkel, S. N., & Critchley, H. D. (2014). Neural correlates of fear: Insights from neuroimaging. *Neuroscience and Neuroeconomics*, 3, 111–125.

Gaskill, R. L., & Perry, B. D. (2014). The neurobiological power of play using the Neurosequential Model of Therapeutics to guide play in the healing process. In C. A. Malchiodi & D. A. Crenshaw (Eds.), *Creative Arts and Play Therapy for Attachment Problems* (pp. 178–194). New York: Guilford Press.

Gough, D., & Lynch, M. A. (2002). Culture and child protection. *Child Abuse Review, 11*, 341–344.

Green, A. H. (1967). Self-mutilation in schizophrenic children. *Archives Gen Psychiatry, 17*, 234–244.

Guarino, K., Soares, P., Konnath, K., Clervil, R., & Bassuk, E. (2009). *Trauma-informed organizational toolkit*. Rockville, MD: National Center on Family Homelessness.

Hambrick, E., Brawner, T., & Perry, B. D. (2018). Examining developmental adversity and connectedness in child welfare-involved children. *Children Australia, 43*(2), 105–115. doi: 10.1017/cha.2018.21

Hambrick, E. P., Brawner, T., Perry, B. D., Brandt, K., Hofeister, C., & Collins, J. (2019). Beyond the ACE Score: Examining relationships between timing of developmental adversity, relational health and developmental outcomes in children. *Archives of Psychiatric Nursing, 33*(3), 238–247. doi: 10.1016/j.apnu.2018.11.001

Harlow, H. F., & Harlow, M. K. (1966). Social deprivation in monkeys. *Scientific American, 207*, 136–146.

Herman, J. (1997). *Trauma and recovery: The Aftermath of Violence—From Domestic Abuse to Political Terror.* New York: Basic Books.

Hildeyard, K. L., & Wolfe, D. A. (2002). Child neglect: Developmental issues and outcomes. *Child Abuse & Neglect, 26*, 679–695.

Hull, A. M. (2002). Neuroimaging finds in Post-Traumatic Stress Disorder. *British Journal of Psychiatry, 181*, 102–110.

Human Rights and Equal Opportunity Commission [HREOC]. (1997). Bringing them home: Report of the National Inquiry into the Separation of Aboriginal and Torres Strait Islander Children from Their Families. Canberra, ACT: Author.

Hummer, V. L., Dollard, N., Robst, J., & Armstrong, M. I. (2010). Innovations in implementation of trauma-informed care practices in youth residential treatment: A curriculum for organizational change. *Child Welfare, 89*(2), 79–95.

Jackson, A., Frederico, M., Cox, A., & Black, C. (2018). The treatment of trauma: The Neurosequential Model and "Take Two." In B. Huppertz (Ed.), *Approaches to Psychic Trauma: Theory and Practice* (pp. 423–456). London: Rowman & Littlefield.

Jackson, A. L., & McConachy, J. E. (2014). Neither here nor there—Revisiting reunification. Melbourne, Victoria: Berry Street Childhood Institute.

Jackson, A. L., & Waters, S. E. (2015). Taking time: A trauma-informed framework for supporting people with intellectual disability. Richmond, Victoria: Berry Street.

Jaggs, D. (1986). *Neglected and criminal: Foundations of child welfare legislation in Victoria.* Bundoora, Victoria: Phillip Institute of Technology.

Kempe, C. H., Silverman, F. N., Steele, B. F., Droegemueller, W., & Silver, H. K. (1962). The battered-child syndrome. *JAMA, 181*(July), 17–24.

Krystal, J. H., Kosten, T., Perry, B. D., Southwick, S. M., Mason, J., & Giller, E. L. (1989). Neurobiological aspects of post-traumatic stress disorder: Review of clinical and preclinical studies. *Behavior Therapy, 20,* 177–198.

Kucherenko, O. (2012). Without a family: Public order, social welfare and street children in the wartime Soviet Union. *Australian Journal of Politics and History*, 421–436.

Kurtz, C. F., & Snowden, D. J. (2003). The new dynamics of strategy: Sense-making in a complex and complicated world. *E-business Management, 42*(3).

Lewis, M. L., & Ghosh Ippen, C. (2004). Rainbows of tears, souls full of hope: Cultural issues related to young children and trauma. In J. D. Osofsky, (Ed.), *Young Children and Trauma: Intervention and Treatment* (pp. 11–46). New York: Guilford Press.

Main, M., Kaplan, K., & Cassidy, J. (1985). Security in infancy, childhood and adulthood. A move to the level of representation. In I. Bretherton & E. Waters (Eds.), *Growing Points of Attachment Theory and Research* (pp. 66–104). Monographs of the Society for Research in Child Development, 50.

MacKenzie, M. J., Kotch, J. B., & Li Ching, L. (2011). Toward a cumulative ecological risk model for the etiology of child maltreatment. *Children and Youth Services Review, 33,* 1638–1647.

Mental Health Coordinating Council [MHCC]. (2013). *Trauma-informed care and practice: Towards a cultural shift in policy reform across mental health and human services in Australia: A national strategic direction, position paper and recommendations of the National Trauma-Informed Care and Practice Advisory Working Group.* Authors: Bateman, J., Henderson, C., & Kezelman, C., NSW, Australia.

Murphy, Y. (2013). Institutional child sexual abuse: The Irish experience [online]. *Judicial Officers Bulletin, 25*(4), 29–33.

Myers, C. S. (1915). A contribution to the study of shell shock. *The Lancet, 185*(4772), 316–320.

National Child Traumatic Stress Network [NCTSN]. (n.d.). https://www.nctsn.org

Newman, L. (2016). Asylum seekers and refugees—How should psychiatry respond? *Australian Psychiatry, 24*(1), 5–7.

O'Connor, T. G., Rutter, M., Beckett, C., Keaveney, L., Kreppnew, J. M., & the English and Romanian Adoptees Study Team. (2000). The effects of global severe privation on cognitive competence: Extension and longitudinal follow-up. *Child Development, 71,* 376–390.

Office of the United Nations High Commissioner for Human Rights. (1989). *Convention on the Rights of the Child.*

Ortega, R., & Coulborn Faller, K. (2011). Training child welfare workers from an intersectional cultural humility perspective: A paradigm shift. *Child Welfare, 90*(5), 27–49.

Perry, B. D. (2019). The Neurosequential Model: A developmentally-sensitive, neuroscience-informed approach to clinical problem solving. In J. Mitchell, J. Tucci, & E. Tronick (Eds.), *The Handbook of Therapeutic Child Care: Evidence-Informed Approaches to Working with Traumatized Children in Foster, Relative and Adoptive Care* (pp. 135–153). London: Jessica Kingsley.

Perry, B. D. (2017). Trauma- and stress-related disorders. In T. P. Beauchaine & S. P. Hinshaw (Eds.), *Textbook of Child and Adolescent Psychopathology: 3rd Ed.* (pp. 683–705). New York: Wiley.

Perry, B. D. (2014). *Creative interventions with traumatized children.* New York: Guilford Publications.

Perry, B. D. (2006). The Neurosequential Model of Therapeutics: Applying principles of neurodevelopment to clinical work with maltreated and traumatized children. In N. Boyd Webb (Ed.), *Working with Traumatized Youth in Child Welfare* (pp. 27–52). New York: Guildford Press.

Perry, B. D. (2002). Childhood experience and the expression of genetic potential: What childhood neglect tells us about nature and nurture. *Brain and Mind, 3,* 79–100.

Perry, B. D. (2001). The neurodevelopmental impact of violence in childhood. In D. Schetky & E.P. Benedek (Eds.). *Textbook of child and adolescent forensic psychiatry* (pp. 221-238). Washington, DC: American Psychiatric Press, Inc. https://www.childtrauma.org/violence-public-health

Perry, B. D. (2000). The neuroarcheology of childhood maltreatment: The neurodevelopmental costs of adverse childhood events. *The Cost of Child Maltreatment: Who Pays? We All Do* (B. Geffner, Ed.). Haworth Press.

Perry, B. D. (1994). Neurobiological sequelae of childhood trauma: Post traumatic stress disorders in children. In M. Murburg (Ed.), *Catecholamine Function in Post Traumatic Stress Disorder: Emerging Concepts* (pp. 253–276). Washington, DC: American Psychiatric Press.

Perry, B. D., Hambrick, E., & Perry, R. D. (2016). A neurodevelopmental perspective and clinical challenges: In R. Fong & R. McRoy (Eds.), *Transracial and Intercountry Adoptions: Culturally Sensitive Guidance for Professionals* (pp. 126–153). New York: Columbia University Press.

Perry, B. D., & Jackson, A. L. (2018). Trauma-informed leadership. In M. Frederico, M. Long, and N. Cameron (Eds.), *Child and Family Practice* (pp. 125–141). London: Routledge.

Perry, B. D., Jackson, A. L., & Waters, S. (2018). Leadership in direct practice. In M. Frederico, M. Long, & N. Cameron (Eds.), *Child and Family Practice* (pp. 71–82). London: Routledge.

Putnam, F. W. (1997). *Dissociation in Children and Adolescents: A Developmental Perspective.* New York: Guilford Press.

Rascovsky, M., & Rascovsky, A. (1950). On consummated incest. *The International Journal of Psycho-Analysis, 31,* 42–47.

Salter, A. C. (1995). *Transforming Trauma: A Guide to Understanding and Treating Adult Survivors of Child Sexual Abuse.* London: Sage Publications.

Selye, H. (1936). A syndrome produced by diverse nocuous agents. *Nature, 138* (July), 2.

Shonkoff, J. P., & Phillips, D. A. (Eds.) (2000). *From Neurons to Neighborhoods: The Science of Early Childhood Development.* Washington, DC: National Academy Press.

Sidebotham, P. (2001). An ecological approach to child abuse: A creative use of scientific models in research and practice. *Child Abuse Review, 10,* 97–112.

Sloane. P., & Karpinsky, E. (1942). Effects of incest on the participants. *American Journal of Orthopsychiatry, 12*, 666–673.

Standing Senate Committee on Social Affairs, Science and Technology. (2018). The shame is ours: Forced adoptions of the babies of unmarried mothers in post-war Canada. Ottawa, Canada: Senate.

Substance Abuse and Mental Health Services Administration [SAMHSA]. (2014). *SAMHSA's Concept of Trauma and Guidance for a Trauma-Informed Approach.* Rockville, MD: Author.

Sweeney, A., Clement, S., Filson, B., & Kennedy, A. (2016). Trauma-informed mental healthcare in the UK: What is it and how can we further its development? *Mental Health Review Journal, 21*(3) 174–192.

Teicher, M. H., & Samson, J. A. (2016). Annual research review: Enduring neurobiological effects of childhood abuse and neglect. *Journal of Child Psychology and Psychiatry 57*(3), 241–266.

Terr, L. C. (1990). *Too scared to cry: How Trauma Affects Children and Ultimately Us All.* New York: Basic Books.

Twardosz, S., & Lutzker, J. R. (2010). Child maltreatment and the developing brain: A review of neuroscience perspectives. *Aggression and Violent Behavior, 15*, 59–68.

United Nations. (1948). *Universal Declaration of Human Rights.*

United Nations. (2009). Guidelines for the alternative care of children, 64/142.

Van der Kolk, B. A., Weisaeth, L., & Van der Hart, O. (1996). History of trauma in psychiatry. In B. A. van der Kolk, A. C. McFarlane, & L. Weisaeth (Eds.), *Traumatic Stress: The Effects of Overwhelming Experience on Mind, Body, and Society* (pp. 47–74). New York: Guilford Press.

Victorian Foundation for Survivors of Torture Inc. (1998). *Rebuilding Shattered Lives.* Parkville: Author.

Winnicott, D. W., Winnicott, C., & Shepherd, R. (2012). *Deprivation and Delinquency.* New York: Routledge.

Wright, K., Swain, S., & McPhillips, K. (2017). The Australian Royal Commission into Institutional Responses to Child Sexual Abuse. *Child Abuse & Neglect, 74*, 1–9.

Zawada, B. (2018). Me Too: The EEOC, workplace sexual harassment, and the modern workplace. *Wisconsin Journal of Law, Gender & Society, 33*(2), 199–121.

Figure Credits

Img. 4.1: Copyright © 2015 Depositphotos/ambrozinio.

Fig. 4.1: Copyright © by CereMetrix/Neurosequential Network/Bruce D. Perry. Reprinted with permission.

Img. 4.2: Copyright © 2017 Depositphotos/lightsource.

Img. 4.3: Copyright © 2016 Depositphotos/photographee.eu.

CHAPTER • 5

Multidimensional Engagement of Families in Child Welfare

Jennifer Bellamy, Michele D. Hanna, Jon D. Phillips, and Rachel Speer

Introduction

Family engagement is a significant challenge for the child welfare system. In order to serve families and optimally achieve the goals of safety, permanency, and child well-being, families must be successfully engaged in the process. The term **multidimensional engagement** is used because engaging families in child welfare is a complex and evolving process that requires the consideration of many dimensions of practice. As illustrated in Figure 5.1, the five dimensions used to describe family engagement in this chapter include: 1) Family Inclusive Practice; 2) Cultural and Linguistic Responsiveness; 3) Delivery Across the Continuum of Child Welfare Services; 4) Developmentally Appropriate Approaches;

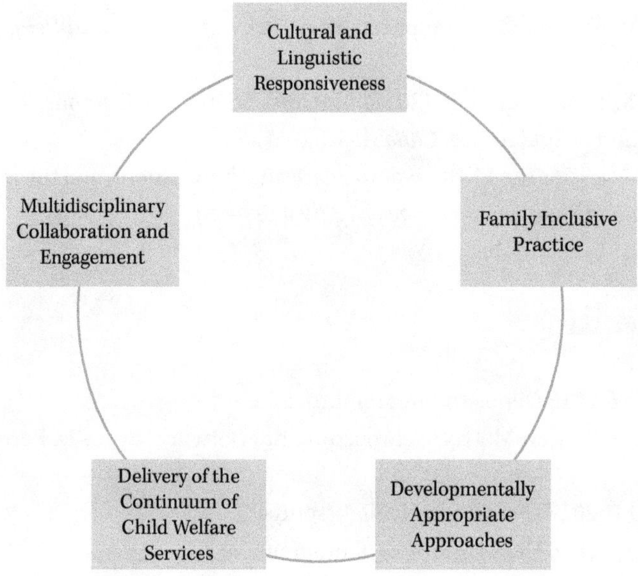

FIGURE 5.1. Multidimensional Engagement

and 5) Multidisciplinary Collaboration and Engagement. Multidimensional engagement is at the intersection of these dimensions, and each is essential to support families' participation in and benefit from child welfare services. This chapter will explore the concept of multidimensional engagement in child welfare by defining engagement broadly and describing each of these five dimensions and providing examples of their application.

Defining Engagement

Before describing each of the five dimensions of engagement, it is important to consider what is meant by *engagement*. Engagement of families in child welfare services may first bring to mind the idea of participation. Families participate in a great variety of types of child welfare services, such as assessments, hearings, court-ordered services, phone calls with caseworkers, home visits, and other activities that are asked or required of them over the course of their involvement with the system. Their participation in these services reflects the mechanisms through which families' needs are identified; progress toward case goals is tracked; needed services and supports are provided; and families' continued involvement, or exit from the child welfare system, is determined.

Engagement is more complicated than participation alone. For example, families may show up for a service, but if they are just "going through the motions" (Yatchmenoff, 2005), these services are not likely to be effective. It is also important to note here that engagement is a two-way street. Families are not solely responsible for their engagement in services, but rather successful engagement is the collaboration between caseworkers and families.

Staudt (2007) developed a model of family engagement with caregivers of at-risk children that includes two major components of engagement. The first component includes behaviors such as attendance at meetings, hearings, or services, as well as follow-through on related tasks like finding safe housing, following through with referrals, or other activities related to case goals. The second component is more attitudinal in nature. This attitudinal component includes the emotional investment in, or commitment to, engaging in services.

There are many factors that can impact both behavioral and attitudinal types of engagement in services. For example, many child welfare–involved families must engage in a variety of services simultaneously. A parent may need to complete parenting classes, substance abuse treatment, and a batterer's program by court order. Each of these services may be delivered by three different agencies, at three different locations, with three different appointment-making processes and three different intake processes. Practical barriers such as lack of transportation, limited available time given work or school schedules, and child care may all make it hard for a parent to participate in the behavior (service participation) that is required. The mandate to participate in these services and tolerate all the practical challenges related just to getting to each one, especially if they do not see the value or need for the service, can also impact a parent's attitudinal engagement.

Family-Inclusive Practice

The term **family-inclusive practice** is used to describe the need for child welfare workers to fully engage families in their many diverse forms and work with all family members who have parenting responsibilities for children. The landscape of U.S. families is no longer dominated by two married biological parents (Bramlett & Blumberg, 2007); and children's living arrangements reflect this diversity. Declines in marriage and increases in nonmarital childbirths have more commonly led to complex parenting arrangements. The majority of children in the United States do not live with two biologically related married parents (Kreider & Ellis, 2011). A mother and father may have a child together and then later re-partner and blend their families with new partners and new children. Blended families are on the rise in Western societies in general; in the United States, 40% of adults have a family member who is not biologically related to them (Kumar, 2017; Zeleznikow & Zeleznikow, 2015). In other cases, children are raised in multigenerational families where grandparents—or even great-grand parents—play an important caregiver role in the life of a child (Ellis & Simmons, 2014). Same-sex partners, single parents, transgender parents, adoptive parents, and a great many other parent identities and family constellations represent the diverse family structures of the United States. Somewhere between 2 million and 3.7 million children under the age of 18 are estimated to have a parent who identifies as lesbian, gay, bisexual, or transgender (Gates, 2015).

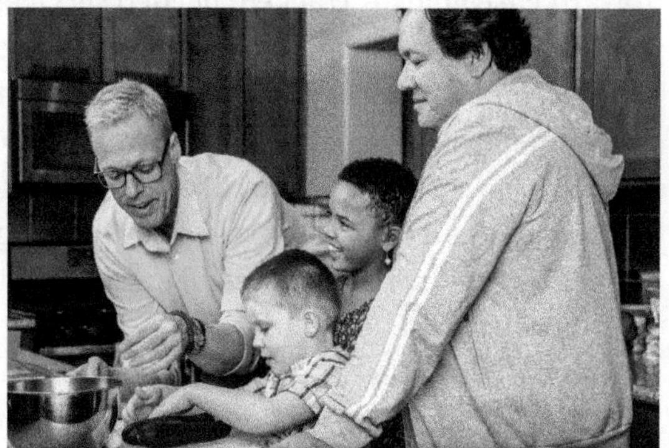

Image 5.1

These demographic trends are often reflected, or even amplified, in child welfare–served populations (Sonenstein, Malm, & Billing, 2002). For example, children in the child welfare system disproportionately come from low-income families (Zilberstein, 2016), and low-income parents are more likely to be unmarried (e.g., Carlson, McLanahan, & England, 2004). Diverse constellations of parenting arrangements in families forged through marriage and other romantic partnerships, biological relationships, legal, or household membership might present distinct challenges related to the successful engagement of families in services. For example, a child might primarily live with a biological mother and her boyfriend and his maternal grandmother but have regular visits with a biological father and his wife. All five adults may play important, but varied, roles in a child's life. Child welfare workers will have to think carefully about how to engage this family and navigate complex parenting arrangements. Each parent in this scenario may have varying levels of relationship with the other parents, and the child's relationship

Image 5.2

with each one is unique. Furthermore, each parent may have a different legal standing in a child welfare case, which may or may not align well with the parenting role played in the family. For example, the maternal grandmother may have primary direct caregiving responsibilities, even though the biological mother and father have legal shared custody. The number and type of diverse family constellations are too great to explore in detail here; however, fathers and **multigenerational parenting** are used in this chapter to illustrate some of the important barriers to, and strategies for, engaging in family-inclusive practice.

Fathers

Mothers are most often engaged in child welfare services (Baum, 2017). Although fathers are increasingly taking on direct caregiving roles in U.S. families today (Jones & Mosher, 2013), mothers more commonly have these parenting responsibilities. As a result, many child welfare policies and procedures were designed with mothers in mind. Recent research findings suggest that fathers are often perceived by workers as less important than mothers, often relatively uninvolved, or even dangerous to families (Bellamy, 2009). However, the majority of child welfare–involved families do have an active father or adult male playing a fathering role involved (Bellamy, 2009). While some men do confer risks to families, these fathers, just like mothers who bring risks to the table, are in need of services and supports.

Father engagement is generally positive for child outcomes (Flouri, 2005). Recent studies indicate that in child welfare cases where fathers have been identified, children experience fewer days of foster care and increased potential for reunification with parents (Burrus, Green, Worcel, Finigan, & Furrer, 2012). Studies on father engagement with children in the child welfare system have found positive effects on child well-being. The successful engagement of fathers in child welfare services may positively affect the externalizing behaviors of children (Leon, Bai, & Fuller, 2016); their cognitive and academic development (Leon et al., 2016); and familial support, including child support, and frequency of visitation (Amato & Gilbreth, 1999; Greene & Moore, 2000; Leon et al., 2016).

There are many barriers to engaging fathers in child welfare cases, especially when fathers are not present at the time of the investigation. Some of these barriers are at the family level. For example, single mothers may be reluctant to name the father, especially when he has not been actively involved in the child's life up to that point. In some families, there is also the possibility that the mother may be fearful of the father, due to a history of violence in the relationship. Many studies have highlighted the overlap between interpersonal violence and child maltreatment. Rates vary, but data from national surveys of families in contact with child welfare indicate that approximately 25–29% of female caregivers report experiencing domestic violence in the past year (Casanueva, Smith, Ringeisen, Dolan, & Tueller, 2014).

Other barriers to engagement of fathers may include caseworker factors. Given that many caseworkers in child welfare are women, some may feel less comfortable and confident about working with men. Prior studies have described their discomfort with, or lack of knowledge of how to work with, men as parents (Baum, 2017). Similarly, fathers may also be less comfortable or trusting of professionals than mothers, making their engagement further challenging (Brown et al., 2009). Other factors that can diminish father engagement are structural in nature. Some data collection tools and systems in child welfare jurisdictions do not allow workers to easily record information about both parents; few child welfare authorities train workers on the importance of working with fathers or strategies for successfully doing so. Working with both parents adds some additional complexity and demands on workers, and if workers feel already burdened by heavy caseloads, they may feel they do not have the time or resources to effectively work with both parents, particularly when they are not coresidential.

While caseworkers may inquire initially about the father's location, they may not actively pursue locating a father when the mother reports that he has not been involved or, in some cases, that he may be unknown or deceased. Active attempts to locate the father or verify information reported by the mother may not be made until prompted by case progression toward a **termination of parental rights** after attempts to reunify with the mother have failed. While focusing on working with the mother, caseworkers will unfortunately miss the opportunity to gather relevant information needed to meet the child's needs, as well as explore viable kinship placement resources and important paternal family connections for the child. Kinship placements are those in which a child is placed with a relative or close family friend. Fathers and paternal relatives can offer an expanded collection of resources and placement opportunities than mothers and maternal relatives alone.

As states and child welfare agencies prioritize kinship, family connections, and permanency for children in care, initiatives to engage fathers as well as their extended family members are increasingly becoming a priority, and improved father engagement is often a targeted outcome for a state's Child and Family Service Review (CFSR) Program Improvement Plans (PIPs). The CFSRs are administered by the Children's Bureau and are used by the federal and state government to identify each state agency's strengths and needed improvements in outcomes of services provided, as well as systematic factors that relate to those outcomes. The federal and state agencies also work together on the PIP that specifies goals and measures toward addressing needed improvements—such as improved father engagement.

Multigenerational Parenting

In many families, multiple adults in different generations share parenting responsibilities. The most recent United States Census indicates that approximately 10% of grandparents live with grandchildren; 2.7 million grandparents are raising their grandchildren; and one-third of grandparents living with grandchildren have two parents in the household as well (Ellis & Simmons, 2014). Recent trends suggest that this pattern of multigenerational households is increasing.

Globally, grandparents commonly play a parenting role for children across communities and cultures (Burnette, Sun, & Sun, 2013; Uhlenberg & Cheuk, 2010). For some families, including many immigrant communities, multigenerational parenting is culturally normative. For example, Chinese American immigrant families may prefer parenting assistance from grandparents due to the important cultural contributions grandparents make to the family through the teaching of language and cultural norms (Chen & Lewis, 2017). The multiple demands of work and school, as well as the high cost of child care, may mean that grandparents are the adults most often providing direct care to children. Some families use multigenerational parenting because multiple families are sharing housing and child care and U.S. adults are living longer on average. Adolescent parents, who are at relatively greater risk for child maltreatment (Lounds, Borkowski, & Whitman, 2006; Putnam-Hornstein, Cederbaum, King, Eastman, & Trickett, 2015), and are often still living at home and going to school, frequently share parenting responsibilities with their own parents. Grandparents often step in to care for children when parents are unable to do so.

Just as it is problematic to focus services on mothers and not address the needs of fathers, it is problematic not to include other adults playing a parenting role who may also need to be supported. A variety of barriers reduce the engagement of extended family in services. Parents may not freely disclose to child welfare workers contact information for grandparents due to estrangement or out of shame or fear of parents' response to the circumstances that led to child welfare involvement. In some cases, there may be multigenerational abuse or neglect preventing grandparent involvement. When grandparents do become involved, cases can become more complex, particularly if they are not in agreement with the goal of reunification between the parent and the children. In addition, some grandparents may struggle navigating the complexity of their ongoing parental relationship with the responsibility of protecting the grandchild. This can become particularly difficult in cases where visitation must be supervised or limited. Kinship families have been found to have more challenges with parenting children with special needs and navigating birth family relationships and visitation than non-kinship families (Christenson & McMurtry, 2007). Overall, research has found that while kinship families may receive some tangible support and training, it is often less than that received by non-kinship families (Cuddeback, 2004). See Chapter 12 for more information on kinship families in child welfare.

Developmentally Appropriate Approaches for Children's Service Delivery

While the primary focus of child welfare is the safety, permanency, and well-being of the child, child welfare caseworkers spend the majority of their time engaging with biological parents, kinship or foster parents, service providers, and the courts. Depending on the stage of the case, caseworkers' engagement with the child varies. Across the course of a case, workers should, as much as possible, engage children and youth in decision-making and case planning, taking into account the child's developmental age and stage (CWIG, 2017). This involves having a strong understanding of a child's physical, emotional, neurobiological, and cognitive development. Regardless of the phase of the case, caseworkers need to be aware of the child's ongoing development and recognize the long-term effects of maltreatment and trauma on child development (see Chapter 4).

The first opportunity to engage with the children involved in a case is at the point of investigation or removal. Caseworkers during this stage are usually focused on gathering factual information needed to determine the most appropriate intervention. Caseworkers are required to observe the child and, if the child is verbal, to interview the child regarding the allegations. Physical abuse allegations most often require a physical examination of the child for evidence of injury. Depending on the age of the child and the location of the injuries, this can be a very awkward and uncomfortable interaction for both the worker and the child. The worker's task is to quickly build rapport with the child so that the child feels both safe and comfortable. Gender is an important consideration, particularly if the worker is of a different gender from the child and the alleged injuries are under clothing.

In cases of alleged sexual abuse, this initial contact can be even more complex. Most jurisdictions offer specialized training for workers who investigate sexual abuse (e.g., Sherrid, 2010). This is necessary for several reasons, including, but not limited to, the need to be sensitive to the child in an effort to not further traumatize the child. Also, many times, sexual abuse cases involve criminal charges and the worker's interview with the child often becomes part of the evidentiary process. Investigating child sexual abuse most often involves collaboration with medical professionals as well as law enforcement. Ongoing cases may require coordination with relatives, foster parents, therapists, victim advocates, and other professionals to best meet the needs of the child, who may be called to testify in criminal proceedings.

Throughout a child's foster care stay, caseworkers' and other professionals' engagement with the child is dependent on several variables, such as the age of the child, extent of trauma the child has experienced, the number of placements the child has experienced, the current placement, the child's mental, emotional, and physical health, the child's developmental stage, and the child's ongoing contact with the birth family, including parents and siblings. Child welfare caseworkers are required to see children on their caseload at minimum once a month (Stoltzfus, 2011). This mandate can be challenging in larger agencies where caseloads include more children then there are workdays in the month and children are placed great distances from one another or from the office, making it geographically and physically difficult for one worker to see all the children on their caseload during the calendar month. As a result, many agencies hire lower-level caseworkers or case aides whose sole responsibility is to visit the child in the foster home.

The Child and Family Services Improvement Act of 2006 (P.L. 109-288) not only provides funding to states to support monthly caseworker visits but also addresses the content of the visits. While the primary intent of visits is to assess and ensure child safety, visits should also be an opportunity to build relationships with the child, youth, and family as well as assess progress on the case plan. See Figure 5.2 for guidance on worker visits with a child in foster care.

Planning	☐ Schedule visits in accordance with state or agency requirements. If possible, schedule the next visit prior to ending the current visit. ☐ Schedule ample time for visit being mindful of travel time. Allow for additional time between appointments in case visits so as not to be rushed. ☐ Visit the child where they currently reside (foster home, kinship home, group home, etc.) at a time that is convenient for both the child and the caregiver. ☐ Plan for individual private time with the child and the caregiver. ☐ Have goals established for the visits that align with the case plan. ☐ Have an agenda that includes identified issues that need discussing or exploration as well as status updates on actions necessary to support children and families in meeting case plan goals.
During Visit	☐ Be open and responsive to child and/or caregiver's need for meaningful consultation. ☐ Observe and explore changes in the child or caregiver's circumstances. ☐ Be supportive and prepared to provide child or caregiver with skill building and tools to deal with change and challenges.
After Visit	☐ Document visit in detail identifying commitments and decisions made with timeline and plan for follow-up. Provide descriptive and specific detail regarding the information gathered during the visit related to the case plan and case plan goals as well as child's current status re: safety, permanence, and well-being.

FIGURE 5.2. Effective Worker Visits with Children in Foster Care
Adapted from: Jordan Institute for Families (2007, April)

It is important that caseworkers and other professionals understand that achieving permanency is a process that occurs over time. Concurrent planning as mandated by the Adoption and Safe Families Act of 1997 (AFSA) requires that workers simultaneously pursue an alternative plan for permanency (guardianship/adoption) while working toward a goal of reunification in case reunification fails (CWIG, 2018b). As children move closer to permanency and exit from foster care, engagement should focus on preparing the child and the family for the transition—whether the goal is reunification or another permanent placement. Caseworkers and other professionals working with children and youth during this time need to help children as they process issues of loss and grief, resulting confusion and anger, and possible divided loyalties they may be experiencing in relationship to their birth parents, foster parents, kinship parents, and possibly new adoptive parents (CWIG, 2013). Preparing children for permanency is a collaborative effort between the caseworker, the biological parents, the foster/kin parents, and in many cases, behavioral health providers. The work requires honesty, consistency, and time on the part of the professionals and should be sensitive to the developmental capacity and needs of the child.

Preparing children for adoption when reunification is not possible begins with helping the child understand that they will not be returning home. There are several models of child preparation for adoption, all of which have a basic three-part structure: 1) helping the child understand the facts of removal; 2) helping the child explore feelings of loss, anger, and confusion; and 3) engaging and empowering the child in plans for their future (Hanna, 2007).

TABLE 5.1. Engagement Opportunities and Activities Across the Stages of a Child Welfare Case

Stage of a Case	Activities Included
Prevention	Community services designed to reduce the risk of child maltreatment.
Hotline and screening	Reports and referrals to child welfare regarding a family and the decision making process designed to determine the level of risk and determine the initial system response, if any. This can also include referrals from other systems such as juvenile justice.
Initial system response	Investigation to determine whether or not child maltreatment has occurred as well as determination of which response the child welfare system will initiate including emergency removal, differential or alternative response, and in-home or out of home services.
Coordination and planning meetings	For those families for whom services are initiated, a number of planning and coordination meetings are used to guide the course of a case, including supportive services and permanency planning.

Continues on next page

Table 5.1: M. D. Hanna, Engagement Opportunities and Activities across the Stages of a Child Welfare Case, from "Preparing School Age Children for Adoption: Perspectives of Successful Adoptive Parents and Caseworkers," *Adoption Quarterly*, vol. 10, no. 2.

Stage of a Case	Activities Included
In-Home and Out of home Services	Families receive services primarily in-home, when children remain with their families, or out of home if children are placed in foster care or another temporary living arrangement.
Visitation	Parents, siblings, and other relatives have supervised or unsupervised visits with children who are in out of home care.
Permanency services	These services are designed to plan for and support permanency for children placed in out of home care including independent living, guardianship, and reunification.

Roughly 25% of the children in foster care are 14 years or older, and on average, 8.8% of children who exit foster care do so by emancipation or "aging out." Outcomes for youth aging out of care at 18 are discouraging across all domains—health, mental health, education, etc. (See Chapter 11 for more information.) Neuroscience has provided valuable insight into the adolescent brain that we can use to inform engagement with adolescents in foster care (Jim Casey Youth Opportunities Initiative, 2011). Recommendations for engaging youth in foster care include:

1. Using a positive youth development approach with youth,
2. Providing "interdependent" as opposed to "independent" services to help youth connect with caring adults in their life,
3. Engage youth in planning and decision-making,
4. Use a trauma informed approach, and
5. Extend developmentally appropriate services for youth to age.

Delivery Across the Continuum of Child Welfare Services

Image 5.3

Across the stages of a child welfare case, child welfare staff have multiple opportunities to engage diverse parents and families in services (see Table 5.1). Engagement of families at each point is impacted by the unique characteristics of that stage of a case—including which professionals are involved (child welfare, judicial, mental health providers, etc.), how long a family may be at a stage, and how the present stage connects to other points in the case. For example, during the initial response stage of a case, the family is primarily interacting with the child welfare investigator and possibly law enforcement. Once the child is placed in out of home care, the number of professionals involved with the family expands, often adding mental health providers, health care providers, and members of the judicial system (judges, lawyers, etc.). Regardless of the stage of intervention, with the exception of prevention, involvement with child welfare services is involuntary on the part of the family and the result of alleged child abuse or neglect. The involuntary nature of the relationship between the family and child welfare presents unique challenges at each stage.

Prevention

The recently passed Family First Prevention Services Act of 2018 provides funding for states to provide services up to 12 months to prevent removal of child(ren) from the family (National Conference of State Legislatures [NCSL], 2018). As outlined in Chapter 1, historically, child welfare has been more reactive than proactive as a system. The move toward developing services that are more preventative in nature is long overdue; however, engaging families in prevention services presents challenges. To successfully engage families in prevention services, workers likely need to coordinate with other service providers in the community, adding complexity as different actors may have varied approaches and goals for services. Although some child welfare agencies provide direct prevention services, many collaborate with a variety of child and family and community-serving agencies such as local health departments or mental health clinics to support prevention efforts.

In addition, access to supportive services, such as mental health or substance abuse treatment, can prove challenging in more rural or socioeconomically depressed areas. Even in cases where services are available, there can be long waitlists or other obstacles like limited transportation options that can result in inequity for some families during this stage. Also, families may receive prevention services for varying lengths of time, depending upon the particular prevention program in which they participate. A family's quality and duration of engagement in these services is likely impacted by their willingness and ability to participate in the program.

Prevention programs are considered "voluntary" in nature; however, depending on the jurisdiction, participation in prevention services is often offered to families in lieu of removal or court involvement. While a family may opt not to participate, depending on the severity of the concerns, this may or may not have negative ramifications should the family come to the attention of child welfare in the future. In addition, accessing some preventive services may be difficult for working parents or those who depend on public transportation. For example, parents may be required to attend weekly nutrition or parenting classes at a local health department—often scheduled on weekdays during regular business hours. Many families offered prevention services are hourly employees who may not easily afford missing work hours. Navigating public transportation to get to and from different agencies may also present a barrier, depending on the family's residence and work location. Prevention workers must work to convey to families that they are truly there to help and maintain or preserve the family and willing to assist parents in problem solving to overcome barriers. Developing rapport and trust with families during this stage is vital to success.

Hotline and Screening

Rarely does this stage involve direct contact with the family themselves. The initial report most often comes from someone outside of the family. This is usually a brief interaction, most often via telephone; however, it can be in person or online. At this stage workers are seeking to rapidly engage the person making the report, focusing on gathering information needed to determine if the concern meets the criteria for child abuse and neglect as defined by state statutes and determining the appropriate response. The majority of reports alleging child abuse or neglect (65.7%) are made by professionals mandated to report by both federal and state statutes (USDHHS, 2018). This includes teachers, police officers, and social workers. The remaining reports are made by family, neighbors, and friends, with a small percentage (17%) made by unknown or anonymous sources (USDHHS, 2018).

Workers will engage with the reporter by asking questions about the child, the perpetrator, and details related to the alleged abuse or neglect. Rarely does this stage of engagement involve gathering data related to nonresident fathers or other extended family or kin. Depending on the reporter, this information may or may not be known. While it would be helpful to gather this information early in the case, most often it is gathered at later stages should the situation warrant removal or out of home placement. In rare cases, a parent may make this initial contact with the system requesting services—such as cases involving a child in need of supervision or a report from a child regarding abuse by the other parent or another caregiver.

While many factors may be at play in determining who is engaged at this stage, it is important that the **hotline** worker engage in a manner that is empathetic and not adversarial, offering solutions—not obstacles—to services. For example, it is not uncommon for adoptive parents to contact child welfare when the child they adopted from foster care is in need of mental health services. Adoptive parents may use the hotline as a strategy to reach out for help, due to often limited post-adoption supports. Unfortunately, adoptive parents have reported that rather than receiving the help they seek, they are often accused of "bad parenting" or treated as though they are perpetrators (Hanna, Boyce, & Mulligan, 2017).

Initial System Response

Beginning with this stage of the child welfare continuum, families have more direct interaction with the system. Depending on the outcome and the jurisdiction, this stage may be relatively brief. Workers must quickly work to engage families, which can be challenging given that most families may experience this initial response as adversarial in nature.

Based on the findings of the original screening, the system response will either be investigation or differential response. Differential response, also known as alternative response, has been a part of child welfare practice since the early 1990s as child welfare social workers seemed conflicted between their roles as investigators of child abuse and neglect and as social workers assessing the family's situation and providing supportive services (CWIG, 2014). In jurisdictions where differential response is an option, an investigation is reserved for those cases that are more serious in nature. **Differential response** is a strengths-based, family-centered approach aimed to support families where the risks of safety for the child(ren) is minimal. It is an approach to child welfare services designed to be less adversarial and engages families through an assessment process (Child and Family Services Reviews Informational Portal, 2018).

The most recent data provided from the National Quality Improvement Center on Differential Response in Child Protective Services (QIC-DR) indicates that the majority of the states and the District of Columbia had either implemented or were in the process of implementing statewide or regional or county differential response initiatives, varying in approach, including structure and decision-making (CWIG, 2014). Common characteristics across state practices include 1) the focus on assessment; 2) the individualization of response dependent on each family's unique needs; 3) a strengths-based approach to family engagement; 4) referrals to community-based services; 5) preserving response for families at minimal risk; and 6) flexibility to change to the more traditional response of investigation should the risk and safety concerns become more serious (Child and Family Services Reviews Informational Portal, 2018).

Many jurisdictions involve law enforcement in investigations, particularly when the alleged abuse meets the criteria of a criminal offense. In cases of severe abuse and imminent threat, law enforcement may be the first responders and have the authority to take the child into emergency custody prior to a child welfare investigation. As discussed in Chapter 1, the investigation may result in an emergency removal of the child from the home and lead to the state or county obtaining temporary custody and the child being placed in out of home care.

The Fostering Connections to Success and Increasing Adoptions Act of 2008 (H.R. 6893/ P. L. 110-351) mandates that within 30 days of removal the state must complete a diligent search to notify adult relatives of the child of the removal and assess them for their capacity to care for the child. During this time, several workers, including the investigative worker, may contact the family or a worker designated to complete the diligent search. Families may also be introduced to a new worker during this time. This new worker is assigned to help them complete the court-ordered tasks necessary to reunite with their child(ren).

Both the worker performing the diligent search and the one assigned to help them complete court-ordered tasks may encounter barriers initially. They may find that the family is reluctant to engage or trust the system to work alongside them but rather see them as agents of an adversarial system that has broken up their family. In some cases, parents may be facing criminal charges and, often on the advice of an attorney, may not cooperate or respond to workers' attempts to engage. In a case study during a 1-year demonstration project, Gibson and Rinkel (2012) found that as a result of the implementation of the Fostering Connections Act, workers in one jurisdiction reported widening their definition of kin, conducting searches earlier in the case, shifting their view of biological fathers as a viable resource, and overall promoting kinship care as vital to child well-being and preservation. These same workers, however, reported barriers, including worker attitudes toward biological parents and family members, lack of cooperation across systems, and familial issues such as discord between paternal and maternal relatives, as well as resistance from custodial parents to participate in the process by providing accurate information on relatives. The skill and ability of a caseworker to engage parents at these early stages often sets the tone and expectations for a parent's engagement with other services within the agency as well as the community. Similarly, the worker responsible for contacting and engaging grandparents or other extended family, including nonresident fathers, often sets the tone for how well the extended family supports the parents in their attempts to achieve case plan goals.

Coordination and Planning Meetings

Families with open child welfare cases may participate in coordination and planning meetings for the duration of their involvement with the system. Different jurisdictions use different approaches or models for their coordination and planning meetings; some of these approaches or models may affect the degree to which families are actively engaged. A good example is **Family Group Decision Making (FGDM)**. An intervention that originated in New Zealand over 20 years ago, FGDM is lauded as a culturally responsive approach to family engagement (National Center for Family Group Decision Making, 2010). "FDGM is a decision-making process to which members of the family group are invited and joined by members of their informal network, community groups and the child welfare agency that has become involved in the family's life" (American Humane Association and the FGDM Guidelines Committee, 2010, p. 8). The frequency of these meetings as well as the participants invited—for service planning, transition planning, and permanency planning—depend on various characteristics of the family, including the age of the child or youth, the nature of the child maltreatment, the degree to which the court is involved, and where the child or youth is residing.

Although child welfare agencies generally initiate and organize these meetings, often providers outside of child welfare and other professionals are involved, and so family engagement is also dependent on the skills and abilities of these other meeting participants. When these professionals work well together, family engagement may benefit. Likewise, poor coordination or relationships between professionals may compromise family engagement. Additional discussion on the impact of these collaborations on engagement is provided later in this chapter.

Other common engagement challenges in this stage of services are related to scheduling, location, and transportation. Often, meetings are scheduled to meet the needs of the professionals (time and/or location) involved rather than in consideration of the family's needs. Many parents involved in child welfare depend on public transportation to attend meetings; therefore, they may have difficulty arriving on time. For some, there is a risk of losing income or employment if they attend the meeting as scheduled, which is often a condition of the case plan. Parents may simply be told to attend the required meeting or risk negative consequences such as having decisions made without their input or being labeled as "uncooperative." These consequences hinder the family's progress toward successful completion of their case's plan. In order to increase family engagement, it is important for the conveners of these meetings to include parents in the scheduling.

In-Home and Out of home Services

Those families with open cases will spend the longest amount of time in this phase of a case. During this phase, children and family members receive services that may or may not be ordered by the court or decided upon by the child welfare agency.

Federal law requires that case plans be completed in collaboration with the family (45 C.F.R. 1356.21). Unfortunately, there are times where the case plan is developed *for* the family rather than *with* the family. Family-centered, strengths-based case planning is best practice (CWIG, 2018a). The Adoption Assistance and Child Welfare Act of 1980 required case plans for any child eligible for Title IV-E foster care. Children are eligible for IV-E (federal) reimbursement to the state for foster care maintenance payments if the family they are removed from meets the eligibility requirement for Assistance to Families with Dependent Children (AFDC) as of 1996 (42 U.S. Code §672(a)(3)(A)). Case plans are written documents that provide guidance to the parents as they work to correct the conditions that led to the child(ren)'s removal. They should be specific to the case, and be clear as to expectations and time frames for completion. Case plans should also address the services that need to be provided to the child(ren) while in care. Engaging the parents in this process is vital to their successful implementation and completion. Case plans are reviewed by the courts at regular intervals throughout the life of the case. The courts look for evidence that parents have progressed on the tasks outlined in the case plan and need updated information related to the child(ren)'s placement, health, education, and other service needs (CWIG, 2018a).

Court-ordered services are a key part of the case plan. They are case specific and often include items such as parenting classes, substance use treatment, counseling, anger management, or therapy to address specific issues such as domestic violence or a mental health diagnosis. The variation in service needs and particular services shapes the length and amount of time a family spends with any one service provider—and therefore the opportunity for engagement also varies. Child welfare caseworkers and others providing specific services are likely to develop relationships with the child(ren) and the family members through the provision of services. Ideally, if services are high quality and successful relationships are built, there is a great opportunity to support family engagement.

Visitation

A very common court-ordered service is **visitation** between the child(ren) and parents. Courts will sometimes extend visitation orders to include extended family and siblings who may have been separated and placed in different foster homes or out of home placements. Visitation between parents and foster children is positively correlated with child well-being and serves as a protective factor against behavioral problems, both externalizing and internalizing (McWey, Acock, & Porter, 2010). Visitation is often observed by child welfare caseworkers or contract agencies and presents a great opportunity for positive engagement with the parents and the child(ren). Efforts to ensure that visits happen with both maternal and paternal family members create a natural opportunity for increasing family engagement, often motivating parents to stay on track in the completion of their case plan, knowing that this may lead to reunification. In cases where there is significant positive progress on the case plan, visitation will often increase, lengthen, and even become unsupervised the closer the family gets to reunification.

The courts as well as the child welfare agency influence visitation. If visits cause the child distress, or the parent(s) are not consistent in attendance, or there are observations of inappropriate parent-child interaction, the courts may restrict or discontinue visits based on the recommendation of the caseworker or the agency supervising the visits. It is not uncommon that if the case plan goal changes or termination of parental rights is pursued, the parent and child(ren) may have a final or "good-bye" visit. These visits can be very difficult, and a caseworker's relationship with the parent(s), child(ren), and other visiting relatives may influence how well the visit goes.

Coordination is paramount with family engagement in visitation. Not only must child welfare staff schedule visits so that the intended individuals can participate, visits also need to occur in locations that are comfortable for and accessible to all—including the caregiver and foster parents. Caseworkers may experience challenges navigating who may visit the child or youth and with what other family members, due to legal or personal relationship reasons. Siblings placed separately, or two or more sets of paternal relatives (when children have different fathers), can make visitation more challenging. Caseworkers may have to prioritize with whom the child(ren) visits, due to logistics based on placement, transportation, schedules, and relationships between the adults involved. Visitation may be even more challenging if parents are in prison or relatives live out of town. Characteristics of visits, such as when and where visitations happen or what forms of interaction are possible, will affect a family's engagement in visitation. It may be possible to use technology—for example, video calls—to facilitate visitation; however, this requires that the caregiver and/or child(ren) have a device that can make video calls and has access to the internet. This may also be complicated by the level of supervision needed; i.e., if the interaction between the child(ren) and the parents needs to be supervised, it may require the foster family or kinship caregiver be available when the child or youth is, and possibly, present physically or online.

Permanency Services

The final stage of a case represents the services aimed at facilitating the child(ren)'s exit from care and the services available. Families with a **permanency** goal of reunification need to successfully complete or graduate from services such as parenting education, substance abuse treatment, or homemaker services. Reunification is a process over time that starts with an increase in unsupervised visitation. Most often there is a period of time post–physical reunification that caseworkers make regular visits with the family to assist in the transition and provide additional services if needed. Engagement during this phase is dependent on the relationship between the family and the assigned caseworker. The family needs to see the caseworker as a resource, someone they can call if needed and be honest with about the challenges of reunification after not having full-time parenting responsibility for a significant length of time. Families may also receive additional services during this time from therapists, home nurses, et al., to aid in the transition.

For children with the permanency goal of adoption, services to the biological parents tend to stop after the final visit with the child(ren), as once parental rights are terminated and the goal changes, the focus of the case is no longer on helping the biological parent correct the conditions that led to removal. However, in cases where the child is being adopted by a relative or kinship placement provider, the caseworker may help the adoptive parent(s) and birthparent(s) redefine their new ongoing relationship, including visitation to ensure ongoing safety for the child while maintaining relationship with the birth parents. In some cases, a birth parent may be counseled and encouraged to relinquish parental rights voluntarily as opposed to an involuntary court action to expedite permanency through adoption by either a current foster parent or kinship/relative provider.

In the case of adoption or guardianship, the worker's focus of engagement shifts from the biological parents to the new prospective parents, preparing them to take care of the child long term. Guardianship policies and procedures vary from state to state. Most often, guardianship is granted to relatives or someone with a close attachment to the child or family (CWIG, 2015). While guardians are expected to make a long-term commitment to the child(ren), a guardianship can be modified or revoked at any time before the child reaches the age of majority (age 18 years) by the court if determined to be in the child's best interest. Most often, parental rights are not terminated prior to a guardianship order. This means that parents may retain visitation rights and the right to consent to an adoption, as well as be ordered to pay child support (CWIG, 2015).

Adoption services vary depending on who is adopting the child and the age of the child. In many child welfare agencies, several caseworkers engage with prospective adoptive parents once identified (see Chapter 14). Sometimes these are caseworkers employed by the public child welfare agency; however, in many states private agencies or individual social workers are contracted for adoption services. This includes pre- and post-placement up to the point of legal finalization of the adoption and possibly post-adoption (see Chapter 15). The Adoption Assistance and Child Welfare Act of 1980 established the Federal Title IV-E adoption assistance program, also known as an adoption subsidy. An adoption subsidy can be in the form of a one-time nonrecurring financial assistance to the family or ongoing financial assistance to help the family meet the needs of the child (see Chapter 15 for more detailed information). Unlike adoption, guardians are not eligible for post-placement subsidies in every state. Currently, 25 states plus the District of Columbia offer a state-funded subsidized guardianship and only 22 states offer federally funded guardianship assistance (CWIG, 2015).

Each exit from child welfare includes a wide range of people, including the family, child welfare agency staff, staff from other agencies, and other professionals, including lawyers and medical and mental health professionals. As with the other phases across the child welfare continuum of services, when the case involves interagency or interprofessional collaboration, engagement with families can be supported or compromised by the multiple organizations and professionals involved. The length of time of engagement for the family is facilitated at this stage will vary by case. Dependent on the case plan goal, the target of engagement may shift from biological parents to alternative permanent family such as guardians or adoptive parents. In this stage, the success of engagement is influenced by the many experiences, professionals, and services provided to the family up to this point. Altman (2008) provides some insight into the importance of engagement from the worker as well as the client perspective. This small study identified honest communication and supportive relationships that foster motivation for change at a sufficient pace as important worker strategies for successful engagement with families. The more successful the engagement early in the case, the easier it can be to engage families throughout the case (Dawson & Berry, 2002).

Cultural and Linguistic Responsiveness

We use the term **cultural and linguistic responsiveness** in this chapter to describe the complex and evolving collection of engagement practices that acknowledge and address the diverse cultures of families served by child welfare. These include language-appropriate services, cultural competence, and cultural humility.

Linguistically Appropriate Services

Many families served by child welfare do not speak English as their primary language. Child welfare services are complex and include a variety of legal processes that are difficult to understand, even for proficient English speakers. Therefore, careful attention to the language needs of families is critical to their successful engagement in services. Linguistic competence is defined as the capacity of an organization and its personnel to effectively communicate and convey information in a way that is easily understood by a diverse audience such as those with limited English proficiency, individuals with disabilities, and those who have low literacy skills or who are not functionally literate (Goode & Jones, 2006). Organizations need to have structures, practices, policies, and procedures that support this capacity, including, but not limited to, staff who are multilingual and multicultural, cross-cultural communication approaches, foreign or sign language interpretation services, TTY and other assistive technology devices, or telehealth technologies (Goode & Jones, 2006).

Cultural Competence

Serving culturally diverse families requires more than language-appropriate services. Families and children involved in child welfare represent an array of racial, ethnic, and cultural backgrounds. While the largest percentage of children entering foster care are White (47%), roughly 51% are children of color (USDHHS, 2018). Black children are overrepresented nationally with 21% entering care, and Hispanic children of any race represent 20% of the children in care. Roughly 11% of the remaining children identify as American Indian/Alaska Native (2%), Asian (1%), Native Hawaiian/Other Pacific Islander (> 1%), or two or more races (7%). These racially and ethnically diverse children represent a myriad of cultures, too numerous to explore here. However, given that approximately 80% of the child welfare workforce are White females (Barth, Lloyd, Christ, Chapman, & Dickinson, 2008) and given the diversity among families in contact with the child welfare systems, child welfare workers must continually engage in cross-cultural practice. **Cross-cultural practice** is any professional relationship in which two or more participants differ with respect to cultural values, lifestyle, and/or background (Pillay, 2003; Sue et al., 1982; Yan, 2008). Cultural competence requires child welfare workers to acquire the knowledge, values, and skills to make services culturally relevant and, in turn, increase their effectiveness in cross-cultural practice (Sue et al., 1982; Yan, 2008).

Image 5.4

Varied cultural frames can impact family engagement and influence the ways families understand and engage in their relationships with child welfare, legal services, mental health, and other types of professionals. Likewise, workers' own cultural lens shapes their expectations of families and influences their capacity to form successful, collaborative relationships with them. Unfortunately, children and families of color are overrepresented in child welfare and experience disparities within the system (Children's Bureau, 2016). Child welfare workers work with diverse families who experience different levels of disparities related to child welfare outcomes, which are due in part to cultural differences between the family and the provider. Unacknowledged and unaddressed, cultural differences can compromise successful engagement of families and further perpetuate disproportionality and disparities. However, culturally competent social workers can help address these important and challenging problems (Lawrence, Zuckerman, Smith, & Liu, 2012).

Cultural competence was developed out of the need to remedy issues related to the multiple forms of oppression that play out within the helping relationship and includes both self-awareness and skills development (Abrams & Moio, 2009). Self-awareness is the development of insight into one's own identities through exploration of identities, including race, ethnicity, sexual orientation, gender identity, socioeconomic status, physical abilities, and cultural background, to name a few (Bender, Negi, & Fowler, 2010). Child welfare workers need to be aware of the origins of their values and worldviews with regard to differences so that any deeply rooted or unconscious beliefs can be managed (Abrams & Moio, 2009). Workers also need to develop a set of practice skills, including engagement skills that build on and are adapted to the customs, styles, needs, and worldviews of the families that they serve (Abrams & Moio, 2009).

Cultural Humility

Focusing exclusively on self-awareness and building knowledge of other cultures, however, is a limited approach (Bender et al., 2010). Cultural competence trainings that simply build knowledge do not hold child welfare workers accountable for the power and privilege that their role entails (Ortega & Faller, 2011). Cultural humility, therefore, represents a more recent approach to cultural and linguistic responsiveness that addresses some of the limitations of cultural competence.

Drawing on the work of Morris, Brotheridge, and Urbanski (2005) as well as Ortega and Faller (2011), the **cultural humility** perspective has three connected but discrete dimensions that are critical to engagement and connecting with oneself and with others: self-awareness, openness, and transcendence.

Self-awareness: Similar to this dimension as described in the cultural competence approach, the use of a cultural humility approach requires that people must appreciate who they are in terms of their cultural perspective and how this perspective shapes their views.

Openness: This dimension departs from the cultural competence approach in that in order to be open, one cannot claim to know all there is to know about the world and those who are in it. Cultural humility requires that one be open to the reality that they do not know how others feel, think, or perceive a situation. It requires that one remain open to those they interact with in order to learn from others' experiences.

Transcendence: Transcendence is the acceptance of something greater than oneself, which comes with an appreciation of others, a recognition of the positive self-worth of others, and an understanding of the small role that one plays in the infinite universe.

In order to employ cultural humility, child welfare workers, therefore, need to not only be aware of how their own views and limitations impact their ability to engage families, as is required for cultural competence, they also need to maintain openness and a humble attitude toward themselves and others. They must value the families' perspective on the issues at hand as well as the families' own approaches to solutions. A cultural humility perspective further encourages child welfare workers to take into account the multiple, intersecting identities of individuals and the way in which their social experiences impact their worldview (Ortega & Faller, 2011).

Cultural Humility Approach to Child Welfare

Ortega and Faller (2011) developed a cultural humility approach specific to child welfare practice that can be used as a framework for implementing cultural humility tenets. In subsequent chapters of this book, you will be introduced to some of the nuances in working with diverse communities and will consider some of these concepts more deeply. This framework, therefore, is intended to provide you with a generalizable approach for how to put this into practice. This framework is intended to actively engage the clients in the service delivery process, inclusive of their cultural differences.

- ☐ Embrace the complexity of diversity
- ☐ "Know thyself" and critically challenge one's "openness" to learn from others
- ☐ Accept cultural differences and relate to children and families in ways that are most understandable to them
- ☐ Continuously engage in collaborative helping
- ☐ Demonstrate familiarity with the living environment of children and families being served
- ☐ Build organizational support that demonstrates cultural humility as an important and ongoing aspect of the work itself

FIGURE 5.3. Ortega and Faller's Cultural Humility Approach (2011)

Figure 5.3 identifies the six principles for a cultural humility approach as developed by Ortega and Faller (2011).

In summary, child welfare workers need to understand the diverse, intersecting identities of child welfare clients and develop an awareness of the power differentials that are at play in their work. They must consistently reflect on their own identity and its relationship to the identities of those with whom they work while also developing the skills required for cross-cultural practice and ensuring that their interactions with the client and family are culturally and linguistically congruent, non-paternalistic, and mutually beneficial. To do so requires regularly appraising the effectiveness of family interventions, dialoguing with the family as to the issues that might be impacting outcomes, and building on family strengths as a means to improve the outcomes for the family. Furthermore, child welfare workers need to assess policies, procedures, knowledge, and skills connected to child welfare worker practice as well as the larger organizational environment. It is not enough for an individual case worker to utilize a cultural humility approach; rather, as social workers and family advocates, child welfare workers need to advocate for the inclusion of a cultural humility approach on a systems level as well.

Multidisciplinary Collaboration and Engagement

Although this chapter has primarily addressed engagement of families and the practice of child welfare workers, much of child welfare practice is carried out in teams of professionals or in collaboration with other service systems and allied professionals—or in the context of multidisciplinary collaboration. Billups (1987) defines multidisciplinary collaboration as the "purposeful sequences of change-oriented transactions between or among representatives of two or more professions who possess individual expertise, but who are functionally interdependent in their collaborative pursuit of commonly shared goals" (p.148). These transactions or collaborative processes include defining roles; working together to assess clients and identify issues requiring intervention; joint creation of goals and action plans; regular communication; resolving conflicts that arise between professionals; and ongoing evaluation of the collaborative process.

As described in Chapter 2, child welfare workers are required to engage and collaborate with various professionals from the different systems that serve child welfare–involved families, including the behavioral health system, the judicial system, and the education system. Child welfare workers work with service providers such as mental health therapists and substance abuse counselors who work with children, parents, and families to address the issues that led to their involvement in the child welfare system and prevent them from exiting the system; attorneys who represent children, parents, or child protective services; Guardians Ad Litem or Court-Appointed Special Advocates (CASAs) appointed by the courts to determine what is in the "best interests of the child" and promote those interests when case decisions are being made inside and outside of the courtroom; and teachers who are responsible for ensuring that the child's academic needs are being met.

The level of engagement and collaboration with the various professionals working with a family may influence a social worker's ability—as well as the ability of other professionals—to engage with the family and provide services that are appropriately matched to a family's unique needs (Green, Rockhill, & Burrus, 2008). For example, when professionals share information (e.g., available resources and assessments) and make decisions together (e.g., what service to provide or whether a child should be reunified), they are better able to monitor families and provide services that align with a family's strengths and needs (Carnochan et al., 2007; Green et al., 2008). In addition, professionals can ensure that families are not given competing or overwhelming demands that could prevent them from achieving their goals or the goals dictated by the child welfare system (Green et al., 2008; Haight, Bidwell, Marshall, & Khatiwoda, 2014).

A lack of culturally appropriate decision-making and services has contributed to the problems of racial disproportionality and disparity in the child welfare system. The sharing of perspectives, knowledge, and skills that occurs when professionals work together may be one way to promote culturally responsive practice. Professionals can draw on one another's knowledge and experience working with diverse populations to enhance their own cultural competence and humility and support culturally informed decisions. At the same time, by making decisions together, professionals can challenge one another to see how their biases, prejudices, or privilege may be influencing their assessment or recommendation. Given child welfare workers' social work training and values, child welfare workers are well positioned to assist other members of an interprofessional team in identifying cultural factors that may be impacting a case. Child welfare workers must advocate for social justice to ensure that the professionals serving a family are providing culturally and linguistically responsive services.

Disagreements between professionals working with child welfare–involved families are not uncommon, given their different training/education, professional values, roles, and mandated goals (Beeman, Hagemeister, & Edleson, 1999; Darlington, Feeney, & Rixon, 2005). When disagreements arise, they must be resolved in a timely manner to prevent delays and to provide unified support to families. However, confronting other professionals and addressing interprofessional conflicts can be uncomfortable and difficult. Some strategies that can be employed to help in these situations include exploring differences to understand the rationale behind each person's point of view and identify common ground; remaining respectful of one another's roles and responsibilities; focusing on what the family needs to be successful; recognizing that conflicts occur because of differences in training, roles, and goals and not taking them personally; and, when necessary, agreeing to disagree and allowing the court to resolve the issue if needed. In many cases, differing perspectives may be offered by different professionals to the court to inform key decisions such as removal or reunification. In general, perhaps the most important thing a child welfare worker can do to prepare for interprofessional collaboration is to work on understanding the roles and mandated goals of the various professionals who must work together in the child welfare system. Doing so will increase mutual understanding of the motivations behind different professionals' actions to improve service coordination for families, which can help prevent or resolve interprofessional conflict.

Conclusion

Efforts to engage families over the course of a case is complex but critically important. A multidimensional approach to engagement in this chapter was presented because successful engagement requires that workers take a family-inclusive approach that is culturally and linguistically responsive, developmentally informed, attended to throughout the life of a case, and done in skillful coordination with other systems and professionals. This is challenging work, but building positive relationships with families and engaging them in services is one of the most important facets of child welfare work.

Fortunately, there are some key elements of engagement that remain consistent across diverse families, life stages, and services. At a basic level, families want workers who are genuine and authentically invested in their best interests. They want workers who are not "just in it for the check." This genuineness and authenticity are often demonstrated through simple gestures of humanity and caring, that can be as basic as learning the names of family members, asking how everyone is doing before jumping into the task at hand, and making meeting rooms as comfortable as possible. Families also want workers to be there for them when they are needed. So, making it clear how families can get in touch, checking in regularly, responding to communication consistently, and following through on any needed information, tasks, and services can be beneficial. These relationship-building skills are the key to successful engagement, whether the goal is to collect information from families in an investigation or to facilitate a successful family meeting. Lastly, if not most importantly, workers must use a cultural humility approach when working with diverse families, recognizing that each family's unique **culture** and past experiences with systems of power such as child welfare, discrimination, racism, and other -isms, impacts how they experience each and every interaction with child welfare.

Case Application

The following case vignette describes the Martin family, the children they are seeking to adopt, the family members involved in the case, and their engagement with the child welfare system. The case is complicated and raises many challenges and opportunities for multidimensional engagement.

Case Vignette

The Martins are an interracial couple with three birth children, Angel, age 8, Brian, age 6, and Mariah, age 4.5. Mrs. Martin identifies herself as Black and her husband, Mr. Martin, identifies himself as White. Recently, they became foster parents to a sibling set of two half brothers, James, age 1, and John, age 3, who were removed from their biological mother, Sraya, who identifies as Indian American. The half brothers were placed with the Martins after Sraya left them alone overnight while she went out with her boyfriend. A neighbor heard James, approximately 2 months old, crying for hours and called the police. Initially, the half brothers were placed separately. James was placed with the Martin family on an emergency placement at removal, and John was placed with his paternal grandmother, who did not want to take James as James had a different father.

John's placement was recently disrupted when his grandmother died and his father was unable to care for him due to inconsistent job hours and no one able to care for him while he worked. John's father requested that John be placed with the Martins as they had met during sibling visitation, and he felt that the Martins would allow him to have continued contact with his son.

The child welfare caseworker assigned to the case has been working with Sraya since the case was adjudicated, as she attempted to complete her case plan and reunify with her children. Visitation with James had been consistent until about 1 month ago when Sraya did not show for two visits in a row because of a lack of transportation. She had not been able to visit with John, as neither the father nor the paternal grandmother would cooperate with bringing John to visits. Sraya has also failed to have a clean drug test the last two times she was required to submit a urine sample. The worker contacted Sraya's drug counselor and found that she has not made her last few office visits and did not attend the most recent weekly group therapy session.

Based on Sraya's recent disengagement from visitation and therapy, the caseworker is recommending that her rights be terminated and that the Martins be allowed to adopt both boys. The caseworker attempted to contact Sraya to discuss a voluntary relinquishment, but Sraya said she just had a temporary setback and that she has contacted an inpatient substance use program and was on the waiting list. She feels strongly that the only proper place for children, especially at such a young age, is with their mother. She also feels it important that her children maintain their Indian identity and connection to their family culture.

John's father has indicated that he would voluntarily relinquish his rights if the Martins adopt the children and allow him to have an ongoing long-term relationship with his son. This week the caseworker received a call from a man claiming to be James's birth father. He stated that he had been away serving overseas for over a year, and when he came home he was told that Sraya had his baby and that the baby and brother were in foster care. He reported that prior to going overseas, he broke up with Sraya because she reported having had an abortion and he did not agree with that decision. He stated his intent to obtain an attorney and fight for custody of his son as well as John, as he stated that John knew him and he was like a "second father" to him. The Martins have always expressed an interest in adopting James and now John; however, they are concerned about the expense of having five children in the home without receiving a foster care payment. The caseworker has made a referral to the adoption worker to begin the adoption process. She told James's alleged birth father that he has no rights to the child since he has never been in the child's life, and she refused his request to visit with the children.

DISCUSSION QUESTIONS

1. What are the opportunities for engagement by the caseworker with the adults who are playing a parenting role, or could be playing a parenting role, for the children involved in this case? Are there opportunities that may have been missed or mishandled? At what stages of the case were these opportunities missed or mishandled? What alternative outcomes may have resulted if the worker had better taken advantage of these opportunities?
2. At this point in the case, what opportunities does the worker have to engage with the adult family members moving forward? Are there any cultural issues that should be explored? What other collaborative agencies or service providers might be useful and potentially lead to positive outcomes for all involved?

References

42 U.S. Code § 672 (a) (3) (A).

45 C.F.R 1356.21.

Abrams, L. S., & Moio, J. A. (2009). Critical race theory and the cultural competence dilemma in social work education. *Journal of Social Work Education, 45*(2), 245–261.

Altman, J. C. (2008). Engaging families in child welfare services: Worker versus client perspectives. *Child Welfare, 87*(3).

Amato, P. R., & Gilbreth, J. G. (1999). Nonresident fathers and children's well-being: A meta-analysis. *Journal of Marriage & the Family, 61*(3), 557–573.

American Humane Association and the FGDM Guidelines Committee. (2010). *Guidelines for Family Group Decision Making in Child Welfare*. Englewood, CO: American Humane Association.

Barth, R. P., Lloyd, E. C., Christ, S. L., Chapman, M. V., & Dickinson, N. S. (2008). Child welfare worker characteristics and job satisfaction: A national study. *Social Work, 53*(3), 199–209.

Baum, N. (2017). Gender-sensitive intervention to improve work with fathers in child welfare services. *Child and Family Social Work, 22*(1), 419–427. doi: 10.1111/cfs.122259

Beeman, S. K., Hagemeister, A. K., & Edleson, J. L. (1999). Child protection and battered women's services: From conflict to collaboration. *Child Maltreatment, 4*(2), 116–126.

Bellamy, J. L. (2009). A national study of male involvement among families in contact with the child welfare system. *Child Maltreatment,14*(3), 255–262.

Bender, K., Negi, N., & Fowler, D. N. (2010). Exploring the relationship between self-awareness and student commitment and understanding of culturally responsive social work practice. *Journal of Ethnic & Cultural Diversity in Social Work,* 19, 34–53.

Billups, J. O. (1987). Interprofessional team processes. *Theory into Practice, 26*(2), 146–152.

Bramlett, M. D., & Blumberg, S. J. (2007). Family structure and children's physical and mental health. *Health Affairs, 26*(2), 549–558.

Brown, L., Callahan, M., Strega, S., Walmsley, C., & Dominelli, L. (2009). Manufacturing ghost fathers: The paradox of father presence and absence in child welfare. *Child & Family Social Work, 14*(1), 25–34.

Burnette, D., Sun, J., & Sun, F. (2013). A comparative review of grandparent care of children in the US and China. *Ageing International, 38*, 43–57.

Burrus, S. W., Green, B. L., Worcel, S., Finigan, M., & Furrer, C. (2012). Do dads matter? Child welfare outcomes for father-identified families. *Journal of Child Custody, 9*(3), 201–216.

Carlson, M., McLanahan, S., & England, P. (2004). Union formation in fragile families. *Demography, 41*, 237–262.

Carnochan, S., Taylor, S., Abramson-Madden, A., Han, M., Rashid, S., Maney, J., Teuwen, S., & Austin, M. J. (2007). Child welfare and the courts: An exploratory study of the relationship between two complex systems. *Journal of Public Child Welfare, 1*(1), 117–136. doi: 10.1300/J479v01n01

Casanueva, C., Smith, K., Ringeisen, H., Dolan, M., & Tueller, S. (2014). Families in need of domestic violence services reported to the child welfare system: Changes in the National Survey of Child and Adolescent Well-Being between 1999–2000 and 2008–2009. *Child Abuse & Neglect, 38*, 1683–1693.

Chen, H. M., & Lewis, D. C. (2017). The role of Chinese grandparents in their adult children's parenting practices in the United States. In K. T. Quek & S. R. Fang (Eds.), *Transition and Change in Collectivist Family Life* (pp. 57–66). Springer, Cham.

Child and Family Services Reviews Information Portal. (2018). *Differential Response.* https://training.cfsrportal.acf.hhs.gov/section-2-understanding-child-welfare-system/3011

Child Welfare Information Gateway. (2018a). Case planning for families involved with child welfare agencies. Washington, DC: U.S. Department of Health and Human Services, Children's Bureau.

Child Welfare Information Gateway. (2018b). Concurrent planning for timely permanence. Washington, DC: U.S. Department of Health and Human Services, Children's Bureau.

Child Welfare Information Gateway. (2017). The Family Engagement Inventory (FEI): A brief cross-disciplinary synthesis. Washington, DC: U.S. Department of Health and Human Services, Children's Bureau.

Child Welfare Information Gateway. (2016). Racial Disproportionality and Disparity in Child Welfare. Washington, DC: U.S. Department of Health and Human Services, Children's Bureau.

Child Welfare Information Gateway. (2015). Kinship guardianship as a permanency option. Washington, DC: U.S. Department of Health and Human Services, Children's Bureau.

Child Welfare Information Gateway. (2014). Differential response to reports of child abuse and neglect. Washington, DC: U.S. Department of Health and Human Services, Children's Bureau.

Child Welfare Information Gateway. (2013). Preparing children and youth for adoption or other family permanency. Washington, DC: U.S. Department of Health and Human Services, Children's Bureau.

Christenson, B., & McMurtry, J. (2007). A comparative evaluation of preservice training of kinship and nonkinship foster/adoptive families. *Child Welfare, 86*(2), 125–140.

Cuddeback, G. S. (2004). Kinship family foster care: A methodological and substantive synthesis of research. *Children and Youth Services Review, 26*(7), 623–639.

Darlington, Y., Feeney, J. A., & Rixon, K. (2005). Interagency collaboration between child protection and mental health services: Practices, attitudes and barriers. *Child Abuse & Neglect, 29*(10), 1085–1098. http://doi.org/10.1016/j.chiabu.2005.04.005

Dawson, K., & Berry, M. (2002). Engaging families in child welfare services: An evidence-based approach to best practice. *Child Welfare, 81*(2).

Ellis, R. R., & Simmons, T. (2014). *Coresident Grandparents and Their Grandchildren.* Report. P20-S76. U.S. Department of Commerce, Economics and Statistics Administration, United States Census Bureau.

Flouri, E. (2005). *Fathering and Child Outcomes.* New York: John Wiley & Sons.

Fostering Connections to Success and Increasing Adoptions Act of 2008 (H.R. 6893/ P. L. 110-351).

Gates, G. J. (2015). Marriage and family: LGBT and same-sex couples. *The Future of Children, 25*(2), 67–87.

Gibson, P. A., & Rinkel, M. (2012). Increased attention to the search process improves the chances of foster kinship placements. *Journal of Family Social Work, 15*(2), 141–156.

Goode, T. D., & Jones, W. (2006). National Center for Cultural Competence. A Definition of Linguistic Competence. https://gucchd.georgetown.edu/products/DefinitionLinguisticCompetence.pdf

Green, B. L., Rockhill, A., & Burrus, S. (2008). The role of interagency collaboration for substance-abusing families involved with child welfare. *Child Welfare, 87*(1), 29–61. http://0search.proquest.com.bianca.penlib.du.edu/docview/621586474?accountid=14608

Greene, A. D., & Moore, K. A. (2000). Nonresident father involvement and child well-being among young children in families on welfare. *Marriage & Family Review, 29*(2/3), 159–171.

Haight, W. L., Bidwell, L. N., Marshall, J. M., & Khatiwoda, P. (2014). Implementing the crossover youth practice model in diverse contexts: Child welfare and juvenile justice professionals' experiences of multisystem collaborations. *Children and Youth Services Review, 39*, 91–100. https://doi.org/10.1016/j.childyouth.2014.02.001

Hanna, M. D. (2007). Preparing school age children for adoption: Perspectives of successful adoptive parents and caseworkers. *Adoption Quarterly 10*(2), 1–32.

Hanna, M. D., Boyce, E., & Mulligan, D. (2017). When love is not enough: Parenting an adopted child with mental illness. *Families in Society, 98*(3), 201–208. doi: 10.1606/1044-3894.2017.98.30

Jim Casey Youth Opportunities Initiative. (2011). The adolescent brain: New research and its implications for young people transitioning from foster care. https://www.aecf.org/resources/the-adolescent-brain-foster-care/

Jones, J., & Mosher, W. D. (2013). *Fathers' involvement with their children: United States, 2006–2010.* National Health Statistics Reports, No. 71. Hyattsville, MD: National Center for Health Statistics.

Jordan Institute for Families. (2007, April). Child welfare worker visits with children in foster care. *Children's Services Practice Notes for North Carolina's Child Welfare Social Workers, 12*(2). http://www.practicenotes.org/vol12_no2/visits.htm

Kreider, R. M., & Ellis, R. (2011). Living arrangements of children: 2009. Current Population Reports No. P70-126, U.S. Census Bureau. Washington, DC.

Kumar, K. (2017). The blended family life cycle. *Journal of Divorce & Remarriage, 58*(2), 110–125.

Lawrence, C., Zuckerman, M., Smith, B. D., & Liu, J. (2012). Building cultural competence in the child welfare workforce: A mixed-methods analysis. *Journal of Public Child Welfare*, 6, 225–241.

Leon, S. C., Bai, G. J., & Fuller, A. K. (2016). Father involvement in child welfare: Associations with changes in externalizing behavior. *Child Abuse and Neglect, 55*, 73–80.

Lounds, J. J., Borkowski, J. G., & Whitman, T. L. (2006). The potential for child neglect: The case of adolescent mothers and their children. *Child maltreatment, 11*(3), 281–294.

McWey, L. M., Acock, A., & Porter, B. E. (2010). The impact of continued contact with biological parents upon the mental health of children in foster care. *Children and Youth Services Review, 32*(10), 1338–1345.

Morris, J. A., Brotheridge, C. M., & Urbanski, J. C. (2005). Bringing humility to leadership: Antecedents and consequences of leader humility. *Human Relations*, 58, 1323–1350. http://dx.doi.org/10.1177/0018726705059929

National Center for Family Group Decision Making. (2010). *Family Group Decision Making: A Solution to Racial Disproportionality and Disparities in Child Welfare.* http://www.ucdenver.edu/academics/colleges/medicalschool/departments/pediatrics/subs/can/FGDM/Documents/FGDM%20Web%20Pages/Resources/Issue%20Briefs/dispfgdm.pd

National Conference of State Legislatures (NCSL). (2018). *Family First Prevention Services Act (FFPSA): Overview.* http://www.ncsl.org/research/human-services/family-first-prevention-services-act-ffpsa.aspx

Ortega, R. M., & Faller, K. C. (2011). Training child welfare workers from an intersectional cultural humility perspective: A paradigm shift. *Child Welfare, 90*(5), 27–48.

Pillay, M. (2003). Cross-cultural practice: What is it really about? *Folia Phoniatrica et Logopaedica, 55*(6), 293–299.

Putnam-Hornstein, E., Cederbaum, J. A., King, B., Eastman, A. L., & Trickett, P. (2015). A population-level and longitudinal study of adolescent mothers and intergenerational maltreatment. *American Journal of Epidemiology, 181*(7), 496–503.

Sherrid, G. L. (2010). *203: Investigative Interviewing in Child Sexual Abuse Cases: Standard Curriculum.* Mechanicsburg, PA: The Pennsylvania Child Welfare Training Program: University of Pittsburgh, School of Social Work.

Sonenstein, F., Malm, K., & Billing, A. (2002). Study of fathers' involvement in permanency planning and child welfare casework. Washington, DC: U.S. Department of Health and Human Services, Assistant Secretary for Planning and Evaluation.

Staudt, M. (2007). Treatment engagement with caregivers of at-risk children: Gaps in research and conceptualization. *Journal of Children and Family Studies, 16*(2), 183–196.

Stoltzfus, E. (2011). *Child welfare: Funding for child and family services authorized under Title IV-B of the Social Security Act.* Washington, DC: Congressional Research Service.

Sue, D. W., Bernier, Y., Durran, A., Feinberg, L., Pedersen, P. B., Smith, E. J., et al. (1982). Position paper: Cross-cultural counseling competencies. *The Counseling Psychologist,* 10, 45–52.

Uhlenberg, P., & Cheuk, M. (2010). The significance of grandparents to grandchildren: An international perspective. In D. Dannefer & C. Phillipson (Eds.), *The Sage Handbook of Social Gerontology.* Thousand Oaks, CA: Sage, pp. 457–1448.

U.S. Department of Health and Human Services, Administration for Children and Families, Administration on Children, Youth and Families, Children's Bureau (USDHHS). (2018). *The AFCARS Report (#25).* Washington, DC: Author.

Yan, M. C. (2008). Exploring cultural tensions in cross-cultural social work practice. *Social Work, 53*(4), 317–328.

Yatchmenoff, D. K. (2005). Measuring client engagement from the client's perspective in nonvoluntary child protective services. *Research on Social Work Practice, 15*(2), 84–96.

Zilberstein, K. (2016). Parenting in families of low socioeconomic status: A review with implications for child welfare practice. *Family Court Review, 54*(2), 221–231.

Zeleznikow, L., & Zeleznikow, J. (2015). Supporting blended families to remain intact: A case study. *Journal of Divorces & Remarriage, 56,* 317–335.

Figure Credits

Img. 5.1: Copyright © 2015 Depositphotos/creatista.

Img. 5.2: Copyright © 2017 Depositphotos/XiXinXing.

Fig. 5.2: Adapted from Jordan Institute for Families, "Effective Worker Visits with Children in Foster Care," Children's Services Practice Notes for North Carolina's Child Welfare Social Workers, vol. 12, no. 2. Copyright © 2007 by University of North Carolina School of Social Work.

Img. 5.3: Copyright © 2018 Depositphotos/IgorVetushko.

Img. 5.4: Copyright © 2017 Depositphotos/Rawpixel.

CHAPTER • 6

Domestic Children of Color in Child Welfare

Aakanksha Sinha, Michele D. Hanna, and Ruth McRoy

Introduction

As of September 30, 2018, there were 437,293 children in foster care in the United States (USDHHS, 2019a). Of that number, 51% were reported to be children of color or non-White—i.e., American Indian/Alaska Native, Asian, Black or African American, Native Hawaiian/Other Pacific Islander, Hispanic,[1] or Two or More Races. Since 1995, states have been federally mandated to submit data on all children in foster care to the Adoption and Foster Care Analysis and Reporting System (AFCARS), including demographic data related to race and ethnicity (Pietrowiak & Schibanoff, 2003). It is important to note that AFCARS excludes children who identify as Hispanic from all other racial categories (i.e., African American, White, Asian), noting that "children of Hispanic ethnicity may be of any race" (USDHHS, 2019a, p. 2), meaning that *Hispanic* is an exclusive category. Using recent and historical data, this chapter provides an overview of all children in the U.S. foster care system. Contributing factors related to the disproportionate representation of domestic (U.S.) children of color, as well as the outcome disparities, will be discussed. Trauma-informed care, practice challenges specific to these diverse populations, and evidence-based and systems approaches to working with this population will also be addressed. Lastly, current policies that impact children and families of color involved with the child welfare system will be reviewed.

Child welfare data prior to 1998 is often considered unreliable as states were given a short period of time to comply with the mandate prior to risking penalties for lack of compliance. However, it was not until fiscal year (FY) 2001 that all states, including the District of Columbia and Puerto Rico, submitted the data. AFCARS data is released publicly twice a year, reporting on two time periods—October 1–March 31 and April 1–September 30 of the previous federal fiscal year (October 1–September 30) (Children's

1 In this chapter, the term *Hispanic* is used as opposed to Latinx or Latino/a to be consistent with the Adoption and Foster Care Analysis and Reporting System (AFCARS) data used throughout the chapter.

Bureau, 2012). AFCARS data includes nationwide estimates on the number of children in foster care and the number of children waiting to be adopted, on the last day of the reporting period, as well as estimates of the number of children who entered foster care, exited foster care, and were adopted during that fiscal year. AFCARS also provides demographic data such as age, sex, and race/ethnicity of the children at each of these pivotal points. Lastly, data related to case plan goals, the reason for removal, reason for discharge, placement type, adoption type, and length of time in care is also publicly available. Historical as well as the most recent AFCARS reports are available on the Children's Bureau website (Children's Bureau, 2019).

Overview of Children in Care

In the United States, there are an estimated 73.4 million children under the age of 18 years (Annie E. Casey Foundation, 2019). Of these, 13 million live below the poverty line and have limited access to basic resources, such as safe living, nutritious food, quality education, and health care (Annie E. Casey Foundation, 2019). In addition to experiencing poverty, a significant number of children are victims of abuse or neglect and as a result are often placed in the foster care system for protection. According to Kim, Wildeman, Jonson-Reid, and Drake (2017), 37% of children in the United States experience a child protective services investigation by the age of 18 years. In 2017, approximately 674,000 of the 3.5 million children involved in either a child abuse or neglect investigation or alternative response were confirmed to be victims of child maltreatment, including 1,720 fatalities (USDHHS, 2019b). The majority of these children were victims of neglect (75%), with approximately 18% physically abused and 9% sexually abused. Many of the children were victims of multiple types of abuse or neglect.

Image 6.1

According to AFCARS data collected since 1998, the foster care population has on average been about 52% male and 48% female. As noted in Figure 6.1, the number of children in foster care has fluctuated over time, with the largest estimate recorded in 1999 as 567,000 and lowest in 2012 of 396,605 (USDHHS, 2006–2019). There was a significant decline in the number of children entering foster care between FY 2005 (311,000, the largest estimate recorded) and FY 2012 (251,352, the smallest estimate recorded), due to efforts made by various states to safely reduce the number of children in care, and federal legislation such as the Fostering Connections to Success and Increasing Adoptions Act (2008). After 2012, the number of children entering foster care, as well as the number in care, began to slowly increase. However, between 2016 and 2018, the number of children entering care decreased slightly (from 272,995 in 2016 to 269,799 in 2017, and to 262,956 in 2018) (USDHHS, 2019a). The number of children exiting care hovered around 263,000 since 1998 with the highest estimate being 294,989 in 2007 and the lowest 235,843 in 2014. However, since then, the number exiting care has been slowly increasing (i.e., in 2018, 250,103).

The number of children waiting to be adopted decreased significantly, and the number of children adopted increased after the passing of the Adoption and Safe Families Act of 1997, which included adoption incentive monies awarded to states who increased the number of children adopted from foster care (Child Welfare Information Gateway, 2019). The number of waiting children reached an all-time high in 2000 of 131,000 and dropped to an all-time low of 101,945 in 2012 and has been steadily increasing since that time (USDHHS, 2006–2019). According to historical AFCARS data, in 1998, only 37,000 children were reported to have been adopted through the public child welfare system. This number has increased incrementally over time, and in 2018 an estimated 63,123 children were adopted through public child welfare (USDHHS, 2006–2019) (See Figure 6.1).

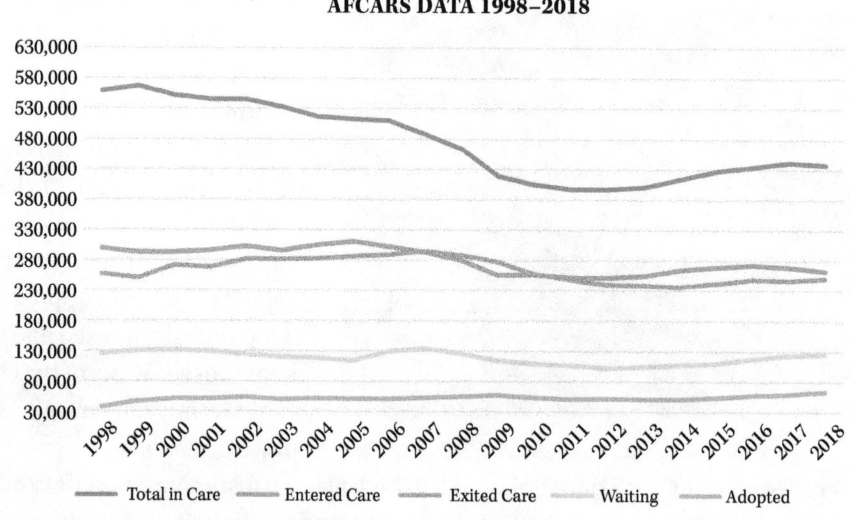

FIGURE 6.1. AFCARS Data (1998–2018)
Data extracted from historical AFCARS reports available from https://www.acf.hhs.gov/cb/research-data-technology/statistics-research/afcars

Racial Disproportionality in the Child Welfare System

Racial disproportionality of children of color, particularly Black/African American children, in the child welfare system has been a concern for several decades (McRoy, 2004) and has been well documented (Ganasarajah, Siegel, & Sickmund, 2017). As stated in Chapter 1, **disproportionality** occurs "when the proportion of people of a certain race or ethnicity in a target population differs from the proportion of people of the same group in a reference population" (Fong, Dettlaff, & Crocker, 2015, p. 5). Historically, the child welfare system was designed to meet the needs of poor White children in the United States (Hill, 2004). Although the system historically served a small number of African American children (Reid & Phillips, 1972) prior to the influx of Black children into the child welfare system after the 1961 Amendment of the Social Security Act of 1961 (P.L. 87-31), the needs of African American children were primarily met by the African American community (Bass, 1997; Hill, 2004; Jeter, 1963). Native American children were served primarily through federal programs under the auspices of the Bureau of Indian Affairs. Other children of color were less than 1% of the population served and counted as "Other Non-White" (Jeter, 1963). As the number of African American children began to increase, the juvenile justice system began to take note and question why this phenomenon was occurring (Derezotes & Poertner, 2005).

The National Council of Juvenile and Family Court Judges (NCJFCJ) annually publishes a report on the disproportionality rates for children of color in foster care (Ganasarajah et al., 2017). A disproportionality index is calculated for each state dividing the proportion of children in foster care, of the different race/ethnic groups, by the proportion of children in the state from the same racial or ethnic group:

$$\frac{\text{Proportion of children in foster care}}{\text{Proportion of children in state population}} = \textbf{Disproportionality Index}$$

Overrepresentation is indicated by a disproportionality index higher than 1.0 and underrepresentation by an index less than 1.0, with a score of 1.0 indicating no disproportionality. For example. according to AFCARS, 23% of the children in U.S. foster care are Black, whereas only 14% of children in the United States are Black, making the disproportionality index approximately 1.6 (Annie E. Casey Foundation, 2019). Between 2010 and 2017, the overall overrepresentation of Black children in foster care nationwide has decreased (improved) from a 2.09 disproportionality index to 1.67, yet the overrepresentation of Native American children has increased from a 2.01 disproportionality index to 2.66 (see Figure 6.2) (Puzzanchera & Taylor, 2019). It is important to note that the disproportionality index of different racial and ethnic groups varies by state. Since 2000, almost every state has an overrepresentation or disproportionate number of Black children in foster care, with the 2017 disproportionality indexes ranging from 1.04 to 3.39 across 43 states (Puzzanchera & Taylor, 2019). The states with the highest overrepresentation of Black children in 2017 were California (3.39), Wisconsin (3.10), New Jersey (2.96), Illinois (2.92), and New York (2.79) (Puzzanchera & Taylor, 2019).

Hispanic children are overrepresented in 21 states, plus Puerto Rico, having disproportionality indexes that range from 1.04 to 2.75. The states with the highest overrepresentation of Hispanic children in 2017 are Maine (2.75), Massachusetts (1.84), Connecticut (1.64), Oklahoma (1.55), and South Dakota (1.51). American Indian/Alaska Native children are overrepresented in Minnesota (16.05), Wisconsin (5.43), North Dakota (4.55), South Dakota (4.10), and Nebraska (3.88). Asian/Pacific Islander children are overrepresented in the state of Hawaii (1.05), and White children are slightly overrepresented (1.02–1.55) in 15 states, the highest being Hawaii (1.55), Mississippi (1.20), Nevada (1.18), Florida (1.13), and Georgia (1.12) (Puzzanchera & Taylor, 2019).

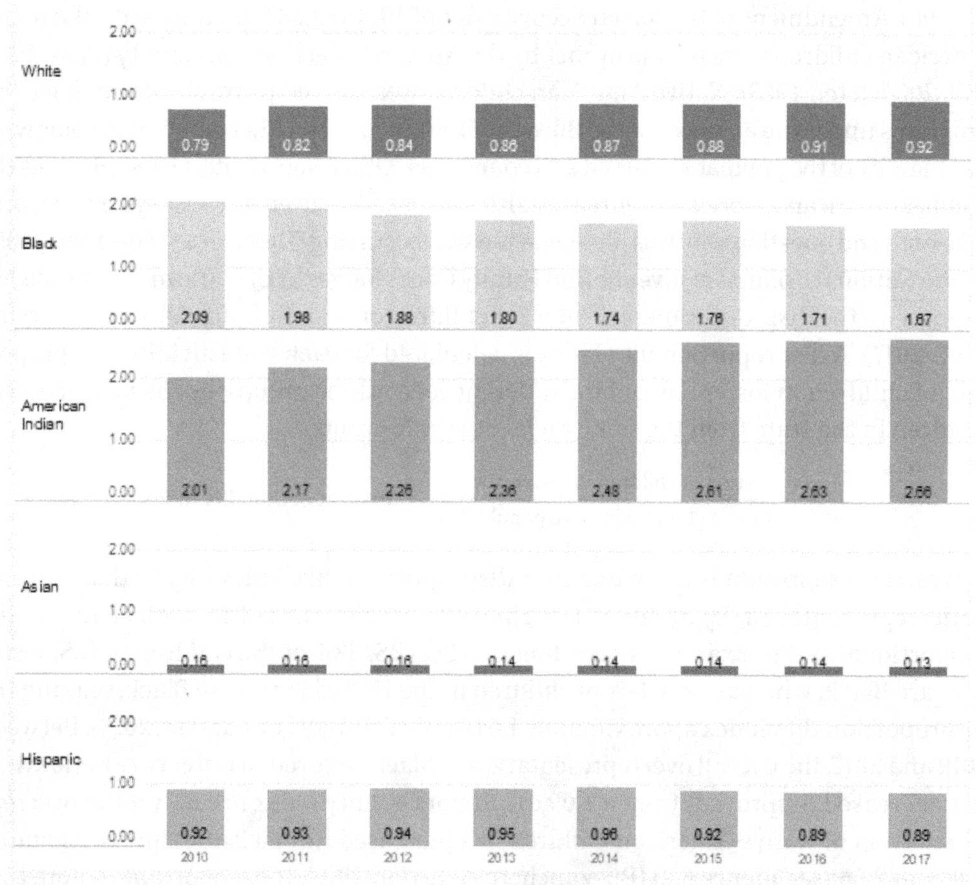

FIGURE 6.2. Trends in Disproportionality Index by Race: Children in Foster Care to Youth Population 2010–2016
Source: Puzzanchera & Taylor, 2019

It is important to note that overrepresentation in and of itself is not necessarily a problem (Fong et al., 2015). If a system is truly responding to a societal issue based on need within a community, some overrepresentation of various groups may emerge and remain over long periods of time. The underlying concern is that this pattern of disproportionality is the result in part of racial biases (implicit or explicit), and historical institutional racism embedded in agency, state, or federal policies that negatively impact minoritized populations (Hill, 2004; Fong, et al., 2015). When coupled with other documented racial disparities that occur within the same system and which negatively impact these same populations, the need to address this issue becomes clear.

Disparity in the Child Welfare System

Disparity occurs when one racial or ethnic group experiences unequal or disparate outcomes as compared to another racial or ethnic group while presumed to be receiving the same or equitable treatment (Fong et al., 2015). Disparities are seen in the child welfare system at multiple decision-making points, including (1) initial report of alleged maltreatment; (2) substantiation of alleged maltreatment; (3) decision to provide services; (4) placement in out of home care; (5) exit from out of home care; and (6) reunification (Dettlaff et al., 2011; Harris & Hackett, 2008; Hill, 2007). Not only are Black, Hispanic, and American Indian/Alaska Native children more likely to be reported as victims of abuse and neglect as compared to White children, they are also more likely to be placed in foster care, spend longer time in the foster care system, and are less likely to reunify with their family (Ards et al., 2012; Dettlaff et al., 2011; Font, Berger, & Slack, 2012; Garcia, Aisenberg, & Harachi, 2012; Harris & Hackett, 2008). American Indian/Alaska Native and Black children are reported to have the highest rate of victimization and having abuse/neglect substantiated (USDHSS, 2019b). African American children have historically been found to have longer lengths of stay in foster care, be less likely to be reunified, and, although they are often more likely to have parental rights terminated, are also less likely to exit care to adoption (Akin, 2011; Alstein & McRoy, 2000; Becker, Jordan, & Larsen, 2007; Lu et al., 2004; Snowden, Leon, & Sieracki, 2008).

Children of color, primarily Black and American Indian/Alaska Native, continue to be overrepresented and experience disparities in child welfare, despite there being no significant difference between the overall maltreatment rates based on race (Dettlaff et al., 2011; Harris, 2014; Hill, 2006). Wildeman and Emanuel (2014) calculated the cumulative risk of children (under the age of 18 in the United States) being placed in foster care and found that while 5.9% (1 in 17) of all U.S. children "will experience foster care placement at some point between birth and 18" (p. 5), the risk of entering foster care between birth and 17 was much higher for American Indian/Alaska Native children (15.44, or 1 in 7) and for Black children (11.53%, or 1 in 9).

The Impact of Trauma on Children in the Child Welfare System

Children who encounter the child welfare system have suffered immense trauma which can negatively impact the physical, emotional, psychological, and mental development of children (Klain & White, 2013). According to the National Conference of State Legislators, "up to 80 percent of children in foster care have significant mental health issues, compared to 18–22 percent of the general population" (NCSL, 2019, para. 1). Research has shown that youth in care have often experienced trauma resulting from frequent moves in care, disrupted family relationships, limited or lack of access to mental health services, and often overutilization of psychotropic medications (National Conference of State Legislators Podcast, Nov. 11, 2019).

It is important for professionals involved in every stage of the child welfare system to provide trauma-informed care to the children and families who come in contact with the child welfare system. The Family First Prevention Services Act, which was signed into law as a part of the Bipartisan Budget Act on February 9, 2018, urges all practitioners to use a trauma-informed approach when providing services. This includes offering appropriate trauma screenings, assessments, and providing trauma-specific treatments. The National Child Traumatic Stress Network (2016) defines trauma-informed system as follows:

> *A trauma-informed child and family service system is one in which all parties involved recognize and respond to the impact of traumatic stress on those who have contact with the system, including children, caregivers and service providers. Programs and agencies with such a system infuse and sustain trauma awareness, knowledge and skills into their organizational cultures, practices and policies. They act in collaboration with all those who are involved with the child, using the best available science, to maximize physical and psychological safety, facilitate the recovery of the child and family, and support their ability to thrive. (para. 1)*

Trauma-informed practices are beneficial, as they focus on treatment of the underlying causes and context of trauma rather than the symptoms. The treatments are designed to help children attain a sense of physical and psychological safety, develop coping strategies, and increase resilience (Klain & White, 2013). The several types of trauma-informed practices include: Child-Parent Psychotherapy, Trauma Affect Regulation, Trauma-Focused Cognitive Behavioral Therapy (TF-CBT), Cognitive Behavioral Interventions for Trauma in School (CBITS), Parent-Child Interaction Therapy (PCIT), and Trauma and Grief Component Therapy for Adolescents. To successfully implement trauma-informed practices, it is imperative for child welfare professionals to receive the adequate training and tools. There are many organizations that have taken the lead in developing trauma-informed frameworks that can be implemented in child welfare. For example, the National Child Traumatic Stress Network (NCTSN) learning collaborative and child welfare trauma training toolkit provides training and resources to educate child welfare professionals regarding trauma-informed practices (National Child Traumatic Stress Network, 2016). Also, the Stark County Family Court in Ohio is another example of utilization of trauma-informed practices in the child welfare system (Howard & Tener, 2008). It is a nationally recognized model of trauma-informed family and juvenile court, which provides trainings related to screening, assessment, and service provision for children who have gone through abuse and neglect. According to the U.S. Department of Health and Human Services, the use of trauma-informed care could lead to fewer children requiring crisis services, decreased use of psychotropic drugs, fewer foster care placements, reduced length of stay in the foster care system, and improved child functioning and overall development.

As noted above, trauma-informed practices are essential to ensure behavioral, emotional, educational, and physical well-being. They have, however, been out of reach for low-income children of color and thus do not provide a comprehensive treatment to many of their presenting problems (Becker, Greenwald, & Mitchell, 2011). As a result, while immediate needs might be met, children of color continue to have negative outcomes, as their trauma has not been addressed. To ensure that culturally responsive trauma-informed practices are provided to children of color, specifically low-income children of color, social workers and other helping professionals should be trained in trauma-informed practices through a cultural humility lens (Fraser et al., 2014). Additionally, systems at all levels that interact with children of color, such as education, health, criminal justice, among others, should integrate culturally responsive trauma-informed practice to ensure that they are equipped to address the complex needs of children of color, who are at a high risk of trauma due to poverty, institutional racism, and violence, among other factors (Becker et al., 2011; Blitz, Anderson, & Saastamoinen, 2016).

As discussed in Chapter 12, another practice that has been found to have a very positive impact on children is kinship care, or placing them with relatives, which can be less traumatic than placing them with "strangers" or nonrelated foster parents. Given the growing number of children needing placement, and often the reduced number of available foster homes, agencies are often seeking potential relative care providers. The federal Fostering Connections Act to Success and Increasing Adoptions Act of 2008 highlights the very important role relatives play in the life of a child in care and encourages agencies to seek relative care providers. Research has shown that kinship care can provide many benefits, including minimizing trauma, improving child well-being, increasing likelihood of relatives becoming the legal guardians of children, decreasing behavioral problems, promoting sibling ties (when children are placed together in the home of a relative), and preserving cultural identity and community connections (Epstein, 2017).

Service and Practice Challenges in the Child Welfare System

Disproportionality in the child welfare system is complex and should be examined based upon (1) parent and family factors; (2) community risk factors; and (3) organizational and systemic factors (McCrory, Ayers-Lopez, & Green, 2006). As mentioned previously, Hispanic,

African American, and American Indian families represent the majority of households in poverty. Many scholars have suggested that the high proportion of children from these ethnic/racial backgrounds in the child welfare system is a result of a lack of substantial economic, social, and emotional support, as well as disproportionately higher needs (Schuck, 2005; Sedlak & Schultz, 2005). Many studies (Chibnall et al., 2003, Sedlak & Broadhurst, 1996, and Pecora et al., 2014) have provided evidence that maltreatment and neglect are not correlated to income or race. However, researchers have found that the number of reported cases, availability of support, and reconciliation efforts do vary by race (Harris, 2014; Hill, 2003; Johnson, Antle, & Barbee, 2009; McRoy, 2005). These studies support the claim that institutionalized or structural racism and its ripple effects are most likely the root cause of the disproportionately high rates of children of color in the child welfare system.

Structural racism is racism at the macro level that serves to generate, perpetuate, and reinforce inequities among racial and ethnic populations (Gee & Ford, 2011). Structural mechanisms—legislation, policies, and procedures—serve to maintain these inequities in collaboration with, and in spite of, individual efforts to eliminate or mediate the underlying inherent racism. Structural racism results in limited accessibility to services that focus on parental support and family preservation and has been the strongest contributor to the disproportionate number of children entering the foster care system (Harris & Hackett, 2008). Children of color and families are less likely to receive services that reduce the impact of poverty, such as health care access, employment support, and housing as compared to White families (Rodenborg, 2004).

Additionally, there can be discrepancies in quality of services provided, the type of agency to which they are referred, the efficiency with which their case is handled, the support the family receives, and the eventual outcomes (Hill, 2003). The Family First Prevention Services Act, passed in 2018, aims to provide preventive services to support families and reduce the risk of children entering the foster care system. This law focuses on providing mental health services, substance abuse treatment, and in-home parenting training, as well as developing a prevention plan for children to remain safely in home. If implemented in an equitable and just manner, this act can help reduce the number of children entering the foster care system dramatically.

Evidence-Based Practices for Children of Color

Evidence-based practices (EBPs) have been traditionally considered a hallmark of effective interventions. EBPs have been supported by policy makers, researchers, and funders to ensure the best outcome for individuals, families, and communities. However, children of color have been often overlooked in the development of EBPs (Annie E. Casey Foundation, 2017; Wells, Merritt, & Briggs, 2009). Although children of color have participated in the clinical trials of the evidence-based programs, they are often not included in the process of designing and conceptualizing the programs. As a result of this, the programs are designed without keeping in mind the unique challenges of these children. Martinez, Callejas, and Hernandez (2010) highlight that one of the biggest challenges in developing EBP for children of color is the narrow definition of evidence, which is based on the expertise of the researcher. Martinez et al. (2010) indicate that for programs and interventions to be effective, specifically for children of color, the unique needs and strengths of the communities in which they reside should be considered. Community-defined evidence extends beyond clinical trials or interventions and is a set of practices that communities have used and determined to yield positive results by community consensus over time, and which may or may not have been measured empirically, but have reached a level of acceptance within the community (Annie E. Casey Foundation, 2017). The report by the Annie Casey Foundation (2017) highlights that to create sustainable and effective solutions for children of color, we need to take a person-in-the-environment perspective and support the children and their caregivers. To be more community focused, the Institute of Medicine has also expanded their definition of EBP to include "the integration of best research evidence with clinical expertise and patient values" (Academy Integrating Behavioral Health and Primary Care, n.d., para. 2). They therefore focus on the need to not only consider empirical research but also the complex realities of communities that children of color are entrenched in.

Some EBPs that have utilized a community-focused lens to improve outcomes for children of color include the following: Strong African American Families Program (SAAF), Familias Unidas, Con Mi Madre, Cultural Wellness Center, Latinos in Action, and Family Connections among others. The SAAF was developed by Gene Brody to address the lack of systematic research and interventions for rural African American families. It is a 7-week interactive educational program for African American parents and their early adolescent children and targets three particular areas: (i) family routines, parent-child relationship quality, racial socialization, and parent involvement in school; (ii) goal setting, self-regulation, resistance skill development; and (iii) the cognitive antecedents of adolescent risk behavior. Two evaluation studies have been conducted to test the effectiveness of SAAF (Futris & Kogan, 2014; Kogan et al., 2016). Both studies were conducted in Georgia. The assessment reported fewer conduct problems, lower alcohol usage, greater positive change in youth protective factors, and greater positive change in parenting after the implementation of SAAF.

Image 6.2

Con Mi Madre: Mothers and Daughters Raising Expectations (conmimadre.org) is a program that engages young Latinas and their mothers to have a shared value for higher education and works with them to make this a reality (Con Mi Madre, n.d.). The program has a curriculum and intervention structure that is based on the challenges that the Hispanic communities face as well as their strengths. For example, the program recognizes the importance of community within the Hispanic culture and utilizes close family to build confidence in both the mother and child simultaneously. Additionally, this program is not limited to ensuring higher enrollment rates. It also looks at structural inequities related to social, cultural, mental, and academic aspects that hinder their enrollment and graduation. The program has not been replicated in other locations currently; however, it is working with organizations such as the Annie E. Casey Foundation to develop a replicable model that can be utilized by other organizations working primarily with Hispanic youth.

The Family Connections project is another relevant example that was developed by Dr. Diane DePanfilis and Dr. Howard Dubowitz (DePanfilis & Dubowitz, 2005) to provide empirically based in-home early intervention services for families living in Baltimore, Maryland. Family Connections is a community-based service program that works with families in their homes and within the context of their communities to help meet the basic needs of children and reduce incidences of neglect (DePanfilis & Dubowitz, 2005). The program has core components or services that address the barriers faced by communities of color, particularly African American communities. The program components include (i) emergency assistance; (ii) home-based family interventions, such as assessment, individual and family counseling, and outcomes-driven service plans; (iii) service coordination with referrals targeted toward risk; and (iv) mutually supportive recreational activities. This project to date has provided services to 1,094 families and supported approximately 3,276 children. This program is being replicated by other agencies in the United States. This includes the Florida Family Connections program and eight programs in the Bronx, Manhattan, and Brooklyn in New York City. Results from the Florida Family Connections program have indicated a positive change in parental attitudes, parenting competencies, and social support. It has also improved child safety and diminished risk factors, such as parental depressive symptoms and parenting stress (DePanfilis, Filene, & Burdowski, 2009).

These examples of EBPs that are informed by the needs of the communities of color show that a systems approach is essential to develop effective solutions to improve outcomes of children of color. The following section addresses how various social systems—educational, legal, and health services, among others—can work in an integrated manner to ensure the well-being of the children who are at risk.

Systems Approach: Integration of Public Systems

The overall well-being of children is dependent on various institutions with which they interact throughout their life span. Some of the most significant institutions include education, criminal justice, and health care. These systems often treat children of color differently, thus negatively impacting their mental, physical, social, emotional, and cognitive growth. These systems and their impact on child well-being are discussed below.

Education System

School success has been correlated with positive short- and long-term outcomes in terms of socioemotional development, physical and health outcomes, as well as economic well-being. Children in various out of home placements are often unable to have a supportive network that positively impacts their educational outcomes. Children of color, particularly African American children, face disproportionately high barriers in school success. With the disproportionately high number of African American children in foster care (23%, or 99,025) (USDDHS, 2019a) and the increased likelihood of having experienced multiple moves in care, there is a greater likelihood that these children experience more educational challenges and more limited school success (Segermark, 2017). Studies have also reported that suspensions and expulsions are also associated with racial bias and cultural misunderstandings, as well as enrollment in special education programs, especially for children diagnosed with emotional, behavioral, or learning disorders (Maydosz, 2014). Children in foster care are more likely to have these diagnoses and therefore may be more likely to not only be enrolled in special education programs, but also be more likely to experience expulsions. A closer look at the implications for African American children reveals that compared to their White peers, they are 2.7 times more likely to be diagnosed with emotional disabilities and twice as likely to be diagnosed with cognitive impairment (Teasley, et al., 2018; Sullivan & Bal, 2013). These factors lead to additional challenges for African American children in foster care to overcome and achieve school success. Educators such as Bowman et al. (2018) suggest that in order to improve the educational outcomes of African American children and other children of color in the foster care system, there is a need to take a more holistic approach, in which educators are trained on issues such as institutional racism, impact of familial and community stressors on education outcomes, historical trauma faced by these students, and lastly effective engagement practices that consider the specific needs of children of color.

Image 6.3

Criminal Justice System

Similar to the education system, children of color are disproportionately impacted by the criminal justice system, including higher rates of arrests, convictions, and incarceration. According to a report by the Annie E. Casey Foundation (2011), out of the 60,500 youth confined in correctional facilities, 2 of every 5 youth are African American, and one-fifth are Hispanic. Non-Hispanic White youth comprised only 37% of the confined youth, even though they are three-fifths of the total youth population in the United States. Research indicates that 1 in 3 African American youth and 1 in 6 Latino youth are expected to go to prison, compared to 1 in 17 White youth (Bonczar, 2003).

Youth, especially youth of color, who are involved in the foster care system have higher risks of being involved in the criminal justice system. These youth are considered *dual jurisdiction youth, or cross-over youth* and are at higher risks of pretrial detention and for commitment into youth correction facilities or other out of home placements (Annie E. Casey Foundation, 2011). The factors that have been attributed to the increased risk are related to unstable living environments, severe punishments or zero tolerance policies practiced within schools, and overall lack of services that support the multidimensional needs of youth in the child welfare system (Bilchik & Nash, 2008; Annie E. Casey Foundation, 2011). The intersection of race and greater likelihood of out of home placement leads to particular mental, emotional, social, and physical challenges that increase the chances of these youth being involved in the juvenile justice system. Additionally, the inequitable treatment of these youth by the criminal justice system has a long-term impact on their psychosocial and emotional well-being as well as overall development. More information on youth involved in both the child welfare system and the juvenile justice system is found in Chapter 16.

It is also important to highlight the continued disproportionately high rates at which children of color come in contact with the juvenile justice system despite decades-long efforts to reduce disparities based on race and ethnicity. As of 2017, non-Hispanic White children accounted for 53% of the juvenile population and 33% of the incarcerated youth, whereas African American youth comprised 14% of the juvenile population, but 40% of the incarcerated youth (Rovner, 2017). In 1988, the Conference of the National Coalition of State Juvenile Justice Advisory Groups highlighted the differential processing of children of color within the juvenile justice system. Based on this, three amendments were made to the Juvenile Justice and Delinquency Prevention Act of 1974, which mandated all states to address disproportionate minority contact (DMC). The first and second amendment directed funds to reduce overrepresentation of minority youth confined in secure detention and other residential treatment settings. The third amendment expanded the focus of overrepresentation from only detention to contact with the system (Kempf-Leonard, 2007). According to a report by the Sentencing Project (Rovner, 2017), although the rates of juvenile arrests have reduced since 1990, the ratio of children of color as compared to White children being arrested has remained largely unchanged. This disproportionate representation of children of color in the juvenile justice system highlights the deep-rooted structural inequities that impact the short- and long-term well-being of children and families of color.

Health and Mental Health Care

Racial disparities are prevalent in the health care system as well. Children of color have a higher likelihood of living in poverty, which is closely related to stunted physical and mental well-being. Living in poverty increases the likelihood of exposure to stressors, such as poor quality of education and housing, unsafe neighborhoods, and reduced access to community resources (American Psychological Association, 2017). Additionally, children of color have an additional challenge of experiencing race- and income-based oppression and discrimination. It is also important to highlight that children of color are disproportionately represented in the child welfare system. Children that enter the child welfare system have a high likelihood of being victims of physical, mental, and emotional abuse and neglect (Stoltzfus, Baumrucker, Fernandez-Alcantara, & Fernandez, 2014). According to a report by the Congressional Research Services (Stoltzfus et al., 2014), approximately 35–60% of children placed in foster care have at least one chronic physical health condition that requires treatment. As many as 75% of the children have some behavioral issues that warrant mental health services to ensure long-term well-being; these children require wraparound mental and physical health services that cater to their unique needs and lead to long term well-being.

A study by the American Psychological Association (APA) (2017) highlighted that while mental health and physical health services might be theoretically available to all children, including children of color, the accessibility and usability are questionable. The services do not take into consideration the intersectionality of various disadvantages that children of color experience. Additionally, children of color are more likely to be misdiagnosed as compared to their White counterparts. Practitioner bias, stereotyping, and prejudice also impact the quality of care that is provided. Additionally, mental health service providers often do not use culturally informed models and acknowledge contextual factors when diagnosing or providing treatments to children of color (APA, 2017).

Overall, policy makers must recognize the presence of deep-rooted structural inequities and how they impact the overall well-being of children of color. Also, service providers should be trained to recognize their implicit bias and work toward providing services that are culturally informed and use an anti-oppressive lens.

Child Welfare Policies: Implications for Children of Color

In general, all child welfare policies—federal and state—impact all children in care regardless of race or ethnicity; however, the two pieces of federal policy that directly impact children of color, specifically American Indian/Alaska Native and African American/Black children are discussed below. The Indian Child Welfare Act of 1978 (ICWA) governs child welfare practice in relation to any child who has or is eligible for membership in a federally recognized tribe. The Multiethnic Placement Act of 1994 as Amended by the Interethnic Adoption Provisions of 1996 (MEPA-IEP) governs policies and procedures related to the placement of all other children in foster care or adoption as well as the recruitment of foster and adoptive parents.

Indian Child Welfare Act of 1978 (ICWA)

As discussed in Chapter 1, ICWA was passed in response to the systematic, forceful removal and placement of Indian[2] children in boarding schools as well as the placement of 395 children for adoption with White families as part of the Indian Adoption project. Four years of deliberation and debate, documented by hundreds of pages of testimony, affirmed that Indian children were being removed from their homes without due process and without thorough investigation or provision of services (Fletcher, 2009). As a result, ICWA not only provides guidance related to the placement of children in foster and adoptive placement but also "provides for minimal procedural guarantees with which each state must comply" when the "state court has jurisdiction in an Indian child custody case" (Fletcher, 2009, p. 5).

According to ICWA, child custody proceedings (cases) include any action, other than an emergency one, that results in one of the following outcomes: (1) foster care placement; (2) termination of parental rights; (3) pre-adoptive placement; and (4) adoptive placement (25 U.S.C. 1903(1); 25 CFR § 23.2). An **Indian child** is defined as "any unmarried person who is under age 18 and either: (1) Is a member or citizen of an Indian Tribe; or (2) Is eligible for membership or citizenship in an Indian Tribe and is the biological child of a member/citizen of an Indian Tribe" (25 CFR § 23.2). Of note, ICWA only applies to those children whose Indian tribe is "federally recognized as eligible for the services provided to Indians by the Secretary because of their status as Indians, including any Alaska Native village as defined in section 3 of the Alaska Native Claims Settlement Act, 43 U.S.C. 1602 (c)" (25 CFR § 23.2). Only the tribe believed to be the child's tribe has the authority to make the determination as to whether or not the child is an Indian child (National Indian Child Welfare Association [NICWA] & Native Rights Fund [NARF], 2016).

In 2016, the Bureau of Indian Affairs provided the first comprehensive regulations and guidance on the implementation of ICWA (NICWA & NARF, 2016). These regulations serve to clarify and strengthen key definitions and provisions of ICWA as it pertains to child welfare matters when they involve Indian children and their families. The provisions of the act ensure that tribes maintain their inherent right to jurisdiction over Indian children. Among the key provisions of the act are:

---

2 Although problematic, the term *Indian* is used when discussing ICWA, as the legislation applies to the "Indian Child" as defined in 25 U.S.C. 1903; 25 CFR § 23.2. See Chapter 7 for additional discussion of terminology when referring to American Indian/Alaska Natives.

Active Efforts—*For Indian children, child welfare agencies must show that they have made active efforts as opposed to reasonable efforts to prevent removal. Culturally specific to Indian families, active efforts are differentiated from reasonable efforts in that when considering removal of a child from the family, caseworkers must actively explore resources within the child and family's tribe and extended family and tailor interventions to be consistent with the cultural values of the child, family, and tribe (Edwards, 2015). If active efforts are unsuccessful, the reasons must be documented and made part of the court record (NICWA & NARF, 2016).*

Notice in Child Custody Proceedings—*ICWA requires that notice be given, not only to the parents of the Indian child, but also to the tribe and/or Indian custodian for any involuntary proceedings seeking placement in either foster care or adoption. Notice is not required for voluntary proceedings or emergency removal. The new regulations increase the Bureau of Indian Affairs' (BIA) role in locating the child's parents, tribe, or Indian custodian, stating that the BIA may be asked to make "reasonable efforts" to assist in the location (NICWA & NARF, 2016).*

Standards of Evidence—*Unlike non-Indian children, the court may only order removal of an Indian child and placement in foster care if clear and convincing evidence is presented (25 CFR § 23.121(a)). For non-Indian children, only a preponderance of evidence is needed for removal or placement (see Box 6.1 for definitions of the standards of proof). Courts may only terminate parental rights for Indian children if the evidence presented is beyond a reasonable doubt (25 CFR § 23.121(b)). For non-Indian children, the standard is clear and convincing. In addition, both placement and termination require "the testimony of one or more qualified expert witnesses, demonstrating that the child's continued custody by the child's parent or Indian custodian is likely to result in serious emotional or physical damage to the child" (25 CFR § 23.121(a)(b)).*

Placement Preferences—*ICWA provides placement preferences for both foster care and adoption, should the removal of an Indian child from their parent or Indian custodian be determined necessary. The preferences for foster care or pre-adoptive placement in descending order are:*

1. A member of the Indian child's extended family;
2. A foster home that is licensed, approved, or specified by the Indian child's Tribe;
3. An Indian foster home licensed or approved by an authorized non-Indian licensing authority; or
4. An institution for children approved by an Indian tribe or operated by an Indian organization which has a program suitable to meet the child's needs. (§ 23.131 (b) (1–4)).

The preferences for adoptive placement in descending order are:

1. A member of the Indian child's extended family;
2. Other members of the Indian child's tribe; or
3. Other Indian families.

Deviation from these preferences may only occur when there is a determination that there is *good cause* to do so. Good cause must be proven by *clear and convincing* evidence and documented on the record. Good cause may be based on any of the following:

1. The request of one or both of the Indian child's parents after they have reviewed the ICWA preferred placement options, if any, that are available;
2. The request of the child if the child is of sufficient age and has the capacity to understand the decision;
3. The presence of a sibling attachment that can only be maintained through a particular placement;
4. The extraordinary physical, mental, or emotional needs of the Indian child; or
5. The unavailability of a suitable placement after a determination by the court that a diligent search was conducted to find suitable placements that meet the placement preferences, but none has been located (NICWA & NARF, 2016, p. 5).

BOX 6.1. Legal Standards of Evidence

A standard of proof refers to the duty of the person responsible for proving the case. There are different standards of proof in different circumstances. The three primary standards of proof are a preponderance of the evidence, clear and convincing evidence, and proof beyond a reasonable doubt.

Preponderance of the Evidence

This is the lowest standard of proof. It is used primarily in civil proceedings. This standard means that it is more likely than not that the facts are what one of the parties claim them to be. In civil cases, the plaintiff bears the burden of proving that all of the legal elements were present in the given case. When deciding whether to rule on behalf of the plaintiff or the defendant, the jury weighs each piece of evidence. Jury instructions often state that the jury can use their own judgment in determining the credibility of each piece of evidence and how much weight to assign to each piece of evidence.

Jurors do not have to be completely convinced of one side. However, the burden requires that the evidence be strong enough that a fair and impartial mind would gravitate toward one side or another.

Although this standard is primarily used in civil cases, it can be used in some aspects of criminal law. For example, if a defendant wants the court to conclude that he or she is not fit to stand trial, the standard of proof is by the preponderance of the evidence.

Clear and Convincing Evidence

This standard is a step up from the preponderance of the evidence standard. This standard requires that the evidence show that it is highly probable or probably certain that the thing alleged has occurred. This standard may apply to civil cases or some aspects of criminal cases. Some states use this standard to determine whether a search was voluntary.

Proof Beyond a Reasonable Doubt

Proof beyond a reasonable doubt refers to the standard of proof in criminal prosecutions. The prosecutor has the duty to convince the jury by proof beyond a reasonable doubt of each and every element of the crime before a jury should convict a defendant. Because a person's freedom is on the line, the highest standard of proof is used. The United States Supreme Court has specifically stated that it is much worse to convict an innocent person than to allow a guilty one to go free. This standard of proof is specifically required by the due process clause of the Fifth Amendment to the federal United States Constitution.

Proof beyond a reasonable doubt does not mean that there can be absolutely no doubt of the defendant's guilt. A jury begins the process of considering a defendant's guilt or innocence by presuming that the defendant is innocent. This standard is comprised of two equal and important parts: the burden of production and the burden of persuasion. The burden of production requires the prosecution to supply adequate evidence to place a fact in issue. If the prosecution does not aptly satisfy the burden of production, the judge can direct a verdict. The burden of persuasion requires the prosecution to persuade the jury of the veracity of each element.

HG.org Legal Resources (2019)

ICWA has been challenged in the courts several times over the years (Trowbridge, 2017). On October 1, 2019, the Fifth Court of Appeals overturned a lower court decision and ruled that ICWA was indeed constitutional (National Indian Child Welfare Association, 2019a). Several entities (including 325 tribes, 57 tribal organizations, 21 states) joined the United States, and four tribes (Morongo, Quinault, Oneida Nation, and Cherokee Nation) appealed a decision rendered by a Texas judge in October 2018 finding ICWA unconstitutional in spite of the fact that two previous United States Supreme Court decisions did not find ICWA unconstitutional (National Indian Child Welfare Association, 2019b). This decision was the result of a lawsuit brought by the State of Texas and a non-Indian foster family who petitioned the court to allow them to deviate from the placement preferences of ICWA so that the family could adopt the child.

The Multiethnic Placement Act of 1994 as Amended by the Interethnic Adoption Provisions (MEPA-IEP)

Concurrently in the 1970s, while American Indian/Alaska Natives were fighting for exclusive jurisdiction over Indian children in child welfare matters, the National Association of Black Social Workers (NABSW) called attention to the rise in transracial placements of Black children with White foster and adoptive parents (Jennings, 2006). As noted above, ICWA was passed in 1978; however, the debate over the transracial placement of Black children in White families continued and culminated in the passage of the Multiethnic Placement Act (MEPA) in 1994 and its amendment by the Interethnic Adoption Provisions in 1996 (MEPA-IEP).

MEPA-IEP is explicitly linked to Title VI of the Civil Rights Act of 1964 (USDHHS, 2009). Violation of MEPA-IEP is deemed to be a violation of Title VI of the Civil Rights Act of 1964 (H.R 6-539, Sec. 553(f)). The stated intentions of MEPA-IEP are to

1. Decrease the length of time that children wait to be adopted;
2. Facilitate the recruitment and retention of foster and adoptive parents who can meet the distinctive needs of children awaiting placement; and
3. Eliminate discrimination on the basis of the race, color, or national origin [RCNO] of the child or the prospective parent. (Hollinger, 1998, p. 2)

Although MEPA-IEP applies to all children of all races, the primary concern of Congress at the time was "that many children, in particular those from minority groups, were spending lengthy periods of time in foster care awaiting placement in adoptive homes" (Children's Bureau, 1995, p. 2). Even more specifically, MEPA was reported to reflect Congress's judgment that "matching children with families of the same race, culture, or ethnicity may result in delaying, or even preventing, the placement for foster care or adoption of children by qualified families" (p. 2). The public media debate as well as the congressional testimony focused primarily on the racial and ethnic preferences of White families who were being denied access to Black children due to policies that gave preference for same-race placements (Herring, 2007; Jennings, 2006; McRoy, Mica, Freundlich, & Kroll, 2007). Creating race-neutral adoption practices and removing the barriers to transracial adoption were seen as a way to reduce the rising disproportionality of Black children in foster care; however, state officials have reported that it has had little effect (Government Accountability Office [GAO], 2007). In fact, several state officials reported that "in some cases child welfare workers may be less likely to place African American children with relatives or in African American adoptive homes, because they mistakenly believed that the law prohibits or discourages same-race adoptions" (GAO, 2007, p. 58).

The Interethnic Adoption Provisions amended the original legislation to "clarify that routine consideration of a child's or a prospective parent's race, color, or national origin is impermissible" (Hollinger, 1998, p. 22) unless it meets the "strict scrutiny" standard of Title IV (Children's Bureau, 2009; Hollinger, 1998). In order to meet the strict scrutiny standard, the state must show that there is a compelling interest to consider **RCNO**, and the only acceptable compelling reason is "advancing the best interests of the child" (Children's Bureau, 2009, p. 5). In summary, under MEPA-IEP:

A state or any other entity in a state that is involved in adoption/foster care placements and receives Title IV- E funds from the federal government may not:

- **Deny an individual the opportunity** to foster or adopt on the basis of the child's or the prospective parent's RCNO or
- **Delay or deny a child's placement** into foster care or adoption on the basis of the child's or the prospective parent's RCNO. (Children's Bureau 2009, p. 9)

Although MEPA-IEP failed to address the systemic racism that led to the disproportionate representation of children of color, primarily Black children, in foster care, a third provision of the law directly addresses the need to diligently recruit families of color as foster and adoptive parents. Specifically, MEPA-IEP requires states to "provide for the **diligent recruitment** of prospective foster/adoptive parents who reflect the race and ethnicity of children currently in the State foster care system for whom homes are needed" (Children's Bureau, 2009, p. 7) as a part of their Title IV-B state plan. Title IV-B state plans are plans that states must submit to receive federal funding under Title IV-B of the Social Security Act (Stoltzfus, 2012). This will be addressed further in Chapter 13.

Interaction of ICWA and MEPA-IEP

As noted above, MEPA-IEP applies to children of all races; however, MEPA-IEP clearly states that it has no effect on the Indian Child Welfare Act (ICWA) (42 U.S. Code § 1996b. Interethnic adoption). This is often confusing to child welfare and adoption professionals, as MEPA-IEP clearly states that RCNO may not be considered in the placement of children in foster care or adoption and, according to the U.S. government, "American Indian/ Alaska Native" is a racial category (U.S. Census, 2018). In short, ICWA acknowledges the political status and sovereignty of the tribes—recognizing them as separate nations with jurisdiction over their citizens (Krakoff, 2014). In doing so, this limits the applicability of the law to those children who are members of tribes affirmed by the U.S. government as sovereign nations—i.e., only members of federally recognized tribes are eligible for the protections of ICWA. MEPA-IEP only addresses discrimination in regard to RCNO of the adoptive parent(s) or child. It does not address cultural considerations such as religion, language, age, or gender; however, federal guidance is clear that culture may not be used as a proxy for race (Hollinger, 1998). ICWA clearly addresses the importance of addressing and maintaining the cultural roots of the Indian child. Children who may be members of Indigenous tribes—those not federally recognized—fall under the jurisdiction of MEPA-IEP.

Similarly, other children of color, including Hispanic, Asian/Pacific Islanders, and others, are under the jurisdiction of MEPA-IEP. In essence, the interaction effect of these two laws is that the majority of the children of color in care are more likely to be placed with White foster and/or adoptive parents because the majority of foster and adoptive parents (those who adopt children from foster care) are White (AdoptUSKids, 2019; Child Welfare Information Gateway, 2016; Kirby, 1997; Vandivere, Malm, Child Trends, & Radel, 2009).

Case Application

The following case vignette is a collective narrative based on real-life situations designed to exemplify the multiple issues facing children and families of color involved in the child welfare system.

Case Vignette

Beth is a 25-year-old, divorced, White, single mother of five children, ages 18 months to 10 years. Beth had her first child, Pryor, when she was 15 years old. Beth was disowned by her parents when she told them she was pregnant by her (then) boyfriend, Jamar, who was African American. Beth moved in with Jamar and his family when she was 6 months pregnant and lived with them until the baby was 2 years old and a month before she graduated from high school. At that time, she moved back in with her parents, who had become attached to baby Pryor. However, they only agreed to let Beth and Pryor move back in their home if she cut off all contact with Jamar and his family. Beth agreed; however, she would periodically meet up with Jamar and his family without her parents' permission or knowledge.

Beth graduated from high school and began attending the local community college, where she met Bobby, a young Native American groundskeeper at the college. She became pregnant and had Bobby Jr. She and Bobby had a rocky relationship, eventually breaking up when Bobby moved back to the

Navajo Reservation. Beth would send Bobby pictures of Bobby Jr. regularly, and Bobby sent birthday cards with $5 every year.

Jamar went on to college on a basketball scholarship and would send Beth $20–50 periodically. Jamar's parents would keep Pryor from time to time when Beth needed to work or wanted to go out. Beth's parents eventually accepted that both of their grandchildren would see their birth fathers; however, they refused to allow any of them to visit in their home and did not have a relationship with either.

Beth met Jacob while working as a waitress at the local diner. She had to drop out of community college and was working two jobs trying to save enough money to move out on her own. Jacob, a White male from out of state, was an auto mechanic who worked for several different auto repair shops around town, but none permanently. Beth and Jacob got married after dating for a year and had three children, Jules and Julia (twins) and Castor. Jacob left Beth when she was pregnant with Castor, and they divorced because he did not believe Castor was his child. When Castor was born, Beth admitted to having an affair with Jacob's best friend, Fernando. Jacob left town and has not had any contact with Beth or any of the children.

At the time of the referral, Beth and her five children were living in an income-restricted apartment complex. Pryor, age 8, and Bobby Jr., age 5, were attending the local elementary school. Jules and Julia, age 3, and Castor, age 18 months, attended the day care on the property where Beth was working during the day. Beth's parents had minimal contact with Beth and the children, seeing them mainly at birthday parties and during the holidays. Pryor spent every other weekend with Jamar and his family. Bobby Jr. continued to receive cards from Bobby and his family and was scheduled to visit his father and family on the reservation the next month. Beth heard a rumor that Jacob was in California but did not know where.

Child welfare became involved because Beth and Fernando were arrested as part of a drug raid at a party in their residential complex. All five children were home asleep and alone at the time of the arrest. The children were all placed in emergency foster homes at the time of removal, as it was around midnight on Saturday night at the time of the removal. Beth refused to give the arresting officers any contact information regarding any next of kin for the children at the time of the arrest. Upon examination, Castor was found to have a severe diaper rash and was slightly dehydrated. Jules and Julia both had bruising on their buttocks and legs and were in various stages of healing. Pryor and Bobby Jr. did not appear to have any physical injuries, but both appeared to be underweight. The apartment was unkempt, and drug paraphernalia was found in the parents' bedroom; minimal food was in the kitchen. Pryor told the police and the caseworkers that his dad and grandparents would come get the children, but he mistakenly transposed two numbers when he gave them the phone number for his dad. The police called the number, but it was a "nonworking" number, so they did not try again, and the children were placed in foster care.

On Monday, the local child welfare office staffed the case and began a diligent search for relatives to take the children. They learned from the police report that this was not Beth or Fernando's first drug arrest, and that Beth would more than likely be in jail for a long period of time and was facing federal charges that may result in serious prison time. The child welfare staff first contacted Beth's parents, who stated they would consider taking Jules and Julia but none of the other children. Pryor's grandparents stated they would be willing to take all five children. Bobby Sr. indicated that he would come get Bobby Jr., and Fernando indicated that his mother would be willing to take Castor, but she was undocumented and afraid to get involved with the authorities.

Additional information discovered during the initial child welfare investigation included the following:

- Pryor has learning disabilities and is delayed in school. He had been often reported as having behavioral problems at school and threatened with suspension. During his weekends with Jamar and family, he spends most Saturdays with Jamar, his girlfriend, and their three children at their apartment, located in another income-restricted complex. Jamar dropped out of college when he tore his ACL, making him ineligible for his basketball scholarship, and he could no longer afford tuition. He works overnight at a warehouse, so when Pryor is visiting, he spends most of the day asleep. Pryor visits his paternal grandparents on Sunday. He goes to church with them, has dinner, and then they drop him off at the apartment complex. Pryor has his own key, so he lets himself in. The grandparents have not actually spoken with or seen Beth in over 3 months.
- Bobby Jr. has a speech delay and is also reported to have behavioral problems at school. He and Pryor are very close and share a bed in the small two-bedroom apartment. Bobby Jr. has an upcoming trip to visit his father and family on the reservation. This is the first time he will actually meet his extended family and, to his memory, his father.
- Jacob is in California in prison serving a 10-year sentence on drug-related charges. Jacob is the one who introduced Beth to meth, and during

their time together, the two of them not only used, but also cooked and sold, meth.

- Fernando is also undocumented. He was deported shortly after his arrest.
- Beth has been in rehab twice, both times paid for by her parents, who have been aware of her drug problem since high school. In high school she mostly drank and smoked marijuana. To their knowledge, she only experimented with harder substances after she met Jacob.

DISCUSSION QUESTIONS

1. Which federal policies discussed in this chapter have an impact on the placement options for these children in the short and long term?
2. What factors need to be considered, and what additional information is needed to make a placement decision for each of the children? Based on this discussion, what is your placement recommendation for the children, and why?
3. What would Beth need to accomplish to have all five children returned to her?
4. Imagine that this case proceeds to the termination of Beth's parental rights, due to her receiving a long-term prison sentence. What are the issues influencing the placement options for each of the children? Why?

References

Academy Integrating Behavioral Health and Primary Care. (n.d). *Evidence-based practices.* https://integrationacademy.ahrq.gov/news-and-events/resources/evidence-based-practices

AdoptUSKids. (2019). *Meet the families.* Adoption Exchange Association. https://adoptuskids.org/for-professionals/adoptuskids-photolisting/meet-the-families

Akin, B. A. (2011). Predictors of foster care exits to permanency: A competing risks analysis of reunification, guardianship, and adoption. *Children and Youth Services Review, 33*(6), 999–1011.

Alstein, H., & McRoy, R. (2000). *Does Family Preservation Serve a Child's Best Interest?* Washington, DC: Georgetown University Press.

American Psychological Association. (2017). *Addressing the Mental Health Needs of Racial and Ethnic Minority Youth: A Guide for Practitioners.* American Psychological Association.

Annie E. Casey Foundation. (2019). 2019 kids count data book: State trends in child well-being. Baltimore: Author.

Annie E. Casey Foundation. (2017). *Considering Culture: Building the Best Evidence-Based Practice for Children of Color.* The Annie E. Casey Foundation.

Annie E. Casey Foundation. (2011). *No Place for Kids: The Case for Reducing Juvenile Incarceration.* The Annie E. Casey Foundation.

Ards, S. D., Myers, S. L., Ray, P., Kim, H. E., Monroe, K., & Arteaga, I. (2012). *Racialized perceptions and child neglect. Children and Youth Services Review, 34*(8)1480–1491.

Bass, S. F. (1997). The public foster care system and the transracial placement of African-American children: Exploring the history and the issue. *Hybrid: The University of Pennsylvania Journal of Law and Social Change* 4, 73–90.

Becker, J., Greenwald, R., & Mitchell, C. (2011). Trauma-informed treatment for disenfranchised urban children and youth: An open trial. *Child and Adolescent Social Work Journal, 28*(4), 257–272.

Becker, M. A., Jordan, N., & Larsen, R. (2007). Predictors of successful permanency planning and length of stay in foster care: The role of race, diagnosis and place of residence. *Children and Youth Services Review, 29*(8), 1102–1113.

Bilchik, S., & Nash, M. (2008). Child welfare and juvenile justice: Two sides of the same coin. *Juvenile and Family Justice Today.*

Blitz, L. V., Anderson, E. M., & Saastamoinen, M. (2016). Assessing perceptions of culture and trauma in an elementary school: Informing a model for culturally responsive trauma-informed schools. *The Urban Review, 48*(4), 520–542.

Bonczar, T. C. (2003). Prevalence of imprisonment in the U.S. population, 1974–2001. Washington, DC: Bureau of Justice Statistics.

Bowman, B. T., Comer, J. P, & Johns, D. J. (2018). Addressing the African American Achievement Gap: Three leading educators call to action. *Young Children, 73*(2).

Chibnall, S., Dutch, N. M, Jones-Harden, B., Brown, A., Gourdine, R., Smith, J., Boone, A., & Snyder, S. (2003). *Children of Color in the Child Welfare System: Perspectives from the Child Welfare Community.* Department of Health and Human services, Children's Bureau, Administration for Children and Families. https://www.childwelfare.gov/pubPDFs/children.pdf

Children's Bureau, Administration for Children and Families, U.S. Department of Health and Human Services, Administration for Children, Youth and Families. (2019). *Adoption & Foster Care Statistics.* https://www.acf.hhs.gov/cb/research-data-technology/statistics-research/afcars

Children's Bureau, Administration for Children and Families, U.S. Department of Health and Human Services, Administration for Children, Youth and Families. (1995, October 11). *Multiethnic placement act: Submission of recruitment plans.* ACYF-PI-CB-95-23. Washington, DC: Author.

Children's Bureau, an Office of the Administration for Children & Families. (2012). *About AFCARS.* https://www.acf.hhs.gov/cb/resource/about-afcars

Children's Bureau, an Office of the Administration for Children & Families. (2009). *Understanding and Complying with Title VI of the Civil Rights Act of 1964 and the Multiethnic Placement Act of 1994, as Amended by the interethnic Provisions (IEP)–PowerPoint.* Washington, DC: Author. https://www.acf.hhs.gov/cb/resource/mepa-powerpoint

Child Welfare Information Gateway. (2019). *Major Federal legislation concerned with child protection, child welfare, and adoption.* Washington, DC: U.S. Department of Health and Human Services, Children's Bureau.

Child Welfare Information Gateway. (2016). *Diligent recruitment of families for children in the foster care system.* Washington, DC: U.S. Department of Health and Human Services, Children's Bureau.

Con Mi Madre (n.d.). *Our Program.* http://www.conmimadre.org/our-program.html

DePanfilis, D., & Dubowitz, H. (2005). Family Connections: A program for preventing child neglect. *Child Maltreatment, 10*(2), 108–123.

DePanfilis, D., Filene, J. H., & Burdowski, L. (2009). Introduction to Family Connections and the national replication effort. *Protecting Children, 24*(3), 4–14.

Derezotes, D., & Poertner, J. (2005). Factors contributing to the overrepresentation of Black children in the child welfare system. In D. Derezotes et al. (Eds.), *Race Matters in Child Welfare: The Overrepresentation of African American Children in the System* (pp. 1–23). Washington, DC: CWLA Press.

Dettlaff, A. J., Rivaux, S. L., Baumann, D. J., Fluke, J. D., Rycraft, J. R., & James, J. (2011). Disentangling substantiation: The influence of race, income, and risk on the substantiation decision in child welfare. *Children and Youth Services Review, 33*(9), 1630–1637.

Edwards, L. (2015). "Active efforts" and "reasonable efforts": Do they mean the same thing? *The Bench, Spring,* 33–34.

Epstein, H. (2017). *Kinship care is better for children and families.* Washington, DC: American Bar Association. https://www.americanbar.org/groups/public_interest/child_law/resources/child_law_practiceonline/child_law_practice/vol-36/july-aug-2017/kinship-care-is-better-for-children-and-families/

Fletcher, M. (2009). The origins of the Indian Child Welfare Act (ICWA): A survey of the legislative history. East Lansing: Michigan State University College of Law: Indigenous Law and Poverty Center. http://www.law.msu.edu/indigenous/papers/2009-04.pdf

Fong, R., Dettlaff, A., Crocker, T. (2015). Introduction to racial disproportionality and disparities. In R. Fong, A. Dettlaff, J. James, & C. Rodriguez (Eds.), *Addressing Racial Disproportionality and Disparities in Human Services: Multisystemic Approaches.* New York: Columbia University Press.

Font, S. A., Berger, L. M., & Slack, K. S. (2012). Examining racial disproportionality in child protective services case decisions. *Children and Youth Services Review, 34*(11), 2188–2200.

Fraser, J. G., Griffin, J. L., Barto, B. L., Lo, C., Wenz-Gross, M., Spinazzola, J., Bodian, R. A., Nisenbaum, J. M., & Bartlett, J. D. (2014). Implementation of a workforce initiative to build trauma-informed child welfare practice and services: Findings from the Massachusetts Child Trauma Project. *Children and Youth Services Review,* 44, 233–242.

Futris, T. G., & Kogan, S. (2014). *The Strong African American Families (SAAF) project: 2010–2014 program impact report.* Athens: University of Georgia Cooperative Extension.

Ganasarajah, S., Siegel, G., & Sickmund, M. (2017). *Disproportionality Rates for Children of Color in Foster Care (Fiscal Year, 2015).* Reno, NV: National Council of Juvenile and Family Court Judges.

Garcia, A., Aisenberg, E., & Harachi, T. (2012). Pathways to service inequities among Latinos in the child welfare system. *Children and Youth Services Review, 34*(5), 1060–1071.

Gee, G. C., & Ford, C. L. (2011). Structural racism and health inequities. *DuBois Review, 8*(1), 115–132.

Government Accountability Office. (2007). African American childing in foster care: Additional HHS assistance needed to help states reduce the proportion in care. (GAO Publication No. 07-816). Washington, DC: U.S. Government Printing Office.

Harris, M. S. (2014). *Racial Disproportionality in Child Welfare.* New York: Columbia University Press.

Harris, M. S., & Hackett, W. (2008). Decision points in child welfare: An action research model to address disproportionality. *Children and Youth Services Review, 30*(2), 199–215.

Herring, D. J. (2007). The Multiethnic Placement Act: Threat to foster child safety and well-being. *University of Michigan Journal of Law Reform, 41*(1) 89–120.

HG.org Legal Resources. (2019). *Different standards of proof.* HG.org Legal Resources—HGExperts.com. https://www.hg.org/legal-articles/different-standards-of-proof-6363

Hill, R. (2004). Institutional racism in child welfare. In J. E. Everett, S. P. Chipungu, & B. R. Leashore (Eds.), *Child Welfare Revisited: An Africentric Perspective* (pp. 57–76). New Brunswick, NJ: Rutgers University Press.

Hill, R. B. (2007) *An analysis of racial/ethnic disproportionality and disparity at the national, state and county levels.* Seattle: Casey Family Programs.

Hill, R. B. (2006). *Synthesis of research on disproportionality in child welfare: An update.* Seattle: Casey Family Programs.

Hill, R. B. (2003). *The Strengths of Black Families.* University Press of America.

Hollinger, J. H. (1998). *A Guide to the Multiethnic Placement Act of 1994 as Amended by the Interethnic Provisions of 1996.* Washington, DC: American Bar Association. https://www.americanbar.org/content/dam/aba/administrative/child_law/GuidetoMultiethnicPlacementAct.pdf

Howard, J. M. L., & Tener, R. R. (2008). Children who have been traumatized: One court's response. *Juvenile and Family Court Journal, 59*(4), 21–34.

Jennings, P. K. (2006). The trouble with the Multiethnic Placement Act: An empirical look at transracial adoption. *Sociological Perspectives, 49*(4), 559–581.

Jeter, H. R. (1963). *Children problems and services in child welfare programs* (No. 403). Washington, DC: U.S. Department of Health, Education, and Welfare, Welfare Administration, Children's Bureau.

Johnson, L. M., Antle, B. F., & Barbee, A. P. (2009). Addressing disproportionality and disparity in child welfare: Evaluation of an anti-racism training for community service providers. *Children and Youth Service Review, 31*, 688–696.

Kempf-Leonard, K. (2007). Minority youths and juvenile justice: Disproportionate minority contact after nearly 20 years of reform efforts. *Youth Violence and Juvenile Justice, 5*(1), 71–87.

Kim, H., Wildeman, C., Jonson-Reid, M., & Drake, B. (2017). Lifetime prevalence of investigating child maltreatment among U.S. children. *American Journal of Public Health, 107*(2), 274–280.

Kirby, K. M. (1997). Foster parent demographics: A research note. *The Journal of Sociology & Social Welfare, 24*(2), 135–141.

Klain, E. J., & White, A. R. (2013). Implementing trauma-informed practices in child welfare. *ABA Center on Children and the Law*. Child Welfare. http://childwelfaresparc.org/wp-content/uploads/2013/11/Implementing-Trauma-Informed-Practices. pdf

Kogan, S. M., Lei, M. K., Brody, G. H., Futris, T. G., Sperr, M., & Anderson, T. (2016). Implementing family-centered prevention in rural African American communities: A randomized effectiveness trial of the Strong African American families program. *Prevention Science, 17*(2), 248–258.

Krakoff, S. (2014). Constitutional concern, membership, and race. *FIU Law Review, 9*(2), 295–330.

Lu, Y. E., Landsverk, J., Ellis-Macleod, E., Newton, R., Ganger, W., & Johnson, I. (2004). Race, ethnicity, and case outcomes in child protective services. *Children and Youth Services Review, 26*(5), 447–461.

Martinez, K., Callejas, L., & Hernandez, M. (2010). Community-defined evidence: A bottom-up behavioral health approach to measure what works in communities of color. *Emotional & Behavioral Disorders in Youth, 10*(1), 11–16.

Maydosz, A. S. (2014). Disproportional representation of minorities in special education. *Journal for Multicultural Education, 8*(2), 81–88.

McCrory, J., Ayers-Lopez, S., & Green, D. (2006). Disproportionality in child welfare. *Protection Connection, 12*(4), 1–16.

McRoy, R. (2004). The color of child welfare. In K. E. Davis & T. B. Bent-Goodley (Eds.), *The Color of Social Policy* (pp. 37–64). Alexandria, VA: Council on Social Work Education.

McRoy, R., Mica, M., Freundlich, M., & Kroll, J. (2007). Making MEPA-IEP work: Tools for professionals. *Child welfare, 86*(2), 49–66.

McRoy, R. G. (2005). Overrepresentation of children and youth of color in foster care. In G. Mallon & P. Hess (Eds.), *Child Welfare for the Twenty-first Century: A Handbook of Practices, Policies and Programs* (pp. 623–634). New York: Columbia University Press.

National Association of Social Workers [NASW]. (2015). Standards and indicators for Cultural Competence in Social Work Practice. Washington, DC: NASW Press.

National Child Traumatic Stress Network. (2016). *What is a trauma-informed child and family service system?* https://www.nctsn.org/resources/what-trauma-informed-child-and-family-service-system

National Conference of State Legislatures Child Welfare Podcast. (11/1/2019). *Mental Health and Foster Care.*

National Conference of State Legislatures Child Welfare Podcast. (2019). *Mental Health and Foster Care.* https://www.ncsl.org/research/human-services/mental-health-and-foster-care.aspx

National Indian Child Welfare Association. (2019a). *Child and family policy update, October 2019.* https://www.nicwa.org/policy-update/

National Indian Child Welfare Association. (2019b). *Child and family policy update, January 2019.* https://www.nicwa.org/policy-update/

National Indian Child Welfare Association & Native American Rights Fund. (2016, June). *Indian Child Welfare Act Final Rule—25 CFR Part 23 Summary of Key Provisions.* Oregon/Colorado: Author.

Pecora, P. J., Sanders, D., Wilson, D., English, D., Puckett, A., & Rudlang-Perman, K. (2014). Addressing common forms of child maltreatment: Evidence-informed interventions and gaps in current knowledge. *Child & Family Social Work, 19*(3), 321–332.

Pietrowiak, D., & Schibanoff, S. L. (2003). Child welfare: Most states are developing statewide information systems, but reliability of child welfare data could be improved. (GAO-03-809). Washington, DC: General Accounting Office.

Puzzanchera, C., and Taylor, M. (2019). Disproportionality rates for children of color in foster care dashboard, National Council of Juvenile and Family Court Judges. http://www.ncjj.org/AFCARS/Disproportionality_Dashboard.aspx

Reid, J. H., & Phillips, M. (1972). Child welfare since 1912. *Children Today, 1*(22), 13–18.

Rodenborg, N. A. (2004). Services to African American children in poverty: Institutional discrimination in child welfare? *Journal of Poverty, 8*(3), 109–130.

Rovner, J. (2017, September 12). Black Disparities in Youth Incarceration. http://www.sentencingproject.org/publications/black- disparities-youth-incarceration/

Sedlak, A., & Schultz, D. (2005). Racial differences in child protective services investigation of abused and neglected children. In D. Derezotes, J. Poertner, & M. F. Testa (Eds.), *Race Matters in Child Welfare: The Overrepresentation of African American Children in the System* (pp. 97–118). Washington, DC: CWLA Press.

Sedlak, A. J., & Broadhurst, D. D. (1996). The national incidence study of child abuse and neglect. Washington, DC: U.S. Department of Health and Human Services, 8730763.

Segermark, D. R. (2017). Students in foster care at risk of school failure: Addressing multiple needs. *Culminating Projects in Special Education, 52*, 1–61.

Schuck, A. M. (2005). Explaining black-white disparity in maltreatment: Poverty, female-headed families, and urbanization. *Journal of Marriage and Family, 67*(3), 543–551.

Snowden, J., Leon, S., & Sieracki, J. (2008). Predictors of children in foster care being adopted: A classification tree analysis. *Children and Youth Services Review, 30*(11), 1318–1327.

Stoltzfus, E. (2012). Child welfare: Funding for child and family services authorized under Title IV-B of the Social Security Act. Washington, DC: Congressional Research Service.

Stoltzfus, E., Baumrucker, E. P., Fernandez-Alcantara, A. L., & Fernandez, B. (2014). *Child Welfare: Health Care Needs of Children in Foster Care and Related Federal Issues.* Congressional Research Services.

Sullivan, A. L., & Bal, A. (2013). Disproportionality in special education: Effects of individual and school variables on disability risk. *Exceptional Children, 74*(4), 475–494. doi: 10.1177/001440291307900406

Teasley, M., McRoy, R. G., Joyner, M., Armour, M., Gourdine, R., Crewe, S., Kelly, M., Franklin, C., Payne, M., Jackson, J., & Fong, R. (2018). *Increasing Success for African American Children and Youth.* Working Paper, American Academy of Social Work & Social Welfare.

Trowbridge, S. (2017). Understanding the 2016 Indian Child Welfare Act regulations. *Child Law Practice, 36*(1), 6–10.

U.S. Census Bureau. (2018). *Race.* https://www.census.gov/topics/population/race/about.html

U.S. Department of Health & Human Services (USDHSS), Administration for Children and Families, Administration on Children, Youth and Families, Children's Bureau. (2019a). The AFCARS Report. *Preliminary Estimates for FY2018 as of August 22, 2019. (No. 26).* Available from https://www.acf.hhs.gov/cb/research-data-technology/statistics-research/afcars

U.S. Department of Health & Human Services (USDHSS), Administration for Children and Families, Administration on Children, Youth and Families, Children's Bureau. (2019b). *Child Maltreatment 2017.* Available from https://www.acf.hhs.gov/cb/research-data-technology/ statistics-research/child-maltreatment

U.S. Department of Health & Human Services (USDHSS), Administration for Children and Families, Administration on Children, Youth and Families, Children's Bureau. (2018). *Trends in foster care and adoption: FY 2008-FY 2017.* Available from https://www.acf.hhs.gov/cb/resource/trends-in-foster-care-and-adoption

U.S. Department of Health & Human Services (USDHSS), Administration for Children and Families, Administration on Children, Youth and Families, Children's Bureau. (2009). *Understanding and Complying with Title VI of the Civil Rights Act of 1964 and the Multiethnic Placement Act of 1994 as Amended by the Interethnic Adoption Provisions (IEP).* Available from https://www.acf.hhs.gov/sites/default/files/cb/mepa_power–point.pdf

U.S. Department of Health & Human Services (USDHSS), Administration for Children and Families, Administration on Children, Youth and Families, Children's Bureau. (2006–2019). The AFCARS Reports. *(No. 10-26).* Available from AFCARS Data: https://www.acf.hhs.gov/cb/research-data-technology/statistics-research/afcars

Vandivere, S., Malm, K., Child Trends, & Radel, L. (2009). Adoption USA. A chartbook based on the 2007 national survey of adoptive parents. Washington, DC: U.S. Department of Health and Human Services, Office of the Assistant Secretary for Planning and Evaluation.

Wells, S. J., Merritt, L. M., & Briggs, H. E. (2009). Bias, racism, and evidence-based practice: The case for more focused development of the child welfare evidence base. *Children and Youth Services Review, 31*(11), 1160–1171.

Wildeman, C., & Emanuel, N. (2014). Cumulative risks of foster care placement by age 18 for US children, 2000–2011. *PLOS ONE, 9*(3), e92785.

Figure Credits

Img. 6.1: Copyright © 2010 Depositphotos/Feverpitch.

Fig. 6.1: Source: https://www.acf.hhs.gov/cb/research-data-technology/statistics-research/afcars.

Fig. 6.2: Source: http://www.ncjj.org/AFCARS/Disproportionality_Dashboard.aspx.

Img. 6.2: Copyright © 2013 Depositphotos/dnf-style.

Img. 6.3: Copyright © 2013 Depositphotos/michaeljung.

CHAPTER • 7

Native Children and Families in Child Welfare

Nancy M. Lucero

Overview of Native Peoples in Child Welfare

The U.S. Census Bureau estimates that in 2017, 6.8 million people in the United States, or 2.0% of the total population, identified as American Indian and Alaska Native, either alone or in combination with one or more other races (U.S. Census Bureau, Population Division, 2018). Approximately 32% of the American Indian and Alaska Native population, or 166,000 individuals, are ages 0–18 (National Congress of American Indians, n.d.). Within this chapter, the terms *Native* and *Native people* will be used by the author to refer collectively to American Indians and Alaska Natives. However, when referring to research findings from other authors, the terminology originally used to refer to the groups under study has been retained (e.g., *American Indian* or *American Indians and Alaska Natives*). Additionally, the Indian Child Welfare Act, Public Law 93-608 (Office of the Law Revision Counsel, n.d.), uses the term *Indian* to refer inclusively to American Indians and Alaska Natives. When referring to elements of the ICWA, the author retains the terminology of the act.

There are 573 **federally recognized tribes** in the continental United States and Alaska located on reservations or within other geographical areas over which they exercise control (National Congress of American Indians, 2019). Tribes vary considerably in the size of their membership, from small tribes with several dozen members to very large tribes with several hundred thousand members. Reservation size varies as well, from less than 2 square miles to the more than 16 million acres that comprise the Navajo Nation (U.S. Dept. of the Interior, n.d.). Census data also indicate that 78% of the American Indian and Alaska Native, alone-or-in-combination population, live outside of American Indian and Alaska Native areas (Norris, Vines, & Hoeffel, 2012).

The Pew Research Center (2015) identified that in 2013, 50% of the multiracial population in the United States identified as White-American Indian; this same study also found 61% of American Indian women and 54% of American Indian men were married to someone from another racial group. The exogenous, or out-marriage, trend, in which American Indians marry members of other racial groups, has been identified as beginning in earnest in the 1960s (Sandefur & McKinnell, 1986), and as the 2015 Pew study confirms, continues in the present. One consequence of this phenomenon is that increasing numbers of Native children are no longer eligible for **tribal membership** (also referred to as tribal enrollment), most often because their blood quantum has fallen below their tribal nation's minimum requirement because of their mixed heritage.

The ICWA uses a specific legal definition of a Native child for purposes of determining those children covered under the act. In the act's language, an "Indian Child" is any unmarried person who is under age 18 and is either: (1) a member of an Indian tribe; or (2) eligible for membership in an Indian tribe and is the biological child of a member of an Indian tribe (25 U.S.C. § 1903). Native children who are not eligible for tribal membership, and thus also not covered by the federal Indian Child Welfare Act[1] (ICWA) (Public Law 95-608), may still be members of families who hold tribal worldviews and values, practice tribal traditions, and structure their families in traditional ways. These children often are still identified by their family and community, or identify themselves, as culturally Indian. State child protective services (CPS) agencies are encouraged to provide these Native children and families with services that are culturally congruent and responsive and "in the spirit of ICWA" (Judicial Council of California, n.d.).

Before moving further into this chapter's content, readers should be aware that two different child welfare systems exist to serve Native children and families—tribal child welfare agencies and state CPS agencies. A Native child's legal domicile and tribal enrollment status are basic determinants of whether a **tribal child welfare agency** or a state CPS agency will handle his or her case. Domicile looks to the person's physical presence in a certain place along with the intent to remain in that place. Children typically are unable to form the requisite intent to establish a domicile, so the domicile of the child is determined by that of the parents. Domicile is important in child custody proceedings because it may affect the jurisdiction of the court. Children who are members of, and *domiciled within,* the boundaries of their tribal nation, when abuse or neglect occurs, fall under the jurisdiction of the tribal nation and are served by the tribe's child welfare agency (Native American Rights Fund, 2007). Native children domiciled outside their tribe's boundaries when abuse or neglect occurs, such as in cities, towns, and non-reservation rural areas, come under the immediate jurisdiction of the state or county child welfare system serving that area, and these children may be afforded the protections of the ICWA[1] if they are members of, or eligible for membership in, a federally recognized tribe.

This chapter will present current statistics on Native children's involvement in child welfare and foster care and discuss disproportionality and disparities for this segment of

1 A detailed explanation of all requirements for ICWA compliance is beyond the scope of this chapter. Many resources are available on this topic. Interested readers may want to begin by visiting the websites of the National Indian Child Welfare Association (www.nicwa.org) or the Native American Rights Fund (www.narf.org/icwa).

the child welfare population. Readers will learn about historical processes and policies that continue to play a part in these child welfare disparities, as well as how current high levels of trauma exposure may also increase the risk of Native caregivers becoming involved in a child welfare action. The chapter will offer information on practice and service delivery considerations when working with Native families and examine evidence-informed practices that show promise in Native child welfare. A case vignette that exemplifies family and caseworker challenges in cases with Native families concludes the chapter.

Statistics on Native Children in Child Welfare

The National Child Abuse and Neglect Data System (NCANDS) revealed that in 2016, 8,861 Native children across the United States were victims of child abuse or neglect (U.S. Children's Bureau, 2018). The actual figure may be higher since this number does not include Native children who were classified as multiple race or those served by some tribal child welfare agencies. A limited number of tribes contribute abuse and neglect data to the NCANDS system, and currently, there is no central source that compiles annual statistics on the total number of Native children nationally who are served by tribal child welfare agencies. State and national statistics indicate that Native children are referred to child welfare significantly more often for neglect than are White children (Casey Family Programs, 2011; Earle & Cross, 2001), and evaluations of urban Native families have also shown them to become involved with child welfare more often for neglect than for abuse (Lucero & Bussey, 2015).

Image 7.1

The 2016 Adoption and Foster Care Reporting System (AFCARS) data indicated that 10,366 Native children, or 2% of the total foster care population, were in care on September 30, 2016. Of all children entering foster care in FY 2016, 6,033 (2%) were Native; of all children exiting foster care for the same period, 5,125 (2%) were also Native children (U.S. Children's Bureau, 2017). Adoption statistics reflect the consistent 2% figure: 2,302 Native children were waiting to be adopted (2% of total children waiting) and 970 (again, 2% of total) were adopted with public child welfare involvement during FY 2016 (U.S. Children's Bureau, 2017).

History of Native Peoples in Child Welfare

Historically, child welfare policies and practices in the United States (and similarly in Canada) have reflected the structural and institutional racism in American society and have functioned to replicate the colonized status of Native people. This has been exemplified by Native people having had an increased likelihood of becoming involved with the child welfare system, and, once involved, finding it extremely difficult to reunify with their children (Halverson, Puig, & Byers, 2002; Horejsi, Craig, & Pablo, 1992; Kessel & Robbins, 1984). The imposition of dominant culture power, along with racial bias, ignorance of Native cultural practices, and the imposition of dominant culture standards of child-rearing and family structure—coupled with poverty, lack of resources in Native communities, and negative stereotypes of reservations—have for decades also contributed to high rates of child welfare involvement for Native children and families (Hull, 1982; Pierce & Pierce, 1996; Siegel, 1994).

Challenges for Native families in the United States began in the early 1800s with Congress's attempts to deal with the "Indian problem": how to civilize Native people, assimilate them into mainstream American society, and transfer lands under tribal control to White settlers (Hoxie, 2001). American Indians and Alaska Natives are the only ethnic group in America toward whom official policies were carried out with the intent of physical annihilation (Hull, 1982). The desire to possess Native lands was the primary driving force, with colonial policy makers envisioning that Native nations would cede their land for American westward expansion in exchange for treaties offering assistance in moving toward civilization (Ostler, 2015). However, when these nations resisted, wars of extermination and forced removals were legally sanctioned and considered morally justified (Innskeep, 2015; Ostler, 2015). Later policy direction shifted to assimilating Native people into the national whole by destroying the social, familial, and community structures of Native nations (Dippie, 1982; Lacey, 1986). Assimilative efforts involved several intentional and organized efforts that relate to child welfare—boarding schools, non-Indian adoptions, and urban relocation.

Image 7.2

Beginning in 1879 with the opening of the Carlisle Indian Industrial School in Carlisle, Pennsylvania, Native children became early assimilation targets when they began to be forcibly removed from their families and communities and placed in government or church-run boarding schools. Boarding schools were a mechanism used to destroy traditional extended family and clan structures and communal childrearing processes and to prevent cultural transmission by forbidding the speaking of Indigenous languages and the practice of social and spiritual traditions (Adams, 1995; Gram, 2016). By 1900, most Native children were being reared in boarding schools and institutions under the control of the Bureau of Indian Affairs (BIA) (Cross, Earle, & Simmons, 2000). Although federal policy on Indian education began to change in the 1920s and mandatory attendance requirements were lessened in the 1930s (Marr, n.d.), large numbers of Native children continued to attend boarding schools on a semi-voluntary basis well into the 1970s (Earle, 2000).

BOX 7.1. Carlisle Indian Industrial School—Carlisle, Pennsylvania

In 1879 the United States government undertook a project aimed at assimilating Native American youth into mainstream American culture. Amid dire predictions of the "extinction" of Native Americans without complete and rapid integration, Civil War veteran Lt. Col. Richard Henry Pratt spearheaded the effort to create an off-reservation boarding school. Pratt instituted a system of forced "Americanization," abandonment of Native languages, required conversion to Christianity, and harsh military discipline, and headed north to create the Carlisle Indian Industrial School.

After Pratt convinced several influential tribal leaders to send their children with him to Pennsylvania, the Carlisle Indian Industrial School opened its doors as the nation's first non-reservation boarding school. Pratt maintained his belief that the only hope for Native American survival was to shed all native culture and customs: thus Pratt's refrain, "Kill the Indian, Save the Man."

The school was in operation for 39 years from 1879–1918. More than 10,000 Native children attended from more than 141 different tribes. Only a fraction ever graduated. Disease and harsh conditions took their toll, and hundreds of children died, with 186 still buried on the site today.

From: Carlisle Indian Industrial School Heritage Center Project
http://www.carlisleindianschoolproject.com/history/

Removal of Native children from their families and their adoption by non-Natives was the second large-scale assimilation effort. These adoptions eventually came to be well planned and systematically executed when, in 1959, the Child Welfare League of America (CWLA), in cooperation with the BIA, initiated the Indian Adoption Project. The project promoted private adoptions of Native children by non-Natives, and adopting out Native children quickly became standard public child welfare practice (Jacobs, 2013; Palmiste, 2011). In the early 1970s, just over a decade after the project began, nearly one in four Native infants under 1 year of age had been placed for adoption; 90% of these were placed in non-Native homes (Earle, 2000).

Assimilation policies of the 20th century also focused on the relocation of Native peoples from their rural communities to large metropolitan areas and other urban settings. The Bureau of Indian Affairs Voluntary Relocation Program of the 1950s–1970s moved large numbers of Indian people from their reservations to the city (Fixico, 2000). Native urbanization continued at a high rate even after the Relocation Program ended in the mid-1970s, so that the percentage of American Indians and Alaska Natives now living in urban areas is greater than the number living in official tribal areas (Norris, Vines, & Hoeffel, 2012). While some Native families quickly established a life in the city, found ways to practice cultural traditions and maintain cultural connections in the urban environment, and even flourished (Lucero, 2013), others experienced cultural dislocation, discrimination, loss of social and familial support networks, and other conditions that put them at high risk of child welfare involvement (Blackhawk, 1995; Jackson, 1998).

By the mid-1970s, Native children were being placed in out of home care at 12–18 times the rate of non-Indian children (Cross, 1986), and statistics such as this contributed to a national call for action to stop the loss of tribal children. The result was passage of the Indian Child Welfare Act in 1978. The ICWA brought with it high expectations that child welfare would take a different approach in its work with Native families and that Native children would remain in their homes and connected to their tribes (Bending, 1997). However, despite the requirements of the ICWA, the number of Native children placed in out of home care increased by 25% in the early-to-mid-1980s (Bending, 1997; Mannes, 1995), and by the end of that decade, placement rates for Native children were 3.6 times higher than for non-Native children (Wares, Wedel, Rosenthal, & Dobrec, 1994). By itself, the ICWA was unable to overcome the effects of institutionalized racism and decades of government-supported assimilation policy on the overrepresentation of Native children in child protection and adoption systems. Thus, disproportionality and disparities for Native children and families remain ongoing problems (Crofoot & Harris, 2012).

Child Welfare Disproportionality and Disparities for Native Children

Both disproportionality, or overrepresentation, and disparity are concepts that apply to involvement of Native people with state CPS agencies. Disproportionality in child welfare refers to the *representation rate of a racial/ethnic group (or other social group) being greater or lesser than its percentage in the general population.* Disproportional representation may occur at one or more points in the child welfare process, such as reports to CPS, investigations or assessments, opened cases, and removals from home (Child Welfare Information Gateway, 2016). Disparity, in contrast, refers to a state of being unequal *in comparison to another racial/ethnic group*, and this statistic represents the likelihood of one group experiencing an event compared to the likelihood of another group experiencing that same event (Shaw, Putnam-Hornstein, Magruder, & Needell, 2008). Disparities in outcomes between Native and other groups also occur at various points throughout the child welfare process (Farrow, Notkin, Derezotes, & Miller, 2010).

The Children's Bureau calculates a racial disproportionality index (RDI) to compare the percentage of Native children in the child welfare system to their percentage in the general population. An RDI of 1.0 would mean Native children are represented proportionately in child welfare to their representation in the general population, and an RDI more than 1.0 would indicate they are overrepresented. For example, an RDI of 2.0 for a particular child welfare process would mean Native children are represented at twice their rate in the general population (U.S. Children's Bureau, 2016). In 2014, Native children comprised 0.9% of the general child population and 1.3% of the children identified by CPS as victims; the corresponding RDI of 1.5 indicates that Native children are represented among victims of child abuse and neglect at 1.5 times their rate in the general population. RDIs calculated for other points in the child welfare process also show Native disproportionality: Native children currently in foster care are overrepresented by 2.8 times, and Native children waiting to be adopted are overrepresented by 2.2 times their rate.

Of special note is that the RDI for Native children in foster care increased from 1.5 in 2000 to 2.7 in 2014 (U.S. Children's Bureau, 2016). A National Council of Juvenile and Family Court Judges study in 2014 found that Native children are not overrepresented in all states but are disproportionately overrepresented in 21 states. Of these states, 24% have a disproportionality index of greater than 4.1, with Minnesota having the highest disproportionality index at 13.9 (National Council of Juvenile and Family Court Judges, 2016).

Native Trauma Exposure and Trauma as a Child Welfare Issue

National statistics indicate that Native people experience traumatic victimization at very high rates: 83.4% of Native women (or more than 4 in 5) and 81.6% of Native men (again, more than 4 in 5) have reported at least one violent experience in their life history (Rosay, 2016). In contrast, lifetime trauma prevalence rates among the U.S. general population are 51.2% for women and 60.7% for men (Kessler, Sonnega, Bromet, Hughes, & Nelson, 1995).

Image 7.3

Whether residing in a tribal area or urban area, Native people are 2.5 times more likely to be the victim of a violent crime than are members of other ethnic groups (NCAI Policy Research Center, 2013), and Natives residing in suburban areas are 2.8 times more likely than the average for suburban residents of other races to have experienced a violent assault and 2.6 times more likely than the average for rural residents of other races to have been violently assaulted (Perry, 2004).

Native women, as compared to women of other races, have higher rates of sexual assault. Thirty-four percent of American Indian/Alaska Native women will be raped in their lifetimes, compared to 19% of African American women, 18% of White women, and 7% of Asian and Pacific Islander women (Bachman, Zaykowski, Kallmyer, Poteyeva, &

Lanier, 2008). Native women also experience intimate partner violence at considerably higher rates than women of other races, and this victimization is most often perpetrated by a partner of a different race (Rosay, 2016).

Native men and women have also been found to be highly likely to have witnessed rape and life-threatening accidents, injury, or death that occurred to loved ones, or to have themselves experienced serious accidents and natural disasters at rates higher than their counterparts in the U.S. population (Manson, Beals, Klein, & Croy, 2005; Sarche & Spicer, 2008). Injuries and violence account for 75% of all deaths among Native children and youth (Wallace, Patel, & Dellinger, 2003), with family and community members often witnessing these losses of life. With American Indian/Alaska Native suicide rates more than 3.5 times higher than those of other racial groups (Leavitt et al., 2018), it is also likely that Native individuals have close family or community connections to someone who has attempted or committed suicide (Gray & McCullagh, 2013).

While there is a good understanding of the prevalence of trauma exposure at the individual level in the general Native population, statistics typically do not reflect trauma exposure at the family or community level or among subgroups within the Native population. The prevalence of trauma among Native caregivers and children involved with child welfare is an example of an area where little research has taken place. However, extrapolating from general trauma statistics, it would follow that among this population of Natives, high levels of trauma also exist.

The results of trauma screenings of urban Native caregivers receiving Indian Child Welfare services from a community-based agency support the findings of studies referenced above. This screening tool was developed for the agency by the author and asked about whether caregivers had experienced seven traumas common in the general population: (1) been in a situation where they feared that they, a loved one, and/or a friend might be killed or seriously injured; (2) been seriously injured in an accident; (3) experienced a serious physical assault attack with a weapon; (4) experienced a natural disaster where they felt they, or someone with them, was in danger of death or injury; (5) seen a loved one, friend, or community member be seriously injured or killed, or commit suicide; (6) as an adult, been sexually assaulted or forced to have sex against their will; and (7) as a child, ever been sexually molested.

More than 94% of caregivers (n=46) had had at least one traumatic experience. The highest percentage of individuals (70.3%) who reported a traumatic event indicated it was a situation where they had feared for their life or safety or the life or safety of someone they knew. Of note in this study was that 80% of individuals reported multiple traumatic experiences during their lifetimes (Denver Indian Family Resource Center, 2016), a good number having taken place when individuals were adults. It was also not uncommon for caregivers receiving services through the agency to experience new traumatic events while their child welfare cases were open.

Both the biopsychosocial effects of a single traumatic event and the cumulative effects of multiple traumas across the life span can disrupt individual functioning, and untreated trauma exposure can also make it difficult for caregivers to meet the demands of parenting. A trauma-informed approach with Native clients begins with caseworkers' recognition that Native people, as a group, experience high rates of trauma exposure, and as such, the Native adults and children with whom they work are likely to be among those who have experienced trauma. Next, workers should be aware that an individual Native person's trauma load may be comprised of three interacting elements: "(a) historical group traumatic events (such as forced relocations and boarding school attendance); (b) intergenerational transmission of trauma; and (c) individual contemporary trauma exposures" (Lucero & Bussey, 2015, p. 108) and thus has an added level of complexity and impact. Additionally, it is essential to create service settings and utilize practice approaches that allow Native clients to experience cultural safety—an environment which is safe for people where there is no assault or challenge on who they are or denial of their identity (Williams, 1999).

Practice and Service Delivery Challenges in Native Child Welfare

To work effectively with Native children and families involved in the child welfare system requires the development of a critical consciousness as to: (a) the historic relationship between Native Nations and the United States; (b) awareness of governmental actions that have created oppressive conditions for Native people; (c) understanding that most contemporary Native people carry with them awareness of how these past governmental actions have directly impacted their own families and tribes; and (d) that the underlying structural, political, and attitudinal conditions that allowed historic abuses have changed very little and, in fact, may still continue in the present (Lucero & Leake, in press). Achieving a critical consciousness involves: (a) gaining in-depth understanding of the ways in which power manifests in political and social structures, as it does when child welfare systems carry out laws and government mandates, to create oppression; and (b) implementing anti-oppressive practices to build new structures that empower historically oppressed groups and enhance human well-being (Freire, 1998; Newark Community Collaborative Board, 2016).

The endemic racism, structural inequalities, and power imbalances identified by critical race theorists as a deeply embedded facet of American society (Abrams & Moio, 2009) manifest in child welfare through practices that create high disproportionality and disparities for Native children and families. Racism and power issues can also be factors underlying poor compliance with the ICWA in state CPS systems, and failure in some jurisdictions to recognize **tribal sovereignty** as the basis for the act and framing

ICWA as unconstitutional race-based legislation giving preferential treatment to Native children (Elder, 2018).

Overarching current challenges in this area of child welfare practice continue to be (a) reducing disproportionality and disparity rates; (b) placing fewer Native children in non-kinship and non-Native out of home placements; (c) keeping Native children who have been removed connected to family and culture; (d) increasing compliance with all provisions of the ICWA; and (e) increasing engagement with families by incorporating culturally respectful and responsive practices and a trauma-informed approach. Each of the two child welfare systems serving Native children and families also has its own context-specific challenges, although the two systems also share some similar challenges, as can be seen in Table 7.1.

TABLE 7.1. Practice Challenges for Tribal and State Child Welfare Agencies

Challenges for state CPS agencies

- Complying with legal and practice provisions of the ICWA
- Developing a culturally responsive workforce
- Working with families across a continuum of cultural knowledge and connectedness
- Effectively serving families with high levels of need
- Incorporating extended family and kin into service plans
- Identifying extended family and kin for out of home placements
- Recruiting a sufficient number of **ICWA-compliant kinship and foster homes**
- Forming a referral network of culturally appropriate service providers
- Collaborating with tribal child welfare agencies

Challenges for tribal child welfare agencies

- Obtaining adequate funding and resources for program infrastructure and operations
- Hiring a sufficient number of workers and filling staff vacancies
- Working with families on a spectrum of cultural knowledge and connectedness
- Effectively serving families with high levels of need
- Recruiting a sufficient number of ICWA-compliant kinship and foster homes
- Ensuring that children and families have access to collateral services that are culturally based
- Responding to large numbers of ICWA notices
- Collaborating with state CPS agencies

Several studies have pointed out specific factors that contribute to disproportionality and disparities for Native children and families. These include resource inequities, geography, cultural misunderstandings and perceptions of Native lifestyles, caseworker characteristics and educational levels, ICWA noncompliance, and even fear of liability (Courtney et al., 1996; Crofoot & Harris, 2012; Fluke, Harden, Jenkins, & Ruehrdanz, 2010; Lucero, 2007; Ryan, Garnier, Zyphur, & Zhai, 2006; Texas Dept. of Family and Protective Services, 2010). Most experts agree, however, that these conditions result from the broad interaction of agency policy and practice, racial biases, and differential decision-making

(Fluke et al., 2010). Implementation of strategies in state CPS systems, including protocols for early identification of Native children, increased oversight of ICWA compliance, intensive case management services for family preservation (Bussey & Lucero, 2013), staff training (Lucero, 2007; Mindell, De Haymes, & Francisco, 2003), and addition of a Native liaison to state CPS agency staff (Richardson, 2008), have shown promise in reducing disproportionality and disparities for Native children and families.

Whether Native people are currently living in an urban or a tribal area, they have been affected by the same historical processes, and similar economic conditions and psychosocial concerns touch both groups. In both tribal and state child welfare practice, workers encounter Native parents and extended family members who carry with them memories of generations of relatives having had their children taken away through governmental actions. Although child welfare involvement is frightening for all families, these memories can create a current challenge in working with Native families when they produce extreme mistrust, resistance, or even disengagement. Caseworkers can find building trust and engagement at the family's pace while still meeting legal and administrative timelines to be a demanding task. Adapting practice to accommodate families that fall along a wide continuum of cultural knowledge and connectedness and integrating into family service plans the preference of some Native families to utilize services that incorporate cultural practices or to seek help from elders or informal service providers can present additional service delivery challenges.

Evidence-Informed Practice for Native Child Welfare

Determining the approaches and intervention models that work most effectively with Native children and families is a relatively new area in child welfare research and evaluation. At present, practices focus on the Native child welfare population that has undergone a series of randomized controlled trials and been found to meet the standards for designation as evidence-*based* are lacking. However, there is a growing body of evidence-*informed* approaches derived from rigorous program evaluation and documented practice experience that can be considered current best practice for achieving positive child welfare outcomes for Native children and families. Several of these approaches being implemented in tribal and state child welfare agencies are presented below.

Image 7.4

Practice-informed child- and family-centered approaches in tribal child welfare include implementing a consistent and planned approach to casework focused on creating family stability. Using this approach, rather than working to remediate each family crisis, caseworkers assist families to recognize and change patterns of maladaptive behaviors that result in frequent family crises. Families receive assistance in meeting their basic needs of daily living while also working on long-term family change and healing (Lucero, Jewett, Bigpond, & Echohawk, 2012). Implementation of a cultural model of trauma-informed care that includes screening for trauma exposure, intensive case management, and access to culturally appropriate mental health, substance abuse, and trauma treatment is another practice approach that has been documented to improve child welfare outcomes for Native children and families (Lucero & Bussey, 2015).

In state CPS agencies, utilizing evidence-informed practice centers on approaches that improve ICWA compliance and culturally responsive practice. These include: (a) implementation of policies for early identification of Native children entering state or county systems; (b) training of child welfare staff about Native history and culturally appropriate practice, in addition to the legalities of ICWA compliance; (c) commitment to kinship placements and supporting extended family systems; (d) commitment to maintaining children's cultural connections; and (e) partnering with community-based agencies and providers skilled at working with Native children and families to develop a referral network (Halverson, Puig, & Byers, 2002; Lucero, 2007; Mindell, De Haymes, & Francisco, 2003).

Child- and family-centered approaches for state CPS agencies that show promise for improving outcomes for Native children and families include focusing contacts in the initial stages of the case process on engagement and trust building with Native parents—rather than on completing paperwork and assessments—and using family decision-making meetings to incorporate extended family members and informal kin into service plans (Bussey & Lucero, 2005). And similar to what is effective in a tribal setting, stabilizing families with supports for basic needs and helping them to engage in culturally appropriate mental health and substance abuse and trauma treatment have been shown to improve the extent to which families are able to complete the requirements of their family services plans (Bussey & Lucero, 2013).

Systems Approaches for Native Child Welfare

Utilizing a systems approach is critical to positive child welfare outcomes for Native children. In this section, a systems approach is defined as: *collaboration between a state or tribal child welfare agency, and governmental agencies, community-based nonprofits, other private agencies, and tribal programs that are intended to meet the needs of Native families involved with child welfare.* Whether Native families are being served by tribal child welfare agencies or in state CPS agencies, during their case they must typically also interface with governmental agencies, the legal system (including attorneys, law enforcement, and corrections), and state and/or **tribal courts**. These Native families also commonly need services such as: (a) behavioral health; (b) health care; (c) Temporary Assistance for Needy Families (TANF), Medicaid, and child health insurance programs; (d) housing, food, and basic needs; and (e) employment, job training, and educational programs.

Within the boundaries of a tribal nation, tribal programs may provide to tribal members certain of these services, such as behavioral health care or housing and food programs. However, few tribes have the resources to provide a full range of social and health services, and the types of services available within a tribal nation vary considerably by tribe. Frequently, tribally based families also need services that must be accessed from non-tribal providers located outside the tribal community. But in most non-tribal cities, towns, and rural areas, few if any community-based agencies exist that are focused on serving the Native population, and there are usually few providers available who are themselves Native.

Urban-based Native families also face the challenge of finding agencies and providers who are skilled in working with members of their cultural group. These families are likely to have to either obtain services from agencies that serve the general population of their area or travel considerable distances to their reservations or tribal communities for help. However, agencies that are structured to serve many ethnic groups have been found to often fail to identify Native clients because they comprise a small percentage of the area's population or to misidentify them as being members of other groups. Furthermore, agencies may also be unfamiliar with the help-seeking behaviors of some Native people or interpret as resistance or denial the reluctance or fear of seeking help from non-Native providers that stems from historical experiences unique to Native people.

Elements of a Systems Approach for Anti-Oppressive and Culturally Responsive Service Delivery to Native Children and Families

Identifying and deconstructing race, racism, and power differentials between dominant culture systems and Native people are required to develop the critical consciousness needed to practice in anti-oppressive and culturally responsive ways. This process is a crucial first step that must involve both agency leadership and staff when creating a collaborative service delivery system and utilizing a systems approach that supports Native children and families as they move through their involvement in a child welfare case. The process should begin with gaining awareness of the continuing impacts of historically traumatic events on contemporary Native individuals, families, communities, and tribes. Additionally, it is crucial that individuals working with Native people understand that the foundational power dynamics, social constructions and stereotypes of Native people, and assimilationist forces that allowed these events to take place are still active, albeit in more modern forms.

Additional elements of a collaborative systems approach include: (a) understanding the cultural values and worldview of the tribe(s) whose members agencies serve; in larger urban areas where there are families from many different tribes, this may involve having an understanding of a set of values shared across tribes; (b) learning skills that allow workers to hear each individual's unique experience of being Native so as to be accepting of differences in the expression of identity and cultural connectedness; (c) incorporating relational and trauma-informed approaches to practice and service delivery; and (d) openness to Native individuals using traditional healing and cultural practices in addition to formal dominant culture systems (Lucero & Bussey, 2015). Ongoing in-service training, coaching, and case consultation provided by individuals experienced in working with Native peoples can also assist agencies participating in collaborative service delivery systems to operationalize these elements in alignment with their own service provision.

Strategically building culturally responsive service delivery networks comprised of private agencies, community-based nonprofits, tribal programs, governmental agencies (including education, entitlement programs, law enforcement, and courts), and child welfare departments who together have the intention of better serving Native children and families is showing promise for improving agencies' responsiveness to Native clients. These networks have been found to also improve access to and receipt of services.

BOX 7.2. The Denver Indian Family Resource Center

For nearly 2 decades, the Denver Indian Family Resource Center (DIFRC) has served urban-based Native families involved with, or at risk of involvement with, CPS agencies in the seven-county Denver metropolitan area. DIFRC collaborates with county child welfare departments and tribal child welfare agencies to provide culturally appropriate case management services. Honoring the tradition of strong Native families drives DIFRC's work to support families to create safe and healthy home environments where children are nurtured and can remain connected to their culture.

In early spring 2015, DIFRC launched an effort to not only develop an integrated service delivery network for Native child welfare families but to also enhance the cultural responsiveness of community agencies' services and offer opportunities for service providers to learn more about the city's Native community. Within the first year, 43 agencies were participating regularly in the Seven Stars Collaborative, representing a wide range of community-based agencies and governmental programs, including behavioral health; domestic violence; housing services; school districts; legal, criminal justice, and victim services; and child welfare (Denver Indian Family Resource Center, 2016).

A 2016 evaluation of the collaborative found that 87% of respondents agreed or strongly agreed that participating in the collaborative had benefited their own agency; 73% agreed or strongly agreed that the trainings received at the collaborative meetings had helped improve their agencies' cultural responsiveness; and 67% agreed or strongly agreed that the collaborative had helped their agency be more accessible to Native clients. Native clients, in turn, shared that knowing non-Native providers were learning about Native people helped them feel supported and have smoother interactions with other service providers (Denver Indian Family Resource Center, 2016).

Policies Relevant to Native Peoples in Child Welfare

Legal constructs and federal, state, and tribal policies that are foundational in understanding child welfare and Native people are presented in this section and listed in Table 7.2. Readers should note that the use of the term *Indian* in the descriptions that follow reflects the language of the laws and policies and refers inclusively to American Indian and Alaska Native tribes and peoples.

TABLE 7.2. Federal, State, and Tribal Policies and Legal Constructs Related to Child Welfare

- Doctrine of Trust Responsibility (recognition of inherent tribal sovereignty)
- Indian Self-Determination and Education Assistance Act of 1975 (P. L. 93-638)
- Indian Child Welfare Act of 1978 (P. L. 95-608)
- State ICWA Statutes
- Tribal Children's Codes
- Social Security Act of 1935 Title IV-B and Title IV-E
- Tribal-State Child Welfare Agreements

Tribal Sovereignty and the Doctrine of Trust Responsibility

Being a member of a Native tribal nation is not only a cultural distinction, but a political status. The United States has a government-to-government relationship with tribal nations that originates from treaties between the parties signed in the 1700s. The U.S. Supreme Court has determined that these early treaties created a trust responsibility between the United States and Native people because they recognized the tribes as sovereign nations independent of the United States; this legal trust responsibility continues to the present. Under its trust responsibility, the United States has a duty to ensure the survival and welfare of Native tribes and people and an obligation to provide services and social programs necessary to raise the standard of living and social well-being of Native people to that comparable to non-Natives (Pevar, 2012).

Indian Self-Determination and Education Assistance Act of 1975 (Public Law 93–638)

The Indian Self-Determination and Education Assistance Act of 1975 (P. L. 93-638) made tribal self-determination the focus of government actions and reversed decades of federal government efforts to terminate its legal obligations to Indian tribes (Harvard Project, 2008). The act gave government agencies authority to directly contract with, and make grants to, federally recognized Indian tribes and allowed tribes increased control over the management of federal programs that impact their resources, governments, and the welfare of their members. Tribal sovereignty gives tribal nations the right to oversee child protection matters within tribal jurisdictions, and many tribal nations have exercised sovereignty and self-determination by choosing to operate a tribal-run child welfare program through a contract under this act.

Indian Child Welfare Act of 1978 (ICWA) and State ICWA Statutes

The Indian Child Welfare Act of 1978 (P. L. 95-608) is the policy most directly connected to Native people and child welfare. This federal legislation was intended to remedy past use of poor standards to justify removal of Indian children from their homes and address adoptions of Indian children into families that did not reflect their cultures. The ICWA is legislation recognizing tribal sovereignty, and understanding and respecting tribal sovereignty is a key factor in ICWA compliance. The purpose of the ICWA is to restore and maintain connections between Indian children, their families, and their tribes and to preserve Indian cultures. The ICWA promotes the best interests of Indian children to be and remain with their families. It also promotes the stability and security of Indian tribes and families by establishing minimum standards for removal of Indian children from their families and outlines an order of foster and adoptive placement preferences that keep Indian children in homes that reflect Indian culture.

The ICWA is enacted in state CPS agencies and state courts through five primary actions: (1) inquiry into whether a child is a member of an Indian tribe or has Indian ancestry, and if so, notice to the child's tribe that the child is involved with the child welfare agency; (2) provision of casework **active efforts** to prevent the breakup of the child's Indian family; (3) if out of home placement is warranted, placement in a setting that is compliant with ICWA's placement standards; (4) concurrent planning for permanency, typically in the form of the two goals of reunification of the Indian child with his/her family and an alternative permanency outcome; and (5) in cases of removal and foster care placement, use of testimony by a qualified expert witness with knowledge of the cultural and community standards of the Indian child's tribe. The most common ways tribes exercise their rights under ICWA are by either choosing to become a party to the case in state court (called "intervening") or motioning to transfer jurisdiction of the case from the state court to the tribal court.

In the past two decades, several states have passed their own state statutes related to the ICWA. Michigan, Minnesota, Nebraska, Oklahoma, and Washington have adopted most of the federal ICWA into their own Indian Child Welfare Act legislation. Other states, among them California, Colorado, New Mexico, and North Dakota, have passed legislation to strengthen ICWA compliance or emphasize certain provisions of the federal law, such as notification requirements, or to recognize special provisions of state law, such as California's recognition of tribal customary adoptions (National Conference of State Legislators, n.d.).

Tribal Children's Codes

Like states, most tribal nations have a set of legal codes intended to ensure the care and protection of children and which form the basis of policies that structure and direct tribal child welfare agencies' operations, as well as the roles of law enforcement and the tribal court in child welfare matters. Tribal codes interact with ICWA by defining tribal membership criteria and therefore guide the legal determination of whether a child is covered under the act.

Social Security Act of 1935

Like state CPS agencies, tribal child welfare agencies may receive funding through Titles IV-B and IV-E of the Social Security Act of 1935. Title IV-B funding is intended to promote child and family services programs to: (a) protect and promote the welfare of children and prevent their neglect, abuse, or exploitation; (b) support children remaining safely with their families and being reunified in a timely manner; (c) promote the safety, permanence, and well-being of children in foster care and adoptive families; and (d) provide training, professional development, and support to ensure a well-qualified child welfare workforce. Title IV-E provides funding for foster care, adoption, and kinship guardianship assistance, and transitional independent living programs for certain eligible children.

Tribal-State Child Welfare Agreements

The ICWA authorizes tribes and states to enter into mutual agreements on Indian child welfare matters, commonly known as "tribal-state agreements." There are no standards for tribal-state agreements, and tribal-state relationships can be tense or even problematic (Brown, Whitaker, Clifford, Limb, & Munoz, 2000). These agreements often address issues such as: (1) the roles of each party in elements of the child welfare and foster care processes, such as who does initial investigations, who licenses Native foster homes, and who pays for foster care placements; (2) how states notify tribes in emergency removals; and (3) how jurisdictional conflicts are to be resolved. Tribal-state agreements are also the vehicle through which most tribes secure Title IV-E funding for their foster care and adoption programs.

Case Application

Case Vignette: The Kills First Family

The following vignette presents the case of the Kills First family, a large Native extended family group from a tribe in the Northern Plains who now live in a suburban neighborhood in a large metropolitan area. The family exhibits attitudes, behaviors, and characteristics that may be seen in Native families who become involved with a state CPS agency. The vignette also presents some cultural elements that state CPS workers may find challenging or frustrating and that can make family engagement difficult. It also incorporates several stereotypes of Native people that may arise during a child welfare case and examples of the worker's lack of understanding of the family's culture.

The Kills First family became involved with the state CPS agency when 10-year-old Mandy was sexually abused by her mother's boyfriend. Mandy and her four younger siblings (one of whom is a 6-month-old baby) were removed from their mother's home and placed in a non-kinship foster home, despite having a large extended family both in the city and on the reservation. As required by the ICWA, the state CPS worker notified the tribe at the time of removal that the children had been taken into the state's custody. The tribal child welfare agency responded back quickly that Mandy and her siblings were enrolled members and that the children should be placed with family members known to the tribe who were living in the city.

Family members are quite distressed that the children still remain in foster care with strangers 2 months later despite the court determining the children's case to be an ICWA case and the tribal child welfare agency recommending at the first court hearing that the siblings be kept together and placed with their maternal grandmother Constance, age 69. Elders in the family, including Constance, have let the caseworker know that for several generations, "too many of our family's children" have been removed by child welfare "simply because we are Indians." Memories of the loss of these relative children remain fresh and powerful for these elders. Mandy's eldest uncle, Conrad, has confronted the worker and informed her that the family "knows its rights through ICWA" and that the law expects the children to be placed with family members who are suitable and available to care for the children, in this case Constance. At times the worker feels "ganged up on," like the family is trying to tell her how to do her job, intimidated by their "anger," and frustrated by their "living in the past." Family members believe she is in violation of the ICWA and feel that she wants to "give our children to a White family."

Constance raised nine of her own children who were "like stair steps in age" and is currently raising three other teenage grandchildren whose mother died after being unable to overcome long-term alcohol addiction. The state worker doesn't feel Constance would be a suitable placement for Mandy and her siblings because she has the other grandchildren in her care and has stated, "eight children would be too much for her." The worker also has concerns about this placement due to Constance's age, because she has diabetes, the young ages of Mandy's siblings, and the severity of Mandy's abuse. The worker has shared privately with coworkers that she wonders what was going on in the way Constance raised her daughter that could have contributed to her being an alcoholic from a young age.

Constance's siblings and adult children have conveyed to the worker that while the children will be residing in Constance's home, extended family members will be having daily contact with Constance and the children to provide support and resources. Several family members have also tried to help the worker understand that traditionally in their tribal culture, children who could not be cared for by their parents were cared for by a grandmother. Despite trying to educate the worker, these family members feel they are not being heard and are frustrated by what they interpret as the worker's dismissal of "our cultural ways."

Members of the Kills First family have maintained strong connections to their tribal culture, and most continue to speak the tribal language, are involved in traditional spiritual practices, and are active in the powwow community, often traveling great distance to compete in powwows that offer prize money. All family members are considered "4/4 degree Indian blood" or what is often termed "full blooded," except for Mandy's younger siblings, who have a Hispanic father and are 1/2 Indian blood. The family is well known both on the reservation and in the city, and their ancestor, Kills First, played a historically significant role in their tribal culture.

Grandma Constance and her siblings came together to the city in the mid-1960s as part of the Bureau of Indian Affairs Voluntary Relocation Program. These family members have maintained residences and raised their children and grandchildren in the city since that time. However, since first arriving, they have frequently traveled back as a family to their reservation and have maintained strong connections to relatives still living on the reservation.

It has been difficult for the worker to reconcile in her mind that members of the Kills First family have lived in the city for several generations yet still talk a lot about being "traditional" and "practicing our culture." In fact, the worker wonders if the family might be trying to "manipulate using cultural stuff" but finds that she doesn't have anyone to help her sort through cultural differences, make sense of the large extended family's presentation and behaviors, and guide her to be more culturally knowledgeable. To avoid mistakenly placing Mandy and her siblings in an unsafe setting where further abuse or neglect could take place, the worker is inclined to err on the side of caution and advocate for continued foster care placement as being in the children's "best interests." She feels more strongly about this course of action after learning recently from Constance that she has experienced multiple traumatic events in her lifetime but has never received any counseling or treatment, choosing instead to "talk to other Indian women in the community" about the experiences.

DISCUSSION QUESTIONS

1. As a caseworker from a different cultural group than the family in the case vignette, how would you begin to engage and build rapport? If you are a Native caseworker, how would you approach your initial work with this family?
2. What kinds of trauma exposure have members of the Kills First family experienced? What could the worker in the vignette do to demonstrate she is using a trauma-informed approach with this family?
3. What is tribal sovereignty, and why is it important in child welfare with Native peoples?
4. What factors make Grandma Constance a suitable placement for Mandy and her siblings? What factors would argue against Constance as an appropriate placement?
5. What are some of the steps agencies might take to help workers build a critical consciousness and increase their cultural responsiveness when serving Native peoples?
6. What are some of the factors that experts consider contribute to child welfare disproportionality and disparities for Native children?

References

Adams. D. W. (1995). *Education for extinction: American Indians and the boarding school experience 1975–1928.* Lawrence: University Press of Kansas.

Abrams, L. S., & Moio, J. A. (2009). Critical race theory and the cultural competence dilemma in social work education. *Journal of Social Work Education, 45*(2), 245–261.

Bachman, R., Zaykowski, H., Kallmyer, R., Poteyeva, M., & Lanier, C. (2008). *Violence against American Indian and Alaska Native women and the criminal justice response: What is known.* Unpublished grant report to the U.S. Department of Justice. www.ncjrs.gov/pdffiles1/nij/grants/223691.pdf

Bending, R. L. (1997). Training child welfare workers to meet the requirements of the Indian Child Welfare Act. *Journal of Multicultural Social Work, 5*(3/4), 151–164.

Blackhawk, N. (1995). I can carry on from here: The relocation of American Indians to Los Angeles. *Wicazo Sa Review, 11*(2), 16–30.

Brown, E. F., Whitaker, L. S., Clifford, C. A., Limb, G. E., & Munoz, R. (2000). *Tribal/state Title IV-E intergovernmental agreements: Facilitating tribal access to federal resources.* Seattle: Casey Family Programs and the National Indian Child Welfare Association.

Bussey, M., & Lucero, N. M. (2013). Re-examining child welfare's response to ICWA: Collaborating with community-based agencies to reduce disparities for American Indian/Alaska Native children. *Children and Youth Services Review, 35*(3), 394–401.

Bussey, M. C., & Lucero, N. M. (2005). A collaborative approach to healing substance abuse and child neglect in an urban American Indian community. *Protecting Children, 20*(4), 9–22.

Casey Family Programs. (2011). *American Indian children in foster care Colorado.* Seattle: Author.

Child Welfare Information Gateway. (2016). *Racial disproportionality and disparity in child welfare.* Washington, DC: U.S. Department of Health and Human Services, Children's Bureau.

Courtney, M. E., Barth, R. P., Berrick, J. D., Brooks, D., Needell, B., & Park, L. (1996). Race and child welfare services: Past research and future directions. *Child Welfare, 75*(2), 99–137.

Crofoot, T. L., & Harris, M. S. (2012). An Indian Child Welfare perspective on disproportionality in child welfare. *Children and Youth Services Review, 34*(9), 1667–1674.

Cross, T. A., Earle, K. A., & Simmons, D. (2000). Child abuse and neglect in Indian country: Policy issues. *Families in Society, 81*(1), 49–58.

Cross, T. L. (1986). Drawing on cultural tradition in Indian child welfare practice. *Social Casework, 67*(5), 283–289.

Denver Indian Family Resource Center. (2016). *ACYF project evaluation findings.* Denver: Author.

Dippie, B. W. (1982). *The vanishing American: White attitudes and U.S. Indian policy.* Lawrence: University of Kansas Press.

Earle, K. A. (2000). *Child abuse and neglect: An examination of American Indian data.* Seattle: National Indian Child Welfare Association and Casey Family Programs.

Earle, K. A., & Cross, A. (2001*). Child abuse and neglect among American Indian/Alaska Native children: An analysis of existing data.* Seattle: National Indian Child Welfare Association and Casey Family Programs.

Elder, A. K. (2018). "Indian" as a political classification: Reading the tribe back into the Indian Child Welfare Act. *Northwestern Journal of Law and Social Policy, 13*(4), 417–438.

Farrow, F., Notkin, S., Derezotes, D., & Miller, O. (2010). Racial equity in child welfare: Key themes, findings and perspectives. In J. Fluke, B. Harden, M. Jenkins, & A. Ruehrdanz (Eds.), *Research Synthesis on Child Welfare Disproportionality and Disparities* (pp. 127–150). Washington, DC: Center for the Study of Social Policy.

Fixico, D. L. (2000). *The Urban Indian Experience in America.* Albuquerque: University of New Mexico Press.

Fluke, J., Harden, B., Jenkins, M., & Ruehrdanz, A. (2010). Research synthesis on child welfare disproportionality and disparities. *Disparities and disproportionality in child welfare: Analysis of the research. Papers from a Research Symposium (pp. 1–93).* Washington, DC: Center for the Study of Social Policy. http://www.cssp.org/publications/child-welfare/alliance/Disparitiesand-Disproportionality-in-Child-Welfare_An-Analysis-of-the-Research-December-2011.pdf

Freire, P. (1998). *Pedagogy of the Oppressed.* New York: Continuum.

Gram, J. R. (2016). Acting out assimilation: Playing Indian and becoming American in the federal Indian boarding schools. *American Indian Quarterly, 40*(3), 251–273.

Gray, J. S., & McCullagh, J. A. (2013). Suicide in Indian Country: The continuing epidemic in rural Native American communities. *Journal of Rural Mental Health, 38*(2), 79–86.

Halverson, K., Puig, M. E., & Byers, S. R. (2002). Culture loss: American Indian family disruption, urbanization, and the Indian Child Welfare Act. *Child Welfare, 81*(2), 319–336.

Harvard Project on American Indian Economic Development. (2008). *The state of the Native Nations: Conditions under U.S. Policies of Self-Determination.* New York: Oxford University Press.

Horejsi, C., Craig, B., & Pablo, J. (1992). Reactions by Native American parents to child protection agencies: Cultural and community factors. *Child Welfare, 71*(4), 329–342.

Hoxie, F. E. (2001). *A final promise: The campaign to assimilate the Indians, 1880–1920.* Lincoln: University of Nebraska Press.

Hull, G. H. (1982). Child welfare services to Native Americans. *Social Casework, 63*(6), 340–347.

Indian Child Welfare Act of 1978, Pub. L. No. 95-608, §2, 92 Stat. 3069 (1978). http://uscode.house.gov/view.xhtml?path=/prelim@title25/chapter21&edition=prelim

Indian Self-Determination and Education Assistance of 1975, Pub. L. No. 93-638, § 5301 *et seq.*, 88 Stat. 2203 (1975). http://uscode.house.gov/view.xhtml?path=/prelim@title25/chapter46&edition=prelim

Jacobs, M. D. (2013). Remembering the “forgotten child”: The American Indian child welfare crisis of the 1960s and 1970s. *American Indian Quarterly, 37*(1–2), 136–159.

Jackson, D. D. (1998). “This hole in our heart”: Urban Indian identity and the power of silence. *American Indian Culture and Research Journal, 22*(4), 227–254.

Judicial Council of California. (n.d.). *Following the spirit of the Indian Child Welfare Act (ICWA).* San Francisco, CA: Author. http://www.courts.ca.gov/documents/Tribal-FollowSpiritICWA.pdf

Innskeep, S. (2015). *Jacksonland: President Andrew Jackson, Cherokee Chief John Ross, and a great American land grab.* New York: Penguin Books.

Kessel, J., & Robbins, S. P. (1984). The Indian Child Welfare Act: Dilemmas and needs. *Child Welfare, 63*(3), 225–232.

Kessler, R. C., Sonnega, A., Bromet, E., Hughes, M., & Nelson, C. B. (1995). Posttraumatic stress disorder in the National Comorbidity Study. *Archives of General Psychiatry, 52,* 1048–1060.

Lacey, L. J. (1986). The white man’s law and the American Indian family in the assimilation era. *Arkansas Law Review, 40,* 327–375.

Leavitt, R. A., Ertl, A., Sheats, K., Petrosky, E., Ivey-Stephenson, A., & Fowler, K. A. (2018). Suicides among American Indian/Alaska Natives —National Violent Death Reporting System, 18 states, 2003–2014. *Morbidity and Mortality Weekly Report, 67*(8), 237–242.

Lucero, N. M. (2013). "Being Indian in the city": Generational differences in the negotiation of Native identity among urban-based American Indians. In E. J. Peters and C. Anderson (Eds.), *Indigenous in the City: Contemporary Identities and Cultural Innovations*, pp. 193–215. Vancouver: University of British Columbia Press.

Lucero, N. M. (2007). *Resource Guide: Working with Urban American Indian Families with Child Protection and Substance Abuse Challenges*. Englewood, CO: American Humane Association. http://www.americanhumane.org/assets/pdfs/children/pc-rmqic-dif-guide.pdf

Lucero, N. M., & Bussey, M. C. (2015). Practice informed approaches to addressing substance abuse and trauma exposure in child welfare involved urban Native families. *Child Welfare 94*(4), 97–117.

Lucero, N. M., Jewett, J., Bigpond, P., & Echohawk, L. (2012). *Denver Indian Family Resource Center Practice Model*. Denver: Denver Indian Family Resource Center.

Lucero, N. M., & Leake, R. (in press). Dual marginalization of urban-based American Indian and Alaska Native children and families. *Child Welfare*.

Mannes, M. (1995). Factors and events leading to the passage of the Indian Child Welfare Act. *Child Welfare, 74*(1), 264–282.

Manson, S. M., Beals, J., Klein, S. A., & Croy, C. D. (2005). Social epidemiology of trauma among 2 American Indian reservation populations. *American Journal of Public Health, 95*, 851–859.

Marr, C. J. (n.d.). Assimilation through education: Indian boarding schools in the Pacific Northwest. Seattle: University of Washington Libraries. https://content.lib.washington.edu/aipnw/marr.html

Mindell, R., De Haymes, M., & Francisco, D. (2003). A culturally responsive practice model for urban Indian Child Welfare services. *Child Welfare, 82*(2), 201–217.

National Conference of State Legislatures. (n.d.). *State statutes related to the Indian Child Welfare Act*. http://www.ncsl.org/research/human-services/state-statutes-related-to-indian-child-welfare.aspx

National Congress of American Indians. (2019). *Tribal nations and the United States: An introduction*. Washington, DC: Author. http://www.ncai.org/tribalnations/introduction/Tribal_Nations_and_the_United_States_An_Introduction-web-.pdf

National Congress of American Indians. (n.d.). *Indian Country demographics*. Washington, DC: Author. http://www.ncai.org/about-tribes/demographics

National Council of Juvenile and Family Court Judges (NCJFCJ). (2016). *Disproportionality rates for children of color in foster care technical assistance bulletin*. Reno, NV: Author. http://www.ncjfcj.org/sites/default/files/NCJFCJ%202014%20Disproportionality%20TAB%20Final.pdf

Native American Rights Fund. (2007). *A practical guide to the Indian Child Welfare Act: Topic 2. Jurisdiction.* Boulder, CO: Author. https://www.narf.org/nill/documents/icwa/faq/jurisdiction.html#Q4

NCAI Policy Research Center. (2013). *Policy insights brief: Statistics on violence against Native Women.* Washington, DC: Author. http://www.ncai.org/attachments/PolicyPaper_tWAjznFslemhAffZgNGzHUqIWMRPkCDjpFtxeKEUVKjubxfpGYK_Policy%20Insights%20Brief_VAWA_020613.pdf

Newark Community Collaborative Board. (2016). *Critical Consciousness Theory.* Newark, NJ: Author. http://newarkccb.org/framework/critical-consciousness-theory/

Norris, T., Vines, P. L., & Hoeffel, E. M. (2012). *The American Indian and Alaska Native population: 2010.* Washington, DC: U.S. Census Bureau.

Office of the Law Revision Counsel, U.S. House of Representatives (n.d.). *Title 25/Chapter 21—Indian Child Welfare.* Washington, DC: Author. http://uscode.house.gov/view.xhtml?path=/prelim@title25/chapter21&edition=preli

Ostler, J. (2015). Genocide and American Indian history. *Oxford Research Encyclopedia of American History.* New York: Oxford University Press. https://oxfordindex.oup.com/oi/viewindexcard/10.1093$002facrefore$002f9780199329175.013.3

Palmiste, C. (2011). From the Indian Adoption Project to the Indian Child Welfare Act: The resistance of Native American communities. *Indigenous Policy Journal, 22*(1), 1–10.

Perry, S. W. (2004). *American Indians and crime: A BJS Statistical Profile, 1992–2002 [NCJ 203097].* Washington, DC: U.S. Department of Justice, Bureau of Justice Statistics. bjs.ojp.usdoj.gov/content/pub/pdf/aic02.pdf

Pew Research Center. (2015). *Multiracial America: Proud, diverse, and growing in numbers.* Washington, DC: Author. http://www.pewsocialtrends.org/2015/06/11/multiracial-in-america/

Pevar, S. L. (2012). *The Rights of Indians and Tribes.* New York: Oxford University Press.

Pierce, R. L., & Pierce, L. H. (1996). Moving toward cultural competence in the child welfare system. *Children and Youth Services Review, 18*(8), pp. 713–731.

Richardson, B. (2008). Comparative analysis of two community-based efforts designed to impact disproportionality. *Child Welfare, 87*(2), 297–317.

Rosay, A. B. (2016). Violence against American Indian and Alaska Native women and men. *NIJ Journal 277,* 38–45. http://nij.gov/journals/277/Pages/violenceagainstamerican-indians-alaska-natives.aspx

Ryan, J. P., Garnier, P., Zyphur, M., & Zhai, F. (2006). Testing the effects of caseworker characteristics in child welfare. *Children and Youth Services Review, 28,* 993–1006.

Sandefur, G. D., & McKinnell, T. (1986). American Indian intermarriage. *Social Science Research, 15,* 347–371.

Sarche, M., & Spicer, P. (2008). Poverty and health disparities for American Indian and Alaska Native children: Current knowledge and future prospects. *Annals of the New York Academy of Science, 1136,* 126–136.

Shaw, T., Putnam-Hornstein, D., Magruder, J., & Needell, B. (2008). Measuring racial disparity in child welfare. *Child Welfare, 87*(2), 23–36.

Siegel, L. (1994). Cultural differences and their impact on practice in child welfare. *Journal of Multicultural Social Work, 3*(3), pp. 87–96.

Texas Dept. of Family and Protective Services. (2010). *Disproportionality in child protective services: The preliminary results of statewide reform efforts in Texas.* Austin, TX: Author. https://repositories.lib.utexas.edu/handle/2152/15377

U.S. Census Bureau, Population Division. (June 2018). *Annual estimates of the resident population by sex, age, race alone or in combination, and Hispanic origin for the United States and States: April 1, 2010 to July 1, 2017.* Washington, DC: Author. https://factfinder.census.gov/faces/tableservices/jsf/pages/productview.xhtml?pid=PEP_2015_PEPASR5H&prodType=table

U.S. Children's Bureau. (2018). *Child maltreatment 2016.* https://www.acf.hhs.gov/cb/research-data-technology/statistics-research/child-maltreatment

U.S. Children's Bureau. (2017). *AFCARS Report #24.* Washington, DC: Author. https://www.acf.hhs.gov/sites/default/files/cb/afcarsreport24.pdf

U.S. Children's Bureau. (2016). *Racial disproportionality and disparity in child welfare.* Washington, DC: Author. https://www.childwelfare.gov/pubpdfs/racial_disproportionality.pdf

U.S. Dept. of the Interior-Bureau of Indian Affairs. (n.d.). *Frequently asked questions.* https://www.bia.gov/frequently-asked-questions

Wallace, L. D. J., Patel, A., & Dellinger, A. (2003). Injuries mortality among American Indian and Alaska Native children and youth—United States, 1989–1998. *Morbidity and Mortality Weekly Report, 52*(30), 697–701. Atlanta: Centers for Disease Control and Prevention.

Wares, D. M., Wedel, K. R., Rosenthal, J. A., & Dobrec, A. (1994). Indian child welfare: A multicultural challenge. *Journal of Multicultural Social Work, 3*(3), 1–15.

Williams, R. (1999). Cultural safety—what does it mean for our work practice? *Australia and New Zealand Journal of Public Health, 23*(2), 213–214.

Figure Credits

Img. 7.1: Copyright © 2011 Depositphotos/MonaMakela.

Img. 7.2: Source: https://commons.wikimedia.org/wiki/File:Carlisle_pupils.jpg.

Img. 7.3: Copyright © 2013 Depositphotos/karelnoppe.

Img. 7.4: Copyright © 2012 Depositphotos/creatista.

CHAPTER • 8

Immigrant Children and Families in the Child Welfare System

Alan Dettlaff, Megan Finno-Velasquez, and Rowena Fong

Overview of Chapter and Population

Changes in immigration patterns and trends over the past 2 decades have considerably shifted the demographic profile of the United States. Not only have the numbers of foreign-born immigrants living in the United States increased, but also a larger proportion of this population consists of children and families. This chapter will review the demographics of the immigrant children and families in the United States and in the public child welfare system. It will discuss disproportionality and disparity issues as well as practice challenges for this population. Evidence-based practices, system approaches, as well as policies at the federal, state, and local levels, will be offered. The chapter will end with a case example highlighting the complexities in working with this population.

As of 2015, a full one-quarter (25%, 18,270,000) of children in the United States were living in immigrant families (Annie E. Casey Foundation, 2018). Of those children, almost one-third (30%) have at least one undocumented parent (Capps, Fix, & Zong, 2016), while 90% of children in immigrant families are themselves U.S. citizens (KIDS COUNT Data Center, 2016). More than half (55%) of immigrant children are of Hispanic origin, followed by 16% non-Hispanic White, 17% non-Hispanic Asian, and 9% non-Hispanic Black (Child Trends Data Book, 2014). Rates of children in immigrant families vary widely by state, ranging from 48% in California to 3% in West Virginia; however, half of all immigrant children in the United States live in just four states—California (4,367,000), Texas (2,427,000), New York (1,527,000), and Florida (1,332,000) (KIDS COUNT Data Center, 2016).

Numbers of unaccompanied children arriving to the United States has also grown in recent years, peaking in 2014 and rising again in 2016, with nearly 60,000 unaccompanied children arriving that year (U.S. Customs and Border Protection, 2016). The greatest numbers of children encountered by U.S. Customs and Border Patrol have arrived from Guatemala, Honduras, and El Salvador, known as the Northern Triangle region of Central

America (Chishti & Hipsman, 2016). Of those children, the majority who have been released to approved sponsors are in California, Texas, New York, and Florida.

Immigrant Children in the Child Welfare System

Data on the involvement of immigrant and refugee children and families involved in the child welfare system has historically been limited, as this data has not been collected uniformly by national or state child welfare reporting systems. This lack of data has resulted in a limited ability to determine the extent to which immigrant children and families become involved in this system, as well as the extent of their experience of child maltreatment. However, following the completion of the first National Survey of Child and Adolescent Well-Being (NSCAW) in 2002, new data became available to understand immigrant children and families' experiences with this system. In the first study to examine the involvement of immigrant children and families using this data, Dettlaff and Earner (2012) found that children living with an immigrant parent comprised 8.6% of all children who come to the attention of the child welfare system in the United States. More than two-thirds (67.2%) of children of immigrants in the child welfare system are Hispanic, followed by non-Hispanic White (14.8%), non-Hispanic Black (10%), and non-Hispanic Asian (7.5%). Consistent with national data, more than 4 out of 5 (82.5%) children of immigrants in the child welfare system are U.S.-born citizens (Dettlaff & Earner, 2012).

Image 8.1

Studies have also used data from NSCAW to examine the maltreatment patterns and risk factors among children in immigrant families, as well as how those differ from children in U.S.-born families. In the study by Dettlaff and Earner (2012), no significant differences were found in overall rates of maltreatment between children with immigrant parents and children with U.S.-born parents. However, studies have also shown that children of immigrants from certain racial/ethnic backgrounds may be vulnerable to specific types of maltreatment. For example, Dettlaff, Earner, and Phillips (2009) found that Latino children of immigrants were more than five times likely to experience sexual abuse than Latino children of U.S.-born parents. Chang, Rhee, and Weaver (2006) found that children in immigrant Korean families were more likely to come to the attention of the California child welfare system for physical abuse than children in other ethnic groups. Similarly, Rhee, Chang, Weaver, and Wong (2008) found that children in immigrant Chinese families were more likely to experience physical abuse compared to the general child welfare population. Yet, although these studies have begun to shed light on the unique maltreatment patterns and experiences among children in immigrant families, it is important to caution that much additional research is needed to fully understand these patterns and draw accurate conclusions.

A small number of studies have examined the risk factors associated with maltreatment among immigrant families, consistently finding that risk factors are more likely to be present in families with U.S.-born parents than in those with immigrant parents. Using data from NSCAW, Dettlaff and Earner (2012) found that U.S.-born parents were three times more likely to be actively abusing alcohol or drugs than immigrant parents and were significantly more likely to have a physical or cognitive impairment or recent histories of arrest. No significant differences were found in the prevalence of several risk factors often associated with immigrant families, including the use of excessive discipline, active domestic violence, low social support, and difficulty meeting their family's basic needs. Subsequently, further studies produce consistent findings concerning the presence of risk. Dettlaff and Johnson (2011) found that U.S.-born Latino children were significantly more likely to be living in homes with active alcohol and drug abuse, active domestic violence, and recent histories of parental arrest, while Johnson-Motoyama, Dettlaff, and Finno (2012) found that Latino children with U.S.-born parents were significantly more likely than those with foreign-born or mixed-nativity parents to be living in homes with active alcohol and drug abuse, recent histories of parental arrest, a history of maltreatment of the primary caregiver, and difficulty meeting basic needs.

The following case vignette provides an example of how an immigrant family may come to the attention of this system.

Case Application

Case Vignette

Eight-year-old Alejandra and her 29-year-old mother, Teresa, attempted to migrate to the United States from Honduras seeking asylum. Teresa had been suffering years of domestic abuse from Alejandra's father, Martin, and Alejandra had suffered from physical abuse at the hands of her father. Teresa now feared for both her and her daughter's life. Unfortunately, at the U.S. port of entry, they were sent back to Mexico to await their immigration hearing on their asylum claim as part of the new Migrant Protection Protocols, also known as the "Remain in Mexico" policy.

While in the asylum camp in Mexico, Teresa was robbed. After the robbery, Teresa no longer felt that it was safe for Alejandra to stay in the camp. So she sent Alejandra with a male they had befriended at the camp to attempt to cross the border again, this time illegally, in the hopes that Alejandra would be able to live with Teresa's relatives in the United States. Alejandra was again stopped by immigration officials at the border, and because she was not related to the man, she was considered an unaccompanied minor and placed in the custody of the Office of Refugee Resettlement (ORR).

After 2 weeks in ORR custody, officials were able to locate Teresa's 32-year-old cousin, Martha, in California. Martha agreed to sponsor Alejandra, and she was released into her custody. Unfortunately, after only a month in Martha's custody, Martha asked Child Protective Services to take custody of Alejandra because she could not handle her, stating that she had serious behavioral issues, would not listen to her, and was violent toward her 4-year-old son. Alejandra was then placed with foster parents in California while Teresa remained in Mexico.

DISCUSSION QUESTIONS

1. What kind of help would you recommend that Alejandra get first?
2. What systems of care are needed for Alejandra, and how can professionals from these systems help in this situation?
3. What is an unaccompanied minor?
4. What is the Office of Refugee Resettlement, and what kinds of services does it offer?
5. What is asylum? What is the eligibility requirement to receive asylum?

Disproportionality and Disparities Impacting Immigrant Children

The meaning of the terms *disproportionality* and *disparity* has evolved over time, and only recently has a common understanding of these terms reached consensus. The term *disproportionality* refers to the state of being out of proportion and describes a condition that exists when the proportion of people of a certain race or ethnicity in a target population differs from the proportion of people of the same group in a reference population (Fong, Dettlaff, James, & Rodriguez, 2015). The term *disparity* refers to a state of being unequal and is typically used to describe unequal outcomes experienced by one racial or ethnic group when compared to another racial or ethnic group (Fong et al., 2015). With immigrant and refugee children and families, both of these terms apply to the respective populations (Dettlaff & Fong, 2016).

Although limited, the data available suggests that children of immigrants are considerably underrepresented among children who become involved with the child welfare system, given that children in immigrant families represent approximately 9% of children in the child welfare system, although they represent 25% of the total child population in the United States. However, some data suggests there may be disparities at later points in the child welfare pathway. One study (Vericker, Kuehn, & Capps, 2007a) examining Latino children involved in the Texas child welfare system found that immigrant children and children of immigrants were significantly less likely to be placed with relatives than children of U.S.-born parents. This study also found that immigrant children were more likely to be placed in group homes than other children. Additionally, immigrant children were less likely to have case goals of reunification or relative adoption than U.S.-born children and were more likely to have goals of long-term foster care or independent living (Vericker et al., 2007a). These findings raise concerns given the previously cited research that demonstrated lower rates of risk among immigrant families, raising the possibility that issues such as immigration status or bias against immigrant families may be interfering with decisions made by child welfare professionals. However, much additional research is needed to understand why these differences exist and to determine whether these patterns hold true in other jurisdictions.

Researchers, educators, practitioners, and policy makers acknowledge that disproportionality and disparity are complex phenomena likely caused by multiple factors. However, some studies have continued to find evidence of racial bias even after controlling for poverty and risk (e.g., Dettlaff, Rivaux, Baumann, Fluke, Rycraft, & James, 2011; Rivaux et al., 2008). Thus, rather than debating which factors contribute most to disproportionalities and disparities, a more useful approach would be to acknowledge the contribution of each and support the continued exploration and understanding of these phenomena.

A useful approach to understanding racial disproportionality and disparities is one that involves critical race theory and cultural humility attitudes and behaviors. This approach can be one of using cultural humility with a lens of critical race theory. Critical race theory asserts that "racism is an ordinary, everyday occurrence for people of color" (Abrams & Moio, 2009, p. 251). Racism is based on a social construction of race and "people in power can racialize groups of people in different ways at different times, depending on historic, social, and economic need" (Abrams & Moio, 2009, p. 251). To counter "people in power racializing other people" advocates for cultural humility; Ortega and Faller (2011) assert that training of child welfare workers or others who have power over clients should be done from an "intersectional cultural humility perspective" (p. 27).

This perspective complements the cultural competence approach and it "liberate[s] workers from expectations of cultural expertise about others, … actively engages the clients, inclusive of their cultural difference …" (2011, p. 27). Using a cultural humility approach would be a very important empowering practice in working with immigrant and refugee children and families:

> *A cultural humility approach advocates for incorporating multicultural and intersectional understanding and analyses to improve practice, since together these concepts draw attention to the diversity of the whole person, to power differences in relationships (especially between workers and families), to different past and present life experiences including microaggressions, and to potential resources or gaps. (Ortega & Faller, 2011, p. 32)*

Immigrant children and families experience many micro-aggressions while living in their countries of origin and also while adjusting to the United States. It is very important that child welfare workers acknowledge these micro-aggressions and be very cautious not to create or impose more micro-aggressions while trying to serve them with non-culturally competent programs and services.

Practice Challenges with Immigrant Children and Families

Once children in immigrant families become involved in the child welfare system, they face unique challenges that threaten the system's ability to facilitate reunification with their parents, as well as positive outcomes related to their health and well-being (Dettlaff et al., 2009; Earner, 2007; Maiter, Stalker, & Alaggia, 2009). Child welfare systems may not be familiar with the complexity of immigration law and policies and may be unprepared to assist children or parents in addressing these issues. Beyond concerns associated with immigration status, child welfare practitioners may be unfamiliar with many of the challenges immigrant families face related to their immigration and acculturation experiences. Although efforts have been made in recent years to increase cultural competence in child welfare agencies, these efforts have largely focused on U.S.-born racial and ethnic groups. This lack of cultural awareness can lead to inaccurate assessments that fail to consider the underlying issues affecting immigrant families.

Of additional concern for immigrant children and families is access to services in their preferred language (Ayón, 2009; Barrios, Suleiman, & Vidal de Haymes, 2004). Language barriers can result in miscommunication and misunderstandings, which can affect families' ability to respond to interventions. Language barriers can also result in delays of service, which can affect parents' abilities to complete required services and place them at risk for termination of parental rights due to the timeframes mandated by the Adoption and Safe Families Act (ASFA) of 1997 (Ayón, 2009). ASFA calls for permanency decisions to be made within 12 months and requires the filing of petitions for termination of parental rights for children who have been in substitute care for 15 of the last 22 months. Beyond language, immigration status can create additional delays or barriers to reunification, as parents may be unable to obtain employment or participate in certain mandated services. Undocumented parents may also be ineligible for certain services that could facilitate reunification, such as those that are federally funded, including housing and public assistance and services requiring Medicaid, like substance abuse services (Siskin, 2016). Given these barriers, the expedited process required by ASFA may place immigrant families at a disadvantage in meeting case requirements, thus placing them at risk for termination of parental rights.

For immigrant children in foster care, a lack of culturally or linguistically appropriate services can also limit their ability to receive services needed to address both their physical and mental health needs. Further, funding for services for immigrant children may be limited due to restrictions within Title IV-E of the Social Security Act, the primary source of federal child welfare funding to states. This funding allows states to receive federal matching funds for the care of children in state custody, but receipt of IV-E funds is restricted to children who meet eligibility requirements, including U.S. citizenship (Vericker, Kuehn, & Capps, 2007b). Undocumented children do not meet the eligibility requirement, so states must bear the total burden of the cost of substitute care. In times of shrinking resources for public child welfare systems, this burden may limit states' abilities to adequately care for ineligible immigrant children.

For children who enter the child welfare system due solely to an immigration enforcement action, the complexities of these cases can be very challenging. Immigrant parents detained in immigration facilities may be unable to meaningfully participate in a reunification plan. In some cases, child welfare staff cannot locate parents, making their participation in decisions concerning their children unlikely. Detained parents are also unlikely to be able to participate in court proceedings related to their children's custody. Deportation proceedings and decisions may last longer than the timeframes under which child welfare agencies must make decisions, further complicating the agencies' ability to act in children's best interests. When children are U.S. citizens, the prospect of parental deportation poses a uniquely difficult situation for children, their parents, and for child welfare systems. Children may remain in the United States and be permanently separated from their parents—or they can leave their home and all they have known to move to an unfamiliar country to remain with their family.

Evidence-Based Interventions for Working with Immigrant Children and Families

Although the number of immigrant children and families involved in the child welfare system continues to grow, the design, implementation, and dissemination of evidence-based practices that are culturally responsive to immigrant families remain relatively underdeveloped (Garcia, Aisenberg, & Harachi, 2012). However, there are a number of interventions with some evidence of success in parent training, early intervention/prevention programs, behavioral health treatments, and child welfare practice models that have been adapted for, or demonstrated to be effective among, Spanish-speaking populations specifically.

Parent Training

Parent training is a common type of intervention used by child welfare agencies when child abuse and neglect are suspected or substantiated. Some evidence-based parent training models have been tested and validated with diverse samples, many of whom are immigrant families. For example, Parent Child Interaction Therapy (PCIT) is a widely used dyadic behavioral intervention for young children and their parents or caregivers that focuses on decreasing externalizing child behavior problems, increasing child social skills and cooperation, and improving the parent-child attachment relationship (Eyberg et al., 2001; Hood & Eyberg, 2003; Chaffin, Funderburk, Bard, Valle, & Gurwitch, 2011). PCIT has been used with multiple settings, has been translated to Spanish, and has been implemented with specific cultural groups, including Hong Kong Chinese (Leung, Tsang, Sin, & Choi, 2015). The Guiando a Niños Activos, or Guiding Active Children program (GANA) (McCabe, Yeh, Garland, Lau, & Chavez, 2005), is a version of PCIT that was specifically designed and tested for use with Spanish-speaking Mexican and Mexican American families. GANA is different from PCIT in that it is presented as an educational program as opposed to a form of psychological treatment in order to reduce the stigma associated with mental health treatment.

SafeCare is an in-home parent training program appropriate for families who have had concerns of neglect and physical abuse in multiple communities throughout the United States and internationally (Chaffin, Hecht, Bard, Silovsky, & Beasley, 2012). It targets parent skills in three areas: (1) positive interactions with children; (2) recognizing home safety hazards; and (3) to recognize and respond to health issues (Self-Brown et al., 2014). SafeCare has manuals for training in Spanish, French, and Hebrew and has been implemented with cultural adaptations made for Spanish-speaking immigrants in Southern California with positive outcomes (Finno-Velasquez, Fettes, Aarons, & Hurlburt, 2014).

Early Intervention/Prevention Programs

Some early intervention programs may also be appropriate for use with immigrant families to prevent child maltreatment. For example, Healthy Families America (HFA) is a widely tested home-visiting program designed for families who are at risk of child abuse or neglect and other **adverse childhood experiences** (Harding, Galano, Martin, Huntington, & Schellenbach, 2007). HFA is designed to work with families who may have histories of trauma, intimate partner violence, mental health issues, and/or substance abuse issues. HFA services are offered voluntarily, intensively, and over the long term and have been found to be effective with Latina immigrants (Sandy, Anisfeld, & Ramirez, 2009).

Mental and Behavioral Health Treatments

Individual and family therapy is often recommended or mandated when concerns of child abuse and neglect are identified in a home. Despite challenges to engagement in treatment that may stem from a mental health stigma that is common in various cultures, several therapeutic models or programs may be appropriate options for use with immigrant parents and children who are involved with the child welfare system.

Some programs have been designed specifically for immigrants to address issues of acculturative stress and prevent or reduce youth behavioral issues. For example, Familias Unidas is a family-based program delivered in schools to prevent behavioral problems in adolescents' lives by increasing parental involvement (Coatsworth, Pantin, & Szapocznik, 2002). Entre Dos Mundos is a similar program designed to alleviate acculturative stress among Latinx immigrant families (Bacallao & Smokowski, 2005). The Mental Health for Immigrants Program (MHIP) is delivered to children in schools to decrease symptoms of depression and PTSD among immigrant children who have been exposed to violence (Kataoka et al., 2003).

These programs designed to address acculturation stress and intergenerational cultural conflicts are especially relevant because mental health treatments provided to children and families in the child welfare system (CWS) typically do not address these issues. There are also family- or group-based programs, offered most often in schools, which may be helpful for developing supportive relationships for immigrant families involved with an unfamiliar child welfare system. However, the children and families who have been part of these programs do not necessarily have mental health issues and also are not involved with the CWS, so it is not known how well these programs would work to address the more serious nature of concerns present in families with CWS involvement.

Some specific therapeutic models may be appropriate for immigrant children and parents to address mental health concerns in CWS settings. Trauma-Focused Cognitive Behavioral Therapy (TF-CBT), for example, has been translated into multiple languages, including Spanish, Mandarin, Korean, German, and Japanese (Deblinger, Thakkar-Kolar, & Ryan, 2006) and may be a good fit for immigrant children who have experienced trauma or violence in their countries of origin or during the migration journey (Kataoka et al., 2003). Motivational Interviewing is a client-centered, directive method designed to enhance client motivation for behavior change (Hohman, 2012). It focuses on exploring and resolving ambivalence by increasing intrinsic motivation to change. MI can be used by itself, as well as in combination with other treatments. It has been utilized in pretreatment work to engage and motivate clients in preparation for other treatment modalities and has been found effective with Latino immigrants (Carroll, Libby, Sheehan, & Hyland, 2001; Mullins, Suarez, Ondersma, & Page, 2004).

Child Welfare Practice Models

It does not appear that any child welfare system practice models have been tested for effectiveness with immigrant families. However, one well-known model, Family Group Decision Making (FGDM), may be an appropriate approach for child welfare work with immigrant groups (Pennell & Burford, 2000). FGDM is a manualized intervention that has translated materials available in Spanish, French, and Inukitut (California Evidence-Based Clearinghouse for Child Welfare, 2009). It may be offered in the family home or in other settings where families feel comfortable, such as a religious organization or church. Its approach especially aligns with groups with collectivist cultural values because it positions the "family group," including kin and extended family members, as leaders in decision-making about their children's safety, permanency, and well-being (Merkel-Holguin, 2003; Wang et al., 2012). Another newer model, called the cultural mediator or cultural broker model, was originally designed to raise and address concerns related to disproportionalities and disparities for African American groups that exist in the child welfare system as well as concerns that involve issues of fairness and equity (Montana, Rondero Hernandez, Siegel, & Jackson, 2010). This model has since been implemented with Latino groups in some communities to strengthen engagement with the community and with families in child welfare service delivery. Despite a lack of rigorous research and evaluation of this model, it may be promising for use with immigrant parents who may need individual support and mentoring to navigate the child welfare system and to ensure that reasonable efforts are made to provide the best possible services in often complex situations.

Image 8.2

Below is a list of promising interventions available on the California Evidence-Based Clearinghouse for Child Welfare (CEBC) that are designed specifically for immigrant populations or have 1) evidence of success in implementation with Spanish-speaking or immigrant samples; 2) specific cultural adaptations made for immigrant samples; or 3) manuals in languages other than English AND studies conducted with samples, including high percentages of Hispanic or Asian groups. (For a detailed description of the CEBC and the criteria to be included in this, refer to Chapter 3.)

Parent Training Models

- Parent Child-Home Program (PCHP)
- Parent Management Training
- Parent Child Interaction Therapy (PCIT)
- Guiando a los Niños Activos (GANA)

- SafeCare
- ACT Raising Safe Kids
- CICC Los Ninos Bien Educados
- Healthy Families America
- Triple P

Child Welfare Practice Models

- Family Group Decision Making (FGDM)
- Cultural Mediators/Cultural Brokers

Behavioral/Mental Health Models

- Trauma Focused Cognitive Behavioral Therapy
- Brief Strategic Family Therapy
- Motivational Interviewing
- Multi-Systemic Therapy
- Entre Dos Mundos
- Familias Unidas
- Mental Health for Immigrants Program (MHIP)

Systems Approach: Integration of Public Systems with Private Agencies

Immigrant children and families interact with a number of public and social service systems, including child welfare, criminal justice, education, mental health, and health. However, barriers to services exist, ranging from fear of using services to outright exclusion from services. These systems and their intersections with the immigrant population are discussed below.

Child Welfare

A family's involvement with the child welfare system has the potential to aid family members in accessing services for wide-ranging needs. However, many immigrant families fear involvement in this system. They worry CWS involvement will lead to detention and deportation or child removal; they also fear the child welfare system as a potentially repressive government entity (Slayter & Križ, 2015; Ayón, Aisenberg, & Erera, 2010). In addition to fear as a barrier to access, immigrant families are likely to encounter obstacles to feeling rapport with their service provider. Their parenting principles may be questioned or misinterpreted; they may feel powerless in comparison to the service provider; or they may have trouble finding a provider who can communicate effectively with them in their language of choice (Ayón et al., 2010).

Criminal Justice

Immigrants face specific challenges in relation to the criminal justice system. For example, a child or adolescent's contact with the criminal justice system can have severe consequences for an immigrant family with an undocumented member. In addition to the typical risks faced by young offenders (i.e., dropping out of school, recidivism), these youth also risk exposing undocumented family members to the courts.

This fear of deportation has a complex impact on immigrants' relationship to the criminal justice system; among other consequences, it lowers the likelihood that immigrants will report crimes to the authorities (Becerra, Wagaman, Androff, Messing, & Castillo, 2017). The underreporting of crime creates difficulties for police trying to control criminal activity. It also increases fear of crime, which, in turn, may decrease quality of life for immigrants (Davis, Erez, & Avitabile, 2001).

Education

Children of immigrants are deeply involved in the public school system in the United States. Indeed, federal law (Title VI of the Civil Rights Act of 1964; McKinney-Vento Act) and Supreme Court decisions (*Plyler v. Doe*) have long underscored the right of an undocumented student in the United States to a public education. As of 2015, 23% of U.S. public school students came from an immigrant household; of these children, between one-fourth and one-third were the children of undocumented immigrants (Camarota, Griffith, & Zeigler, 2017).

Immigrant children face a number of barriers to success within the K–12 school system. An academic performance gap persists between children with an immigrant background and nonimmigrant children; this gap is likely due to disparities in opportunity (Schnepf, 2007). As well, students from immigrant families have a lower sense of belonging at school when compared to native students (Ham, Yang, & Cha, 2017).

Once immigrant children become college-age, the barriers to further education become outright exclusionary, in particular for undocumented students. Some universities adhere to state laws that restrict admission of undocumented students; others permit admission but stick undocumented students with out-of-state tuition rates, even those that are long-standing local residents. And since federal work study programs require proof of legal status or citizenship, undocumented students are limited in their ability to find employment (Frum, 2007).

Not having the right documents restricts undocumented students in other ways, too: they face barriers in signing up for internships, participating in college-backed insurance programs, and going on a semester abroad or international travel opportunities (Gámez, Lopez, & Overton, 2017). The Obama-era immigration policy **Deferred Action for Childhood Arrivals (DACA)** offered temporary protection against deportation and work authorization to many undocumented college students, but the Trump administration's repeated pushes to end the program leave many undocumented students in a perpetual state of stress and uncertainty about their futures. While challenges related to education exist for all children entering foster care, these additional challenges related to citizenship status increase the likelihood of negative educational outcomes for undocumented children.

Mental Health

In addition to stress stemming from uncertainty about educational opportunities, immigrant children can experience anxiety from stressors, including discrimination or stigma, uncertainty about immigration laws, trauma stemming from their own migration experiences, and caregiver immigration status. And if fears come to fruition and caregivers are deported, these children are significantly more likely to display behavioral and mental health problems than children whose parents were not deported (Allen, Cisneros, & Tellez, 2015).

There are clear intersections between the mental health and child welfare systems. In one study of over 800 adolescents who were investigated as victims of child abuse or neglect, nearly half reported at least one mental health problem (Heneghan et al., 2013). However, when a child referred to the child welfare system is a member of a family with an undocumented parent, that child is significantly less likely to receive mental health services when compared to a child whose parents are U.S. citizens (Finno-Velasquez, Berger Cardoso, Dettlaff, & Hurlburt, 2016). Finno-Velasquez et al. suggest that "caregivers' vulnerable legal status may deter parents from seeking services for their children" (2016, p. 196).

Health

Children in households with noncitizen parents experience worse health and less access to care, including lower frequency of doctor and dentist visits (Ziol-Guest & Kalil, 2012). There are several possible explanations for this. For one, undocumented immigrants are not eligible for health insurance under the Affordable Care Act and therefore must pay out-of-pocket for most health care services. This may mean that many immigrant families avoid the health care system whenever possible, only going to providers as a last resort.

In addition to the high cost of health care, barriers include lack of culturally competent and bilingual providers and mistrust of the health care system due to fear of discrimination and deportation. For example, the most frequently reported obstacle to health care for Korean immigrants and their families is a language barrier (Jang, 2016). However, beyond a lack of bilingual and bicultural health care providers, immigrant families may fear exposure of their immigration status as a result of bias or vulnerable data collection systems.

Private Agencies

Increasingly, policy and other decision-makers view **privatization** as a vital means of meeting the country's social obligations toward providing care-oriented services.

In terms of the immigrant population, privatization creates a lucrative opening for turning undocumented immigrants into a source of revenue. Indeed, private prison corporations stand to profit significantly from private immigration detention centers (Ackerman & Furman, 2013). There is also a bustling business in housing, transporting, and otherwise detaining immigrant children along the southwestern border; one company has won at least $955 million in federal contracts since 2015 to run shelters and provide other services to immigrant children in federal custody (Fernandez & Benner, 2018). Whether these companies focus more on profit than on the safety and security of the immigrants they house is a hotly debated topic.

Child welfare is increasing its use of public-private partnerships and the contracting out of services to private vendors. One can see why this is an attractive option; private agencies tend to be more nimble than public bureaucracies in their ability to be innovative and adaptable. Many of the innovative programs for immigrants discussed earlier in this chapter are run through some version of privatization. For example, SafeCare is run through the nonprofit National SafeCare Training and Research Center, and Healthy Families America is run through the nonprofit Prevent Child Abuse America.

This section is by no means exhaustive but provides a brief window into the complexities of working with immigrant families and children and the many tangled systems with which they interact.

Policies That Impact Immigrants Involved with the Child Welfare System

Public policy impacts program funding, service access, and benefits eligibility, making it one of the most complex levers to improve outcomes for immigrant children, youth, and families (LeBrun et al., 2015). Over the past several decades, major policy developments at the federal level have impacted immigrant children and families, affecting their likelihood of coming into contact with the child welfare system as well as their experiences once involved. Table 8.1 below highlights a selection of policies, which generally fall into one of three categories:

- **Benefits Eligibility:** These policies restrict or expand individual eligibility for services, or federal reimbursement to states for services delivered, based on recipient immigration status. Utilization of benefits such as Temporary Assistance for Needy Families (TANF) has been associated with lower rates of child maltreatment, suggesting that limiting access to these supports may increase the likelihood that a family will encounter the child welfare system (LeBrun et al., 2015). Similarly, access to and utilization of prevention and support services is often vital to parents' ability to safely care for their child and meet court-mandated requirements to regain custody.

- **Procedural and Practice Guidance:** While most federal child welfare policies systems do not provide guidance for work with immigrant children and families, they often have a unique impact on them. Many policies aim to improve the permanency and well-being of children, such as efforts to speed the adoption process by shortening the timeline for termination of parental rights. However, most policies fail to account for the unique barriers that an immigrant family may face; for example, in meeting requirements to regain custody, which can hamper reunification if children are in foster care. Other policies emphasize the maintenance of family connections, something that may be particularly vital in the context of immigrant family and community bonds. This can become particularly challenging if federal immigration enforcement officials are involved and parents are deported, resulting in complicated international reunification processes involving local social service agencies and foreign governments.
- **Cultural Competency and Addressing Disparity:** The federal government has implemented several policies designed to combat racial and ethnic disparities. While not specifically addressing immigrants, some of these efforts can have a positive impact on immigrant children in the child welfare system. For example, recruitment of diverse foster parents may result in less trauma for children when they are placed with a family who shares their language and cultural background. Yet federal government efforts are often less impactful than county and state government efforts, such as softening licensing regulations for relatives of immigrant children, including relatives that are undocumented. Additionally, requirements for collection of data capturing racial and ethnic disparities or language(s) spoken at home provide useful—albeit imperfect—proxies in the face of all but absent data regarding immigrant status.

TABLE 8.1. Federal Policies Impacting Immigrant Families in Child Welfare

Policy	Purpose and Impact
Benefits Eligibility	
Personal Responsibility and Work Opportunity Reconciliation Act of 1996 (PRWORA)	Select provisions significantly restricted eligibility for public benefits among legal immigrants, refugees, citizen children, and other populations who had previously been eligible, in an effort to disincentivize illegal immigration.

Policy	Purpose and Impact
Temporary Assistance for the Needy (TANF)	TANF was significantly impacted by PRWORA, with a dramatic decline in aided-adult cases and an increase in child-only cases, as well as the addition of a new categorization of ineligible immigrant parents (IIPs), with 25% of the country's child-only cases being children of IIPs.
U.S. Department of Health and Human Services	Federal policies impacting children in foster care prevent federal reimbursement of some costs to states for undocumented immigrant children, including Medicaid and Title IV-E payments.
Child Welfare Procedural and Practice Guidance	
Fostering Connections to Success and Increasing Adoptions Act of 2008	Designed to promote permanency for children in foster care by encouraging maintaining family connections, supporting youth transitioning from foster care, ensuring health and educational well-being for foster youth.
Adoption and Safe Families Act of 1997	Decreased the time required for the termination of parental rights (TPR) by requiring states to file a TPR petition for any child in out of home care for 15 of the last 22 months.
Trafficking Victims Protection Reauthorization Act of 2008 (TVPRA)	Intended to ensure the safety and well-being of apprehended Unaccompanied Alien Children (UAC), a provision speeds up the timeline for transfer to 72 hours after determining a child is unaccompanied.
Cultural Competency and Addressing Disparity	
Civil Rights Act of 1964 (Title VI)	Established that all services provided in public systems (e.g., education, child welfare) must be linguistically and culturally available and appropriate.
Multiethnic Placement Act of 1994, as amended by the Interethnic Adoption Provision of 1996 (MEPA-IEP)	Requires the recruitment of foster care and adoptive parents that are representative of the ethnic and racial diversity of the children in care.

Immigration Policy and Its Impact on Children and Families

In addition to how policy influences benefit eligibility, practice guidelines, and efforts to reduce disparities, federal immigration policy also plays a critical role in the experiences of immigrant families with child welfare involvement. These policies tend to address either immigration enforcement or immigration relief, both of which can have a significant impact on the lives of immigrant families. A selection of major immigration enforcement policies is summarized in Table 8.2.

TABLE 8.2. Select Federal Immigration Enforcement Policies

Policy	Purpose and Impact
Secure Communities	Creates a partnership between U.S. Immigration and Customs Enforcement (ICE) and state or local law enforcement to share data and fingerprints from arrests to FBI database and an ICE database.
287(g) Program	Creates a partnership between ICE and state or local law enforcement to screen individuals in local jails and state prisons to identify deportable noncitizens.
An Executive Order to the U.S. Immigration and Customs–Parental Interests Directive	Intended to aid ICE in enforcing immigration laws fairly and with respect for parents' rights and responsibilities by outlining policies and procedures for the handling of cases involving primary caretakers, parents, or legal guardians of minor children, and particularly those involved in family court or child welfare proceedings.

Immigration Enforcement

Immigration enforcement activities conducted by Immigration and Customs Enforcement (ICE) have resulted in an unprecedented number of deportations over the past decade. In 2007, a strategy was adopted to prioritize the apprehension of immigrants who committed criminal offenses, which resulted in the merging of several programs under the ICE Agreements of Cooperation in Communities to Enhance Safety and Security (ACCESS) initiative. One of the best-known of these is the 287(g) program, which established collaborations between ICE and local officials that allow local police to be deputized to enforce immigration laws. Currently, ICE has 287(g) agreements with 76 law enforcement agencies in 20 states, and ICE officers have certified more than 1,800 local officers to enforce immigration law (U.S. Department of Homeland Security, 2017).

A related program, Secure Communities, uses local jails to identify immigrants for deportation by forwarding fingerprint data from the FBI to ICE, which determines the arrested person's immigration status. If the arrested person is identified as a noncitizen, ICE can request that local authorities detain that person until ICE moves him or her to an immigration detention center. Secure Communities has resulted in the deportation of thousands of immigrants who do not have criminal convictions at all, or whose only crimes are simple misdemeanors such as driving without a license (U.S. Immigration and Customs Enforcement, 2012). This resulted in a decrease in removals of parents of children legally present in the United States (Trevizo, 2016). In 2011, ICE created policy that directs ICE personnel to avoid arresting individuals at certain "sensitive locations," including churches, schools, and child care programs (Morton, 2011).

In 2013, ICE's 2013 Parental Interests Directive was implemented with the aim of helping ICE balance the enforcement of immigration laws with respect for a parent's/guardian's rights and responsibilities. As a result, it also increased the ability of detained parents to make decisions for the care of their children and participate in child welfare proceedings. With the implementation of the Parental Interests Directive, while families continued to be separated by immigration enforcement, the chances that a family would become involved with the child welfare system as a result of immigration enforcement decreased.

In addition to these federal enforcement programs, a number of state and local immigration enforcement initiatives have been fueled by anti-immigrant sentiment, such Arizona's Senate Bill 1070 and other copycat laws. Arizona Senate Bill 1070 (2010) imposed penalties on immigrants who failed to provide immigration documentation and allowed law enforcement to ask suspected undocumented immigrants about their immigration legal status. Following the adoption of Arizona's law, many other states considered copycat laws, while Utah, Georgia, Indiana, Alabama, and South Carolina passed SB1070-style legislation (Lacayo, 2011). In 2012, the U.S. Supreme Court blocked three of four provisions in SB 1070 as well as in other copycat laws (Wang, 2012; National Immigration Law Center, 2014).

Unaccompanied Minors

In addition to increased immigration enforcement and anti-immigrant policies, the past decade has also seen growing migration to the United States among unaccompanied alien children (UAC) fleeing poverty and violence in the Northern Triangle countries of El Salvador, Guatemala, and Honduras (Chen & Gill, 2015). When encountered by law enforcement, most children are initially placed in the custody of the Office of Refugee Resettlement (ORR) and eventually released to relatives while awaiting the immigration court decisions for their case.

Image 8.3

However, harsh enforcement strategies were elevated along the border in 2014 when unaccompanied immigrant children began to flee to the United States in large numbers to escape violence and persecution in their countries of origin (Kandel, 2017). As a result, the Obama administration publicly committed to an aggressive deterrence strategy, which resulted in increased apprehensions of children and individuals seeking asylum from Mexico and other Central American countries (White House, Office of the Press Secretary, 2014). This surge resulted in an expansion of immigrant detention, including the detention of children and mothers, and increases in the separation of children from their parents when crossing the border (Detention Watch Network, n.d.). Through the Office of Refugee Resettlement, many thousands of unaccompanied children are released to parents or relatives willing to sponsor the children while they are waiting for decisions in their immigration cases. As currently funded, the ORR licensing and monitoring process for unaccompanied minor sponsor cases is generally less stringent than the regulation and oversight of state foster care licensing. In most cases, federal protective jurisdiction of unaccompanied children ends after a short home study and release to sponsors. Once released to sponsors, these placements are not subject to any oversight or monitoring, and the children do not have access to health insurance, public assistance, or any health or support services normally afforded to children in state foster care, situating the placements at risk of disruption, exploitation, and maltreatment.

Current policy around unaccompanied minors presents several challenges, including a cursory approval process for sponsors, minimal ongoing monitoring for child well-being, and a lack of support services or resources for the youth or relatives. These shortcomings can impact a child's safety and well-being, as well as the likelihood that there will be a placement disruption and subsequent involvement with the local public child welfare system. Additionally, increased immigration enforcement has begun to target undocumented parents, guardians, and relative sponsors of unaccompanied children, creating additional trauma and instability.

Among undocumented youth and **mixed-status families** in particular, policies governing immigration enforcement may impact many aspects of life, including encounters with the child welfare system. Limited research has explored child outcomes associated with parental detention and deportation and the barriers to family reunification that can result from immigration status. A selection of these policies is found in Table 8.3.

TABLE 8.3. Select Immigration Relief Policies

Policy	Purpose and Impact
Special Immigrant Juvenile Status (SIJS)	SIJS provides lawful permanent residency to children who are under the jurisdiction of a juvenile court and who will not be reunified with their parents due to abuse, neglect, or abandonment.

Policy	Purpose and Impact
U Visa	Victims of certain designated crimes, including domestic violence and sexual assault, may be eligible for a U Visa. The victim must be willing to work with law enforcement to cooperate in the investigation and prosecution of the crime.
T Visa	Victims of human trafficking may be eligible for a T Visa allowing them to live and work temporarily in the United States, generally upon agreeing to aid in the prosecution of their traffickers.
Asylum	Asylum status is provided to those who can prove past persecution or fear of future persecution due to race, religion, nationality, membership in a particular social group, or political opinion.
Deferred Action for Childhood Arrivals (DACA)	DACA provides temporary work authorization and reprieve from deportation for some individuals brought to the United States as children. This policy is currently facing potential changes.
Violence Against Women Act (VAWA)	VAWA provides a self-petition process to protect immigrant victims married to an abuser who is a U.S. citizen or legal permanent resident who uses the victim's undocumented status to exert power and control.
Cancellation of Removal (CoR) for Non-Permanent Residents	Some youth faced with immigration enforcement may receive permanent residence if they have lived in the United States for at least 10 years and have a parent, spouse, or child who is a legal resident or citizen who would suffer hardship if they were deported.
Citizenship and Family Immigration	Some youth may be citizens based on the U.S. citizenship of parents or grandparents. Some may gain lawful permanent residency through family members with U.S. citizenship or lawful permanent residency.

Some legal scholars argue that immigration law operates in ways that intentionally hinder family unity and ignore the best interests of children, the effects of which are in direct conflict with child welfare principles (Morrison & Thronson, 2010). For example, parental immigration status is sometimes used as a basis for terminating parental rights by arguing that parents' status will result in instability for the child (ibid, 2010). Additionally, family courts are rarely equipped to address the complex issues that mixed-status families face, and historically have discriminated against undocumented immigrant parents (Rogerson, 2012). Discrimination can also extend to undocumented family members who would otherwise be able to serve as kin caregivers, who might be afraid to come forward due to fears of deportation. In the worst scenarios, when parents are deported, their children may either become exiles (i.e., children who leave with their parents to another country, often one they do not know), or orphans (i.e., children whose parents leave them in the United States in the care of others, sometimes the child welfare system).

Immigration Relief

Once involved with the child welfare system, immigrant children and families may qualify for several forms of immigration relief, which are outlined above in Table 8.3. Familiarity with these different relief options is important, as child welfare workers can screen for eligibility for various forms of relief, which can lead to legal permanent residency and citizenship.

Case Application

This case is about a 17-year-old Honduran youth who does not have a permanent home or legal residence and is placed in detention.

Case Vignette

Carlos is a 17-year-old boy and recent migrant to the United States. In Honduras, he lived with his father, younger sister, and grandmother. After his father was killed by a street gang, it fell to Carlos to support his grandmother and sister. He thought he would find better jobs in the United States, so he attached himself to a band of men who were also migrating in search of work. They arrived (illegally) in the United States, and Carlos found a job at a car wash. However, the car wash was raided by ICE. Carlos sat in detention for 6 months. Finally, he was referred to a social worker at the Office of Refugee Resettlement.

Carlos is now rapidly approaching his 18th birthday. He has been sitting cooling his heels in forced detention for so long, when quicker processing would have greatly improved his chances of getting placed in a foster home. Now there is only so much that can be done for him before he ages out.

Carlos also reveals that while in detention, one of the other boys raped him. Now he is suffering from classic post-traumatic stress symptoms, including night terrors that cause him to wake up screaming at night. The night terrors will make him difficult to place in a group home, and there is not a long list of foster parents eager to take older teenagers who have been sexually abused for a short-term placement. Carlos is considering going back to Honduras. It would have been easier for Carlos to be placed before the ICE raid. Time is quickly running out for Carlos.

DISCUSSION QUESTIONS

1. What kind of help would you recommend that Carlos get first?
2. What systems of care are needed for Carlos, and how can professionals from these systems help his situation?
3. What is the difference between the terms *disproportionality* and *disparity*?
4. What does SIJS stand for, and to whom does it apply?
5. What is a T Visa? What is the eligibility requirement to get one?

References

Abrams, L., & Moio, J. (2009). Critical race theory and the cultural competence dilemma in social work education. *Journal of Social Work Education, 45*(2), 245–261.

Ackerman, A. R., & Furman, R. (2013). The criminalization of immigration and the privatization of the immigration detention: Implications for justice. *Contemporary Justice Review, 16*(2), 251–263. doi: 10.1080/10282580.2013.798506

Allen, B., Cisneros, E., & Tellez, A. (2015). The children left behind: The impact of parental deportation on mental health. *Journal of Child & Family Studies, 24*(2), 386–392. doi: 10.1007/s10826-013-9848-5

Annie E. Casey Foundation. (2018). KIDS COUNT Data Center. *Children in Immigrant Families.* http://datacenter.kidscount.org/data/tables/115-children-in-immigrant-families?loc=1&loct=1#detailed/1/any/false/870,573,869,36,868/any/445,446

Ayón, C. (2009). Shorter time-lines, yet higher hurdles: Mexican families' access to child welfare mandated services. *Children and Youth Services Review, 31*, 609–616.

Ayón, C., Aisenberg, E., & Erera, P. (2010). Learning how to dance with the public child welfare system: Mexican parents' efforts to exercise their voice. *Journal of Public Child Welfare, 4*(3), 263–286. doi: 10.1080/15548732.2010.496077

Bacallao, M. L., & Smokowski, P. R. (2005). "Entre dos mundos" (between two worlds): Bicultural skills training with Latino immigrant families. *Journal of Primary Prevention, 26*(6), 485–509.

Barrios, L., Suleiman, L., & Vidal de Haymes, M. (2004). Latino population trends and child welfare services: Reflections on policy, practice, and research from the Latino Consortium roundtable discussions. *Illinois Child Welfare, 1*, 106–114.

Becerra, D., Wagaman, M. A., Androff, D., Messing, J., & Castillo, J. (2017). Policing immigrants: Fear of deportations and perceptions of law enforcement and criminal justice. *Journal of Social Work, 17*(6), 715–731. doi: 10.1177/1468017316651995

California Evidence-Based Clearinghouse for Child Welfare. (2009). Family Group Decision Making (FGDM). http://www.cebc4cw.org/program/family-group-decision-making/detailed

Camarota, S. A., Griffith, B., & Zeigler, K. (2017, January). *Mapping the impact of immigration in public schools.* Center for Immigration Studies. https://cis.org/Report/Mapping-Impact-Immigration-Public-Schools

Capps, R., Fix, M., & Zong, J. (2016, January). *Fact sheet: A profile of U.S. children with unauthorized immigrant parents.* Migration Policy Institute. https://www.migrationpolicy.org/research/profile-us-children-unauthorized-immigrant-parents

Carroll, K. M., Libby, B., Sheehan, J., & Hyland, N. (2001). Motivational interviewing to enhance treatment initiation in substance abusers: An effectiveness study. *The American Journal on Addictions, 10,* 33--339.

Chaffin, M., Funderburk, B., Bard, D., Valle, L. A., & Gurwitch, R. (2011). A combined motivation and Parent-Child Interaction Therapy package reduces child welfare recidivism in a randomized dismantling field trial. *Journal of Consulting and Clinical Psychology, 79,* 84–95.

Chaffin, M., Hecht, D., Bard, D., Silovsky, J. F., & Beasley, W. H. (2012). A statewide trial of the Safe-Care home-based services model with parents in child protective services. *Pediatrics, 129*(3), 509–515. doi: 10.1542/peds.2011-1840

Chang, J., Rhee, S., & Weaver, D. (2006). Characteristics of child abuse in immigrant Korean families and correlates of placement decisions. *Child Abuse & Neglect, 30,* 881–891.

Chen, A., & Gill, J. (2015). Unaccompanied children and the US immigration system: Challenges and reforms. *Journal of International Affairs, 68*(2), 115.

Child Trends Data Bank. (2014). *Immigrant children: Indicator of child and youth well-being.* https://www.childtrends.org/?indicators=immigrant-children

Chishti, M., and Hipsman, F. (2016). *Increased Central American migration to the United States may prove an enduring phenomenon.* Washington, DC: Migration Policy Institute. www.migrationpolicy.org/research/border-metrics-how-effectively-measure-border-security-and-immigration-control

Coatsworth, J. D., Pantin, H., & Szapocznik, J. (2002). Familias Unidas: A family-centered ecodevelopmental intervention to reduce risk for problem behavior among Hispanic adolescents. *Clinical Child and Family Psychology Review, 5*(2), 113–132.

Davis, R. C., Erez, E., & Avitabile, N. (2001). Access to justice for immigrants who are victimized: The perspectives of police and prosecutors. *Criminal Justice Policy Review, 12,* 183–196.

Deblinger, E., Thakkar-Kolar, R., & Ryan, E. (2006). Trauma in childhood. In V. M. Follette & J. Ruzek J(Es.), *Cognitive Behavioral Therapies for Trauma.* New York: Guilford Press.

Detention Watch Network. (n.d.). Family Detention: The unjust policy of locking up immigrant mothers with their children. https://www.detentionwatchnetwork.org/issues/family-detention

Dettlafff, A., & Fong, R. (2016). *Immigrant and Refugee Children and Families: Culturally Responsive Practice*. New York: Columbia University Press.

Dettlaff, A. J., & Earner, I. (2012). Children of immigrants in the child welfare system: Characteristics, risk, and maltreatment. *Families in Society: The Journal of Contemporary Social Services, 93*, 295–303.

Dettlaff, A. J., Earner, I., & Phillips, S. D. (2009). Latino children of immigrants in the child welfare system: Prevalence, characteristics, and risk. *Children and Youth Services Review, 31*, 775–783.

Dettlaff, A. J., & Johnson, M. A. (2011). Child maltreatment dynamics among immigrant and U.S. born Latino children: Findings from the National Survey of Child and Adolescent Well-Being (NSCAW). *Children and Youth Services Review, 33*, 936–944.

Dettlaff, A. J., Rivaux, S. R., Baumann, D. J., Fluke, J. D., Rycraft, J. R., & James, J. (2011). Disentangling substantiation: The influence of race, income, and risk on the substantiation decision in child welfare. *Children and Youth Services Review, 33*, 1630–1637.

Earner, I. (2007). Immigrant families and public child welfare: Barriers to services and approaches to change. *Child Welfare, 86*(4), 63–91.

Eyberg, S. M., Funderburk, B. W., Hembree-Kigin, T., McNeil, C. B., Querido, J., & Hood, K. K. (2001). Parent-child interaction therapy with behavior problem children: One- and two-year maintenance of treatment effects in the family. *Child & Family Behavior Therapy, 23*, 1–20.

Fernandez, M., & Benner, K. (2018, June 21). The billion-dollar business of operating shelters for migrant children. *The New York Times*, p. A15.

Finno-Velasquez, M., Berger Cardoso, J., Dettlaff, A. J., & Hurlburt, M. S. (2016). Effects of parent immigration status on mental health service use among Latino children referred to child welfare. *Psychiatric Services, 67*, 192–198. doi: 10.1176/appi.ps.201400444

Finno-Velasquez, M., Fettes, D. L., Aarons, G. A., & Hurlburt, M. S. (2014). Cultural adaptation of an evidence-based home visitation programme: Latino clients' experiences of service delivery during implementation. *Journal of Children's Services, 9*(4), 280–294.

Fong, R., Dettlaff, A., James, J., & Rodriguez, C. (2015). *Addressing Racial Disproportionality and Disparities in Human Services: Multisystemic Approaches*. New York: Columbia University Press.

Frum, J. L. (2007). Postsecondary educational access for undocumented students: Opportunities and constraints. *American Academic, 3*(1), 81–108.

Gámez, R., Lopez, W., & Overton, B. (2017). Mentors, resiliency, and *ganas*: Factors influencing the success of DACAmented, undocumented, and immigrant students in higher education. *Journal of Hispanic Higher Education, 16*(2), 144–161.

Garcia, A., Aisenberg, E., & Harachi, T. (2012). Pathways to service inequalities among Latinos in the child welfare system. *Children and Youth Services Review, 34*(5), 1060–1071.

Ham, S., Yang, K., & Cha, Y. (2017). Immigrant integration policy for future generations? A cross-national multilevel analysis of immigrant-background adolescents' sense of belonging at school. *International Journal of Intercultural Relations, 60*, 40–50. doi: 10.1016/j.ijintrel.2017.06.001

Harding, K., Galano, J., Martin, J., Huntington, L., & Schellenbach, C. J. (2007). Healthy Families America effectiveness: A comprehensive review of outcomes. *Journal of Prevention and Intervention in the Community, 34*(1/2), 149–179.

Heneghan, A., Stein, R. E. K., Hurlburt, M. S., Zhang, J., Rolls-Reutz, J., Fisher, E. ... McCue Horwitz, S. (2013). Mental health problems in teens investigated by U.S. child welfare agencies. *Journal of Adolescent Health, 52*, 634–640.

Hohman, M. (2012). *Motivational Interviewing in Social Work Practice.* New York: Guilford Press.

Hood, K. K., & Eyberg, S. M. (2003). Outcomes of parent-child interaction therapy: Mothers' reports on maintenance three to six years after treatment. *Journal of Clinical Child and Adolescent Psychology, 32*, 419–429.

Jang, S. H. (2016). First-generation Korean immigrants' barriers to healthcare and their coping strategies in the US. *Social Science & Medicine, 168*, 93–100. doi: 10.1016/j.socscimed.2016.09.007

Johnson-Motoyama, M., Dettlaff, A. J., & Finno, M. (2012). Parental nativity and the decision to substantiate: Findings from a study of Latino children in the second National Survey of Child and Adolescent Well-being (NSCAW II). *Children and Youth Services Review, 34*, 2229–2239.

Kandel, W. A. (2017). Unaccompanied alien children: An overview. *Congressional Research Service, January, 18.* http://www.nnirr.org/drupal/sites/default/files/uac_overview_january_2017_r43599.pdf

Kataoka, S. H., Stein, B. D., Jaycox, L. H., Wong, M., Escudero, P., Tu, W., ... Fink, A. (2003). A school-based mental health program for traumatized Latino immigrant children. *Journal of the American Academy of Child & Adolescent Psychiatry, 42*(3), 311–318.

KIDS COUNT Data Center. (2016). *Children in immigrant families* [data set]. http://datacenter.kidscount.org/data/tables/115-children-in-immigrant-families#detailed/1/any/false/573,869,36,868,867/any/445,446

Lacayo, A. E. (2011). *One year later: A look at SB 1070 and copycat legislation.* Washington, DC: National Council of LaRaza

LeBrun, A., Hassan, G., Boivin, M., Fraser, S. L., Dufour, S., & Lavergne, C. (2015). Review of child maltreatment in immigrant and refugee families. *Canadian Journal of Public Health, 106*(7), eS45–eS56.

Leung, C., Tsang, S., Sin, T. C., & Choi, S. Y. (2015). The efficacy of Parent-Child Interaction Therapy with Chinese families randomized controlled trial. *Research on Social Work Practice, 25*(1), 117–128.

Maiter, S., Stalker, C. A., & Alaggia, R. (2009). The experiences of minority immigrant families receiving child welfare services: Seeking to understand how to reduce risk and increase protective factors. *Families in Society, 90*, 283–286.

McCabe, K. M., Yeh, M., Garland, A. F., Lau, A. S., & Chavez, G. (2005). The GANA program: A tailoring approach to adapting parent-child interaction therapy for Mexican Americans. *Education and Treatment of Children*, 111–129.

Merkel-Holguin, L. (Ed.) (2003). Promising results, potential new directions: International FGDM research and evaluation in child welfare, special issue of *Protecting Children, 18*(1–2).

Montana, S., Rondero Hernandez, V., Siegel, D., & Jackson, M. (2010). *Cultural brokers research project: An approach to community engagement with African American families in child welfare*. Report. California Social Work Education Center (CALSWEC). Berkeley: University of California.

Morrison, A. D., & Thronson, D. B. (2010). Beyond status: Seeing the whole child. *Evaluation and program planning, 33*(3), 281–287.

Morton, J. (2011). Exercising prosecutorial discretion consistent with the civil immigration priorities of the agency for the apprehension, detention, and removal of aliens [Memorandum]. *U.S. Immigration and Customs Enforcement*. http://www.ice.gov/doclib/secure-communities/pdf/prosecutorial-discretion-memo.pdf

Mullins, S. M., Suarez, M., Ondersma, S. J., & Page, M. C. (2004). The impact of motivational interviewing on substance abuse treatment retention: A randomized control trial of women involved with child welfare. *Journal of Substance Abuse Treatment, 27*, 51–58.

National Immigration Law Center. (2014). SB 1070 Four Years Later. https://www.nilc.org/issues/immigration-enforcement/sb-1070-lessons-learned/

Ortega, R., & Faller, K. (2011). Training child welfare workers from an intersectional cultural humility perspective: A paradigm shift. *Child Welfare, 90*(5), 27–49.

Pennell, J., & Burford, G. (2000). Family Group Decision Making: Protecting children and women. *Child Welfare, 79*(2), 131–158.

Rhee, S., Chang, J., Weaver, D., & Wong, D. (2008). Child maltreatment among immigrant Chinese families: Characteristics and patterns of placement. *Child Maltreatment, 13*, 269–279.

Rivaux, S. L., James, J., Wittenstrom, K., Baumann, D., Sheets, J., Henry, J., & Jeffries, V. (2008). The intersection of race, poverty, and risk: Understanding the decision to provide services to clients and to remove children. *Child Welfare, 87*, 151–168.

Rogerson, S. (2012). Unintended and unavoidable: The failure to protect rule and its consequences for undocumented parents and their children. *Family Court Review, 50*(4), 580–593.

Sandy, J. M., Anisfeld, E., & Ramirez, E. (2009). Effects of a prenatal intervention on breastfeeding initiation rates in a Latina immigrant sample. *Journal of Human Lactation, 25*(4), 404–411.

Schnepf, S. V. (2007). Immigrants' educational disadvantage: An examination across ten countries and three surveys. *Journal of Population Economics, 20*(3), 527–545.

Self-Brown, S., McFry, E., Montesanti, A., Edwards-Guara, A., Lutzker, J., Shanley, J., & Whitaker, D. (2014). SafeCare: A prevention and intervention program for child neglect and physical abuse. In R. Reece, R. Hanson, & J. Sargent (Eds), *Treatment of Child Abuse: Common Ground for Mental Health, Medical and Legal Practitioners* (2nd ed.). Baltimore: Johns Hopkins University Press.

Siskin, A. (2016). Noncitizen Eligibility for Federal Public Assistance: Policy Overview. *Congressional Research Service*. https://fas.org/sgp/crs/misc/RL33809.pdf

Slayter, E., & Križ, K. (2015). Fear factors and their effects on child protection practice with undocumented immigrant families—"A lot of my families are scared and won't reach out." *Journal of Public Child Welfare, 9*(3), 299–321. doi: 10.1080/15548732.2015.1044765

Trevizo, P. (2016, February 3). Arivaca residents monitoring Border Patrol checkpoint on AZ 286. *Arizona Daily Star*. http://tucson.com/news/arivacaresidentsmonitoring-border-patrol-checkpoint-on-az/article_e3a9e9e1-0706-5c59-bdf7-fae183140a29.html

U.S. Customs and Border Protection. (2016, October 18). *United States Border Patrol Southwest Family Unit Subject and Unaccompanied Alien Children Apprehensions Fiscal Year 2016.* https://www.cbp.gov/newsroom/stats/southwest-border-unaccompanied-children/fy-2016

U.S. Department of Homeland Security. (2017). Delegation of Immigration Section 287(g) Immigration and Nationality Act. https://www.ice.gov/factsheets/287g-reform

U.S. Immigration and Customs Enforcement. (2012). Secure communities. https://www.ice.gov/secure-communities

Vericker, T., Kuehn, D., & Capps, R. (2007a). *Foster care placement settings and permanency planning: Patterns by child generation and ethnicity.* http://www.urban.org/publications/311459.html

Vericker, T., Kuehn, D., & Capps, R. (2007b). *Title IV-E funding: Funded foster care placements by child generation and ethnicity.* https://www.urban.org/research/publication/title-iv-e-funding-funded-foster-care-placements-child-generation-and-ethnicity

Wang, C. (2012). What's Next for Arizona's SB 1070 and Other Copycat Laws. *American Civil Liberties Union "Speak Freely" Blog.* https://www.aclu.org/blog/whats-next-arizonas-sb-1070-and-other-copycat-laws

Wang, W. E., Lambert, M. C., Johnson, L. E., Boudreau, B., Breidenbach, R., & Baumann, D. (2012). Expediting permanent placement from foster care systems: The role of Family Group Decision-Making. *Children and Youth Services Review, 34,* 845–850.

The White House, Office of the Press Secretary. (2014). A Letter from the President to the Speaker of the House of Representatives, Majority Leader of the Senate, Republican Leader of the Senate and the Democratic Leader of the House of Representatives. www.aila.org/File/DownloadEmbeddedFile/58154

Ziol-Guest, K. M., & Kalil, A. (2012). Health and medical care among the children of immigrants. *Child Development, 83*(5), 1494–1500. doi: 10.1111/j.1467-8624.2012.01795.x

Figure Credits

CHAPTER • 9

Victims of Human Trafficking and Child Welfare

Joan Blakey, Rowena Fong, and Georgina Petronella

Overview of Chapter and Population

This chapter will provide an overview of children who are sex trafficked. It will discuss the prevalence of child sex trafficking among vulnerable populations such as youth involved with the child welfare system and identify the ways in which vulnerable children are identified and groomed by traffickers. The chapter will identify practice challenges associated with this population. Additionally, it will explore evidence-based practices for working with youth who have histories of sex trafficking and what a systems approach would look like. Moreover, the chapter will examine policies related to this population and end by discussing a case vignette that highlights the complexities associated with child sex trafficking cases among child welfare–involved populations. As the numbers continue to grow, particularly among child welfare–involved populations, it is crucial that there is more understanding about the challenges facing this population and more learning about promising practices and services needed to address the myriad challenges that trafficked children involved with the child welfare system experience.

Definitions

Commercial sexual exploitation, sex trafficking, and forced prostitution are often used interchangeably to describe circumstances under which individuals are forced, tricked, or coerced to engage in prostitution, exotic dancing, and pornography, usually for money (Albanese, 2007). Prostitution, or survival sex (i.e., using sex in exchange for shelter, food, or other basic needs), is distinguished from sex trafficking in that prostitution or survival sex are considered voluntary or describe someone who engages in this behavior of their own volition. Whereas sex trafficking "is induced by force, fraud, or coercion, or in which a person induced to perform sexual acts has not attained 18 years of age" (U.S. Department of State, 2008, p. 6). A primary factor that distinguishes prostitution from sex trafficking is "consent." Children and youth under 18 years of age cannot legally consent to engage in prostitution because they often are believed to be emotionally and physically immature (Albanese, 2007). Since consent requires a person to have an adult level of understanding, children under the age of 18 are believed to lack the ability to understand the full scope of decisions. Therefore, most forms of sex (e.g., prostitution, exotic dancing/stripping, pornography) involving children under 18 are considered illegal (Annitto, 2011).

Equating prostitution and other types of sex work with sex trafficking can cause several problems. Blurring the two diverts attention away from structural conditions that make prostitution and other sex work a necessity. It also leads to a lack of clarity over who trafficking victims are, thereby leading organizations, agencies, and groups to become unsure about what to "fund" or who to "rescue" (Brennan, 2008).

Commercial sexual exploitation and child sexual abuse can also be associated with prostitution and sex work with sex trafficking. While these are problematic concerns in child welfare, this chapter will focus primarily on sex trafficking. More information on sexual abuse can be found in Chapter 4.

Prevalence

There has been increased attention and concern internationally and nationally regarding sex trafficking among children and youth, particularly among those who are involved in state child welfare systems (Bounds, Julion, & Delaney, 2015; Fong & Berger Cardoso, 2010; United States Department of Health and Human Services, 2009). Globally, sex trafficking is becoming the most popular and lucrative form of organized crime, garnering from $7–10 billion dollars worldwide annually (Brinlee, 2018; McClain & Garrity, 2011; Schauer & Wheaton, 2006). Sex trafficking is more profitable, easier to conceal, and has lower prison sentences, if convicted, than drug trafficking (Schauer & Wheaton, 2006). It is believed that within 10 years, sex trafficking will replace drug trafficking as the number one international crime (Brinlee, 2018; Schauer & Wheaton, 2006). The United Nations found that 28% of the more than 17,000 sex trafficking victims were minors from 106 countries (Greenbaum, 2017; United Nations, 2016). Due to the high prevalence of sex trafficking globally, the United States Department of State created a tier system in which countries are ranked from one to three based on the size of the country's sex trafficking problem and the country's efforts toward complying with the Victim of Trafficking and Violence Protection Act (TVPA) of 2000 (United States Department of State-USDS, 2018).

Tier 1 is the most desirable tier in that these countries fully comply with minimum standards of TVPA, which seek to eliminate trafficking (USDS, 2018). In order to be in Tier 1, countries must show that they are making progress annually to combat trafficking. The United States and 38 other nations are in Tier 1. Eighty-one countries are considered Tier 2. These countries are making significant efforts to comply with the minimum standards of TVPA but are not quite there. Additionally, 43 countries also are Tier 2, but are on probation and in danger of losing Tier 2 status. These countries are different from Tier 2 countries because there is a significant rise in the number of victims, and the country must provide evidence that they have increased efforts to combat sex trafficking in the next year (USDS, 2018). Twenty-three countries are in Tier 3 because they are not making any effort to comply with the minimum standards of TVPA (USDS, 2018).

While the actual prevalence of sex trafficking is unknown, between 2004 and 2013, the number of suspects referred to U.S. law enforcement for commercial sexual exploitation of children (CSEC) increased by 54%, from 2,972 to 4,579 suspects (Adams & Flynn, 2017). In an attempt to convey the gravity of the situation, studies report that "more US citizens than foreign nationals are victims of sex trafficking" (Hughes, 2007, para. 4). Studies estimate that 100,000 to 2 million American youth are at risk of being or are sexually exploited each year (Estes & Weiner, 2002; Hughes, 2007; Laczko & Gramegna, 2003; National Coalition to Prevent Child Sexual Abuse and Exploitation, 2012; Schauer & Wheaton, 2006; Smith, 2008). **Studies report that 33% of human trafficking investigations in the United States involve minors** (Banks & Kyckelhahn, 2011; Kyckelhahn, Beck, & Cohen, 2009). Hughes (2007) estimates that 70% or more of women who engage in prostitution were trafficked as children.

While it is known that the numbers of sexually trafficked children are growing, the actual number of domestic children who are sexually exploited is unknown (Stransky & Finkelhor, 2008). There are several reasons why it is difficult to determine the actual number of individuals regardless of age that are sexually exploited. The first reason is that there are no uniform definitions of what is considered sex trafficking or sexual exploitation. Until recently, sex exploitation among juveniles was viewed as prostitution and not a form of sexual victimization (Mitchell, Finkelhor, & Wolak, 2010). The second reason is the hidden nature of the crime. Until youth or adults come to the attention of the criminal justice or some other system, they often remain unknown (Countryman-Roswurm & Bolin, 2014). The third reason is that those who come to the attention of a system such as child protection often are incorrectly identified as homeless or runaway youth rather than as victims of sexual exploitation (Countryman-Roswurm, 2006).

A fourth reason why it is difficult to determine actual numbers is because commercially exploited young people are moved frequently, taken to different states, and sold or traded frequently to other traffickers (Countryman-Roswurm & Bolin, 2014). These are strategies traffickers use to keep sex-trafficked minors disoriented and completely dependent upon them. A fifth reason that has increased the difficulty of identifying victims is glamorization of pimp culture that dominates social media, music, videos, movies, and television (Bounds et al., 2015). Kotrla (2010) identifies this as a culture of tolerance, which condones and celebrates pimp culture. Being constantly bombarded with these messages desensitizes youth such that they do not see certain kinds of treatment as being exploitative. A sixth reason is that sexually exploited youth have to feel safe enough to reveal to adults that they are being trafficked. Fear, violence, and intimidation are frequently used tactics that make individuals afraid to disclose abuse and sexual victimization (Countryman-Roswurm & Bolin, 2014). The FBI considers sex trafficking of minors the "most overlooked and under-investigated form of child sexual abuse" facing American society today (Annitto, 2011, p. 6).

Disproportionality and Disparities Related to the Population

Disparity is typically used to describe unequal outcomes experienced by one racial or ethnic group when compared to another racial or ethnic group. However, unequal outcomes and risk factors are major concerns for women and girls, who are trafficked regardless of race and ethnicity.

While all children are susceptible to being sexually exploited or trafficked, girls are most at risk of being sex trafficked (Bounds et al., 2015). Studies report that girls from 10 to 17 years old are among the most vulnerable children to be sex trafficked (Bounds et al., 2015; Kotrla & Wommack, 2011). These studies found that 8% to 30% of the youth who are trafficked are 10 to 13 years old and 30% to 92% of them are 14 to 17 years old. However, children as young as 5 were trafficked, as there is high demand for virgins (Bounds et al., 2015; Reid, 2010; Smith, 2008; USDOJ, 2007). Boys make up about 2% of sexually trafficked children within the United States. Youth who have mental health diagnoses, lower intelligence quotients, cognitive or physical disabilities, and histories of involvement with the criminal justice system also are more likely to be sexually exploited (Brawn & Roe-Sepowitz, 2008).

Certain circumstances make youth vulnerable to being domestically sex trafficked. Living near international borders and large cities with thriving adult prostitution markets or cities that have a lot of transient men also increases the likelihood that youth will experience commercial sexual exploitation (Ugarte, Zarate, & Farley, 2004). Research shows that there are places where the majority of sex-trafficked victims come from (i.e., recruitment countries/cities), places where the majority of victims are taken (i.e., destination countries/cities), and places where victims are both recruited and taken to work (i.e., bidirectional countries/cities) (Williamson & Prior, 2009). Sex trafficking occurs in every city, state, and country (Countryman-Roswurm & Bolin, 2014). Nonetheless, there are cities where sex-trafficked victims are heavily recruited. Smaller cities, particularly those in the Midwest (i.e., Toledo), have been identified as recruitment areas (Davis, 2006; Williamson & Prior, 2009). Larger cities tend to be destination or bidirectional cities (Wilson & Dalton, 2008). Estes and Weiner (2002) found that 17 cities throughout the United States are known to have a high prevalence of domestic minor sex trafficking. Among these cities are Chicago (bidirectional), Dallas-Fort Worth, Detroit (bidirectional), El Paso, Honolulu, Las Vegas (bidirectional), Los Angeles, Miami, New York, New Orleans, Oakland, Philadelphia, San Antonio, San Diego, San Jose, San Francisco, and Seattle (Fong & Cardoso, 2010; Williamson & Prior, 2009).

Youth who are homeless or runaway are most at risk of being sex trafficked (Fong & Cardoso, 2010; Kotrla, 2010; Logan, Walker, & Hunt, 2009; Mitchell et al., 2010; Reid, 2010; Schauer & Wheaton, 2006). There are a disproportionate number of homeless youth (20%

to 40%) who identify as lesbian, gay, bisexual, or transgender (Ray, 2006). For many of these youth, the coming-out process can cause them to run away or be homeless (Walsh & Donaldson, 2010). For example, 40% to 75% of runaways and homeless youth have been sex trafficked by a pimp/trafficker (United States Department of Justice [USDOJ], 2007). Most domestic minor sex-trafficked victims ran away at least one time prior to being trafficked (Williamson & Prior, 2009). Many of these youth were running away from situations that were intolerable (i.e., excessive responsibility and being overwhelmed with family problems). Agencies who track runaways reported that 33% of youth who run away from home or have unstable living situations will be trafficked within 48 hours of being homeless or living on the street (National Runaway Switchboard, 2005). While youth who run away or lack supportive relationships are more vulnerable to being trafficked, studies have found that sex trafficking can happen to any child (Fong & Cardoso, 2010). Countryman-Roswurm and Bolin (2014) found that among youth who were sex trafficked, 57% lived with a biological parent; 52% indicated that they could count on their parent; and 57% reported having a good support system.

Recent studies have found that being in out of home care also makes youth vulnerable to being sex trafficked (Countryman-Roswurm, 2012; Kotrla, 2010). Sometimes youth are recruited while in placement. They are recruited by other residents, women who assume a "mothering" role, or men who can sense their vulnerability. Many of these youth feel unsettled physically and emotionally. Their desire for love makes them susceptible to traffickers (Williamson & Prior, 2009). Other times, the fact that youth do not have a stable home, have to constantly adjust to different parental figures, and have very little input into where they are placed puts minors in foster care at increased risk of being sex trafficked (Coy, 2009; McLeod, 2007). According to Coy (2009), almost 15% of youth had over 35 placements over 4 to 7 years in care. These destabilizing circumstances cause youth to run away from placements and limit their ability to develop trusting relationships, which increases the likelihood that they will be trafficked (Williamson & Prior, 2009).

Studies report that poverty, domestic violence, substance abuse, and households involved with criminal activity such as the drug trade also are associated with increased risk of being sexually exploited (Herman, 2003; Reid, 2010; Tyler & Johnson, 2004). Countryman-Roswurm and Bolin (2014) indicated that physical abuse by a caregiver (61% of youth), domestic violence (83% of youth), and use of drugs and alcohol by youth (70%–74% of youth) were risk factors associated with domestic minor sex trafficking. According to Countryman-Roswurm and Bolin (2014), teen relationship violence is a notable risk factor for being sexually trafficked because the risk factors are similar and closely associated with signs of someone being groomed for trafficking.

The early effects of abuse and neglect and intimate partner violence laid the groundwork for youth to be groomed for sex trafficking because it often is a continuation of violence and victimization the youth are used to, as well as normalizes and desensitizes youth to violence. Moreover, sexual abuse reinforces that individuals' bodies are not their own and that their bodies are there for someone else's pleasure (Dworkin, 1997). Therefore, when youth experience violence often associated with trafficking, they may not recognize that anything is wrong.

Trauma-Informed Care

In order to address the complex needs of sexually trafficked children, a trauma-informed approach is necessary. Trauma-informed care recognizes the symptoms of trauma in a client and looks for ways to reduce symptoms, acknowledges the impact of past trauma on an individual's life and coping skills, maximizes youths' sense of safety, helps youth find meaning in their trauma histories, and incorporates this understanding into practices to both empower and avoid retraumatizing the individual (Ko et al., 2008).

For youth who have been victims of sexual trafficking, a trauma-informed approach means first and foremost that these youth should be considered and treated as victims who need care and protection, not prosecution (Williamson & Prior, 2009). If a sexually trafficked minor is treated as a criminal and placed in a juvenile justice facility, the system of care at the facility may exacerbate trauma symptomatology. Procedures that include the loss of privacy or the use of seclusion and restraints may be a trigger or reenactment of previous sexual trauma.

In addition, mental health professionals who come into contact with youth they suspect are being trafficked should create an environment in which youth feel safe disclosing (Ko et al., 2008; McClain & Garrity, 2011). If youth indicate that they are ready to talk to someone, it is important to make that happen as quickly as possible. The longer youth have to wait, the more likely they are to change their minds. If professionals are lucky enough to see youth multiple times, they may have a better chance of getting the youth to talk about the situation.

Practice Challenges Working with Victims of Human Trafficking

There are myriad challenges when working with youth who have histories of sex trafficking. These challenges include: 1) relational challenges; 2) preexisting and extensive histories of trauma; 3) physical and mental health challenges; and 4) limited services equipped to meet their unique constellation of needs.

Relational Challenges

Many youth have been introduced to sex trafficking by relatives, friends, or men who gained their trust as boyfriends and gradually began exploiting them (ECPAT, 2012).

Consequently, youth may have difficulty trusting professionals based on past betrayal and violations of trust.

Preexisting and Extensive Histories of Trauma

Youth who have a history of sex trafficking often have histories of child maltreatment, including physical and sexual abuse as well as other types of trauma, such as rape, physical assault, or witnessing violence (Fong & Berger Cardoso, 2010; Kotrla, 2010). The use of violence is a common scare tactic used by pimps and traffickers to intimidate and discourage youth from fighting back. Trafficking experiences often retraumatize and compound preexisting histories of trauma.

Many sex trafficking survivors experience physical and mental health challenges. Physically, they have sustained injuries from being beaten by pimps and/or johns (Gajic-Veljanoski & Stewart, 2007; Hodge, 2008). They often do not have a say in terms of their sexual health, so they are commonly exposed to sexually transmitted and other infectious diseases (McClain & Garrity, 2011). They also may suffer from malnutrition as a result of an unhealthy diet or simply not eating because of ongoing substance use (McClain & Garrity, 2011). Raymond and Hughes (2001) found that sex-trafficked individuals have high rates of health problems and infections.

Mentally, many youth have preexisting histories of depression and anxiety, which are exacerbated by the mental injuries they sustain from being trafficked. Consequently, many youth who have histories of sex trafficking also end up developing severe and debilitating **post-traumatic stress disorder (PTSD)**, suicidal ideation, and panic attacks (Flowers, 2001; Fong & Berger Cardoso, 2010; McClain & Garrity, 2011; Raymond & Hughes, 2001).

Substance abuse is common among sex trafficking survivors as it often is used by sex traffickers as a method to maintain control over their victims (McClain & Garrity, 2011). Moreover, ongoing substance use often is a way to cope with their experiences of victimization and abuse (Clawson, Dutch, Solomon, & Goldblatt Grace, 2009a; Raymond & Hughes, 2001).

Limited Services Equipped to Meet the Unique Constellation of Needs

Finally, there is limited knowledge regarding effective treatments for sex trafficking survivors. The lack of effective treatments makes it difficult for individuals to leave this past behind, which increases the likelihood that they will go back to traffickers (Fong & Berger Cardoso, 2010; Reid, 2010). In order to successfully create a new life, youth who have histories of sex trafficking require holistic services, including housing, counseling, and mental and physical health, as well as educational opportunities and job preparedness (Clawson & Goldblatt Grace, 2007; Fong & Berger Cardoso, 2010; Kotrla, 2010). Nonetheless, there is a dearth of social service and mental health service providers that are able to meet the complex needs of sex-trafficked individuals who may have experienced torture, rape, assault, abuse, and other kinds of humiliating and stigmatizing experiences (Fong & Berger Cardoso, 2010).

Sex Trafficking Process

Becoming a victim of sex trafficking is a process. There are five basic stages in this process. Brayley, Cockbain, and Laycock (2011) created a visual diagram of the process.

Stage One: Identifying and Targeting a Victim

Traffickers identify victims who have some vulnerability, such as needing a place to live or money, low self-esteem, and cognitive disabilities. Traffickers will drive around or frequent places where children hang out, like movie theaters, malls, or arcades (Boxill & Richardson, 2007; Brayley, Cockbain, & Laycock, 2011). They tend to target youth who are alone, have run away, look hungry, lost, or without money (Albanese, 2007). They also identify youth online through websites or social media sites such as Facebook® and Instagram®. Through these websites, adolescents can be tricked into sharing personal information or pictures, which increases the liklihood of them becoming sexually trafficked victims (Kotrla, 2010). Some youth are kidnapped and lured from public places, but many youth go with traffickers willingly because of trickery or enticement (Schauer & Wheaton, 2006). Once a victim is identified, the information gained in stage two often determines what grooming tactic the trafficker uses. The trafficker often studies the victim to determine the best approach.

Stage Two: Gaining Trust and Gathering Information

Traffickers often befriend the individual with the sole purpose of gathering information and gaining trust. They may ask an individual what they want to be when they grow up. If a youth says they want to be a model, the trafficker may create a modeling scam to entice the victim. For some youth, they gather information about the individual's home life or parents. They begin to plant seeds that they would be better off leaving home and staying with the trafficker. For example, if a young woman has a low self-esteem, the trafficker may assume the role of the potential victim's boyfriend, uncle, or father figure. They complement, flirt with, treat them as a grown-up (i.e., offering them an alcoholic drink), or profess their love to the individual, which makes the person feel special (Brayley et al., 2011). Each ruse is individualized and tailored for the victim they are trying to coerce, manipulate, or trick.

Stage Three: The Grooming Process Begins

Grooming, "softening," or "seasoning" is a process whereby traffickers take complete physical, mental, and emotional control over individuals in order to manipulate, force, or coerce youth to do what they want them to do (Schauer & Wheaton, 2006). During the grooming process, traffickers begin to normalize sexual activity. They may make sexually explicit jokes, expose the youth to pornography, ask about the youth's sexual experiences and sexual preferences, and repeatedly talk about sex. If the trafficker poses as the youth's boyfriend, they may sleep with them and begin teaching them tricks or techniques. They begin to manipulate the individual, suggesting that if they really loved them, they would do things to repay their love. Over time, they cajole, coerce, manipulate, and as a last resort, force individuals into sex trafficking (Tyler & Johnson, 2004).

There are two most common forms of grooming: "finesse pimping" or "guerrilla pimping" (Williamson & Prior, 2009). ***Finesse pimping*** tends to be a kinder and gentler form of grooming (McClain & Garrity, 2011). The trafficker manipulates individuals by showing kindness, generosity, love, and affection (Williamson & Prior, 2009). Traffickers become the individual's romantic partner. Studies found that 28% of individuals who were trafficked reported being trafficked by someone they were romantically involved with prior to being trafficked (Bounds et al., 2015; Raymond & Hughes, 2001). Consequently, individuals feel compelled to repay traffickers' kindness.

The most common tactic used by "finesse" pimps is filling a need. If the individual needs love and reassurance, the trafficker will be very loving toward their victims. If the youth needs money or a place to live, they provide them with these things. They shower the youth with gifts, praise, and compliments, all of which are intended to gain their victim's loyalty and trust. They often begin to convince the youth that they are the only one who can fill the need. During this stage, the trafficker convinces the individual that they love them. They often do not try to touch or harm them in any way. Another tactic within finesse pimping is promising someone a gift or opportunity that fulfills their wishes and desires. The opportunities are known as bait-and-switch and often are too good to be true (Williamson & Prior, 2009). Finesse pimping is intended to gain someone's trust or create a situation where the individual feels cared for or indebted to the trafficker.

The other most common type of grooming is known as ***guerrilla pimping***, which involves violence, fear, intimidation, threats to loved ones, and drugs or substance abuse (Williamson & Prior, 2009). Youth often are subjected to horrific abuse that compels them to comply with all demands. Individuals who are groomed guerrilla style describe being gang raped, severely beaten, confined/imprisoned, tortured, and watching someone else be beaten or killed. (Richard, 2000). They may sodomize the youth or prepare them for other degrading experiences such as a customer urinating on them. The trafficker does anything they can to break the individual so that they are obedient and realize that fighting back is futile. Guerrilla pimping utilizes violent measures to gain and maintain control (McClain & Garrity, 2011). Sometimes these tactics are used on individuals in order to set an example to others as to what could happen if they do not obey.

Stage Four: Isolation

Over time, they begin to isolate the individual from their parents, family, or anyone who cares about them. Part of the reason that traffickers target runaways and homeless youth is because they are less likely to have people in their lives who are looking for them. Traffickers tell individuals that their parents, friends, and family do not care about them. This is much easier when youth have troubled relationships with their family. They become the central figure in the youth's life by monopolizing all of their time. If individuals are in school, they often convince them that school is a waste of time. Individuals who are trafficked often are moved constantly, never remaining in one place more than a few weeks. This prevents them from making attachments or establishing friendships. The goal is to keep them disoriented, unfamiliar with their surroundings, and fearful to contact the police or escape (Schauer & Wheaton, 2006). The goal of this stage is to isolate individuals from anyone who cares about them and could potentially disrupt the relationship between the trafficker and individual. The trafficker taints every relationship the youth has so that they become completely dependent upon them for everything.

Stage Five: Maintain Control

Once control is established, the trafficker will do anything that will allow them to maintain control. Traffickers have been known to threaten to harm family members or children, destroy passports or immigration documents, take driver's licenses or bank cards, lock them in a room or chain them to the bed or toilet, and perpetrate physical assault, rape, and other demeaning acts to maintain control over victims (Richard, 2000; Williamson & Prior, 2009). Violence used to maintain control is often severe (Fong & Berger Cardoso, 2010).

Impact of Being Trafficked

Unsurprisingly, the consequences of such brutal treatment can be severe. Children who have histories of sex trafficking often report adverse mental and physical health effects, some of which are outlined below.

Mental Health

Researchers have identified a number of mental health issues among sexually exploited youth, including depression, anxiety, anger problems, attachment issues, self-harming behavior, inability to trust, suicide attempts, shame, guilt, low self-esteem, and a sense of hopelessness (WestCoast Children's Clinic, 2012; Clawson & Goldblatt Grace, 2007; Flowers, 2001; Clarke, Clarke, Roe-Sepowitz, & Fey, 2012).

Substance Use

Drug use is common among this population. For example, in a study with sexually exploited youth in New York, more than 50% of the sample reported regular marijuana use as well as the use of cocaine and alcohol (Curtis, Terry, Dank, Dombrowski, & Khan, 2008).

Reproductive and Physical Health

High rates of unsafe sex make sexually exploited youth particularly vulnerable to sexually transmitted diseases and pregnancy (Willis & Levy, 2002). As well, these youth have higher rates of malnutrition, general infections, and untreated chronic medical conditions such as asthma and diabetes (Greenbaum, 2014).

Reluctance to Disclose

When youth are being trafficked, there are many reasons why they may be reluctant to disclose the abuse. They fear getting their trafficker or pimp in trouble. They fear they will be placed in foster care or made to participate in services against their will. They also fear the unknown and what could happen if adults know what is happening to them.

Professionals must understand that no matter what they do, some youth may not disclose that they are being trafficked. Nonetheless, there are many signs that youth are being trafficked, even if the youth fail to disclose it. These signs include:

- Bruising, cuts, and injuries that youth are unable to explain
- Inappropriately dressed
- Overly sexualized behavior
- Excessive tiredness or falling asleep anytime they are sitting still
- Withdrawn, depressed, anxious, checked out, distant
- Access to things that are difficult for a youth to afford
- Has a lot of money or new expensive items but does not have a job
- New tattoos or markings (used by traffickers to mark their property)
- Dating older men, older boyfriend with a huge disparity in age, or whole new friend group that tends to be older than they
- Appears emaciated or sickly
- Has no personal belongings or identification
- Poor school performance
- Details seem scripted, rehearsed, or inconsistent history
- Unwilling or resistant to answering questions about injuries or disappearances
- Accompanied by an adult who does not let them answer or speak for themselves
- Unrealistic or excessive concerns about pleasing a boyfriend or family member
- Unable to provide details about where they are staying and with whom they are staying
- Homelessness
- Chronic running away
- Visible or invisible signs of violence, such as being jumpy, fidgety, or exhibiting nervousness or fear
- Repeated sexually transmitted diseases or pregnancy
- History of abortions
- Early involvement with the criminal justice system, such as curfew violations, truancy, or other types of criminal behavior
- Substance use
- Travel with an older male who is not their legal guardian

Image 9.1

- Frequently missing school or change in grades (McClain and Garrity, 2011; Torres-Carlson, 2018)

There are many warning signs that youth may be in a situation where they are trafficked.

It is possible that youth are not being trafficked and are still experiencing these things. Professionals need to look at the totality of responses, including safety needs, the reason(s) that youth may be seeking help, and their professional intuition to determine if someone is a sex-trafficked victim (Vera Institute of Justice, 2014). These are possible signs that youth are being trafficked. These signs should be an indication to professionals to dig deeper or look out for other signs that might provide confirmation.

Questioning individuals that professionals may suspect are being trafficked should be integrated into the intake process. Professionals should familiarize themselves with possible signs and find ways to word questions in ways that make individuals feel at ease. The Vera Institute of Justice (2014) has created a Trafficking Victim Identification Tool (TVIT) tip sheet for conducting interviews as well as a trafficking victim identification tool. There is a long and short version that can help professionals identify sex-trafficked victims, which can be found at: https://www.vera.org/downloads/publications/human-trafficking-identification-tool-and-user-guidelines.pdf

The TVIT is reliable and will help in the identification of victims of sex and labor trafficking. It is important to remember that negative responses to the questions does not mean that individuals are not being trafficked. It just means that more trust and rapport may be needed before individuals feel safe disclosing. The screening tool should be used to guide the interaction with potential victims (Vera Institute, 2014).

Criminal Justice System's Response to Children Arrested for Prostitution

The most common criminal justice response to domestic sex-trafficked minors is to arrest, incarcerate, detain, and prosecute minors who are prostituting (Annitto, 2011; Fong & Berger Cardoso, 2010; Urbina, 2009; Williamson & Prior, 2009). Arresting domestic sex-trafficked minors is a common response for several reasons. The first reason is a lack of awareness among the local and state police departments (Schauer & Wheaton, 2006). Klueber (2003) reported that 83 of the largest police departments throughout the United States were unaware that trafficking even existed. The second reason is that there is no consensus regarding how to deal with youth who are caught prostituting.

Some jurisdictions view youth involved with prostitution as victims of child abuse and believe these youth need protection. In these instances, cases are handed off to child welfare agencies that work with the youth to get them the necessary services. Other jurisdictions see sex-trafficked youth as delinquents (Kotrla, 2010; Williamson & Prior, 2009). It is believed that if the law does not intervene by incarcerating and processing them through the criminal justice system, they could escalate to more serious offenses.

Professionals working in the criminal justice system are not the only ones confused. Helping professionals also may have difficulty determining if a youth is being sex trafficked, particularly if the youth possesses adult capacities or acts or dresses in seductive ways. Helping professionals also may incorrectly believe that the youth are acting of their own volition if a way out is being offered and the youth is unsure or unwilling to take it. It is difficult for many helping professionals to understand why youth would rather go back to their traffickers than go to a shelter. Professionals must understand that they have been indoctrinated and brainwashed by their trafficker. The psychological abuse sex-trafficked youth endure often has them so afraid that they will go back to the trafficker (Brennan, 2008).

Another reason that the criminal justice system is uncertain about how to handle sex-trafficked victims is because these individuals often do not fit squarely in the victim or offender categories. They are both victims *and* offenders. For example, the bottom women often started as victims. They were trafficked. They were and are still subjected to abuse and intimidation. Since the bottoms often have been with the trafficker the longest, they have figured out how to survive. If they recruit others, then they are no longer the sole target of the trafficker's abuse. The more they help the trafficker, the less abuse they tend to experience. Through this process, the bottoms become offenders because they are doing to others what was done to them. What is the alternative? If they do not comply, then they could be hurt or killed. Another example are minors who started off as sex-trafficked victims and now willingly engage in prostitution. Williamson and Prior (2009) found that 64% of girls began prostituting for themselves once they were no longer under the control of a trafficker. Moreover, they found that if minors did not receive the proper services, over time, 77% of them return to prostitution (Ventura et al., 2007).

There are no easy answers to these difficult conundrums. Historically, there has been disagreement regarding what situations warrant child protection versus juvenile justice involvement (Bounds et al., 2015). Some jurisdictions are dealing with domestic sex-trafficked minors in promising ways. In these jurisdictions, sex-trafficked youth are placed in special group homes that employ trauma counselors and other resources that youth need to begin to heal.

Lack of Appropriate, Trauma-Informed, Age-Appropriate Services

Given its secrecy and ruthlessness, sexual exploitation of children is challenging to study, which results in a lack of knowledge related to trauma, and how best to develop specific services that effectively engage and meet the needs of young survivors. Indeed, few programs emphasize the unique experiences and special needs of this population (Fong & Berger Cardoso, 2010).

The lack of tailored services for this population is problematic because, if providers could demonstrate a sensitivity to and understanding of the complexity of the physical and psychological trauma experienced by this population, that may over time increase the likelihood of trafficking victim disclosures. This would in turn allow health and mental health providers the opportunity to recognize and address the full spectrum of victims' acute and long-term health and mental needs.

Evidence-Based Practices with Victims of Human Trafficking

The research literature on effective interventions for trafficked minors is limited, both in terms of the number of empirical studies done with this group and the number of evidence-informed practice models that have been tested with this population. Fong and Berger Cardoso (2010) offer an explanation: "In the American child welfare system, public child welfare workers depend on licensed private therapists and providers who are knowledgeable in treating child sexual abuse but who struggle with treatment modalities available for child victims of human trafficking because of poor 'best practice fit'" (p. 314).

Image 9.2

Therefore, professionals may have to examine evidence-based interventions used with other vulnerable youth populations and adapt them as necessary to meet the service needs of sexually trafficked youth. Several of these practices are discussed below.

Multisystemic Therapy (MST)

MST was developed to help youth with serious social, emotional, and behavioral problems. The MST framework posits that problem behaviors are associated with the interplay of individual, family, and community characteristics; thus, intervention must occur between multiple systems. One can see how this framework would apply to trafficked minors, as it is often an interplay of characteristics that lead to youth falling prey to sexual traffickers. MST has been found to be effective with physically abused youth involved with child welfare services (Swenson, Schaeffer, Henggeler, Faldowski, & Mayhew, 2010), a population with similar characteristics to victims of sexual trafficking.

Cognitive Behavioral Therapy (CBT)

For traumatized youth, one of the most used treatments is CBT, which works to change attitudes and behavior by focusing on the thoughts, images, beliefs, and attitudes that a person holds and how these processes relate to the way the person behaves. Trauma-focused CBT (TF-CBT) is a promising approach to treating youth who have been sexually exploited. One recent randomized controlled trial of trauma-focused CBT, delivered to sexually exploited girls in the Democratic Republic of Congo, demonstrated a reduction in trauma symptoms, decreased anxiety and depression, and improved prosocial behavior (O'Callaghan, McMullen, Shannon, Rafferty, & Black, 2013).

Current Programs for Youth Who Have Histories of Sex Trafficking

Below is a description of currently operating programs that specialize in treating young people who have been sexually trafficked.

Girls Educational & Mentoring Services (GEMS)

GEMS is the only organization in New York State specifically designed to serve girls and young women who have experienced commercial sexual exploitation and domestic trafficking. It was founded in 1998 by Rachel Lloyd, who had been sexually exploited as a teenager. GEMS services include prevention and outreach, direct intervention (including short-term and crisis care, court advocacy, transitional and supportive housing, and holistic case management), and empowering survivors (GEMS, 2018). It serves over 400 girls and young women a year (Lloyd, 2017).

Rapha House

Rapha House a/k/a Rapha International "seeks to: prevent the trafficking of children before it starts; provide healing, hope, and freedom through quality care for children who have been rescued from trafficking; train and reintegrate children who come into our care; and educate, engage, and empower advocates to rise up and fight this injustice" (Rapha International, n.d., para. 1). In 2003, Rapha House began a safe house program for girls who had been rescued from slavery and sexual exploitation. At these houses, located around the world, girls receive foundational needs (shelter, food, clothing, etc.), counseling and medical care, personalized educational and vocational training plans, social services, and legal advocacy.

Children of the Night

Children of the Night is an organization dedicated to rescuing children and young people from prostitution. It was established in 1979. Since its founding, the organization has rescued over 10,000 children from prostitution in the United States. Children of the Night has a caseload of over 2,500 children on their outpatient case management program. These children receive confidential social services, shelter and housing referrals, medical and mental health services, psychiatric evaluations, school tutoring, and other advocacy services. In addition to the United States, the organization works in the Dominican Republic, the Philippines, Cambodia, Thailand, Vietnam, Laos, India, and Nepal (Children of the Night, 2018).

youthSpark

Founded in 2000 in Atlanta, youthSpark combats sexual trafficking through a combination of services for youth, investigative research, policy advocacy, court advocacy, and training. In the past, they offered housing for girls recovering from sex trafficking through Angela's House, but the organization has since pivoted from residential solutions to community-based services. In 2016, youthSpark served over 130 youth and families across all programs. The children they serve demonstrate a decrease in running away and an increase in school attendance (youthSpark, 2016).

Systems Approach: Integration of Public Systems

Multiple systems of care work with victims of sex trafficking and CSEC. These systems often overlap, meaning that trafficked minors may be involved with more than one system at the same time. Collaboration is key for the child welfare, mental health, health, school, and juvenile justice system providers to successfully offer comprehensive, coordinated, and effective services. Additional guidelines and best practices for each system working with this population follow.

Child Welfare

Since a large percentage of trafficked youth have a history of involvement with the child welfare system prior to entry into CSEC (Estes & Weiner, 2002), Child Protective Services (CPS) employees are in a unique position to identify CSEC victims and flag children at risk for falling prey to a trafficker. With training, CPS employees can improve their ability to identify the risk factors for entry, increase their knowledge of relevant laws and services, and increase their willingness to refer trafficked minors and those at risk to specialized services (McMahon-Howard & Reimers, 2013).

Criminal Justice

Youth who have experienced sexual exploitation often become entangled in the juvenile justice system. Their treatment varies considerably, depending on whether they are viewed as abused or delinquent. Although the most common response is still for these youth to be arrested, some jurisdictions are becoming more victim centered. For example, the District of Columbia has created legislation mandating the development and implementation of CSEC screening in juvenile court defendants (Andretta, Woodland, Watkins, & Barnes, 2016). In Sacramento, service providers were trained to recognize potential trauma triggers and responses that might occur in the courtroom (Liles, Blacker, Landini, & Urquiza, 2016).

Education

There is a correlation between sexual exploitation of children and school-related problems (Clawson, Dutch, Solomon, & Goldblatt Grace, 2009). One possible explanation for this relationship is that when children, in particular girls, do poorly in school, their self-esteem plummets, which in turn makes them more vulnerable to recruitment by a trafficker or pimp. However, many sexually exploited youth continue to attend school, albeit sporadically. Therefore, schools have responsibilities in identifying and helping victims of sexual exploitation, including increasing staff awareness, increasing parent and student awareness of the risks and realities of CSEC, and developing policies for what should happen if a disclosure occurs (Goldblatt Grace, Starck, Potenza, Kenney, & Sheetz, 2012).

Mental Health

As discussed earlier, sexually exploited youth are at risk for a range of mental health issues, from depression to anger problems to self-harming behavior. Treatment should therefore involve a thorough mental health assessment to guide the delivery of services, including trauma-informed care and culturally relevant mental health services. Above all, this population needs individualized care that recognizes a hierarchy of needs.

Health

Health and safety standards in exploitative settings are typically dismal, further compromising a child's well-being. In addition, sexually exploited youth who are still being victimized may not access health services because of concerns about confidentiality, worries about feeling judged, and fears about traffickers and the police (Ijadi-Maghsoodi, Bath, Cook, Textor, & Barnert, 2018). Because of these factors, trafficked minors may emerge with health issues ranging from sexually transmitted diseases to substance use to malnutrition. Thus, it is important to conduct a referral for a medical assessment to identify any medical issues.

Private Agencies

Combating the sexual trafficking of children requires a comprehensive, coordinated effort to meet the full range of young trafficking victims' needs. According to the U.S. Department of State, "within government, this means the participation and coordination among agencies with a range of responsibilities that include criminal enforcement, labor enforcement, victim outreach and services, public awareness, education, trade policy, international development and programs, immigration, intelligence, and diplomacy" (2017a, para. 1). Coordinated federal efforts should also incorporate state, local, and tribal entities, along with the private sector, survivors, academia, and faith communities in order to best leverage resources and amplify results (U.S. Department of State, 2017a).

An Integrated Approach to Sexual Trafficking

What would an integrated approach to sexual trafficking look like for this population? Several promising approaches are outlined below.

Interagency Collaboration

Because young victims of sexual trafficking usually have multiple needs, lack of communication and collaboration between agencies prevents victims from receiving all the services they require. Interagency collaboration can take many forms: establishing task forces so that multiple agencies can share information; developing shared protocols, policies, memorandums of understanding and data-sharing policies; or establishing informal relationships between professionals from different agencies to facilitate coordination of efforts and referrals.

For example, 13 agencies, organizations, and departments in Florida created the Miami CARES initiative to collectively address the trafficking of minors by, among other goals, institutionalizing a system of collaboration among groups, creating and implementing a comprehensive data system to gather and track information, and increasing utilization of multidisciplinary interventions (Miami CARES, 2016). As an example of a success story, Miami CARES collaborated with the judicial system to implement a new protocol in which all dependency judges now alert Miami CARES if they have a case that might involve human trafficking. Within 24 hours, a Miami CARES staffing convenes, determines if the case meets criteria for human trafficking, and, if so, transfers the case to a particular experienced judge's division. The consolidation of cases has helped ensure streamlined services and processes for all involved in a case (OurKids, n.d.).

Image 9.3

Specialized Child Welfare Units

Young victims have unique needs and are often unaware of the rights they are entitled to in the legal system. For example, young victims may not be aware that they can halt questioning from law enforcement and request that a guardian or lawyer be present. The guidance these victims require is often very specific, and thus requires professionals who have specialized training when this population intersects with child welfare services. In 2018, Arizona's Department of Child Safety created a special unit to protect child victims' rights—the first child welfare agency in the nation to do so. The members of the unit will work with the DPS police agencies, case managers, and prosecutors as criminal cases move through the court system. The unit's members will advocate for children who have been crime victims (getting their voices heard in court if appropriate, making sure these victims are being treated with respect and dignity, etc.) (DaRonco, 2018).

Training Intake and Emergency Workers to Screen for Child Sexual Exploitation

The first step in prosecuting sexual exploitation cases and assisting victims is being able to identify the victims. Too often, victims are labeled criminals and shunted into the juvenile justice system. As well, many service providers and nonprofit staff are unaware that youth who qualify as domestic minor sex trafficking victims should be considered a separate population of victims.

Lack of training on how to screen for child sexual exploitation directly affects the identification and handling of a child sex trafficking case. For example, victim-centered interviewing techniques are typically used for any traumatized population, but especially for children. When a domestically trafficked minor is not recognized as a child victim, these precautions are not taken during interviews.

In 2012, the Georgia Department of Family and Children's Services (DFCS) made a webinar training on recognizing child sexual exploitation mandatory for all social service staff in the state. The purpose of the training was to make Georgia's child welfare personnel aware of the risk factors, the "red flags," and the laws and services that are in place within the state to protect those who have become victims. McMahon-Howard and Reimers (2013) tested the effectiveness of this training. They found that participation in the training had a significant positive impact on CPS employees' beliefs and knowledge on child sexual exploitation.

Policies Related to Human Trafficking and Child Welfare

Federal Level

Increased Government Spending

The federal government has increased spending on issues related to sex trafficking, particularly as it relates to minors. According to federalspending.gov, from 2008 through 2016, the federal government spent over 10 million more dollars ($10,446,734) on research and services to sex-trafficked individuals ($31,567,467.61) than individuals with histories of prostitution ($21,120,733.91).

Laws

The Trafficking Victims Protection Act (TVPA) of 2000 was the first comprehensive federal law to address trafficking of persons. Under the TVPA, sexually exploited minors are considered victims rather than perpetrators, regardless of the absence of force, fraud, or coercion that is applicable to adult victims. The TVPA has been reauthorized several times, but it was not until 2013 that it specifically addressed the domestic sexual trafficking of minors (Roby & Vincent, 2017).

In 2015, Congress passed the Justice for Victims of Trafficking Act (JVTA), which, among other things, enhanced services for runaway and homeless victims of youth trafficking, provided for training for child protective services workers on identifying, assessing, and providing comprehensive services for children who are sex trafficking victims, and replaced the term "child prostitution" with "child sex trafficking" (Roby & Vincent, 2017).

State Level

Laws

At least 34 states have adopted safe harbor laws that assure consistencies in how commercial sex–exploited children/youth are treated and go beyond identifying victims to funding intervention services (Edinburgh, Huemann, Richtman, Marboe, & Saewyc, 2012). In addition, 36 states have laws that allow survivors to seek a court order vacating or expunging criminal convictions that resulted from their trafficking situation (U.S. Department of State, 2017b).

The content of safe harbor laws varies; some states have more protections in place than others. For example, Minnesota's safe harbor law explicitly removes the requirement of the victim's cooperation with law enforcement in the investigations or trials of their pimps, directly addressing the Stockholm-type bond that victims can form with perpetrators (Roby & Vincent, 2017).

Court Systems

Texas, California, New York, and other states have created prostitution/sex trafficking courts to protect and assist juvenile victims of sex trafficking. These courts also try to minimize the trauma youth experience resulting from the criminal justice system. In addition, the Texas Supreme Court decided that children under the age of 14 should not be prosecuted because they cannot legally consent to sex (Fong & Berger Cardoso, 2010).

Local Level

Task Forces

Tasks forces and coalitions have been created to find, identify, and assist more sex-trafficked victims. Over the last 10 years, at least 42 anti-trafficking task forces throughout the United States were created. The task forces often are made up of law enforcement, staff from social service agencies, or community-based agencies that work with refugee and immigrant populations (Brennan, 2008).

Although strides have been made in combating sexual exploitation of minors in federal, state, and local legislation, more needs to be done. The U.S. Department of Justice (2010) has put forward the following policy recommendations: continued funding for CSEC-specific initiatives; across-the-board agreement on definitions of CSEC-related terms; support and funding of data collection at the state and local levels; and heightened funding that gives victims access to specialized services.

Case Application

The following case is about a 14-year-old minor who is sex trafficked by an "uncle" and has her child taken away from her and placed for adoption by child protective services. She ends up committing suicide.

Case Vignette

Dominique[1] is a 14-year-old who was reported to child protection services by her "uncle" because she was reportedly bringing her newborn baby to calls where she was having sex with men. Dominique has been in and out of the system since she was 7. Initially, Dominique entered the child protection system because of sexual abuse by her mother's boyfriend. Her mother ended this relationship, and Dominique was allowed to return home. Dominique came into the system again at the age of 11 because of domestic violence. Dominique's mother was arrested for stabbing her boyfriend after one of his almost fatal beatings. Dominique witnessed her mother in and out of abusive relationships. After several failed placements, Dominique was placed in a group home. While at the group home, Dominique was bullied by residents. Angelique, a resident, befriended Dominique and protected her from the other youth. One day Angelique introduced Dominique to her uncle Frank. Angelique told Dominique all about how her uncle Frank would take care of her.

1 This is a true story. All names and some details have been changed to protect the participant.

Angelique and Dominique ran away from the group home to live with Uncle Frank. He bought her nice clothes, took her places, and made sure she had the latest cell phone and Jordans. Dominique felt loved for the first time in her life. Uncle Frank told her how special she was and how much he loved her. After a couple of months, Uncle Frank convinced Dominique that if she really loved him, she would have sex with him. Dominique willingly engaged in sex. In fact, she liked having sex with Uncle Frank. Gradually, Dominique began having sex with Uncle Frank's friends and then random strangers. Dominique routinely had sex with six to ten men per night. This went on for a year. Dominique intentionally got pregnant by Uncle Frank, hoping that she would no longer have to sleep with other men. This only pissed Frank off, and he began to beat her. Dominique had seen violent relationships growing up, so she did not realize that Frank did not love her until he forced her to have sex with men 48 hours after giving birth to their daughter. Dominique was never allowed to leave with the baby. Frank threatened to call child protection to have her baby taken away if she did not do what he said. One day she managed to escape, and Frank called child protection on her. Frank told CPS that he was her uncle and he was worried about her. He said that she took her newborn baby on "jobs" with her and that he believed that Dominique's daughter was in danger. Once child protection caught up with Dominique, her daughter was placed in foster care. Dominique ended up going back to Uncle Frank, as the child welfare system did not have an appropriate place for her to live, except the group home she once left. Dominique had no familial support, as her mother was in prison for attempted manslaughter. She was isolated and alone. Dominique was angry and combative and refused to do anything her child protection case worker asked of her. Child protection professionals believed Uncle Frank's story that Dominique willingly engaged in prostitution. Eventually, Dominique's rights were terminated, and her daughter was listed as available for adoption. Dominique was lost and felt empty without her child. Unable to bounce back after her rights were terminated, Dominique overdosed on heroin and died 6 months after losing custody of her daughter. It wasn't until years later that the child protection caseworker realized that Dominique was being trafficked. Uncle Frank was a predator who used the child protection system to punish Dominique for attempting to escape. Unfortunately, many group homes are becoming ideal places for recruiting new girls. Within the last 2 years, a specialized unit that only handles sex trafficking cases has been created to address the influx of child welfare cases involving the sex trafficking of minors.

DISCUSSION QUESTIONS

1. How did Angelique recruit Dominique?
2. How did Uncle Frank groom Dominique? Did he use finesse pimping, guerrilla pimping, or both?
3. What risk factors did Dominique exhibit for becoming a victim of sex trafficking?
4. How did Uncle Frank keep Dominique under his control?
5. How could child protective services have handled this case differently to prevent such a tragic outcome?

References

Adams, W., & Flynn, A. (2017). *Federal prosecution of commercial sexual exploitation of children cases, 2004–2013.* http://www.bjs.gov/index.cfm?ty=pbdetail&iid=6086

Albanese, J. (2007). Commercial sexual exploitation of children: What do we know and what do we do about it? http://www.ncjrs.gov/pdfFilesl/nij/215733.pdf

Andretta, J. R., Woodland, M. H., Watkins, K. M., & Barnes, M. E. (2016). Towards the discreet identification of commercial sexual exploitation of children (CSEC) victims and individualized interventions: Science to practice. *Psychology, Public Policy, and Law, 22*(3), 260–270. http://dx.doi.org/10.1037/law0000087

Annitto, M. (2011). Consent, coercion, and compassion: Crafting a commonsense approach to commercial sexual exploitation of minors. *Yale Law and Policy Review, 30*(1), 1–70.

Banks, D., & Kyckelhahn, T. (2011). *Characteristics of suspected human trafficking incidents, 2008–2010.* Washington, DC: U.S. Department of Justice, Office of Justice Programs, Bureau of Justice Statistics.

Bounds, D., Julion, W. A., & Delaney, K. R. (2015). Commercial sexual exploitation of children and state child welfare systems. *Policy, Politics, & Nursing Practice, 16,* 17–26.

Boxill, N., & Richardson, D. (2007). Ending sex trafficking of children in Atlanta. *Affilia, 22,* 138–149.

Brawn, M., & Roe-Sepowitz, D. (2008). Female juvenile prostitutes: Exploring the relationship to substance use. *Children and Youth Services Review, 30,* 1395–1402.

Brayley, H., Cockbain, E., & Laycock, G. (2011). The value of crime scripting: Deconstructing internal child sex trafficking. *Policing: A Journal of Policy and Practice, 5*(2), 132–143.

Brennan, D. (2008). Competing claims of victimhood? Foreign and domestic victims of trafficking in the United States. *Sexuality Research & Social Policy, 5*(4), 45.

Brinlee, M. (2018, November 13). "13 Sex Trafficking Statistics That Put The Worldwide Problem Into Perspective." *Bustle,* Bustle, www.bustle.com/p/13-sex-trafficking-statistics-that-put-the-worldwide-problem-into-perspective-9930150

Children of the Night. (2018). *Mission statement.* https://www.childrenofthenight.org/mission-statement/

Clarke, R. J., Clarke, E. A., Roe-Sepowitz, D., & Fey, R. (2012). Age at entry into prostitution: Relationship to drug use, race, suicide, education level, childhood abuse, and family experiences. *Journal of Human Behavior in the Social Environment, 22*(3), 270–289. doi: 10.1080/10911359.2012.655583

Clawson, H. J., Dutch, N., Solomon, A., & Goldblatt Grace, L. (2009). Human trafficking into and within the United States: A review of the literature. Washington, DC: U.S. Department of Health and Human Services. http://aspe.hhs.gov/hsp/07/HumanTrafficking/LitRev/

Clawson, H. J., Dutch, N. M., Solomon, A., & Goldblatt Grace, L. (2009a). Human trafficking into and within the United States: A review of the literature. http://aspe.hhs.gov/hsp/07/ humantrafficking/litrev/

Clawson, H. J., & Goldblatt Grace, L. (2007). *Finding a path to recovery: Residential facilities for minor victims of domestic sex trafficking.* https://aspe.hhs.gov/report/finding-path-recovery-residential-facilities-minor-victims-domestic-sex-trafficking

Countryman-Roswurm, K. (2012). Girls like you, girls like me: An analysis of domestic minor sex trafficking and the development of a risk and resiliency assessment for sexually exploited youth. Doctoral dissertation, Wichita State University, Kansas.

Countryman-Roswurm, K. (2006). Human trafficking of homeless, runaway, and throwaway youth: Working with victims of sexual exploitation. Paper presented at the Department of Health and Human Service (DHHS) Pathways to Adulthood Conference, Portland, OR.

Countryman-Roswurm, K., & Bolin, B. L. (2014). Domestic minor sex trafficking: Assessing and reducing risk. *Child and Adolescent Social Work Journal, 31*(6), 521–538.

Coy, M. (2009). "Moved around like bags of rubbish nobody wants": How multiple placement moves can make young women vulnerable to sexual exploitation. *Child Abuse Review, 18*, 254–266.

Curtis R., Terry, K., Dank, M., Dombrowski, K., & Khan, B. (2008). *Commercial Sexual Exploitation of Children in New York City, Volume One: The CSEC Population in New York City: Size, Characteristics, and Needs* (NIJ Doc. No. 225083). Washington, DC: U.S. Department of Justice.

DaRonco, D. (2018, May 15). DCS creates unit to protect child victims' rights. *Arizona Department of Child Safety*. https://dcs.az.gov/news/may-15-2018-dcs-creates-unit-protect-child-victims-rights

Davis, K. (2006). Human trafficking and modern day slavery in Ohio. Polaris Project. Washington, DC: Polaris Project. http://www.ccv.org/wp-content/uploads/2010/04/Ohio-Report-on-Tracking.pdf

Dworkin, A. (1997). *Life and Death: Unapologetic Writings on the Continuing War against Women.* New York: Free Press.

ECPAT. (2012). Global monitoring status of action against commercial sexual exploitation of children: United States. http://www.ecpat.net/sites/default/files/a4a_v2_am_usa_2.pdf

Edinburgh, L., Huemann, E., Richtman, K., Marboe, A. M., & Saewyc, E. M. (2012). The Safe Harbors Youth Intervention Project: Intersectoral collaboration to address sexual exploitation in Minnesota. *Nursing Reports, 2*(1), 18–24.

Estes, R. J., & Weiner, N. A. (2002). *The Commercial Sexual Exploitation of Children in the U.S., Canada and Mexico.* Philadelphia: University of Pennsylvania, School of Social Work, Center for the Study of Youth Policy.

Flowers, R. B. (2001). The sex trade industry's worldwide exploitation of children. *Annals of the American Academy of Political and Social Science, 575*(1), 147–157.

Fong, R., & Berger Cardoso, J. (2010). Child human trafficking victims: Challenges for the child welfare system. *Evaluations and Program Planning, 33*, 311–316.

Gajic-Veljanoski, O., & Stewart, D. E. (2007). Women trafficked into prostitution: Determinants, human rights and health needs. *Trans-cultural Psychiatry, 44*, 338–358. doi: 10.1177/1363461507081635

Girls Educational and Mentoring Services. (2018). *Our services*. http://www.gems-girls.org/about/what-we-do/our-services

Goldblatt Grace, L., Starck, M., Potenza, J., Kenny, P. A., & Sheetz, A. H. (2012). Commercial sexual exploitation of children and the school nurse. *The Journal of School Nursing, 28*(6), 410–417. doi: 10.1177/1059840512448402

Greenbaum, V. J. (2017). Child sex trafficking in the United States: Challenges for the healthcare provider. *PLOS medicine, 14*(11), e1002439.

Greenbaum, V. J. (2014). Commercial sexual exploitation and sex trafficking of children in the United States. *Current Problems in Pediatric Adolescent Health Care, 44*(9), 245–269.

Herman, J. L. (2003). Hidden in plain sight: Clinical observations on prostitution. In M. Farley (Ed.), *Prostitution, Trafficking, and Traumatic Stress* (pp. 1–13). Binghamton, NY: Haworth Press.

Hodge, D. R. (2008). Sexual trafficking in the United States: A domestic problem with transnational dimensions. *Social Work*, 53, 143–152. doi: 10.1093/sw/53.2.143

Hughes, D. (2007). *Enslaved in the USA*. https://www.nationalreview.com/2007/07/enslaved-usa-donna-m-hughes/

Ijadi-Maghsoodi, R., Bath, E., Cook, M., Textor, L., & Barnert, E. (2018). Commercially sexually exploited youths' health care experiences, barriers, and recommendations: A qualitative analysis. *Child Abuse & Neglect, 76*, 334–341.

Klueber, S. A. (2003). *Trafficking in human beings: Law enforcement response*. Doctoral dissertation, University of Louisville.

Ko, S. J., Ford, J. D., Kassam-Adams, N., Berkowitz, S. J., Wilson, C., Wong, M., ... Layne, C. M. (2008). Creating trauma-informed systems: Child welfare, education, first responders, health care, juvenile justice. *Professional Psychology: Research and Practice, 39*(4), 396 –404.

Kotrla, K. (2010). Domestic minor sex trafficking in the United States. *National Association of Social Workers, 55*(2), 181–187.

Kotrla, K., & Wommack, B. (2011). Sex trafficking of minors in the U.S.: Implications for policy, prevention and research. *Journal of Applied Research on Children: Informing Policy for Children at Risk, 2*(1), 5.

Kyckelhahn, T., Beck, A. J., & Cohen, T. H. (2009). *Characteristics of suspected human trafficking incidents*. https://www.bjs.gov/content/pub/pdf/cshti0810.pdf

Laczko, F., & Gramegna, M. A. (2003). Developing better indicators of human trafficking. *The Brown Journal of World Affairs, 10*, 179–194.

Liles, B. D., Blacker, D. M., Landini, J. L., & Urquiza, A. J. (2016). A California multidisciplinary juvenile court: Serving sexually exploited and at-risk youth. *Behavioral Sciences and the Law, 34*, 234–245.

Lloyd, R. (2017, September 28). I thought working in the sex industry gave me control–I was wrong. *The Telegraph*. https://www.telegraph.co.uk/women/life/thought-working-sex-industry-gave-control-wrong/

Logan, T. K., Walker, R., & Hunt, G. (2009). Understanding human tracking in the United States. *Trauma, Violence, and Abuse, 10*(3), 3–30. doi: 10.1177/15249=838008327262.

McClain, N. M., & Garrity, S. E. (2011). Sex trafficking and the exploitation of adolescents. *Journal of Obstetric, Gynecologic, & Neonatal Nursing, 40*, 243–252. doi: 10.1111/j.1552-6909.2011.01221.x

McLeod, A. (2007). Whose agenda? Issues of power and relationships when listening to looked-after young people. *Child and Family Social Work, 12*, 278–286.

McMahon-Howard, J., & Reimers, B. (2013). An evaluation of a child welfare training program on the commercial sexual exploitation of children (CSEC). *Evaluation and Program Planning, 40*, 1–9. doi: 10.1016/j.evalprogplan.2013.04.002

Miami CARES. (2016). *Project summary*. http://www.ourkids.us/getinvolved/Site%20Assets/Grants-Summaries/MiamiCARESProjectSummary.pdf

Mitchell, K., Finkelhor, D., & Wolak, J. (2010). Conceptualizing juvenile prostitution as child maltreatment: Finding from the national juvenile prostitution study. *Child Maltreatment, 15*(1), 18–36.

National Coalition to Prevent Child Sexual Abuse and Exploitation. (2012). National Plan to Prevent the Sexual Abuse and Exploitation of Children. http://www.preventtogether.org/Resources/Documents/NationalPlan2012FINAL.pdf

National Runaway Switchboard. (2005). http://www.1800runaway.org/default.html

O'Callaghan, P., McMullen, J., Shannon, C., Rafferty, H., & Black, A. (2013). A randomized controlled trial of trauma-focused cognitive behavioral therapy for sexually-exploited, war-affected Congolese girls. *Journal of the American Academy of Child & Adolescent Psychiatry, 52*(4), 359–369. https://doi.org/10.1016/j.jaac.2013.01.013

OurKids. (n.d.). *Quality management plan: 2017–2018*. http://centerforchildwelfare.org/qa/QAC-BCPlans/OurKidsQMPlanFY17-18.pdf

Rapha International (n.d.) *What we do*. https://rapha.org/what-we-do

Ray, N. (2006). *Lesbian, gay, bisexual, and transgender youth: An epidemic of homelessness*. https://www.thetaskforce.org/lgbt-youth-an-epidemic-of-homelessness/

Raymond, J., & Hughes, D. (2001). *Sex trafficking of women in the United States: International and domestic trends*. (Grant number 98-WT-VX-0032 awarded by the National Institute of Justice).

Reid, J. (2010). Doors wide shut: Barriers to the successful delivery of victim services for domestically trafficked minors in a southern U.S. metropolitan area. *Women & Criminal Justice, 20*(1–2), 147–166. doi: 10.1080/0897/4451003641206

Richard, A. O. (2000). *International trafficking in women to the United States: A contemporary manifestation of slavery and organized crime*. Washington, DC: DCI Exceptional Intelligence Analyst Program, Bureau of Intelligence and Research, United States Department of State.

Roby, J. L., & Vincent, M. (2017). Federal and state responses to domestic minor sex trafficking: The evolution of policy. *Social Work, 62*(3), 201–209.

Schauer, E. J., & Wheaton, E. M. (2006). Sex trafficking into the United States: A literature review. *Criminal Justice Review, 31*(2), 146–169.

Smith, L. (2008, July). *Keynote address.* Delivered at Catholic Charities Anti-Human Trafficking Training, San Antonio, TX.

Stransky, M., & Finkelhor, D. (2008). *How many juveniles are involved in prostitution in the U.S.?* http://www.unh.edu/ccrc/prostitution/Juvenile_Prostitution_factsheet.pdf

Swenson, C. C., Schaeffer, C. M., Henggeler, S. W., Faldowski, R., & Mayhew, A. M. (2010). Multisystemic therapy for child abuse and neglect: A randomized effectiveness trial. *Journal of Family Psychology, 24*(4), 497–507. doi: 10.1037/a0020324

Torres-Carlson, A. (2018). How to Recognize the Signs of Human Sex Trafficking. https://humantraffickingsearch.org/resource/how-to-recognize-the-signs-of-human-sex-trafficking/?gclid=Cj0KCQiAqY3zBRDQARIsAJeCVxNAY6DYkcJEm40QTvuzAe_GoxKv1FW-6mCnShRaxEKFWNeoofWARVcaAk4dEALw_wcB

Tyler, K. A., & Johnson, K. A. (2004). Victims and offenders: Accounts of paybacks, invulnerability, and financial gain among homeless youth. *Deviant Behavior, 25,* 427–449. Taylor & Francis Group.

Ugarte, M. B., Zarate, L., & Farley, M. (2004). Prostitution and trafficking of women and children from Mexico to the United States. *Journal of Trauma Practice, 2*(3–4), 147–165.

United States Department of Health and Human Services, & Administration for Children and Families. (2009). Fact sheet: Child victims of human trafficking. http://www.acf.hhs.gov/trafficking/about/children_victims.html

United States Department of State, *2018 Trafficking in Persons Report–Australia,* 28 June 2018. https://www.refworld.org/docid/5b3e0bb2a.html [accessed 21 January 2019]

Urbina, I. (2009, October 26). For runaways, sex buys survival. *New York Times.* Retrieved October 29, 2009, from http://nytimes.com/2009/10/27/us/27runaways.html

U.S. Department of Justice. (2010). *Effects of federal legislation on the commercial sexual exploitation of children.* http://www.ncjrs.gov/pdffiles1/ojjdp/228631.pdf

U.S. Department of Justice. (2007). *Child exploitation and obscenity section: Child prostitution.* Retrieved December 11, 2011, from http://www.justice.gov/criminal/ceos/prostitution.html

U.S. Department of State, Office to Monitor and Combat Trafficking in Persons. (2017a). *U.S. Government entities combating human trafficking.* https://www.state.gov/j/tip/rls/fs/2017/272160.htm

U.S. Department of State, Office to Monitor and Combat Trafficking in Persons. (2017b). *United States of America: Tier 1.* https://www.state.gov/j/tip/rls/tiprpt/countries/2017/271309.htm

U.S. Department of State, Office to Monitor and Combat Trafficking in Persons. (2008). *Trafficking in persons report (TIP).* http://www.state.gov/g/tip/rls/tiprpt/2008/

United Nations Office on Drugs and Crime. (2016). Global report on trafficking in persons. United Nations publications, Sales No. E16IV6. 2016.

Ventura, C., Williamson, C., Cox, J., Moe, J., Dupuy, P., Lambert, E., et al. (2007). *Female Offenders in the Justice System: Needs of and Services for Mothers and their Children: Summary and Recommendations.* Toledo, OH: University of Toledo.

Vera Institute of Justice. (2014). Screening for human trafficking: Guidelines for administering the trafficking victim identification tool. New York: Vera Institute of Justice. (www.vera.org)

Walsh, S. M., & Donaldson, R. E. (2010). Invited commentary: National safe place: Meeting the immediate needs of runaway and homeless youth. *Journal of Youth and Adolescence, 39*, 437–445. doi: 10.1007/s10964-010-9522-9

WestCoast Children's Clinic. (2012). *Research to action: Sexually exploited minors (SEM) needs and strengths.* Oakland, CA: WestCoast Children's Clinic.

Williamson, C., & Prior, M. (2009). Domestic minor sex trafficking: A network of underground players in the Midwest. *Journal of Child and Adolescent Trauma, 2*, 1–16. doi: 10.1080/19361520802702191

Willis, B. M., & Levy, B. S. (2002). Child prostitution: Global health burden, research needs, and interventions. *Lancet, 359*(9315), 1417–1422.

Wilson, J. M., & Dalton, E. (2008). Human trafficking in the heartland: Variation in law enforcement awareness and response. *Journal of Contemporary Criminal Justice, 24*(3), 296–313.

youthSpark. (2016). 2015–2016 Annual Report. https://youth-spark.org/wp-content/uploads/2016/10/Annual-Report-2016-WEB.pdf

Figure Credits

Img. 9.1: Copyright © 2012 Depositphotos/Kuzmafoto.

Img. 9.2: Copyright © 2017 Depositphotos/AndreyPopov.

Img. 9.3: Copyright © 2012 Depositphotos/cidepix.

CHAPTER • 10

Trauma-Informed Approaches to Competent Practice with Lesbian, Gay, Bisexual, Transgender, and Questioning (LGBTQ) Youth and Their Families in Child Welfare Systems

Gerald P. Mallon

Overview of Chapter and Population

This chapter is designed to help child welfare, social work, and youth care professionals increase their knowledge about trauma-informed approaches to competently practice with **lesbian**, **gay**, **bisexual**, **transgender**, and questioning (LGBTQ) youth and their families, in particular those within child welfare systems (for further information about LGBTQ youth, see also Mallon, 2018a). LGBTQ children and youth, and families affected by issues of **sexual orientation** and/or **gender identity expression**, are present in every child welfare system in this country. Although much has changed in the past 3 decades (Lorthridge, Evans, Heaton, Stevens, & Phillips, 2018; Mallon, 1994, 2018a), many professionals continue to not have adequate or culturally responsive knowledge about an LGBTQ orientation (Paul, 2018), and as such, LGBTQ youth—maybe even more so their families—continue to be an often-invisible population. Consequently, most professionals (including direct-care child welfare staff, supervisors, managers, and administrators), unless they are LGBTQ themselves or have a highly developed knowledge base about working with these clients, are not usually well prepared to address or respond to their trauma-informed practice needs.

This chapter, using individual and systemic case examples, will provide social workers and child welfare professionals with knowledge needed for practice with LGBTQ youth with a focus on practice and policy development through a trauma-informed lens, and offering guidelines for practice within that framework within six domain areas:

1. Building trauma-informed knowledge and skills;
2. Promoting trauma-informed procedures and policies;
3. Establishing guidelines for safe and supportive relationships and environments;
4. Providing assessments and corresponding services that are trauma informed;
5. Involving youth and families in decision-making; and
6. Encouraging collaboration across systems.

Child Welfare History and Prevalence for LGBTQ Youth

Most LGBTQ young people are not placed in child welfare settings. In fact, the majority of LGBTQ youth live with their families and never rely on a foster home, a group home, or a shelter at all. Those adolescents who do come to the attention of child welfare are young people who have experienced difficulties within their family system to such a degree that they cannot or should not continue to live at home.

Image 10.1

Although some LGBTQ youth are thrown out of their homes when they disclose their sexual orientation or gender identity expression or when they are "found out" by their families, not all of them enter the child welfare system because of issues directly related to their identity. Like their heterosexual counterparts, the majority of LGBTQ young people were placed there before or during the onset of adolescence. Many were placed for the same reasons that other young people are: family disintegration; divorce, death, or illness of a parent; parental substance abuse or alcoholism; or physical abuse and neglect.

Living apart from one's family is seldom easy. The structure of the different types of child welfare programs varies widely and can take many forms. They range from small community-based group homes and short-term respite care or shelter facilities to large congregate care institutions that provide long-term or custodial care. Some facilities have a juvenile justice component to them (Irvine & Canfield, 2016), some are foster care programs (Clements & Rosenwald, 2007), and others still are programs designed for runaway and homeless youth (Maccio & Ferguson-Colvin, 2016). All of these different types of services share one common feature, however: they provide care for children and youth on a 24-hour-a-day basis, which is very different from other youth services that are not residential in nature.

Generally, most group homes, juvenile justice facilities, and shelters are staffed by individual youth care workers or counselors who are employed by an agency to work in shifts to cover the facility 24 hours a day. The youth care workers who work in group home settings play a very important role in the lives of the young people in their care. Nevertheless, they are generally the lowest paid—and in many cases, have obtained the least education and training—in the youth services system. The daily stress of working with adolescents in these settings, combined with the poor pay, can make it difficult for staff to be empathetic and compassionate in their dealings with the young people, and these factors also account for a high staff turnover.

Most child welfare settings for adolescents focus on preparing these young people for the transition to adulthood—on or before their 18th birthday, or 21st birthday in some states. Some group homes are warm, loving, and accepting of diversity, and some are cold, poorly maintained, and rigid. LGBTQ young people live in and speak about both.

LGBTQ Youth in Out of home Settings

Historically, data on the sexual orientation and gender identity of youth in foster care have not been collected and tracked, but this is slowly changing. Data on youth who are LGBTQ show that among 18- to 26-year-olds in the sample of youth in the general population, approximately 12% report same-sex attraction and/or identify as LGBTQ, and approximately 10% report identifying as LGBTQ (Poirier, Wilkie, Sepulveda, & Uruchima, 2018). In comparison, one study examining the Los Angeles County foster care system found that 19.1% of a random sample of young people ages 12 to 21 years old identified as LGBTQ (Wilson, Cooper, Kastanis, & Nezhad, 2014).

Disproportionality and Disparity Related to LGBTQ Youth

The challenges are greatest for young people overrepresented in the child welfare system—young people of color and those who have diverse sexual and gender identities (e.g., LGBTQ). In the United States, the rate of foster care placement among young people who are Black/African American, non-Hispanic, and over 14 years old is 2.74 times as high as the rate of foster care placement among their peers who are White, non-Hispanic. Among young people who are Hispanic, the rate is 1.34 times as high (Jim Casey Youth Opportunities Initiative, 2016). To adequately address the complex universe of issues that increase disproportionality, in addition to the collection of data points required by federal law, training of staff, recruitment of diverse staff and foster parents, including resources dedicated to promoting family preservation and reunification and additional

Image 10.2

support to relative caregivers are some of the strategies which could and should be employed to combat such disproportionality (Wilson & Kastanis, 2015).

Youth who identify as LGBTQ, on average, face more barriers to permanency and well-being in comparison to their non-LGBTQ peers in foster care (Wilson et al., 2014). These youth are at increased risk for negative health outcomes, such as high levels of depression, substance abuse, unprotected sexual contact, and attempted suicide (Ryan, Huebner, Diaz, & Sanchez, 2009; Ryan et al., 2010). Studies have found that youth who identify as LGBTQ are 1.2 times more likely to experience physical abuse compared to youth who are heterosexual (Friedman et al., 2011). Gender expansiveness in childhood also may increase the risk of child maltreatment (Roberts, Rosario, Corliss, Koenen, & Austin, 2012a, 2012b). A recent national study on youth in detention found that youth who are LGBTQ were approximately seven times more likely to have been previously removed from their homes and placed in foster care than youth who are heterosexual. Youth who identify as transgender or gender expansive were five times more likely to have a foster care history than youth who are **cisgender** or gender conforming (Irvine & Canfield, 2016). Identifying as LGBTQ alone does not mean a young person will experience any negative outcomes; however, the higher proportion of youth who identify as LGBTQ and who have these experiences in comparison to youth who do not identify as LGBTQ demonstrates the importance of ensuring that youth who identify as LGBTQ in vulnerable situations such as foster care have supports available to meet their needs.

Although youth who identify as LGBTQ enter the child welfare system for a variety of reasons, not always related to their sexual orientation or gender identity, many do not find themselves any safer in foster care due to anti-LGB and anti-transgender bias and/or lack of knowledge about how to serve these youth. For example, a survey of youth who identified as LGBTQ and were in foster care, living in New York City Administration for Children's Services group homes, found that 78% of youth had been removed or had run away from their foster placements because of hostility toward their sexual orientation or gender identity (Feinstein, Greenblatt, Hass, Kohn, & Rana, 2001). This study also found that of the youth who identify as LGBTQ and had lived in group homes, 70% reported experiencing physical violence, and 100% had experienced verbal harassment. Furthermore, youth who identify as LGBTQ had disproportionately longer stays in care, greater placement instability, and a greater risk of mistreatment and neglect in their care setting as compared to their peers who identify as heterosexual and cisgender.

Significantly, family acceptance and support has been shown to be critical to better outcomes for youth who identify as LGBTQ. Recent research shows that families of youth who identify as LGBTQ typically become more accepting over time, even when family members had religious or cultural beliefs that rejected LGBTQ identities (Ryan et al., 2009, 2010). These important findings suggest that anti-gay and anti-transgender bias could be remedied given time and education, opening new possibilities for reunification and kinship placements.

"Best practices" are often shaped by social policies existing at multiple levels and may have differential impacts on the systems serving vulnerable youth and families involved with child welfare systems (Aarons & Palinkas, 2007; Shireman, 2015). The majority of child welfare jurisdictions still do not routinely inquire about youth's sexual orientation or gender identity, nor do they consistently integrate this information and other aspects of youth's identities into case and permanency planning (Dettlaff, Washburn, Vogel, & Carr, 2017; Martin, Down, & Erney, 2016). There remains vast diversity at the agency, county, and state levels concerning LGBTQ-related policies, such as sex-based placement and the use of affirming names and gender pronouns. There is also great variability concerning LGBTQ-inclusive nondiscrimination policies, and how these policies are implemented and enforced within various child welfare jurisdictions (Mallon, 2018a; Washburn et al., 2018; Wilber, 2013; Winter, 2013; Yarbrough, 2012). Moreover, even in jurisdictions with affirming policies, many youth who identify as LGBTQ continue to experience adverse outcomes.

These concerns are complicated further by institutional bias and systemic discrimination, along with providers' individual bias. Concerns about bias are not limited to a particular jurisdiction, nor to child welfare alone, but rather extend to all child-, youth-, and family-serving systems. As a result, many who are a part of these systems lack the requisite knowledge and skills to effectively serve youth identifying as LGBTQ (Gandy, McCarter, & Portwood, 2013; Martin et al., 2016; Sikerwar & Rider, 2015; Toner, 2013).

Trauma-Informed Care

What Does Trauma Look Like for an LGBTQ Youth in a Child Welfare Setting?

The majority of children and youth who are part of the foster care system have experienced multiple traumas, making this a vulnerable population with an increased risk for emotional, behavioral, and life-long challenges. LGBTQ children and youth are even further challenged by additional traumas that are directly related to their sexual orientation and/or gender identity expression. A lack in trauma-informed care within the child welfare system tends to create additional traumatic experiences that should be addressed (Butler, Critelli, & Rinfrette, 2011). Heightened awareness of the occurrence and impact of trauma has drawn attention to the need for trauma-informed care, which has resulted in the development of trauma-focused practices and initiatives (National

Child Traumatic Stress Network, 2013). However, the implementation of such practices as they relate to LGBTQ children and youth has only just begun. This chapter strives to educate all involved, including practitioners and policy makers, about this need by highlighting trauma prevalence rates and consequences for LGBTQ youth in foster care and by providing examples, such as those highlighted below, of what has been done so far as well as specific areas for improvement.

Hamid's Narrative

My family was always a mess. My mom could barely provide for us—we were always hungry, I went to school dirty, and when she wasn't drunk or high, she was verbally and physically abusive to us.

She always had a string of boyfriends—all of whom were disgusting. Most times they beat on her; sometimes they beat on me—physically or emotionally. One of them was always ragging on me about being a "fag"—he was relentless, it really bothered him that I was different—"Why do you walk like that?" "Why do you hold your books like that?" "Why can't you be more like other boys?"—I was only 9 and didn't really know myself—but he seemed to be obsessed with the idea that I was gay. Another one of them molested me for years, starting when I turned 11. I didn't tell my mother—I mean she couldn't even help herself, how was she gonna help me?

My life from the time I was 5 until the time I left home at 15 was a nightmare. I left when I realized that things were never gonna change and I just couldn't take it anymore. Believe it or not, running away from home was the best thing that ever happened to me.

When I ran away, I went into foster care. Even though ultimately, it was the best thing for me, until I found the right placement, it was a pretty harsh experience as well. The first foster home I was in I was with this lady who had like six other kids and clearly didn't really care about any of us. Being gay didn't even matter. Then, I went to this foster home with really religious people and they kept saying they were OK with me being gay, but then they were always trying to get me to go to their church and to change who I was. Next, I went into this family where the older son kept trying to molest me—it was all pretty bad. Finally, after these three places I went to a foster home with this woman named Mary, who was like a saint. She was so genuinely nice and compassionate and good, at first, I couldn't believe that anyone could be that good—but after I developed some trust in her and saw for myself that she was really as good as she seemed—I relaxed and I felt like I could be myself.

I wasn't just a kid that someone got paid to take care of, like in the other foster homes I was in. I was someone that Mary loved and cared for, she made me part of her family. Even though there were eight of us living in her house—she cared for each one of us individually—unconditionally. Mary saved my life, to me she is the only mother I have ever had—and when I was 20, she adopted me.

Even though I feel like I have a good life now, I still have a lot of bad shit that haunts me about all the stuff that happened to me—I guess I will have that for the rest of my life.

Josie's Narrative

I couldn't live at home with my family once they found out that I was a lesbian so I was sent to live in a group home. But that was worse than living at home. I didn't fit in at home and then I didn't fit in at the group home either. I was living in my fourth group home in like 6 months and it was horrible. The teasing, the tormenting, the harassment really got to me and one day I just decided that I couldn't take it anymore and I tried to hurt myself. I didn't really want to kill myself, I just wanted someone to see that I was hurting. They put me in the psych hospital, and no one there knew how to deal with an out lesbian. They let me go when I said I wouldn't try to hurt myself anymore. I went back to the same group home, and nothing changed—it was hopeless—after 3 days, I left. I had no place to stay, but I didn't even care. I knew that I just couldn't stay one more minute in that group home. I lived with friends, I stayed on people's sofas, I prostituted—I'm not proud of that, but I did what I had to do—to get money to rent a place. I even lived in an abandoned trailer truck with 10 other people, slept in railroad tunnels, and anywhere that was warm. As bad as things got on the streets—it was better than the group homes that I had lived in—at least on the streets, people cared for me.

Martin's Narrative

One day my father heard me talking on the telephone to a guy who I had met. When I got off the phone he just went crazy on me, he started slapping me and saying that he didn't raise me to be no faggot. He told me to get the hell out of his house and literally threw me out the front door. I was devastated. I didn't know where to go, I had no place to go. I walked the streets for a long time and then I called a friend who let me stay at his house. My friend told me about a shelter for young people and I went there. They helped me to get into a group home.

I went from group home to group home, I didn't seem to fit in anywhere. In the last group home I was in somebody tried to set me on fire. I was sleeping and they put lighter fluid on my bed and threw a match on me, I got burned on the leg (he points to an eight-inch burn mark). The staff didn't do nothing, they knew about it, they just moved my bed. I didn't feel safe there, you kinda had to sleep with one eye open. I finally left. I was tired of that shit.

Mauri's Narrative

I always knew I was different from a very young age. At first, I thought I was gay, then I realized, I was not. I had no idea at first what it meant to be trans, I was born into a body of a boy, but I always knew I was a girl. The more I told people, including my family, that I was not a boy, I was a girl, the more they tried to convince me that I was not. I had literally no support for who I was in my family. I tried to express what I felt by dressing like a girl, I tried to wear my hair more like a girl would, but I just kept getting beat up at school, in my neighborhood, and verbally harassed by my family. My parents became physically abusive, trying to force me to change, my life was hell. I finally at 15, entered foster care, and I was lucky, I went to this group home that was known for being cool with LGBTQ kids.

In that place, the first place where anyone told me I could be myself, I went to school, I felt safe, and I felt like they "got" me. This place was a real home, for a short time. This place gave me a sense of stability that I had lacked, the support that was desperately needed, provided me with lessons that needed to be taught to young, impressionable youth. Because I felt safe and understood, I was able to be a carefree child for a short time again.

When we lacked a father and a mother the Director of the program, Jerry, who was a kind and wonderful man, was our parent. In retrospect, a part of me had wished that Jerry had been my father or that my father could have learned from him. I can say now that I love myself, I know my self-worth, I value myself and that I can have a healthy relationship despite all I went through because Jerry guided me through this time of my life. Thanks to him I learned to not be afraid of social workers and while there are good and bad ones, having now seen a good one, I know there are many more out there that are good than there are bad ones. Thanks to his goodness I was able to find therapists and interview them well to make sure they would suit my needs. I am a little cracked in some spots because of all this trauma in my life, but I am proud that I have emerged as a whole person.

A Trauma-Informed Approach

Children and families become known to the child welfare system primarily because of suspected abuse or neglect. Experiences which—in combination with domestic violence, mental health issues, substance abuse, under a huge umbrella of poverty, and other stressors—can result in traumatic stress reactions. Given the prevalence of trauma and traumatic stress reactions among child welfare system–involved children, families, caregivers, professionals, and other stakeholders, it is critical that child welfare professionals link families with trauma-informed treatment and services and integrate an understanding of trauma into their own practice, especially as they relate to LGBTQ children and youth (Dorsey et al., 2012).

Before discussing what a trauma-informed child welfare system might look like for LGBTQ youth, one must define the elements of a trauma-informed child welfare system. According to the National Child Traumatic Stress Network, there are six broad elements of a Trauma-Informed Child Welfare System (National Child Traumatic Stress Network, 2013).

- To maximize physical and psychological safety for children and families.
- To identify trauma-related needs of children and families.

- To enhance child and family well-being and resilience.
- To enhance the well-being and resilience of those working in the system.
- To partner with youth and families.
- To partner with agencies and systems that interact with children and families.

Agencies that are committed to adopting a trauma-informed approach from a system-wide child welfare perspective means a commitment to changing the entire organization's practices, policies, and culture in order to ensure that all youth—but in this case LGBTQ youth and their families—get the support they need to thrive in the face of experienced adversity. SAMHSA (2014a) offers the following outline as a framework for adopting a trauma-informed approach across six core domains, which are used in this chapter in a slightly different order and illustrated with case examples. These identified domains are:

1. Building trauma-informed knowledge and skills;
2. Promoting trauma-informed procedures and policies;
3. Establishing guidelines for safe and supportive relationships and environments;
4. Providing assessments and corresponding services that are trauma informed;
5. Involving youth and families in decision-making; and
6. Encouraging collaboration across systems.

This framework reflects the common core elements of a trauma-informed approach across child welfare, social work, and youth-serving settings (Guarino, Soares, Konnath, Clervil, & Bassuk, 2009; SAMHSA, 2014a).

Practice Challenges and Evidence-Based Practices for Addressing the Needs of LGBTQ Youth

First Domain: Build Trauma-Informed Knowledge and Skills

My life at home with my family and then in foster care, was full of trauma. I couldn't talk about who I was with my family, even after I came out to them. Then, when I entered the foster care system, things were even worse. I don't think the staff or foster parents ever received any training about even basic LGBTQ issues

—Foster Care Youth

All professionals working with LGBTQ youth in child welfare systems need to be trained on a variety of topics, including:

1. The current and ever changing lexicon of LGBTQ youth and relevant professionally oriented definitions (e.g., sexual orientation, gender identity expression);
2. Issues related to identity development and accompanying stressors;
3. The range of myths and stereotypes regarding LGBTQ youth;

4. A clear identification of the types of trauma specific to LGBTQ youth, such as verbal harassment, emotional abuse, physical violence, peer difficulties, family issues, and/or rejection;
5. The impact of traumatic stress on all aspects of one's development and life; the specific effects of trauma on LGBTQ youth, such as: parental ostracizing; homelessness (Shelton, Poirier, Wheeler, & Abramovich, 2018); suicidal ideation and/or expression, depression, anxiety, isolation, loneliness, substance abuse, sexually transmitted diseases, and the core basic principles of a trauma-informed approach.

In addition to the basic LGBTQ 101 training (which everyone needs, even those who claim they understand), child welfare staff should receive training on the unique issues and challenges experienced by particular subgroups of LGBTQ youth (Weeks, Altman, Stevens, Lorthridge, & Heaton, 2018). For example, transgender youth have specific risk factors related to their gender and/or sexual orientation expression, including even higher rates of exposure to trauma than their sexual minority peers (Mallon, 2009; 2017). By tailoring their responses appropriately, staff can better meet the needs of these young people and not add to their trauma by engaging these young people with outmoded "homo-ignorant" practices. All staff members should be required to participate in training on specific skills and strategies for working with LGBTQ youth in a trauma-informed way. Some skills may be specific to particular professionals such as clinicians, while others will be applicable to all staff who come in contact with LGBTQ youth.

Training topics may include the following:

- Recognizing that gender is a nonbinary construct that may not correspond to gender assigned at birth.
- Understanding that sexual orientation is distinct and different from gender identity expression.
- Understanding the role that stigma, prejudice, discrimination, and violence may play in the health and well-being of LGBTQ youth.
- Identifying elements necessary to creating an LGBTQ-affirming environment.
- Crisis intervention and techniques to deescalate a crisis, which include LGBTQ-affirming practices.
- Targeted safety planning for all youth, including LGBTQ youth, with agencywide anti-bullying approaches that address safety issues for all young people, not just LGBTQ young people.
- Strategies for helping LGBTQ youth self-identify trauma triggers.
- Understanding the intersection of gender identity, race, and other cultural identities through the lens of cultural humility and critical race theory.
- Helping staff to recognize the types of care that may be needed in addition to counseling, including physical, emotional, cultural, spiritual, and financial support.
- Development of strengths-based approaches for working with LGBTQ youth.

- Evidence-based clinical interventions for trauma conducted by LGBTQ-affirming clinicians and adapted when possible with fidelity for LGBTQ youth (Weiner, Schneider, & Lyons, 2009).
- Meaningful engagement with LGBTQ youth.
- Engaging the families of LGBTQ youth in meaningful ways.
- Specific strategies for working with trans and gender-expansive youth.

Training all personnel ensures a more complete agency-led (as opposed to an individually led) understanding. It also helps staff identify potential trauma-related responses and can enhance staff's capacity to respond in ways that are LGBTQ affirming, respectful, and appropriate. Training about trauma as it relates to LGBTQ youth permits child welfare staff to step back, take things less personally, and respond in a more informed and professional manner. It is critical to remember that not all LGBTQ youth experience significant adversity and trauma, and that for those who are distressed, not all difficulties are related to **sexual orientation** or **gender identity expression**. Adopting a trauma-informed approach ensures that the potential role of trauma is considered, though it may not always be the underlying issue.

Second Domain: Promote Trauma-Informed Policies and Practices

In the absence of clear, written, approved, and sanctioned policies, workers create their own policies, usually based in their own personal values rather than the values of the authorizing agency (Gerrity & Folcarelli, 2008). This is, in this researcher's experience, especially true as it relates to LGBTQ youth in child welfare settings. As this young person from foster care so clearly articulated:

> *These staff, just make up rules as they are going along. If there isn't some sort of agency policy, they just make one up on the spot. I can tell you from my experience, sometime the staff in the group home or the foster parents were more punitive and restrictive than my parents were. And there were definitely different rules for gay kids than there were for straight kids.* —Foster Care Youth

Trauma-informed agencies that are interested in competent practice with LGBTQ youth need to establish policies and procedures that are aligned with the core principles of trauma-informed care and continuously review existing practices to eliminate those practices and policies that are retraumatizing. Potentially retraumatizing practices for LGBTQ youth who have been traumatized include creating rigid, punishment-driven environments; employing harsh approaches to discipline or programming that mimic abusive experiences; adopting crisis intervention practices or emergency procedures that are further traumatizing; treating youth disrespectfully; and establishing policies that minimize youth voice, choice, and control. Continued review of policies and procedures is required, and it should be done with staff and youth input.

Policies Related to LGBTQ Youth in One State

The State of Louisiana's Department of Children and Family Services (DCFS) is one example of a system which has made a statewide commitment to changing LGBTQ practices and policies. Before launching into a staff training curriculum on trauma-informed practice with LGBTQ youth, as many organizations have done in the past, they convened an in-house group of key staff to examine how all of the agency's policies impacted on competent practice with LGBTQ youth (Kramer, Sigel, Conners-Burrow, Savary, & Tempel, 2013). They made a commitment to review every one of DCFS's policies and procedures by asking the following questions:

1. Is this policy relevant to LGBTQ children or youth?
2. If the policy was not relevant (i.e., a policy on buying diapers for an infant in a foster home) it was left intact, but a note was made to document that no change was needed.
3. If the policy was relevant, it was amended to identify its specific relevance to sexual orientation and/or gender identity expression.
4. Consideration was given to whether or not the policy as written could hurt an LGBTQ youth.
5. Consideration was given to whether the existing policy or rule could retraumatize LGBTQ youth or their families.

After the policies were rewritten and considered, they were reviewed in the usual manner in which DCFS policies were reviewed and approved by the secretary of the Department of Children and Family Services and enacted as new policies. Considering the above can allow systems to determine whether existing policies should be changed or eliminated and if new policies should be included.

To support policy implementation, Louisiana was committed not only to making sure that policies were implemented, but to ensuring that support for practice was offered. To ensure this, the state was committed to developing a *Practice Guide for Working with LGBTQ Youth in the Child Welfare System* (Mallon, 2018a) and a complementary guide for foster parents, *Practice Guide for Foster Parents Caring for LGBTQ Youth* (Mallon, 2020). Statewide training, beginning with the core administration staff in Baton Rouge, was rolled out to all nine regions in the state. Individualized clinical case consultation services were offered to any DCFS staff and/or foster parents who were in need of additional assistance.

Third Domain: Developing Safe and Supportive Environments and Relationships

> *I wasn't safe at home, in school, in my neighborhood, and definitely not in the group homes and foster homes where I lived. Basically, I was told, if I had just shut my mouth about who I was, I wouldn't have gotten beat up. It seemed I was blamed every time for just being myself. It is one of the reasons why I think I am always very guarded with people, even now, until I get to know them, I don't tell them anything about my life. Safety is always a big issue for me*
>
> —Foster Care Youth

As evidenced by the narrative above, LGBTQ youth come to the child welfare system with past experiences that include being mistreated, ignored, silenced, and rejected by others because of their sexual orientation and/or gender identity expression. These experiences negatively affect their willingness to connect with and trust adults. Emotional safety involves feeling protected, comforted, in control, heard, and reassured. Creating LGBTQ-affirming environments for LGBTQ youth requires strategies that demonstrate respect and reduce the potential for trauma (Mallon, 1994; Paul, 2018).

Image 10.3

Demonstrate Respect

Showing youth respect is critical to positive engagement. The following elements should be considered in demonstrating this:

- If youth allege verbal, emotional, or physical abuse, it is the obligation and duty of staff to explore those allegations and act on them.
- Never excuse bullying behavior of peers or staff.
- Ensure that youth are not treated differently because of their sexual orientation or gender identity expression.
- Use current, affirming, gender-neutral language that acknowledges a youth's chosen identity expression.
- Address issues such as bedroom/bathroom privacy up front and unambiguously with policies that support these decisions.
- Allow transgender or gender-nonconforming youth to safely express their gender identity expression through clothing, personal appearance, and preferred pronoun use, as applicable to the setting.

- Maintain confidentiality and privacy related to a youth's disclosure of personal information about sexual orientation and/or gender identity expression.
- Provide opportunities for youth to date and to openly discuss their romantic relationships.
- Demonstrate an open, positive attitude in interactions with LGBTQ youth.

Reduce the Potential for Trauma

Reducing the potential for further traumatization is key to positive engagement. Consider the following elements to minimize the potential for trauma:

- Be aware of the possibility of traumatic triggers in the environment.
- Integrate an awareness of LGBTQ-specific trauma and its impact into all crisis intervention and prevention practices.
- Set a tone of zero tolerance for slurs or negative comments based on sexual orientation, gender identity expression, race, ethnicity, religion, body size, and physical abilities.
- Provide youth with referrals and accompany them when necessary for support on where to go for information and support about their sexual orientation and/or gender identity expression.
- Create safe zones (including the use of visible safe zone stickers or posters), which can signal to youth that they are safe to talk about their gender identity expression and sexual orientation, if they choose to do so.

Efforts to increase competence in working with LGBTQ youth cannot be sustained in an environment that does not explicitly encourage such undertakings. As agencies struggle to demonstrate their commitment to diversity, they must also be willing to include sexual orientation and gender identity expression in their diversity continuum. In doing so, they begin the work necessary for creating a safe and welcoming environment for all clients, not just LGBTQ youth. Once this orientation is set, and the organization's culture shifts to clearly include LGBTQ concerns, it becomes possible for youth workers to learn about, advocate for, and provide affirming services to LGBTQ youth.

Fourth Domain: Provide Trauma-Informed Assessments and Services

The majority of LGBTQ youth do not struggle with significant mental health or adjustment issues (Mallon, 1994; Paul, 2018). However, as evidenced by the narratives in this chapter, they are at increased risk of exposure to trauma and its effects.

Trauma-Informed Assessment Practices for LGBTQ Youth

> *It took me a while to actually come to terms with my lesbian identity. I struggled with decisions about who to tell, when to tell, and if to tell. The hardest was telling my family—and when I finally did tell them—it was like the worst nightmare came true—it didn't go well. I didn't get beat or thrown out like some kids I knew, but I just got the cold freeze—it was like I became invisible—I stopped existing in my family. It was horrible. Even after many years, the strain between me and my family has never been fully resolved—it really hurts—when your own family cannot accept you—how can you expect the world to accept you?*
>
> —Foster Care Youth

LGBTQ youth often face shame and rejection at home, at school, in their communities, and in child welfare settings. LGBTQ youth also face a heightened risk of violence. Stigma-induced shame and guilt can contribute to mental illnesses. Research shows that chronic emotional upset physically damages the brain and impedes decision-making.

Greater anxiety and depression that is sometimes common among LGBTQ youth can also lead to self-loathing. Use of substances, engaging in unsafe sexual practices to numb the pain, quell the isolation, or to self-medicate may also be present for many LGBTQ youth. Stress levels for LGBTQ youth, as for all youth, depend on how much support and acceptance they experience in everyday settings (home, school, community) as opposed to pain and rejection. Rural LGBTQ youth (De Pedro, Lynch, & Esqueda, 2018) and LGBTQ youth of color (Perez-Carrillo, 2018) face even greater risks. They may totally lack visible LGBT adult role models and may be significantly challenged to come out to anyone.

Conversely, acceptance of LGBTQ youth engenders more positive opportunities for health (Ryan, 2009a, 2009b). LGBTQ youth who are fully supported by their parents, by their schools, and by mentors, and who have not experienced bullying and physical violence have much greater chances of positive outcomes.

So how does an agency begin to conduct trauma-informed practice? Trauma Screening is the first step in this process. Screening usually refers to a tool or process that is a brief, focused inquiry to determine whether an individual has experienced one or more traumatic events, has reactions to such events, has specific mental or behavioral health needs, and/or needs a referral for a comprehensive trauma-informed mental health assessment (Copeland, Keeler, Angold, & Costello, 2007). Screening is a process of casting a wide net to gather initial information.

Once the initial screening is conducted, a fuller assessment is the next step. Staff conducting these assessments must consider the potential impact of trauma, and all individualized plans consider ways to address trauma if applicable. To ensure quality of care for all, including LGBTQ youth, family engagement, school and child welfare providers should ensure that all intake forms and screeners include gender-neutral language and offer options for various sexual orientations and/or gender identity expression. Assessments should be conducted in a trauma-informed manner that upholds the core principles of safety, choice, control, and cultural awareness (NCTSN, 2013). Conducting trauma-informed assessments for an LGBTQ youth should first begin with a practitioner who is trained in trauma-informed practice and who has clear experience in practice with LGBTQ youth. Families, when possible, must be included in the assessment process; for youth who are not out to their families, this will not be possible. Assessment should lead the professional to developing measurable goals, objectives, and treatment interventions.

Trauma-Informed Mental Health Services for LGBTQ Youth

LGBTQ youth face unique and potentially traumatic experiences related to their sexual orientation and/or gender identity expression that place them at greater risk of a number of mental health issues, including depression, anxiety, and post-traumatic stress disorder, as well as substance abuse and suicide-related behaviors (Horvath, Remafedi, Fisher, & Walrath, 2012; Roberts et al., 2012a, 2012b). Levels of risk may vary among LGBTQ youth.

Historically, LGBTQ individuals have reported lower satisfaction with mental health and child welfare services, and research suggests that negative attitudes toward LGBTQ individuals among clinicians significantly affect quality of care (Lazear, Pires, Forssell, & Mallery, 2012). Worth noting is that additional practices within the mental health system that have compromised care include:

1. labeling same-gender sexual orientation and variations in gender identity expression as a mental health disorder (Nguyen & Lau, 2018);
2. employing practices such as conversion therapy in an attempt to change identity or orientation (Mallory, Brown, & Conron, 2018; SAMSHA, 2015).

Mental health professionals should be aware of changes in practice related to understanding and treating LGBTQ youth, enabling them to eliminate potentially traumatizing or retraumatizing practices and adopt current standards of care and best practices for working with a diverse group of LGBTQ youth.

It is important to remember that not all LGBTQ youth require more intensive mental health services, and that when services are needed, sexual orientation or gender identity are not always the central issues (Greeson et al., 2011). The majority of LGBTQ youth do not experience negative outcomes, and in many cases, difficulties do not arise from LGBTQ status itself, but from negative responses within families or communities that are not accepting of LGBTQ youth. Adopting a trauma-informed approach ensures that all LGBTQ youth feel safe and supported and that those with more intensive needs are identified and have access to the highest quality of care.

Fifth Domain: Involving Youth and Families

Involving Youth

As suggested within the narratives at the beginning of this chapter, traumatic experiences leave youth feeling helpless, vulnerable, and not in control of their lives. Moving youth from trauma to an opportunity to thrive and to assist them in regaining control over their lives is critical to building resilience and promoting healing. LGBTQ youth are uniquely vulnerable to experiences that include being marginalized, isolated, and silenced. Maintaining a youth-driven focus—"nothing about us, without us"—includes providing formal and informal opportunities for LGBTQ youth to have a voice in the organizations that are supposed to care for them.

Strategies for involving LGBTQ youth include the following (Helfgott & Gonsoulin, 2012; Mallon, 2009):

- Include LGBTQ youth in hiring of appropriate staff.
- Find ways to seek regular input from LGBTQ youth, such as client satisfaction surveys, eliciting feedback when appropriate, and making sure to provide them with aggregated feedback from these mechanisms.
- Encourage LGBTQ youth to offer suggestions on cultural responsiveness policies, procedures, and practices that agencies and schools should adopt.
- Allow LGBTQ youth to express themselves in ways that resonate with their sexual orientation and/or gender identity expression.
- Provide safe places and opportunities for LGBTQ youth to express themselves (e.g., support groups).
- Meaningfully engage LGBTQ youth in the development of policies, practices, and programming.
- Encourage other LGBTQ youth and adults with similar life experiences to share their life narratives—which can provide youth with the hope for a future as a healthy adult.

Engaging Families

Parents or caregivers play a critical role in mitigating the impact of adversity on their children and fostering resilience (NCTSN, 2012). Among LGBTQ youth, family acceptance and support helps protect children from potential stressors related to sexual orientation and/or gender identity expression (Ryan & Diaz, 2011). Although many families may be unprepared for the disclosure of an LGBT youth, not all parents are completely rejecting of their child's sexual orientation or gender identity expression. Many parents affected by the child welfare system are burdened with their own histories of trauma or become the source of trauma, and the effects of this on their children are particularly devastating. Some parents known to the child welfare system may have their own histories of trauma that may be triggered by interactions with staff. It is also important to consider the ways in which issues related to a child's sexual orientation or gender identity expression may be traumatic for parents, particularly if this goes against their cultural or religious upbringing or beliefs (Heiden-Rootes, Wiegand, & Bono, 2018). Given the risk of trauma resulting from family rejection among LGBTQ youth, engaging families and helping them support their LGBTQ children is critical to success (SAMHSA, 2014b).

Trauma-sensitive agencies need to find ways to educate and to work with parents about trauma and its impact on their child and their families. Adopting a trauma-informed approach to working with parents who may have experienced trauma involves being flexible, maintaining a respectful and empathic tone, and ensuring that parents understand the process and have opportunities to give their opinions. Trauma-sensitive agencies also consider cultural factors when engaging with youth and their families, such as how to greet families; what topics may be difficult to address; what a staff member does or does not know about a family's cultural norms, values, or beliefs; and a particular group's experiences with systems, including education and behavioral health. Specific strategies for engaging with families of LGBT youth, as identified by the Family Acceptance Project, include the following (Ryan, 2009a; Ryan, 2009b; Ryan & Diaz, 2011; SAMHSA, 2014a):

- Do not buy into the myth that all families are unaccepting of their child's sexual orientation and/or gender identity expression. Meet families where they are.
- Permit and encourage parents and caregivers to tell their story.
- Educate parents and caregivers about the development of sexual orientation and gender identity.
- Educate families on the important role they play in protecting and supporting their LGBT child.
- Provide additional resources and be prepared to go with the family if they feel uncomfortable attending alone.
- Assess the level of family rejection or acceptance.
- Help families identify how to utilize supportive behaviors and language.
- Work to support positive changes or adjustments among families who are more ambivalent toward or are rejecting of their child's gender identity or sexual orientation.

Systems Approaches

Sixth Domain: Collaborate Across Systems

Exposure to trauma is common across all child welfare and youth-serving systems. LGBTQ youth exposed to trauma often have complex needs that cross multiple service systems. Collaboration and integration of care across service systems is a key component of trauma-informed care. When one system is trauma informed but another is not, there is likely to be a discrepancy in the quality of care that can compromise success for youth. For LGBTQ youth, a negative experience in one system can erode trust and decrease the likelihood that they will seek out additional support in any service settings and may—as some of the youth in the narratives above suggested—resort to living on the streets rather than engaging in systems designed to "care" for them.

Recognizing that the environment outside the organization is often actively hostile to LGBTQ youth, child welfare agencies must also be committed to external change and advocacy efforts as well. This may mean participating in an advocacy campaign to end discriminatory language in contracts and/or attending mainstream conferences to insert content and language about LGBTQ issues. Affirming organizations must also be prepared to advocate for LGBTQ youth in community schools, in local adolescent treatment settings, in juvenile justice settings, and in family agencies. Further, organizational leaders must also be prepared to educate local, state, and national politicians and policy makers and funders about the needs of LGBTQ youth.

As the 21st century progresses, child welfare and youth workers continue to play a critical role in developing young people. Child welfare has historically had a cyclical interest in certain subjects: youth suicide, violence, substance abuse, and homelessness. All are worthwhile issues that require our best efforts, but the needs of LGBTQ youth should not be viewed as the "issue du jour" of child welfare work. Sexual orientation and gender identity expression issues are too vital to continue to be overlooked. A particular LGBTQ client might trigger a plethora of attention at the time, only to fade from view when the next issue presents itself. Dealing with LGBTQ youth issues in an intermittent manner is a mistake. Organizations must continue to diligently develop training, assess their own ability or inability to respond to the needs of LGBTQ youth, and address new approaches to competent practice with these youths and their families. For an organization to be consistently sensitive to the needs of its clients, efforts to create affirming environments and to transform existing ones must be realized. If organizations are guided by the same principles that embrace diversity and can translate these into concrete action, LGBTQ youth will be better served.

Providers looking to deliver the highest-quality care for LGBTQ youth must commit to ensuring that all systems understand the unique needs of this group. Strategies for collaborating to serve LGBTQ youth across sectors include the following (Helfgott & Gonsoulin, 2012; Lazear et al., 2012):

- Establish a joint commitment to supporting LGBTQ youth.
- Ensure consistent language and a consistent level of understanding and support for LGBTQ youth across service systems.
- Support cross-system awareness and knowledge building related to trauma and its impact on LGBTQ youth.
- Foster a shared commitment to improving outcomes for LGBTQ youth across youth-serving systems.

- Promote consistent policies and practices across youth-serving systems (e.g., non-discrimination policies, affirmative services and supports).
- Share resources across service systems.
- Create partnerships with providers in the community who specialize in LGBTQ youth.
- Help youth connect to and navigate various service settings.

Conclusion

Although LGBTQ youth in child welfare systems have experienced greater acceptance and understanding in the past 30 years, many child welfare organizations may still actively discriminate against LGBTQ youth. In other cases, the organization's inattentiveness to the trauma-informed needs of LGBTQ youth will send a clear signal that they are not welcome.

An organization's commitment to LGBTQ youth involves more than one-shot training, affirming posters, and books. It is critical to recognize that the internal structure of the organization, as reflected in its policies and public information materials, also need to be evaluated. Training and educational efforts may assist staff in developing their competence in working with a particular population, but written policies and what the outside community knows about the organization may also need to be altered in order to affect real change.

However, regardless of the organizational changes that must occur, the most powerful influence in an LGBTQ young person's life is the individual contact and the ability to form a relationship with a competent and caring adult. While the organizational structure can set the stage for an LGBTQ-affirming environment where a young LGBTQ person can heal from trauma, socialize, learn, and find a safe place to be themselves, it is the individual, LGBTQ- and trauma-competent worker with whom they will engage, connect, and possibly disclose the most personal information.

Trauma-informed child welfare and youth-serving systems seek to remove trauma as a barrier to success by cultivating environments where youth can be most fully and authentically themselves. This mission is vital for supporting LGBTQ youth, who so often experience additional trauma within their families, communities, and systems that are designed to protect them.

DISCUSSION RELATED TO CASE APPLICATION

1. What are three elements of trauma experienced by Hamid that you can cull from reading his narrative?
2. How would you work with Josie to assist her in dealing with the trauma she experienced within her family system?

3. What two things could an organization do to address the trauma which Martin experienced?
4. What interventions would you encourage the agency to use in helping Mauri address his long-standing trauma from foster care?

References

Aarons, G. A., & Palinkas, L. A. (2007). Implementation of evidence-based practice in child welfare: Service provider perspectives. *Administrative Policy Mental Health, 34*(4), 411–419.

Butler, L., Critelli, F., & Rinfrette, E. S. (2011). Trauma-informed care and mental health. *Directions in Psychiatry, 31*(3), 197–212.

Clements, J. A., & Rosenwald, M. (2007). Foster parents' perspectives on LGB youth in the child welfare system. *Journal of Gay & Lesbian Social Services, 19*(1), 57–69.

Copeland, W. E., Keeler, G., Angold, A., & Costello, E. (2007). Traumatic events and posttraumatic stress in childhood. *Archives of General Psychiatry, 64*(5), 577–584.

De Pedro, K. T., Lynch, J., & Esqueda, M. (2018). Understanding safety, victimization and school climate among rural lesbian, gay, bisexual, transgender, and questioning (LGBTQ) youth. *Journal of LGBT Youth, 15*(4), 265–279.

Dettlaff, A. J., Washburn, M., Vogel, N., & Carr, L. C. (2017). *Sexual minority youth in the child welfare system: Prevalence, characteristics and risks for a nationally representative sample.* Manuscript submitted for publication.

Dorsey, S., Burns, B. J., Southerland, D. G., Cox, J., Wagner, H., & Farmer, E. Z. (2012). Prior trauma exposure for youth in treatment foster care. *Journal of Child and Family Studies, 21*(5), 816–824.

Feinstein, R., Greenblatt, A., Hass, L., Kohn, S., & Rana, J. (2001). *Justice for All? A Report on Lesbian, Gay, Bi-Sexual and Transgendered Youth in the New York Juvenile Justice System.* New York: Urban Justice Center (citing Joint Task Force of New York City's Child Welfare Administration and the Council of Family and Child Caring Agencies, Improving Services for Gay and Lesbian Youth in NYC's Child Welfare System: A Task Force Report).

Friedman, M. S., Marshal, M. P., Guadamuz, T. E., Wei, C., Wong, C. F., Saewyc, E. M., & Stall, R. (2011). A meta-analysis of disparities in childhood sexual abuse, parental physical abuse, and peer victimization among sexual minority and sexual nonminority individuals. *American Journal of Public Health, 10* (8), 1481–1494.

Gandy, M. E., McCarter, S. A., & Portwood, S. G. (2013). Service providers' attitudes toward LGBTQ youth. *Residential Treatment for Children & Youth, 30*(3), 168–186.

Gerrity, E., & Folcarelli, C. (2008). *Child traumatic stress: What every policymaker should know.* Durham, NC, and Los Angeles: National Center for Child Traumatic Stress.

Greeson, J. K. P., Briggs, E. C., Kisiel, C. L., Layne, C. M., Ake, G. S., Ko, S. J., ... Fairbank, J.A. (2011). Complex trauma and mental health in children and adolescents placed in foster care: Findings from the National Child Traumatic Stress Network. *Child Welfare, 90*(6), 91–108.

Guarino, K., Soares, P., Konnath, K., Clervil, R., & Bassuk, E. (2009). Trauma-informed organizational toolkit. Rockville, MD: Center for Mental Health Services, Substance Abuse and Mental Health Services Administration, Daniels Fund, National Child Traumatic Stress Network, and W. K. Kellogg Foundation.

Heiden-Rootes, K., Wiegand, A., & Bono, D. (2018). Sexual minority adults: A national survey on depression, religious fundamentalism, parent relationship quality & acceptance. *Journal of Marital and Family Therapy, 2*(15), 112–121.

Helfgott, K. P., & Gonsoulin, S. G. (2012). Standards of care for LGBT youth. In S. K. Fisher, J. M. Poirier, & G. M. Blau (Eds.), *Improving Emotional and Behavioral Outcomes for LGBT Youth: A Guide for Professionals* (pp. 141–158). Baltimore: Brookes.

Horvath, K. J., Remafedi, G., Fisher, S. K., & Walrath, C. (2012). Addressing suicide and self-harming behaviors among LGBT youth in systems of care. In S. K. Fisher, J. M. Poirier, & G. M. Blau (Eds.), *Improving Emotional and Behavioral Outcomes for LGBT Youth: A Guide for Professionals* (pp. 189–206). Baltimore: Brookes.

Irvine, A., & Canfield, A. (2016). The overrepresentation of lesbian, gay, bisexual, questioning, gender nonconforming and transgender youth within the child welfare to juvenile justice crossover population. *Journal of Gender, Social Policy & the Law, 24*, 243–261.

Jim Casey Youth Opportunities Initiative. (2016). *Accelerating race equity, inclusion, and well-being for young people: A data packer to support the conversation.* Baltimore: Author.

Kramer, T. L., Sigel, B. A., Conners-Burrow, N. A., Savary, P. E., & Tempel, A. (2013). A statewide introduction of trauma-informed care in a child welfare system. *Children and Youth Services Review, 35*(1), 19–24.

Lazear, K. J., Pires, S. A., Forssell, S. L., & Mallery, C. J. (2012). Building systems of care to support effective therapeutic and programmatic interventions and resources for LGBT youth and their families. In S. K. Fisher, J. M. Poirier, & G. M. Blau (Eds.), *Improving Emotional and Behavioral Outcomes for LGBT Youth: A Guide for Professionals* (pp. 111–126). Baltimore: Brookes.

Lorthridge, J., Evans, M., Heaton, L., Stevens, L., & Phillips, L. (2018). Strengthening family connections and support for youth in foster care who identify as LGBTQ: Findings from the PII-RISE evaluation. *Child Welfare, 96*(1), 53–78.

Maccio, E. M., & Ferguson-Colvin, K. (2016). Services to LGBTQ runaway and homeless youth: Gaps and recommendations. *Children and Youth Services Review, 63*, 47–57.

Mallon, G. P. (2020). *A Practice Guide for Foster Parents Caring for LGBTQ Youth.* Baton Rouge: Louisiana Department of Children and Family Services.

Mallon, G. P. (2018a). *A Practice Guide for Working with LGBTQ Youth in the Child Welfare System.* Baton Rouge: Louisiana Department of Children and Family Services.

Mallon, G. P. (Ed.). (2017). *Social Work Practice with Lesbian, Gay, Bisexual, and Transgender People* (3rd ed.). New York: Routledge.

Mallon, G. P. (Ed.). (2009). *Social Work Practice with Transgender and Gender Variant Youth* (2nd ed.). New York: Routledge.

Mallon, G. P. (1994). *We Don't Exactly Get the Welcome Wagon: The Experiences of Gay and Lesbian Adolescents in Child Welfare Systems*. New York: Columbia University Press.

Mallory, C., Brown, C. N. T., & Conron, K. J. (2018). *Conversion therapy and LGBT youth*. Los Angeles: The Williams Institute.

Martin, M., Down, L., & Erney, R. (2016). *Out of the Shadows: Supporting LGBTQ Youth in Child Welfare through Cross-System Collaboration*. Washington, DC: Center for the Study of Social Policy.

National Child Traumatic Stress Network. (2013). *Child Welfare Trauma Training Toolkit*. http://www.nctsn.org/products/child-welfare-trauma-training-toolkit-2008

National Child Traumatic Stress Network. (2012). *Child-Parent Psychotherapy (CPP)*. http://www.nctsn.org/sites/default/files/assets/pdfs/cpp_general.pdf

Nguyen, A., & Lau, B. D. (2018). Collecting sexual orientation and gender identity information: Filling the gaps in sexual and gender minority health. *Medical Care, 56*(3), 205–207.

Paul, J. (2018). Under the radar: Exploring support for lesbian, gay, bisexual transgender, queer and questioning (LGBTQ) young people transitioning from foster care to emerging adulthood. Doctoral dissertation. University of Wisconsin–Madison.

Perez-Carrillo, S. (2018). *Youth Survey Reveals Significant Disparities for Youth of Color and LGBT Youth*. Denver: Colorado Children's Campaign.

Poirier, J., Wilkie, S., Sepulveda, K., & Uruchima, T. (2018). The Jim Casey Youth Opportunities Initiative: Experiences of and disparities related to youth who are LGBTQ. *Child Welfare, 96*(1), 1–26.

Roberts, A. L., Rosario, M., Corliss, H. L., Koenen, K. C., & Austin, S. B. (2012a). Childhood gender nonconformity: A risk indicator for childhood abuse and posttraumatic stress in youth. *Pediatrics, 129*, 410–417.

Roberts, A. L., Rosario, M., Corliss, H. L., Koenen, K. C., & Austin, S. B. (2012b). Elevated risk of posttraumatic stress in sexual minority youths: Mediation by childhood abuse and gender nonconformity. *American Journal of Public Health, 102*(8), 1587–1593.

Ryan, C. (2009a). Helping families support their lesbian, gay, bisexual, and transgender (LGBT) children. Washington, DC: National Center for Cultural Competence, Georgetown University Center for Child and Human Development.

Ryan, C. (2009b). Supportive families, healthy children: Helping families with lesbian, gay, bisexual and transgender children. San Francisco: Family Acceptance Project, Marian Wright Edelman Institute, San Francisco State University.

Ryan, C., & Diaz, R. (2011). Family Acceptance Project: Intervention guidelines and strategies. San Francisco: Family Acceptance Project.

Ryan, C., Huebner, D., Diaz, R. M., & Sanchez, J. (2009). Family rejection as a predictor of negative health outcomes in white and Latino lesbian, gay, and bisexual young adults. *Pediatrics, 123*, 346–352.

Ryan, C., Russell, S. T., Huebner, D. M., Diaz, R., & Sanchez, J. (2010). Family acceptance in adolescence and the health of LGBT young adults. *Journal of Child and Adolescent Psychiatric Nursing, 23*(4), 205–213.

Shelton, J., Poirier, J., Wheeler, C., & Abramovich, A. (2018). Reversing erasure of youth and young adults who are LGBTQ and access homelessness services: Asking about sexual orientation, gender identity, and pronouns. *Child Welfare, 96*(2), 1–28.

Shireman, J. F. (2015). *Critical Issues in Child Welfare.* New York: Columbia University Press.

Sikerwar, P., & Rider, E. (2015). *Transgender youth in child welfare settings.* New York: National Center for Child Welfare Excellence at the Silberman School of Social Work at Hunter College.

Substance Abuse and Mental Health Services Administration (SAMHSA). (2014a). SAMHSA's concept of trauma and guidance for a trauma-informed approach (HHS Publication No. [SMA] 14-4884). Rockville, MD: Substance Abuse and Mental Health Services Administration.

Substance Abuse and Mental Health Services Administration (SAMHSA). (2014b). A practitioner's resource guide: Helping families to support their LGBT children (HHS Publication No. PEP14-LGBTKIDS). Rockville, MD: Author.

Substance Abuse and Mental Health Services Administration (SAMHSA). (2015). Ending conversion therapy: Supporting and affirming LGBTQ youth (HHS Publication No. [SMA] 15-4928). Rockville, MD: Author.

Toner, J. (2013). Rural social workers' perceptions of training needs for working with LGBTQ-identified youth in the foster care system. *Contemporary Rural Social Work, 5,* 65–84.

Washburn, M., Good, M., Lucadamo, S., Weber, K., Bettancourt, B., & Dettlaff, A. J. (2018). Yes We Can Allegheny: Implementing SOGIE Inclusive System Improvements in Child Welfare. *Child Welfare, 96*(1), 99–124.

Weeks, A., Altman, D., Stevens, A., Lorthridge, J., Heaton, L. (2018). Strengthening the workforce to support youth in foster care who identify as LGBTQ+ through increasing LGBTQ+ competency: Trainers' experience with bias. *Child Welfare 96*(2), 125–177.

Weiner, D. A., Schneider, A., & Lyons, J. S. (2009). Evidence-based treatments for trauma among culturally diverse foster care youth: Treatment retention and outcomes. *Children and Youth Services Review, 31,* 1199–1205.

Wilber, S. (2013). *Guidelines for managing information related to the sexual orientation and gender identity and expression of children in child welfare systems.* Oakland, CA: Putting Pride into Practice Project, Family Builders by Adoption.

Wilson, B. D. M., Cooper, K., Kastanis, A., & Nezhad, S. (2014). Sexual and gender minority youth in foster care: Assessing disproportionality and disparities in Los Angeles. Los Angeles: The Williams Institute, UCLA School of Law.

Wilson, B. D. M., & Kastanis, A. A. (2015). Sexual and gender minority disproportionality and disparities in child welfare: A population-based study. *Children and Youth Services Review, 58,* 11–17.

Winter, E. A. (2013). *Lesbian, gay, bisexual, transgendered, questioning, and queer youth: The challenge for child welfare.* In H. Cahalane (Ed.), *Contemporary Issues in Child Welfare Practice* (pp. 127–157). New York: Springer-Verlag.

Yarbrough, J. (2012). *LGBTQ youth permanency.* New York: National Resource Center for Permanency and Family Connections.

Figure Credits

Img. 10.1: Copyright © 2015 Depositphotos/marcbruxelle.
Img. 10.2: Copyright © 2018 Depositphotos/NeydtStock.
Img. 10.3: Copyright © 2014 Depositphotos/jakubzak92.

CHAPTER • 11

Aging Out

Transitioning Youth to Adulthood

Jessica Yang and Michele D. Hanna

Overview of Chapter and Population

Of the 250,103 children and youth who exited foster care in 2018, a large percentage achieved permanency through reunification with a parent or primary caretaker (49%), followed by adoption (25%), or guardianship (11%) (USDHHS, 2019). A small yet alarming number exited foster care through legal ***emancipation*** or aging out (7%, or 17,844) (U.S. Department of Health and Human Services [USDHHS], 2019). According to the **Adoption and Foster Care Analysis Reporting System (AFCARS)** data, the remaining 8% exit foster care through non-adoptive relative care (7%), transfer of custody to an agency outside of the state or tribe (1%), running away (<1%), or death while in foster care (<1%). Emancipation is a legal term meaning that the child has reached the legal age of majority (usually 18 years) according to the law, or through marriage, entering the military, or judicial determination—legally becoming an adult and supposedly no longer in need of a legal guardian (USLegal, n.d.). Although the terms are used interchangeably, this chapter focuses on youth who exit foster care due to age or *aging out* (National Data Archive on Child Abuse and Neglect [NDACAN], 2019). Since the passing of the Fostering Connections to Success and Increasing Adoptions Act of 2008, which is discussed in more detail later in this chapter, approximately 46 states, the District of Columbia, and American Samoa provide services to youth after the age of 18, including, but not limited to, continuation in foster care, supervised independent, or transitional living as long as the youth is pursuing educational or employment goals (Child Welfare Information Gateway, 2017). Eligibility for extended care varies from state to state, as do the services provided (Juvenile Law Center, 2018). In some states youth may opt to extend their stay in foster care until 21 with no conditions, while in other states the youth must meet criteria such as needing to complete high school, having special needs, or a disability. Services and supports often center around education, employment, and health care; however, they may vary on the extent, the criteria or access, and the limitations. The Juvenile Law Center has created a searchable tool, the National Extended Foster Care Review, for youth and child welfare professionals to learn about the extended foster care policies in their state (Juvenile Law Center, 2019).

Unfortunately, the majority of the youth turning 18 opt not to take advantage of extended foster care services (Fryar, Jordan, & DeVooght, 2017). While these youth may legally be adults with the legal right to make decisions they presume to be in their own best interest, the decision not to enroll in an extended foster care program, when available, is troubling. Decades of research affirm that overall outcomes for this population are less than ideal (Festinger, 1983; Barth, 1990; Courtney & Barth, 1996; Courtney, Piliavin, Grogan-Kaylor, & Nesmith, 2001; Courtney, Dworsky, Lee, & Raap, 2010; Gypen, Vanderfaeillie, De Maeyer, Belenger, & Van Holen, 2017). Youth who age out of care are at greater risk of experiencing negative outcomes in many domains of psychosocial functioning, including education, employment, homelessness, relationships, physical health, mental health, and criminal justice involvement (Barth, 1990; Courtney, Dworsky, Cusick, Havlicek, Perez, & Keller, 2007; Pecora et al., 2006).

This chapter provides a brief history of youth aging out of care and relevant policies designed to address the needs of this population. An overview of the population, including relevant disproportionality and disparate outcomes across domains of psychosocial functioning, is discussed. Current child welfare practices, pre– and post–aging out, including an integrated systems approach, is presented and applied through a case study example and discussion questions.

Terminology

In this chapter, the term *foster care alumni* will be used to refer to those who have aged out of the system. In addition, the term **independent living** will be applied to services and programs that are provided to youth prior to their aging out of the system that seek to increase the skills of foster youth to prepare them for successful adulthood. Conversely, the term **extended foster care** describes programs and services that meet the needs of youth who are older than 18 years of age but have voluntarily signed themselves back into the jurisdiction of the child welfare system. Lastly, the term **extended care** describes programs and services that are available to youth after they have been discharged from foster care without a permanent home, designed to aid and assist youth with navigating early adulthood, but the youth are not governed by the child welfare system and receive services on a strictly volunteer basis.

History of Foster Care and Older Youth

Foster care in the United States is rooted in the colonial practices of indentured servitude and the later iteration of practice, placing out (Hacsi, 1995). In early America, society's response to the needs of orphaned and dependent children was often to *indenture* or send them to live with other families where they could be raised to adulthood, while simultaneously working and earning a trade. It was also commonplace for children from all class backgrounds to be sent to live in other homes around the age of 13 or 14, formally and informally, to learn a trade, as a primary way of transitioning youth to adulthood (Hacsi, 1995). This practice became less popular as the concept of childhood began to change. Childhood gradually became seen as a time of innocence to be nurtured and cultivated as opposed to simply a biological imperative to be monitored until a child was old enough to work, learn a trade, and contribute to society (Hacsi, 1995). Over time, childhood came to be seen as a period of dependence, and the culture of the family in the United States became one where parents were seen as having primary responsibility and control over their own children (Cunningham, 1998; Rodham, 1973).

In the mid-1800s, as social ills, specifically poverty, began to rapidly increase in the country's urban centers, young children who were either orphaned or whose families were unable to care for them were *placed* with families as opposed to orphanages, where they could receive individual care. Orphanages, or *asylums*, then quickly became crowded with older children and met with criticism from those who felt that children would best be served when placed with families. In an effort to resolve the problem, Charles Loring Brace founded the New York Children's Aid Society (CAS) in 1853 and began the process of *placing out* children with families in the Midwest in what he considered "the best remedy for juvenile pauperism" (Brace, 1872, p. 223).

In his book *The Dangerous Classes of New York*, Brace (1872) provides details of CAS's placing-out program and what came to commonly be known as *orphan trains*—the means by which several thousands of children were taken from urban communities and placed with rural families, primarily farmers. Despite the name, many of these children were not actually orphans, but rather street children and vagrants (Cook, 1995; Hacsi, 1995). While young children were often placed with families and treated as members of the family, older children were more often than not placed for the sole purpose of working the farms. These families were not compensated for taking in the children but rather considered "free" homes. Unlike the previous indenture system, the rationale for placing out children was not so that they could learn a trade or prepare for adulthood but rather that they needed rescuing or protection from their impoverished environment, including their parents, who were often deemed as unworthy and incapable of parenting properly (Brace, 1872; Hacsi, 1995). Over time, Brace placed over 150,000 children (Cook, 1995). A few of the younger children were adopted by the families they were placed with either formally or informally; however, the majority of the children were over 10 years old and only stayed with the placement families until they were old enough to return to their families on their own within a few years of being placed out (Hacsi, 1995).

Near the end of the century and shortly after the turn of the century, the country began to recognize child abuse and neglect as a societal problem that needed to be addressed. Many city governments began passing laws, and agencies were created to aid in the removal of children from homes deemed unfit. Most of these children were placed in free homes, similar to the ones used by CAS. While younger children were most often loved and cared for as new members of the family, older children were expected to work in exchange for being taken in; however, some agencies began to pay adults "board payments" so that these children would not be exploited (Hacsi, 1995). There were many debates through the years as to whether or not homes should be paid for taking in these youth. By the 1920s, many cities were *boarding out* children (i.e., paying adults to board the child) and few were placing out with free families. Boarding out eventually became known as "foster care," and the ages of children placed in care became younger (Hacsi, 1995). Foster care expanded nationwide, especially after the passage of the Social Security Act of 1935 made federal funds available to states to create public child welfare systems. The use of orphanages and institutions gradually decreased, and the use of foster homes increased. Increasingly large numbers of children were being removed from homes, primarily due to poverty and neglect, and growing up in relatively stable nonrelative family homes—some free and some board. Amendments to the Social Security Act in 1961 effectively ended the use of free foster homes when matching federal funds became available to states for children removed and placed in foster care by the courts from families who met the criteria for Aid to Families with Dependent Children (AFDC). Shortly after, the number of children in foster care grew exponentially. Between 1962 and 1972, the foster care population grew by 18% from 272,000 to 319,800, and then it grew by another 67% to 502,000 in 1977 (Barbell & Freundlich, 2001). As the number of children in care continued to rise, child welfare researchers became increasingly concerned about the outcomes for children in foster care (Mnookin, 1973).

The term *foster care drift* was coined to describe the experience of children in long-term foster care, drifting from placement to placement with no real permanency (Maas & Engler, 1959). Maas (1969) reported that children tended to remain in foster care longer when their parents had little to no contact with either the child or the child welfare agency. These children remained in foster care for 10 years or longer, and the majority of them (91%) left care at age 15 or older. Of those children, only 16% returned home, and only 3% were adopted. The majority of the remaining children were reported to leave care for independent living (54%) or under the care of other public agencies, such as mental health, correctional, or other public welfare (22%). These findings, as well as the growing number of children in care, led to a shift in philosophy regarding the use of foster care from an alternative living arrangement to a temporary situation with a focus on *permanency planning*, assuming that children would either return home or be adopted within allotted relatively shortened timeframes (Festinger, 1983).

Long-Term Foster Care

The Adoption Assistance and Child Welfare Act (AACWA) of 1980 was passed to address these issues. AACWA required states to make *reasonable efforts* to 1) prevent the removal of children; and 2) to reunify children removed as soon as possible. AACWA also required that every child receiving foster care maintenance funded through Title IV-E of the Social Security Act have a case plan approved and periodically reviewed by the court no longer than 18 months after the original placement (see Chapter 1). At that time, the courts were charged with determining the child's future plan as either 1) reunification with a parent; 2) continuation in foster care for a specified time; 3) adoption; or 4) continued care on a permanent or long-term basis (aka long-term foster care) (AACWA, 1980; Renne & Mallon, 2005). Unfortunately, this last option became the reality far too often for older children whose parents were unable to correct the conditions that led to removal in a timely fashion or who passed the age assumed at the time to be "adoptable."

It was not until 1997, when the Adoption and Safe Families Act (ASFA) was passed, that the concept of long-term foster care was challenged legislatively. Focusing on permanency, ASFA strongly promoted adoption of children who could not return safely to their parents within much shorter timeframes than AACWA. Reasonable efforts no longer focused on the preservation of family or parental rights but rather on meeting these goals of permanency. For children who were not reunified with parents, adopted, or exited care through guardianship, ASFA replaced the case plan goal of long-term foster care, with the new concept of ***another planned permanent living arrangement*** **(APPLA)**. The intent was that child welfare and the courts would work to identify and make a plan based on the unique individual needs of the child that may not be as permanent as reunification, guardianship, or adoption but more stable than regular foster care. Unfortunately, the nebulousness of the definition of AAPLA did little to change practice—as with the goal of long-term foster care, APPLA became the default goal for older youth for whom a more permanent plan was not viable. In response, the Preventing Sex Trafficking and Strengthening Families Act of 2014 set forth specific requirements for the agencies and the courts when choosing APPLA as a permanency goal and restricted the use of APPLA as a permanency option to youth age 16 or older (Capacity Building Center for States, 2016) (see Box 11.1).

BOX 11.1. Agency and Court Requirements When APPLA Is the Selected Permanency Plan

When APPLA Is the Selected or Continued Permanency Plan

At each permanency hearing, the agency must:

- Document the intensive, ongoing, and unsuccessful efforts for family placement, including efforts to locate biological family members using search technologies such as social media.

Box 11.1: The Children's Bureau, Selection from "Pathways to Permanancy: Expanding on APPLA Provisions and Youth Engagement to Improve Permanency."

- Ensure youth are asked about their desired permanency outcome.
- Explain why APPLA is the best permanency plan for the youth and why reunification, adoption, guardianship, or placement with a fit relative is not in the youth's best interest.
- Specify steps the agency is taking to ensure the reasonable and prudent parent standard (RPPS) is being followed and provide regular, ongoing opportunities for the youth to engage in age-appropriate and developmentally appropriate activities.

At each permanency hearing, the court must:

- Determine whether the agency has documented the intensive, ongoing, unsuccessful efforts to achieve reunification, adoption, guardianship, or placement with a fit and willing relative.
- Ask youth about their desired permanency outcome.
- Make a judicial determination explaining why, as of the date of the hearing, APPLA is the best permanency plan and provide compelling reasons why reunification, adoption, legal guardianship, or placement with a fit and willing relative is not in the youth's best interest.
- Confirm that the agency is taking steps to ensure the RPPS is being exercised and the agency has documented that the youth has regular and ongoing opportunities to engage in age-appropriate and developmentally appropriate activities.

For more information on the specific changes P.L. 113-183 made to APPLA, see "Pathways to Permanency: Collaborating on the APPLA Provisions of P.L. 113-183."

Source: Capacity Building Center for States. (2016, pp. 1–2)

Overview of Older Youth in Foster Care

The percentage of children exiting foster care without legal permanency has averaged 8.85% since 1998, although peaking at 11% in 2009 and declining again steadily since 2012 to the most recent 8% (2016–2017) (USDHHS, 2006–2019). There was no systematic collection of data on foster youth collected prior to AFCARS; however, research indicates that the number of youth exiting via aging out has consistently hovered around 20,000 since at least the late 1980s. In total, since 1998, approximately 421,899 youth have exited care through aging out. Data made available by the National Data Archive on Child buse and Neglect[1] (NDACAN) indicates that annually (2013–2017), on average, 42% of the youth who age out of care are non-Hispanic White, 29% non-Hispanic Black or African American, 20% Hispanic, 5% two or more races, 2% American Indian, 1% Asian,

1 The data used in this publication was made available by NDACAN, Cornell University, Ithaca, NY, and has been used with permission. Data from the AFCARS was originally reported to the Children's Bureau. Funding for the project provided by the Children's Bureau, Administration on Children, Youth and Families, Administration for Children and Families, U.S. Department of Health and Human Services.

and less than 1% Pacific Islander, with the remaining 1% unknown. As noted below in Table 11.1, in this data African American or Black youth age 17 are only 16% of the U.S. youth population, meaning that they are overrepresented in the aging-out population as are American Indians (2% vs. 1.5%), Pacific Islanders (1% vs. .3%), and youth who identify as two or more races (5% vs. 3%). Hispanic or Latino youth appear to be representative (20% vs. 19.9%) and Whites underrepresented (42% vs. 59%).

National Youth in Transition Database (NYTD)

The National Youth in Transition Database (NYTD), created as part of the Foster Care Independence Act (P.L. 106-169), collects both demographic data and data on outcomes for youth who have aged out of foster care by surveying youth who receive independent living services through child welfare. States began submitting data in May 2011 with the first Database Brief published in October 2012 (Children's Bureau, 2019).

The NYTD Database Brief #7 provides information on the cohort of youth surveyed at ages 17, 19, and 21 between 2014 and 2018 (NYTD, 2019). Of this cohort, approximately 16,480 (69%) of the 23,780 youth eligible completed the survey responded at baseline (age 17). This cohort was surveyed while still in foster care during FY 2014,[2] meaning that they more than likely aged out of care during FY 2015. At age 19, 72% of 12,309, or 8,898 youth, completed the survey, and at age 21, 7,799 (64%) of the 12,273 eligible completed the survey. The response rate varied by state, ranging from 14%–100% for all age groups. To account for this wide discrepancy in response rates, results are "weighted" so that they may be more representative of the youth population as a whole. The reasons for the lack of participation included the youth being incapacitated, incarcerated, missing, unable to locate, deceased, or refusal to participate.

Table 11.1 provides racial and ethnic demographic data of the youth from the NYTD cohort data, in comparison to the U.S. Census data and the NDACAN data for the comparable age group. Highlighted within the table is the *disproportionality* as it relates to youth of color. In reviewing this data, it is important to note that 1) the NYTD demographic data is relatively similar for all races across the three points in time, even though the number of respondents decreases with each survey; and 2) American Indians and Blacks are disproportionately *overrepresented* in all of the foster care and aged-out data. Interestingly, Pacific Islanders are not overrepresented in the NDACAN data; however, they are overrepresented in the NYTD data. Youth who identify as being two or more races are also *overrepresented* in the NDACAN data; however, the NYTD data does not account for this racial categorization.

2 FY refers to the Federal Fiscal Year. FY 2014 runs from October 1, 2013, to September 30, 2014.

TABLE 11.1. **Race and Ethnicity of Youth Emancipating from Care**

	U.S. Population Age 17	Aged Out of Foster Care FY2015	Cohort 2 Age 17 (in Foster Care) N=16,480	Cohort 2 Age 19 N=8,898	Cohort 2 Age 21 N=7,799
Source	U.S. Census	NDACAN	NYTD	NYTD	NYTD
American Indian or Alaska Native	**.9%**	**1.8%**	**3%**	**3%**	**4%**
Asian	4.8%	.8%	2%	2%	2%
Black or African American	**14.2%**	**28.3%**	**35%**	**36%**	**34%**
Hispanic or Latino	22.3%	19.9%	21%	20%	21%
Native Hawaiian or Pacific Islander	**.2%**	.2%	1%	1%	1%
Two or More	**3.3%**	**5.5%**	–	–	–
Unknown/ Declined	–	1.1%	8%	7%	6%
White	54.4%	42.5%	59%	58%	61%

Sources: NYTD (2019); U.S. Census Bureau (2016). NDACAN.

Trauma-Informed Care

Youth who age out of foster care carry with them immense trauma from childhood, including the abuse and neglect that resulted in their placement in foster care initially. Sadly, many of these youth also encounter abuse or neglect at the hands of foster parents or kinship providers as they move through the foster care system (Havlicek & Courtney, 2016). The process and immediate aftermath of emancipating from care may compound the trauma experiences that are carried by these individuals. For some, the experience of leaving care is traumatic as they are often discharged from the system with little to no communication or preparation and exit into homelessness because they are simply grossly underprepared for the future that awaits them (McCoy, McMillen, & Spitznagel, 2008). Moreover, these youth are highly likely to attempt to reestablish the connections with their biological families, even if those bonds were terminated or severed years prior by the system or the courts. This may prove to be a potentially dangerous decision, as often youth will find that when they return home they are simply reintegrating into the abusive and neglectful patterns that existed before their entry into foster care (Yang, 2017). Finally, many youth carry with them the shame or stigma of having been a foster child and seek desperately to hide this label at all costs. This may result in an open refusal of help from the system (including the use of extended foster care) because they so greatly desire to be free from the label and the associated stigma.

Mitigating the trauma faced by these youth is not easy, given the scope and complexity of the compound trauma that many have experienced since early childhood. However, some approaches, such as ensuring that the youth have safe and stable natural mentors (Greeson, Garcia, Kim, & Courtney, 2015) to fall back on, may make it less likely that they will try to return home or reignite potentially negative relationships with biological family members. Working with youth to provide adequate mental health care prior to their emancipation can help to reduce the weight and stigma of the foster child label (Yang, 2017). Sadly, for many, the negative impact of childhood trauma may last well into adulthood, potentially shaping relationships and decisions for decades to come and require years of therapeutic intervention.

Practice Challenges with the Population

Research exploring the needs, experiences, and outcomes of youth aging out of care is vastly expanding over several decades and clearly demonstrates that youth who age out of care are a high-needs population. Youth who age out of care are at greater risk of experiencing negative outcomes in many domains of psychosocial functioning, including education, employment, homelessness, relationships, physical health, mental health, and criminal justice involvement (Barth, 1990; Courtney et al., 2007; Pecora et al., 2006). There are a myriad of reasons that youth age out of foster care, including but not limited to, inability to reunite with caregivers, not being selected or matched for adoption, or because they chose not to be adopted. There is also considerable stigma about older youth in care, such as the notion that they are harder to adopt or that they have greater levels of need compared to younger children in foster care (Avery, 2010). Regardless of the reason why the youth aged out of care, federal legislation dictates that certain services should be provided to these young people prior to their exit from care. The primary service offered to youth who are aging out of foster care is independent living programs (ILPs). The primary mechanism for facilitating ILPs is the John H. Chafee Foster Care Independence Program, or as it is commonly referred to, the "Chafee program."

Image 11.1

The Chafee program is part of Title IV-E of the Social Security Act and was codified under the Foster Care Independence Act (FICA) in 1999 (P.L. 106-169). The Chafee program provides federal funding and programmatic stipulations for the services to be provided to youth in preparation for aging out (P.L. 106-169). These services vary widely and can include, but are not limited to, life skills education (such as budgeting, preparing meals, self-care skills, etc.), mental health education and support, housing education and support, assistance with obtaining and maintaining transportation, gathering legal documents (birth certificate, social security card, etc.), and other skills necessary for independence after their exit from foster care. Additionally, the Chafee program contains a separate provision that specifically provides funding and support for educational supporting, mentoring, and coaching (Fernandes-Alcantara, 2019). This component, known as the Educational Training Vouchers program, awards up to $5,000 per year for a young person to obtain postsecondary education at a qualified institution of higher learning.

Finally, youth aging out of foster care are also afforded the option to extend their stay in care. Extended foster care enables the child to stay under the care of the state, thereby providing comprehensive care and services to youth beyond their 18th birthday, using federal dollars provided through the Title IV-E program. This practice has been shown to reduce the likelihood of experiencing negative outcomes typically associated with aging out of foster care (such as homelessness, substance use, unemployment, etc.); however, the availability and eligibility for this program varies tremendously by state (Fernandes-Alcantara, 2017).

Health and Mental Health

The short-term and lifetime prevalence rates of mental illness among youth who emancipate from the foster care system range between 15% and 65% (Brandford & English, 2004; Villegas & Pecora, 2012). Depression, PTSD, and substance use disorders are among the most common mental health conditions that these youth face, with males more likely to experience struggles with substance use (Courtney et al., 2007). In comparison, youth exiting care are more likely than youth who were never in care to meet diagnostic criteria for a substance use disorder (Stott, 2013), and as many as 12% of former foster youth meet diagnostic criteria for a substance use disorder (Courtney et al., 2007).

Nearly 20% of youth aging out of foster care report that their health is subpar (Courtney et al., 2007), with 12% indicating that their health severely affects their daily living (Courtney et al., 2007; Zlotnick, Tamm, & Soman, 2012). Research has consistently shown that up to 75% of females who emancipate from care will experience an unplanned pregnancy (if they haven't already) in the first 4 years after they leave foster care (Pecora et al., 2006; Scannapieco et al., 2016).

Education

Perhaps one of the best-studied psychosocial domains with regard to emancipated foster youth is education. Over the last several decades, the number of foster youth who exit high school with a diploma has remained steadily near 50% (Yang, 2017). However, the range varies tremendously, as some studies report as few as 40% of emancipating youth have a high school diploma (or equivalency), and some report as many as 97% (Gypen, Vanderfaeillie, De Maeyer, Belenger, & Holen, 2017). This stands in stark contrast to the nearly 85% of youth from the general population, on average, who will obtain a high school diploma each year in the United States. Many foster youth will eventually obtain a diploma or a GED (Courtney et al., 2007; Pecora et al., 2006), but the time lost obtaining a GED—as well as the stigma associated with a GED over a diploma—can cost these youth many career opportunities and earning potential (Atkinson, 2008). Many foster youth indicate that they wish to attend college; however, due to difficulties and delays in obtaining a high school education, barriers to attending college, and lack of support once enrolled, the collegiate graduation rate among former foster youth is quite low (Courtney, Terao, & Bost, 2004; Courtney et al., 2011a; Jones, 2010; Wiltz, 2017). Of the youth who enter into college, an alarming number will drop out before completion, many within the first year (Gypen et al., 2017). Youth who aged out of foster care often face tremendous barriers once enrolled in postsecondary institutions that will prevent them from completing their degrees. Lack of degree completion is due in part to the individual's lack of preparation prior to entering college. Many aged-out youth had tumultuous educational experiences during their tenure in foster care, resulting in less educational continuity, less representation in college preparatory courses, and less opportunity for mentorship and support from a stable and consistent adult (Day, Dworsky, Fogarty, & Damashek, 2011; Geiger, Hanrahan, Cheung, & Lietz, 2016). Additionally, many foster alumni face issues with continuity once enrolled in a postsecondary institution due to transferring institutions, experiencing academic probation and suspension, and lack of financial resources to continue. In fact, financial difficulties are one of the single most impactful factors regarding whether or not an alumnus graduates from college. Youth struggle to navigate the world of higher education and financial aid, often require a job while in college to support basic needs such as food and transportation, and many are homeless without the use of a dormitory and require additional housing support during breaks and summer vacations (Day et al., 2011; Geiger et al., 2016).

Employment

On average, less than a quarter of foster care alumni will graduate with a college degree by the time they are in their mid-to-late twenties (Courtney et al., 2010; Day et al., 2011). This lack of formal education at the secondary and postsecondary levels often limits the type of job as well as the earning potential creating barriers to the quality and stability of employment available to people who aged out of foster care (Atkinson, 2008). Furthermore, many former foster youth report underemployment and difficulty in meeting their financial needs (Dworsky, 2005; Goerge et al., 2002; Pecora et al., 2006). Emancipated foster youth earn, on average, nearly $9,000 less per year than their peers without a history of foster care and live well below the federal poverty line (Courtney et al., 2010; Gypen et al., 2017; Naccarato, Brophy, & Courtney, 2010). Because of the immense financial difficulties that these individuals face upon their exit from foster care, many former foster youth engage in criminalized activities such as survival sex (Atkinson, 2008) to meet their needs.

Homelessness

Nearly half of the youth exiting care are likely to experience homelessness at some point after they leave the foster care system (Dworsky & Courtney, 2009; Snyder et al., 2016). In fact, many youth will experience homelessness immediately upon exit from care due to poor discharge planning and subsequently will engage in couch surfing or sleeping in their car to obtain shelter (Barth, 1990). Interestingly, many youth who are technically homeless do not consider themselves to be homeless and will likely avoid services because they do not want to be associated with that label. For many, homelessness is temporary; however, research indicates that 46% of former foster youth experience homelessness up to age 26, well past the age of exit from care (Dworsky, Napolitano, & Courtney, 2013). Additionally, approximately 20% of all former foster youth are likely to experience chronic homelessness, lasting well into adulthood (Fowler, Toro, & Miles, 2009). Sadly, once a former foster youth has experienced homelessness, they are likely to remain homeless longer than youth without a history of foster care (Bender, Yang, Ferguson, & Thompson, 2015). Foster alumni who experience homelessness often struggle to exit into stable housing for a myriad of complex and interconnected reasons. Many alumni have a high school diploma or less, limiting the types and availability of employment opportunities. Furthermore, many youth who experience homelessness struggle with substance abuse and other mental health diagnoses. Due to lack of health care and stable housing, they are unable to experience long periods of sobriety or recovery from their conditions, decreasing the likelihood of exiting homelessness (Bender et al., 2015).

Criminal Activity

Youth who have aged out of the foster care system are at an increased risk of experiencing legal trouble after exiting the system. Up to 33% of these youth are arrested at least once, and nearly 41% have spent one night in jail (Courtney et al., 2001; Courtney et al., 2005; Crawford, Pharris, & Dorsett-Burrell, 2018; Reilly, 2003). For some, these challenges may be temporary struggles stemming from chaos or struggle immediately after exit. For others, exposure to law enforcement is because of substance use or petty crime to facilitate substance use. Yet others are engaging in destructive activities such as property damage or violence to others (Courtney et al., 2005). Approximately 37.2% were arrested for a felony crime within 3 years of leaving care (Hook & Courtney, 2011), and many former foster youth (38% to 45%) report ongoing legal trouble or involvement with the law (Benedict, Zuravin, & Stallings, 1996; Reilly, 2003). Roughly 22% of youth respondents to the NYTD surveys reported having been incarcerated in the previous 2 years prior to completing the survey at ages 19 and 21 (Kids Count Data Center, 2018).

These outcomes paint a picture of a population that is experiencing chaotic upheaval, frequent moves, separation from other family members, significant instability, and great needs. However, it is plausible that the chaos associated with aging out of foster care could be the unique expression of the emerging adulthood phase of development for this population. Emerging adulthood is a phase in the span of human development that is characterized by considerable exploration, chaos, and upheaval as a young person settles into an independent adult identity (Arnett, 1998). For non–foster involved youth, this process often takes place during college, where the largely unregulated environment allows for youth to explore who they want to be in their personal and professional lives and the opportunity to develop their worldviews. During this phase of development, behaviors such as casually dating, starting and stopping jobs as part of career exploration, participating in travel, participating in civic activities, and experimenting with worldviews are developmentally normal. Furthermore, during emerging adulthood, many non–foster care affiliated young people have ongoing support (emotional, financial, housing, etc.) from their biological families, often extending into the mid-to-late twenties. In contrast, during this stage, many foster care alumni are struggling to meet and maintain their basic needs. They may or may not have the mental or emotional bandwidth to explore identity, challenge previously held worldviews, or explore what they would desire in a romantic relationship while focusing on where their next meal may come from or where they may be sleeping that night. Finally, the lack of or limited education and subsequent limited employment opportunities means that many former foster youth are unable to explore career paths and often find themselves stuck in minimum wage jobs with little to no mobility.

Relationships and Social Network Needs

Lastly, many of the youth who are emancipating from care lack social networks, and many missed out on pivotal developmental experiences during adolescence, further isolating them from their peers (Yang, 2017). Because of the child welfare system's focus on the protection of vulnerable youth rather than facilitating normalcy, many youth in foster care are not allowed to participate in normal teenage activities because the liability on the youth and the foster care system is far too great (Bruskas, 2008). As these youth move through adolescence without experiencing the normative teenage experiences, such as dating, spending the night with friends, creating normal and healthy social relationships, identifying and engaging with natural mentors, and building social capital, these youth are severely compromised in their ability to navigate social situations in adulthood (Scannapieco, Smith, & Blakeney-Strong, 2016).

Evidence-Based Practices for Working with Youth Who Age Out

Addressing the needs of youth who are aging out or who have aged out of foster care is daunting and challenging under the best of circumstances. The wide array of challenges these youth face, in tandem with their diffuse nature and discontent for the system, makes targeting these individuals after they have left care difficult at best. Since the mid-1980s, states have been charged with providing services to these youth prior to aging out; however, it was not until the late 1990s that funds were provided to assist states with provision of aftercare services. Unfortunately, the services provided have minimal empirical evidence to guide states and caseworkers as to what works and what doesn't. Research continues to indicate dismal outcomes for this population, indicating that more research is needed. This section highlights the services that are most often provided to these youth and a summary of how well these approaches are empirically supported, and suggestions to improve the efficacy of current approaches.

Transition to Adulthood: A Spectrum of Services

The term *independent living services* in child welfare applies to a wide range of services provided to youth to help them as they transition to adulthood. It is important to note that independent living is not a permanency goal (see Chapter 13). Independent living programs are considered age-appropriate services to be provided concurrently while the child's permanency goal is being pursued (Child Welfare Information Gateway, 2019). However, for many youth who reach the age of 16 without having obtained legal permanency, independent living services play a significant role in the case plan designed to successfully help that youth transition to adulthood and prepare them to age out of foster care.

Independent living services have been supported by federal funds since 1985; however, it was not until the passage of the Foster Care Independence Act of 1999 (FCAI) that significant funding was provided to help states provide independent living services through the John H. Chafee Foster Care Independence Program and the federal government was required to develop outcome measures to assess a state's performance related to independent living programs (Barth, Greeson, Zlotnik, & Chintapalli, 2011;

Child Welfare Information Gateway, 2019). Contrary to popular belief, the FCAI did not provide a minimum age requirement for when services were to be provided, other than to state that the purpose of the act was to help youth who were "likely to remain in foster care until 18 years of age" (Sec. 477(a)(2)); however, many states opted to begin services around age 16. FCAI did state that youth could only receive services up to age 21. The Preventing Sex Trafficking and Strengthening Families Act of 2014 gave children ages 14 and up the right to participate in transitional planning to adulthood, and the Family First Prevention Services Act of 2018 extended services to age 23.

Independent living programs, while they vary tremendously between states, counties, and local child welfare offices, all seek to provide youth the skills they will need to function as competent and productive adults. The focus of these programs is often on building skills like financial literacy, healthy and safe relationships, housing, and employment. Specifically, states are to work on preparing these youth for the transition to adulthood by creating, implementing, and supporting case plans in collaboration with teenage youth while addressing issues like financial health, housing, and education. Independent living is also used by some to refer to the idea of "extended foster care"; describing services that are provided to youth after they have aged out and voluntarily signed themselves into the foster care system. These individuals are typically between the ages of 18–23 and still under the jurisdiction of the foster care system. These youth may or may not be placed in a "foster home" of some type where they receive additional services. Independent living programs may also provide services to youth who have legally emancipated from foster care and are not under the jurisdiction of the foster care system, yet are eligible to receive services from the child welfare department based on their status as an "emancipated foster child."

McDaniel, Courtney, Pergamit, and Lowenstein (2014) created a typology of Independent Living Programs as part of their research and evaluation of several Independent Living programs (see Box 11.2). It is important to note that they do not include as a typology programs that focus on the relational needs of youth, a psychosocial need that many programs focus on within the context of the various program types (McDaniel et al., 2014).

The Independent Living Plan

Serving the needs of the youth begins with the creation of an independent living plan. The **independent living plan** is essentially a case plan for the youth that outlines the goals and objectives necessary for that youth to enter into adulthood as self-sufficiently as possible. The Adoption and Safe Families Act (ASFA) requires that an independent living plan be created for every youth age 16 or older in foster care (ASFA, 1997, 42 U.S.C. § 675 (1)(D)). Plans are expected to be created in collaboration between the caseworker and the youth. Together, the youth and caseworker develop a plan with established goals, objectives, and tasks to help the youth become self-sufficient. Plans should use objective criteria, ensure fair and equitable treatment, and assist youth in various stages of achieving independence. Special attention is provided to education, housing, and employment as states are encouraged to assist youth in preparing for ongoing education, stable housing, and employment if needed. In addition, caseworkers are now charged with helping youth to identify and establish adult networks and supports to assist them after they exit from care (see Fostering Connections to Success and Increasing Adoptions Act in Policy section).

The manner in which child welfare staff can help youth in meeting their goals for self-sufficiency varies greatly, although most independent living programs provided to youth are in the form of classroom-based instruction. Typically, youth will come to a central location, often the child welfare office, and they will learn about various topics, such as healthy eating, relationships, budgeting and finances, employment (including résumés and job hunting), and housing. Sometimes these classes will include guest speakers, hands-on activities (such as cooking or shopping), or excursions in the community (such as visiting a local bank). However, the implementation of these programs may differ drastically as they are based on funding, worker capacity, and the needs of the specific youth.

The Fostering Connections to Success and Increasing Adoptions Act of 2008 (P.L. 110-351) requires that child welfare programs work with a youth to develop and have in place a **transition plan** within 90 days of a youth aging out of care (Epstein, 2011). This includes providing them with important documents like their birth certificate, social security card, health insurance card, driver's license or state identification card, and any medical or educational records. In addition, Fostering Connections mandates that the worker use the transition plan as the opportunity to help the youth identify permanent connections or stable adults they can rely on for advice and in case of emergencies (Epstein, 2011).

BOX 11.2. Typology of Independent Living Programs

Typology of Independent Living Programs

	Independent living programs and services	Description
1	Education services	Education services fall broadly into three categories: (1) high school completion programs; (2) college access programs; and (3) college success programs. These programs are designed to (1) increase high school graduation, (2) increase college readiness and enrollment, and (3) increase college retention and graduation.

Box 11.2: Marla McDaniel, et. al., "Typology of Independing Living Programs," *Preparing for a 'Next Generation' Evaluation of Independent Living Programs for Youth in Foster Care*, pp. 6, U.S. Department of Health and Human Services, 2014.

2	Employment services	Employment services help youth prepare for the workforce, identify careers or jobs or interests, and gain and maintain employment during or after leaving care. Some programs only target employment; others integrate these services with broader intervention approaches.
3	Housing	Housing interventions fall into two general domains: (1) programs to help youth find and apply for existing community housing and (2) programs that provide or subsidize housing for current or former foster youth. Many of these programs also provide ongoing case management and may be limited to specific populations (e.g., pregnant or parenting girls).
4	Mentoring	These programs seek to provide youth with a caring and supportive nonparental adult. Programs often differ in the relationship between the mentor and the youth (e.g., some mentors are young adults with whom the youth has had a previous relationship with; others are similarly aged youth in transition). These programs are implemented in many settings, most commonly school- or community-based settings.
5	Behavioral health services	Behavioral health services for youth in foster care are delivered through many modalities and settings, ranging from inpatient residential care to multisystem, community-based models. Some public child-welfare agencies directly provide psychotherapeutic and trauma-informed services to foster youth in transition and contract for such services. Agencies play an important role in educating and linking transitioning youth to behavioral health services to which they are entitled.
6	Permanency enhancement	Permanency-enhancement interventions focus primarily on identifying, developing, and supporting relationships with immediate and extended family and other adults to whom youth feel a connection.
7	Pregnancy prevention	Pregnancy prevention programs take on many forms and take place in different settings. Many of these programs use a group milieu to educate youth (primarily females) about the consequences of risky sexual behavior and to empower youth to make thoughtful decisions about sexual behavior and pregnancy.

8	Parenting support	Most parenting support programs provide support and parenting skills training that promote health and well-being for young parents and their children. Services are commonly delivered as individual or family sessions, multifamily group sessions, or home-based observations and interventions. They may take place in the home, community, or a clinical setting.
9	Financial literacy and asset building	Asset-building programs commonly focus on the administration of individual development accounts, which help participants accumulate assets by matching their contributions to an account used for a prespecified purpose. Individual development accounts usually provide matches on savings made for three primary purposes: postsecondary education, small business development, and home purchase. Financial literacy programs aim to increase financial knowledge and skills, often through education, training, or direct experience with mainstream financial services.
10	Multicomponent services	Multicomponent services reflect the fact that foster youth can experience challenges across multiple domains. These programs offer a "one-stop shop" approach that may both reduce service duplication and avoid instances where needs are not identified and addressed.

Extended Care Services

Through FCIA as well as the Family First Prevention Services Act, once youth have reached 18 years old, a different set of services becomes available to them. States have the option of extending foster care to youth until age 21 and providing services up until the youth is 23 years old. Youth are eligible to retain their Medicaid coverage until age 21, and they are able to use vouchers to help cover the costs of higher education, technical education, or housing. The majority of these services are available to the youth who left foster care through a kinship, guardianship, or adoption arrangement after their 16th birthday, even if they were not in foster care when they turned 18.

There are some benefit-specific requirements. For example, in some states, in order to receive housing assistance, a youth must be enrolled in a full-time educational program (or vocational program). Some states will provide services to youth on an individualized basis, evaluating the unique context and needs of each youth, whereas others require that all youth must participate in certain programs or housing options in order to receive services. In a survey of 26 states, it was found that states consider factors such as the youth's ability to handle finances and budget, schedule doctors' appointments, education and employment status, availability of housing, affordability, and other special circumstances such as pregnancy or parenthood when deciding whether or not to place a youth in an independent housing situation (Government Accounting Office [GAO], 2019).

To date, the efficacy of programs designed to meet the needs of youth aging out or in extended foster care remains sparse and somewhat inconclusive (Barth, Greeson, Zlotnik, & Chintapalli, 2011; McDaniel et al., 2014). Early research (Scannapieco, Schagrin, & Scannapieco, 1995) indicated that preparing youth for independence may be beneficial in promoting a successful transition. This trend has been echoed in recent literature, demonstrating that programs that focus on relationship building as a means to improve self-sufficiency skills increase financial literacy, educational attainment, and employment (Scannapieco, Smith, & Blakeney-Strong, 2015). However, retrospective studies with middle-aged foster care alumni have shown that these programs were not viewed as helpful, as they did not provide timely or relevant information to the youth at the time (Yang, 2017).

Many youth choose not to remain in foster care after their 18th birthday simply because they are frustrated with the complexity of the child welfare bureaucracy and seek independence. Therefore, finding youth who are able, willing, and eligible to participate in research has proven challenging. However, the studies that have been conducted have largely shown that extended foster care and post-emancipation programs are overall ineffective at producing long-term positive outcomes (Courtney, Zinn, Koralek, & Bess, 2011; Greeson et al., 2015). These evaluations have shown that in some instances there were short-term gains or minor improvements in specific psychosocial domains, but overall these effects were not substantial, significant, or persistent.

Mentoring: The Importance of Adult Relationships

It is noteworthy that above and beyond any specific program or plan to address the needs of youth emancipating from care, the importance of relationships is critical. The importance of strong social connections for emancipating youth has been well documented and has been shown to improve overall odds of a successful transition to adulthood (Osgood, Foster, Flanagan, & Ruth, 2005). In fact, scholars have known about how important these relationships are for decades, as large studies on the needs and experiences of youth who emancipated from care demonstrated this as far back as the early 1990s (Cook, 1995). Few will argue the importance of strong and supportive relationships to the health and well-being of emancipating and emancipated youth; strategies to promote, support, and maintain these relationships are still not well understood. One randomized control trial was conducted looking at a post-aging-out program specifically designed to foster supportive networks and relationships; however, findings from this study did

Image 11.2

not yield successful results beyond the standard approach (Greeson et al., 2015). A systematic review found that natural mentors (meaning adults who were present in the youths' lives organically, not placed through a matching or other program) who were not parents of the youth had meaningful impacts on the transition to adulthood. The most important characteristics of these natural relationships were that they were consistent (Thompson, Greeson, Brunsink, 2016). Since publication of this review, numerous studies have been published highlighting these findings and illuminating that meaningful natural relationships can exist between a youth and members of the biological family, former caseworkers, even employees and roommates; but consistent access to a supportive individual in times of need was the pervasive key trait of these relationships (Duke, Farruggia, & Germo, 2016; Singer, Berzin, & Hokanson, 2013; Yang, 2017).

Systems Approach: Integration of Services for Youth Who Age Out

The number of services, programs, and domains of need that former foster youth encounter may seem overwhelming and difficult to generalize. Given that the majority of research studies exploring effective ways in which to provide services to youth who have aged out have illuminated methods that are largely ineffective, in order to conceptualize the needs of these individuals from a systems approach, this chapter will utilize a different lens. The policies that guide system practice with this population help to create a narrative and ideological approach toward engaging with youth who have aged out, one where independence rather than interdependence is prized. Instead of focusing on the services and programs themselves, we offer an alternative perspective, a critique of the current approach and proposed reframe of the needs of alumni in which the narrative is shifted from one of independence to one of interdependence.

FCIA explicitly states, in the title of the legislation, that it intends to support former foster youth in obtaining independence and promoting self-sufficiency in adulthood. This goal manifests in the numerous provisions of FCIA intended to provide funding for independent living programs and services for youth aged 18–21. In an effort to keep former foster youth from "succumbing to a life of poverty" (Guinn, 2000, p. 403), the FCIA was designed to build upon prior independent living programs with the goal of ensuring all eligible youth are provided assistance in securing employment, postsecondary education, and personal and emotional support (Guinn, 2000). The educational and vocational training program provides employment and postsecondary education services to youth aged 18–21 through funding from Title IV-E of the Social Security Act (P.L. 106-169) to ensure that they have the means to support themselves upon aging out of the child welfare system.

Additionally, this act calls for personal support and connections for former foster youth and stipulates that for youth for whom adoption is not possible and aging out is imminent, connections should be made with agencies like Big Brothers/Big Sisters to promote self-sufficiency and connectedness (Allen & Nixon, 2000). This is troubling given the vast body of literature that demonstrates that naturally occurring relationships are far more advantageous than artificially created ones (Thompson et al., 2016).

The FCIA clearly seeks to promote the independence and self-sufficiency of former foster youth by providing programs and services designed to prevent youth from continued reliance on federal programs. American social welfare policies have long favored the neoliberal values of independence and self-sufficiency (Schelbe, 2011), and as such it is not surprising that these values are so heavily embedded in FCIA. However, there are scholars who believe that promoting independence in these youth may be harmful or even prevent a successful transition to adulthood (Collins, 2004; Propp, Ortega, & NewHeart, 2003; Szilagyi, 1998). Research clearly shows that youth exiting foster care have higher rates of mental health and behavioral health needs than youth without a history of foster care involvement (Barth, 1990; Courtney et al., 2007; McMillen et al., 2005). As such, encouraging these youth to become prematurely independent and limiting the reliance on federal programs that could be of assistance may exacerbate these mental health conditions (Szilagyi, 1998). Furthermore, many adults in modern society are not independent from one another. Many rely on assistance from family, neighbors, and friends to cope with the ever-changing demands of life. Therefore, promoting the message to former foster youth that independence is a highly desirable characteristic may be setting them up for failure in the future, as they will lack the necessary connections and supports to cope with normal stressors throughout their lives (Avery & Freundlich, 2009; Mendes & Moslehuddin, 2006; Propp et al., 2003).

Furthermore, for many youth of color, independence is not a culturally or realistically appropriate goal. African American and Hispanic youth often reconnect with their families after leaving the child welfare system, but many report these relationships are often strained and not a source of significant support (Iglehart & Becerra, 2002). African American youth are also more likely to be homeless due to these familial conflicts as well as lack of access to support programs than other youth (Dworsky et al., 2010; Iglehart & Becerra, 2002). For many White youth, postsecondary education is a gateway to independence (Arnett, 1998). However, many youth of color report that higher education is often not accessible, as the need to work and support oneself or one's family takes priority over educational pursuits (Dworsky et al., 2010; Iglehart & Becerra, 2002). Additionally, the strong push for independence embedded in FCIA also causes frustration for many youth, particularly Native American youth, whose cultures espouse values of interdependence and connectedness to one's community (Downs, Gillette, & Konen, 2006). Given the cultural incompatibility and risk of negative outcomes raises questions about the efficacy of FCIA for all foster youth, but particularly youth of color.

A similar narrative of independence is also seen in Fostering Connections and its arguably most important connection for youth who age out: the extension of foster care services. As the extension of foster care services helps to create a support network that facilitates the transition to adulthood, this is somewhat related to permanency. However, this relationship with child welfare is not a stable, long-term relationship throughout life. Instead, this relationship exists to temporarily bolster support in an effort to prevent youth from experiencing the myriad of well-documented struggles associated with aging out of foster care. Despite good intentions, many of these efforts fall short of genuinely creating a safety net for these youth. For example, one of the biggest struggles that youth face upon aging out of foster care is housing. By remaining in care, youth have the option of taking advantage of supervised housing options paid for and monitored by the child welfare system. However, these housing programs often have regulations and prices that youth find difficult to maintain once they no longer receive support from the child welfare system (Stott, 2013). As such, many youth still may experience homelessness despite ongoing assistance from the child welfare system (Schelbe, 2011; Stott, 2013). Additionally, many youth are encouraged to address their housing concerns by enrolling in college and living in on-campus housing. At face value, this solution seems to address both the need for housing and higher education, as well as many other services provided as part of the collegiate experience. However, it is an often overlooked fact that on-campus housing is only available during the academic year, and when that is over or the campus is closed for holiday breaks, these youth often find themselves with nowhere to go (Schelbe, 2011).

In addition to struggling with housing, many youth struggle with access to health care after aging out (Courtney et al., 2007; Reilly, 2003). Fostering Connections contained provisions that enabled states to expand Medicaid funding to these youth; however, many states have failed to formally change their policies to enact these provisions (Schelbe, 2011). This deficit-based approach highlights the fact that many youth struggle with the transition to adulthood as they lack the necessary support network and services to make the transition in the same manner as their peers (Schelbe, 2011; Stott, 2013).

Just as with FCIA, there are many scholars who question the validity of valuing independence for former foster youth (Avery & Freundlich, 2009; Mendes & Moslehuddin, 2006; Propp et al., 2003). As previously discussed, successful adulthood in our society is rarely attained by individuals without connections to others. Therefore, stressing to youth who are aging out of foster care that independence is valuable and that the inability to transition off support from child welfare and other government programs is a personal failure is a true disservice to these youth. Additionally, many youth—particularly youth of color—find that independence is a value contrary to the cultural norms and expectations of their own communities. One strength of Fostering Connections is that youth who are in the legal guardianship of their relatives remain eligible for independent living services (P.L. 110-351). This helps to strengthen the kinship networks, family relationship, and ongoing support for youth for whom returning to their biological parents is not an option. In time, this may help reduce negative outcomes for youth of color, particularly for African American youth, where kinship ties are incredibly strong (Gipson Rankin, 2012; Iglehart & Becerra, 2002). However, as many of the provisions of Fostering Connections were not enacted until the 2011 fiscal year, long-term data on outcomes for these youth is still presently unknown.

Policies Related to Youth Aging Out of Care

Between the passing of the Adoption Assistance and Child Welfare Act of 1980 (AACWA) and the Adoption and Safe Families Act (ASFA) in 1997, scholars began to note that outcomes for youth who aged out of foster care were quite abysmal. In 1983, Festinger published *No One Ever Asked ... A Postscript to Foster Care*, summarizing results from a comprehensive research project exploring the status of over 250 young adults who had left foster care in 1975. In addition, to emphasize the need for the system to involve them in the decisions that greatly impacted their lives, the young adults in this study identified three areas where they felt the system needed to do a better job for preparing them for adulthood, including 1) how to pursue additional training/education; 2) planning for job/career; and 3) finances. In 1985, the Consolidated Omnibus Budget Reconciliation Act (P.L. 99-272) amended section 477 of Title IV-E of the Social Security Act and created Independent Living Initiatives—services designed to assist youth in foster care, age 16 or older, in transitioning out of foster care into *independent living*. Services funded included educational, job skills, vocational training, daily living skills, and counseling. These federal funds were reauthorized indefinitely in 1993; however, they were limited in that they could not be used to pay for room and board or any services provided after the child left foster care. In 1999, the Foster Care Independence Act (FCIA), also known as the Chafee program, was enacted, ushering in the modern era of policy and practice to help youth transition to adulthood.

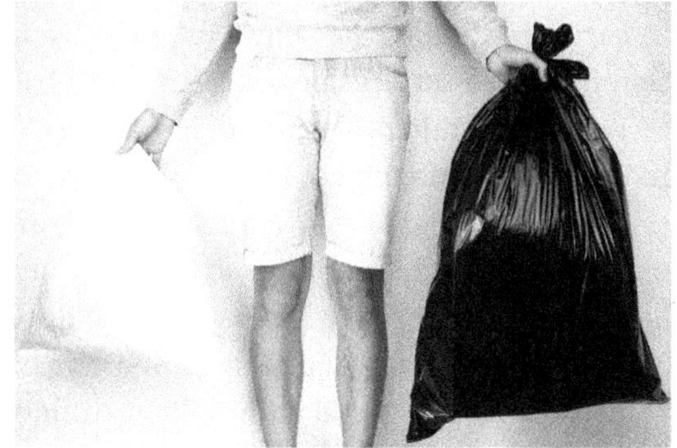
Image 11.3

The Foster Care Independence Act (P.L. 106–169)

Signed into law by President Bill Clinton on December 14, 1999, FCIA further amended Title IV-E of the Social Security Act expanding funding and proving greater flexibility to states operating independent living programs for foster youth aging out of care. The act increased the number of services available to youth in transition specifically through the provision of numerous services for youth between the ages of 18 and 21 (Fernandes, 2006).

For youth still under the care of the child welfare system, FCIA increased funding for adoption incentive payments in order to increase the likelihood that the youth will find legal permanency before emancipating from foster care on their 18th birthday (CWIG, 2019). However, the bulk of this act affects former foster youth after the age of 18. FCIA expanded the existing provisions of Title IV-E to raise the funding available for former foster youth from $70 million to $140 million per year. This funding can be used to help former foster youth address vocational needs, mental and physical health needs, employment services, financial management, housing, and expanded Medicaid eligibility. Unlike previous funding, FCIA allowed federal funds to be used to assist youth ages 18–21 who had left foster care and allowed youth to retain up to $10,000 in personal assets (as opposed to $1,000). While the provisions of FCIA also expanded the funding available for independent living programs, this act was explicit in that independent living is intended to be a *service* to all foster youth, not an alternative living arrangement or permanency plan. This fact was made even clearer with the passage of the Family First Prevention Services Act in 2018 that renamed the John H. Chafee Foster Care Independence Program to the Chafee Foster Care Program for Successful Transition to Adulthood (CWIG, 2019).

Fostering Connections to Success and Increasing Adoptions Act of 2008 (P.L. 110–351)

The Fostering Connections to Success and Increasing Adoptions Act of 2008 (aka Fostering Connections) placed increased attention on helping youth develop and maintain greater prosocial bonds with adults as well as providing services to increase educational attainment and access to behavioral and mental health care (Krinsky & Liebmann, 2011). Fostering Connections is multifaceted and affects many areas of service delivery within child welfare, including the identification and approval of kinship families for children in care (see Chapter 12); however, this discussion focuses on the provisions of the act that impacted services provided to youth transitioning to adulthood from foster care.

Two of the main provisions of Fostering Connections impact youth who are expected to age out or emancipate from foster care in the near future. First, Fostering Connections requires that all youth must have a transition plan in place within 90 days of their expected emancipation. It is expected that social workers, foster parents, and other key adults collaborate with the youth to develop this plan. The plan consists of specific actions that the youth and other supportive individuals can take to ensure that the youth transitions to adulthood with as little difficulty as possible (Stoltzfus, 2008).

Arguably, the largest provision of Fostering Connections is that youth who have reached the age of 18 may elect to remain in foster care until the age of 21, effectively extending foster care for these youth (Krinsky & Liebmann, 2011). Funding for this voluntary extension of foster care comes from an expansion of the eligibility requirements of Title IV-E for youth who are still in school, a job readiness program, or employed (Stoltzfus, 2008). This act additionally extended eligibility for Title IV-E assistance to youth who exited foster care through adoption or legal guardianship after the age of 16 who were not yet age 19, 20, or 21 (at the discretion of the state). Similar to youth who opt to remain in foster care, these former foster youth must be in school, employed, or engaged in activities designed to remove barriers to employment. The only exception to these criteria being if the youth is incapable of participating in such activities due to a medical reason. This portion of Fostering Connections encourages permanency through the adoption of older youth and providing incentives of ongoing services to these youth and their families. Additionally, this echoes the sentiment captured in both ASFA and FCIA, that emancipation from foster care is not an appropriate permanency plan for youth (Stoltzfus, 2008).

Preventing Sex Trafficking and Strengthening Families Act (P.L. 113–183)

The Preventing Sex Trafficking and Strengthening Families Act of 2014 amended the Social Security Act and was primarily designed to prevent children in foster care from falling victim to sex trafficking; however, a significant portion of the act addressed the right for youth in foster care to have the opportunity to engage and participate in developmentally and age-appropriate activities (CWIG, 2019). Important for youth exiting care through emancipation at age 18 or older, the act requires that these youth be provided with their medical records, health insurance information, birth certificate, social security card, and state-issued identification card/driver's license—vital records that all adults need to successfully navigate adulthood.

Family First Prevention Services Act (P.L. 115–123)

Section 50753 of the Family First Prevention Services Act (FFPSA), passed in 2018, focused on improving the John H. Chafee Foster Care Independence Program. The act changed the name of the program to the "John H. Chafee Foster Care Program for Successful Transition to Adulthood," clearly indicating a focus on transition to adulthood as opposed to independence. In addition, the Family First Prevention Services Act revised the program to

- assure that the program is available to youth who experienced foster care at age 14 or older;
- make education and training vouchers (ETV) available to youth ages 14–26, limiting participation in the ETV program to a total of 5 years;

- allow states and tribes to extend the Chafee program to youth up to the age of 23, if Title IV-E foster care extended to age 21 or if comparable services are provided to non–Title IV-E youth;
- clarify that youth who age out of foster care at an age other than 18 are eligible for the Chafee program as long as they do so before age 21 (or 23 if foster care extended to 21 in that state or tribe);
- ensure that youth who age out of care are given official proof that documents they were in foster care;
- require ongoing tracking and analysis of outcomes of youth who age out of care or who exit through adoption or kinship guardianship for comparison.

(Children's Defense Fund, 2018)

Case Application

The following case vignette is quite typical, as it reflects much of the literature on the experience of youth who age out of foster care. The vignette shows the chaos that many youth face when they immediately exit care and the importance of strong adult supports in the lives of these youth.

Case Vignette

Gabrielle, or "Gabby," as her friends call her, is a 17-year-old female currently in foster care. Gabby turns 18 in 3 weeks, and she is excited to be able to move out of the group home where she has lived for the last 3 years. Gabby hasn't seen her social worker in several months, but she has been working with the staff at the group home to plan for what will happen to her after she turns 18.

The group home staff has worked to build a strong relationship with Gabby and one of her teachers over the last 6 months. Gabby had plans to move in with her teacher, Ms. Jacobson, on her 18th birthday. After a small celebration at the group home, all of Gabby's things were packed up, and Ms. Jacobson picked her up shortly after 5:00 p.m. that day. Initially, Gabby was very overwhelmed, but she found that this move reminded her of all the other times she had moved when she was in foster care, and she quickly remembered all of the tricks to make moves easier. Gabby's first rule when moving to a new place is to wait at least 3 weeks to unpack because "you never know if the placement will work out or not." The second rule is to never be too open or honest with your thoughts or feelings, because if the placement ends up not working, the foster parents or staff may use it against you. Finally, Gabby was always polite, but never put on a "show" for new placements because they were going to find out who she was anyway; it was just a matter of time.

The first week with Ms. Jacobson and her family went like most new placements do; everyone was polite, things were calm, and even though she felt very out of place in this environment, Gabby admittedly felt safe. Then Gabby went on a weeklong vacation with her friends to celebrate her 18th birthday. This vacation was planned prior to her aging out of care, and everyone knew that Gabby would be at the beach for a week with her three closest friends. During that week, Gabby experienced freedom for the first time as she was able to do whatever she wanted whenever she wanted, and this feeling proved to be irresistible to Gabby.

When she returned from vacation, she became more and more defiant to Ms. Jacobson. When Ms. Jacobson tightened down on the rules in an attempt to curb Gabby's defiant behavior, Gabby ran away. Gabby is now homeless and sleeping on friends' couches. She has no car, no job, and very little money. Gabby was always a good student and was supposed to start college in the fall. The start of the fall semester is only 3 weeks away, but Gabby has no idea where she will live until school starts, or even if she will be able to find a ride to college, as the school is over 4 hours away from where she is crashing now.

Gabby's future is uncertain, but she knows she wants to go to college and be different from her "deadbeat parents," who never did anything with their lives. The days and weeks ahead will prove to be some of the most challenging she has ever faced.

DISCUSSION QUESTIONS

1. What activities might Gabby's social worker have completed to better prepare her to transition out of foster care?
2. Identify and discuss three strategies a social worker could use to help Gabby get back on track and succeed in meeting her goals.

References

Adoption Assistance and Child Welfare Act of 1980, Pub. L. No. 96–272, 94 Stat. 500. (1979).

Adoption and Safe Families Act of 1997, Pub. L. No. 105-89. (1997).

Allen, M., & Nixon, R. (2000). Foster Care Independence Act and John H. Chafee Foster Care Independence Program: New catalysts for reform for young people aging out of foster care. *Clearinghouse Rev., 34,* 197.

Arnett, J. J. (1998). Learning to stand alone: The contemporary American transition to adulthood in cultural and historical context. *Human development, 41*(5–6), 295–315.

Atkinson, M. (2008). Aging out of foster care: Towards a universal safety net for former foster care youth. *Harvard Civil Rights-Civil Liberties Law Review, 43,* 183.

Avery, R. J. (2010). An examination of theory and promising practice for achieving permanency for teens before they age out of foster care. *Children and Youth Services Review, 32*(3), 399–408.

Avery, R. J., & Freundlich, M. (2009). You're all grown up now: Termination of foster care support at age 18. *Journal of Adolescence, 32,* 247–257.

Barbell, K., & Freundlich, M. (2001). *Foster Care Today.* Washington, DC: Casey Family Programs.

Barth, R. P. (1990). On their own: The experiences of youth after foster care. *Child and Adolescent Social Work Journal, 7,* 419–440.

Barth, R. P., Greeson, J. K. P., Zlotnik, S. R., & Chintapalli, L. K. (2011. Evidence-based practice for youth in supervised out of home care: A framework for development, definition, and evaluation., *Journal of Evidence-Based Social Work, 8*(5), 501–528. doi: 10.1080/15433710903269529

Bender, K., Yang, J., Ferguson, K., & Thompson, S. (2015). Experiences and needs of homeless youth with a foster care history. *Children and Youth Services Review, 55,* 222–231.

Benedict, M. I., Zuravin, S., & Stallings, R. Y. (1996). Adult functioning of children who lived in kin versus nonrelative family foster homes. *Child Welfare: Journal of Policy, Practice, and Program, 75,* 529–549.

Brace, C. L. (1872). *The Dangerous Classes of New York and Twenty Years' Work among Them.* New York: Wynkoop & Hallenbeck.

Brandford, C., & English, D. (2004). Foster youth transition to independence study. Seattle, WA: Office of Children's Administration Research, Washington State Department of Social and Health Services.

Bruskas, D. (2008). Children in foster care: A vulnerable population at risk. *Journal of Child and Adolescent Psychiatric Nursing, 21,* 70–77.

Capacity Building Center for States. (2016). *Pathways to permanency: Expanding APPLA provisions and youth engagement to improve permanency.* Washington, DC: U.S. Department of Human Services, Administration for Children and Families, Children's Bureau. (pp. 1–2).

Child Welfare Information Gateway. (2019). *Definitions of child abuse and neglect.* Washington, DC: U.S. Department of Health and Human Services, Children's Bureau.

Child Welfare Information Gateway. (2019). *Major federal legislation concerned with child protection, child welfare, and adoption.* Washington, DC: U.S. Department of Health and Human Services, Children's Bureau.

Child Welfare Information Gateway. (2017). *Extension of foster care beyond 18.* Washington, DC: U.S. Department of Health and Human Services.

Children's Bureau. (2019, June 10). NYTD. https://www.acf.hhs.gov/cb/research-data-technology/reporting-systems/nytd

Children's Defense Fund. (2018, February). The Family First Prevention Services Act. [PDF file] Retrieved November 21, 2019, from https://www.childrensdefense.org/wp-content/uploads/2018/08/family-first-detailed-summary.pdf

Collins, M. E. (2004). Enhancing services to youths leaving foster care: Analysis of recent legislation and its potential impact. *Children and Youth Services Review, 26,* 1051–1065.

Cook, J. F. (1995). A history of placing-out: The orphan trains. *Child Welfare, 74*(1), 181–197.

Consolidated Omnibus Budget Reconciliation Act of 1985, Pub. L. No. 99-272, 100 Stat. 82. (1986).

Courtney, M., Dworsky, A., Lee, J., & Raap, M. (2010). *Midwest evaluation of the adult functioning of former foster youth: Outcomes at ages 23 and 24.* Chapin Hall Center for Children at the University of Chicago.

Courtney, M., Dworsky, A., Ruth, A., Keller, T., Havlicek, J., & Bost, J. (2005). *Midwest evaluation of the adult functioning of former foster youth: Outcomes at age 19.* Chicago: Chapin Hall Center for Children at the University of Chicago.

Courtney, M., Zinn, A., Koralek, R., & Bess, R. (2011b). Evaluation of the Independent Living Employment Services Program, Kern County, California: Final Report. OPRE Report # 2011 13. Washington, DC: Office of Planning, Research and Evaluation, Administration for Children and Families, U.S. Department of Health and Human Services.

Courtney, M. E., & Barth, R. P. (1996). Pathways of older adolescents out of foster care: Implications for independent living services. *Social Work, 41(*1), 75–83.

Courtney, M. E., Dworsky, A., Brown, A., Cary, C., Love, K., & Vorhies, V. (2011a). *Midwest evaluation of the adult functioning of former foster youth: Outcomes at age 26.* Chicago: Chapin Hall at the University of Chicago.

Courtney, M. E., Dworsky, A. L., Cusick, G. R., Havlicek, J., Perez, A., & Keller, T. E. (2007). Midwest evaluation of the adult functioning of former foster youth: Outcomes at age 21. Chicago: Chapin Hall Center for Children at the University of Chicago.

Courtney, M. E., Piliavin, I., Grogan-Kaylor, A., & Nesmith, A. (2001). Foster youth transitions to adulthood: A longitudinal view of youth leaving care. *Child Welfare, 80,* 685–718.

Courtney, M. E., Terao, S., & Bost, N. (2004). *Midwest evaluation of the adult functioning of former foster youth: Conditions of youth preparing to leave state care.* Chicago: Chapin Hall Center for Children at the University of Chicago.

Crawford, B., Pharris, A. B., & Dorsett-Burrell, R. (2018). Risk of serious criminal involvement among former foster youth aging out of care. *Children and Youth Services Review, 93,* 451–457.

Cunningham, H. (1998). Histories of childhood. *The American Historical Review, 103*(4), 1195–1208.

Day, A., Dworsky, A., Fogarty, K., & Damashek, A. (2011). An examination of post-secondary retention and graduation among foster care youth enrolled in a four-year university. *Children and Youth Services Review, 33*(11), 2335–2341.

Downs, A. C., Gillette, B., & Konen, E. I. C. (2006). Assessing cultural life skills of American Indian youth. In *Child and Youth Care Forum* (Vol. 35, No. 4, pp. 289–304). Springer US.

Duke, T., Farruggia, S. P., & Germo, G. R. (2017). "I don't know where I would be right now if it wasn't for them": Emancipated foster care youth and their important non-parental adults. *Children and Youth Services Review, 76,* 65–73.

Dworsky, A. (2005). The economic self-sufficiency of Wisconsin's former foster youth. *Children and Youth Services Review, 27*(10), 1085–1118.

Dworsky, A., & Courtney, M. E. (2009). Homelessness and the transition from foster care to adulthood. *Child Welfare, 88*, 23.

Dworsky, A., Napolitano, L., & Courtney, M. (2013). Homelessness during the transition from foster care to adulthood. *American Journal of Public Health, 103*(S2), S318–S323.

Dworsky, A., White, C. R., O'Brien, K., Pecora, P., Courtney, M., Kessler, R., ... Hwang, I. (2010). Racial and ethnic differences in the outcomes of former foster youth. *Children and Youth Services Review, 32*, 902–912.

Epstein, H. R. (2011). Judicial guide to implementing the Fostering Connections to Success and Increasing Adoptions Act of 2008 (PL 110-315). Washington, DC: ABA Center on Children and the Law.

Fernandes, A. L. (2006). Child Welfare: The Chafee Foster Care Independence Program (CFCIP). *Congressional Research Service*, 1–6.

Fernandes-Alcantara, A. L. (2019). John H. Chafee Foster Care Program for successful transition to adulthood. *Congressional Research Service* (1–2).

Fernandes-Alcantara, A. L. (2017). Youth transitioning from foster care: Background and federal programs. *Congressional Research Service* (1–37).

Festinger, T. (1983). *No One Ever Asked Us: A Postscript to Foster Care.* New York: Columbia University Press.

Foster Care Independence Act of 1999, Pub. L. No. 106–169, 113 Stat. 1822. (1999).

Foster Care Independence Act of 1999: Hearings before the committee on Rules and Administration, House, 106th Cong. 1 (1999).

Fostering Connections to Success and Increasing Adoptions Act of 2008, Pub. L. No. 110-351, 112 Stat. 3949. (2008).

Fowler, P. J., Toro, P. A., & Miles, B. W. (2009). Aging-out of foster care: Pathways to and from homelessness and associated psychosocial outcomes in young adulthood. *American Journal of Public Health*, 99, 1453–1458.

Fryar, G., Jordan, E., & DeVooght, K. (2017). *Supporting young people transitioning from foster care: Findings from a national survey.* Bethesda, MD: Child Trends.

Geiger, J. M., Hanrahan, J. E., Cheung, J. R., & Lietz, C. A. (2016). Developing an on-campus recruitment and retention program for foster care alumni. *Children and Youth Services Review, 61*, 271–280.

Gipson Rankin, S. M. (2012). Black kinship circles in the 21st century: Survey of recent child welfare reforms and how it impacts black kinship care families. *Whittier Journal of Child & Family Advocacy, 12*, 1.

Goerge, R. M., Bilaver, L., Lee, B. J., Needell, B., Brookhart, A., & Jackman, W. (2002). Employment outcomes for youth aging out of foster care. Chicago: Chapin Hall Center for Children, University of Chicago.

Government Accounting Office. (2019). *Foster care: States with approval to extend care provide independent living options for youth up to age 21.* Washington, DC: Government Printing Office. https://www.gao.gov/assets/700/699219.pdf

Greeson, J. K., Garcia, A. R., Kim, M., & Courtney, M. E. (2015). Foster youth and social support: The first RCT of independent living services. *Research on Social Work Practice, 25,* 349–357.

Guinn, R. P. (2000). Passage of the Foster Care Independence Act of 1999: A pivotal step on behalf of youth aging out of foster care and into a life of poverty. *Georgia Journal on Poverty Law & Policy, 7*(2), 403–421.

Gypen, L., Vanderfaeillie, J., De Maeyer, S., Belenger, L., & Van Holen, F. (2017). Outcomes of children who grew up in foster care: Systematic review. *Children and Youth Services Review, 76,* 74–83.

Hacsi, T. (1995). From indenture to family foster care: A brief history of child placing. *Child Welfare, 74*(1), 162–180.

Havlicek, J., & Courtney, M. E. (2016). Maltreatment histories of aging out foster youth: A comparison of official investigated reports and self-reports of maltreatment prior to and during out of home care. *Child Abuse & Neglect, 52,* 110–122.

Hook, J. L., & Courtney, M. E. (2011). Employment outcomes of former foster youth as young adults: The importance of human, personal, and social capital. *Children and Youth Services Review, 33,* 1855–1865.

Iglehart, A. P., & Becerra, R. M. (2002). Hispanic and African American youth: Life after foster care emancipation. *Journal of Ethnic and Cultural Diversity in Social Work, 11*(1–2), 79–107.

Jones, L. P. (2010). The educational experiences of former foster youth three years after discharge. *Child Welfare, 89*(6), 7–22.

Juvenile Law Center. (2019). National extended foster care review. Retrieved November 22, 2019, from https://jlc.org/issues/extended-foster-care

Juvenile Law Center. (2018, May). National extended foster care review: Executive summary. [PDF file]. Retrieved November 22, 2019 from https://jlc.org/resources/national-extended-foster-care-review-50-state-survey-law-and-policy

Kids Count Data Center. (2018). Youth transitioning out of foster care: Incarcerated in the past two years by race/ethnicity in the United States. The Annie E. Casey Foundation. Retrieved November 21, 2019, from https://datacenter.kidscount.org/data/tables/10214-youth-transitioning-out-of-foster-care-incarcerated-in-the-past-two-years-by-race-ethnicity?loc=1&loct=1#detailed/1/any/false/1698,1697/6285,4411,4039,2638,2597,4880,4758,6286,1353|6259/19762,19763

Krinsky, M., & Liebmann, T. (2011). Charting a better future for transitioning foster youth: Executive summary of report from a national summit on the Fostering Connections to Success Act. *Family Court Review*, 49, 292–300.

Maas, H. S. (1969). Children in long-term foster care. *Child Welfare, 48*(6), 321–347.

Maas, H.S. & Engler, R.E. (1959). *Children in need of parents. New* York: Columbia University Press.

McCoy, H., McMillen, J. C., & Spitznagel, E. L. (2008). Older youth leaving the foster care system: Who, what, when, where, and why? *Children and Youth Services Review, 30,* 735–745.

McDaniel, M., Courtney, M. E., Pergamit, M. R., & Lowenstein, C. (2014). *Preparing for a "next generation" evaluation of independent living programs for youth in foster care: Project overview.* OPRE Report #2014-71. Washington, DC: Office of Planning, Research and Evaluation, Administration for Children and Families, U.S. Department of Health and Human Services.

McMillen, J. C., Zima, B. T., Scott Jr., L. D., Auslander, W. F., Munson, M. R., Ollie, M. T., & Spitznagel, E. L. (2005). Prevalence of psychiatric disorders among older youths in the foster care system. *Journal of the American Academy of Child & Adolescent Psychiatry, 44*, 88–95.

Mendes, P., & Moslehuddin, B. (2006). From dependence to interdependence: Towards better outcomes for young people leaving state care. *Child Abuse Review, 15*(2), 110–126.

Mnookin, R. (1973). Foster care—In whose best interest? *Harvard Educational Review, 43*(4), 599–638.

Naccarato, T., Brophy, M., & and Courtney, M. (2010). Employment outcomes of foster youth: The results from the Midwest Evaluation of the Adult Functioning of Foster Youth. *Children and Youth Services Review,* 32, 551–559.

National Data Archive on Child Abuse and Neglect (NDACAN). (2019). *AFCARS Foster Care Annual File: Codebook.* Ithaca, NY: Author.

Osgood, D. W., Foster, E. M., Flanagan, C., & Ruth, G. R. (2005). *On Your Own without a Net: The Transition to Adulthood for Vulnerable Populations.* University of Chicago Press.

Pecora, P. J., Kessler, R. C., O'Brien, K., White, C. R., Williams, J., Hiripi, E., ... Herrick, M. A. (2006). Educational and employment outcomes of adults formerly placed in foster care: Results from the Northwest Foster Care Alumni Study. *Children and Youth Services Review, 28*, 1459–1481.

Propp, J., Ortega, D. M., & NewHeart, F. (2003). Independence or interdependence: Rethinking the transition from "ward of the court" to adulthood. *Families in Society: The Journal of Contemporary Human Services, 84*, 259–266.

Reilly, T. (2003). Transition from care: Status and outcomes of youth who age out of foster care. *Child welfare–New York, 82*, 727–746.

Renne, J., & Mallon, G. P. (2005). Facilitating permanency for youth: The overuse of long-term foster care and the appropriate use of another planned permanent living arrangement as options for youth in foster care. *Child Welfare for the Twenty-First Century: A Handbook of Practices, Policies, and Programs*, 488–503.

Rodham, H. (1973). Children under the law. *Harvard Educational Review, 43*(4), 487–514.

Scannapieco, M., Schagrin, J., & Scannapieco, T. (1995). Independent living programs: Do they make a difference? *Child and Adolescent Social Work Journal, 12*, 381–389.

Scannapieco, M., Smith, M., & Blakeney-Strong, A. (2016). Transition from foster care to independent living: Ecological predictors associated with outcomes. *Child and Adolescent Social Work Journal, 33*, 293–302.

Schelbe, L. A. (2011). Policy analysis of Fostering Connections to Success and Increasing Adoptions Act of 2008. *Journal of Human Behavior in the Social Environment, 21*, 555–576.

Singer, E. R., Berzin, S. C., & Hokanson, K. (2013). Voices of former foster youth: Supportive relationships in the transition to adulthood. *Children and Youth Services Review, 35*, 2110–2117.

Snyder, S. M., Hartinger-Saunders, R., Brezina, T., Beck, E., Wright, E. R., Forge, N., & Bride, B. E. (2016). Homeless youth, strain, and justice system involvement: An application of general strain theory. *Children and Youth Services Review, 62*, 90–96.

Stoltzfus, E. (2008, October). Child welfare: The Fostering Connections to Success and Increasing Adoptions Act of 2008. In *CRS Report for Congress*. Retrieved November 22, 2019 (Vol. 10, p. 2008).

Stott, T. (2013). Transitioning youth: Policies and outcomes. *Children and Youth Services Review, 35*(2), 218–227.

Szilagyi, M. (1998). The pediatrician and the child in foster care. *Pediatric Review, 19*, 39–50.

Thompson, A. E., Greeson, J. K., & Brunsink, A. M. (2016). Natural mentoring among older youth in and aging out of foster care: A systematic review. *Children and Youth Services Review, 61*, 40–50.

U.S. Census Bureau, Population Division. (2016, June) Annual Estimates of the Resident Population by Sex, Single Year of Age, Race, and Hispanic Origin for the United States: April 1, 2010 to July 1, 2015. https://factfinder.census.gov/faces/tableservices/jsf/pages/productview.xhtml?src=bkmk#

U.S. Department of Health and Human Services, Administration for Children and Families, Administration on Children, Youth and Families, Children's Bureau. (2019). *Adoption and Foster Care Analysis and Reporting System (Report No. 26).* http://www.acf.hhs.gov/sites/default/files/cb/afcarsreport25.pdf

U.S. Department of Health and Human Services (USDHHS), Administration for Children and Families, Administration on Children. Youth and Families, Children's Bureau. (2006–2019). *AFCARS Reports #12-26,* Washington, DC: Author.

USLegal. (n.d.). *Emancipation law and legal definition.* https://definitions.uslegal.com/e/emancipation/

Villegas, S., & Pecora, P. J. (2012). Mental health outcomes for adults in family foster care as children: An analysis by ethnicity. *Children and Youth Services Review, 34*(8), 1448–1458.

Wiltz, T. (2017). For foster care kids, college degrees are elusive. The Pew Charitable Trust. https://www.pewtrusts.org/en/research-and-analysis/blogs/stateline/2017/12/07/for-foster-care-kids-college-degrees-are-elusive

Yang, J. L. (2017). *The Rest of The Story: Exploring the Overall Functioning and Maturational Experiences of Former Foster Youth in Middle Adulthood.* Doctoral dissertation, University of Denver.

Zlotnick, C., Tam, T. W., & Soman, L. A. (2012). Life course outcomes on mental and physical health: The impact of foster care on adulthood. *American Journal of Public Health, 102*, 534–540.

Figure Credits

Img. 11.1: Copyright © 2017 Depositphotos/monkeybusiness.

Img. 11.2: Copyright © 2012 Depositphotos/photography33.

Img. 11.3: Copyright © 2015 Depositphotos/NikolayShubin.

CHAPTER · 12

Kinship Foster Care

Maria Scannapieco and Alan Kunz Lomelin

Overview of Chapter and Population

Children may not be able to stay with their parents for various reasons such as abuse and neglect, substance abuse by the parent, parental death, military deployment, serious mental or physical illness of the parent and/or child, or serious disability. Relatives or other individuals who maintain a significant relationship with the child may step in and provide a home for the child. Kinship care as an alternative to foster care may be a valuable resource, as it may provide a sense of belonging and security for the child.

Kinship foster care has become an integral part of the child welfare system since the early 1990s in the United States as well as many other countries (Burgess, Rossvoll, Wallace, & Daniel, 2010; Strozier, Elrod, Beiler, Smith, & Carter, 2004). From 1986 to 1990, the number of children placed with a kinship caregiver, as a foster care placement option, went from 18% in 1986 to 31% in 1990 (Hong, Algood, Chiu, & Lee, 2011). Child welfare systems at that time experienced an increase in the number of children coming into care, a decrease in the number of foster homes available, and a philosophical shift to a more family-centered approach, all influencing the increase in the use of kinship foster care. In 1978, the passage of the Indian Child Welfare Act (ICWA, 1978) (discussed in more detail later in the chapter) began a shift to understanding family-centered approaches which were more advantageous for children. It was acknowledged that children were best cared for by their families in their own communities or tribes (Weiss, Oberleitner, & Easton, 2013). This trend in the use of relatives as a placement option for children in state custody has continued. In the latest estimates, there were 437,283 children in foster care, with 32% (139,004) in kinship foster care (USDHHS, 2019).

The focus in this chapter will specifically be on those children entering the child welfare system because of state intervention due to child abuse or neglect and in either voluntary kinship care or formal kinship care (hereafter referred to as *kinship foster care*). The chapter will 1) present the current state of knowledge about kinship foster care through a review of the empirical literature; 2) review what services and evidence-based practices are available for this population; 3) discuss the social policies related to kinship foster care; and 4) provide a case study as well as a discussion of the application of the chapter materials to the case vignette.

Types of Kinship Care

Most scholars characterize four types of kinship care (Scannapieco & Hegar, 2002; CWLA, 2018; Child Welfare Information Gateway, 2016): formal kinship care, voluntary kinship care, informal/private kinship care, and temporary guardianship. Kin can be persons related by blood, such as grandmother/father, aunt/uncle, sister/brother, or fictive kin. **Fictive kin** are those persons related by a significant relationship with the child, including a godmother/father, tribal or clan member, or close friend. Persons related by blood and fictive kin are represented in all four types of kinship care.

Voluntary kinship care involves the child welfare system but not the court system. A parent may become involved with the child welfare system because there may be signs of abuse and/or neglect by a parent or other adult in the home (e.g., a boyfriend). The parent voluntarily allows the child welfare agency to place the child with a relative, but there is no court intervention, and the child welfare agency does not maintain custody or pay support for the child in the home. Formal kinship care is when a child is placed into kinship care by a child welfare agency whereby the child welfare agency has legal custody of the child. Legal custody requires the child welfare agency to take responsibility for the child's well-being financially, medically, educationally, emotionally, and socially.

Informal/private kinship care occurs when a parent makes an arrangement with a family member to care for their child. Informal kinship care does not involve the child welfare or the court system; it is a private arrangement among family members. Temporary guardianship is similar to informal kinship care in that it does not involve the child welfare system, but it does involve the court system. A parent would consult an attorney to develop a guardianship agreement among the relative and the parent, and it would be sent to the court system to be approved by a judge. In making this type of arrangement, the relative is given decision-making ability for medical and educational purposes. An example of a situation might be when a single parent needs to undergo inpatient treatment for substance abuse and wants their child cared for by a relative.

Image 12.1

Overview of Kinship Care

In the next section, the current state of knowledge in kinship care is reviewed by examining the empirical literature over the past 10 years in the context of the chapter-specific discussion areas.

Disproportionality and Disparities Related to Kinship Care

The child welfare system in the United States serves a heterogeneous group of clients, and as a result, must be mindful of their individual differences, beliefs, cultures, and practices. These differences create unique barriers, disproportionate representations, and disparity among different groups participating in kinship care. African Americans, Latinos, and Native Americans are among the groups that have been adversely affected by these (Ayón, Aisenberg, & Cimino, 2013; Cross, Day, & Byers, 2010; Foster, Hillemeier, & Bai, 2011; Knott & Donovan, 2010; Koh, 2010; Liao & White, 2014; Ryan, Sung Hong, Herz, & Hernandez, 2010).

Unfortunately, Asian Americans and Pacific Islanders have been excluded from this analysis because there is a significant gap in the literature. Although studies have demonstrated disparities within these groups in the child welfare system, in areas such as rates of childhood physical abuse, research has not been done on the disparities specifically found on kinship care and how placement selection and stability might be different for these populations (Rhee, Chang, Weaver, & Wong, 2008; Dakil, Cox, Lin, & Flores, 2011; Mokuau, Garlock-Tuiali'i, & Lee, 2008). Researchers have identified the need to not only address these gaps in the literature but also to avoid the trap of placing Asian Americans and Pacific Islanders under a single category, as each group has distinct and unique views and values (Mokuau et al., 2008). As gaps in the literature are filled, focus must also remain on being culturally aware and consider the role that differences between Eastern and Western cultural values might have in the disparities found in the child welfare system and specifically in kinship care (Vakalahi, Heffernan, & Johnson, 2007; Weng & Nguyen, 2011).

African Americans

Important disparities have been found between African Americans and Whites in areas such as caregiver well-being, placement types, placement stability, and juvenile delinquency (Boyd, 2014; Kim, Chenot, & Ji, 2011; Liao & White, 2014). Evidence shows that African American children are more likely to receive out of home care placements, be placed in foster care, or be placed with kin when compared to White children (Foster et al., 2011; Knott & Donovan, 2010; Liao & White, 2014). However, research also shows that race might not be the only determinant of these placement decisions, but rather other intersecting factors that differentiate African Americans from Whites (e.g., presence of biological father/mother, number of children in household, identity of perpetrator, parental/household risk factors, and informal placements arranged by the police), which are associated with placement decisions (Woodmass, Weisberg, Shlomi, Rockymore, & Wells, 2017).

In an analysis of five states, researchers found that African American children were more likely to be placed in kinship care than White children in two (Missouri and Ohio), whereas White children were more likely to be placed in kinship care than African

American in one (Arizona), with the final two states (Connecticut and Tennessee) showing similar rates of kinship care placement for African American and White children (Koh, 2010). These findings show that each state has its own unique needs and challenges, which means that a general one-size-fits-all solution might not be appropriate. As social workers, advocating for interventions that are mindful of the unique disparities, challenges, and needs of each state is essential. Instability factors (factors affecting children's ability to remain in a placement) were also different between these groups. Factors that led to placement instability in African American children included older age, an initial placement that was not with kinship, and more **externalizing behaviors** before their placement. In contrast, placement instability in White children was only predicted by initial placement in a foster care setting. (Foster et al., 2011). Finally, research also shows that African American and White adolescent males in kinship care are at an increased risk for juvenile delinquency when compared with their non-kinship counterparts; however, no effects were found for African American and White females (Ryan et al., 2010). It is important for social workers to try to identify what it is about kinship placements or children placed in kinship care that puts these children at increased risk for criminal behavior. Overall, disparities between African Americans and White clients are significant and must be considered in the development of new policies, programs, and interventions that aim to provide better kinship services to these groups.

Latinos

Latinos have a unique set of cultural beliefs, traditions, and challenges that should be understood when looking at child welfare disparities. While kinship care seems like a viable and useful service for Latino families, their providers (caregivers and child protective services) will likely encounter barriers in their attempts to provide services (Ayón et al., 2013). For instance, licensing requirements in the foster care system were developed based on "Anglo middle-class values," which might differ from the values and practices of other groups (Latinos, African Americans, etc.) (Ayón et al., 2013). The barriers faced by Latinos can also be attributed to structural inequalities and can also include things like immigration status, fear of deportation, and language barriers (Ayón et al., 2013). The child welfare system introduced international kinship care placements to overcome the immigration status barrier faced by undocumented Latinos in the United States (Cardoso, Gomez, & Padilla, 2009). However, there are other barriers associated with international kinship placements (Cardoso et al., 2009; Scott, Faulkner, Cardoso, & Burstain, 2014). Accuracy of information, conflicting agency policies, and a lack of child protective services (CPS) policy enforcement are only a few of the obstacles Latino children might face when trying to secure an international kinship placement (Cardoso et al., 2009). Child welfare professionals must remain culturally aware and gain a better understanding of the unique barriers faced by Latinos so that they can offer services that can address their specific needs.

American Indians

A third ethnic group that has been disproportionately impacted by disparities in the child welfare system is American Indians (Cross et al., 2010; Kopera-Frye, 2009; Limb, Shafer, & Sandoval, 2014). Cross et al. (2010) interviewed American Indian caregivers to find out the reasons why they chose to provide sole care for their grandchildren with or without the intervention of the child welfare system. One of the main reasons was that they wanted to raise their grandchildren within the tribal nation's traditions and culture. Another reason was that American Indian caregivers wanted to protect their grandchildren from the "harsh" and "punitive" services offered by the child welfare system. They were reluctant to seek aid from non-Indian/non-tribal service programs because they have had negative traumatic experiences in the past with the boarding school system, which to them is parallel to the child welfare system. They wanted to prevent their grandchildren from having to go through a similar traumatic experience. Finally, American Indian grandparents may choose to provide sole care because it gives them an increased sense of purpose to know that they played a role in ending the cycle of past trauma, dissolution of families, and dissolution of tribal traditions.

Policies have been passed to help address some of the injustices and disparities that American Indians face in the child welfare system; however, the extent to which these are successful depends on people's knowledge of these services and their ability to seek them out. Cross et al. (2010) also studied the custody status of American Indians and their knowledge of the Indian Child Welfare Act (ICWA). He found that out of the grandparents who were interviewed, 20 had no legal documentation for the child's custody, 7 had legally adopted the child, 3 obtained guardianship, and 1 became a foster parent. In addition, 9 didn't know about the Indian Child Welfare Act (ICWA), 15 were aware of it but didn't find it helpful, and 7 were aware of it and found it helpful (6 out of these 7 adopted their grandchildren). Based on these findings, an argument could be made that the ICWA was successful in helping grandparents adopt their grandchildren; however, several American Indian families still struggle in navigating the child welfare system, getting over past trauma and stigma, and knowing what their rights are and what they are entitled to. New interventions must be implemented that look for ways to solve these concerns and assist American Indian families in navigating and understanding the child welfare system.

Trauma-Informed Care

A lot of children involved with the child welfare system have experienced trauma at some point in their lives, and that is why it is important that caregivers, child welfare workers, and policy makers be aware of how this might impact the child's well-being and ability to find a secure and stable placement. Research shows that increased trauma experiences can be associated with things like increased risk behaviors and caregiver stress and that post-permanency outcomes can be negatively impacted by children's behavioral problems (Blakely, Leon, Fuller, & Jhe Bai, 2017; Liao & White, 2014; Sprang, Choi, Eslinger, & Whitt-Woosley, 2015). Failing to address a child's mental health needs before, during, and after their kinship placement could lead to increased caregiver stress, unstable placements, and a negative impact to the child's long-term development. Therefore, it is important to understand the role that trauma plays in a child's well-being in order to prevent the need for multiple placements or a negative impact in the child-caregiver relationship.

Practice Challenges with Kinship Care

In the child welfare system, kinship care is often offered as an alternative to traditional foster care, but this type of placement brings unique challenges that are experienced by child welfare workers, caregivers, and children in care. Policies and interventions must be geared toward addressing these challenges and providing services that target the specific needs of each group involved in kinship care (e.g., child, caregiver, biological parents, child welfare workers, etc.). The following sections will outline what is known about some of these challenges and what can be done to help improve the well-being of children, caregivers, and families involved in kinship care.

Image 12.2

Mental Health in Foster/Kinship Care

Child welfare interventions and kinship care can provide better services if they have a good understanding of the prevalence of mental illness in children entering care. Tarren-Sweeney (2013) provides an overview of some of the mental health disorders children in kinship care might experience and how these might manifest themselves. He believes that most of these difficulties arise as a result of social and interpersonal difficulties and while many of these are problematic, they do not necessarily manifest in the same way as they would in an adult or in a *Diagnostic and Statistical Manual of Mental Disorders* (DSM) diagnosis. DSM diagnoses are based on clinical criteria capturing the experiences and symptoms of the more severe disorders children experience. Tarren-Sweeney found that out of a sample of 347 children in foster or kinship care, 35% of children manifested noncomplex clinical difficulties that could be categorized as discrete mental disorders or comorbidity, and that 20% experienced complex attachment- and trauma-related symptoms that cannot be accurately categorized by the DSM or International Classification of Disease (ICD) classifications. As a result, these children experienced more severe developmental adversity, greater placement instability, and were in greater need of mental health services than children with less complex disorders. That is why it is important for child welfare workers and policy makers to develop and implement interventions that can provide appropriate services for children who have been victims of trauma and their caregivers.

Kinship Versus Non-Kinship Foster Care

The type of placement a child gets in the child welfare system could be indicative of their accessibility to mental health services that can help address childhood trauma. Research shows that children raised by kin were less likely to receive mental health services than children raised in non-kinship care, and they were more likely to have to wait longer to receive these services (Liao & White, 2014; Swanke, Yampolskaya, Strozier, & Armstrong, 2016). In addition, research on adult mental health outcomes found that kinship care was not a predictor of fewer mental health issues when compared with children in non-kinship foster care, which contradicts the idea that kinship care might be more conducive to positive mental health outcomes than non-kinship care (Fechter-Leggett & O'Brien, 2010). This study also found predictive factors of positive mental health outcomes, which included being male, having a stable placement, not having parents with psychological problems, having accessibility to school services, few changes of school, having positive relationships with adults, not having a history of sexual abuse, not experiencing maltreatment in care, and not running away. These factors must be looked at when trying to determine a child's risk for developing trauma-like symptoms or to develop interventions that might help address these symptoms. Therefore, it might not be the type of placement in itself which affects a caregiver's ability to address and work with trauma, but rather their accessibility to services. When working with kinship care families, social workers must be aware of the limitations and barriers that these families might face when trying to access needed services.

Stability of Placements

A challenge in all foster care placements is to provide a safe and stable environment for children in the child welfare system. A variety of studies have looked at this issue and tried to determine the effectiveness of kinship care in providing stable placements for children (Andersen & Fallesen, 2015; Bramlett, Radel, & Chow, 2017; Koh & Testa, 2008; Koh, 2010; Liao & White, 2014). Studies have found that children in kinship care experienced greater placement stability than children in non-kinship placements and were significantly more likely to end in legal guardianship than in adoption (Koh & Testa, 2008; Koh, 2010). Other studies contradict these findings and report that for the most part, children in kinship care did not experience greater stability when compared to other types of care (Andersen & Fallesen, 2015; Bramlett et al., 2017; Koh & Testa, 2008; Liao & White, 2014). However, they found that children with high-quality kin (characterized by empathy and dutifulness) were less likely to experience placement instability when placed with kin (Andersen & Fallesen, 2015).

Risk Behaviors and Child Competence

Another important challenge in kinship care is to provide services that identify and reduce children's risk behaviors, as well as identify services, interventions, and placements that will increase a child's competence (Blakely et al., 2017; Taussig & Clyman, 2011; Washington, Cryer-Coupet, Coakley, Labban, Gleeson, & Shears., 2014). Research has found that age, kin involvement, and fictive kin involvement (e.g., phone calls, visits, etc.) were associated with lower-risk behavior (Blakely et al., 2017). In contrast, Taussig and Clyman (2011) found that longer length of time living with kin was associated with increased risk behavior, such as illegal behaviors, poor grades, sexual risk behaviors, substance abuse, and total risk behaviors. However, this study also found that time living with kin had no significant relationship with competence or behavioral problems of a child. When looking at child competence, changes in family resources (e.g., food, clothes, transportation, and time to sleep) were significantly and positively related to changes in total competence of children. In other words, children had higher levels of competence when their families had more adequate resources (Washington et al., 2014). In addition, a caregiver's education, child's age, caregiver's social support, and healthy family functioning were also significantly and positively associated with competence (Washington et al., 2014).

Biological Parent Relationships

Figuring out what level of involvement, if any, biological parents should have with their children is another challenge in kinship care. Research shows that children's relationship with their biological parents is a significant predictor of that child's competence (Washington, Gleeson, & Rulison, 2013). Similarly, they found that paternal involvement had a significant positive relationship with the competence of African American children placed in informal kinship care. It was found that fathers' increased contact and good relationship with their children and their caregivers led to increased competence levels in the child (Washington et al., 2013). In addition, they found that a good father-child relationship was more commonly found in non-kinship placements (Washington et al., 2013). These findings demonstrate the importance of maintaining and protecting the biological parent's relationship with their children whether they are placed in kinship or non-kinship care

A positive trend was also found between children's competence and mothers' increased contact and good relationship with their children and their caregivers. This trend was not statistically significant, but the quality of a mother's relationship did serve as a predictor for a child's competence levels (Washington et al., 2014). However, one study found that non-kinship placements demonstrated better outcomes in aspects of contact with and attitudes of parents. Mothers were more likely to respond positively to a non-kinship placement, allow the child to remain in that placement, and get along better with the non-kinship parents in that placement (Vanschoonlandt, Vanderfaeillie, Van Holen, De Maeyer, & Andries, 2012).

Green and Goodman (2010) identified three factors that increased the probability of having high birth parent involvement. Factors that increased this probability were when the birth parent had a close relationship with the grandmother and the grandmother was satisfied with her life, when there was a younger child living with the grandmother and there was no CPS involvement, and when families had informal kinship arrangements (twice as likely for birth parents to be highly involved). These factors should be taken into consideration when selecting a child's placement and when developing care strategies that focus on protecting and maintaining the biological parent's relationship with their child.

Caregiver Well-Being

Another challenge in kinship care is to provide services and interventions that not only target the well-being of the child but also the well-being of the caregiver. Caregivers in kinship care, as compared to foster parents, are more likely to be "older, unmarried, have less formal education, and lower income" (Koh, 2010; Liao & White, 2014). Liao and White (2014) also found that children with unmarried caregivers were more likely to experience placement disruption than children with married caregivers, which might demonstrate the importance of having a partner as an emotional or financial support. Caregiver stress and emotional strain is an important area in the literature (Denby, Testa, Alford, Cross, & Brinson, 2017; Garcia, O'Reilly, Matone, Kim, Long, & Rubin, 2015; Sprang et al., 2015). The literature shows that there is a negative relationship between child-grandparent conflicts and the emotional well-being of custodial grandparents (Sprang et al., 2015), which is to say the more conflict, the less emotional well-being. It also found that kinship caregivers were more likely to become or remain depressed than non-kinship caregivers (Garcia et al., 2015). However, caregivers of children who were doing well reported low levels of stress and strain, and it was found that the well-being of children in kinship care increased when they did not have special needs and were not receiving Supplemental Security Income (SSI) (Denby et al., 2017). Protective factors against the strain of caring for children with special needs, caring for multiple children, having low income or high stress included a caregiver's "readiness/capacity, childrearing/parenting skills, motivation/sustainability, and family involvement/support" (Denby et al., 2017). A caregiver's relationship with a child in kinship care, accessibility to resources, and health (physical and psychological) are important areas of a caregiver's well-being that must be addressed by kinship services and interventions.

In terms of service needs, kinship families had a lower number of needed services when compared to non-kinship (Liao & White, 2014). Child disability and caregiver's education level had a positive relationship with number of service needs and services sought. Adoption placement was also found to be associated with more service needs, services sought, and higher discontinuity than guardianship placements (Liao & White, 2014). Therefore, ensuring a caregiver's accessibility to needed services and resources is an important area in kinship care that should be targeted. Understanding these demographics and unique challenges that kinship caregivers face will help ensure their emotional stability and well-being, which might in turn help improve a child's placement stability and well-being.

Effects of Kinship Care on Child Well-Being

One of the challenges in kinship care is to demonstrate that this type of placement is equally as or more effective than non-kinship care placements. As social workers, there is ethical responsibility to identify what types of interventions, policies, or placements would be conducive to the most positive outcomes for clients. In this case, the literature has found significant positive outcomes that support the idea that kinship care is better than non-kinship care placements (Vanschoonlandt et al., 2012; Wu, White, & Coleman, 2015). They have found that kinship care is associated with better child outcomes, fewer behavioral problems, lower levels of mental health problems, and better functioning than non-kinship care. However, one study found that the type of placement was not a significant factor when other variables were taken into account. It was rather the number of out of home placements that was the main predictor of behavioral problems (Vanschoonlandt et al., 2012). In addition, the researchers found that older children had significantly lower levels of problem behaviors in kinship care when compared to non-kinship care, while younger children in kinship care did not demonstrate a significant relationship between kinship care and behavioral problems (Wu et al., 2015). These findings suggest that the impact of kinship care might vary across age groups and developmental stages, and these factors must be looked at when trying to determine the type of placement that would be most beneficial for a child.

Disproportionality and Disparities

Scholars have debated what would be the most appropriate and effective way to deal with disproportionality in the child welfare system. The perspective used will determine what the focus will be when selecting a placement for a child. Anyon (2011) provides an overview of four long-standing perspectives that have been used in child welfare to determine where a child should be placed and what characteristics must be emphasized when selecting a placement. The first perspective is called "expedient permanency," and its main focus is on providing permanent placements to youth in the least amount of time possible by helping youth establish a stable and secure attachment with their caregivers. The second perspective is "cultural continuity," which focuses on the idea that children should be placed where their connections to their racial and ethnic communities can be maximized. The third perspective is "family preservation," and it highlights the importance of children maintaining contact and preserving a relationship with their biological families. "Social advantage" is the fourth perspective, and it focuses on the idea that youth need environments where conditions will be conducive to youth becoming more productive and self-sufficient adults, who do not engage in illegal activities or seek out welfare dependency. These are the main child welfare perspectives that guide placement selections.

Cultural Humility/Critical Race Theory

Historically, the field of social work has encouraged the use of cultural competence in practice and research; however, new research has been done which outlines the limitations of this approach and introduces a new theory that expands upon cultural competence (Abrams & Moio, 2009; Ortega & Faller, 2011). Critical Race Theory (CRT) introduces the idea that cultural diversity is not just limited to a distinction and understanding of racial origins (cultural competence), it is also an understanding of the many subcultures (sexuality, religion, ability, etc.) that may exist within a particular ethnic group (Abrams & Moio, 2009). Placing all individuals of one ethnic group under a single umbrella limits the ability to see the larger picture and understand the client's unique beliefs, needs, and challenges.

It is not enough to understand the ethnic characteristics that have historically been associated with those groups; it is important to look at the individual differences that make each of the clients unique and which make them part of other subcultures within their ethnic group (Ortega & Faller, 2011). Incorporating CRT in practice and research will better address the disparity and disproportionality problems in the child welfare system, so that social workers do not remain blind to the unique obstacles and challenges that may be associated with subcultures within each ethnic group.

Policies Related to the Kinship Foster Care

In the 1980s, the foster care system and federal and state child welfare policy did not include kinship care (Hegar & Scannapieco, 2014). At the time, it was not child welfare practice to place children in kinship homes but rather to place them in non-kin foster homes, group care, or institutions. Much of the thinking at the time was that abusive parents come from dysfunctional homes, and therefore placing children with relatives was not appropriate. Jurisdictions choosing to assist kinship care providers who were caring for relative children did so through income assistance programs. It was not until the late 1970s and early 1980s that there was a shift in child welfare practice and federal policy began to evolve to include kinship care.

Several things occurred to precipitate this shift in child welfare policy. The number of children needing foster care increased dramatically across the United States, particularly in urban areas (Spar, 1993), and at the same time there was a shortage of foster homes. States began to consider kinship homes as a practical option. Child welfare theoretical perspective was moving more toward family-centered practice.

Another catalyst was the U.S. Supreme Court case *Miller v. Youkim* (1979), which mandated that states make federal foster care dollars available to relatives who meet foster care licensing standards, have a placement of a child in state custody, and are eligible for Aid to Families with Dependent Children (AFDC), which made them eligible for Title IV-E funding. After these events, a number of federal policies were enacted.

The Indian Child Welfare Act (1978) was the first federal policy to emphasize relative (tribal) placements as a preferred, valuable, and beneficial option for placement of an Indian child. This legislation has its own history not directly related to the above. American Indian children were disproportionately being removed from their homes and tribes and placed in non-native homes even when willing relatives were available (Mannes, 1995). The act's goal was to "protect the best interests of Indian children and to promote the stability and security of Indian tribes and families" (ICWA, 1978).

Shortly thereafter, the Adoption Assistance and Child Welfare Act of 1980 mandated states should find "the least restrictive, most family-like setting available located in close proximity to the parent's home, consistent with the best interests and special needs of the child" (AACWA, 1980). Although not explicitly stating kinship care, many states interpreted this act as indicating a preference for kinship care and enacted state laws on kinship foster care. Since these initial policies addressing kinship care, more recent federal policies have been explicit and more comprehensive. The following is a summary of the most significant as they relate to kinship care policy.

The Social Security Act was amended in 1994, giving the Department of Health and Human Services (HHS) authority to approve child welfare demonstration projects waiving certain federal legislative and regulatory requirements under Titles IV-E and IV-B. Some states opted to use the waivers to provide guardianship subsidies to relatives as a permanency option. Historically, this is important because through the strength of evidence of the effectiveness of guardianship assistance programs (Testa, 2012; Shlonsky, 2013), later policy (2008), which will be discussed, allowed relatives to receive guardianship subsidies across the country.

The Adoption and Safe Families Act of 1997 (ASFA) was the first federal legislation acknowledging the distinctive role of kin within the foster care system—specifically, two provisions of the law. The first indicated a fit and willing relative could provide a planned permanent living arrangement, and the second, that unlike children in non-kin foster care, the state did not need to pursue termination of parental rights within the allotted amount of time if the child was being cared for by a relative. In order to be eligible for reimbursement under Title IV-E, the act defined a foster home, whether kin or non-kin, as fully licensed by the state. At the time, some states were licensing or approving foster homes and kinship homes differently, waiving some licensing requirements for kinship homes. This act mandated states do not exclude relative homes, as a group, from any requirements if they wanted Title IV-E reimbursement. The act also established a federal Kinship Care Advisory Panel (Hegar & Scannapieco, 2017).

Fostering Connections to Success and Increasing Adoptions Act (FCSIA) was enacted in 2008 and had far-reaching opportunities for children and kinship care. Key provisions in the law provided federal funding for Guardianship Assistance Programs (GAPs) for states and federally recognized Indian tribes interested in expanding kinship assistance programs. As previously indicated, guardianship subsidies have increased permanency for children placed with kin (Testa, 2012).

In the most recent evolution of kinship care policy, the Family First Prevention Services Act of 2018 further strengthens supports and resources for relative care. Family First's main purpose is to provide prevention services to help keep children safely with their families and avoid the traumatic experience of entering foster care. Emphasis is on the importance of children growing up in families and ensuring children are placed in the least restrictive, most family-like setting (Family First, H.R. 1892). Key aspects of the law relating to kinship care are:

- Kinship care families are eligible for prevention and family services and programs if the child in their care is a candidate for foster care, or the guardianship arrangement is at risk of disruption or dissolution that would result in reentry into foster care.
- Eligible children, youth, parents, and kin caregivers are eligible for prevention services and programs regardless of whether they meet AFDC income-eligibility requirements required for Title IV-E reimbursement.
- A child who is with a kin caregiver for more than 6 months and meets the Title IV-E eligibility requirements will continue to be eligible for Title IV-E foster care payments at the end of the 12 months.
- States and tribes can receive Title IV-E reimbursement for up to 50% of the state's expenditures on evidence-based kinship navigator programs.
- Establish model licensing standards for relative foster family homes and require states to demonstrate that the state standards are in accord with the corresponding national model standards.

States and tribes vary on how they embrace and implement the federal policies discussed. As an example, the Guardianship Assistant Program (GAP) is not implemented by all states. There are various reasons for variation, particularly when a provision is not mandated by the law, like GAP. As of 2017, 43 Title IV-E agencies have submitted Title IV-E plan amendments to enable them to make claims for federal support of eligible guardianship assistance. (Please refer to the Child Welfare Information Gateway [https://www.childwelfare.gov/] for the most up-to-date information.)

- 35 states and the District of Columbia have been given final approval of those GAP amendments (Alabama, Alaska, Arkansas, California, Colorado, Connecticut,

District of Columbia, Hawaii, Idaho, Illinois, Indiana, Louisiana, Maine, Maryland, Massachusetts, Michigan, Minnesota, Missouri, Montana, Nebraska, New Jersey, New Mexico, New York, Nevada, North Carolina, Oklahoma, Oregon, Pennsylvania, Rhode Island, South Dakota, Tennessee, Texas, Vermont, and Washington, West Virginia, and Wisconsin).

- 8 tribes or tribal consortia have been given final approval of the GAP amendment (Confederated Salish and Kootenai Tribe, Eastern Band of Cherokee Indians, the Keweenaw Bay Indian Community, Navajo Nation, Pascua Yaqui Tribe, Port Gamble S'Klallam Tribe, the South Puget Intertribal Planning Agency, and Tolowa Dee-ni' Nation of Smith River, California (formerly Smith River Rancheria) (U.S. Children's Bureau, 2018).

Additionally, individual states passed laws related to kinship care but only for the particular state enacting the law. In the last reported legislative report (National Conference of State Legislatures, 2018):

- In 2016, 20 states enacted more than 30 bills addressing kinship care. General themes are locating and notifying relatives and giving relatives priority as guardians for a child who has been removed from their home, financial assistance to relative caregivers, and successor guardianship.
- Three states (California, Illinois, and New Mexico) enacted legislation to ensure that all efforts have been taken to identify, locate, and notify relatives and/or fictive kin of a child in out of home care.
- Other legislation in three states (Connecticut, Georgia, and Michigan) prioritized the placement of a child with an adult who is a relative or fictive kin of the child, amended the definition of relative, added a definition of half sibling, and required notification of support services for foster parents and relative caregivers.
- Five states (Arizona, Colorado, Georgia, Michigan, and Wisconsin) enacted legislation to extend or clarify the accessibility of financial assistance for relative caregivers. Additionally, five bills from five states addressed successor guardianships and the transfer of guardianship to a relative caregiver (NCSL, 2018).

Federal and state policies guide and authorize the development and implementation of programs and services in child welfare and specifically kinship care programs. The Family First Prevention Services Act is an example of how research influences policy, which then influences practice. The process continues as each new initiative is implemented and evaluated, which thus continues to influence and update policy and practice. In the next section, practice and services in kinship care will be presented with an emphasis on the evidence base for each of the programs or services.

Evidence-Supported and Evidence-Based Kinship Foster Care: Supports and Services from a Systems Perspective

As indicated in the empirical review of the literature examining kinship care families presented above, kinship families receive less support and fewer resources than other foster care non-relative families while having the same level of need. That, coupled with the fact that while kinship caregivers are caring for related children, they often have less time for social activities, feel isolated, and less supported by their community (Gordon, McKinley, Satterfield, & Curtis, 2003). Given the lack of formal and informal support kinship care families receive, interventions and support services are needed to ensure the well-being of the caregiver and the children, with an emphasis on the integration of systems such as the legal, mental and physical health, and education.

Types of Services

Image 12.3

Services to kinship foster families generally fall into four categories that focus on the integration of systems: kinship navigator programs, financial assistance, support services, and training and educational programs. Each general area of service will be discussed and the supporting evidence presented. Services may vary, depending on the type of kinship foster care (voluntary or formal). If differences exist in the delivery of services, it will be discussed.

Kinship Navigator Programs

Kinship navigator programs were created over 15 years ago as a result of the unmet needs of relatives caring for their children. These early programs were community initiatives created by states and counties to help relative caregivers access financial resources, needed information, and provide supports to families caring for children they often took in during a crisis with little assistance and great need. Based on the early success of these programs, a national effort was undertaken, which resulted in the passage of the Fostering Connections to Success and Increasing Adoptions Act of 2008. This act created Family Connection Grants, funding two rounds of Kinship Navigator grants to states, tribes, and county jurisdictions. Evaluation of these grants found positive outcomes as a result of receiving services through the kinship navigator programs (James Bell Associates, Inc., 2011; Nelson-Dusek & Gerrard, 2012). Some of the positive outcomes indicated in these and other studies were:

- Kinship care providers achieved safety goals for their families.
- Caregivers and children were more involved with the services provided through the kinship navigator program.
- Caregivers reported less intense needs after the intervention compared to those caregivers who did not receive the services.
- Children in kinship care receiving navigator services had higher rates of permanency through legal guardianship and reunification with parents.
- Lower rates of reentry into the child welfare system.
- Caregivers reported improvement in mental health for the relative children they were caring for.
- Caregivers in the navigator programs experienced support, felt their needs were met, and their problems were eliminated (California Evidence-Based Clearinghouse, 2013; James Bell Associates, Inc., 2011; Nelson-Dusek & Gerrard, 2012; Woodruff, Murray, & Rushovich, 2014).

Resulting from the continued evidence supporting the impact of kinship navigator programs, in 2018 the federal government passed the Family First Prevention Services Act, which provides federal funds to all states to continue the growth and expansion of kinship navigator programs.

Kinship navigator programs' features vary by community but generally are initiatives providing information, referral, and follow-up services to kinship families raising children. Programs are designed to connect the families to benefits and services in their communities that the family and children need. Through the kinship navigator programs, coordination and connections are provided among and between the many entities a kinship family needs to negotiate, such as financial, legal, educational, and medical. Underlying all of the kinship navigator programs is a culturally sensitive approach to the unique needs of relatives caring for their kin.

As was discussed in the policy section, kinship navigator programs are defined by federal law and most recently reestablished under the Family First Prevention Services Act (Family First, 2018), which allows states and tribes to be reimbursed for up to 50% of their expenditures to provide kinship navigator programs. The Family First Prevention Services Act specifies that kinship navigator programs meet the following requirements (42 U.S.C. 627):

- Kinship navigator programs must be coordinated with other state or local agencies that promote service coordination or provide information and referral services, including the entities that provide 2-1-1 or 3-1-1 information systems where available, to avoid duplication or fragmentation of services to kinship care families.
- Must be planned and operated in consultation with kinship caregivers and organizations representing them, youth raised by kinship caregivers, relevant government agencies, and relevant community-based or faith-based organizations.

- Must establish information and referral systems that link kinship caregivers, kinship support group facilitators, and kinship service providers:
  - To each other;
  - Eligibility and enrollment information for federal, state, and local benefits;
  - Relevant training to assist kinship caregivers in caregiving and in obtaining benefits and services;
  - Relevant legal assistance and help in obtaining legal services.
- Must provide outreach to kinship care families by establishing, distributing, and updating a kinship care website or other relevant guides or outreach materials.
- Must promote partnership between public and private agencies, including schools, community- or faith-based organizations, and relevant government agencies, to increase their knowledge of the needs of kinship care families and to promote better services for those families.
- Under federal law, these programs may also establish and support a kinship care ombudsman with authority to intervene and help kinship caregivers access services and support any other activities designed to assist kinship caregivers in obtaining benefits and services to improve their caregiving.

As of April 2018, there are currently 73 kinship navigator programs throughout the United States. The following is an example of the kinship navigator program of one state. To view the complete list, please go to grandfamilies.org.

Arkansas Voices for the Children Left Behind

Arkansas Voices for the Children Left Behind's Mission is to advocate for children left behind because of a parent's incarceration or any other reason and to provide mentoring, services and supports for children, their caregivers, and incarcerated parent with the goal of strengthening and empowering the family unit (http://www.arkansasvoices.org).

Examples of Arkansas Voices services are:

- Parenting classes: Arkansas State Hospital, ACC units, ADC prisons, and Pulaski County Jail;
- Development of co-parenting agreements between incarcerated parents and the caregivers of the children;
- Support groups and services for kinship caregivers;
- School-based services for children whose lives have been impacted by incarceration of a parent, relative or other significant person; children with a parent returning home, and children in the foster care system;
- Reunification and re-entry services for prisoners and their families;
- Family literacy services, including financial literacy and health literacy;
- Referrals to services and supports provided by the State and the community.

Financial and Health Services

The second category of services provided to kinship families is financial services. Financial services are quite different for kinship care families, contingent on varying factors, such as the legal status of the kinship care family (voluntary versus formal), the income of the family and child, the number of children in the home, and if the child has a disability. The needs of the children are often the same, but voluntary kinship care providers, particularly grandparents, may face greater challenges than non-kinship care providers, such as being older, lower income, and lack of access to information and resources (Sakai, Lin, & Flores, 2011; Lin, 2014).

Voluntary kinship care families are eligible to receive child-only grants through the Temporary Assistance to Needy Families Program (TANF) but are not eligible to receive the higher foster care maintenance payments formal kinship care providers and non-kinship care providers receive. Kinship caregivers do not need to have custody of the child in order to receive financial assistance. Caregiver families, if meeting the criteria, may also be eligible to receive assistance based on their income, but the child-only grant is based on the child's income, not the families.

Along with TANF, kinship care families below a certain income level may be eligible for the Federal Food Stamps program, Supplemental Nutrition Assistance Program (SNAP). The relative child can be counted toward the household size and income in determining eligibility for SNAP. There is not a similar TANF child-only eligibility for SNAP.

Kinship caregivers and relative children may be eligible for Supplemental Security Income (SSI) through Title XVI of the Social Security Act. The SSI program makes cash assistance payments to aged, blind, and disabled persons who have limited income and resources. Many states pay a supplemental benefit to persons in addition to their federal benefits (Social Security Administration, retrieved May 2, 2018, https://www.ssa.gov/redbook/eng/overview-disability.htm).

Various states have financially supplemented kinship care families in order to provide initial funding to the family to ensure the safety and well-being of the child (Baumann, Esterline, Henry, Sheets, & Witttenstrom, 2008; Lin, 2014). Kinship caregivers may need assistance purchasing products to ensure the child has a place to sleep or live, such as a mattress, crib, and/or rent money for a larger apartment. As indicated earlier, many kinship care families take in more than one child in order to keep siblings together and may need accommodations to care for the children.

Only formal kinship caregivers are eligible to receive guardianship or foster care payments. Requirements for receiving these payments differ from state to state, tribe to tribe, and in the U.S. Territories (Child Welfare Information Gateway, 2016). As discussed in the policy section, states and tribes, through the Fostering Connections Act, have the option to provide payment to children placed with relatives through a guardianship arrangement. Kinship caregivers who become licensed foster parents and have children placed with them through the child welfare and court systems are eligible for foster care maintenance payments.

Along with these financial services, children living in kinship care arrangement are eligible for health insurance as well. Children usually receive health care through Medicaid or the Children's Health Insurance Program (CHIP). Often, the types of services are similar, but with CHIP, states have different rules for eligibility and coverage. Both programs are based on the child's income only (Centers for Medicaid and Medical Services [CMS], 2018: https://www.medicaid.gov/federal-policy-Guidance/index.html).

Support Services

When thinking about the support services kinship care families require, it is important to approach it through a systems perspective in order to access the array of services needed. Support services include support groups, mental health services, legal services, and respite. It is through the integration of these multiple public systems that the needs of the kinship caregiver and children will be met.

Support Groups

There are a number of support group models that have been found to be effective with kinship caregivers. The traditional support group model, which takes place in the community and is relatively easy and inexpensive to implement, has been found to be highly effective and highly valued by the kinship caregiver (Smith & Monahan, 2006; Strozier, 2012). Support groups provide caregivers with emotional and community support, relaxation, and respite. Additionally, kinship caregivers and children who participated in support groups increased their social support (Strozier, 2012).

Another effective approach to support groups with kinship caregivers is a peer-to-peer model (Denby, 2011). Based on social cognitive theory, kinship caregivers are paired with a full-time, paid kinship liaison who is either a current or former kinship care provider. Kinship liaisons are assigned to a kinship caregiver at the time the related child is placed in the home. Kinship liaisons provide the kinship caregiver with information and referral service as needed by the family. The level of intensity of the peer-to-peer interaction is based on the need of the kinship caregiver and child. The peer-to-peer approach increased the kinship caregivers' knowledge of accessing services and the permanency process, increased the kinship caregiver's coping ability, and increased the willingness to be a long-term resource for the children (Denby, 2011).

Mental Health Services

As discussed in the challenges section above, there is clearly a need for mental health services for children in kinship care, many of whom experience multiple adverse childhood experiences. In a comprehensive review of the literature on effective mental health interventions for children in care (Hambrick, Oppenheim-Weller, N'zi, & Taussig, 2016), 10 efficacious interventions were identified demonstrating positive mental health outcomes for children. Common across all the interventions was that they addressed outcomes of behavioral, internalizing, cognitive/academic, and physiological domains (Hambrick et. al, 2016). The following are the interventions (if wanting more information for specific intervention, please refer to the professional literature):

- Attachment and Biobehavioral Catchup (ABC)
- Child-Parent Psychotherapy (CPP)
- Fostering Healthy Futures (FHF)
- Incredible Years (IY)
- Keeping Foster Parents Trained and Supported (KEEP)
- Kids in Transition to School (KITS)
- Parent-Child Interaction Therapy (PCIT)
- Short Enhanced Cognitive-Behavioral Parent Training (CEBPT)
- Trauma-Focused Cognitive Behavioral Therapy (TF-CBT), and
- Treatment Foster Care Oregon for Preschoolers (TFCO-P)

Legal Services

Kinship caregivers, depending on whether they are in an informal or formal kinship care arrangement, need assistance in understanding the legal process. Resources available to kinship caregivers vary by state, tribe, or jurisdiction. There are national organizations and websites, such as Generations United, the Child Welfare Information Gateway, and AARP, for kinship caregivers to access. Kinship caregivers may have difficulty finding an affordable lawyer if they decide they want representation in the legal process. In most communities, there are low- or no-cost alternatives available, such as Area Agencies on Aging, legal aid clinics, and local law schools. Older kinship caregivers may be about to access referral service through AARP Legal Services Network. Kinship navigator programs and support groups may also provide legal guidance.

Respite

The last general type of support service need is respite care. Kinship caregivers may at times want a break from caring for their related child. Respite care refers to programs giving kinship caregivers a break by caring for children for short periods of time when the caregivers request the service. Respite care is provided by a respite caregiver, either in the home or the children visit the respite home during the time the kinship caregiver is taking a break. These services are often provided to the kinship caregiver by the child welfare agency.

Training and Education Services for Kinship Caregivers

Kinship caregivers raising related children have unique training and education needs. Often, kinship caregivers do not feel like they require training to take care of their grandchild, niece, nephew, or other relation. Kinship caregivers may benefit from training, especially if they are raising a child who has experienced trauma or who has developmental challenges. Parenting skills training and other forms of information on parenting have been found to be helpful for kinship caregivers (Kicklighter, Whitley, Kelley, Shipskie, Taube, & Berry, 2007; Strozier et al., 2004).

Similar to other areas, the training and educational programming for kinship caregivers varies by state, tribe, or jurisdiction. Some states and tribes require formal kinship caregivers to go through a series of trainings as part of the foster care licensing process. These trainings usually focus on child development, effects of child abuse and neglect, substance abuse issues, the child welfare system, court system, and other areas related to fostering a child. Informal kinship caregivers are usually not required to go through a series of trainings but may be offered the opportunity.

Some examples of what state offerings are (Child Welfare Information Gateway):

- Oregon Department of Human Services has Foster Parent and Relative Caregiver Training, which includes links to videos on parenting foster youth and covers the importance of birth families and child development, as well as the impact of abuse, behavior management, and discipline versus punishment.
- Washington State Department of Social and Health Services provides Kinship Care: Raising Children. Information is provided on what services are available, including information and training on caregiving, available through several resources in Washington.
- In Maryland, through the University of Maryland at Baltimore, In-Service Training for Resource and Adoptive Parents and Kinship Caregivers is provided. The training program is designed to equip kinship and adoptive parents with the education, resources, and tools they need to help their children with complex situations or caregiving issues.
- Tennessee Department of Children's Services has Foster Parent Training Course Catalog: Parent Learning and Development. They offer learning opportunities that help kinship parents in Tennessee to provide a safe, nurturing, and loving environment for the children in their care. Information is provided on medical care, education, problem solving, and teamwork skills.

Case Application

The following kinship care case vignette is based on real situations that exemplify the challenges and opportunities faced by families and children in kinship care. Please apply the knowledge you have gained from the chapter to the case vignette. Questions are provided to help guide you through the case.

Additionally, there are several general questions for the overall chapter.

Case Vignette

Sixty-one-year-old Gloria Stewart has been caring for her two grandchildren, Robert, 7, and Marie, 4, for the past 2 years. They live in a small metropolitan area. She has a two-bedroom apartment, which, up until recently, she shared with her single son, Martin, 31, who is a school bus driver for the local district. Ms. Stewart was granted guardianship of Robert, but not Marie, by dependency court. This situation has prevented Ms. Stewart from adequately addressing Marie's school and medical needs. Marie's custody is with the state child welfare agency.

Robert's father is incarcerated; Marie's father lives in the city and has a job at a clothing factory. Once a month, he visits her home and gives Ms. Stewart $30 toward the care of Marie. This is his only contact with his daughter, although he has expressed an interest in seeking custody of her. When asked what prevents his assuming the care of his child, he cites the obstacles of child care, his lack of parenting skills, and his living arrangements. In spite of his failure to address these issues, he has prevented Ms. Stewart from securing custody of Marie.

Robert has had serious problems for a few years. For a short time, he attended therapy at a local mental health center. However, his visits stopped for several reasons: the center was an hour's bus ride each way; the waiting room was filled with all the center's clients; and the wait was too long. Ms. Stewart discontinued the visits because she believes that Robert will outgrow his problems. Meanwhile, Robert continues to become involved in neighborhood fights, he steals, and he is a chronic bed wetter.

Marie is experiencing problems, also. As an infant, she was diagnosed with physical problems as a result of her mother's drug use during pregnancy. She is developmentally delayed in the area of social and cognitive skills. Ms. Stewart does not seek wellness visits for either child, only medical treatment for emergencies or symptomatic problems. Robert is on medical assistance and is assigned to a local HMO, and Marie has medical assistance coverage. The children appear to be attached to their grandmother, who loves them dearly but is beginning to show signs of impatience with Robert. She also is frustrated because she has had to forfeit several of her favorite activities, including singing in the church choir and her Wednesday Bible studies.

Ms. Stewart receives $230 a month from Temporary Assistance for Needy Families (TANF) payments for Robert and $820 a month in foster care payments for Marie. She does not receive food stamps. Ms. Stewart works at a part-time job for which she earns $700 each month but does not receive medical or leave benefits. The child welfare agency provides day care money for Marie; however, Robert is ineligible for Title IV-A day care funds since Ms. Stewart is not a part of his TANF case. Finally, Ms. Stewart is considering allowing the child welfare agency to take custody of Robert because the financial allowance for foster care would be much greater. But she is not happy with the requirements of foster care.

DISCUSSION QUESTIONS

1. Is Ms. Stewart the appropriate placement option for Robert and Marie? Why?
2. Thinking about the Family First Policy, what additional services might the child welfare social worker suggest to Ms. Stewart?
3. As the child welfare worker, what would a person do to enhance this placement for Robert, Marie, and Ms. Stewart?
4. Should Marie's father be considered as a placement option? Why?
5. What is the importance of kinship navigator programs?

References

Abrams, L. S., & Moio, J. A. (2009). Critical race theory and the cultural competence dilemma in social work education. *Journal of Social Work Education 45*(2), 245–261.

Adoption Assistance and Child Welfare Act. (1980). Public Law 96-272.

Andersen, S. H., & Fallesen, P. (2015). Family matters? The effect of kinship care on foster care disruption rates. *Child Abuse & Neglect, 48*, 68–79.

Anyon, Y. (2011). Reducing racial disparities and disproportionalities in the child welfare system: Policy perspectives about how to serve the best interests of African American youth. *Children and Youth Services Review, 33*, 242–253.

Ayón, C., Aisenberg, E., & Cimino, A. (2013). Latino families in the nexus of child welfare, welfare reform, and immigration policies: Is kinship care a lost opportunity? *Social Work, 58*(1), 91–94. https://doi-org.ezproxy.uta.edu/10.1093/sw/sws014

Baumann, D., Esterline, J., Henry, J., Sheets, J., & Wittenstrom, K. (2008). Overview and Preliminary Evaluation of the Relative Caregiver Assistance Program. Texas Department of Family and Protective Services.

Blakely, G., Leon, S., Fuller, A., & Jhe Bai, G. (2017). Foster care children's kinship involvement and behavioral risks: A longitudinal study. *Journal of Child & Family Studies, 26*(9), 2450–2462. doi: 10.1007/s10826-017-0746-0

Bramlett, M. D., Radel, L. F., & Chow, K. (2017). Health and well-being of children in kinship care: Findings from the National Survey of Children in Nonparental Care. *Child Welfare, 95*(3), 41–60.

Boyd, R. (2014). African American disproportionality and disparity in child welfare: Toward a comprehensive conceptual framework. *Children and Youth Services Review 37*, 15–27.

Burgess, C., Rossvoll, F., Wallace, B., & Daniels, B. (2010). "It's just like another home, just another family, so it's nae different." Children's voices in kinship care: A research study about the experience of children in kinship care in Scotland. *Child and Family Social Work, 15*(3), 297–306. http://dx.doi.org/10.1111/j.1365-2206.2009.00671.x

California Evidence-Based Clearinghouse for Child Welfare. (2013, June). Kinship Navigator Program. http://www.cebc4cw.org/program/kinship-navigator-program

Cardoso, J. B., Gomez, R. J., & Padilla, Y. C. (2009). What happens when family resources are across international boundaries? An exploratory study on kinship placement in Mexican immigrant families. *Child Welfare, 88*(6), 67–84. http://search.ebscohost.com.ezproxy.uta.edu/login.aspx?direct=true&db=pbh&AN=49717649&site=ehost-live

Child Welfare Information Gateway. (2016). Kinship Caregivers and the Child Welfare System. Washington, DC: U.S. Department of Health and Human Services, Children's Bureau.

Child Welfare League of America. (2018). *Kinship Care: Traditions of Caring and Collaborating Model of Practice*. Washington, DC: Author.

Cross, S. L., Day, A. G., & Byers, L. G. (2010). American Indian grand families: A qualitative study conducted with grandmothers and grandfathers who provide sole care for their grandchildren. *Journal of Cross-Cultural Gerontology, 25*(4), 371–383. doi: 10.1007/s10823-010-9127-5

Dakil, S. R., Cox, M., Lin, H., & Flores, G. (2011). Racial and ethnic disparities in physical abuse reporting and child protective services interventions in the United States. *Journal of the National Medical Association, 103(*9–10), 926–931. https://doi-org.ezproxy.uta.edu/10.1016/S0027-9684(15)30449-1

Denby, R. W. (2011). Kinship liaisons: A peer-to-peer approach to supporting kinship caregivers. *Children and Youth Services Review, 33*, 217–235.

Denby, R. W., Testa, M. F., Alford, K. A., Cross, C. L., & Brinson, J. A. (2017). Protective factors as mediators and moderators of risk effects on perceptions of child well-being in kinship care. *Child Welfare, 95*(4), 111–136.

Family First Prevention Services Act of 2018 (H.R. 1892).

Fechter-Leggett, M. O., & O'Brien, K. (2010). The effects of kinship care on adult mental health outcomes of alumni of foster care. *Children and Youth Services Review, 32*, 206–213.

Foster, E. M., Hillemeier, M. M., & Bai, Y. (2011). Explaining the disparity in placement instability among African-American and white children in child welfare: A Blinder-Oaxaca decomposition. *Children and Youth Services Review, 33*, 118–125.

Garcia, A., O'Reilly, A., Matone, M., Kim, M., Long, J., & Rubin, D. (2015). The influence of caregiver depression on children in non-relative foster care versus kinship care placements. *Maternal & Child Health Journal, 19*(3), 459–467. doi: 10.1007/s10995-014-1525-9

Gordon, A. L., McKinley, S. E., Satterfield, M. L., & Curtis, P. A. (2003). A first look at the need for enhanced support services for kinship caregivers. *Child Welfare, 8*(1), 77–96.

Green, Y. R., & Goodman, C. C. (2010). Understanding birthparent involvement in kinship families: Influencing factors and the importance of placement arrangement. *Children and Youth Services Review, 32*, 1357–1364.

Hambrick, E. P., Oppenheim-Weller, S., N'zi, A., & Taussig, H. N. (2016). Mental health intervention for children in foster care: A systematic review. *Children and Youth Services Review, 70*, 65–77.

Hegar, R. L., & Scannapieco, M. (2017). Foster care to kinship adoption: The road less traveled. *Adoption Quarterly Journal, 20*(1), 83–97.

Hegar, R. L., & Scannapieco, M. (2014). Preservation of the extended family. In G. P. Mallon & P. McCartt Hess (Eds.), *Child Welfare for the Twenty-First Century: A Handbook of Practices, Policies, and Programs*, 2nd ed. New York: Columbia University Press.

Hong, J. S., Algood, C. L., Chiu, Y., & Lee, S. A. (2011). An ecological understanding of kinship foster care in the United States. *Journal of Child and Family Studies ,20*(6), 863–872.

Indian Child Welfare Act of 1978, P.L. 95-608, 92 Stat. 3069.

James Bell Associates Inc. (2011). Family Connection Discretionary Grants. 2009-Funded grantees year 2 cross-site evaluation report. Kinship Navigator Program area summary. Arlington, VA: Author.

Kicklighter, J. R., Whitley, D. M., Kelley, S. J., Shipskie, S. M., Taube, J. L., & Berry, R. C. (2007). Grandparents raising grandchildren: A response to a nutrition and physical activity intervention. *Journal of the American Dietetic Association, 107*(7), 1210–1213.

Kim, H., Chenot, D., & Ji, J. (2011). Racial/ethnic disparity in child welfare systems: A longitudinal study utilizing the Disparity Index (DI). *Children and Youth Services Review, 33*, 1234–1244. 10.1016/j.childyouth.2011.02.021

Knott, T., & Donovan, K. (2010). Disproportionate representation of African-American children in foster care: Secondary analysis of the National Child Abuse and Neglect Data System, 2005. *Children and Youth Services Review, 32*, 679–684.

Koh, E. (2010). Permanency outcomes of children in kinship and non-kinship foster care: Testing the external validity of kinship effects. *Children & Youth Services Review, 32*(3), 389–398. doi: 10.1016/j.childyouth.2009.10.010

Koh, E., & Testa, M. F. (2008). Propensity score matching of children in kinship and nonkinship foster care: Do permanency outcomes still differ? *Social Work Research, 32*(2), 105–116.

Kopera-Frye, K. (2009). Needs and issues of Latino and Native American nonparental relative caregivers: Strengths and challenges within a cultural context. *Family and Consumer Sciences Research Journal, 37*(3), 394–410. https://doi-org.ezproxy.uta.edu/10.1177/1077727X08329563

Liao, M., & White, K. R. (2014). Post-permanency service needs, service utilization, and placement discontinuity for kinship versus non-kinship families. *Children and Youth Services Review, 44*, 370–378.

Limb, G. E., Shafer, K., & Sandoval, K. (2014). The impact of kin support on urban American Indian families. *Child & Family Social Work, 19*(4), 432–442. https://doi-org.ezproxy.uta.edu/10.1111/cfs.12041

Lin, C-H. (2014). Evaluating services for kinship care families: A systematic review. *Children and Youth Services Review, 36*, 32–41.

Mannes, M. (1995). Factors and events leading to the passage of the Indian Child Welfare Act. *Child Welfare, 74, 1*, 264.

Miller v. Youakim, 44 U.S. 125, 99 S. Ct. 957. (1979).

Mokuau, N., Garlock-Tuiali'i, J., & Lee, P. (2008). Has social work met its commitment to Native Hawaiians and other Pacific Islanders? A review of the periodical literature. *Social Work, 53*(2), 115–121. http://search.ebscohost.com.ezproxy.uta.edu/login.aspx?direct=true&db=pbh&AN=31951662&site=ehost-live

National Conference of State Legislatures. (2018). http://www.ncsl.org/research/human-services/2016-child-welfare-legislative-enactments-summary

Nelson-Dusek, S., & Gerrard, M. D. (2012). Minnesota Kinship Navigator Project: Final progress report. Family Connections Discretionary Grants, Reporting Period October 2009-September 2012. St. Paul, MN: Wilder Research. http://www.wilder.org/Wilder-

Office of the Administration for Children & Families. (2013). Title IV-E Guardianship Assistance. *Children's Bureau*. Washington, DC: Author.

Ortega, R. M., & Faller, K. C. (2011). Training child welfare workers from an intersectional cultural humility perspective: A paradigm shift. *Child Welfare 90*(5), 27–49.

Rhee, S., Chang, J., Weaver, D., & Wong, D. (2008). Child maltreatment among immigrant Chinese families: Characteristics and patterns of placement. *Child Maltreatment, 13*(3), 269–279. https://doi-org.ezproxy.uta.edu/10.1177/1077559507313461

Ryan, J. P., Sung Hong, J., Herz, D., & Hernandez, P. M. (2010). Kinship foster care and the risk of juvenile delinquency. *Children and Youth Services Review, 32*, 1823–1830.

Sakai, C., Lin, H., & Flores, G. (2011). Health outcomes and family services in kinship care: Analysis of a national sample of children in the child welfare system. *Archives of Pediatrics and Adolescent Medicine, 165*(2), 159–165.

Scannapieco, M., & Hegar, R. L. (2002). Kinship care providers: Designing an array of supportive services. *Child and Adolescent Social Work Journal, 19*(4), 315–327.

Scott, J., Faulkner, M., Cardoso, J. B., & Burstain, J. (2014). Kinship care and undocumented Latino children in the Texas foster care system: Navigating the child welfare-immigration crossroads. *Child Welfare, 93*(4), 53–69. http://search.ebscohost.com.ezproxy.uta.edu/login.aspx?direct=true&db=pbh&AN=110870806&site=ehost-live

Shlonsky, A. (2013). Evaluations of subsidized legal guardianship. In B. Kerman, M. Freundlich, & A. N. Maluccio (Eds.), *Achieving Permanence for Older Children and Youth in Foster Care*, 2nd ed. New York: Columbia University Press.

Smith, C. J., & Monahan, D. J. (2006). KinNet: A Demonstration Project for a National Support Network for Kinship Care Providers. *Journal of Health and Social Policy, 22*(3–4), 215–231. doi: 10.1300/J045v22n03_14.

Social Security Administration. Retrieved May 2, 2018, https://www.ssa.gov/redbook/eng/overview-disability.htm

Spar, K. (1993). "Kinship" Foster Care: An Emerging Federal Issue. U.S. Report for Congress.

Sprang, G., Choi, M., Eslinger, J. G., & Whitt-Woosley, A. L. (2015). The pathway to grandparenting stress: Trauma, relational conflict, and emotional well-being. *Aging & Mental Health, 19*(4), 315–324. doi: 10.1080/13607863.2014.938606

Strozier, A. L. (2012). The effectiveness of support groups in increasing social support for kinship caregivers. *Children and Youth Services Reviews, 34*(5), 876–881.

Strozier, A. L., Elrod, B., Beiler, P., Smith, A., & Carter, K. (2004). Developing a network of support for relative caregivers. *Children and Youth Services Review, 26*(7), 641–656.

Swanke, J. R., Yampolskaya, S., Strozier, A., & Armstrong, M. I. (2016). Mental health services utilization and time to care: A comparison of children in traditional foster care and children in kinship care. *Children and Youth Services Review, 68*, 154–158.

Tarren-Sweeney, M. (2013). An investigation of complex attachment- and trauma-related symptomatology among children in foster and kinship care. *Child Psychiatry and Human Development, 44*(6), 727–741. doi: 10.1007/s10578-013-0366-x

Taussig, H. N., & Clyman, R. B. (2011). The relationship between time spent living with kin and adolescent functioning in youth with a history of out of home placement. *Child Abuse & Neglect, 35*(1), 78–86. doi: 10.1016/j.chiabu.2010.09.001

Testa, M. F. (2012). Support the alternative care of children by relatives: The U.S. guardianship assistance program. Paper presented at the Joint World Conference on Social Work and Social Development, Stockholm, Sweden, 8–12 July 2012.

U.S. Department of Health and Human Services, Administration for Children and Families, Administration on Children, Youth and Families, Children's Bureau. (2019). The AFCARS Report: Preliminary FY 2018 estimates as of August 22, 2019. Washington, DC: Author.

U.S. Department of Health and Human Services, Administration for Children and Families, Administration on Children, Youth and Families, Children's Bureau. (2018). Kinship Guardianship as a Permanency Option. Washington, DC: Author.

Vakalahi, H. F. O., Heffernan, K., & Johnson, R. N. (2007). Pacific Island elderly: A model for bridging generations and systems. *The Journal of Baccalaureate Social Work, 12*(2), 26–41. http://search.ebscohost.com.ezproxy.uta.edu/login.aspx?direct=true&db=psyh&AN=2007-17812-001&site=ehost-live

Vanschoonlandt, F., Vanderfaeillie, J., Van Holen, F., De Maeyer, S., & Andries, C. (2012). Kinship and non-kinship foster care: Differences in contact with parents and foster child's mental health problems. *Children and Youth Services Review, 34*, 1533–1539.

Washington, T., Cryer-Coupet, Q. R., Coakley, T. M., Labban, J., Gleeson, J. P., & Shears, J. (2014). Examining maternal and paternal involvement as promotive factors of competence in African American children in informal kinship care. *Children and Youth Services Review*, 449–515. doi: 10.1016/j.childyouth.2014.05.019

Washington, T., Gleeson, J. P., & Rulison, K. L. (2013). Competence and African American children in informal kinship care: The role of family. *Children and Youth Services Review, 35*, 1305–1312.

Weiss, R. A., Oberleitner, L., & Easton, C. J. (2013). Preservation Versus Child Wellbeing Under the Indian Child Welfare Act. *The Journal of the American Academy of Psychiatry and the Law, 41*(1), 12–127.

Weng, S., & Nguyen, P. (2011). Factors affecting elder caregiving in multigenerational Asian American families. *Families in Society: The Journal of Contemporary Social Services, 92*(3), 329–335. http://search.ebscohost.com.ezproxy.uta.edu/login.aspx?direct=true&db=swh&AN=81497&site=ehost-live

Woodmass, K., Weisberg, S., Shlomi, H., Rockymore, M., & Wells, S. J. (2017). Examining the potential for racial disparity in out of home placement decisions: A quantitative matched-pair study. *Children and Youth Services Review, 75*, 96–109.

Woodruff, K., Murray, K., & Rushovich, B. (2014). Kinship caregiver perception of a state-supervised kinship navigator program. *Journal of Family Social work*, 17(2), 136–153. doi: 10.1080/10522158.2014.880984

Wu, Q., White, K. R., & Coleman, K. L. (2015). Effects of kinship care on behavioral problems by child age: A propensity score analysis. *Children & Youth Services Review*, 57, 1–8. doi: 10.1016/j.childyouth.2015.07.020

Figure Credits

Img. 12.1: Copyright © 2013 Depositphotos/londondeposit.
Img. 12.2: Copyright © 2015 Depositphotos/Tanya.Ru.
Img. 12.3: Copyright © 2012 Depositphotos/stillfx.

CHAPTER · 13

Permanency Planning in Child Welfare

Foster and Adoptive Parents

Michele D. Hanna, Megan H. Piel, and Ruth McRoy

Overview of Chapter

The need for more foster and adoptive parents for children in the child welfare system continues, as the number of children in foster care each year hovers around 435,000 and the number waiting to be adopted hovers around 125,000 (USDHHS, 2019). The Chronicle of Social Change (2017) staff conducted a multi-state case study, including Washington, DC, reviewed state by state Adoption and Foster Care Analysis and Reporting System (AFCARS) data, Child and Family Service Review data, and interviewed key state officials in several states, focusing on the years between 2012 and 2017. Key findings indicated that while some states had succeeded in increasing the number of foster care beds, half of the states (n=25) had decreased in capacity between 2012–2017, despite diligent recruitment efforts. Of the 20 states that had an increase in non-relative foster home beds, for over half (n=11), the increase in foster youth far exceeded the increase in foster homes or beds. In some states, the decrease in nonrelated foster homes was offset by an increase in the use of kinship or related homes; however, this was not true for all states. In some states, the overall increase was localized, meaning that for some children, the only available foster beds were far from home (Chronicle of Social Change, 2017). The need for adoptive parents is clear—the over 100,000 children in care waiting to be adopted are in care because they have been abused, neglected, or abandoned and, as a result, may have special needs. Finding an adoptive family for a child requires thorough consideration of the behavioral, emotional, educational, cultural, linguistic, and physical needs of the child and the prospective parent(s)' capacity to meet these needs long term (Hanna & McRoy, 2011).

The concept of **permanency planning** became a part of child welfare practice in the late 1970s as social workers and society became increasingly concerned about the growing numbers of children in foster care and the long periods of time these children were spending in foster care with no clear plan of reunification or other plans of **permanency**, i.e., **foster care drift** (Adler, 2001; Maluccio & Fein, 1983; Pike, Downs, Emlen, Downs, & Case, 1977). The idea of **permanence**—placing a child in a home that is intended to last indefinitely (Pike et al., 1977)—continues to drive the practice of permanency planning in child welfare. Foster care was never meant to be permanent (Meisels & Loeb, 1956). From the moment a child is legally placed in the temporary custody of the state or county child welfare agency, the child welfare worker is mandated to identify and work toward a permanency plan goal for that child and family (Maluccio & Fein, 1983). This chapter will provide a brief legislative history of permanency planning and review various permanency planning options for children in foster care.

In addition, this chapter includes a discussion of the role and services provided to foster and adoptive parents as part of the permanency planning process prior to the child exiting care. Other forms of permanency are discussed in other chapters throughout this text. For example, engaging birth families is discussed in Chapter 5, kinship families are discussed in Chapter 12, and while not a permanency plan, services to children aging out of foster care are discussed in Chapter 11. Chapter 15 focuses on services to families formed by adoption and guardianship after they exit care.

Permanency Planning

Legislative History of Permanency Planning

The Child Abuse Prevention and Treatment Act of 1974 was passed in part as a means to allow the federal government authority to intervene and protect children from abusive and neglectful parents. Foster care was seen as a temporary intervention, with the idea that services could be provided to families to correct the conditions that led to removal, and the children would return home through reunification—permanently (Jimenez, 1990). By 1980, when the Adoption Assistance and Child Welfare Act (AACWA) was passed, it had become abundantly clear that reunification was not always feasible and that foster care was not a viable permanency plan. The AACWA was the first federal legislation to emphasize the need for permanence and permanency planning in child welfare (Adler, 2001). The AACWA required all children placed in out of home care (a home other than the one from which they were removed) to have a case plan, and required that the case plan address services to facilitate reunification with the family or an alternative permanent placement of the child (Atwell, 1992). The status of every child who was not in a permanent placement was required to be reviewed regularly by the court or a case review system, with the court making a determination within 18 months of the child's initial removal from care, as to whether not a child would be reunited with the parents, placed for adoption or legal guardianship, or remain in long-term foster care (Child Welfare Information Gateway, 2019a). Although AACWA included the creation of the Federal Adoption Assistance Program to assist adoptive parents of children with special needs, the emphasis of the act was clearly on preserving or reunifying the family (Adler, 2001). This emphasis was reinforced by the requirement that states receiving federal funding make reasonable efforts to either prevent removal of a child from the home or to reunite the family as soon as possible (Adler, 2001). Over time, some felt that the mandate to make reasonable efforts, in practice, resulted in parents being afforded an *unreasonable* number of opportunities over many years to work toward correcting the conditions that led to the child's removal (Adler, 2001).

The number of children in foster care rose from 302,000 in 1980 to 507,000 in 1996, with over half of those children waiting to be adopted (Johnston, 2017). In response to this increase, Congress passed the Adoption and Safe Families Act (ASFA) in 1997 with the express intent to expedite permanency, specifically adoption, for the over 250,000 children waiting to be adopted (Townsend, Hignight, & Rubovits, 2008). While not changing the definition of reasonable efforts per se, ASFA emphasized the health and safety of the child as paramount in determining reasonable efforts and required that reasonable efforts "be made to place the child in a timely manner in accordance with the permanency plan, and to complete whatever steps are necessary to finalize the permanent placement of the child" (ASFA, H.R. 867-3 Sec. 101(a)(E)(ii)). Reunification remained the primary permanency plan for children; however, ASFA extended services to families to include time-limited reunification services, as well as promote adoption and support services, with an emphasis on child safety, renaming the previously named *Family Preservation and Support Services Program* to the *Safe and Stable Families Program* (Child Welfare Information Gateway, 2019a).

ASFA also expedited time frames for permanency, requiring a permanency planning hearing no later than 12 months after the child was placed in out of home care, as opposed to the 18-month review previously required by AACWA. In addition, ASFA required states to initiate termination of parental rights (TPR) if a child was in foster care for 15 of the previous 22 months (not necessarily consecutive). Termination of parental rights is required in order for a child to be legally adopted by new parents. In addition, ASFA identified extreme circumstances in which reasonable efforts to preserve and reunify the family are *not* required. In these cases, states may proceed directly to termination of parental rights and pursue a permanency plan other than reunification, thereby expediting the timeframe to permanence for the child (See Box 13.1).

ASFA also included the Adoption Incentive Program, which rewarded states financially if they increased the number of adoptions completed within the fiscal year. Although adoptions from foster care had been steadily on the rise at the time ASFA was passed, the combination of these two major provisions resulted in a relatively quick exit from care to adoption of several children who had been in foster care for an extremely long period of time shortly after the act was passed (Wulczyn, 2002). The Adoption Incentive Payment program, now known as the **Adoption and Legal Guardianship Incentive Payment program**, has been reauthorized several times, most recently funded through fiscal year 2021 for $43 million under the Family First Prevention Services Act of 2018. The program now includes incentives to states that increase permanency through legal guardianship as well as adoption (Child Welfare Information Gateway, 2019a).

BOX 13.1. Adoption and Safe Families Act (ASFA) H.R. 867 Reasonable Efforts

TITLE I—REASONABLE EFFORTS AND SAFETY REQUIREMENTS FOR FOSTER CARE AND ADOPTION PLACEMENTS

SEC. 101. CLARIFICATION OF THE REASONABLE EFFORTS REQUIREMENT.

(a) IN GENERAL.—Section 471(a)(15) of the Social Security Act (42 U.S.C. 671(a)(15)) is amended to read as follows:

"(15) provides that—

"(A) in determining reasonable efforts to be made with respect to a child, as described in this paragraph, and in making such reasonable efforts, the child's health and safety shall be the paramount concern;

"(B) except as provided in subparagraph (D), reasonable efforts shall be made to preserve and reunify families—

"(i) prior to the placement of a child in foster care, to prevent or eliminate the need for removing the child from the child's home; and

"(ii) to make it possible for a child to safely return to the child's home;

"(C) if continuation of reasonable efforts of the type described in subparagraph (B) is determined to be inconsistent with the permanency plan for the child, reasonable efforts shall be made to place the child in a timely manner in accordance with the permanency plan, and to complete whatever steps are necessary to finalize the permanent placement of the child;

"(D) reasonable efforts of the type described in subparagraph (B) shall not be required to be made with respect to a parent of a child if a court of competent jurisdiction has determined that—

"(i) the parent has subjected the child to aggravated circumstances (as defined in State law, which definition may include but need not be limited to abandonment, torture, chronic abuse, and sexual abuse);

"(ii) the parent has—

"(I) committed murder (which would have been an offense under section 1111(a) of title 18, United States Code, if the offense had occurred in the special maritime or territorial jurisdiction of the United States) of another child of the parent;

"(II) committed voluntary manslaughter (which would have been an offense under section 1112(a) of title 18, United States Code, if the offense had occurred in the special maritime or territorial jurisdiction of the United States) of another child of the parent;

Box 13.1: 105th Congress, Selection from "Adoption and Safe Families Act of 1997," 1997.

"(III) aided or abetted, attempted, conspired, or solicited to commit such a murder or such a voluntary manslaughter; or

"(IV) committed a felony assault that results in serious bodily injury to the child or another child of the parent; or H. R. 867—3

"(iii) the parental rights of the parent to a sibling have been terminated involuntarily;

"(E) if reasonable efforts of the type described in subparagraph (B) are not made with respect to a child as a result of a determination made by a court of competent jurisdiction in accordance with subparagraph (D)—

"(i) a permanency hearing (as described in section 475(5)(C)) shall be held for the child within 30 days

after the determination; and

"(ii) reasonable efforts shall be made to place the child in a timely manner in accordance with the permanency plan, and to complete whatever steps are necessary to finalize the permanent placement of the child; and

"(F) reasonable efforts to place a child for adoption or with a legal guardian may be made concurrently with reasonable efforts of the type described in subparagraph (B);"

Concurrent Planning

ASFA intentionally promotes adoption as a preferred permanency plan should attempts to reunify fail (White, 2016), and some concerns have been voiced that the time constraints on reunification efforts, the emphasis on concurrent planning, as well as the financial incentives provided to states who increase adoptions, actually serve to disincentivize and work against reunification efforts (Coupet, 2005; Hollingsworth, 2000; Lowry, 2004; White, 2016). ASFA legislatively mandated the practice of **concurrent planning**, meaning that efforts toward a permanent placement through adoption or guardianship are to be made *concurrently*, with reasonable efforts to preserve and reunify the family (White, 2016). Questions have been raised as to whether or not it is possible to work concurrently toward these two seemingly polar opposite goals.

Concurrent planning is not a new concept, having first been introduced through a demonstration project completed by Lutheran Social Services (LSS) in the late 1980s (Katz, 1990). Called the "Two-pronged Casework Approach," LSS designed the project based on the concept that if "birth parents were given the dual message that because of the child's need for permanency, the options to return home and adoption must be considered simultaneously, not sequentially," this would greatly reduce the time to case resolution (Katz, 1990, p. 221). Katz noted that the success of the project was in part due to reduced caseloads, intensive services to parents, and special training with foster parents. Unlike the requirements of ASFA, only children who were from families deemed "untreatable" participated in the program, meaning that only children whose cases were identified early, as more than likely not to result in reunification, were included. Currently, 38 states and the District of Columbia address concurrent planning under various circumstances in their state statutes (Child Welfare Information Gateway, 2017). For example, while 19 states require that the agency include concurrent planning be a part of the family case plan, only 6 states require that the agency fully disclose the concurrent plan to the family. Full text excerpts of state laws related to concurrent planning are available through the Child Welfare Information Gateway (Child Welfare Information Gateway, 2017).

Alternative Permanency Plans

As stated earlier, the primary permanency plan for most children who enter out of home care is reunification. Should the reunification plan fail or, in cases where reunification is not an option, the alternative permanency plans per ASFA are adoption, legal guardianship, or another planned permanent arrangement (APPLA), each of which will be discussed below.

Image 13.1

Adoption

Adoption is "the social, emotional, and legal process through which children who will not be raised by their birth parents become full and permanent legal members of another family, while maintaining genetic and psychological connections to their birth family" (Child Welfare Information Gateway, 2019b). Children are legally free for adoption when all parental rights are terminated or have consented to the adoption of the child (Child Welfare Information Gateway, 2016a). States vary regarding the minimum qualifications of adoptive parents regarding age, residency, and marital status (Child Welfare Information Gateway, 2016a). Currently, all 50 states allow same-sex married couples to legally adopt.

Prior to the 1960s, adoption practice, through both private and public agencies, focused primarily on finding healthy, White infants for infertile, White couples who could not have children (Sokoloff, 1993); however, by the mid-1950s, the demand for healthy, White infants far exceeded the supply. In 1961, approximately 7,500 children were being assessed to see if they should be placed for adoption in public child welfare agencies (Jeter, 1963). By 1990, this number had risen to 19,918 (Johnston, 2017). Since the late 1990s, the vast number of adoptions of children involved with the public child welfare system have been by foster parents and relatives (88%), with a small percentage by nonrelated persons (12%) (USDHHS, 2019) (see Figure 13.1 for a breakdown of relationship to adoptive parents, 1998–2018). Within the child welfare system, the type of adoption is determined by the relationship the child had with the adoptive parent at the time of adoption (Electronic Code of Federal Regulations [e-CFR], 2020).

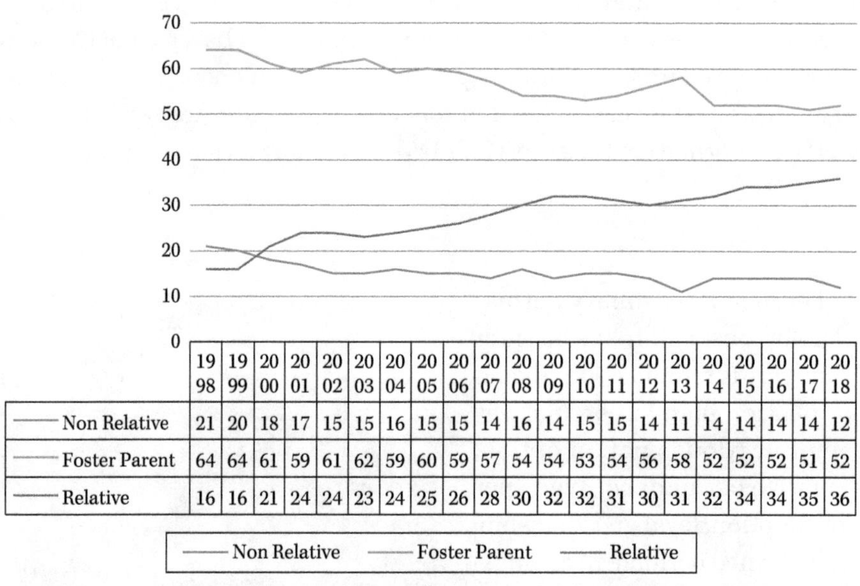

	1998	1999	2000	2001	2002	2003	2004	2005	2006	2007	2008	2009	2010	2011	2012	2013	2014	2015	2016	2017	2018
Non Relative	21	20	18	17	15	15	16	15	15	14	16	14	15	15	14	11	14	14	14	14	12
Foster Parent	64	64	61	59	61	62	59	60	59	57	54	54	53	54	56	58	52	52	52	51	52
Relative	16	16	21	24	24	23	24	25	26	28	30	32	32	31	30	31	32	34	34	35	36

FIGURE 13.1. Relationship to Adopted Children (%) 1998–2018
Source: AFCARS Report #12-26.

Foster parent adoptions are those in which the child is initially placed in a nonrelative foster home through a foster parent agreement, contract, or license. The foster parent(s) may or may not have intended to adopt at the time of the initial placement. The official decision to adopt the child is made at some point after the child was placed in the home when the child's permanency plan changes from reunification to adoption.

Until the early 1970s, states considered foster homes as a temporary living situation for children and did not consider foster parents as viable resources for permanency or adoption (Gill, 1975; Meezan & Shireman, 1982). Festinger (1974) found in a national survey of states that of the 44 states that responded, 27 (61%) either prohibited foster parent adoption or highly cautioned against it. The shift in philosophy and attitudes toward allowing foster parents to adopt became preference in both practice and policy in the late 1970s, after foster parents and child development experts began to challenge agency practices in court (Proch, 1981). By 1981, preference was given to foster parents by legislation (9 states and Washington, DC), agency policy (15 states), or in practice (19 states) (Proch, 1981). In 2018, 52% of the children were adopted by a foster parent (USDHHS, 2019).

Other relative adoptions are those in which the child is adopted by someone related to them through their birth parents by blood or marriage (kinship). In 2018, 36% of children adopted through public child welfare were adopted by a relative (USDHHS, 2019). A very small number of children (n=55 in 2018) involved in the public child welfare system are adopted by a **stepparent**, defined as the spouse of the child's birth mother or birth father (Electronic Code of Federal Regulations [e-CFR], 2020).

Nonrelative adoptions are those who do not fit any of the above categories. In the majority of these cases, the first time the child and family meet is when the child is placed in the home for adoptive purposes (Electronic Code of Federal Regulations [e-CFR], 2020).

Legal Guardianship

ASFA defines legal guardianship as

> *judicially created relationship between child and caretaker which is intended to be permanent and self-sustaining, as evidenced by the transfer to the caretaker of the following parental rights with respect to the child: protection, education, care and control of the person, custody of the person, and decision making. (Sec. 101(b))*

Taylor (1966) was the first to suggest child welfare consider legal guardianship as a means of closing a child's case when neither reunification or termination of parental rights is feasible, once a satisfactory, appropriate placement had been achieved. Guardianship can be an appropriate permanency plan when

- The child has been in a stable placement with the caregiver for a period of time.
- The child is unwilling to be adopted.
- Parental rights cannot be terminated.
- The child continues to benefit from the relationship with the birth family.
- The caregiver is able and willing to provide a permanent home for the child but is unwilling to adopt the child (Child Welfare Information Gateway, 2019c, p. 2).

Both Taylor (1966) and Krymow (1979) discussed the need for agencies to broaden their concept of guardianship to include relative or kin, especially with African American children (Taylor, 1966). In addition, both discussed the need to provide financial assistance to families who opt to become legal guardians. Krymow (1979) stated that in order for legal guardianship to truly become a viable option, "the question of subsidy, if needed, would have to be resolved" (p. 102).

Legal guardianship was identified as an alternative plan to reunification in the Adoption Assistance and Child Welfare Act (AACWA) of 1980. At that time, legal guardianship was rarely used (Berrick, 1998), with the majority of the children who exited care to legal guardianship placed with relatives or kin; however, only non-kin foster parents were eligible to receive financial assistance through state-funded subsidy (Berrick, 1998). Although the Adoption and Safe Families Act (ASFA) gave legislative preference to relatives over nonrelative caregivers and further solidified legal guardianship as a permanency plan, it did not address the issue of subsidized legal guardianship for relative kin. It was not until the passage of the Fostering Connections to Success and Increasing Adoptions Act of 2008 that states were given the option to use federal funds for kinship guardianship assistance programs (Child Welfare Information Gateway, 2019c). Kinship Guardianship Assistance provides the guardian with an array of services, including a monthly subsidy payment, health care coverage for the children, and reimbursing the caregiver for legal fees and costs related to obtaining guardianship.

As of 2018, while all states have statutes allowing for legal guardianship of a child, not all states have statutes that provide for Kinship Guardianship Assistance (Child Welfare Information Gateway, 2019c). Legal guardianship requires the guardian to provide the child with a "safe, stable, and appropriate home; adequate food and clothing; education; and basic health, mental health, and dental health" (Child Welfare Information Gateway, 2019c, p. 2). In addition to the authority to consent to school enrollment, health, and mental health services, states vary in the rights and authority afforded to the guardian. For example, approximately a quarter of the states allow for the guardian to consent to marriage, approximately 18 states allow the guardian to consent to enlistment in the armed forces, and 16 allow the guardian to consent to the adoption of the child (Child Welfare Information Gateway, 2019c).

Another Planned Permanent Living Arrangement (APPLA)

ASFA eliminated long term foster care as a permanency goal and replaced it with APPLA (another planned permanent living arrangement), defined by federal regulations as any permanent arrangement not identified in the statute (Fiermonte & Renne, 2002). The primary difference between APPLA and long-term foster care is that APPLA is meant to be "planned" and "permanent," whereas long-term foster care simply meant that the child would remain in foster care until they reached adulthood. Preferably, APPLA would involve a plan for the child to remain with an adult who would commit to the child, beyond the child reaching the age of majority and the closure of the child welfare case. APPLA would not require termination of parental rights or a change in custody; however, the court would reflect the arrangement as permanent (Fiermonte & Renne, 2002).

The Preventing Sex Trafficking and Strengthening Families Act of 2014 (P.L.113-183) includes language designed to limit the use of APPLA, as it was believed that APPLA was being misused and becoming a default permanency goal for any child who was difficult to place in a permanent home, especially older youth (Capacity Building Center for States, 2017). Section 112 states that APPLA may only be used as a permanency plan for children age 16 or older. It further requires that ongoing case review include documentation of "intensive, ongoing, and unsuccessful efforts" to locate biological family and pursue family placement for the child. In addition, the youth must be present at every hearing and asked what they desire their permanency plan to be. The agency must also provide to the court ongoing evidence as to why APPLA is in the best interest of the child and why other permanency plan options are not as good as ensuring that the child is engaging in age and developmentally appropriate activities (P.L. 113-183, Sec. 112).

The Indian Child Welfare Act (ICWA) and the Multi-Ethnic Placement Act as Amended by the Interethnic Provisions (MEPA-IEP)

Both ICWA and MEPA-IEP impact foster and adoptive parents in child welfare and are discussed in great detail in other chapters of this text (Chapters 1, 6, and 7). Both address placement of children related to race and culture, and both impact children who are disproportionately represented in the child welfare system. Although the two laws are similar, they are mutually exclusive. MEPA-IEP does not apply to a child who meets the definition of an Indian child under ICWA, and MEPA-IEP applies to all children who do not meet the definition of an Indian child under ICWA.

Racial Disproportionality and Disparity in Adoption and Permanency

AFCARS data indicate that the same racial disproportionality seen in the percentage of children in foster care exists in the percentages of children waiting to be adopted (USDHSS, 2018). African American children are overrepresented, with 22% waiting to be adopted as compared to being approximately 14% of the child population in the United States (USDHHS, 2018). Similarly, Native American children are approximately 1% of the child population, yet 2% of the waiting child population (USDHHS, 2018). With the exception of African American children, the percentage of children adopted of all races is roughly the same as the percentage of children in care, entering care, exiting care, and waiting to be adopted (see Table 13.1). The percentage of African American children adopted is noticeably lower.

TABLE 13.1. Race and Ethnicity of Children at Key Points in Child Welfare System FY 2008–FY 2017

	% In Care	% Entered	% Exited	% Waiting	% Adopted
American Indian/Native American	2%	2%	2%	2%	2%
Asian	0%	1%	1%	0%	0%
Black/African American	**23%**	**21%**	**21%**	**22%**	**17%**

Continues on next page

	% In Care	% Entered	% Exited	% Waiting	% Adopted
Native Hawaiian/Pacific Islander	0%	0%	0%	0%	0%
Hispanic	21%	20%	21%	22%	21%
White	44%	47%	46%	44%	49%
Unknown	1%	2%	1%	1%	1%
Two or more	8%	7%	7%	8%	9%

Although research varies related to racial disparities regarding permanency outcomes, it is clear that disparities continue to exist for children of color and must be addressed. Akin (2011) found no statistical significance in the rate of reunification or guardianship comparing African American children to White; however, Shaw (2010) found that African American children were significantly less likely to reunify with their families within 2 years than White children. Shaw's findings echo many others as cited in Akin (i.e., Connell, Katz, Saunders, & Tebes, 2006; Courtney, 1994; Courtney, Piliavin, & Wright, 1997; Courtney & Wong, 1996; Wells & Guo, 1999; Wulczyn, 2003). Shaw also found that Hispanic children had significantly lower odds of reunification than White children; however, Asian children were found to have significantly higher odds of reunification than White children. Native American children are often not included in studies looking at permanency outcomes due to low numbers; however, Landers, Bellamy, Danes, McLuckie, & Hawk (2019) found that they were neither more nor less likely to reunify than their White peers. Akin (2011) did find that African American children were 38% less likely to experience adoption than White children. This finding was consistent with most of the prior research as cited in Akin (i.e., Barth, 1997; Courtney & Wong, 1996; McDonald, Poertner, & Jennings, 2007; Smith, 2003; Snowden, Leon, & Sieracki, 2008; Wulczyn, 2003).

History of Foster and Adoptive Families in Child Welfare

As outlined in Chapter 1, the history of foster care and adoption in the United States is interconnected. Early foster parents were often assumed to be altruistic, and therefore these were considered "free" foster homes with no monetary compensation provided (Cook, 1995; Hacsi, 1995). Many took children in to help around the home or the farm in exchange for room and board; however, as child labor laws evolved, the role of children in the home changed. Children were to be nurtured and cared for as opposed to being viewed as adults in small bodies, making the idea of taking a child into one's home to earn their keep by working the farm increasing unacceptable (Hardesty, 2018). Organizations reported having children returned—not because they were bad children, but because the children were unable to keep their end of the bargain by doing the labor expected of them in return for being allowed to stay in the home (Hardesty, 2018). To counter this phenomenon, states and other social service agencies began to issue board payments to foster families as incentives to families willing to take children into their homes. These payments served two purposes: 1) to "offset the child's inability to contribute to the household"; and 2) to serve as a "mechanism to shelter children from the labor market and keep them in school" (Hardesty, 2018, p. 99).

Today, "foster parent maintenance payments" are defined in the Social Security Act as "payments to cover the cost of (and the cost of providing) food, clothing, shelter, daily supervision, school supplies, a child's personal incidentals, liability insurance with respect to a child and reasonable travel to the child's home for visitation and reasonable travel for the child to remain in the school in which the child is enrolled at the time of placement" (SSA, Sec. 475(4)). States vary in the amount paid per child and often vary by child's age and sometimes level of need (DeVooght, Child Trends, & Blazey, 2013).

Foster parents play a key role in a child's permanency planning process (Casey Family Programs, 2018; Milwaukee Child Welfare Partnership, 2014; Pasztor, 1985). Whether the permanency plan is reunification, adoption, or kinship guardianship, best child welfare practices include the foster parent as a team member, a resource, and partner in the process. The foster parent's knowledge of the child's daily routine, behavioral, educational, emotional, medical, and physical needs is vital to ensuring that these needs are met by a new caregiver should the case plan involve a change in placement. In 2018, 52% of children adopted from foster care were adopted by their foster parents (USDHSS, 2019). Many of these foster parents were part of a concurrent permanency planning process mandated by the Adoption and Safe Families Act of 1997, meaning that the children were placed in their home with the understanding that should reunification fail, they would adopt the child (White, 2016). The two plans were pursued concurrently, thereby shortening the time to permanency for the child.

Foster parenting requires a unique set of skills, as not only is the foster parent parenting a child that they most likely have not had since birth, they are also not parenting the child alone. They are parenting the child in collaboration with the child welfare system, which includes the courts, an array of caseworkers, therapists, and a multitude of other service providers as well as birth parents and extended family. Craft (2015) identifies the following knowledge and skills that foster parents need to have to be successful:

- Know how to communicate and work well with different professionals and to be a part of a team. Foster parents must be prepared to have a seat at the table, to advocate for the child, and to support the permanency plan.

- Know that working with foster children and the foster care system can be challenging, depending on the child's abuse and neglect history and behaviors.
- Know how to successfully manage behaviors of challenging children using alternative discipline methods. Corporal punishment is not allowed for children in foster care. It is important to understand trauma and risk factors associated with abuse and neglect.
- Know how to manage a child's losses as well as your own. Children in foster care experience grief and loss. Foster care is temporary; reunification is the primary goal. Foster parents need to be prepared to manage their grief when a child leaves their home.

The majority of foster parents open their home to a set number of children who become temporary members of their family and an integral part of the household. This type of foster care, often referred to as **family foster care**, is a single-family home that provides the child with full-time parenting in a home setting, as well as collaborating with the agency to meet the child's educational, medical, and mental health needs. Other types of foster parenting include:

- **Emergency Foster Care**—Foster parents who take children short term on an emergency basis; they are on call and must be prepared to take children at any time (including nights and weekends) with little notice.
- **Kinship Foster Care**—Foster parents who are related to the child or family, such as grandparents, aunts/uncles, adult siblings, etc. See Chapter 12 for more information on kinship foster families in Child Welfare.
- **Respite Foster Care**—Foster parents who provide respite or a break to foster parents who need some time off—a few hours, a day, a weekend, or more; respite is most often a scheduled event.
- **Therapeutic or Treatment Foster Care**—Foster parents who receive special training and support to take care of children in need of intensive services to meet their social, behavioral, and mental health needs.
- **Foster to Adopt Care**—Foster families who become foster parents with the intention to adopt; this is a form of concurrent planning in which children are placed with these families with the understanding that should reunification fail, they will adopt. (AdoptUSKids, n.d.)

Practice Challenges

The nature of foster care and adoption has changed over time, yet challenges have remained consistent, particularly related to recruitment and retention of foster and adoptive families, addressing trauma and promoting resilience, and supporting children and families during transitions. There remains significant progress to be made through intentional recruitment efforts, enhanced training for foster and adoptive families, and additional support during periods of transition and changing family dynamics.

Recruitment of Foster and Adoptive Families

Foster parents serve a critical role in the child welfare system, caring for nearly half (46%) of children in out of home or foster care placements in the United States (USDHHS, 2019). These families provide a safe and stable home for children and youth who are unable to reside with their family of origin for various reasons. The number of children in foster care has steadily increased in recent years, as the number of children entering foster care continues to be higher than the number of children exiting care (USDHHS, 2018); at the same time, the number of resource families available to address this need has not significantly increased, and there is a great need for more foster and adoptive homes to meet the need of children in foster care across the country.

The Dave Thomas Foundation for Adoption periodically commissions a survey on attitudes toward adoption and foster care across the United States (Harris Poll, 2017). In January 2017, of the 1,448 adults surveyed, only 28% had considered becoming a foster parent. Those most likely to consider being a foster parent were between the ages of 18–44, Hispanic, parents, also considering private infant and/or foster care adoption. Similarly, 25% of those who had never adopted were considering adoption and, of that group, 79% were considering adopting from foster care. Those considering adopting were more likely to be between the ages of 18–44, Black or Hispanic, single/never married or living with someone, know someone who had been adopted, have children, and have a high opinion of adoption (Harris Poll, 2017).

The reasons given for considering fostering or adopting from foster care are very similar to one another (see Table 13.2); however, infertility is often a reason given for adopting but not for fostering. Foster parents often report choosing to provide care based on a desire to help children in need, to give back to their community, or related to a spiritual calling (Rodger, Cummings, & Leschied, 2006; Geiger, Hayes, & Lietz, 2013). Others chose to become a licensed foster parent based on personal experience, as a path to adoption and family growth, or after previously serving as a kinship provider and learning about increased accessibility of resources with licensure (Geiger, Piel, & Julien-Chinn, 2016). Knowing someone with a successful adoption experience was also a factor in deciding to pursue adoption from foster care (Harris Poll, 2017). Although foster parents generally report preferring to foster younger children, one study found that foster parents who were older and had a personal history of foster care were more willing to foster a teenager (Geiger, Hayes, & Lietz, 2014).

TABLE 13.2. Reasons for Considering Foster Parenting or Adopting a Child from Foster Care

Reasons for Considering Foster Parenting	%	Reasons for Considering Adoption	%
Help a child in need	72	Help a child in need	77
Aware of need for foster parents	52	Aware of need for adoptive parents	64
Religious faith	22	Friend of family member adopted from foster care	23
Personal experience with foster care	20	Personal experience with foster care	13
Know a foster child in need	17	Unable to have biological children	10
Increase income	10	Know foster child in need	7
Other	5	Other	5

Source: Harris Poll (2017).

Despite these compelling motivations, the increased physical, behavioral, and emotional needs of children entering the foster care system is well documented and can be an additional barrier to recruitment of foster and adoptive parents (e.g., Deutsch & Fortin, 2015; Hayes, Geiger, & Lietz, 2015). Most youth are exposed to at least one childhood adversity, but youth involved in the child welfare system are more likely than their same-age peers to experience multiple adversities, such as maltreatment, economic hardship, parental substance abuse, domestic violence, and separation from family (McLaughlin, Green, Gruber, Sampson, Zaslavsky, & Kessler, 2012). Youth in foster care have higher rates of acute and chronic health issues than their same-age peers (Ahrens, Garrison, & Courtney, 2014; Steele & Buchi, 2008) and are more likely to experience compounding risk factors like homelessness, parental substance abuse, and mental disorder (Forkey & Szilagyi, 2014), which can be intimidating to families without an understanding of trauma and supports available to families.

In 2017, the Harris Poll included an oversample of 202 Blacks/African Americans and 201 Hispanics (p. 5) and found that a higher percentage of Hispanics (36%) and Blacks (35%) were considering adoption than Whites (24%). This was a trend across the three surveys conducted over 10 years (2007, 2012, and 2017) (Harris Poll, 2017, p. 25). Other than stating that Hispanics were more likely to consider foster parenting, the researchers did not present similar data related to those considering foster parenting; however, it is reported that Whites were more likely to have a favorable opinion of foster parents than Blacks or Hispanics. When asked about preferences regarding the child they wished to adopt, younger children (under 5) were preferred, and adults of all races were significantly more likely to prefer to adopt a child of their own race.

It has been well documented that children of color are overrepresented in the foster care system (See Chapter 6). Recruitment of foster and adoptive families of color has historically presented challenges, as lack of culturally sensitive recruitment strategies and bias in application processes continues to impact families (Brown, 2015; Rycus, Freundlich, Hughes, Keefer, & Oakes, 2006; Scheetz & Flavin, 2015). Historical trauma and systemic oppression also play a role in how families view the child welfare system and can negatively impact the diligent recruitment efforts required by the Multiethnic Placement Act of 1994 as Amended by the Interethnic Adoption Provisions of 1996 to increase the number of foster and adoptive families who reflect the racial, ethnic, and cultural characteristics of children in care (Hanna, Boyce, & Yang, 2017).

Becoming a Foster or Adoptive Parent

Families who choose to engage in the process of becoming foster or adoptive parents must also go through a lengthy series of steps before placement of children as part of the licensing and/or matching process. Home studies are used to assess the safety of the home and readiness of the prospective families to provide care for children with early experiences of trauma (Chanmugam, Madden, Hanna, Cody, Ayers-Lopez, McRoy, & Ledesma, 2017). After the series of background checks, interviews, orientations, and **preservice training** is completed, the family is then eligible for potential placement of a child. Minimally, all states require that foster homes comply with local zoning, building, and fire and safety codes (Child Welfare Information Gateway, 2018). States vary in other requirements related to safety, including those regarding firearms and smoke and carbon monoxide detectors. Generally, states require foster homes have ample space for all occupants and that foster children have their own bed and space that allows for their safety and privacy. The approval process varies from state to state as does the timeframe. Foster parents who choose to adopt the child placed in their home may or may not have to go through an additional application and approval process (Child Welfare Information Gateway, 2018).

Image 13.2

The adoption home study process is similar to that of the foster parent process when adopting through a public child welfare system; however, there are several information resources for prospective adoptive parents. AdoptUSKids is a national project operated by the Adoption Exchange Association and funded by the U.S. Children's Bureau that helps families interested in adopting children from the public child welfare system as they navigate through the adoption process (AdoptUSKids, 2002). The website offers a wealth of resources to families as well as adoption professionals. In addition, the website is home to a national adoption exchange photolisting for prospective adoptive families to search and view children waiting to be adopted. As with foster care, the policies and process for being approved for adoption, as well as being matched with a child for placement, varies from state to state. Matching a child to an adoptive family requires a thorough consideration of the behavioral, emotional, educational, cultural, and physical needs of the child and the parent(s)' capacity to meet these needs long term (Hanna & McRoy, 2011). It is a process that can often be time consuming and even frustrating to waiting families; however, when done well, the end result is a permanent, lifelong relationship for the child and family.

Once a child is matched with a prospective adoptive family with whom they have not lived prior, there is most often a time of visitation prior to the actual placement of the child with the family. Once placed in the home, there is a period of post-placement supervision, during which the child remains in the custody of the county or state and the family receives services from the child placing agency. This timeframe varies from jurisdiction to jurisdiction. During this time, the agency often assists the adoptive family with the transition of becoming a family, setting up services to meet the child's and family's needs post adoption (see Chapter 15), and working with a lawyer and the courts to legally finalize the adoption. Part of this includes sharing detailed information about the child and their birth family. All states have statutes that require that information regarding the adopted child and their birth relatives be shared with the adoptive parents (including foster and kinship adoptive parents); however, states vary on exactly what information must be shared, by whom, and when in the adoption process (Child Welfare Information Gateway, 2016).

Retention and Resilience of Foster and Adoptive Families

In addition to diligent recruitment efforts and support through preservice and licensure preparation, retention of foster and adoptive families can also be challenging and presents a barrier to consistency in placement for children. Caring for children who have experienced abuse and neglect is not without challenges, and many foster parents contemplate or discontinue fostering within the first 12–18 months (Chipungu & Bent-Goodley, 2004; Geiger et al., 2013; Gibbs, 2005; Rhodes, Orme, Cox, & Buehler, 2003). Several studies have examined foster parent retention, indicating the importance of formal and informal supports, having a voice on the decision-making team, and the importance of maintaining healthy family functioning, despite the challenges inherent in foster care and adoption.

Foster and adoptive families serve an important role as caregivers for children who have experienced maltreatment, yet they are also professional members of the team, and their perspective should be considered in decision-making for children in their care (MacGregor, Rodger, Cummings, & Leschied, 2006; Blythe, Halcolmb, Wilkes, & Jackson, 2012). They can provide unique insight into behaviors, progress, and service needs as they interact with children and often service providers on a regular basis. Foster and adoptive parents who feel they are heard, consulted, and included in decision-making are more satisfied with their experience and more likely to continue providing care.

Comprehensive training is also important so families have realistic expectations and are able to understand the impact of trauma and the complexity of needs they may encounter. Although some parents feel that the training they received adequately prepared them for navigating child welfare and health care systems, many parents feel they needed more support in understanding the impact of trauma in various relationships and experiences and in navigating behavioral health services (Cooley & Petren, 2011; Hayes et al., 2015). Others have described the need for more training focused on cultural competency and identity development to adequately support cross-racial placements (Hanna, Tokarski, Matera, & Fong, 2011; Chipungu & Bent-Goodley, 2004).

Foster parents also report appreciating caseworkers who provide ongoing concrete and emotional support and believe there is a need for improved communication and enhanced teamwork (Geiger et al., 2016; Cooley & Petren, 2011). Tangible resources, such as respite or relief care and transportation for children's visits with family, are important, as are emotional support and open communication from caseworkers (Cooley, Farineau, & Mullis, 2015; Piel, Geiger, Julien-Chinn, & Lietz, 2017). Both formal and informal supports can serve as protective factors, especially when managing challenging behaviors of children with a history of trauma.

Despite the stressors foster and adoptive families encounter, many families maintain health family functioning and provide care to our nation's most vulnerable children for many years. This resilience is not an outcome, but rather a culture of coping and adaptation that remains responsive to the changing circumstances that accompany each transition and obstacle encountered in the child welfare system. In the process of achieving family resilience (Lietz, Julien-Chinn, Geiger, & Piel, 2016), foster families progress beyond survival to create changes to the structure, schedule, and daily functioning of their family unit (see Figure 13.2). They continue to rely on the connectedness of the family, social support, and shared beliefs.

In the final phase of family resilience, foster families are able to give social support to others in a reciprocal transaction (Lietz et al., 2016). In this way, foster families with experience overcoming the adversities of fostering are able to support others and are important sources of support. This may serve as an important resource for recruitment, training, family preparation, and post-placement activities to support and nurture new foster—and possibly adoptive—families through the system.

Transitions in Foster Care and Adoption

Transitions of children within foster and adoptive homes can be particularly challenging for both the child and birth family involved, as well as for the foster and/or adoptive families. Removal and separation from families can be traumatic for children, compounding early experiences of maltreatment and impacting behavior and emotions in their foster care or adoptive placement. As a new child enters a foster or adoptive family, the dynamics of the family change during a period of adjustment to the circumstances that led to

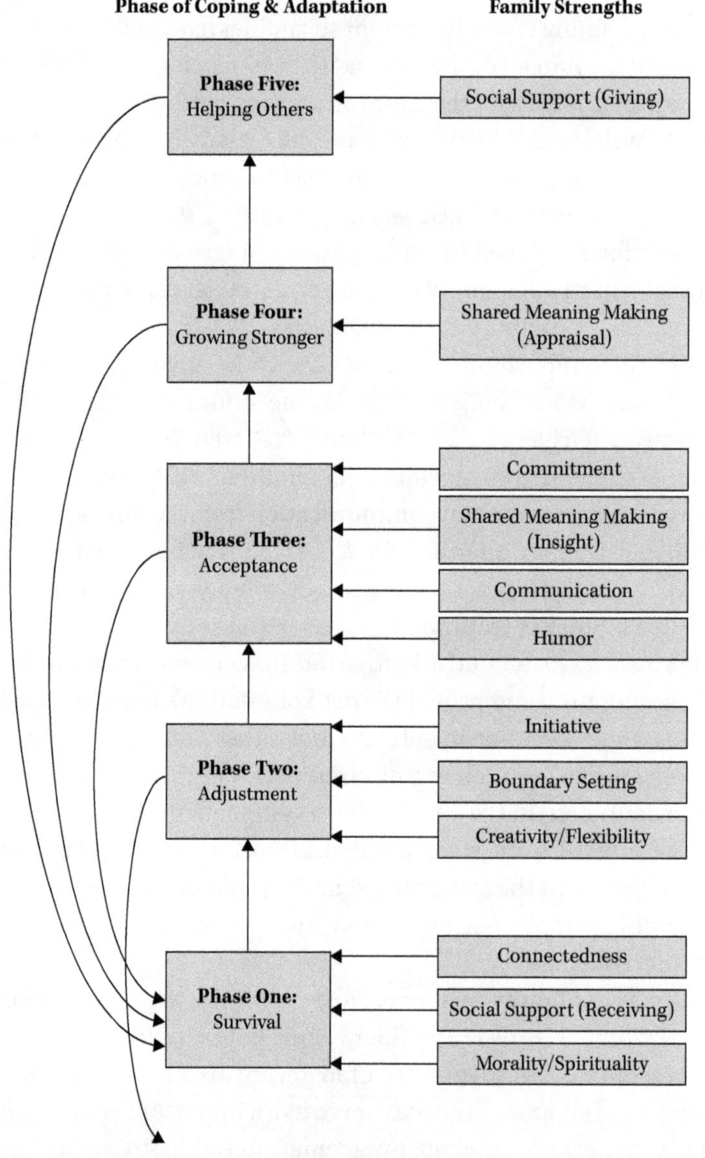

FIGURE 13.2. Process of Family Resilience (Lietz et al., 2016)

placement and in managing changing roles within families. This adjustment is ongoing, as each family member learns to adapt to changing circumstances and accommodate the needs of all family members (Piel et al., 2017). Birth order and age of children may be important when considering changing family dynamics, as children entering the family may be older or younger than existing children in the family. Transitions to new families temporarily or in more permanent circumstances such as adoption or returning home can be difficult for all parties involved. It is natural for foster families to develop attachment to the children in their care and experience a sense of loss when that relationship changes and the children leave the foster home to either return to their birth parents, for a placement in another foster family, or an adoptive placement (Geiger et al., 2013).

In addition to managing their own feelings and changing family dynamics, foster and adoptive parents are also responsible for supporting children's feelings about placement and separation. Children may have an array of feelings related to removal and placement. Although they have experienced abuse and/or neglect with their birth family, they may feel conflicting loyalties between birth and foster or adoptive families, a sense of loss, or guilt about their circumstances (Wojciak, McWey, & Waid, 2018). Remaining connected with birth family or foster parents provides more consistency while also offering permanence. Including birth parents in fostering and other decisions about children, involvement in shared parenting, and advocating when possible for birth parents to be a part of communication can all help support the child during this time (Lietz et al., 2016). Children are also likely changing schools and neighborhoods with the transition, which requires foster and adoptive parents to help them develop new support systems and some continuity in services and support.

When children are removed from their birth parents as a result of abuse or neglect, they may also be separated from siblings, which can cause additional trauma and a sense of loss. Although keeping families together is a goal of child welfare agencies, siblings are not always able to be placed together, especially if they are large sibling groups or there are differential behavioral needs that cannot be managed in a single placement (Leathers, 2005). Terminating parental rights, which is necessary for a child to be eligible for adoption, can also end the legal relationship between siblings, and postadoption contact should be facilitated. Placement with nonrelated foster and adoptive families increases the likelihood that children of color will be placed in transracial foster or adoptive placements, which can have a significant impact on youth's racial identity development and cultural connections (Coakley & Gruber, 2015). Maintaining connections with birth families during foster placement or postadoption is important to helping children maintain cultural connections to support identity development.

Working with Foster and Adoptive Families

Although a variety of programs exist that aim to address the previously mentioned challenges in foster and adoptive families, more rigorous research studies are needed to evaluate the effectiveness of emerging practices for foster care and adoptive families. Training for foster parents aims to orient foster parents to their role and supports development of knowledge, attitudes, and skills necessary to cope with the demands of their role. Federal law requires training of foster and adoptive parents. Nearly all states require training for foster and adoptive parents prior to placement of children (preservice), and more than half of states require a specific curriculum (Dorsey, Farmer, Barth, Greene, Reid, & Landsverk, 2008). Preservice training is important to prepare foster and adoptive parents for their new role, but it is also used to provide agency guidance on screening and matching of children with families to help prevent placement disruptions due to inappropriate fit and retention issues.

Preservice Training

The two most widely used preservice training curricula for foster and adoptive parents are Parent Resources for Information, Development, and Education (PRIDE) and Trauma Informed Partnering for Safety and Permanence—Model Approach to Partnerships in Parenting (TIPS-MAPP). PRIDE was developed in 1993 by the Child Welfare League of America as a competency-based model of practice focused on underlying values of protecting and nurturing children, meeting their developmental needs, and connecting them to family and other supportive relationships. MAPP was originally developed in the 1980s (Mayers-Pasztor, 1987) but has been adapted to include group preparation and selection (MAPP/GPS), and most recently attention specifically to the impact of trauma (TIPS-MAPP; NCTSN 2013). TIPS-MAPP focuses on similar competencies as PRIDE but focuses more heavily on preparing parents for the challenges associated with fostering, including understanding the impact of trauma and culturally responsive service provision. Although most states and agencies require some preservice training, states vary in the requirements for both foster and adoptive parents, and in some states, the requirements vary by county (Child Welfare Information Gateway, 2018; Child Welfare Information Gateway, 2015).

Ongoing Parent Training

Despite the paucity of research evidence for preservice trainings, there are ongoing (in-service) models of parent training that have either well-supported or emerging evidence of effectiveness with foster and adoptive families. Elements of effective parent training programs include increasing positive parent-child interactions and teaching consistency in boundaries and discipline (Kaminski, Valle, Filene, & Boyle, 2008).

Image 13.3

The Treatment Foster Care Oregon for Adolescents (TFCO-A; previously referred to as Multidimensional Treatment Foster Care-MTFC) is well supported by empirical research evidence, meaning it has rigorous research evidence published in peer-reviewed literature and demonstrated sustainable impact when compared to a control group not receiving the intervention (Chamberlain, Leve, & DeGarmo, 2007). TFCO-A aims to provide support to treatment foster care families of adolescents with significant emotional and behavioral health needs by focusing on consistent reinforcement, clear boundaries, structured and close supervision, and the development of prosocial peer relationships (Chamberlain et al., 2007). This is in comparison to preservice trainings that focus on skill building related to application of behavioral modification and social learning principles needed in highly structured treatment foster care settings. There are other versions of TFCO for preschoolers and children (TFCO-P and TFCO-C, respectively), which are still building research evidence to demonstrate impact.

Based on the relative success of TFCO, Chamberlain and colleagues (2008) modified the model for foster and kinship care parents who were caring for children with challenging behaviors, but not in a therapeutic setting such as treatment foster care. Keeping Foster Parents Trained and Supported (KEEP) was developed and has shown promising evidence for improving outcomes for foster care and kinship families by reducing disruptive behaviors and parental stress and generally decreasing placement disruptions (Chamberlain et al., 2008; Greeno, Lee, Uretsky, Moore, Barth, & Shaw, 2015); KEEP SAFE is the adaptation of this model for foster and kinship parents of adolescents, which is supported by research evidence in reducing placement disruption and preventing substance use and other health-risk behaviors (Kim, Buchanan, & Price, 2017; Smith, Leve, & Chamberlain, 2011).

Together Facing the Challenge (TFTC) was created in response to the criticism that some agencies did not have the capacity or resources to hire clinicians with the extensive training required of the TFCO and KEEP models (Southerland, Farmer, Murray, Stambaugh, & Rosenberg, 2018). TFTC is a hybrid model that aims to enhance existing practices within agencies by incorporating evidence-based practices of behavior management and relationship building. The training is for both treatment foster care parents and child welfare agency staff, focusing on practical parenting and supervisory skills to create structure, boundaries, and cultural sensitivity to improve outcomes (Farmer, Burns, Wagner, Murray, & Southerland, 2010).

The Triple P—Positive Parenting Program (PPP) is a multi-tiered training program for parents and caregivers of children and adolescents, which is supported by research evidence (Sanders, Kirby, Tellegen, & Day, 2014). The training is used more broadly than just with foster and adoptive parents, but the focus on family functioning, self-regulation, and behavior modification are relevant to working with children who have experienced abuse and neglect. Triple P provides a variety of strategies and tools to effectively respond to moderate-to-severe behavior problems, which are frequently displayed by children and youth with a history of trauma and separation from families.

Research indicates models that integrate both preservice and ongoing training can positively impact child behaviors, foster parent satisfaction, and retention, and therein placement permanency (e.g., Piescher, Schmidt, & LaLiberte, 2008; Chamberlain et al., 2007). Several of the models with rigorous research evidence are focused on high-needs placements such as treatment foster care, but the principles are likely useful in multiple family-based settings. The threshold of evidence required for training to be considered evidence based is particularly important in light of recent FFPSA legislation, which requires evidence-based practices in federal reimbursement to states for programs and services. More research is needed, particularly related to the inclusion of cultural competence in training models.

Systems Approach

Addressing the complex needs of children and families involved in foster care and adoption requires multisystem collaboration. It requires understanding system priorities, responsively engaging with professionals across systems, and increasing public awareness and advocating for policy reform to implement larger systems change. Navigating a complicated child welfare system can be confusing, in addition to managing complex medical, educational, and mental health needs of children in their care (Hayes, et al., 2015). Despite common goals of improving child and family well-being, each system has differing priorities and views their responsibility in meeting child and family needs differently.

Criminal Justice System

Child protection cases may be involved in civil court, criminal court, or both. Although foster parents are not often legally involved in court cases, they are often managing the logistics to ensure children are meeting with all parties involved, such as caseworkers, attorneys, guardians ad litem, and court-appointed special advocates, as well as managing the emotional consequences of ongoing legal involvement. In addition to the causes for court involvement, lengthy court cases and time delays can result in added emotional stress for both children and resource families (Lipovsky, 1994). The uncertainty and delays can cause significant stress and behavioral and emotional challenges in the foster home. More intensive court involvement is required for criminal prosecution of egregious occurrences of maltreatment. Criminal prosecution for child sexual abuse entails more appearances in court, and the assault must often be relived, which can cause additional emotional stress.

Youth in the foster care system are more likely to be involved in the juvenile justice system than their same-age peers (Yampolskaya, Armstrong, & McNeish, 2011; Dierkhising, Ko, Woods-Jaeger, Briggs, Lee, & Pynoos, 2013). Juvenile court also requires more appearances and typically more requirements related to probation or community service, which must be managed by resource (foster/kin/pre-adoptive) parents while the youth are in their care. Depending on the offense, there may also be more restrictions as to the ages and gender of children with whom the youth can be placed, which impacts other potential placements. In response to the unique needs of youth involved in both child welfare and juvenile justice systems, more states are recognizing the need for collaborative system involvement and crossover youth practice models in diverse contexts (Haight, Bidwell, Marshall, & Khatiwoda, 2014). See Chapter 16 for more information on crossover youth.

Educational System

Schools are integral to child development and can be a source of stability for children in foster care. However, unfortunately, many youth experience placement disruptions, which often also disrupt educational stability. It is estimated that 31–75% of youth in foster care change schools when entering care (Clemens, Klopfenstein, Tis, & Lalonde, 2017; Frerer, Sosenko, & Henke, 2013). Research has shown that while in care, children tend to change schools more than they change placements (Olsen & De Montgomery, 2018). These youth are more likely to struggle with enrollment issues, low test scores, having to repeat a grade, or miss school due to suspension or expulsion than their same-age peers (Okpych, 2012). Olsen and Montgomery (2018) found that negative educational outcomes were strongly associated with children ages 11 and up, with a stronger relationship between school instability and negative educational outcomes for adolescents ages 15 and up. Foster and adoptive parents serve as an important resource to help advocate for the educational needs of children in their care and possibly mediate these outcomes by providing a stable environment, especially for older youth.

Although there is a growing awareness of the prevalence of exposure to trauma among youth, teachers and other educational professionals typically receive little formal training on the impact of trauma and how to support students involved in the child welfare system (Ko et al., 2008; Sass & Henderson, 2000). Children respond to trauma in different ways. They may struggle with inattentiveness, inappropriate boundaries, the ability to self-regulate, or have unexpected reactions or triggers, which are often viewed as behavioral issues requiring disciplinary action, rather than responses to trauma. Foster and adoptive parents can serve as advocates and can help educate school professionals on their individual needs, as well as facilitate communication between school and child welfare professionals.

Health/Behavioral Health Systems

It is well documented that children in the foster care system demonstrate a variety of medical and behavioral health conditions. Youth in foster care have higher rates of acute and chronic health issues than their same-age peers (Ahrens et al., 2014; Steele & Buchi, 2008) and are more likely to experience compounding risk factors such as homelessness, parental substance abuse, and mental disorder (Forkey & Szilagyi, 2014). In one study, 93% of foster parents report caring for children with medical health needs, and 80% report caring for children with behavioral health needs (Hayes et al., 2015). Although most foster parents felt medical and physical health services were easy to navigate, there was some concern about delays in getting the appropriate authorizations for specialized services and surgeries. With regard to behavioral health care, delays in authorizations and acquiring services can result in increased problematic behaviors and placement disruptions.

Medical and behavioral health teams are also hierarchical in structure and decision-making. Provider decisions are often made quickly, based on brief interactions with patients and their caregivers (Ko et al., 2008). Foster parents serve an important role in advocating for the physical and behavioral health needs of children in their care. Having basic medical information, such as prior exams, immunization records, family medical history, and psychological evaluations, passed along foster and adoptive parents from child welfare agencies in a timely manner is important to avoid repetition of services.

State and Private Child Welfare Agencies

Child welfare agencies continue to provide the primary coordinating and decision-making role related to permanency. Foster and adoptive parents serve an important role as primary caregivers in which they coordinate services, visits, and the overall routine for the children in their care, but more importantly they provide a source of consistency and often best know the needs of the children in their care from daily interactions and rapport building. These parents provide a personal yet professional support in the child's team, and their perspective is important to consider in decision-making (Geiger et al., 2013; Blythe et al., 2012). Child welfare agencies can serve as a strong formal support for foster and adoptive families, which also increases the likelihood they continue providing care.

Despite the important role child welfare agencies can provide to foster parents and in permanency planning, agencies and staff are often overburdened with high caseloads and families with complex needs, which can result in turnover and staff shortages. Staff turnover often contributes to delays in services and can negatively impact foster and adoptive placements (e.g., Chanmugam et al., 2017; Hayes et al., 2015). More states are also beginning to privatize aspects of their child welfare systems, many starting with foster and adoption services. Research indicates mixed results in terms of safety outcomes for children (Huggins-Hoyt, Mowbray, Briggs, & Allen, 2019); however, one study found that while on one hand children of color, primarily African American children, remained in care longer waiting for permanency, on the other hand, they had fewer placement moves; i.e., stability while in care when under the care of a private agency as opposed to the public agency (Huggins-Hoyt, Briggs, Mowbray, & Allen, 2019). The researchers stress the need for further research to assess the long-term impact of privatization on child outcomes.

Implications for Systems Change

The future of child and family permanency depends on the preparation, collaboration, and public perception of child and family well-being. The needs of children and families involved in the child welfare system are complex and require multidisciplinary solutions and broad systems changes to have a measurable impact.

Training and Continuing Education

Foster and adoptive parents need adequate preparation to effectively support children who have experienced maltreatment and trauma. This includes preservice and ongoing training that involves partners from the systems of care in which they will engage; moving beyond interaction with child welfare partners to also include interactions with partners from medical and behavioral health systems, family and juvenile justice court systems, and educational systems (Ko et al., 2008). Training needs to be trauma informed and culturally competent. Foster and adoptive parents must understand the impact of trauma, and common behavioral and emotional challenges that may result from trauma, to better advocate for the needs of the children in their care (Cooley & Petren, 2011). Considering the high number of cross-racial foster and adoptive placements, there also needs to be significant attention placed on helping children retain their cultural identity (Carter-Black, 2002; Hanna et al., 2011). Parents and other professionals should actively seek to understand the perspectives, traditions, and strengths of culturally diverse populations.

Responsive Engagement

As part of ongoing education and support, caseworkers and other professionals involved in the case need to responsively engage with foster and adoptive parents to meet their highly individualized needs. Ensuring families are prepared for placement and receiving tailored, ongoing support allows families to maintain healthy family functioning (Lietz et al., 2016). Creating an ecological system of support—including, but not limited to, the caseworker, therapist, medical professionals, education specialists—for families creates a network of multidisciplinary support and recognizes that families' resources and strengths can change over time (Piel et al., 2017). Ensuring resource families are respected members of the professional team reinforces consistency in communication and case planning. Supporting individual and family needs during transitions and involving both youth and parents in decision-making is important to reduce placement disruptions (Geiger et al., 2013).

Community Responsibility for Well-Being

Effectively meeting the needs of foster and adoptive families requires a shift in community perception of child and family well-being. It involves increasing awareness of community responsibility for child protection and family support, as well as helping families to build social and emotional capital within neighborhoods. This includes helping families before they become known to the child welfare system. A comprehensive approach includes both investing in direct assistance to parents, as well as investing in changing community perceptions of child protection and permanency (Daro & Dodge, 2009). This requires a long-term investment as well as a commitment to engaging diverse sectors of the community and potentially conflicting values of child protection and well-being efforts. Targeted recruitment of foster and adoptive families of color is important, but these efforts must also be supported with ongoing commitment to collaboration and attention to implicit bias in decision-making (Hanna et al., 2017; Rycus et al., 2006). Systems reform begins with engagement of stakeholders and creating a community of child welfare that engages both informal and formal supports to enhance the resilience and healthy functioning of families.

Case Application

The following case application is reflective of some of the challenges child welfare workers face in permanency planning for children in foster care. The case is fictional, drawn from the practice experience of the authors.

Case Vignette

Bobby, age 12, is a young African American male who has been in foster care on and off since he was approximately 8 years old. He was removed from his birth mother due to severe neglect and substance use. His mother, Sarah, was originally resistant to services; however, she eventually entered rehab and appeared to be doing well. Sarah completed her treatment, had obtained a job and housing, and was reunified with Bobby on two separate occasions. Sarah had no biological family around to help as she was a runaway who became involved in prostitution at a young age. She has not been in contact with her family since running away and refused to provide caseworkers with any contact information, stating that they were better off thinking she was dead. Bobby's birth father was unknown as he was one of her clients.

During the second time of reunification, she gave birth to a second child, Jaida. Jaida's father was living with her, and they planned to marry. The first time she relapsed, Sarah stated that Jaida's father had tricked her into using, and she promised the courts she would get clean again. She testified against Jaida's father who is now serving a 30-year sentence for vehicular homicide while driving under the influence. Recently, Sarah relapsed for the third time, and both Bobby and Jaida were placed in foster care. The judge told Sarah she was out of chances and that this time he was terminating her parental rights. Jaida was placed with a new foster-to-adopt family at the time of removal when she was 2 months old; she is now 10 months old. Bobby was initially placed in an emergency foster home and is now in his third foster home in 8 months. Initially, Bobby was allowed to visit Jaida regularly; however, Jaida's foster parents have recently requested that visitation stop as they state that it upsets Jaida every time she visits with Bobby, as his behavior is extremely disruptive to her routine. When asked specifically, they state that he attempts to step in and take care of her and is constantly telling them that they are not her real parents.

This time Sarah provided the name and location of her parents since she did not want her children to be separated and she did not want Jaida's father's family involved, as she said they were all drug dealers and gangbangers. In doing a diligent search, a kinship care worker informed the caseworker that she had located a relative of Sarah's who was interested in taking both children. The relative is a maternal cousin who has not seen Bobby since he was about 6 years old and only recently learned that the children were in foster care. She stated that she had done her best to keep up with Sarah for those first few years and then Sarah cut off all contact. The relative lives in another state, is stable, is in a committed relationship, and has started the application process to become a kinship caregiver. The relative is planning a trip to visit the children in 2 weeks.

DISCUSSION QUESTIONS

1. What are the permanency options for Bobby and Jaida?
2. What are the pros and cons of each permanency option?
3. What additional information would the caseworker need to know to make a permanency recommendation for Bobby and Jaida?

References

Adler, L. S. (2001). The meanings of permanence: A critical analysis of the Adoption and Safe Families Act of 1997. *Harvard Journal on Legislation, 38* (1), 1–36.

Adoption and Safe Families Act of 1997 (ASFA). H.R. 867 (Public Law 105-89). http://www.acf.hhs.gov/sites/default/files/cb/pi9802.pdf

AdoptUsKids. (2002). Who we are. https://www.adoptuskids.org/about-us/who-we-are

AdoptUSKids. (n.d.) About foster parenting. https://www.adoptuskids.org/adoption-and-foster-care/overview/foster-parenting

Ahrens, K. R., Garrison, M. M., & Courtney, M. E. (2014). Health outcomes in young adults from foster care and economically diverse backgrounds. *Pediatrics, 134*(6), 1067–1074.

Akin, B. A. (2011). Predictors of foster care exits to permanency: A competing risks analysis of reunification, guardianship, and adoption. *Children and Youth Services Review, 33*(6), 999–1011.

Atwell, B. L. (1992). A lost generation: The battle for private enforcement of the Adoption Assistance and Child Welfare Act of 1980. *University of Cincinnati Law Review, 60*(3), 593–648.

Barth, R. P. (1997). Effects of age and race on the odds of adoption versus remaining in long-term out of home care. *Child Welfare, 76*(2), 285.

Berrick, J. D. (1998). When children cannot remain home: Foster family care and kinship care. *The future of children*, 72–87.

Blythe, S. L., Halcomb, E. J., Wilkes, L., & Jackson, D. (2012). Perceptions of long-term female foster-carers: I'm not a carer, I'm a mother. *British Journal of Social Work, 43*(6), 1056–1072.

Brown, D. (2015). Initiative serves as a culturally responsive community outreach and recruitment model for foster care and adoption with African heritage communities. *Culturally Responsive Child Welfare Practice, Winter*, p. 23.

Capacity Building Center for States. (2017). *Pathways to permanency: Expanding on APPLA provisions and youth engagement to improve permanency*. Washington, DC: U.S. Department of Health and Human Services, Administration for Children and Families, Children's Bureau.

Carter-Black, J. (2002). Transracial adoption and foster care placement: Worker perception and attitude. *Child Welfare, 81*(2), 337–370.

Casey Family Programs. (2018). What are some effective strategies for achieving permanency? Author.

Chamberlain, P., Leve, L. D., & DeGarmo, D. S. (2007). Multidimensional treatment foster care for girls in the juvenile justice system: 2-year follow-up of a randomized clinical trial. *Journal of Consulting and Clinical Psychology, 75*(1), 187.

Chamberlain, P., Price, J., Leve, L. D., Laurent, H., Landsverk, J. A., & Reid, J. B. (2008). Prevention of behavior problems for children in foster care: Outcomes and mediation effects. *Prevention Science, 9*, 17–27.

Chanmugam, A., Madden, E. E., Hanna, M. D., Cody, P. A., Ayers-Lopez, S. J., McRoy, R. G., & Ledesma, K. J. (2017). Agency-related barriers experienced by families seeking to adopt from foster care. *Adoption Quarterly, 20*(1), 25–43.

Children's Bureau. (2013). *The children's bureau legacy: Ensuring the right to childhood.* Washington, DC: Children's Bureau, U.S. Department of Health & Human Services.

Child Welfare Information Gateway. (2019a). *Major legislation concerned with child welfare, child protection, and adoption.* Washington, DC: U.S. Department of Health and Human Services, Children's Bureau.

Child Welfare Information Gateway. (2019b). *Glossary.* Washington, DC: U.S. Department of Health and Human Services, Children's Bureau. https://www.childwelfare.gov/glossary/glossarya/

Child Welfare Information Gateway. (2019c). *Kinship guardianship as a permanency option.* Washington, DC: U.S. Department of Health and Human Services, Children's Bureau.

Child Welfare Information Gateway. (2018). *Home study requirements for prospective foster parents.* Washington, DC: U.S. Department of Health and Human Services, Children's Bureau.

Child Welfare Information Gateway. (2017). *Concurrent planning for permanency for children.* Washington, DC: U.S. Department of Health and Human Services, Children's Bureau.

Child Welfare Information Gateway. (2016a). *Who may adopt, be adopted, or place a child for adoption.* Washington, DC: U.S. Department of Health and Human Services, Children's Bureau.

Child Welfare Information Gateway. (2016b). *Providing adoptive parents with information about adoptees and their birth families.* Washington, DC: U.S. Department of Health and Human Services, Children's Bureau.

Child Welfare Information Gateway. (2015). *Adoption options: Where do I start?* Washington, DC: U.S. Department of Health and Human Services, Children's Bureau.

Child Welfare Information Gateway. (2015). *The adoption home study process.* Washington, DC: U.S. Department of Health and Human Services, Children's Bureau.

Chipungu, S. S., & Bent-Goodley, T. B. (2004). Meeting the challenges of contemporary foster care. *The Future of Children*, 75–93.

Chronicle of Social Change. (2017). *The foster care housing crisis.* Children and Youth, Front and Center. https://chronicleofsocialchange.org/child-welfare-2/chronicle-report-least-25-states-lost-foster-care-capacity-since-2012/28575

Clemens, E. V., Klopfenstein, K., Tis, M., & Lalonde, T. L. (2017). Educational stability policy and the interplay between child welfare placements and school moves. *Children and Youth Services Review, 83,* 209–217.

Coakley, T. M., & Gruber, K. (2015). Cultural receptivity among foster parents: Implications for quality transcultural parenting. *Social Work Research, 39*(1), 11–22.

Cook, J. F. (1995). A history of placing-out: The orphan trains. *Child Welfare, 74*(1), 181–197.

Cooley, M. E., Farineau, H. M., & Mullis, A. K. (2015). Child behaviors as a moderator: Examining the relationship between foster parent supports, satisfaction, and intent to continue fostering. *Child Abuse & Neglect, 45,* 46–56.

Cooley, M. E., & Petren, R. E. (2011). Foster parent perceptions of competency: Implications for foster parent training. *Children and Youth Services Review, 33(*10), 1968–1974.

Connell, C. M., Katz, K. H., Saunders, L., & Tebes, J. K. (2006). Leaving foster care—The influence of child and case characteristics on foster care exit rates. *Children and Youth Services Review, 28* (7), 780–798.

Coupet, S. (2005). Swimming upstream against the great adoption tide: Making the case for impermanence. *Loyola University of Chicago School of Law 34,* 405–458.

Courtney, M. E. (1994). Factors associated with the reunification of foster children with their families. *Social*

Courtney, M. E., Piliavin, I., & Wright, B. R. E. (1997). Transitions from and returns to out of home care. *Social Service Review, 71*(4), 652–667.

Courtney, M. E., & Wong, Y. L. I. (1996). Comparing the timing of exits from substitute care. *Children and Youth Services Review, 18*(4–5), 307–334.

Craft, C. (2015). 6 foster care skills you need to know before becoming a foster parent. Norfolk, VA: The Up Center. https://www.theupcenter.org/6-foster-care-skills-you-need-to-know-before-being-a-foster-parent/

Daro, D., & Dodge, K. A. (2009). Creating community responsibility for child protection: Possibilities and challenges. *The Future of Children/Center for the Future of Children, the David and Lucile Packard Foundation, 19*(2), 67.

Department of Health & Human Services. (2005, August). *ASPE issue brief: Federal foster care financing.* Office of the Secretary. Washington, DC.

Dorsey, S., Farmer, E. M. Z., Barth, R. P., Greene, K. M., Reid, J., & Landsverk, J. (2008). Current status and evidence base of training for foster and treatment foster parents. *Children and Youth Services Review, 30*(12), 1403–1416.

Deutsch, S. A., & Fortin, K. (2015). Physical health problems and barriers to optimal health care among children in foster care. *Current Problems in Pediatric and Adolescent Health Care, 45*(10), 286–291.

DeVooght, K., Child Trends, & Blazey, D. (2013). Foster family care reimbursement rates in the U.S.: A report from a 2010 national survey on family foster care provider classifications and rates. Publication #2013-19. Child Trends.

Dierkhising, C. B., Ko, S. J., Woods-Jaeger, B., Briggs, E. C., Lee, R., & Pynoos, R. S. (2013). Trauma histories among justice-involved youth: Findings from the National Child Traumatic Stress Network. *European Journal of Psychotraumatology, 4*(1), 20274. doi:10.3402/ejpt.v4i0.20274

Electronic Code of Federal Regulations (e-CFR). (2020). Title 45, Subtitle B, Chapter XIII, Subchapter G, Part 1355. Appendix B to Part 1355–Adoption Data Elements. https://www.ecfr.gov/cgi-bin/textidx?SID=0ee0652afa4e03ff12528b91fc120f2b&mc=true&node=pt45.4.1355&rgn=div5#se45.5.1355_120

Farmer, E. M. Z., Burns, B. J., Wagner, H. R., Murray, M., & Southerland, D. G. (2010). Enhancing "usual practice" treatment foster care: Findings from a randomized trial on improving youth outcomes. *Psychiatric Services, 6*, 555–561.

Festinger, T. B. (1974). Placement agreements with boarding homes: A survey. *Child welfare, 53*(10), 643–652.

Fiermonte, C., & Renne, J. L. (2002). Making it permanent: Reasonable efforts to finalize permanency plans for foster children. Washington, DC: American Bar Association, Center on Children and the Law/National Resource Center on Legal and Judicial Issues.

Forkey, H., & Szilagyi, M. (2014). Foster care and healing from complex childhood trauma. *Pediatric Clinics, 61*(5), 1059–1072.

Frerer, K., Sosenko, L. D., & Henke, R. R. (2013). At greater risk: California foster youth and the path from high school to college. Report. http://www. stuartfoundation.org/docs/default-document-library/at-greater-risk-california-fosteryouth-and-the-path-from-high-school-to-college.pdf

Geiger, J. M., Hayes, M. J., & Lietz, C. A. (2014). Foster parents' perspectives on providing foster care for adolescents: Barriers and opportunities. *Child and Youth Services, 35*(4), 237–254. http://dx.doi.org/10.1080/0145935X.2014.938736

Geiger, J. M., Hayes, M. J., & Lietz, C. A. (2013). Should I stay or should I go? A mixed methods study examining the factors influencing foster parents' decisions to continue or discontinue providing foster care. *Children and Youth Services Review, 35*(9), 1356–1365. http://dx.doi.org/10.1016/j.childyouth.2013.05.003

Geiger, J. M., Piel, M. H., & Julien-Chinn, F. J. (2016). Improving relationships in child welfare practice: Perspectives of foster care providers. *Child and Adolescent Social Work, 34*(1), 23–33. http://dx.doi.org/10.1007/s10560-016-0471-3

Gibbs, D. (2005). *Understanding foster parenting: Using administrative data to explore retention.* Washington, DC: U.S. Department of Health and Human Services, Office of the Assistant Secretary for Planning and Evaluation.

Gill, M. (1975). The foster care/adoptive family: Adoption for children not legally free. *Child Welfare, 54*(10), 712–720.

Greeno, E. J., Lee, B. R., Uretsky, M. C., Moore, J. E., Barth, R. P., & Shaw, T. V. (2015). Effects of a foster parent training intervention on child behavior, caregiver stress, and parenting style. *Journal of Child and Family Studies, 25*(6), 1991–2000. doi: 10.1007/s10826-015-0357-6

Hacsi, T. (1995). From indenture to family foster care: A brief history of child placing. *Child Welfare, 74*(1), 162–180.

Hanna, M. D., Boyce, E. R., & Yang, J. (2017). The impact of historical trauma and mistrust on the recruitment of resource families of color. *Adoption Quarterly, 20*(1), 65–82.

Hanna, M. D, & McRoy, R. G. (2011) Innovative practice approaches to matching in adoption. *Journal of Public Child Welfare, (5)*1, 45–66.

Hanna, M., Tokarski, K., Matera, D., & Fong, R. (2011). Happily ever after? The journey from foster care to adoption. *Adoption Quarterly, 14(*2), 107–131.

Haight, W. L., Bidwell, L. N., Marshall, J. M., & Khatiwoda, P. (2014). Implementing the Crossover Youth Practice Model in diverse contexts: Child welfare and juvenile justice professionals' experiences of multisystem collaborations. *Children and Youth Services Review, 39*, 91–100.

Hardesty, M. (2018). "It's not a job!" Foster care board payments and the logic of the profiteering parent. *Social Service Review, 92*(1), 93–133.

Harris Poll (2017). U.S. Adoption Attitudes Survey: 2017. https://www.davethomasfoundation.org/wp-content/uploads/2018/02/2017-adoption-attitudes-survey-us.pdf

Hayes, M. J., Geiger, J. M., & Lietz, C. A. (2015). Navigating a complicated system of care: Foster parent satisfaction with behavioral and medical health services. *Child and Adolescent Social Work, 32*(6), 493–505. http://dx.doi.org/10.1007/s10560-015-0388-2

Hollingsworth, L. D. (2000). Adoption policy in the United States: A word of caution. *Social Work, 45*(2), 183–186.

Huggins-Hoyt, K. Y., Briggs, H. E., Mowbray, O., & Allen, J. L. (2019). Privatization, racial disproportionality and disparity in child welfare: Outcomes for foster children of color. *Children and Youth Services Review, 99*, 125–131.

Huggins-Hoyt, K. Y., Mowbray, O., Briggs, H. E., & Allen, J. L. (2019). Private vs public child welfare systems: A comparative analysis of national safety outcome performance. *Child Abuse & Neglect, 94*, 1–12.

Jeter, H. R. (1963). *Children, problems and services in child welfare programs* (No. 403). Washington, DC: U.S. Department of Health, Education, and Welfare, Welfare Administration, Children's Bureau.

Jimenez, M. A. (1990). Permanency planning and the Child Abuse Prevention and Treatment Act: The paradox of child welfare policy. *J. Soc. & Soc. Welfare, 17*, 55–72.

Johnston, W. R. (2017). Historical statistics on adoption in the United States, plus statistics on child population and welfare. http://www.johnstonsarchive.net/policy/adoptionstats.html

Kaminski, J. W., Valle, L. A., Filene, J. H., & Boyle, C. L. (2008). A meta-analytic review of components associated with parent training program effectiveness. *Journal of Abnormal Child Psychology, 36*(4), 567–589.

Katz, L. (1990). Effective permanency planning for children in foster care. *Social Work, 35*(3), 220–226.

Kim, H. K., Buchanan, R., & Price, J. M. (2017). Pathways to preventing substance use among youth in foster care. *Prevention Science, 18*(5), 567–576. doi: 10.1007/s11121-017-0800-6

Ko, S. J., Ford, J. D., Kassam-Adams, N., Berkowitz, S. J., Wilson, C., Wong, M., ... Layne, C. M. (2008). Creating trauma-informed systems: Child welfare, education, first responders, health care, juvenile justice. *Professional Psychology: Research and Practice, 39*(4), 396–404.

Krymow, B. L. (1979). Obstacles encountered in permanent planning for foster children. *Child Welfare, 58*(2), 97–104.

Landers, A. L., Bellamy, J. L., Danes, S. M., McLuckie, A., & Hawk, S. W. (2019). The reunification of American Indian children in long-term foster care. *Journal of the Society for Social Work and Research, 10*(4), 501–528.

Leathers, S. J. (2005). Separation from siblings: Associations with placement adaptation and outcomes among adolescents in long-term foster care. *Children and Youth Services Review, 27*(7), 793–819.

Lietz, C. A., Julien-Chinn, F. J., Geiger, J. M., & Piel, M. H. (2016). Cultivating resilience in foster families: Understanding how families cope and adapt over time. *Family Process, 55*(4), 660–672. http://dx.doi.org/10.1111/famp.12239

Lipovsky, J. A. (1994). The impact of court on children: Research findings and practical recommendations. *Journal of Interpersonal Violence, 9*(2), 238–257.

Lowry, M. R. (2004). Putting teeth into ASFA: The need for statutory minimum standards. *Children and Youth Services Review, 26*(11), 1021–1031.

Maluccio, A. N., & Fein, E. (1983). Permanency planning: A redefinition. *Child Welfare, 62*(3), 195–201.

Mayers-Pasztor, E. (1987). Model approach to partnerships in parenting/group preparation and selection of foster and/or adoptive families. Atlanta: Child Welfare Institute.

McDonald, T. P., Poertner, J., & Jennings, M. A. (2007). Permanency for children in foster care: A competing risks analysis. *Journal of Social Service Research, 33*(4), 45–56.

MacGregor, T. E., Rodger, S., Cummings, A. L., & Leschied, A. W. (2006). The needs of foster parents: A qualitative study of motivation, support, and retention. *Qualitative Social Work, 5*(3), 351–368.

McLaughlin, K. A., Green, J. G., Gruber, M. J., Sampson, N. A., Zaslavsky, A. M., & Kessler, R. C. (2012). Childhood adversities and first onset of psychiatric disorders in a national sample of US adolescent childhood adversities and psychiatric disorders. *Archives of General Psychiatry, 69*(11), 1151–1160.

Meezan, W., & Shireman, J. F. (1982). Foster parent adoption: A literature review. *Child Welfare, 61*(8), 525–536.

Meisels, J. F., & Loeb, M. B. (1956). Foster-care and adoption: Unanswered questions about foster care. *Social Service Review, 30*(3), 239–246.

Milwaukee Child Welfare Partnership. (2014). *Caregivers Fostering Permanency: A Resource Guide for Child Welfare Workers*. Milwaukee, WI: Author.

Olsen, R. F., & De Montgomery, C. J. (2018). Revisiting out of home placed children's poor educational outcomes—Is school change part of the explanation? *Children and Youth Services Review, 88*, 103–113.

Okpych, N. (2012). Policy framework supporting youth aging-out of foster care through college: Review and recommendations. *Children and Youth Services Review, 34*(7), 1390–1396.

Pasztor, E. M. (1985). Permanency planning and foster parenting: Implications for recruitment, selection, training, and retention. *Children and Youth Services Review, 7*(2-3), 191–205.

Piel, M. H., Geiger, J. M., Julien-Chinn, F. J., & Lietz, C. A. (2017). An ecological systems approach to understanding social support in foster family resilience. *Child and Family Social Work, 22*(2), 1034–1043. http://dx.doi.org/10.1111/cfs.12323

Piescher, K. N., Schmidt, M., & LaLiberte, T. (2008). *Evidence-based practice in foster parent training and support: Implications for treatment foster care providers.* St. Paul, MN: Center for Advanced Studies in Child Welfare at the University of Minnesota.

Pike, V., Downs, S. , Emlen, A., Downs, G., & Case, D. (1977). Permanent planning for children in foster care: A handbook for social workers. Publication No. (OHDS) 78-30124. Washington, DC: Department of Health, Education and Welfare.

Preventing Sex Trafficking and Strengthening Families Act of 2014 (P.L.113-183).

Proch, K. (1981). Foster parents as preferred adoptive parents: Practice implications. *Child Welfare, 60*(9), 617–625.

Rhodes, K. W., Orme, J. G., Cox, M. E., & Buehler, C. (2003). Foster family resources, psychosocial functioning, and retention. *Social Work Research, 27*(3), 135–150.

Rodger, S., Cummings, A., & Leschied, A. W. (2006). Who is caring for our most vulnerable children?: The motivation to foster in child welfare. *Child Abuse & Neglect, 30*(10), 1129–1142.

Rycus, J. S., Freundlich, M., Hughes, R. C., Keefer, B., & Oakes, E. J. (2006). Confronting barriers to adoption success. *Fam. Ct. Rev., 44*, 210–230.

Sanders, M. R., Kirby, J. N., Tellegen, C. L., & Day, J. J. (2014). The Triple P-Positive Parenting Program: A systematic review and meta-analysis of a multi-level system of parenting support. *Clinical Psychology Review, 34*(4), 337–357.

Sass, D. A., & Henderson, D. B. (2000). Adoption issues: Preparation of psychologists and an evaluation of the need for continuing education. *Journal of Social Distress and the Homeless, 9*(4), 349–359.

Scheetz, M., & Flavin, G. (2015). The importance of rice pudding. *Culturally Responsive Child Welfare Practice, Winter*, p. 24.

Shaw, T. V. (2010). Reunification from foster care: Informing measures over time. *Children and Youth Services Review, 32*(4), 475–481.

Smith, B. D. (2003). After parental rights are terminated: Factors associated with exiting foster care. *Children and Youth Services Review, 25(*12), 965–985.

Smith, D. K., Leve, L. D., & Chamberlain, P. (2011). Preventing internalizing and externalizing problems in girls in foster care as they enter middle school: Impact of an intervention. *Prevention Science, 12*(3), 269–277. doi: 10.1007/s11121-011-0211-z

Snowden, J., Leon, S., & Sieracki, J. (2008). Predictors of children in foster care being adopted: A classification tree analysis. *Children and Youth Services Review, 30*(11), 1318–1327.

Sokoloff, B. Z. (1993). Antecedents of American adoption. *The Future of Children*, 17–25.

Southerland, D. G., Farmer, E. M., Murray, M. E., Stambaugh, L. F., & Rosenberg, R. D. (2018). Measuring fidelity of empirically-supported treatment foster care: Preliminary psychometrics of the together facing the challenge—fidelity of implementation test (TFTC-FIT). *Child & Family Social Work, 23*(2), 273–280.

Steele, J. S., & Buchi, K. F. (2008). Medical and mental health of children entering the Utah foster care system. *Pediatrics, 122*(3), e703–e709.

Taylor, H. B. (1966). Guardianship or "permanent placement" of children. *California Law Review, 54*(2), 741–747.

Townsend, S., Hignight, A., & Rubovits, D. (2008). Factors affecting permanency outcomes for foster children before and after passage of the Adoption and Safe Families Act of 1997. *Illinois Child Welfare, 4*(1), 59–73.

U.S. Department of Health and Human Services (USDHHS), Administration for Children and Families, Administration on Children, Youth and Families, Children's Bureau. (2018). *Trends in foster care and adoption: FY 2008–FY 2017,* Washington, DC: Author.

U.S. Department of Health and Human Services (USDHHS), Administration for Children and Families, Administration on Children, Youth and Families, Children's Bureau. (2019). *The AFCARS Report, No. 26,* Washington, DC: Author.

U.S. Department of Health and Human Services (USDHHS), Administration for Children and Families, Administration on Children. Youth and Families, Children's Bureau. *AFCARS Report #12-26,* Washington, DC: Author.

Wells, K., & Guo, S. (1999). Reunification and reentry of foster children. *Children and Youth Services Review, 21*(4), 273–294.

White, K. R. (2016). Placement discontinuity for older children and adolescents who exit foster care through adoption or guardianship: A systematic review. *Child and Adolescent Social Work Journal, 33*(4), 377–394.

Wojciak, A. S., McWey, L. M., & Waid, J. (2018). Sibling relationships of youth in foster care: A predictor of resilience. *Children and Youth Services Review, 84,* 247–254.

Wulczyn, F. (2003). Closing the gap: Are changing exit patterns reducing the time African American children spend in foster care relative to Caucasian children? *Children and Youth Services Review, 25*(5–6), 431–462.

Wulczyn, F. (2002). Adoption dynamics: The impact of the Adoption and Safe Families Act. (U.S. DHHS, ASPE) http://aspe.hhs.gov/HSP/fostercare-issues02/ASFA/index.htm

Yampolskaya, S., Armstrong, M. I., & McNeish, R. (2011). Children placed in out of home care: Risk factors for involvement with the juvenile justice system. *Violence and Victims, 26*(2), 231–245.

Figure Credits

Img. 13.1: Copyright © 2014 Depositphotos/szefei.

Fig. 13.1: AFCARS Reports #12-26.

Img. 13.2: Copyright © 2018 Depositphotos/belchonock.

Fig. 13.2: C. A. Lietz, et. al., The Process of Family Resilience, from "Cultiviating Resilience in Foster Families: Understanding How Families Cope and Adapt Over Time," Family Process, vol. 55, no. 4, pp. 664. Copyright © 2016 by John Wiley & Sons, Inc.

Img. 13.3: Copyright © 2012 Depositphotos/mangostock.

CHAPTER • 14

Children with Mental Health Needs in Child Welfare

Adeline Wyman Battalen, Christina M. Sellers, Catherine LaBrenz, Rowena Fong, and Ruth McRoy

Overview of Chapter and Population

The mental health and well-being of children within the child welfare system continues to be an area requiring greater attention. This chapter will provide an overview of children with mental health needs in the child welfare system, as well as address current practice challenges, innovative and evidence-based approaches, and a discussion of related systems and policies. Over 500,000 children are involved with the child welfare system on any given day (U.S. Department of Health and Human Services, 2017) and prevalence rates of mental health issues are alarmingly high, with up to 80% of all children who are child welfare–involved needing mental health interventions (Child Welfare League of America, 2017; Pecora, Jensen, Romanelli, Jackson, & Ortiz, 2009). As the circumstances of child welfare involvement are often traumatic, youth involved with the child welfare system, compared to other youth, may be more prone to have mental health disorders, particularly due to experiencing abuse, neglect, parental substance abuse, and for many youth, multiple moves while in care. Although not all youth involved with the child welfare system are diagnosed with mental health conditions, research on the prevalence of mental health disorders of children and adolescents in the child welfare system has found that about half met the diagnostic criteria for a mental disorder (Bronsard et al., 2016). This is almost four times that of the general population (Burns et al., 2004).

Despite the high need for mental health services due to emotional or behavioral challenges, developmental delays, or for other reasons (Pecora et al., 2009), fewer than one out of four children in care receive adequate mental health services (DeNard, Garcia, & Circo, 2017; Halfon, Zepeda, & Inkelas, 2002). This is concerning because a lack of mental health treatment can contribute to impaired functioning in multiple domains and cause problems at home, school, and in the community, as well as detract from the ability of children to learn and form healthy relationships with peers and adults (Dore, 2014). These types of challenges, such as difficulty in school due to mental health concerns, contribute to longer-term problems and are associated with serious implications for adulthood, such as increased court involvement (Mallett, Stoddard-Dare, & Seck, 2011). Youth of color, particularly those who are Black or Latino, who also have mental health problems are especially at risk for later court involvement within the juvenile justice system and possible incarceration (Mallett et al., 2011).

Disproportionality and Disparity

Reflective of our greater society, systems of oppression (e.g., racism) permeate the child welfare system, resulting in disproportionality and disparity of treatment for children based on their social demographic characteristics. As discussed in previous chapters, disproportionality refers to different proportions of racial or ethnic groups in a particular system (e.g., child welfare) than the proportion of that same racial or ethnic group in the general population (Fong, Dettlaff, & Crocker, 2015). Children of color continue to be overrepresented in the child welfare system as a whole (McRoy, 2011; Smedley, Stith, & Nelson, 2003; U.S. Department of Health and Human Services, 2017; Wells, Merritt, & Briggs, 2009). While disproportionality focuses on the proportions of diverse racial and ethnic groups, disparities reflect unequal outcomes. In regard to race and ethnicity, significant disparities exist. For example, in the child welfare system, there are disparities for Black, Pacific Islander, and Native American or Alaskan Native children in terms of referrals, substantiation of maltreatment, removals, and discharges from foster care (Fong et al., 2015). Several explanations exist for the possible causes of racial disparity. Researchers credit the disproportionate needs of children and families of color, attributed to higher rates of poverty, as a key contributor to racial disparity within the child welfare system (Fluke, Harden, Jenkins, & Ruehrdanz, 2011). Furthermore, racial bias and discrimination within the child welfare system serve to exacerbate involvement at an interpersonal level (e.g., by caseworkers) and systemic (e.g., few resources for families of color) (Fluke et al., 2011).

Black, Native American, and other children of color have been found to have the highest rates of reported maltreatment (U.S. Department of Health and Human Services, 2016), although rates may be skewed because of referral patterns found among racial and ethnic minority groups and the tendency of caseworkers to over-report racial minority parents (Dakil, Cox, & Flores, 2011). Moreover, racial bias often exists among service providers, which is demonstrated through attitudes toward families, use of language, decision-making, and difficulty fully understanding the consequences of structural racism (DeNard et al., 2017; U.S. Department of Health and Human Services, 2016). As a result, children in the child welfare population are often differentially diagnosed (Morgan, Staff, Hillemeier, Farkas, & Maczuga, 2013) and medicated (Raghavan et al., 2005) regardless of race compared to children who are not child welfare–involved. Children of color in the general population were found to be less likely to be medicated, whereas child welfare–involved children across *all* races were 2–3 times more likely to be medicated (Raghavan et al., 2005).

Mental Health Disparities Among Diverse Racial and Ethnic Groups in Child Welfare Systems

Although children and youth placed in foster care have an increased need for mental health services, prior research has found disparities in the utilization of mental health services by children of color (Garland, Landsverk, & Lau, 2003). For example, some studies have found that children involved in child welfare who identified as Black or Latino were less likely to receive mental health services than their White, non-Latino counterparts (Burns et al., 2004; Gudiño, Martinez, & Lau, 2012; Marrast, Himmelstein, & Woolhandler, 2016) and less likely to receive mental health services than their Latino counterparts (Hurlburt et al., 2004). Latino children and youth also have had lower rates of mental health service utilization while in child welfare than their White, non-Latino counterparts (Hulburt et al., 2004).

Image 14.1

Racial and ethnic disparities in mental health service utilization among children and youth involved in child welfare systems vary by mental health problem. For example, while overall rates of mental health service utilization are lower among minority children and youth, disparities may be less pronounced in service utilization for externalizing behaviors than internalizing behaviors (Gudiño, Lau, Yeh, McCabe, & Hough, 2009). Immigrant status among Latino and Asian and Pacific Islander youth has also been found to impact the relationship between mental health problem and service utilization; prior research found that Latino and Pacific Islander immigrants were more likely to receive services for externalizing behaviors and less likely to receive services for internalizing behaviors than non-immigrant youth (Gudiño, Lau, & Hough, 2008).

There may be cultural factors that impact mental health service utilization among families of color, which could impact initial diagnoses and recognition of the need to seek services for children and youth with mental health needs. For example, Latino children are considered at high risk for not receiving mental health services because of the disproportionate numbers of Latino families without health insurance, and other factors such as an unrecognized need for services and variations in help-seeking behaviors (Kataoka et al., 2003). Different cultures may attribute children and youth problems to cultural beliefs instead of mental health problems (Roberts, Alegria, Roberts, & Chen, 2005), and certain child externalizing behaviors might conflict with cultural values of obedience (Gudiño et al., 2008).

Disparities by Socioeconomic Status, Child's Gender, Child's Age, and Parental Drug Use

The intersection of social demographics adds to the complexity of racial disparities in child welfare. Lower social economic status and poverty have been associated with poorer mental health of children (Yoshikawa, Aber, & Beardslee, 2012), and some research suggests racial disparities in the child welfare system reflect inequality in housing and employment (Wells et al., 2009). However, other research has found that differences exist across race in regard to referral and quality of services provided, regardless of social class (Wells et al., 2009).

Disparities in the child welfare system also occur based on gender, as young boys are more likely than young girls to be abused, with infant boys having the highest rate of victimization (U.S. Department of Health and Human Services, 2016). However, after age 6, girls are at higher risk of victimization. Boys are more likely to be diagnosed with externalizing disorders, such as attention-deficit/hyperactivity disorder (ADHD), whereas girls are more likely to be diagnosed with internalizing disorders like depression and anxiety (Rutter, Caspi, & Moffit, 2003).

In regard to age, children under the age of 6 appear to be particularly vulnerable, as they are the least likely to receive mental health services (U.S. Department of Health and Human Services, 2016). Even more concerning is the fact that among families who are welfare-involved, the most likely age group is children under 3 years (Cooper, Banghart, & Aratani, 2010), with younger children (0–4 years) accounting for the majority (75%) of children who die from child abuse (U.S. Department of Health and Human Services, 2017). Moreover, young children are particularly reliant on their caregivers to protect and provide for them (De Young, Kenardy, & Cobham, 2011).

Substance abuse among caregivers is a risk factor for child maltreatment, and with the opioid epidemic, increasingly high numbers of children and youth are entering the child welfare system due to parental substance abuse. A 2016 study found that 11 states in the United States had almost a 50% increase of maltreatment as a result of substance abuse among their caretaker (Administration on Children, Youth and Families, 2016). Additionally, between 2004 and 2013, there was a sixfold increase in the number of babies born with neonatal abstinence syndrome, a syndrome caused by exposure to opioids prenatally (França, Mustafa, & McManus, 2015). Given the mandated reporting statutes, when a child is born exposed to opioids, a report is often made to the public child welfare system and the family is often investigated for the newborn's safety. Consequently, half of babies born with neonatal abstinence syndrome are removed from their caregivers and placed in out of home care (França et al., 2015). Research has demonstrated that the majority of families afflicted by parental opioid addiction with newborns having neonatal abstinence syndrome are White and middle class (França et al., 2015).

Trauma-Informed Care

A trauma-informed approach is especially important for children with a mental health diagnosis. Child maltreatment is associated with mental health issues over time (Rizvi & Najam, 2014), and many children within the welfare system have experienced complex trauma (Greeson et al., 2011; Ko et al., 2008). Some researchers propose that almost every child in the child welfare system has encountered trauma "by definition"—that the very act of being removed from one's family of origin is a traumatic event, and as such, any child in foster care has therefore experienced trauma (Ko et al., 2008, p. 397). Complex trauma is the phrase used to define the often multitude of traumas a child may experience when involved within the child welfare system, including the "chronic and cumulative experience of abuse, neglect, and parental loss prevalent among children involved with child welfare ... because of its invasive interpersonal nature and deleterious impact on children's self-regulatory functioning and capacity to form healthy attachments and relationships" (Fraser et al., 2014, p. 233). In a study by the National Child Traumatic Stress Network, over 70% of children in their sample reported at least two types of the traumas that constitute complex trauma (e.g., physical abuse) (Greeson et al., 2011). Types can include the chronic and cumulative experience of abuse, neglect, and parental loss prevalent among children involved with child welfare. Clinically, many children are diagnosed with post-traumatic stress disorder (PTSD) following a traumatic experience (American Psychiatric Association, 2013; De Young et al., 2011). Even children who do not receive a PTSD diagnosis or meet the full criteria often experience symptoms of involuntary reexperience (i.e., nightmares, flashbacks), avoidance, negative affect, and hyperarousal, resulting in impaired functioning (American Psychiatric Association, 2013; Bath, 2008).

A child's ability to form healthy attachments, regulate their affect, and control behavior can all be impacted by early trauma exposure (Bath, 2008; Perry, 2009). The experiences of early trauma by a young child and potential separation from their primary caregiver compounds the impact. Bowlby (1969) identified the importance of early attachment and considered this time period of early childhood to be critical to healthy development, as the first relationship a child forms is with his/her mother (this theory has since evolved to now include any parent or primary caregiver; e.g., Gross, Stern, Brett, & Cassidy, 2017) and provides the secure base needed to safely explore the world. This base serves as a template for healthy relationship formation. Disruption to this relationship during the first 2 years of life is associated with long-term problems in social and emotional functioning (Bowlby, 1969; Gross et al., 2017). In fact, over 80% of major structural changes in brain development occur during the first 4 years of life (Ludy-Dobson & Perry, 2010). Consequently, the impact of trauma can be even more pervasive among infants, toddlers, and preschoolers (De Young et al., 2011). This can also inhibit a child's ability to meet normal developmental milestones, such as exploration (Pittman, Keiley, Kerpelman, & Vaughn, 2011). Because of the likelihood of children in the child welfare system to have experienced trauma and its deleterious effects, a trauma-informed approach is critical to effective treatment of mental health in children across all ages.

Trauma-informed care is the primary approach to care recommended for children in the child welfare system due to the widespread rates of trauma exposure experienced by the children and youth and, often, the parents (Greeson et al., 2011). Given that complex trauma was often sustained over time, it is understandable that the treatment must be multifaceted and long-lasting (Bath, 2008). On an agency level, trauma-informed care includes a framework that consists of service delivery with provider training, routine screenings for exposure to trauma, collecting a comprehensive history of trauma, and reliance upon evidence-based practices, consistency across the treatment team, and evaluation (Greeson et al., 2011; Ko et al., 2008). Fortunately, a trauma-informed approach is accessible to providers and can be implemented by even beginner clinicians (Bath, 2008). There are three key components widely accepted for use during individual therapy: 1) development of safety; 2) promotion of healing relationships; and 3) teaching self-management and coping skills (Van der Kolk & Courtois, 2005). These three components each address the need for a child to develop a sense of safety, learn how to form healthy connections with others, and manage their emotions (Bath, 2008).

A systematic review of evidence-based treatments for children who experienced maltreatment recommended trauma-informed cognitive behavior therapy (TF-CBT) as the best supportive treatment (Leenarts, Diehle, Doreleijers, Jansma, & Lindauer, 2013). Notably, incorporation of parent involvement in treatment, whether through coaching, training, or therapy, was encouraged (Leenarts et al., 2013). Leenarts et al. (2013) identified challenges with treatment retention and encourage treatment completion to continue to be explored, as the reasons why clients discontinued treatment were unclear and ways to further engage families are needed. Importantly, TF-CBT was found to be effective among children of color (Weiner, Schneider, & Lyons, 2009), including Latino children (Kataoka et al., 2003). Evidence-based practices (EBPs), practices which have been shown through extensive research to be safe and effective, are especially lacking in services to racial/ethnic minority children and result in gaps in quality service delivery (DeNard et al., 2017; Smedley et al., 2003).

The Office of Justice Programs at the U.S. Department of Justice has also categorized the following interventions for trauma-exposed children and youth as effective or promising in improving mental health: Child-Parent Psychotherapy (CPP); Trauma Affect Regulation: Guide for Education and Therapy (TARGET); Trauma-Focused Cognitive-Behavior Therapy (TF-CBT); Cognitive Behavioral Intervention for Trauma in Schools (CBITS); Parent-Child Interaction Therapy (PCIT); and Trauma and Grief Component Therapy for Adolescents (TGC T-A) (Pilnik & Kendall, 2012). These interventions include tools to determine whether individuals have experienced events that could cause trauma, measure potentially traumatic events a child may have experienced or witnessed, and screen for distress and depression. Additionally, these therapeutic approaches have shown effectiveness in treating children with PTSD, depression, and experiencing grief and loss. Several of these approaches, such as CPP, emphasize the effectiveness of family therapy to address the impact of trauma on the whole family's mental health.

It is especially important to assess the impact of trauma on birth/first parents, foster and adoptive parents, caregivers, siblings, or other extended family members of children in child welfare systems, and provide trauma-related services for those affected (Klain, White, & ABA Center on Children and the Law, 2013). For example, the experience of parents having a child in care can be traumatic in itself (Hanna, Boyce, & Mulligan, 2017). Two recent qualitative studies examined the experiences of adoptive parents who had adopted both from the child welfare system and via private adoption, who felt they could no longer parent their child in-home due to mental illness or problematic behaviors (Brown, LaBrenz, & Fong, 2018; Hanna et al., 2017). These two studies helped shed light on often-overlooked perspectives (Hanna et al., 2017). Findings from both studies revealed parents experienced discrepancies within the systems (e.g., child welfare, education) designed to support their families (Brown et al., 2018; Hanna et al., 2017). Notably, challenges navigating these systems resulted in *parents* beginning to show signs of trauma based on their experiences and misguided support (Hanna et al., 2017). Hanna and colleagues (2017) recommended the following: 1) parenting a child with a mental illness, especially from the child welfare system, impacts the whole family, and a holistic view must be taken into consideration; and 2) providers must partner with parents in treatment planning.

Practice Challenges

The diagnostic criteria for mental health disorders for all children continue to evolve and be refined (American Psychiatric Association, 2013). Understanding the complexity of a child's rapid developmental growth and their environmental context can be a challenge within the fast-paced child welfare system. Children in foster care often have difficulty accessing appropriate mental health screening, assessment, and treatment (McCrae, Barth, & Guo, 2010; Pecora et al., 2009). Service utility and diagnoses look different for child welfare–involved youth. Children in foster care are much more likely to receive a mental health diagnosis than children not in foster care (50% for those in care versus 11% for those not in care) (Center for Mental Health Services and Center for Substance Abuse Treatment, 2013). Common diagnoses among youth involved with the child welfare system include adjustment disorders; mood disorders; anxiety disorders; and attention-deficit, conduct, and disruptive behavior disorders (Center for Mental Health Services and Center for Substance Abuse Treatment, 2013).

In addition, children in care are two to three times more likely than children in the general population to receive mental health–related prescription medication (Raghavan et al., 2005), including antipsychotic medication and attention-deficit/hyperactivity disorder

(ADHD) drugs (Center for Mental Health Services, & Center for Substance Abuse Treatment, 2013). While psychopharmacological medication as an intervention has shown to be effective with some children, the majority of testing is conducted by adults, and when used, are accompanied by a caution of close and consistent monitoring (Zito et al., 2008). Further exploration of the role demographics plays in diagnoses and medication of children in foster care is needed. Additionally, medication should always be used in conjunction with other interventions, such as psychotherapy, parent training, and family therapy.

Image 14.2

Children in foster care receiving mental health treatment generally had many more outpatient visits than their non–foster care peers. Among children and adolescents requiring inpatient stays, children living in foster care averaged longer stays, with adolescents (12–17) in the inpatient level of care having an average of 30 days longer in treatment compared to adolescents not living in foster care (Center for Mental Health Services and Center for Substance Abuse Treatment, 2013).

Service Access

Access to services is a major barrier to mental health treatment, with racial disparities persisting in service access (Burns et al., 2004). Specifically, factors such as being a Black child living at home, an adolescent living at home, or a young child (2–5) not dealing with sexual abuse decreases the likelihood of receiving mental health services. Conversely, having a parent with a significant mental illness increased the chances of a child receiving mental health treatment. School-based mental health services often are the only type of service received (Langer et al., 2015). Part of the challenge of beginning to reduce access limitations is the lack of identification of the reasons *why* service access is a problem. While inadequate resources, overworked child welfare workers, and insufficient training of mental health interventions are contributing factors to service access, more understanding is needed to fully address the problem (Burns et al., 2004).

Caregiver Role

As children do not typically seek out mental health services for themselves (nor should they be expected to!), one study examined how caregiver type was associated with access to mental health services by children in care (Villagrana, 2010). Researchers found that children living in kinship care were half as likely to receive services as compared to those living with nonrelatives (Villagrana, 2010). This may be due to a kinship care provider's desire to avoid the child welfare and related systems or the provider's own barriers to access services, such as because of their age (kinship providers are typically older than non-kinship providers), finances, or own health status (Villagrana, 2010). On the other hand, children living in kinship care may present with less mental health issues than those in non-kinship care, and thus caregiver response may be driven by need rather than other factors (Villagrana, 2010).

Very little research exists regarding the role of birth parents and mental health utilization, although some research suggests children are less likely to receive mental health services while living with their birth parent, as parents may want to avoid involvement with social service agencies or face challenges in access (e.g., financial, transportation) (Burns et al., 2004). In a recent study that examined adoptive families' experiences (the majority of whom had adopted through the child welfare system) with placement in residential treatment centers after adoption because of mental health or behavior issues, Brown and colleagues (2018) concluded that there was a need for more community-based resources for families with children previously in child welfare systems. Moreover, families voiced their desire for help identifying and accessing services early on as problems emerge. Notably, in this study, while the sample size was small, all 10 families reported using multiple services before seeking residential placement for their adopted children, suggesting there may be a need not only for accessible services, but also for those that can adequately address complex trauma (Brown et al., 2018). Thus, interventions should also be evaluated for their evidence base in supporting children and youth in families with child welfare involvement, given the complex trauma and subsequent trauma-informed care they may require.

Evidence-Based Practices for Working with Children with Mental Health Needs

In the past decade, an increasing number of evidence-based practices for child welfare–involved youth have been established. Evidence-based practices are practices or interventions that are supported by empirical research and include evaluating the best intervention for a client system given prior research and the client's own preferences (McNeece & Thyer, 2004). While gaps exist in funding, dissemination, and implementation, there are key tenets that have been identified, including planning, increasing parent collaboration, and streamlining a trauma-informed approach. A case study of one such effort is outlined below as an example of this type of comprehensive approach.

In response to the lack of evidence-based practices (EBPs) access and provision of services for children in the child welfare system, Hanson, Self-Brown, Rostad, and Jackson (2016) conducted a comprehensive review to increase systemic implementation of EBPs.

Their review highlighted frameworks that can provide guidance throughout all phases of treatment of children facing mental health needs in the child welfare system. Of the 10 major programs analyzed, the majority emphasized the importance of planning and preparation, as well as incorporating the context of the program. An important early stage is identifying the target population, selecting the program that will best meet the needs of this target population, and then ensuring there are appropriate funding and referral streams in place to provide the services (Hanson et al., 2016). Subsequently, identification, preparation, and training of the practitioners is needed, followed by ongoing training and evaluation of the services once the program is underway (Hanson et al., 2016).

Best practices include provision of a range of services to 1) provide interventions to address a history of child maltreatment if needed; and 2) provide services to support the current situation of the child. The first key component required is a thorough assessment to evaluate the potential for a history of maltreatment and/or multiple placements, and should include determination of medical, mental health, and developmental needs of the child (Cooper et al., 2010). To better understand the child's current functioning and environment, the nature of the child–caregiver relationship must be examined, along with assessment of the caregivers' strengths, limitations, competencies, and evaluation of risk. Intervention/services to improve and support the caregiver–child relationship and healthy attachment must be prioritized and may include family therapy, parent coaching, and/or other relationship-based skill-building approaches (Cooper et al., 2010).

However, despite extensive research, implementation of EBP is often a challenge because of inadequate practitioner resources, support, and insufficient training and understanding of practices (Glasgow, Lichtenstein, & Marcus, 2003). For example, social workers are often working with large caseloads and may not have the time to implement a thorough cognitive behavior therapy (CBT) intervention as recommended. The complexity of child welfare cases and the heterogeneity of client family situations further contribute to difficulty in applying EBP across systemic and interpersonal factors (Aarons & Palinkas, 2007). Historically, the focus has been on safety and placement rather than meeting the more comprehensive developmental needs of the child (Cooper et al, 2010). However, increasingly, states are developing programs that extend beyond the initial goal of safety and address longer-term solutions.

Weiner et al. (2009) offer tangible solutions to provide culturally competent services and reduce or limit common barriers to treatment of children of color, particularly those for whom a language other than English is spoken at home. As language, transportation, and poor rapport can impact the effectiveness of EBTs, "flexible adaptations" (Weiner et al., 2009, p. 1204) are suggested, such as including an extended family member or caregiver in treatment when parents are unavailable, providing transportation or meeting off-site in a more accessible location, and providing treatment in languages beyond English. In response to the limited research on families with limited English proficiency who are involved with the child welfare system, one study explored how to improve services and reduce language barriers (Maiter, Alaggia, Chan, & Leslie, 2017). They identified four steps organizations can take, including support for bilingual staff, education to service providers on how to use interpreter services, ongoing evaluation of interpreter services, and a commitment to evaluate services to families with limited English proficiency on an ongoing basis (Maiter et al., 2017).

Systems Approach: Integration of Public Systems with Children with Mental Health and Developmental Needs

Child welfare service delivery varies greatly by state, county, and jurisdiction, which creates gaps. Gaps in service delivery are seen across initial screenings, treatment, and follow-up care. Notably, agencies lack a systemic approach for identifying children with mental health and developmental needs. Identification of child maltreatment and/or of a child needing mental health services is often first recognized by pediatricians, school staff, or other providers (Dore, 2014), which calls for a multidisciplinary approach. Despite this need, agencies lack a systemic approach for identifying children with mental health and developmental needs. One way to improve identification of children and youth who have experienced child maltreatment and/or are in need of mental health services is to develop an integrative screener that providers could easily disseminate to children in their well-visits. The following section highlights some of the major gaps prevalent within the child welfare system while providing recommended solutions to develop a more streamlined approach to care.

Image 14.3

It is imperative to incorporate a systems approach because of the different systems a child needing mental health treatment is involved with, such as the court system, substance use treatment facility, school systems, and health systems, among others. This involvement translates into many persons, including, but not limited to, teachers, lawyers, guardians ad litem (GAL), court-appointed special advocates (CASA), therapists, psychiatrists, pediatricians, and caseworkers. Additionally, a child's school team may include a school counselor, educational advocate, and special education coordinator. And of course, the family, which can include the birth family, extended kin, fictive kin, foster family, and/or an adoptive family. As these organizations are interrelated and interactive, a holistic approach is necessary to ensure common goals (Wulczyn et al., 2010).

At the federal level, the United States has tried to create a comprehensive system of care that encompasses the multiple agencies serving children involved with child welfare (Child Welfare Information Gateway, 2018). The Children's Bureau oversees child welfare in the United States with the overarching goal of promoting safety and well-being for children, youth, and families. The mission of the Children's Bureau is to connect social workers and related professionals with resources across the field of child welfare. Additionally, the Children's Bureau is tasked with the overall determination of funding, evaluation of child welfare, maintaining of databases, and dissemination of research findings related to critical issues within the field of child welfare (Child Welfare Information Gateway, 2018).

Policies Related to Children with Mental Health Needs

There are several major policies that impact services in relation to the mental health of children in the child welfare system. The primary policy is the Child Abuse Prevention and Treatment Act (CAPTA), which is the key federal legislation addressing child abuse and neglect. The purpose of CAPTA is to provide federal funding and structure to states in support of prevention, assessment, and treatment, as well as crime-related services such as investigation and prosecution. Additionally, CAPTA provides grants to local agencies for programming, projects, and related research. CAPTA was originally enacted in 1974 and has been amended several times, most recently in 2015, when a section of child trafficking was added, and in 2016, when a section on addiction and recovery was added (Child Welfare Information Gateway, 2017).

Also important are federal and state health insurance programs that directly impact access and funding of mental health services. Medicaid and the Children's Health Insurance Program (CHIP) are two federal and state health insurance and services programs for low-income children, youth, and families, many of whom are children involved with the child welfare system. Understanding the service utilization and limitations of private health insurance is essential as well and typically varies by state. For further information related to state health insurance, visit your state's government website and available plans. This information changes frequently, so checking for changes on a regular basis is important.

Additional federal legislation that has impacted mental health policies for children and youth in child welfare systems includes the Fostering Connections to Success and Increasing Adoptions Act of 2008 and the Family First Prevention Services Act of 2018. Specifically, the Fostering Connections to Success and Increasing Adoptions Act of 2008 provided grants to state, local, and tribal child welfare agencies and nonprofit organizations to implement on-site mental health services or referrals for mental health services for families with children involved in child welfare systems (National Resource Center for Permanency and Family Connections, n.d.). More recently, in 2018, the Family First

Prevention Services Act expanded federal reimbursement for mental health services for families with child welfare involvement (First Focus Campaign for Children, 2018).

At the state level, the National Conference of State Legislatures (2016) tracked legislation enacted at state legislatures between 2011 and 2015. During this timeframe, it registered 27 bills enacted across 17 states that focused on improving mental health outcomes for children and youth in foster care. This ranged from legislation that required mental health screenings within 10 working days of placement to expanding mental health court programs and convening stakeholder groups to identify and address barriers to accessing mental health services (National Conference of State Legislatures, 2016).

As state bills can directly impact child welfare policies, it is important to be familiar with the laws in your state. For example, in Massachusetts, one such state-level policy related to mental health services was proposed in 2019 to help reduce loopholes related to health insurance coverage. This type of bill is common in many states. The intent of the bill, An Act Relative to Mental Health Parity Implementation H.D 1417 (2019) (Representative Balser)/S.D. 1493 (2019) (Senator Friendman), is to help achieve mental health parity and reduce barriers to mental health services; this bill is designed to develop more equitable access to behavioral health care for children and families by streamlining the health insurance coverage process and ensuring consistent definitions of medical necessity criteria, such that coverage of mental health issues will be comparable to medical health issues. This bill stems from the federal legislation enacted in 2008 to target improving health insurance coverage of mental health conditions and substance use disorders on a par with medical treatment (Chiaramida & Linzer, 2016).

At the policy level, Hanson et al. (2016) recommend prioritizing the planning period of an intervention because of the ramifications for multiple agencies, families, and children who will be impacted. Allowances need to be made for troubleshooting and refining the intervention because of its widespread audience (Hanson et al., 2016). Additional considerations at the policy level include relationships between policy-program contexts, such as service reimbursement, opportunities for low-cost dissemination of training, referrals, and agency/practitioner buy-in.

Case Application

Case Vignette

Cedar (12) and her older brother Myles (15) have lived with their grandfather in Massachusetts since their parents lost custody 7 years earlier. The family identifies as Latinx and speaks both English and Spanish fluently. The first 5 years of Cedar's life were filled with the everyday struggle of living with two parents addicted to opiates. As a result, Cedar's parents were unable to keep a consistent job or housing. As their addiction progressed, Cedar's parents' behavior toward their children worsened, and Cedar and Myles were subjected to chronic abuse and neglect. At the age of 5, after multiple reports of abuse were filed, Cedar and her brother were placed with their maternal grandfather, and parental rights were terminated. While the adjustment took some time, Cedar and Myles functioned well enough to remain in their local public school and live with their grandfather.

When Cedar began middle school, she began to skip class, get in trouble at school for explosive behavior, and experiment with drugs and alcohol. The crux of Cedar's behavior came when she showed up intoxicated at school and was arrested for property destruction. Her pro bono lawyer was able to get the charges dropped upon agreement of community service that would be completed by Cedar, involving cleaning up school property. Additionally, Cedar and her grandfather attended several school meetings, so she was not expelled. School staff, including the guidance counselor and school social worker, recommended that Cedar receive individual therapy and the family participate in family therapy. Cedar's grandfather was hesitant to begin therapy, as he preferred to keep their problems "buried in the past" and was not interested in revisiting a hard time in all of their lives. He believed discussing past trauma would only exacerbate their problems and potentially put the children at risk for removal again—not to mention money was tight and he did not want to "waste" what little money they did have.

DISCUSSION QUESTIONS

1. What state or federal policies could help with the finances of Cedar's mental health services?
2. How might the proposed bill in Massachusetts help families like Cedar's?
3. How might Cedar's entry into middle school have triggered/set off/served as a transition point in her behaviors escalating?
4. What services could have been provided to Cedar's parents?
5. What strengths exist within the family (e.g., sibling pair kept together, kinship adoption, not in residential program)?

References

Aarons, G. A., & Palinkas, L. A. (2007). Implementation of evidence-based practice in child welfare: Service provider perspectives. *Administration and Policy in Mental Health and Mental Health Services Research, 34*(4), 411–419. https://doi-org.ezproxy.cul.columbia.edu/10.1007/s10488-007-0121-3

Administration on Children, Youth and Families. (2016). ACYF activities. (Retrieved from Washington, DC).

American Psychiatric Association. (2013). *Diagnostic and Statistical Manual of Mental Disorders* (5th ed.). Arlington, VA: American Psychiatric Publishing.

An Act Relative to Mental Health Parity Implementation, H.910, 191st. (2019).

Bath, H. (2008). The three pillars of trauma-informed care. *Reclaiming Children and Youth, 17*(3), 17.

Bowlby J. (1969). *Attachment. Attachment and loss: Vol. 1. Loss.* New York: Basic Books.

Bronsard, G., Alessandrini, M., Fond, G., Loundou, A., Auquier, P., Tordjman, S., & Boyer, L. (2016). The prevalence of mental disorders among children and adolescents in the child welfare system: A systematic review and meta-analysis. *Medicine, 95*(7).

Brown, K., LaBrenz, C. A., & Fong, R. (2018). From adoption to residential treatment centers. *Adoption Quarterly, 21*(3), 182–200. doi: 10.1080/10926755.2018.1488331

Burns, B. J., Phillips, S. D., Wagner, H. R., Barth, R. P., Kolko, D. J., Campbell, Y., & Landsverk, J. (2004). Mental health need and access to mental health services by youths involved with child welfare: A national survey. *Journal of the American Academy of Child & Adolescent Psychiatry, 43*(8), 960–970. doi: 10.1097/01.chi.0000127590.95585.65

Center for Mental Health Services and Center for Substance Abuse Treatment. Diagnoses and Health Care Utilization of Children Who Are in Foster Care and Covered by Medicaid. HHS Publication No. (SMA) 13-4804. Rockville, MD: Center for Mental Health Services and Center for Substance Abuse Treatment, Substance Abuse and Mental Health Services Administration, 2013.

Chiaramida, S. G., & Linzer, E. (2016). *Understanding the Massachusetts and federal mental health parity laws.* (Volume IV). https://www.mahp.com/wp-content/uploads/2017/05/MAHP_OnPoint_April2016_Mental-HealthParity.pdf

Child Welfare Information Gateway. (2018). Systems of care and child welfare. Washington, DC: U.S. Department of Health and Human Services, Children's Bureau.

Child Welfare Information Gateway. (2017). About CAPTA: A legislative history. Washington, DC: U.S. Department of Health and Human Services, Children's Bureau.

Child Welfare League of America. (2017). *The nation's children 2017.* https://www.cwla.org/wp-content/uploads/2017/03/2017-National-factsheet-final.pdf

Cooper, J. L., Banghart, P. L., & Aratani, Y. (2010). Addressing the mental health needs of young children in the child welfare system: What every policymaker should know. doi.org/10.7916/D8B56SPM.

Dakil, S. R., Cox, M., & Flores, G. (2011). Racial and ethnic disparities in physical abuse reporting and child protective services interventions in the United States. *Journal of the National Medical Association, 103*(9/10), 926. doi: 10.1016/S0027-9684(15)30449-1

De Young, A. C., Kenardy, J. A., & Cobham, V. E. (2011). Trauma in early childhood: A neglected population. *Clinical Child and Family Psychology Review, 14*(3), 231–250. doi:http://dx.doi.org.ezproxy.cul.columbia.edu/10.1007/s10567-011-0094-3

DeNard, C., Garcia, A., & Circo, E. (2017). Caseworker perspectives on mental health disparities among racial/ethnic minority youth in child welfare. *Journal of Social Service Research, 43*(4), 470–486. doi.org/10.1080/01488376.2017.1299827

Dore, M. M. (2014). Mental health care for children and youth. In G. P. Mallon & P. M. Hess (Eds.), *Child Welfare for the Twenty-First Century: A Handbook of Practices, Policies, and Programs* (pp. 115–144). New York: Columbia University Press.

First Focus Campaign for Children (2018). *Family First Prevention Services Act: Section by section.* Washington, DC: First Focus Campaign for Children.

Fluke, J., Harden, B. J., Jenkins, M., & Ruehrdanz, A. (2011). Research synthesis on child welfare: Disproportionality and disparities. *Disparities and Disproportionality in Child Welfare: Analysis of the Research,* 1.

Fong, R., Dettlaff, A., & Crocker, T. (2015). Introduction to racial disproportionality and disparities. In R. Fong, A. Dettlaff, J. James, & C. Rodriguez, *Addressing Racial Disproportionality and Disparities in Human Services* (pp. 3–20). New York: Columbia University Press.

França, U. L., Mustafa, S., & McManus, M. L. (2015). The growing burden of neonatal opiate exposure on children and family services in Massachusetts. *Child Maltreatment, 21*(1), 80–84. http://dx.doi.org/10.1177/1077559515615437

Fraser, J. G., Griffin, J. L., Barto, B. L., Lo, C., Wenz-Gross, M., Spinazzola, J., ... Bartlett, J. D. (2014). Implementation of a workforce initiative to build trauma-informed child welfare practice and services: Findings from the Massachusetts Child Trauma Project. *Children and Youth Services Review, 44,* 233–242. doi.org/10.1016/j.childyouth.2014.06.016

Garland, A. F., Landsverk, J. A., & Lau, A. S. (2003). Racial/ethnic disparities in mental health service use among children in foster care. *Children and Youth Services Review, 25*(5/6), 491–507.

Glasgow, R. E., Lichtenstein, E., & Marcus, A. C. (2003). Why don't we see more translation of health promotion research to practice? Rethinking the efficacy-to-effectiveness transition. *American Journal of Public Health, 93*(8), 1261–1267.

Greeson, J. K., Briggs, E. C., Kisiel, C. L., Layne, C. M., Ake III, G. S., Ko, S. J., ... Fairbank, J. A. (2011). Complex trauma and mental health in children and adolescents placed in foster care: Findings from the National Child Traumatic Stress Network. *Child Welfare, 90*(6), 91.

Gross, J. T., Stern, J. A., Brett, B. E., & Cassidy, J. (2017). The multifaceted nature of prosocial behavior in children: Links with attachment theory and research. *Social Development.* doi-org.ezproxy.cul.columbia.edu/10.1111/sode.12242

Gudiño, O. G., Lau, A. S., Yeh, M., McCabe, K. M., & Hough, R. L. (2009). Understanding racial/ethnic disparities in youth mental health services: Do disparities vary by problem type? *Journal of Emotional and Behavioral Disorders, 17*(1), 3–16. doi.org/10.1177/1063426608317710

Gudiño, O. G., Lau, A. S., & Hough, R. L. (2008). Immigrant status, mental health need, and mental health service utilization among high-risk Hispanic and Asian Pacific Islander youth. *Child & Youth Care Forum, 37,* 139–152.

Gudiño, O. G., Martine, J. I., & Lau, A. S. (2012). Mental health service use by youths in contact with child welfare: Racial disparities by problem type. *Psychiatric Services, 63*(10), 1004–1010. doi: 10.1176/appi.ps.201100427

Halfon, N., Zepeda, A., & Inkelas, M. (2002). Mental health services for children in foster care. *UCLA Center for Healthier Children, Families and Communities, 4*(9), 1–13.

Hanna, M. D., Boyce, E., & Mulligan, D. (2017). When love is not enough: Parenting an adopted child with mental illness. *Families in Society, 98*(3), 201–208. doi: 10.1606/1044-3894.2017.98.30

Hanson, R. F., Self-Brown, S., Rostad, W. L., & Jackson, M. C. (2016). The what, when, and why of implementation frameworks for evidence-based practices in child welfare and child mental health service systems. *Child Abuse & Neglect, 53*, 51–63. doi: 10.1016/j.chiabu.2015.09.014

Hurlburt, M. S., Leslie, L. K., Landsverk, J., Barth, R. P., Burns, B. J., Gibbons, R. D. ... Zhang, J. (2004). Contextual predictors of mental health service use among children open to child welfare. *Archives of General Psychiatry, 61*(12), 1217–1224. doi: 10.1001/archpsyc.61.12.1217

Kataoka, S. H., Stein, B. D., Jaycox, L. H., Wong, M., Escudero, P., Tu, W., ... Fink, A. (2003). A school-based mental health program for traumatized Latino immigrant children. *Journal of the American Academy of Child & Adolescent Psychiatry, 42*(3), 311–318. doi: 10.1097/00004583-200303000-00011

Klain, E. J., White, A. R., & ABA Center on Children and the Law. (2013). *Implementing trauma-informed practices in child welfare*. www.centerforchildwelfare.org/kb/TraumaInformedCare/ImplementingTraumaInformedPracticesNov13.pdf

Ko, S. J., Ford, J. D., Kassam-Adams, N., Berkowitz, S. J., Wilson, C., Wong, M., ... Layne, C. M. (2008). Creating trauma-informed systems: Child welfare, education, first responders, health care, juvenile justice. *Professional Psychology: Research and Practice, 39*(4), 396.

Langer, D. A., Wood, J. J., Wood, P. A., Garland, A. F., Landsverk, J., & Hough, R. L. (2015). Mental health service use in schools and non-school-based outpatient settings: Comparing predictors of service use. *School mental health, 7*(3), 161–173. doi: 10.1007/s12310-015-9146-z

Leenarts, L. E., Diehle, J., Doreleijers, T. A., Jansma, E. P., & Lindauer, R. J. (2013). Evidence-based treatments for children with trauma-related psychopathology as a result of childhood maltreatment: A systematic review. *European Child & Adolescent Psychiatry, 22*(5), 269–283. doi: 10.1007/s00787-012-0367-5

Ludy-Dobson, C. R., & Perry, B. D. (2010). The role of healthy relational interactions in buffering the impact of childhood trauma. In E. Gil (Ed.), *Working with Children to Heal Interpersonal Trauma: The Power of Play* (pp. 26–43). New York: Guilford Press.

Maiter, S., Alaggia, R., Chan, A. S., & Leslie, B. (2017). Trial and error: Attending to language barriers in child welfare service provision from the perspective of frontline workers. *Child & Family Social Work, 22*(1), 165–174. doi.org/10.1111/cfs.12214

Mallett, C. A., Stoddard-Dare, P., & Seck, M. M. (2011). Explicating correlates of juvenile offender detention length: The impact of race, mental health difficulties, maltreatment, offense type, and court dispositions. *Youth Justice, 11*(2), 134–149. doi: 10.1177/1473225411406383

Marrast, L., Himmelstein, D. U., & Woolhandler, S. (2016). Racial and ethnic disparities in mental health care for children and young adults: A national study. *International Journal of Health Services, 46*(4), 810–824. doi.org/10.1177/0020731416662736

McCrae, J. S., Barth, R. P., & Guo, S. (2010). Changes in maltreated children's emotional–behavioral problems following typically provided mental health services. *American Journal of Orthopsychiatry, 80*(3), 350–361.

McNeece, C. A., & Thyer, B. A. (2004). Evidence-based practice and social work. *Journal of Evidence-based Social Work, 1*(1), 7–25. doi: 10.1300/J394v01n01_02

McRoy, R. (2011). Contextualizing disproportionality. Challenging racial disproportionality in child welfare, 67–71. In D. K. Green, K. Belanger, R. G. McRoy, & L. Bullard (Eds.), *Challenging Racial Disproportionality in Child Welfare* (pp. 67–71). Washington, DC: Child Welfare League of America Press.

Morgan, P. L., Staff, J., Hillemeier, M. M., Farkas, G., & Maczuga, S. (2013). Racial and ethnic disparities in ADHD diagnosis from kindergarten to eighth grade. *Pediatrics, 132*(1), 85–93. doi: 10.1542/peds.2012-2390

National Conference of State Legislatures. (2016). *Mental health and foster care*. Washington, DC: National Conference of State Legislatures.

National Resource Center for Permanency and Family Connections. (n.d.). *Fostering connections.* www.nrcpfc.org/fostering_connections/health_care_services.html

Pecora, P. J., Jensen, P. S., Romanelli, L. H., Jackson, L. J., & Ortiz, A. (2009). Mental health services for children placed in foster care: An overview of current challenges. *Child Welfare, 88*(1), 5.

Perry, B. D. (2009). Examining child maltreatment through a neurodevelopmental lens: Clinical applications of the neurosequential model of therapeutics. *Journal of Loss and Trauma, 14*(4), 240–255. doi: 10.1080/15325020903004350

Pilnik, L., & Kendall, J. R. (2012). *Victimization and trauma experienced by children and youth: Implications for legal advocates.* Moving from Evidence to Action: The Safe Start Series on Children Exposed to Violence, Issue Brief # 7. North Bethesda, MD: Safe Start Center, Office of Juvenile Justice and Delinquency Prevention, Office of Justice Programs, U.S. Department of Justice.

Pittman, J. E., Keiley, M. K., Kerpelman, J. L., & Vaughn, B. E. (2011). Attachment, identity, and intimacy: Parallels between Bowlby's and Erikson's paradigms. *Journal of Family Theory & Review, 3,* 32–46. doi: 10.1111/j.1756-2589.2010.00079.x

Raghavan, R., Zima, B. T., Andersen, R. M., Leibowitz, A. A., Schuster, M. A., & Landsverk, J. (2005). Psychotropic medication use in a national probability sample of children in the child welfare system. *Journal of Child & Adolescent Psychopharmacology, 15*(1), 97–106. doi.org/10.1089/cap.2005.15.97

Rizvi, S. F. I., & Najam, N. (2014). Parental psychological abuse toward children and mental health problems in adolescence. *Pakistan Journal of Medical Sciences, 30*(2), 256. doi: http://dx.doi.org/10.12669/pjms.302.4593

Roberts, R. E., Alegria, M., Roberts, C. R., & Chen, I. G. (2005). Mental health problems of adolescents as reported by their caregivers: A comparison of European, African, and Latino Americans. *Journal of Behavioral Health Services and Research, 30,* 176–189.

Rutter, M., Caspi, A., & Moffitt, T. E. (2003). Using sex differences in psychopathology to study causal mechanisms: Unifying issues and research strategies. *Journal of Child Psychology and Psychiatry, 44*(8), 1092–1115. doi.org/10.1111/1469-7610.00194

Smedley, B. D., Stith, A. Y., Nelson, A. R. (2003). Unequal treatment: Confronting racial and ethnic disparities in health care. Institute of Medicine, Committee on Understanding and Eliminating Racial and Ethnic Disparities in Health Care, Washington, DC.

U.S. Department of Health and Human Services. (2017). The AFCARS report: Preliminary FY 2016 Estimates as of July 2017. No. 24.

U.S. Department of Health and Human Services, Administration on Children, Youth and Families. (2016). *Child maltreatment 2014.* Washington, DC: U.S. Government Printing Office. http://www.acf.hhs.gov/programs/cb/resource/child-maltreatment-2014

Van der Kolk, B. A., & Courtois, C. A. (2005). Editorial comments: Complex developmental trauma. *Journal of Traumatic Stress: Official Publication of the International Society for Traumatic Stress Studies, 18*(5), 385–388. doi.org/10.1002/jts.20046

Villagrana, M. (2010). Mental health services for children and youth in the child welfare system: A focus on caregivers as gatekeepers. *Children and Youth Services Review, 32*(5), 691–697. doi.org/10.1016/j.childyouth.2010.01.005

Wells, S. J., Merritt, L. M., & Briggs, H. E. (2009). Bias, racism and evidence-based practice: The case for more focused development of the child welfare evidence base. *Children and Youth Services Review, 31*(11), 1160–1171.doi.org/10.1016/j.childyouth.2009.09.002

Weiner, D. A., Schneider, A., & Lyons, J. S. (2009). Evidence-based treatments for trauma among culturally diverse foster care youth: Treatment retention and outcomes. *Children and Youth Services Review, 31*(11), 1199–1205. doi.org/10.1016/j.childyouth.2009.08.013

Wulczyn, F., Daro, D., Fluke, J., Feldman, S., Glodek, C., & Lifanda, K. (2010). Adapting a systems approach to child protection: Key concepts and considerations. New York: UNICEF.

Yoshikawa, H., Aber, J. L., & Beardslee, W. R. (2012). The effects of poverty on the mental, emotional, and behavioral health of children and youth: Implications for prevention. *American Psychologist, 67*(4), 272. doi.org.ezproxy.cul.columbia.edu/10.1037/a0028015

Zito, J. M., Derivan, A. T., Kratochvil, C. J., Safer, D. J., Fegert, J. M., & Greenhill, L. L. (2008). Off-label psychopharmacologic prescribing for children: History supports close clinical monitoring. *Child and Adolescent Psychiatry and Mental Health, 2*(1), 24. doi: 10.1186/1753-2000-2-24

Figure Credits

CHAPTER • 15

Families Formed Through Adoption and Guardianship

Nancy Rolock, Kevin White, Alfred Pérez, Rowena Fong, and Roni Diamant-Wilson

Overview of Chapter

In the United States children often exit foster care through reunification with their birth family, adoption, or guardianship. If children are not placed into one of these three permanent living arrangements, then they age out of foster care (usually at 18 years old, or the legal age of adulthood). Children are adopted through a number of different avenues, including private domestic agencies, international agencies, stepparent adoptions, and adoptions through the child welfare system. For Native American children, there is also customary tribal adoption (see Chapter 7 for additional information on Native Americans). Sometimes children enter foster care and are discharged to guardianship. Other times guardianship occurs outside the formal foster care system through the courts or informal arrangements made without child welfare or court involvement. The focus of this chapter will be on adoptions and guardianships from foster care, although there are many types of adoption as indicated in Table 15.1.

A central goal of the child welfare system is to "promote the well-being of children by ensuring safety, achieving permanency, and strengthening families to care for their children successfully" (CWIG, 2013, p. 1). The primary path to achieving these goals is through legal permanence—transferring legal custody from the state to adoptive parents or guardians. Historically, adoption or guardianship also means that the day-to-day involvement of the child welfare system ends. Thus, families formed through adoption and guardianship are often left without the services and supports they need to facilitate healthy family formation and development and reduce the risk for poor outcomes, including dissolution (Atkinson & Gonet, 2007; Dhami, Mandel, & Sothmann, 2007; Festinger, 2002; Hartinger-Saunders, Trouteaud, & Matos Johnson, 2014; Reilly & Platz, 2004). Although adoption, and to a lesser extent guardianship, have been the primary paths to permanency for children involved in the child welfare system who are unable to be safely returned to their family of origin, little is known about their long-term outcomes.

TABLE 15.1. Types of Adoption in the United States

Type of Adoption	Description
Domestic Adoption	The adoption of children in the United States by a family that lives in the United States.
Public Agency Adoption	The adoption of children from the public child welfare system or a licensed private agency contracted as a child placement agency by the public agency. Child(ren) most often in foster care due to abuse or neglect, range from ages 0–18 years, may or may not have experienced significant trauma, may have special needs (physical, emotional, mental health, developmental, etc.), may be part of a sibling group, etc. Parental rights are most often terminated involuntarily due to the parents' inability to correct the conditions that led to the child(ren)'s removal from the family of origin.
Private Agency Adoption (Licensed)	The adoption of children—most often infants ages 0–12 months—facilitated by a licensed child-placing agency that works with birth parents who relinquish their rights to the agency and prospective adoptive parents who work with the agency to adopt a child. For the majority of these adoptions, the adoption decision and plans are made while the birth mother is pregnant; however, the adoption is not final until after the child's birth. Social workers employed by the agency often serve as intermediaries between birth parents and adoptive parents, sharing information about both to the other (biographical profiles) to assist in the matching or decision-making process. These adoptions may be open, semi-open, or closed, depending on the level of information shared and whether or not the two sets of parents meet one another face to face and/or have ongoing contact after the child is adopted.
Independent Adoption	The adoption of children—most often an infant placed directly from the hospital at birth—without the assistance of an agency, public or private. The laws vary from state to state, with some states not allowing independent adoptions, others limiting them to facilitation by attorneys, and others allowing them to be completed directly from birth parent(s) to adoptive parent(s) with no third-party involvement.
Facilitated/ Unlicensed Agency	Adoption of children facilitated by an individual or unlicensed agency that may or may not be regulated by state statutes or policy. These adoptions are considered some of the riskiest to all involved as there is no legal recourse should anything go wrong.

Continues on next page

Type of Adoption	Description
Intercountry Adoption	The adoption of children born in a different country through legal means in that country, then brought to the country of residence of the adoptive family to live with them permanently. Intercountry adoptions in the United States are governed by the Hague Convention on Protection of Children and Co-operation in Respect of Intercountry Adoption (2008). The Hague Convention was ratified to protect both the children and families involved in intercountry adoption. Prospective adoptive families have the option of adopting from non-Hague countries; however, there are still certain governmental rules and policies that must be met in order for them to bring the child into the country.
Tribal Customary Adoption	For Native Americans, customary tribal adoption is an alternative to the standard adoption practices listed here. Tribal customary adoption is the transfer of custody of a child to adoptive parents without terminating the rights of the birth parents. Based on native or tribal customs and practices, it is a more appropriate permanency placement for Native children. This practice exercises tribal sovereignty and helps to maintain family connections (http://www.nrc4tribes.org/Tribal-Customary-Adoption-Resources.cfm).

Adapted from Child Welfare Information Gateway (2015) and http://www.nrc4tribes.org/Tribal-Customary-Adoption-Resources.cfm

For several decades, child welfare policy and practice have focused on the achievement of legal permanence for children in foster care, a key ingredient to ensuring the well-being of children and families involved with the child welfare system. While Chapter 1 of this book provides a detailed account of significant child welfare policies and legislation, this chapter focuses on how policies impact families formed through adoption or guardianship. Federal legislation such as the Adoption and Safe Families Act of 1997 (ASFA) was designed to prioritize legal permanence for children in foster care while also ensuring their safety, with the expectation that children and youth would live "happily ever after" (Hanna, Tokarski, Matera, & Fong, 2011) after adoption or guardianship was legally finalized. The intention, and even assumption, was that these new family relationships would endure, and that children would have life-long familial connections and a sense of belonging. Research has shown that for the vast majority of families, these familial relationships have endured. However, there is a subset of families for whom this is not the case (Rolock, 2015; Rolock & Pérez, 2016; Rolock & White, 2016; Testa, Snyder, Wu, Rolock, & Liao, 2015; White, 2016). This chapter explores what is known about the long-term enduring nature of these familial relationships after adoption or guardianship.

Adoption and Guardianship Practice

The largest percentage of children and youth adopted from foster care are adopted by a foster parent (51%) or a relative (35%), and the vast majority of children who exit foster care through guardianship are in the care of relatives (U.S. Department of Health and Human Services, 2018). Similar to the "adoption triad," strengthening existing relationships in the "kinship triad" (the child/youth, the birth parent, and the kin or relative) is also vital for the health and well-being of families (Testa, 2010). In the past, the belief that kin should care for a relative child ("take care of their own") without any assistance from the state was the norm (Testa, Lee, & Ingram, 2017). However, while the bonds between a relative (grandparent, aunt, uncle, etc.) and a birth parent can vary depending on the family's history and connectedness, relationships can become easily frayed from the responsibilities of caring for a child (Hegar & Scannapieco, 2017). Legislation such as the Fostering to Connections to Success and Increasing Adoptions Act and the Kinship Guardian Assistance Payment Program (Kin-Gap) acknowledges that financial assistance and support services provided to relatives, who adopt or assume guardianship of a child, can relieve some of the stress incurred in raising a child and encourage greater cohesiveness among and between families (Testa, Lee, & Ingram, 2017).

Legal guardianship and adoption by relatives are permanency options for children in foster care. In these situations, a relative of the child (e.g., grandparent, aunt, uncle, or stepparent) assumes full-time care, nurturing, and protection for a child or youth. Legal guardianship is a judicially created relationship where a judge decides that an adult—not the child's parents—can assume the rights typically associated with a child's parents. For instance, when a child's parents die, their will may list a person who will take over the care of the child. In child welfare practice, a similar arrangement can be made when a child's parents can no longer care for them. In these situations, the guardian assigned by the judge is often a relative, but it does not need to be. Furthermore, when a guardian is assigned, parental rights do not need to be terminated, and parents can petition the court to reinstate their parental rights. In contrast, adoption by a relative involves the same legal process as adoption by a nonrelative. Parental rights are terminated before the adoption, and the parental rights and responsibilities are then transferred to the relative adoptive parent(s). Relatives help children maintain cultural norms, family traditions, and community continuity (Crumbley, 2017).

When children exit foster care with relatives, through adoption or guardianship, the needs of children run along a continuum. Being adopted by, or placed with, a relative caregiver can be less traumatizing for a child and is often the preferred permanency option over nonrelative placement (Crumbley, 2017). However, the challenges adoptive or guardianship parents and families experience in raising a biologically related child can be as overwhelming as those of nonrelative adoptive parents (Ornelas, Silverstein, & Tan, 2007). In addition, many states do not offer resources or support to relatives who have adopted or assumed guardianship. This lack of services, particularly for adoption- and guardianship-competent mental health services, compounds the problems that may occur in these families (Casey Family Programs, 2012).

The field recognizes that relative caregivers have a unique set of needs. For children who continue to live with relatives, in either an adoptive or guardianship home, after adoption or guardianship, their relationship with their family of origin (see Box 15.1) changes, and these new relationships need to be attended to. This is especially true for children who are old enough to remember and know their birth family, or in rural communities where everyone knows everyone. To meet these unique needs, new workers must work to understand the concerns and priorities of relatives and support them in obtaining the resources and services that will meet their needs. In addition, social workers need to know that legal guardianship is not adoption because children may return to their biological parents if their biological parents successfully petition the court. Kin caregivers may need help balancing the two opposing possibilities—that a child will return to their biological parent(s) or remain indefinitely with them. Special attention and services may also be needed for relatives who have adopted kin and must negotiate the changing familial relationships associated with kinship adoption (e.g., termination of parental rights and establishing new parental rights for the adoptive parent).

Birth Parent Contact After Adoption or Guardianship

Since the last century, practice related to whether children and youth should have a continued relationship with their birth parents after adoption or guardianship has dramatically changed. As recent as 40 years ago, closed adoptions, where an adopted child had no contact with his/her birth family, were the norm. The notion that each member of the "adoption triad" (adopted child or youth, birth parent, and adoptive parent) communicated with one another was not part of common practice and was considered harmful to the child. Current studies on open adoptions indicate that just the opposite may be the case. Maintaining ongoing contact with birth parents has been shown to have a positive impact on a child or youth's identity formation (Von Korff & Grotevant, 2011); better grief resolution for birth mothers (Henney, Ayers-Lopez, McRoy, & Grotevant, 2007); and high levels of satisfaction among the members in the adoption triad (Grotevant, Perry, & McRoy, 2005). In response, a majority of states now have adoption laws that include written and enforceable contact agreements (Child Welfare Information Gateway, 2018c). The internet has also enabled more widespread information and resources in finding and contacting birth families.

BOX 15.1. Family Terminology

Young people may want to have a relationship with their family of origin after adoption or guardianship. They may need assistance in negotiating these relationships, including using language to differentiate between birth parents and adoptive parents or guardians (Neil, 2012). Social workers can assist young people with terminology to discuss these relationships.

Some terms currently in use include: *forever family, adoptive family,* or *guardian* to refer to the caregiver or family that has assumed guardianship or adopted the young person. In discussing family the child was born into, the following terms are common: *birth family, family of origin,* or *biological family.* There is no consensus that one term is the best; rather, social workers can work with individuals to figure out what terminology fits each person. Nonjudgmental, open discussions in which all parties can comfortably express their opinions are encouraged.

The level of contact between adoptive families and birth parents is on a continuum, varying from little to no contact (closed adoptions) to semi- and full contact (open adoptions) (Child Welfare Information Gateway, 2013). When children and youth are adopted from foster care, there is a unique and often complex set of circumstances that make connections with biological parents challenging. Prior to adopting a child, parental rights are terminated with birth parents, which can impede relationships. Prospective adoptive parents may also shy away from open adoptions if birth parents have a history of mental illness, substance use, or domestic violence. In addition, because the majority of children and youth in foster care are adopted by their foster parent or a family relative, the impact of open adoptions broadens to not only include birth parents, but also other significant people in a child's or youth's life, such as extended relatives and siblings in other adoptive or foster care homes (Hanna, Tokarski, Matera, & Fong, 2011).

How Often Do Children and Families Experience Post-Permanency Discontinuity (PDD) After Adoption or Guardianship?

As stated above, once a child leaves foster care through adoption or guardianship, the daily work of the child welfare system with families ends. While families may continue to receive subsidy payments and services, the well-being of children and families is not tracked. For children who have been adopted, parental rights are terminated, children's names are often changed, and the identification numbers used to track children through the data systems usually change. These challenges make it difficult to track and know how many children reenter foster care after an adoption. For guardianship, it is usually easier. Parental rights have not been terminated, names have not been changed, and the same tracking issues are not relevant.

BOX 15.2. Definitions

These definitions provide common language for understanding common conditions for children after adoption or guardianship.

Permanence vs. permanency: Although often used interchangeably, permanence is a noun that describes the legal state of adoption or guardianship, and permanency is an adjective used to describe whether something is characterized by permanence (e.g., a permanency goal).

Permanency planning: A model of practice in which child welfare agents assess the long-term placement plan for a child in foster care on an ongoing basis based on a child's best interests. Practice includes planning for alternative long-term permanent plans, such as adoption or guardianship, in cases where reunification is not feasible.

Post-permanency discontinuity (PPD): This is a broad term used to describe a condition where a child or youth who has left foster care through adoption or placement with a legal guardian, but no longer lives with that adoptive parent or legal guardian. PPD can take several forms; the most common types of PPD are listed below:

Dissolution: A child reenters foster care, and the adoptive parental rights or the legal guardianship is terminated.

Displacement (also known as **post-adoption placement**): This is when a child is temporarily placed in foster care to get services and later returns to her or his adoptive parent or legal guardian once treatment is complete.

Unregulated custody transfer (also known as **rehoming**): This occurs when the physical custody of a child is transferred by a parent to a person who is not the child's parent, stepparent, grandparent, or another adult relative; an adult friend of the family with whom the child is familiar; or a member of the child's tribe with the intent of permanently avoiding responsibility for the child's care and without taking reasonable steps to ensure the safety of the child or the permanency of the placement (CWIG, 2017). In these situations, the child welfare authorities are not consulted about, or informed of, the change in living arrangement.

Relational permanence: This is defined as a "mutually committed, life-long, family connection to an adult–parental figure" (Cushing et al., 2014, p. 74). This idea keeps the focus of a permanent relationship on the youth's perspective. It is the youth, rather than legal documents, who defines which relationships are important, whom they feel connected to, and who provides them with support (Pérez, 2017; Samuels, 2008; Sanchez, 2004).

Post-permanency discontinuity (PPD) is a term used to describe when a child or youth who was adopted or placed with a legal guardian no longer lives with that adoptive parent or legal guardian. PPD can take several forms (see Box 15.2 for additional information). A reasonable estimate of PPD is somewhere between 5% and 20%, depending on the type of population or sample examined, and how long children and families are observed (Rolock, Pérez, White, & Fong, 2018; Rolock, 2015; White, 2016; White, Rolock, Testa, Ringeisen, Childs, Johnson, & Diamant-Wilson, 2018). Formal legal dissolutions of adoptions and guardianships are much less likely to occur, with estimates ranging between 1–10% (Bergeron & Pennington, 2013; CWIG, 2012a; Jones & LaLiberte, 2010). Perhaps the most rigorous evaluation of PPD to date found that 2%, 6%, and 11% of children or youth experienced PPD 2, 5, and 10 years after finalization, respectively (Rolock & White, 2016). Finally, some studies have estimated slightly higher estimates of PPD for guardianship cases as compared to adoption ones, but evidence suggests that the discrepancy between these two types of permanency options are difficult to compare because children, youth, and caregivers who enter into guardianship are different in meaningful ways (Rolock & White, 2017; Testa, 2010). For example, children who exit foster care to guardianship are more likely to be African American, older, and biologically related to their caregiver than those who exit to foster care (Testa, 2010). Also, guardianship caregivers often have lower incomes and are less integrated into formal service networks than adoptive caregivers (Corman & Coon, 2007; Hinterlong & Ryan, 2008; Testa, 2010).

The literature indicates that most children and youth do not experience PPD. Further, surveys of post-adoption and guardianship caregivers generally report that most caregivers are satisfied with their adoptions and guardianships. Surveys find that a majority of adoptive and guardianship caregivers are content to have the children placed in their homes, with most caregivers reporting high satisfaction and overall positive impact with the adoption or guardianship (Erich & Leung, 2002; Groze, 1996; Rycus, Freundlich, Hughes, Keefer, & Oakes, 2006; Smith, 2014).

However, even when children and youth in foster care find permanent homes through adoption or guardianship, they bring the psychological, emotional, behavioral, or relational issues they may have developed from experiences with birth families and the child welfare system. Specifically, children who exit foster care to adoption or guardianship have typically experienced trauma and emotional difficulties due to maltreatment or dependency, years of uncertainty about their living arrangements in foster care (and multiple placements and school moves), and perhaps limited preparation for their placement into new adoptive and guardianship families (Bruskas, 2008; Newton, Litrownik, and Landsverk, 2000; Schwartz, Cody, Ayers-Lopez, McRoy, & Fong, 2014; Simmel, Barth, & Brooks, 2007). For example, one study found that over 50% of a sample of over 1,700 adopted children between the ages of 5 and 17 had participated in at least some type of mental health service since adoption (Tan & Marn, 2013). Children adopted from foster care, as compared to those adopted privately, tend to be older, have much higher rates of prenatal drug exposure, have experienced more child maltreatment (and lived longer with caregivers who mistreat them), and exhibit much higher rates of behavior problems (Faulkner & Madden, 2012; Simmel et al., 2007). As one example, Lloyd and Barth (2011) examined data for over 350 infants for over 5 years after adoption from foster care and found that 24% and 76% of the sample had clinical and subclinical scores, respectively, on the Child Behavior Checklist, a standardized measure of behavioral difficulty (Achenbach & Rescorla, 2001). Thus, even though most children do not experience substantial placement moves after adoption or guardianship placement, they continue to struggle with issues that affect post-permanency adjustment, and caregivers frequently report difficulties meeting the needs of children placed in their homes.

Disproportionality and Disparity

Research indicates complicated relationships between a child's race, the race of his or her caregivers, and post-permanency discontinuity (Orsi, 2015). However, although youth who experience a transracial adoption may struggle with issues related to their identity and peer acceptance, particularly in adolescence (Samuels, 2009), no strong evidence from previous research suggests that transracial adoptions or guardianships are at significantly higher risk for worse post-permanency outcomes than same-race adoptions or guardianships (Orsi, 2015; Rosenthal & Groze, 1994).

Research examining caregiver race explored the experiences of African American caregivers. Many studies have found largely positive outcomes for African American caregivers adopting African American children, such as high parental satisfaction (Gillum & O'Brien, 2010; Smith-McKeever, 2006), with prevalence rates of PPD as low as zero (Belanger, Cheung, & Cordova, 2012; Houston & Kramer, 2008), and cumulative incidence rates of PPD comparable to those of other races (e.g., 8% over 4 years; Liao, Dababnah, & Park, 2017). However, one study found that African American adoptive parents reported less satisfaction with their adoptions than non-African American adoptive parents (Nalavany, Glidden, & Ryan, 2009).

Trauma-Informed Care

The responsibility of nurturing a child physically, emotionally, socially, and intellectually from birth to adulthood can be daunting. Parenting or assuming legal guardianship of a child who may have experienced trauma is that much more challenging. The following section describes the unique needs of families formed through adoption or guardianship and how trauma-informed care may assist with some of these challenges. There is additional information on trauma in Chapter 4 of this book.

All caregivers (parents and guardians) experience the normal ups and downs of childrearing, but adoptive parents and guardians have two additional responsibilities. The first is sharing information with their child about being adopted or in guardianship with a relative. In the past, children were often told they were adopted when they became adults, but studies show they have healthier outcomes when they are provided information earlier in childhood rather than later (Wydra, O'Brien, & Merson, 2012). The "telling" is also a process rather than a one-time conversation, and children need to be informed in ways they can relate to and understand (i.e., in a developmentally appropriate manner) (Brodinsky, 2011). The second and related responsibility all caregivers have is to help their child process the experience of adoption or guardianship. Children may have feelings of loss and separation (Siegel & Strolin-Golzman, 2017). It is not uncommon for children, particularly during adolescence, to seek out contact with their birth parents or other family members (Von Korff & Grotevant, 2011). This contact often stems from a desire to try to make sense of how they came to be in the family, understand where they came from, and to discuss their feelings about being adopted or in guardianship (Wiley & Baden, 2005). In addition, these subjects are not typically openly discussed outside of the family (Brodinsky, 2011). Disclosing this status to others has been compared to a "coming-out" process. Shame and stigma persist in discussing one's adoptive or guardianship identity (Grotevant, Lo, Fiorenzo, & Dunbar, 2017; PACT, 2018; Silverstein & Roszia, 1998).

Informing children that they are adopted or in guardianship and supporting their experience of not residing with their birth parents can be stressful for parents, guardians, and children (Wydra, O'Brien, & Merson, 2012). The amount of support families may need spans a continuum (Riley & Singer, 2016). On one end of the spectrum, a family may successfully navigate the ups and downs of adopting a child with little outside support. On the other end of the spectrum, the family may need a significant amount of support to prevent post-permanency discontinuity. Along this continuum, there are different factors unique to individual families that may affect the child-caregiver relationship. For example, in a closed adoption, a child may not be provided any information about his or her birth parents. On the other end is an open adoption, where a child may have regular contact with her or his birth family (Wiley & Baden, 2005), or a guardianship where the child knows her or his birth parents well. When a youth seeks out contact with her birth family, it may (or may not) create stress in the family. Being aware of these potential stressors is critical to providing services to adoptive and guardianship families.

Families will have different experiences, depending on their individual situations. Experiences that may (or may not) affect the relationship between the caregiver and her or his child include whether: the adoption was voluntary or involuntary on the part of the birth parents; the child was adopted from another country (i.e., intercountry) or within the United States; there are racial, ethnic, and/or cultural differences between the child and the adoptive family; the child was in the foster care system prior to being adopted; the closeness of the relationship with other family members in a guardianship case; and the family dynamics related to the adoption or guardianship (Barth, Crea, John, Thoburn, & Quinton, 2005; Brodinsky, 2011; Burke, Schuleter, Vandercoy, & Authier, 2015; Fong, McRoy, & McGinnis, 2016).

Overwhelming evidence suggests that the experience of past trauma can also affect a child's growth and development and interfere with building strong relationships in adopted and guardianship families (Baden et al., 2016; Liao, 2016; Tan et al., 2015). Perry's (2009) groundbreaking work on brain development and neurodevelopmental functioning applies to adopted children who have experienced trauma (see Chapter 4). Perry proposes that exposure to trauma in early childhood shapes brain development and has lasting effects throughout a person's life. Strengthening frayed relationships among adoptive and guardianship families is critical and may mean the difference between a temporary disruption in the family or dissolution of the adoption/legal guardianship. Having clinically trained professionals with adoption-specific knowledge and skills available to evaluate a child's behaviors is an important prevention measure. For example, specially trained therapists can help children recover from trauma by assessing its impact on the developing brain and prescribing specific activities that stimulate normal patterns of cortical functioning (Perry, Hambrick & Perry, 2016). Adoption-competent therapists have extensive knowledge and training working with children who have a history of abuse, neglect, trauma, or loss (Riley & Singer, 2016) and are part of a case management team that help adoptive families access additional, more intensive services (Atkinson & Riley, 2017). Services are specific to their child's needs and are culturally competent, strength-based, and family-centered (Burke, Schuleter, Vandercoy, & Authier, 2015).

Practice Challenges with Post-Adoption and Guardianship and Well-Being

Supporting adoptive and guardianship families' life-long commitment to a child means ensuring they have access to adoption-sensitive services and the tools they need in helping children and youth feel they are loved, secure, and have a sense of belonging. As a social worker or service provider working with families who have adopted or assumed guardianship of children formerly in foster care, research tells us that there are factors related to the long-term well-being and stability of families that can help us understand the needs and strengths of these families. Common challenges, or risks, for families after they have adopted or assumed guardianship can be generally be divided into three levels: child, family, and services. These are described below and help us understand issues related to this population.

Child and Adolescent Level

Three of the most frequently cited child-level risk factors for post permanency discontinuity and child well-being are: 1) an older-aged child; 2) a child history of more serious types of abuse, such as sexual or physical abuse, or a history of multiple types of abuse; and 3) a child with challenging behavior (White et al., 2018). "Externalizing" behavioral problems, including aggression, hyperactivity, and oppositional behavior, tend to be the most difficult for families to manage (Liu, 2004; White, 2016). Externalizing behaviors strain family resources and burden caregivers who may be surprised if serious behavior problems do not manifest until years after adoption or guardianship, such as when children in foster care enter late childhood and adolescence (Rolock & White, 2016). Other child-level risk factors may include child mental health difficulties, substance abuse, and problems stemming from a higher number of previous child placements in foster care (White et al., 2018).

Image 15.1

Legal permanence is attained through reunification with the family of origin. When reunification is not possible, legal permanence is achieved through adoption or guardianship. However, young adults with foster care histories consider having close relationships more important than their legal permanency status (Pérez, 2017). Specifically, young adults report that their identity is formed through close relationships, and having those close ties is of greater value than their legal status. This idea is referred to as "relational permanence." Relational permanence is fluid and may change over time, as one relationship becomes more important than another; it ebbs and flows as people go through life and developmental stages. One study found that youth who left an adoptive home needed and wanted authentic relationships and a strong desire to feel "normal" (Faulkner, Belseth, Adkins, & Pérez, 2018). These were key factors in promoting well-being and emotionally sustaining relationships during and after legal permanency. Although research points to life-long connections as critical to thrive and reach self-sufficiency during young adulthood and beyond (Pérez, 2017; Samuels, 2008), the child welfare system does not have the legal authority to ensure life-long connections for children and youth who have been involved in the child welfare system.

Family Level

Family level post-permanency discontinuity and poor post-permanency adjustment are often due to limited preparation and information given to caregivers prior to and after placement (Coakley & Berrick, 2007; CWIG, 2013, 2015; Jones & LaLiberte, 2010; White, 2015). Another reason for post permanency problems is unrealistic caregiver expectations and poor parent-child communication (Barth & Miller, 2000; Mariscal, Akin, Lieberman, & Washington, 2015; White, 2016). Other family characteristics that may be associated with post-adoption and guardianship problems such as post permanency discontinuity include single-parent families, poor caregiver mental health or inconsistent caregiver commitment to the child, weak parent-child attachment, and problematic family functioning or cohesion at the time of child placement (Bergeron & Pennington, 2013; CWIG, 2015; Faulkner, Adkins, Fong, & Rolock, 2017; Groze, 1996; Howard, Smith, Zosky, & Woodman, 2006; Lavner, Waterman, & Peplau, 2014; Nalavany, Ryan, Howard, & Smith, 2008; Rosenthal & Groze, 1990; Testa, Snyder, Wu, Rolock, & Liao, 2015). Potential family-level risk factors needing further research include caregiver disability or physical limitations, a lack of life transition preparation for older caregivers, low father involvement, full-time employment of primary caregiver, and weak informal support from spouses/partners (Bergeron & Pennington, 2013; Corman & Coon, 2007; Faulkner et al., 2017; Rosenthal & Groze, 1990; White, 2016; Westhues & Cohen, 1990).

Protective factors that may help ensure post-adoption and guardianship stability as well as more positive well-being include a kinship relationship between a caregiver and child, familiarity between a caregiver and child (such as in foster-parent adoptions), and higher religiosity or calling for adoption or guardianship (for both the child and caregiver) (Berry, Propp, & Martens, 2007; Gillum & O'Brien, 2010; Leung & Erich, 2002; Rosenthal & Groze, 1990; Testa et al., 2015).

Service Level

Several service level risk factors for post-permanency discontinuity and diminished well-being after adoption and guardianship have also been identified. Risk factors include unmet service needs of families and complex child welfare bureaucracies, such as confusing policies, poor communication, delays to adoption, and inflexible mandates (Mariscal et al., 2015; Rosenthal, Groze, & Aguilar, 1991; Rycus et al., 2006). On the positive side, caseworkers can help children and families after adoption or guardianship when they provide strong support for the family, exhibit cultural competency, and have extensive knowledge of local services (Belanger et al., 2012; Mariscal et al., 2015). A child's experiences at school can also significantly impact post-adoption and guardianship families by facilitating or inhibiting child and family adjustment after permanency (Groze, 1996;

Rosenthal et al., 1991). Youth formally in foster care are overrepresented among those who receive special education services, with one survey finding that over half of children who are adopted received special education services (Groze, 1996). Finally, the relationship between financial subsidies and post-adoption and guardianship outcomes is somewhat complex. Although adequate subsidies are needed by families to prevent post-permanency difficulties, providing subsidies that are too high may "crowd out" more altruistic motivations to care for children, such as religious calling or family duty (Testa et al., 2015).

Evidence-Based Practice for Working with Families Formed through Adoption and Guardianship

According to the National Association of Social Workers (2018), the three main components of evidence-based social work practice include: 1) using the best research evidence available, 2) obtaining the best clinical expertise possible; and 3) working within client values, preferences, and culture. All three considerations should be used when planning for services with post-adoption and guardianship families. However, several practice and service barriers or challenges also exist when working with families.

Barriers and Facilitators for Effective Practices

Barriers to Effective Practice

First, there are few evidence-based service models available to child welfare practitioners working with post-adoptive and guardianship families. Child welfare cases are often closed after adoption or guardianship finalization, and families may no longer be under the purview of the child welfare system to receive services (Barth & Miller, 2000; Festinger, 2002; Rolock & White, 2016). Other than a subsidy, families are frequently not provided services unless a crisis occurs. Obtaining support may be difficult if families move out of the child welfare administrative district where the adoption or guardianship was legalized. Another significant barrier to effective practice is when children and families require services years after adoption or guardianship (Faulkner et al., 2017). For example, children may seek out biological families when they become older, which may be a challenge for adoptive families. Children may also begin to exhibit challenging externalizing behaviors during adolescence, long after child welfare authorities have closed the adoption or guardianship case (Berry et al., 2007). Many studies have also reported that post-adoption or guardianship programs lack reliable funding to sustain effective services, particularly over extensive geographic distances (Atkinson & Gonet, 2007; Egbert, 2015; Reilly & Platz, 2004; Rycus et al., 2006).

Other barriers or challenges to effective practice with post-adoption and guardianship families include children with multiple disabilities/needs, inadequate health care coverage (e.g., Medicaid may not cover all the costs of clinical services), caregivers who are older and unfamiliar with the local services available to children and families, and bureaucratic social services systems (e.g., child welfare, juvenile justice, educational institutions) that are difficult to access and/or navigate (Corman & Coon, 2007; Liao & Testa, 2016; Reilly & Platz, 2004; Rycus et al., 2006). In addition, kinship caregivers may be less likely to access formal services than non-kinship caregivers if they feel they should be able to carry out their family duty to care for children (Merrit & Festinger, 2013). However, a kinship relationship to the child may also facilitate access to more informal services and supports, such as extended family members, churches, or community-based organizations.

Facilitators for Effective Practice

Factors that facilitate effective practice with post-adoption and guardianship children and families have also been identified in the research literature. For instance, families report that adequate subsidies and financial assistance may facilitate access to services and supports (Testa et al., 2015). Access to adoption or guardianship "competent" professionals (e.g., mental health therapists, special education teachers) has also enabled families to receive the help they need for children (CWIG, 2015; Freundlich, 2007; National Resource Center for Adoption, 2012; Testa et al., 2015). Other notable facilitators to effective practice include federal, state, and local policies that encourage adoption and guardianship; flexible, unlimited access to services; and connection with, and support from, other post-adoption or guardianship families (Atkinson & Gonet, 2007; Egbert, 2015).

Image 15.2

Promising Programs and Service Models

A review of the current literature on instability and services for post-adoption and guardianship families found that several states, including California, Utah, Virginia, Texas, Missouri, and Illinois, have adopted innovative post-adoption or guardianship services and programs in recent years (White et al., 2018). Below are highlights of some of these programs that have been evaluated and/or discussed in previous research. However, the level of evidence and the continuation of these programs is unclear. These are provided as possible ideas of the types of services available to adoptive and guardianship families.

- *Virginia Adoptive Family Preservation (AFP) program:* Integrated adoption services provided by several private agencies across the state. AFP services included information and referral, counseling, crisis intervention, case management, caregiver and child support groups, training, and small amounts of financial assistance (Atkinson & Gonet, 2007).

- *Intensive Family Preservation Services (IFPS) in Missouri:* Implemented for over 10 years with post-adoptive families at risk for post-permanency discontinuity (Berry et al., 2007). Based on the Homebuilders model, IFPS services included intensive casework, short-term counseling, parenting and other skills-based training, and limited financial assistance for some services. An evaluation of the IFPS program by Berry and colleagues (2007) found families who received more days of services reported less post-permanency discontinuity.
- *The Bennett Chapel Experience:* A unique, culturally competent post-adoption initiative in rural eastern Texas that provided a number of services, including specialized adoption casework, 24-hour post-adoption worker crisis intervention support, enhanced resources, Medicaid, counseling services, respite care, support groups, post-adoption training, psychiatric services, and enhanced post-adoption subsidies to support over 50 post-adoptive African American families. Belanger and associates (2012) evaluated the Texas program and found none of the children in the sample who received the enhanced services experienced post-permanency discontinuity.
- *UCLA TIES (University of California, Los Angeles Training, Intervention, Education, and Services) for Adoption:* Designed for families in Los Angeles who adopted a child from foster care (UCLA TIES Website; Waterman, Nadeem, Paczkowski, Foster, Lavner, Belin, & Miranda, 2013). Adoptive parents enrolled in TIES were offered educational meetings and enhanced services, such as multidisciplinary pre-adoption consultation, child and parent counseling, support groups, and educational, medical, and psychiatric consultation (Lavner et al., 2012, 2014; Waterman et al., 2013).
- *The Adoptive and Foster Couples Retreat and Support Network Program (AFCRSNP) in Texas:* Facilitated weekend retreats for adoptive parents to help adoptive caregivers maintain strong relationships, obtain respite, learn about resources, and develop connections with other adoptive parents (Schwartz et al., 2014).
- *Post-adoption support services in Utah:* A large-scale effort to improve state services delivered to adoptive families based on input from providers, stakeholders, and clients (Egbert, 2015). Revised services included a resource-connection website, parent education and training, respite care, and mental health treatment/crisis intervention provided by clinically trained Department of Children and Family Services (DCFS) post-adoption workers or other agencies (Egbert, 2015).
- *The Illinois Adoption Preservation, Assessment, and Linkages Program (APAL):* A brief post-adoption and guardianship outreach, needs assessment, and referral program in the Chicago area. A recent evaluation of APAL by Liao and Testa (2016) found that services reduced caregivers' perceptions of child behavior problems and enhanced caregiver commitment to the children. Of the adoptive families who received the services, almost 60% were less likely to experience placement discontinuity compared to those who did not receive services.

Future Directions for Effective Practice with Post-Adoption and Guardianship Families

Adoptive and guardianship parents consistently report wanting a wide variety of services available to them, including medical assistance, educational/tutoring, mental health and substance abuse services or counseling (for children and families), informational services, parent training, respite care, and enrichment programs (e.g., cultural events or summer camps for children) (Child Welfare Information Gateway, 2012b, 2018). Although surveys of post-adoption and guardianship caregivers indicate that they generally perceive these services as valuable, less than 50% of caregivers typically use each service overall (Dhami, Mandel, & Sothmann, 2007; Fuller, Bruhn, Cohen, Lis, Rolock, & Sheridan, 2006; Hartinger-Saunders et al., 2014). Further, caregivers use more intensive services, such as in-home counseling or respite care, less often (Barth & Miller, 2000; Reilly & Platz, 2004). Therefore, a key challenge for future programs that serve post-adoption and guardianship families is to figure out how to engage children and caregivers in services more effectively that they report are valuable.

Characteristics of effective post-permanency programs include those that focus on broader systems (e.g., family, school, and community), as well as services available to children who reach adolescence and beyond. Effective programs also provide families with sufficient material resources (e.g., subsidies and medical insurance) to meet their child's needs and unanticipated difficulties that arise. Successful programs that support diverse adoptive or guardianship caregivers provide culturally competent services, respect their spiritual beliefs and practices, and build on community's strengths (Belanger et al., 2012; Festinger, 2002; Gillum & O'Brien, 2010; Orsi, 2015). In addition, effective programs include networks of adoption and guardianship-competent clinicians, as well as support groups or mentoring networks with experienced post-adoptive or guardianship parents (Atkinson & Gonet, 2007; Egbert, 2015). As post-permanency services become more readily available to adoptive and guardianship families in the future, practitioners should avoid deficit-oriented approaches that assume the child is the source of family problems (Freundlich, 2007; Rycus et al., 2006). Rather, effective practice requires a family systems approach that takes the long-term view of family relationships and the interactions that occur with informal and formal systems, such as extended family networks, community organizations, medical and mental health organizations, and child welfare authorities.

Outcomes Across Public Systems with This Population

After families finalize adoption or guardianship, some never meaningfully intersect with the child welfare system again. Other families rely on the child welfare system for substantial post-adoption or post-guardianship services. Regardless of whether the family reconnects with the child welfare system, adoptive and guardianship families are often involved with other broad-based systems like education, mental health, and health. Some of these intersections are described below. The existing research is more likely to focus on youth who were adopted rather than youth placed in guardianship.

Criminal Justice

Although there is not an abundance of research on involvement with the juvenile justice system for children who are adopted or have exited care through guardianship, the studies that do exist highlight particular subsets of youth who are more likely to come in contact with the police. For example, Agnich, Schueths, James, and Klibert (2016) found that in foster care adoptions, boys had significantly higher odds of police contact than adopted girls. Hjern, Lindblad, and Vinnerljung (2002) found that intercountry adoptees (born outside Europe but adopted by parents in Sweden) were more likely to commit crimes than peers born in Sweden.

Education

The relationship between children who exit care through adoption or guardianship and the educational system is nuanced. Meta-analyses have shown that children who are adopted perform better than their peers who remained in pre-adoptive environments but perform worse academically than current environmental peers (who have never been in foster care) (Ijzendoorn, Juffer, & Poelhuis, 2005). Some exceptions to this pattern exist: Chinese girls in transracial adoptions with White parents display very high academic functioning (Tan & Jordan-Arthur, 2012). Fortunately, delays in learning or poor performance can be mitigated by parents who show a high level of involvement in their adopted children's learning (Tan, Kim, Baggerly, Mahoney, & Rice, 2017).

Mental Health

Many families adopt or assume guardianship of children with major mental health concerns, or children who struggle with issues related to not being cared for by their biological parents. Finding mental health providers who are skilled in adoption, guardianship, and managing complex kinship relationships can help children heal from the trauma and loss they may have experienced is vital to long-term adoption stability. Mental health services are also important for caregivers; research shows that the risk of dissolution is lower for parents who attend support groups (Hartinger-Saunders, Trouteaud, & Matos Johnson, 2015).

There is a considerable range in the depth and breadth of mental health services offered to adoptive and guardianship families by different states. In Nebraska, "Permanency Support Specialists" provide families with connections to mental health services in their communities (Burke, Schlueter, Bader, & Authier, 2018). In Utah, over a dozen post-adoption workers are points of contact for adoptive families and provide mental health services that vary from crisis intervention to referral and support for obtaining needed mental health treatment (Egbert, 2015). While many states offer services targeted at adoptive families, fewer offer services targeted at guardianship families.

Health

Several subsets of post-adoptive families report a greater need for medical services. For example, families who have adopted children with special needs report prioritizing financial/health benefits, dental care, and routine medical care (Reilly & Platz, 2004). Families whose adopted children come from abroad report higher usage of medical care than families with domestic adoptions (Le Mare, Audet, & Kurytnik, 2007). This is likely explained by differences in the pre-adoptive care of children adopted domestically and those adopted internationally. In the case of some internationally adopted children, pre- and perinatal care were deficient, and early childhood conditions were at best characterized by poverty and a lack of access to medical attention; at worst by severe global deprivation.

Image 15.3

Private Agencies

Multiple states have contracted out post-adoption and post-guardianship services to private companies or nonprofit agencies to improve child, family, and system outcomes. For example, the previously discussed Texas Health and Human Services Commission contracted with several private agencies to implement AFCRSNP, including Lutheran Social Services, Inc. (to organize and conduct the weekend retreats) as well as Public Strategies, Inc. and the University of Texas at Austin (to evaluate the retreats and support networks) (Schwartz et al., 2014). The Illinois child welfare department funded the APAL intervention discussed above and implemented by three private agencies in the Chicago area (Liao & Testa, 2016). Finally, the AFP program in Virginia was created through a statewide public-private partnership.

Relevant Policies

In 1980, the **Adoption Assistance and Child Welfare Act** (AACWA) (Pub. L. No. 96-272) established the Title IV-E Adoption Assistance program and was crucial to post-permanency practices because it was the first time that federal child welfare legislation specifically prescribed timeframes aimed toward safely moving a child into a legal permanent status (termed *permanency planning*) through adoption, which required judicial proceedings terminating biological parental rights.

During the 1990s, the child welfare caseload rose to an all-time high despite permanency planning becoming widespread child welfare practice. In response to the high number of children in foster care, several child welfare policy reforms were enacted. During the Clinton administration, the following changes occurred: First, Child Welfare Demonstration Waivers were authorized to permit states to experiment with new policy and practice approaches. As a consequence, some states, such as Illinois, implemented a **subsidized guardianship** program. This program permitted the use of legal guardianship as an alternative permanency outcome. Subsidized guardianship differed from adoption in important ways. First, relatives, or kin (e.g., grandparent, aunt, uncle, or stepparent), were recruited in place of nonrelative foster parents to assume legal custody of a child. Second, depending on the case, subsidized guardianship preserved parental biological rights while legally transferring custody to another family member. For families who opted for subsidized guardianship, children exited the legal foster care system to live permanently with relatives and other caregivers who became their legal guardian. These families were also eligible for monthly subsidies equal or comparable to monthly foster care payments. However, when a child reached the age of majority, the monthly subsidy stopped and the legal guardianship dissolved.

In 1997, the **Adoption and Safe Families Act** (ASFA) (Pub. L. No. 105-89) influenced post-permanency practices by shortening the timeframes for moving children into legal permanent status. The goal was established to safely return children home to their families of origin or find an alternative permanency goal such as adoption.

During the first decade of the 21st century, two federal reforms reaffirmed the nation's goal of moving children from foster care to legal permanence. The George W. Bush administration enacted the **Adoption Promotion Act** (Pub. L. No. 108-145) of 2003, which provided financial incentives to states to increase adoptions for special-needs adoptions and older children in foster care. The **Fostering Connections to Success and Increasing Adoptions Act** of 2008 (Pub. L. No. 110-351) expands available permanency options by codifying kinship guardianship as a legal permanency outcome and modifies the adoption incentive program. In addition to expanding discrete permanency outcomes, the act emphasizes the importance of relational permanence—a mutually beneficial parent-child relationship that endures beyond child welfare supervision—regardless of legal status (e.g., adoption or guardianship) (Cushing & Kerman, 2009). These policy changes have coincided with an increased number of children moving from foster care to legally permanent adoptive or judiciary-created guardianship families.

In 2013, President Barack Obama signed the **Preventing Sex Trafficking and Strengthening Families Act** that included several provisions related to increasing permanency for children and adolescents in foster care. The act reauthorized the Adoption Incentive Program, preserves eligibility for kinship guardianship assistance payments, and provides incentives for states to increase adoptions and awards incentives for the first time for guardianship placements through the Adoption and Legal Guardianship Incentive

Program. The act also requires states to track and report through AFCARS disrupted and dissolved adoptions, which will provide new data about post-adoption discontinuity.

The **Family First Prevention Services Act** of 2018 (FFPSA) fundamentally reforms child welfare services by redirecting federal funds to focus on prevention services, family support and reunification services, and congregate care placements. As for permanency policy, FFPSA freezes the Title IV-E Adoption Assistance program authorized through the Fostering Connections and Increasing Adoptions Act of 2008 by requiring a government study (GAO) to ensure states reinvest in post-adoption services. The Adoption and Legal Guardianship Incentive Program authorized through the Preventing Sex Trafficking and Strengthening Families Act is extended, which will continue to provide incentives to states to increase exits of children and youth from foster care to adoption and guardianship.

Case Application

The following two case vignettes are from a research study that sought to understand post-permanency from the perspective of young adults, who reported exiting foster care through adoption or guardianship (Pérez, 2017). Each case vignette provides examples of the different types of post permanency experiences a child welfare practitioner might encounter. The names and other identifying information have been changed to protect confidentiality.

Case Vignettes

James—Subsidized Guardianship

James is a 27-year-old White male who reported exiting foster care at the age of 17 through subsidized guardianship with his maternal grandparents. James entered out of home placement with his grandparents at birth after being abandoned by his birth mother. James's birth mother regained custody of him and his younger sister when he was 6 years old. After being returned to the care of his mother, James characterized this period of his life as being "robbed of my childhood" because of the turbulence, trauma, and insecurity he experienced with his birth mother. "I had to grow up fast because my mother was a drug addict, and you know, never around ... [There] was never any consistency." His relationship with his birth mother remains tenuous. The sense of consistency James desperately yearned for resumed when his grandparents, the only supportive parental figures he had ever known, regained custody of him at age 12 and became his guardians at 17.

When describing his relationship with his grandparents, he explained that they provided him with a sense of "peace and consistency." He further asserted, "I have always felt at home here. And I always, you know, I always called my gramma, 'Gramma,' but to me, you know, she's my mother and grandmother." James attributed his sense of belonging to his grandparents because he viewed them as his primary parental figures. Although he is clear about the love he feels from his grandparents, he points out that the love is not always "a warm, a fuzzy feeling." He explains, "My grandparents are loving and caring, but it's not always mushy. They yell at [me] sometimes. It's because they care and love me. If they didn't care, they wouldn't say anything."

James desired a relationship with his birth father, despite his birth father's absence before James achieved legal permanence. He explains, "My dad, you know, he always wanted what was best for me. There was more stability and consistency here [with my grandparents] than he can provide, so, he always went with what my grandparents said [in terms whom to live with]." While James occasionally saw his father during childhood, his decision at age 17 to choose subsidized guardianship over adoption was, in large part, influenced by his desire to retain a tie to his father's family and a way of legitimizing his belonging to this father through name. James feared that a change in his legal affiliation and last name through adoption might have dire implications for his desired relationship and identity with his birth father. He explains,

> [My grandparents] asked me and my sister [if we wanted to be adopted], and I said, "Well, I don't wanna change my last name." I wanted to keep my father's last name. I've always had it. It would be unusual or weird for me to most of my life know that name and then change to another one.

James's grandparents entered into legal guardianship with him and adopted his younger sister. Because of James's feelings and the security of their relationship, he and his grandparents can be open, retain their family ties, and respect James's need to connect to paternal family. James played an active role in his permanency decision and his preference was honored. As a consequence, he was able to remain with his grandparents through legal permanence, and his tie to his father through name remains intact, further engendering James's sense of relational permanence with both his grandparents and his birth father. James related that his father remains an "important part of my life" and they see each other regularly.

James expressed that his grandparents have provided him unwavering support before, during, and after achieving legal permanence through subsidized guardianship. To illustrate, James recalls he got into a great deal of trouble after graduating from high school and described himself during this period as the neighborhood's "Dennis the Menace." His grandparents, worrying that the trouble he found himself in at age 18 would lead to dire consequences, intervened. He explained,

> [My grandparents] would get on my case so I wouldn't, you know, be lazy or get into trouble. They were worried if I stayed here, I'd keep gettin' into trouble. So that's why they made me make a choice to find an alternative to do something. They told me, "You gotta work. You're not gonna sit around here and do nothing ... You can't keep gettin' into trouble." So, they looked into options for me, and I went away to Job Corps for a couple of years.

James's grandparents' intervention might have put him at risk of feeling like he was being rejected and sent away. Instead, he believed his grandparents' "tough love" approach demonstrated their long-term commitment to him. He reported that going to Job Corps afforded him a break from his environment and an opportunity to gain vocational and academic training in a structured environment. Today, James is an auto mechanic and continues to reside with his grandparents.

Andrea—Adoption

Andrea is a 29-year-old African American single parent of three daughters (ages 13, 11, and 1) who works full-time. Andrea's mother died when she was 10 years old. Initially, Andrea was placed in relative foster care with two of her six siblings. At age 12, Andrea transitioned to foster care placement with a cousin. Although separated from her siblings, Andrea believed that her placement with her cousin was ideal because of their relationship, which developed before her mother's death. Andrea remembers,

> It was just the better choice [to live with my cousin], you know. I had already knew 'em. I was there with her almost every summer, Even after my mom died and I lived with my aunt, I would still go and visit my cousin a lot. I think my cousin asked, "Hey would you mind living, you know coming to live with me?" I was like, "Oh, that would be perfect."

Andrea's preexisting bond with her cousin was strengthened because she felt fully integrated into her cousin's family. She began referring to her cousin as an "aunt," reflecting her sense of belonging, security, and integration into her cousin's family. Andrea and her cousin's relationship would further be legally legitimized through adoption, which Andrea recalls occurred at age 15. Andrea explains,

> You know what, I kinda just went with the flow ... Believe it or not, we never sat down and talked about it. She didn't ask, "Hey is this what you want? Is this what you'd like" or, you know. It's pretty much like, "I'm gonna adopt you today, come on sign these papers," and that's that.

Andrea's foster care record tells a somewhat different story: she exited foster care at age 13 through guardianship and her subsidy ended when she was 16 years old. Despite the type of legal permanency outcome Andrea experienced, she recalled once achieving legal permanence things changed. Andrea recollects two specific incidents that changed her feelings of being loved, sense of belonging, and integration into her cousin's family. The first incident she tells is a story about how her cousin referred to her while looking for a bigger house to live in:

> The landlord asked, "Well, how many children do you have?" And she says, uh, "Well, I have two kids. I have a daughter and a son." And then she turned around and was like, "Oh, my foster kid." Oh, I could've kicked her in her ass. (*laughs*) It was like, "Ohhh, the little runt back there in the back." Aww I was pissed, you know. I was like, you could've just said "your cousin," or, you know? I thought that was ruuude ...
>
> She described another incident where she was excluded from a family portrait:
>
> [My cousin] want[ed] to us to match. I got an outfit, too, but mine didn't look like theirs, you know? I'm like, "Aww man, I can't wear the same?" and she's like, "Aww, this is just for us this time." "What you mean 'just for us'?" "Like, you know, just for them this time." That's how, you know, how it all went down. So this time, I had to sit out, while y'all do the family thing, although we are, you know, technically, we all family, but, they just wanted to do they little family thing. You feel like, damn, you know? It's like ... she just wanted her family picture, I guess, you know. Her and her, her children, you know?

Andrea reported that these incidents alienated her and led her to questioning her status in the family. As communication between Andrea and her cousin diminished, Andrea responded by seeking love and attention through dating relationships. She became pregnant with her first child at the age of 15, the same year in which she believed she achieved legal permanence through adoption. In response to the pregnancy, her cousin kicked Andrea out of the house and severed their relationship.

Andrea was left to fend for herself and believes that her legal status as an adoptee made her ineligible for transitional/independent living services to prepare her for young adulthood. She explains, "I got the short end of the stick because I was with my people or my family" and "my sisters got transitional housing [that] I didn't 'cause, you know, I was adopted and they weren't." Andrea relied on her boyfriend's family until she was able to get on her feet.

Despite her severed relationship, she still yearns to repair the relationship with her cousin, the one person she views as a parental figure. She explained:

> I wanna go and just sit down and talk to her woman-to-woman, because now that I'm grown, you know, I wanna tell her I understand. I don't agree with everything she did, but man I understand now, you know? I understand. I kinda just wanna clear up.

Andrea reports being unable to have this conversation because of her cousin's unwillingness to stay involved. Nonetheless, Andrea further explained why she desires a continued relationship with her cousin:

> I feel like, that I'm lacking, goodness, you know. You wanna feel like, okay, like ... I know her kids. Her kids have kids now. She a grandma, she has grandbabies. And I know she do events and she has things and she only want the grandbabies. Well my kids are never included, you know. And I, I don't have a mom, you know. My mom died, so my kids don't have no one ... I don't feel like I can just get up and say, "Let's go over to gramma's house," you know, I may be, won't be able to say, "Aww, let's go check on my mom," you know? "Yeah, I'm coming over. Cook the dinner—make that pot roast you always make." I don't, I don't have that. I think stuff like that would be important, you know? Making sure they feel comfortable. "Hey, if you need to, you come on back. Visit me. Let's have dinner or sit and talk and ..." That's something I would like that I don't have.

Today, Andrea's relationship with her cousin remains severed and she piecemeals support through her sisters.

DISCUSSION QUESTIONS

1. What additional information would be useful for you to assess each of the cases presented above fully?
2. What are the ways that young people can be involved in, and informed of, key decisions about exiting foster care through legal permanence?

3. Describe how each case exhibits the interplay between young adults' perceptions of relational permanence with their adoptive parents or guardians and their legal permanence outcome (e.g., adoption or guardianship).
4. What are the consequences of post-permanence discontinuity?
5. How do these two cases support and challenge the current framework for pursuing legal permanence for older adolescents who are unable to be reunified with their birth families?
6. Describe the practical strengths and challenges involved with pre- and post-permanency experiences.
7. What are the ways the child welfare system can intervene to ensure the well-being of young people after legal permanence is achieved?

References

Achenbach, T. M., & Rescorla, L. A. (2001). *Manual for the ASEBA School-Age Forms & Profiles*. Burlington: University of Vermont, Research Center for Children, Youth, & Families.

Agnich, L. E., Schueths, A. M., James, T. D., & Klibert, J. (2016). The effects of adoption openness and type on the mental health, delinquency, and family relationships of adopted youth. *Sociological Spectrum, 36*(5), 321–336. doi: 10.1080/02732173.2016.1198950

Atkinson, A., & Gonet, P. (2007). Strengthening adoption practice, listening to adoptive families. *Child Welfare, 86*(2), 87–104.

Atkinson, A., & Riley, D. (2017). Training for adoption competency: Building a community of adoption-competent clinicians. *Families in Society: The Journal of Contemporary Social Services, 98*(3), 235–242. http://familiesinsocietyjournal.org/doi/10.1606/1044-3894.2017.98.23

Baden, A., Mazza, J., Kitchen, A., Harrington, E., & White, E. (2016). Mental health issues. In R. Fong & R. G. McRoy (Eds.), *Transracial and Intercountry Adoptions: Culturally Sensitive Guidance for Professionals* (pp. 193–236). New York: Columbia University Press.

Barth, R. P., Crea, T. M., John, K., Thoburn, J., & Quinton, D. (2005). Beyond attachment theory and therapy. Towards sensitive and evidence-based interventions with foster and adoptive families in distress. *Child and Family Social Work, 10*, 257–268. doi: 10.1111/j.1365-2206.2005.00380.x

Barth, R. P., & Miller, J. M. (2000). Building effective post-adoption services: What is the empirical foundation? *Family Relations, 49(*4), 447–455. http://dx.doi.org/10.1111/j.1741-3729.2000.00447.x

Belanger, K., Cheung, M., & Cordova, W. (2012). The role of worker support and religious support in African American special needs adoption: The Bennett Chapel Experience. *Adoption Quarterly, 15(*3), 185–205. http://dx.doi.org/10.1080/10926755.2012.700299

Bergeron, J., & Pennington, R. (2013). Supporting children and families when adoption dissolution occurs. *Adoption Advocate, 62*, 1–11.

Berry, M., Propp, J., & Martens, P. (2007). The use of intensive family preservation services with adoptive families. *Child & Family Social Work, 12(*1), 43–53. http://dx.doi.org/10.1111/j.1365-2206.2006.00426.x

Brodinsky, D. M. (2011). Children's understanding of adoption: Developmental and clinical implications. *Professional Psychology: Research and Practice, 42*(2), 200–207. doi: 10.1037/a0022415

Bruskas, D. (2008). Children in foster care: A vulnerable population at risk. *Journal of Child and Adolescent Psychiatric Nursing, 21*(2), 70–77. http://dx.doi.org/10.1111/j.1744-6171.2008.00134.x

Burke, R. V., Schlueter, C., Bader, E., & Authier, K. J. (2018). Post-adoption services for high-risk families and their children: Preliminary results of a state-wide intervention. *American Journal of Family Therapy, 46*(2), 122–138. doi: 10.1080/01926187.2018.1450687

Burke, R. V., Schlueter, C., Vandercoy, J., & Authier, K. J. (2015). Post-adoption services for families at risk of dissolution: A case study describing two families' experiences. *Clinical Case Studies 14*(4), 291–306. doi: 10.1177/1534650114556696

California Evidence-Based Clearinghouse for Child Welfare. Homebuilders. https://www.cebc4cw.org/program/homebuilders/detailed

Casey Family Programs. (2012). *USA: Stepping up for kids: What government and communities should do to support kinship families.* Annie E. Casey Foundation. http://www.aecf.org/resources/stepping-up-for-kids/

Coakley, J. F., & Berrick, J. D. (2007). Research review: In a rush to permanency: Preventing adoption disruption. *Child & Family Social Work, 0*(0), 070125002455002- http://dx.doi.org/10.1111/j.1365-2206.2006.00468.x

Corman, D. L., & Coon, L. S. (2007). *DCFS pilot program: Permanency and stability for children in the care of elderly/frail adoptive parents and subsidized guardians* (interim report to the majority leader, Illinois House of Representatives). Chicago: Dept. of Children and Family Services, Center for Law and Social Work.

Crumbley, J. (2017). *Engaging kinship caregivers with Joseph Crumbley.* http://www.aecf.org/blog/engaging-kinship-caregivers-with-joseph-crumbley/

Cushing, G., & Kerman, B. (2009). Permanence is a state of security and attachment. In B. Kerman, M. Freundlich, & A. Maluccio (Eds.), *Achieving Permanence for Older Children and Youth in Foster Care* (pp. 109–122). New York: Columbia University Press.

Cushing, G., Samuels, G. M., & Kerman, B. (2014). Profiles of relational permanence at 22: Variability in parental supports and outcomes among young adults with foster care histories. *Children and Youth Services Review, 39,* 73–83. https://doi.org/10.1016/j.childyouth.2014.01.001

CWIG. (2018). *Providing adoption support and preservation services.* Washington, DC: U.S. Department of Health and Human Services, Children's Bureau.

CWIG (2018a). *Child welfare demonstration waivers.* Washington, DC: U.S. Department of Health and Human Services, Children's Bureau.

CWIG (2018b). *Subsidized guardianship.* Washington, DC: U.S. Department of Health and Human Services, Children's Bureau.

CWIG. (2018c). *Postadoption contact agreements between birth and adoptive families.* Washington, DC: U.S. Department of Health and Human Services, Children's Bureau.

CWIG. (2017). *Unregulated custody transfers of adopted children.* Washington, DC: U.S. Department of Health and Human Services, Children's Bureau.

CWIG. (2015). *Impact of adoption on adoptive parents.* Washington, DC: U.S. Department of Health and Human Services, Children's Bureau.

CWIG. (2013). *Preparing and supporting foster parents who adopt.* Washington, DC: U.S. Department of Health and Human Services, Children's Bureau.

CWIG. (2012a). *Adoption disruption and dissolution.* Washington, DC: U.S. Department of Health and Human Services, Children's Bureau.

CWIG. (2012b). *Finding and using postadoption services.* Washington, DC: U.S. Department of Health and Human Services, Children's Bureau.

Dhami, M. K., Mandel, D. R., & Sothmann, K. (2007). An evaluation of post-adoption services. *Children and Youth Services Review, 29*(2), 162–179. http://dx.doi.org/10.1016/j.childyouth.2006.06.003

Egbert, S. C. (2015). Supporting and strengthening foster adoptive families: Utah's story of post-adoption service development, delivery, and ongoing evaluation. *Journal of Public Child Welfare, 9*(1), 88–113. http://dx.doi.org/10.1080/15548732.2014.1001936

Erich, S., & Leung, P. (2002). The impact of previous type of abuse and sibling adoption upon adoptive families. *Child Abuse & Neglect, 26*(10), 1045–1058.

Faulkner, M., Adkins, T., Fong, R., & Rolock, N. (2017). *Promoting permanency in adoption: A review of the literature.* Southfield, MI: Quality Improvement Center for Adoption & Guardianship Support and Preservation and Spaulding for Children.

Faulkner, M., Belseth, T., Adkins, T., & Pérez, A. (2018). *Texas youth permanency project: Preliminary findings.* Austin: University of Texas at Austin.

Faulkner, M., & Madden, E. E. (2012). Open adoption and post-adoption birth family contact: A comparison of non-relative foster and private adoptions. *Adoption Quarterly, 15*(1), 35–56. http://dx.doi.org/10.1080/10926755.2012.661333

Festinger, T. (2002). After adoption: Dissolution or permanence? *Child Welfare, 81*(3), 515–533.

Freundlich, M. (2007). *Postadoption services: Meeting the mental health needs of children adopted from foster care.* St. Paul, MN: North American Council on Adoptable Children.

Fuller, T. L., Bruhn, C., Cohen, L., Lis, M., Rolock, N., & Sheridan, K. (2006). *Supporting adoptions and guardianships in Illinois: An analysis of subsidies, services, and spending.* Illinois: University of Illinois at Urbana-Champaign.

Fong, R., McRoy, R. G., & McGinnis, H. (2016). Overview of intercountry adoptions. In R. Fong & R. G. McRoy (Eds.), *Transracial and Intercountry Adoptions: Culturally Sensitive Guidance for Professionals* (pp. 19–37). New York: Columbia University Press.

Gillum, N., & O'Brien, M. (2010). Adoption satisfaction of Black adopted children. *Children and Youth Services Review, 32*(12), 1656–1663. http://dx.doi.org/10.1016/j.childyouth.2010.07.005

Grotevant, H., Lo, A., Fiorenzo, L., & Dunbar, N. (2017). Adoptive identity and adjustment from adolescence to emerging adulthood: A person-centered approach. *Developmental Psychology, 53*(11), 2195–2204. doi: 10.1037/dev0000352

Grotevant, H. D., Perry, Y. V., & McRoy, R. G. (2005). Openness in adoption: Outcomes for adolescents within their adoptive kinship networks. *Psychological issues in adoption: Research and practice*, 167–186.

Groze, V. (1996). A 1 and 2 year follow-up study of adoptive families and special needs children. *Children and Youth Services Review, 18(*1–2), 57–82. http://dx.doi.org/10.1016/0190-7409(95)00054-2

Hanna, M., Tokarski, K., Matera, D., & Fong, R. (2011). Happily ever after? The journey from foster care to adoption. *Adoption Quarterly, 14*(2), 107–131. doi: 10.1080/10926755.2011.560789

Hartinger-Saunders, R. M., Trouteaud, A., & Matos Johnson, J. (2015). Post adoption service need and use as predictors of adoption dissolution: Findings from the 2012 National Adoptive Families Study. *Adoption Quarterly, 18*(4), 255–272. doi: 10.1080/10926755.2014.895469

Hartinger-Saunders, R. M., Trouteaud, A., & Matos Johnson, J. (2014). The effects of postadoption service need and use on child and adoptive parent outcomes. *Journal of Social Service Research, 41*(1), 75–92. http://dx.doi.org/10.1080/01488376.2014.953286

Hegar, R. L., & Scannapieco, M. (2017). Foster care to kinship adoption: The road less traveled. *Adoption Quarterly, 20*(1), 83-97.

Henney, S. M., Ayers-Lopez, S., McRoy, R. G., & Grotevant, H. D. (2007). Evolution and resolution: Birthmothers' experience of grief and loss at different levels of adoption openness. *Journal of Social and Personal Relationships, 24*(6), 875-889.

Hinterlong, J., & Ryan, S. (2008). Creating grander families: Older adults adopting younger kin and nonkin. *Gerontologist, 48*(4), 527–536.

Hjern, A., Lindblad, F., & Vinnerljung, B. (2002). Suicide, psychiatric illness, and social maladjustment in intercountry adoptees in Sweden: A cohort study. *The Lancet, 360*(9331), 443–448. doi: 10.1016/S0140-6736(02)09674-5

Houston, D. M., & Kramer, L. (2008). Meeting the long-term needs of families who adopt children out of foster care: A three-year follow-up study. *Child Welfare, 87*(4), 145–170.

Howard, J. A., Smith, S. L., Zosky, D. L., & Woodman, K. (2006). A comparison of subsidized guardianship and child welfare adoptive families served by the Illinois Adoption and Guardianship Preservation Program. *Journal of Social Service Research, 32*(3), 123–134. http://dx.doi.org/10.1300/J079v32n03_07

Ijzendoorn, M. V., Juffer, F., & Poelhuis, C. K. (2005). Adoption and cognitive development: A meta-analytic comparison of adopted and nonadopted children's IQ and school performance. *Psychological Bulletin, 131*(2), 301–316. doi: 10.1037/0033-2909.131.2.301

Jones, A. S., & LaLiberte, T. (2010). *Adoption disruption and dissolution report.* Minneapolis: University of Minnesota.

KidsCount. (2017). Children in kinship care. https://datacenter.kidscount.org/data/tables/7172-children-in-kinship-care#detailed/1/any/false/1652,1564,1491,1443,1218,1049,995/any/14207,14208

Lavner, J. A., Waterman, J., & Peplau, L. A. (2014). Parent adjustment over time in gay, lesbian, and heterosexual parent families adopting from foster care. *American Journal of Orthopsychiatry, 84*(1), 46–53. http://dx.doi.org/10.1037/h0098853

Lavner, J. A., Waterman, J., & Peplau, L. A. (2012). Can gay and lesbian parents promote healthy development in high-risk children adopted from foster care? *American Journal of Orthopsychiatry, 82*(4), 465–472. http://dx.doi.org/10.1111/j.1939-0025.2012.01176.x

Le Mare, L., Audet, K., & Kurytnik, K. (2007). A longitudinal study of service use in families of children adopted from Romanian orphanages. *International Journal of Behavioral Development, 31*(3), 242–251. doi: 10.1177/0165025407076436

Leung, P., & Erich, S. (2002). Family functioning of adoptive children with special needs: Implications of familial supports and child characteristics. *Children and Youth Services Review, 24*(11), 799–816.

Liao, M. (2016). Factors affecting post-permanency adjustment for children in adoption or guardianship placements: An ecological systems analysis. *Children and Youth Services Review, 66*, 131–143. http://dx.doi.org/10.1016/j.childyouth.2016.05.009

Liao, M., Dababnah, S., & Park, H. (2017). Relationship between disabilities and adoption outcomes in African American children. *Journal of Child and Family Studies, 26*(9), 2438–2449. http://dx.doi.org/10.1007/s10826-017-0747-z

Liao, M., & Testa, M. (2016). Postadoption and guardianship. *Research on Social Work Practice, 26*(6), 675–685. http://dx.doi.org/10.1177/1049731514564600

Liu, J. (2004). Childhood externalizing behaviors: Theory and implications. *Journal of Child and Adolescent Psychiatric Nursing, 17*(3), 93–103. http://dx.doi.org/10.1111/j.1744-6171.2004.tb00003.x.

Lloyd, E. C., & Barth, R. P. (2011). Developmental outcomes after five years for foster children returned home, remaining in care, or adopted. *Children and Youth Services Review, 33*(8), 1383–1391. http://dx.doi.org/10.1016/j.childyouth.2011.04.008

Mariscal, E. S., Akin, B. A., Lieberman, A. A., & Washington, D. (2015). Exploring the path from foster care to stable and lasting adoption: Perceptions of foster care alumni. *Children and Youth Services Review, 55*, 111–120. http://dx.doi.org/10.1016/j.childyouth.2015.05.017

Merritt, D. H., & Festinger, T. (2013). Post-adoption service need and access: Differences between international, kinship and non-kinship foster care. *Children and Youth Services Review, 35*(12), 1913–1922. http://dx.doi.org/10.1016/j.childyouth.2013.09.013

Nalavany, B. A., Glidden, L. M., & Ryan, S. D. (2009). Parental satisfaction in the adoption of children with learning disorders: The role of behavior problems. *Family Relations, 58*(5), 621–633. http://dx.doi.org/10.1111/j.1741-3729.2009.00579.x

Nalavany, B. A., Ryan, S. D., Howard, J. A., & Smith, S. L. (2008). Preadoptive child sexual abuse as a predictor of moves in care, adoption disruptions, and inconsistent adoptive parent commitment. *Child Abuse & Neglect, 32*(12), 1084–1088. http://dx.doi.org/10.1016/j.chiabu.2008.07.001

National Association of Social Workers. (2018, April). *Evidence-based practice: NASW practice snapshot.* Washington, DC: National Association of Social Workers. https://www.socialworkers.org/News/Research-Data/Social-Work-Policy-Research/Evidence-Based-Practice

National Resource Center for Adoption. (2012). *Adoption support and preservation services: A continuing public interest.* Southfield, MI: Spaulding Center for Children.

Neil, E. (2012). Making sense of adoption: Integration and differentiation from the perspective of adopted children in middle school. *Children and Youth Services Review, 34*(2), 409–416. https://doi.org/10.1016/j.childyouth.2011.11.011

New York Office of Children and Family Services (OCFS) (2011). Kinship guardianship assistance practice guide. http://www.ocfs.state.ny.us/kinship/KinGAP_Practice_Guide.pdf

Newton, R. R., Litrownik, A. J., & Landsverk, J. A. (2000). Children and youth in foster care: Disentangling the relationship between problem behaviors and number of placements. *Child Abuse & Neglect, 24*(10), 1363–1374. http://dx.doi.org/10.1016/s0145-2134(00)00189-7

Ornelas, L. A., Silverstein, D. N., & Tan, S. (2007). Effectively addressing mental health issues in permanency-focused child welfare practice. *Child Welfare, 86*(5), 93–112.

Orsi, R. (2015). Predicting re-involvement for children adopted out of a public child welfare system. *Child Abuse & Neglect, 39,* 175–184. http://dx.doi.org/10.1016/j.chiabu.2014.10.005

PACT, An Adoption Alliance. (2018). *Shame and secrecy in adoption.* http://www.pactadopt.org/resources/shame-and-secrecy-in-adoption.html

Pérez, A. G. (2017). Classifying relational permanence among young adults who exited foster care through legal permanence as adolescents. *Families in Society: The Journal of Contemporary Social Services, 98*(3), 179–189.

Perry, B. (2009). Examining child maltreatment through a neurodevelopmental lens: Clinical applications of the neurosequential model of therapeutics. *Journal of Loss and Trauma, 14*(4), 240–255. doi: 10.1080/15325020903004350

Perry, B., Hambrick, E., & Perry, R. (2016). A neurodevelopmental perspective and clinical challenges. In R. Fong & R. G. McRoy (Eds.), *Transracial and Intercountry Adoptions: Culturally Sensitive Guidance for Professionals* (pp. 126–153). New York: Columbia University Press.

Reilly, T., & Platz, L. (2004). Post-adoption service needs of families with special needs children. *Journal of Social Service Research, 30*(4), 51–67. http://dx.doi.org/10.1300/J079v30n04_03

Riley, D., & Singer, E. (2016). The need for adoption-competent mental health professionals. In R. Fong & R. G. McRoy (Eds.), *Transracial and Intercountry Adoptions: Culturally Sensitive Guidance for Professionals* (pp. 315–358). New York: Columbia University Press.

Rolock, N. (2015). Post-permanency continuity: What happens after adoption and guardianship from foster care? *Journal of Public Child Welfare, 9*(2), 153–173. http://dx.doi.org/10.1080/15548732.2015.1021986

Rolock, N., & Pérez, A. G. (2016). Three sides to a foster care story: An examination of the lived experiences of young adults, their foster care case record, and the space in between. *Qualitative Social Work, 17*(2), 195–215. doi: 10.1177/1473325016666410

Rolock, N., Pérez, A. G., White, K. R., & Fong, R. (2018). From foster care to adoption and guardianship: A 21st century challenge. *Child & Adolescent Social Work Journal,* 1–10. http://dx.doi.org/10.1007/s10560-017-0499-z

Rolock, N., & White, K. R. (2017). Continuity for children after guardianship versus adoption with kin: Approximating the right counterfactual. *Child Abuse & Neglect, 72,* 32–44. http://dx.doi.org/10.1016/j.chiabu.2017.07.001

Rolock, N., & White, K. R. (2016). Post-permanency discontinuity: A longitudinal examination of outcomes for foster youth after adoption or guardianship. *Children and Youth Services Review, 70,* 419–427. http://dx.doi.org/10.1016/j.childyouth.2016.10.025

Rosenthal, J. A., & Groze, V. (1990). Special-needs adoption: A study of intact families. *Social Service Review, 64*(3), 475–505. http://dx.doi.org/10.1086/603782

Rosenthal, J. A., & Groze, V. K. (1994, November-December). A longitudinal study of special-needs adoptive families. *Child Welfare, 73*(6), 689–706.

Rosenthal, J. A., Groze, V., & Aguilar, G. D. (1991). Adoption outcomes for children with handicaps. *Child Welfare, 70*(6), 623–636.

Rycus, J. S., Freundlich, M., Hughes, R. C., Keefer, B., & Oakes, E. J. (2006). Confronting barriers to adoption success. *Family Court Review, 44*(2), 210–230. http://dx.doi.org/10.1111/j.1744-1617.2006.00081.x

Sanchez, R. M. (2004). *Youth perspectives on permanency.* Oakland, CA: California Permanency for Youth Project.

Samuels, G. M. (2009). "Being raised by White people": Navigating racial difference among adopted multiracial adults. *Journal of Marriage and Family, 71*, 80–94.

Samuels, G. (2008). *A Reason, a Season, or a Lifetime: Relational Permanence among Young Adults with Foster Care Backgrounds.* Chicago: Chapin Hall, University of Chicago.

Schwartz, A. E., Cody, P. A., Ayers-Lopez, S. J., McRoy, R. G., & Fong, R. (2014). Post-adoption support groups: Strategies for addressing marital issues. *Adoption Quarterly, 17*(2), 85–111. http://dx.doi.org/10.1080/10926755.2014.891544

Siegel, D., & Strolin-Goltzman, J. (2017). Adoption competency and trauma-informed practices with adoptive families. *Families in Society, 98*(3), 167–168. doi: 10.1606/1044-3894.2017.98.22

Silverstein, D., & Roszia, S. (1998). Adoptees and the seven core issues of adoption. *Adoptive Families Magazine.* https://vanish.org.au/media/17323/lifelong-issues-in-adoption-by-silverstein-and-kaplan.pdf

Simmel, C., Barth, R. P., & Brooks, D. (2007). Adopted foster youths? Psychosocial functioning: A longitudinal perspective. *Child & Family Social Work, 12*(4), 336–348. http://dx.doi.org/10.1111/j.1365-2206.2006.00481.x

Smith, S. L. (2014). *Keeping the promise: The case for adoption support and preservation.* New York: The Donaldson Adoption Institute.

Smith-McKeever, C. (2006). Adoption satisfaction among African-American families adopting African-American children. *Children and Youth Services Review, 28*(7), 825–840. http://dx.doi.org/10.1016/j.childyouth.2005.08.009

Substance Abuse and Mental Health Services Administration [SAMHSA]. (2014). Trauma-informed care in behavioral health services. https://store.samhsa.gov/shin/content//SMA14-4816/SMA14-4816.pdf

Tan, T. X., & Jordan-Arthur, B. (2012). Adopted Chinese girls come of age: Feelings about adoption, ethnic identity, academic functioning, and global self-esteem. *Children & Youth Services Review, 34*(8), 1500–1508. doi:10.1016/j.childyouth.2012.04.001

Tan, T. X., Kim, E. S., Baggerly, J., Mahoney, E. E., & Rice, J. (2017). Beyond adoption status: Post-adoptive parental involvement and children's reading and math performance from kindergarten to first grade. *American Journal of Orthopsychiatry, 87*(3), 337–346. doi: 10.1037/ort0000216

Tan, T. X., Major, D., Marn, T., Na, E., & Jackson, A. L. (2015). Adopted children's country of origin and post-adoption parent-child relationship quality: Findings from the United States National Survey of Adoptive Parents (NSAP). *Children and Youth Services Review, 48,* 117–125. http://dx.doi.org/10.1016/j.childyouth.2014.12.001

Tan, T. X., & Marn, T. (2013). Mental health service utilization in children adopted from US foster care, US private agencies and foreign countries: Data from the 2007 National Survey of Adoption Parents (NSAP). *Children and Youth Services Review, 35*(7), 1050–1054. http://dx.doi.org/10.1016/j.childyouth.2013.04.020

Testa, M. F. (2010). Evaluation of child welfare interventions. In M. F. Testa & J. Poertner (Eds.), *Fostering Accountability: Using Evidence to Guide and Improve Child Welfare Policy* (pp. 195–230). New York: Oxford.

Testa, M.F., Lee, E. & Ingram, C. (2017). Kinship care and child welfare: New directions for policy and practice [Two volume special issue]. *Child Welfare, 95*(3,4).

Testa, M. F., Snyder, S. M., Wu, Q., Rolock, N., & Liao, M. (2015). Adoption and guardianship: A moderated mediation analysis of predictors of post-permanency continuity. *American Journal of Orthopsychiatry, 85*(2), 107–118.

University of California, Los Angeles Training, Intervention, Education, and Services (UCLA TIES). https://www.uclahealth.org/mattel/ties-for-families/

U.S. Department of Health & Human Services. (2011) ASPE Office for the Assistant Secretary for Planning and Evaluation. Children adopted from foster care: Child and family characteristics, adoption motivation and well-being. https://aspe.hhs.gov/basic-report/children-adopted-foster-care-child-and-family-characteristics-adoption-motivation-and-well-being

Von Korff, L., & Grotevant, H. D. (2011). Contact in adoption and adoptive identity formation: The mediating role of family conversation. *Journal of Family Psychology, 25*(3), 393–401. doi: 10.1037/a0023388

Waterman, J. M., Nadeem, E., Paczkowski, E., Foster, J. C., Lavner, J. A., Belin, T., & Miranda, J. (2013). Pre-placement risk and longitudinal cognitive development for children adopted from foster care. *Child Welfare, 92*(4), 9–30. https://www.ncbi.nlm.nih.gov/pmc/articles/PMC4772770/

Westhues, A., & Cohen, J. S. (1990). Preventing disruptions of special-needs adoptions. *Child Welfare, 69*(2), 141–155.

White, K. (2015). *An Examination of Post-Permanency Adjustment and Discontinuity for Older Foster Youth in Adoptive and Guardianship Homes.* Chapel Hill, NC: University of North Carolina at Chapel Hill Graduate School. https://doi.org/10.17615/5q2c-4889

White, K. R. (2016). Placement discontinuity for older children and adolescents who exit foster care through adoption or guardianship: A systematic review. *Child and Adolescent Social Work Journal, 33*(4), 377–394. http://dx.doi.org/10.1007/s10560-015-0425-1

White, K. R., Rolock, N., Testa, M. F., Ringeisen, H., Childs, S., Johnson, S., & Diamant-Wilson, R. (2018). *Understanding post adoption and guardianship instability for children and youth who exit foster care: Literature review and conceptual framework* (report submitted to the Office of

Planning, Research, & Evaluation, Administration for Children and Families, U.S. Department of Health and Human Services).

Wiley, M. O., & Baden, A. L. (2005). Birth parents in adoption: Research, practice, and counseling psychology. *Counseling Psychologist, 33*(1), 13–50. doi: 10.1177/0011000004265961

Wydra, M., O'Brien, K., & Merson, E. (2012). In their own words. Adopted persons' experiences of adoption disclosure and discussion in their families. *Journal of Family Social Work, 15*(1), 62–77.

Figure Credits

Img. 15.1: Copyright © 2014 Depositphotos/petrograd99.
Img. 15.2: Copyright © 2013 Depositphotos/Wavebreakmedia.
Img. 15.3: Copyright © 2018 Depositphotos/Rawpixel.

CHAPTER • 16

Crossover Youth

Youth Involved in Child Welfare and Juvenile Justice

Hui Huang and Joseph P. Ryan

Overview of Chapter and Population

The term *crossover youth* is used to describe a population of youth involved in both the child welfare and juvenile justice systems. Most studies on crossover youth focus on the youth who had child welfare records prior to being involved in juvenile delinquency (Halemba, Siegel, Lord, & Zawacki, 2004; Runyan & Gould, 1985; Ryan & Testa, 2005; Widom, 1991) and reported that of the children who had child maltreatment records, between 11% and 50% later engaged in juvenile delinquency. These studies vary in their measures of juvenile delinquency, sample selections (age, jurisdiction), the length of time following up delinquency, and the study year.

Previous literature used the terms "crossover youth," "dually involved youth," and "dually adjudicated youth" to indicate this population (Herz, 2010). Herz (2010) explained the differences between these three terms. **Crossover youth** refers to youth who experienced maltreatment and also engaged in delinquency but did not necessarily receive services from the child welfare and the juvenile justice systems. **Dually involved youth** refers to youth who receive services from both the child welfare and the juvenile justice systems. **Dually adjudicated youth** refers to youth who are concurrently adjudicated by both the child welfare and the juvenile justice systems. Adjudication refers to formal court processing, through which a youth becomes a formal "dependent" or "delinquent" case.

This chapter uses the term *crossover youth*, the mostly commonly used term among all three terms. Most literature used the term crossover youth loosely to refer to any of the three types of youth. The chapter starts with an overview of crossover youth, including history, statistics, and related disproportionality and disparity. The second section illustrates practice challenges with working with crossover youth. The third section presents evidence-based practice for working with crossover youth. The fourth section presents systems approach through the integration of public systems with this population. The fifth

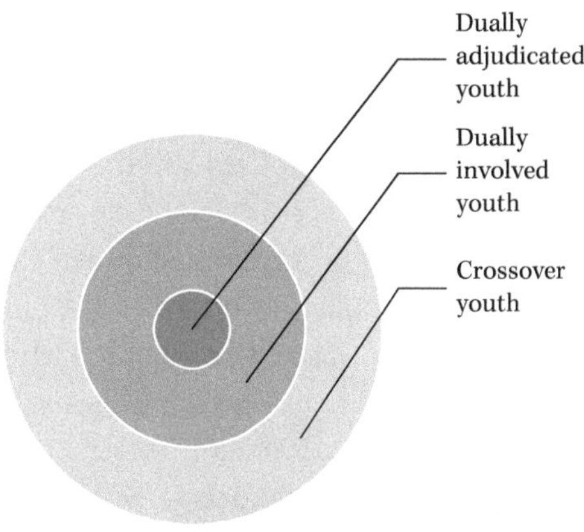

FIGURE 16.1. Three Related Terms

section presents policies related to crossover youth at three stages: policies on identifying crossover youth, policies on serving crossover youth during their involvement with and after their discharge from the juvenile justice system, and policies on serving crossover youth after their discharge from juvenile justice.

History of Child Welfare, Delinquency, and the Juvenile Court

The juvenile court has been a part of the U.S. court system for more than 100 years with the purpose of rehabilitating juvenile offenders through individualized justice. During the Progressive Era at the turn of the 20th century, Jane Addams and other pioneers of the Settlement House movement believed that trying adolescents who committed crimes in adult courts was not just and therefore led the efforts to separate juvenile justice from criminal justice (Lundblad, 1995). In 1899, the first juvenile court in the United States was established in Cook County, Illinois. Different from the criminal court's focus on punishment, juvenile justice focused on rehabilitation. Dr. William Healy, director of the Juvenile Psychopathic Institute located at Hull House in Chicago, conducted an early study of 823 juvenile offenders (Healy, 1915). Healy reported that delinquency was caused by multiple environmental and social factors rather than the explanation of heredity. Healy found that the most prevalent cause was the lack of parental discipline and involvement, usually due to the loss of one or both parents.

BOX 16.1. Settlement House Movement

The Settlement House Movement started in the United States in the late 19th century. The movement was in response to economic and health disparities at the time following the Industrial Revolution. Many immigrants moved to the United States to pursue job opportunities while they could only afford to live in slums in urban areas. Their children and families had limited access to health and education resources. Leaders of the Settlement House Movement aimed to alleviate poverty in city slums. To achieve the goal, the workers of this movement settled in (i.e., lived in) the slums to reach out to residents in a friendly way and decide with them what services were needed. The services often included education, recreation, child care, and health services. At the macro level, many leaders of this movement also advocated for antipoverty-related policy changes, such as housing reform and minimum wage laws (Scheuer, 1985).

FIGURE 16.2. Young Women's Union Dining Room in Philadelphia, in Which the Settlement House Workers Provided Meal Services to Immigrant Children

Subsequent studies using different samples and measurements have consistently documented the maltreatment-delinquency relationship (English, Widom, & Brandford, 2002; Fang & Corso, 2007; Hussey, Chang, & Kotch, 2006; Ryan & Testa, 2005; Smith & Thornberry, 1995; Widom, 1989; Zingraff, Leiter, Myers, & Johnsen, 1993). As a pioneer in this area, Widom (1989) compared delinquency rates between a sample of maltreated children (N=908) and matched controls (N=667) from a metropolitan area in the Midwest. The match was based on sex, age, race, and approximate socioeconomic status of the families. Widom (1989) used official records to measure both maltreatment and juvenile delinquency/adult criminal behavior. Results indicated that 26% of maltreated children had juvenile delinquency records as compared with 16.8% of matched controls.

In a replicate study, English et al. (2002) reported that maltreated children had statistically significantly higher delinquency rates than matched controls (19.6% versus 4.1%). A third study (Ryan & Testa, 2005), using administrative data from the child welfare and

FIGURE 16.3. Greater Arrest Rates Among Youth Abused or Neglected

the juvenile justice systems from Cook County, Illinois, also found that delinquency rates of maltreated children were 47% higher than for non-maltreated children.

Although victims of child maltreatment showed higher rates of juvenile delinquency than the general youth population, many victims were not involved in the juvenile justice system. Certain life experiences may limit the consequences commonly associated with maltreatment. One of the experiences is child welfare services. Many victims of child maltreatment receive child welfare services such as foster or group care. Findings on the effects of child welfare services are mixed. Some authors (Jonson-Reid, 2002; Jonson-Reid & Barth, 2000a) reported that both in-home and foster/group care might actually help reduce the risk of juvenile justice involvement for minority youth.

In contrast, other authors reported the deleterious effects of placement experiences in general foster/group care. Using administrative data from Cook County, Illinois, Ryan and Testa (2005) investigated the relationship between placement, placement instability, and juvenile delinquency. Studying male and female samples separately, their findings indicated that children in placement were at an increased risk of delinquency as compared with children not entering placement. Using similar administrative data on 15,039 children from Illinois, Doyle (2007) reported that children on the margin of removal from home achieved better outcomes when they remained at home as compared with children removed from the biological family. Specifically, Doyle concluded that children removed from home had significantly higher delinquency rates and higher teen birth rates.

Retrospective studies (Halemba, Siegel, Lord, & Zawacki, 2004; Halemba & Lord, 2005) examined the prevalence of the child welfare involvement among delinquent youth and reported that the more in-depth involvement in the juvenile justice system, the greater the percentage of youth with prior child maltreatment records. The term *Adverse Childhood*

Experiences (ACEs) was used to describe all types of abuse, neglect, and other potentially traumatic experiences that occur to people under the age of 18 (Centers for Disease Control and Prevention, 2019b). In the ACEs studies, the definition of abuse includes emotional, physical, and sexual abuse; the definition of neglect includes emotional and physical neglect (e.g., medical neglect); the definition of household challenges includes mother treated violently, household substance abuse, mental illness in household, parental separation or divorce, and criminal household member (Centers for Disease Control and Prevention, 2019c). The ACEs studies measured the prevalence of self-reported childhood abuse and neglect, as well as household challenges among juvenile offenders. In Florida, Baglivio and colleagues (2014) studied the prevalence of ACEs among 64,329 offenders who completed risk assessment between 2007 and 2012. The authors reported that 96.9% of males and 92.2% of females reported at least one ACE. In fact, 27.4% of males and 45.1% of females reported five or more ACEs. In closing, a history of trauma, either formally recognized by child welfare systems or not, is common for adolescents involved with the juvenile justice system.

Disproportionality and Disparity Related to Crossover Youth

Crossover youth are disproportionally youth of color and female as compared with the distribution of juvenile offenders in general (Herz & Fontaine, 2012; Herz & Ryan, 2008; Ryan, Herz, Hernandez, & Marshall, 2007). This finding is consistent across almost all studies of maltreatment and delinquency. In King County, Washington, African Americans are overrepresented in crossover youth (51%) than their presentation in child welfare (41%) and juvenile justice (32%) populations (Herz & Fontaine, 2012). Using administrative data from Los Angeles, Ryan et al. (2007) reported that the child welfare system is a significant source of overrepresentation for African American youth in juvenile justice. Specifically, African Americans comprise 46% of the first-time offenders with dependency background and 21% of the ones without dependency background; dependency cases comprise 14% of new juvenile arrests for African Americans and 7% of new juvenile arrests of all races. In addition, the study showed the overrepresentation of females in crossover youth. Specifically, females comprise 37% of the

Image 16.1

first-time offenders with dependency background and 24% of the offenders without dependency background. The difference was statistically significant. Studies using Los Angeles data (Herz & Ryan, 2008) and the data from Peoria and DuPage Counties in Illinois (Ryan, Chiu, Williams, 2011) reported similar findings.

Consistent with finding of the overrepresentation of African Americans among crossover youth, most studies have shown that maltreated African Americans were more likely to become delinquent than maltreated Whites, after controlling for confounding variables, such as maltreatment type, age, and gender (Jonson-Reid, 2002; Jonson-Reid & Barth, 2000a, b; Ryan & Testa, 2005; Ryan, Marshall, Herz, & Hernandez, 2008; Ryan, Hong, Herz, & Hernandez, 2010). Theoretically, researchers (Jonson-Reid, 2002; Ryan et al., 2008; Ryan et al., 2010) suggested that neighborhood differences between residences of different racial groups might explain differences in delinquency rates. Studies of general populations (Guerra & Williams, 2006; Sampson & Wilson, 1995) found that African American children were more likely to live in dysfunctional neighborhoods, characterized by high crime rates, high unemployment rates, and limited community resources. Exposure to these risks increased their likelihood of delinquency.

Regarding the overrepresentation of females, researchers have not identified clear explanations why females are overrepresented in crossover youth as compared with their percentage in the population of delinquency youth. Most studies examined gender difference within the children with maltreatment experience and have shown that maltreated males were more likely to become delinquent than maltreated females (Fang & Corso, 2007; Jonson-Reid, 2002; Jonson-Reid & Barth, 2000a; Jonson-Reid & Barth, 2000b; Jonson-Reid & Barth, 2003; Ryan et al., 2008). Researchers suggested that the difference in delinquency between males and females is due to their different reactions to abuse (Bender, 2010; Maschi, Morgen, Bradley, & Hatcher, 2008). Generally, males tend to respond to child maltreatment externally, such as with aggression and conduct problems, while females tend to respond internally, such as with depression and suicidal ideation.

Trauma-Informed Care

The initiation of trauma-informed care is in response to research on the enduring negative impacts of trauma in individuals. For example, the Centers for Disease Control and Prevention (2019a) reports that a larger number of ACEs is associated with the greater risk of a variety of physical, mental, and behavioral health problems, such as depression, chronic illness, substance abuse, intimate partner violence, and poor work performance. In 2012, as part of the Defending Childhood Initiative created by the former attorney general Eric H. Holder, the Attorney General's National Task Force on Children Exposed to Violence (Listenbee et al., 2012) released a report on recommendations for ending children's exposure to violence. The recommendations were organized into prevention, identification, treatment, systematic approaches at home, community, and organizational levels. The organizational level approach focused on orienting the juvenile justice system to be more trauma informed. Specifically, the task force recommended 1) making trauma-informed screening, assessment, and care the standard in juvenile justice services; 2) abandoning correctional practices that traumatize children and further reduce their opportunities to become productive members of society; 3) providing ethnoculturally appropriate services, addressing the special circumstance and needs of girls, LGBTQ youth, and victims of sex-trafficking; 4) orienting school police to keep children in school rather than implementing suspension and expulsion; 5) guaranteeing legal representation for juvenile offenders; and 6) limiting the transfer of juveniles to adult courts.

To clarify the elements of trauma-informed care, in 2013 the National Child Traumatic Stress Network (NCTSN) hosted a 2-day Juvenile Justice Roundtable meeting. The NCTSN Trauma-informed Service Systems Working Group developed the definition of the trauma-informed child and family serving system (Dierkhising, Ko, & Halladay Goldman, 2013):

> *A service system with a trauma-informed perspective is one in which programs, agencies, and service providers: (1) routinely screen for trauma exposure and related symptoms; (2) use culturally appropriate evidence-based assessment and treatment for traumatic stress and associated mental health symptoms; (3) make resources available to children, families, and providers on trauma exposure, its impact, and treatment; (4) engage in efforts to strengthen the resilience and protective factors of children and families impacted by and vulnerable to trauma; (5) address parent and caregiver trauma and its impact on the family system; (6) emphasize continuity of care and collaboration across child-service systems; and (7) maintain an environment of care for staff that addresses, minimizes, and treats secondary traumatic stress, and that increases staff resilience. (p. 2)*

The roundtable also suggested important elements of a trauma-informed juvenile justice system (Dierkhising, Ko, & Halladay Goldman, 2013):

- Utilize trauma screening and assessment and evidence-based trauma treatments designed for justice settings
- Partner with families to reduce the potential traumatic experience of justice involvement
- Collaborate across systems to enhance continuity of care
- Create a trauma-responsive environment of care
- Reduce disproportionate minority contact and address disparate treatment of minority youth (p.2)

To prepare the workforce, NCTSN has created several curricula to train professionals to be trauma responsive. The Child Welfare Trauma Training Toolkit (Child Welfare

Committee, National Child Traumatic Stress Network, 2013) is a curriculum for training child welfare caseworkers. The curriculum aims to increase caseworkers' understanding of trauma, provide strategies to address traumatic stress, and guide them to introduce families to appropriate interventions. Think Trauma (Marrow, Benamati, Decker, Griffin, & Lott, 2012) is a four-module trauma-informed milieu training for frontline staff, educators, administrators, and others who work with adolescents in juvenile justice residential settings. It aims to increase trainees' understanding of trauma and its impact, provide strategies for working with youth with trauma, and teach strategies to cope with the secondary trauma that comes with working with traumatized youth and families. NCTSN also developed trauma-responsive curriculum for parents (e.g., Caring for Children Who Have Experienced Trauma: a Workshop for Resource Parents), law enforcement (e.g. Cops, Kids, & Domestic Violence), educators (the Child Trauma Toolkit for Educators), and judges (e.g., Ten Things Every Juvenile Court Judge Should Know About Trauma and Delinquency, the NCTSN Bench Card for the Trauma-Informed Judge).

However, it is still unclear how to implement each element. Dierkhising and Branson (2016) suggested a future research and policy agenda for creating trauma-informed juvenile justice systems. Regarding the element on screening, the authors suggested that future research should examine the appropriate timing for screening, the incorporation of trauma exposure and related impairment in screening, and the appropriate ratio of subsequent services in relation to the youth's trauma experiences versus criminogenic risk factors. As for the element on intervention, the authors recommended that future research should compare the effectiveness of trauma-informed services with other evidence-based intervention in reducing both criminogenic risk and post-traumatic stress impairment, tailor the trauma-informed intervention for different juvenile justice settings of different durations, and examine the cost-effective way of delivering the trauma-informed intervention through the front-line justice staff. Regarding the element on workforce development, the authors suggested that future research should evaluate the effectiveness of each trauma-informed training curriculum and intervention models on different positions (judges, probation/correctional officers, case managers) and settings (court, secure facilities, community-based programs), and measure outcomes, including both the knowledge and skills around working with traumatized youth among professionals and the skills for coping with their own secondary traumatic stress reactions. With respect to the element on vulnerable populations, the authors maintained that future research should examine the impact of discrimination and fairness on outcomes among trauma-exposed youth in the juvenile justice system, especially minority youth; study the needs for gender-responsive programming and the program elements; and study the assessment and interventions for commercial sexual exploitation of children. Regarding system reform, the authors suggested that future research should focus on youth voices and their perceptions of safety during their institutional and justice-related experiences, explore strategies to identify and serve crossover youth, and explore strategies to engage families in the treatment. Lastly, the authors recommended that future research develop and evaluate strategies for increasing organizational readiness for change and promoting the adoption and continuation of trauma-informed practice.

Practice Challenges with Crossover Youth

Working with crossover youth presents three practice challenges. First, practitioners need to address disproportionality and disparity identified above. To address the over-representation of African Americans and females among crossover youth, practitioners should implement culturally responsive practices through cultural humility and the critical race theory lens. A cultural humility perspective incorporates multicultural and intersectional understanding and analysis to improve practice (Ortega & Coulborn, 2011). This perspective places workers in a learning mode as opposed to an expert mode. Workers are encouraged to learn about a client's multiple identities and the ways in which their social experiences impact their worldview. Child welfare workers and their clients have different positions and power. To bridge the differences, workers need to use active listening, reflecting, reserving judgment, and placing him- or herself in the context of the client's world. Workers should establish mutually beneficial, non-paternalistic and respectful working relationships with families. Moreover, workers should advocate for their clients to change environmental factors such as policies that disempower their clients. Cultural humility should also be integrated into child welfare agency culture (Ortega & Coulborn, 2011).

Critical race theory (CRT) presents an explicit and aggressive critique of the larger structures and ideologies around race. Abrams and Moio (2009) summarized six basic tenets of CRT: 1) assert that racism is an ordinary, everyday occurrence for people of color; 2) regard race as a social construction; 3) recognize that dominant social discourses and people in power can racialize groups of people in different ways at different times, dependent on their needs; 4) recognize that progressive change regarding race occurs only when the interest between the racial majority and minorities converge; 5) advocate to rewrite history to include the perspectives of oppressed groups; 6) acknowledge the intersectionality of oppression based on various reasons, such as race, sexuality, and social classes. In practice, CRT offers practitioners the skills to challenge institutional oppression. The skills include identifying and analyzing the problem from the client's perspective, providing emotional and/or political support, critiquing institutional oppression, and advocating for change (Abrams & Moio, 2009).

Second, many crossover youth experience multiple adverse events in addition to physical abuse and neglect. Studying a sample of 581 crossover youth in Los Angeles County, Herz and Ryan (2008) report that crossover youth often stay in the child welfare system for a long period of time (average 7.41 years) prior to their initial arrest. For those in out of home placement, many of them experience numerous placement changes, including multiple episodes in congregate care (average 3.22 congregate care placement for the 62% of the sample who had ever stayed in congregate care). Crossover youth also perform poorly at school and are involved in truancy (Herz & Ryan, 2008). The majority of crossover youth have at least one mental health or substance use problem (Halemba et al., 2004; Herz & Ryan, 2008). Herz and Ryan (2008) reported that only 17% of crossover youth had no mental health or substance use problems, 28% had only mental health problems, 17% had only substance use problems, and 38% had both mental health and substance use problems. Even as compared with their peers involved in only the juvenile justice system, higher percentages of crossover youth have mental health problems (Ryan, Williams, & Courtney, 2013). Prevalent mental health and substance use problems are particularly concerning, since they can interfere with an individual's response to treatment/services (Taylor, Fedoroff, Koch, Thordarson, Fecteau, & Nicki, 2001) and are associated with a greater risk of juvenile recidivism (Herz & Ryan, 2008; Herz, Ryan, & Bilchik, 2010).

Third, although limited in scope, there are several studies that focused on justice processing after arrest (Conger & Ross, 2001; Ryan, Herz, Hernandez, & Marshall, 2007). These studies identified more restrictive treatment toward dually involved youth. That is, dually involved youth were more likely to receive detention (Conger & Ross, 2001) and to be incarcerated (Ryan et al., 2007). Findings from qualitative analyses showed overwhelmingly negative perceptions of system and personal deficits related to dually involved youth. Aiming to examine whether and why foster children were overrepresented in juvenile detention centers, Conger and Ross (2001) at the Vera Institute of Justice collected quantitative and qualitative data to address the question. The findings from their interview showed that police officers have difficulty getting the contact information of caseworkers, and dually involved youth often fail to provide such information. When law enforcement cannot connect with caseworkers who can perform the function of legal guardian, dually involved youth are more likely to be placed in detention (Conger & Ross, 2001). Morris and Freundlich (2004) interviewed dually involved youth and the adults around them, including child welfare and juvenile justice professionals, judges, foster parents, and child welfare administrators. The authors reported that many adults perceived dually involved youth as future adult criminals. Dually involved youth face numerous obstacles, such as a lack of advocates from child welfare agencies and a lack of communication between systems (Morris & Freundlich, 2004).

The high prevalence of crossover youth's continuous involvement in the justice system reflected the limited collaboration between the child welfare and juvenile justice systems. Herz et al. (2012) indicated that the two systems hold fundamentally different views on crossover youth. That is, the child welfare system views crossover youth as victims, while the juvenile justice system views them as perpetrators. Their difference limits their interests in building infrastructure to facilitate communication and collaboration with each other. As a result, crossover youth's child welfare background and past trauma are often left unrecognized. As a result, the youth receive conflicting case planning and are disconnected from other services, such as educational, physical health, and mental health systems, all of which become lost opportunities for intervention.

Evidence-Based Practice for Working with Crossover Youth

Evidence-based practices related to crossover youth were developed for traumatized youth in the juvenile justice system. In a recent review, Ford and colleagues (2016) identified four models of trauma-focused psychosocial therapeutic interventions (TF-PTI) for traumatized youth in the juvenile justice system: Trauma Affect Regulation: Guide for Education and Therapy (TARGET), Trauma and Grief Components Therapy for Adolescents (TGCTA), Cognitive Processing Therapy (CPT), and Trauma-Adapted Multidimensional Treatment Foster Care (TA-MTFC). The following section presents each model.

Image 16.2

Trauma Affect Regulation: Guide for Education and Therapy (TARGET) is a 4- to 12-session educational and therapeutic intervention to be provided in either an individual or group (4–10 youth per group) format by behavioral health clinicians (Ford, Kerig, Desal, & Felerman, 2016). Nonclinical line staff are trained to co-lead the group modality in juvenile justice settings or to deliver TARGET on a 24/7 basis as a milieu intervention in congregate care. In milieu interventions, congregate care environment is part of the intervention, which provides a stable environment for individuals to have therapeutic interaction with other residents, caregivers, and therapists to promote personal growth and behavior change (Colman, 2015). TARGET teaches a seven-step sequence of self-regulation skills with the acronym **FREEDOM**. The foundational skills are **F**ocusing and **R**ecognizing triggers, which help participants to change their reactions from stress reactions driven by hypervigilance to proactive emotion regulation. The four subsequent skills enable participants to differentiate **E**motions, **E**valuate cognitions, **D**eliberate Goals, and **O**ptions for action, and to determine whether they are based on stress reactions or are grounded in the participants' core personal values. The final skill, **M**aking a contribution, enhances participants' reflective skill by providing a practical approach to monitor the day-to-day applications of the first six **FREEDOM** skills and how they enrich the lives of participants and others. Although the same skills are taught in all TARGET programs, discussion topics and activities in TARGET vary with gender, with the purpose to match with the specific interests and needs of each gender. A study by Ford, Steinberg, Hawke, Levine, and Zhang (2012) reported that when being used among justice-involved girls with dual diagnosis of PTSD, substance use, and other disorders, TARGET is more effective in reducing PTSD and depression and improving emotion regulation than relational psychotherapy, in which therapists work with patients to help them become aware of their unconscious, self-defeating relational patterns and participate in a new type of relational experience. Two studies (Ford & Hawke, 2012; Marrow, Knudsen, Olafson, & Bucher, 2012) reported that after detained male and female youth received TARGET in a group and milieu intervention, they showed reduced violent behavioral incidents and related physical restraints used to stabilize their behaviors, reduced PTSD and depression symptoms, and increased hope/engagement in rehabilitation.

Trauma and Grief Components Therapy for Adolescents (TGCTA) (Ford et al., 2016) is a four-module 8- to 24-session group psychosocial intervention. Each group comprises 8–10 youth and are led by two co-leaders. The four models are: 1) foundational knowledge and skills to enhance posttraumatic emotional, cognitive, and behavioral regulation and to improve interpersonal skills; 2) group sharing and processing of traumatic experiences; 3) group sharing and processing of grief and loss experiences; and 4) resumption of adaptive developmental progression by improving their capacity to work on developmental tasks (e.g., schoolwork) and future orientation by working with them to create positive, yet realistic, future aspirations and plans. Each session contains step-by-step instructions for implementation, which include suggested scripts for group leaders. Although it is recommended to form groups of a single gender, some practitioners reported success with mixed-gender groups. As compared with TARGET, which focuses on processing current episodes of post-traumatic stress reactions, TGCTA is more focused on processing memories of past traumatic experiences. The rationale is that processing these memories will help participants to reduce the distress elicited by those memories and reduce the self-defeating avoidance. TGCTA is also unique in its module on group sharing and processing of grief and loss experiences. TGCTA was first developed for adolescent war survivors in Bosnia in the 1990s (Layne et al., 2008). Recently, TGCTA was applied to detained youth in Ohio (Olafson et al., 2016), gang-involved and at-risk youth in Urban, California (Saltzman, Pynoos, Layne, Steinberg, and Aisenberg, 2001), and delinquent youth in Delaware schools (Grassetti et al., 2015). These related studies reported that receiving TGCTA is associated with reduced PTSD, depression, maladaptive grief reactions, and improved behaviors.

Cognitive Processing Therapy (CPT) (Ford et al., 2016) is a 12-session intervention to be provided in either an individual or group format. It teaches cognitive restructuring skills to enable clients to examine their beliefs about their own identity, relationships, the world, and their future and examine the impacts of their traumatic experiences on their existing beliefs. The two components of CPT are cognitive therapy and written trauma accounts. Written trauma accounts are implemented through two sessions that include writing about the worst traumatic event, reading it back to the therapist, and processing emotions. Clients are asked to read the account at home between sessions on a daily basis.

The therapist uses Socratic questioning to challenge the clients' erroneous conclusion about the event. The goal is to develop a participant's abilities to recall the event without avoidance, hyperarousal, and intolerable emotional distress. CPT was later adapted into the cognitive therapy only (CPT-C) condition, which eliminated the two exposure sessions and presents a greater focus on Socratic questioning. Two studies (Ahrens & Rexford, 2002; Matulis, Resick, Rosner, & Steil, 2014) tested the use of CPT among adolescents. Ahrens and Rexford (2002) reported that CPT can help to reduce depression and trauma-related symptoms. More recently, Matulis and colleagues (2014) adapted the traditional CPT for the adolescents in Germany who experienced childhood sexual abuse and physical abuse, and named the adapted version Developmentally Adapted Cognitive Processing Therapy (D-CPT) and reported that the 12 adolescents receiving D-CPT showed reduced PTSD symptoms and reduced co-occurring mental disorders (Matulis et al., 2014).

Trauma-Adapted Multidimensional Treatment Foster Care (TA-MTFC, also called MTFC+T) is an adaptation of multidimensional treatment foster care (MTFC) for treating girls with co-occurring trauma and delinquency (Ford et al., 2016). The traditional MTFC is a community-based intervention for serving chronically delinquent adolescents and their families. MTFC provides training and clinical support to therapeutic foster parents to coach them to implement a highly structured behavioral program at home that includes active adult monitoring, fair and consistent discipline, healthy bonding, and redirection toward prosocial activities and away from antisocial activities. The traditional MTFC was effective for reducing subsequent delinquency, improving school engagement, and reducing pregnancy rates, while not for reducing trauma-related outcomes (e.g., mental health functioning).

To adapt MTFC for the treatment of co-occurring trauma and delinquency, the developers (Smith, Chamberlain, & Deblinger, 2012) integrated Trauma-Focused Cognitive Behavior Therapy (TF-CBT) into MTFC and named it (MTFC+T). The basic components of the adapted model included: (a) daily (Monday-Friday) telephone contact with MTFC+T parents using the Parent Daily Report (Chamberlain & Reid, 1987). These data are used to adjust treatment in the foster home during weekly foster care supervision and support sessions; (b) weekly MTFC+T parent group supervision and support meetings led by the program supervisor; (c) an individualized daily point-and-level program[1] that reinforced adaptive behavior; (d) individual therapy focused on delinquency and trauma treatment; (e) weekly skill building focused on practicing new skills in real-world settings; (f) family therapy for the family of origin, focused on parent management strategies, understanding the impact of trauma, and effective emotion regulation and coping strategies; (g) close monitoring of school attendance, performance, and homework completion; (h) case management to coordinate the interventions in the MTFC+T home, family, peer, and school settings; (i) on-call program staff availability to the MTFC+T and biological

1 The point-and-level program offers participants points for their adaptive behavior skills, effective emotion regulation, coping, and problem-solving skills.

parents; and (j) psychiatric consultation as needed. In their pilot study of 30 delinquent girls with traumatic experiences, the authors (Smith, Chamberlain, & Deblinger, 2012) reported that at 12 months post-baseline, the MTFC-T girls had significantly lower levels of delinquency and trauma-related mental health symptoms than the girls who did not receive MTFC-T (Smith et al., 2012).

BOX 16.2. Trauma-Focused Cognitive Behavior Therapy (TF-CBT)

TF-CBT is an evidence-based treatment model for children and youth showing post-traumatic stress disorder (PTSD) symptoms and diagnosis. It includes 8–25 sessions with the child/adolescent and their caregiver. Research reports TF-CBT helps children and youth reduce trauma symptoms and responses and addresses many other trauma impacts, including affective (e.g., depressive, anxiety), cognitive and behavioral problems, as well as improving the participating parent's or caregiver's personal distress about the child's traumatic experience, effective parenting skills. TF-CBT components are summarized by the acronym PRACTICE: Psychoeducation, Parenting skills, Relaxation skills, Affective modulation skills, Cognitive coping skills, Trauma narrative and cognitive processing of the traumatic event(s), In vivo mastery of trauma reminders, Conjoint child-parent sessions, and Enhancing safety and future developmental trajectory (Cohen & Mannarino, 2008).

It is important to note that although the four models were tested to be effective for improving outcomes of juvenile offenders, they were tested in only a limited number of trials and therefore were still at an early stage of development (Ford et al., 2016). Future research should test these models with different populations to better assess their generalizability. Given the overrepresentation of minority youth and girls in crossover youth, future research needs to include a proportionate number of minority youth and girls in their samples to test the effectiveness of these models on reducing their recidivism rate and mental health symptoms. Moreover, three out of the four models do not include families in the intervention. Only TA-MTFC involves family through weekly MTFC+T parent group supervision, family therapy (for the family of origin), and on-call support availability to the MTFC+T and biological parents, given that family involvement was reported to help reduce future delinquency (Garfinkel, 2010), and future research should test the effectiveness of adding family involvement. The implementation of these evidence-based practice models will need buy-ins from stakeholders from multiple systems that serve crossover youth, including juvenile justice, juvenile court, school, mental health, child welfare, and so on (Ford et al., 2016).

Systems Approach: Integration of Public Systems with Crossover Youth

Crossover youth's background of involvement in multiple systems implies the importance of integrating services from multiple systems: legal, educational, court, mental health, and health (both public and private agencies). The essence of this systems approach is to share information and resources and to coordinate service provisions and evaluations. For example, using the Wave 3 (2002–2003) data on 178 youth from 51 agencies from the National Survey of Child and Adolescent Well-Being, a national survey of families engaged with the child welfare system, Chuang and Wells (2010) examined the effects of interagency collaboration on facilitating behavioral health service access for crossover youth. The authors reported that youth having a single agency accountable for care have higher odds of receiving outpatient and inpatient behavioral health services than youth concurrently involved in both systems. The authors suspected this related to the clear designation of responsibilities to a particular agency. In addition, the authors reported that the agencies that shared administrative data led to youth more likely receiving inpatient behavioral health service.

BOX 16.3. National Survey of Child and Adolescent Well-Being (NSCAW)

The National Survey of Child and Adolescent Well-Being (NSCAW) is a nationally representative, longitudinal survey of children and families who have been the subjects of investigation by Child Protective Services. There have been two cohorts of children enrolled in the survey. Most recent studies focus on data from the second cohort. The second cohort includes 5,872 children, aged birth to 17.5 years old, who had contact with the child welfare system within a 15-month period that began in February 2008. Baseline data was collected between March 2008 and September 2009. The second wave of data was collected 18 months after baseline, and the third wave was collected 36 months after baseline. The survey measures the well-being of children involved with child welfare agencies, including their health, mental health, and developmental risks; captures information about their families; provides information about child welfare interventions and other services; and describes key characteristics of child development (RTI International, 2014).

Models for Change Initiative

Serving crossover youth through system integration has received a lot of attention since 2004, when the National Center for Juvenile Justice (NCJJ) published a paper titled "When Systems Collide: Improving Court Practices and Programs in Dual Jurisdiction Cases."

The paper (Siegel & Lord, 2005) identified promising court-based or court-linked practices and programs that were effective for addressing challenges posed by dual jurisdiction cases. The authors suggested that the juvenile court should assume a leadership role in prompting intervention and practices to serve this population. The authors collected these promising practices and programs through a survey of 94 jurisdictions across the country, their own experiences from working with numerous juvenile and family courts, and a review of the literature. The authors grouped the promising practices and programs into five steps: screening and assessment, case assignment, case flow management, case planning and supervision, and interagency collaboration. Regarding interagency collaboration, the authors presented five strategies, including: broad statutory authority, court-facilitated interagency planning meetings, formal written agreements between agencies regarding each agency's roles, responsibilities, and expected measurable outcomes, collaborative funding arrangements, and integrated or shared information systems or databases. The authors presented the unique statutory structure in California related to dual jurisdiction. California's Welfare and Institutions Code Section 241.1 requires the court to determine the status of crossover youth (dependent or delinquent) based on which status will best serve the interests of the juvenile and best protect the community. Meanwhile, this law allows the court some flexibility for time needed to determine status and dispositions.

Also in 2004, the Models for Change Initiative was launched with the funding from the John D. and Catherine T. MacArthur Foundation. The multistate initiative promotes system reform to make juvenile justice more fair, effective, rational, and developmentally appropriate. The initiative engages a network of government and court officials, legal advocates, educators, community leaders, and families in the reform and provides stakeholders research-based tools and techniques to implement the reform. In 2012, the U.S. Department of Justice's Office of Juvenile Justice and Delinquency Prevention (OJJDP) and the MacArthur Foundation jointly provided $2 million to support the reforms (OJJDP, 2012). One of the reform areas was dual-status youth. As shown in Table 16.1, the initiative published several related tools.

TABLE 16.1. Tools Developed from the Models for Change Initiative

Tools	Summaries
Addressing the Needs for Multi-System Youth: Strengthening the Connection between Child Welfare and Juvenile Justice (Herz, Lee, Lutz, Stewart, Tuell, & Wiig, 2012)	This paper provided a summary of research on crossover youth. More importantly, it presented two initiatives to improve services for crossover youth: The first was the work of the Systems Integration Initiative launched at the Child Welfare League of America in 2000, and the second was the Crossover Youth Practice Model (CYPM) by the Center for Juvenile Justice Reform (CJJR) at Georgetown University in partnership with Casey Family Programs in 2009.

Continues on next page

Tools	Summaries
Guidebook for Juvenile Justice and Child Welfare System Integration and Coordination (Wiig, Tuell, & Heldman, 2013)	This guidebook provides practical guidance on how to integrate the juvenile justice and the child welfare systems. It presents guidelines for each phase of the strategic planning process and introduces promising, practical approaches that jurisdictions around the nation have used to overcome barriers and obstacles.
Dual Status Youth-Technical Assistance Workbook (Tuell, Heldman, & Wiig, 2013)	This Technical Assistance Workbook lays out the 12 to 15 months from pre-launch to implementation procedures, including a month-by-month set of activities. It presents tools, resources, and examples. It also recommends a specific schedule for the 1½-day on-site consultative activity and the tasks and activities covered during each of the on-site visits. The guidebook above (Wiig et al., 2013) and this Technical Assistance Workbook (Tuell et al., 2013) are suggested to be used together to develop policy and practice for dual-status youth.
From Conversation to Collaboration: How Child Welfare and Juvenile Justice Agencies Can Work Together to Improve Outcomes for Dual Status Youth (Robert F. Kennedy National Resource Center for Juvenile Justice, 2014)	This paper describes some of the challenges facing dual-status youth, outlines the benefits of collaboration between the juvenile justice and the child welfare systems, and provides guidance for practitioners to begin a conversation.

These tools facilitated the collaboration between systems in numerous jurisdictions (Robert F. Kennedy National Resource Center for Juvenile Justice, 2014). Moreover, OJJDP and the MacArthur Foundation have cosponsored demonstration sites of systems integration through the Robert F. Kennedy Children's Action Corps and the Center for Juvenile Justice Reform (CJJR) at Georgetown University. CJJR (2018a) provides a week-long intensive certificate program named Multi-System Integration Certificate Program for organization and system leaders working with crossover youth. Collectively, the Robert F. Kennedy Children's Action Corps and CJJR have reached over 100 jurisdictions to provide systems integration education and technical assistance (Fromknecht, 2014).

The Models for Change Initiative also aims to reduce disproportionate minority contact with the juvenile justice system. The initiative supported several jurisdictions in Pennsylvania to successfully reduce racial disparities through a series of reforms, including improved data gathering and analysis, increased cultural competence, implementation of objective screening instruments, development of alternatives to detention and out of home placement, improved probation practices, work with the faith-based community, and training and collaboration with law enforcement (Shoenberg, 2012).

BOX 16.4. Multi-System Integration Certificate Program

The Center for Juvenile Justice Reform (CJJR) at Georgetown University provides a week-long intensive certificate program named the Multi-System Integration Certificate Program for organization and system leaders working with crossover youth. Participants receive training on multisystem approaches, cost efficiency procedures, collaborative leadership techniques, and proactive communication strategies. The training modules include building a multisystem approach, leadership, behavioral health and trauma, education, disproportionality, family and youth engagement, measurement and data analysis, communication strategies, and financing. CJJR (2018b) provides this certificate program and the Crossover Youth Practice Model (CYPM) to prepare jurisdictions to improve their services for crossover youth.

In summary, NCJJ and the Models for Change Initiative provide tools for jurisdictions to implement the integration between the child welfare and juvenile justice systems. CJJR provides training on these tools to prepare jurisdictions to improve their services for crossover youth. In addition, the Models for Change Initiative supports jurisdictions to reduce racial disparities through data-driven reforms.

Progress Until 2016

Ten years after its publication, *When Systems Collide* (Siegel & Lord, 2005), the NCJJ started tracking state progress on systems coordination through their project Juvenile Justice GPS (Geography, Policy, Practice, Statistics) (JJGPS) (Fromknecht, 2014). The JJGPS website (http://www.jjgps.org/systems-integration) organizes the progress in four aspects: agency integration, coordination, reported data, and progressive data.

BOX 16.5. Statistics on System Integration

On the website of Juvenile Justice GPS (Geography, Policy, Practice, Statistics) (JJGPS) (http://www.jjgps.org/systems-integration), the 2016 statistics show that seven states have centralized administration of child welfare and juvenile corrections through a single state-level department; eight states have a general public welfare agency overseeing child welfare and juvenile corrections, often in separate divisions; 11 states have separate state-level organizations responsible for child welfare, juvenile corrections, and probation; 24 states and District of Columbia have decentralized child welfare and/or juvenile probation and are organized at the local level. Regarding coordination, the 2014 statistics showed that 27 states use the statewide information systems to allow for data sharing between systems; 22 states have formal committees or advisory groups that focus on dual-status youth and hold regular meetings to brainstorm ways to improve system integration; 19 states have formal interagency memorandums of understanding (MOUs); and 18 other states have informal interagency agreements to guide systems integration; 15 states have state and/or court rules that mandate systems integration efforts. As for reported data, there is still no national statistic available on dual-status youth. The authors of the website provided state-level statistics gathered from a mixture of state child welfare reports: Child and Family Services Plans (CFSP), Annual Progress and Services Reports (APSR), and Child Abuse Prevention and Treatment Act (CAPTA) Plans. States vary in the amount of detail and time periods available in their reports. For example, only six states (Delaware, Florida, Massachusetts, Oregon, Tennessee, and Washington) publish statewide prevalence statistics on a regular basis. For example, Washington updates sophisticated research databases that link administrative records for youth across juvenile and criminal justice systems, child welfare, risk/need assessment data, and education data. The linked databases are used to examine the trajectories of dual-status youth and promote ongoing research (National Center for Juvenile Justice, 2018).

In addition to the statistical report (Fromknecht, 2014), NCJJ (Thomas, 2015) published a paper on case studies of three jurisdictions' approaches on handling dual-status cases. Both San Diego County (San Diego, California) and Lehigh County (Allentown, Pennsylvania) show exemplary system integration practices at front-end screening and identification and probation-child welfare case coordination, respectively.

In summary, NCJJ (2018) reported that the progress on systems coordination varies between jurisdictions. Specifically, jurisdictions made different levels of progress in four aspects: agency integration, coordination, reported data, and progressive data. Another NCJJ report (Thomas, 2015) also presented exemplary system integration practices at the stages of front-end screening and identification and probation-child welfare case coordination.

BOX 16.6. Case Studies of Approaches on Handling Dual-Status Cases in San Diego County (San Diego, California) and Lehigh County (Allentown, Pennsylvania)

San Diego County shows exemplary practices in front-end screening and identification (Thomas, 2015). In San Diego County, juvenile justice intake probation officers have full access to the database of the child welfare system and therefore can read all details on a youth's child welfare system history and involvement and their caseworker's contact information. Depending on whether a crossover youth is detained or not, he/she can be timely identified of their involvement in the child welfare system by either the intake probation officer or the law enforcement officer. In the juvenile probation department, a specialized Dual Jurisdiction Unit of four probation officers was created in 2013 to serve only crossover youth, with each officer maintaining a caseload of 10 crossover youth. Other strategies used in San Diego include their efforts to divert crossover youth from formal involvement in the juvenile justice system, and the service plan formulated by the collaboration team comprised of representatives from probation, child welfare, education, mental health, guardians/parents, and the youth. Moreover, the readiness hearings and dual jurisdiction docket (or dual calendar) are held by the presiding judge.

Lehigh County shows exemplary practices in probation-child welfare case coordination (Thomas, 2015). In Lehigh County, the Juvenile Probation Department and the Office of Children and Youth Services (i.e., child welfare administration) established a joint probation officer/caseworker protocol to serve crossover youth. The protocol specifies a process for regularly identifying dually involved youth and strategies for collaboration between juvenile probation officers and caseworkers, including shared home or placement visits and shared court appearances. For example, the protocol indicates that juvenile probation officers, caseworkers, and their supervisors meet within 10 days of the date of notification of a shared case to review the case and determine whether it will be handled jointly or separately. Also, to determine if closing is appropriate, both juvenile probation officers and caseworkers are expected to communicate prior to closing a case.

At the beginning of the collaboration, the two sides of administrations convened a day-long workshop to strengthen the relationship. The workshop served multiple purposes: first, both agency directors presented rationales for a collaborative response to youth and families involved in both systems. Second, probation officers and caseworkers were asked to voice their ideas and concerns, which helped the agencies explore a broad range of potentially contentious issues and generate resolutions. Third, the workshop also provided an opportunity for cross-training each side on the other agency's missions, goals, and daily work. Since the workshop, the cross-training has been sustained. Part of the training for the new hires at both agencies includes shadowing their counterparts to get to know employees from the other agency and to learn about their roles and responsibilities. In Lehigh County, judges play a critical role in the cross-agency collaboration. Judges established a court order mandating two agencies to share pertinent case information. The court also adjusted scheduling practice to accommodate a youth's delinquency and dependency hearings occurring jointly. This visible partnership assured youth and their family that a team of professionals would work together to support the youth.

Crossover Youth Practice Model (CYPM): The New Post-Arrest Intervention

The Crossover Youth Practice Model (CYPM) is a post-arrest intervention model tailored to the needs of crossover youth. The CYPM is an innovative model for service integration. The model shows how child welfare and juvenile justice systems can collaborate with each other and partner with families, service providers, and other stakeholders to achieve positive outcomes for crossover youth and their families (Lutz, Stewart, Legters, & Herz, 2015). The key components are early identification of crossover youth and community conferencing that involves multiple stakeholders. The CYPM was developed by the Center for Juvenile Justice Reform at Georgetown University. Until June 2018, the CYPM has been implemented in 103 counties in 21 states (CJJR, 2018c).

As shown in Figure 16.4, the model includes three implementation phases consisting of five practice areas (Lutz et al., 2015).

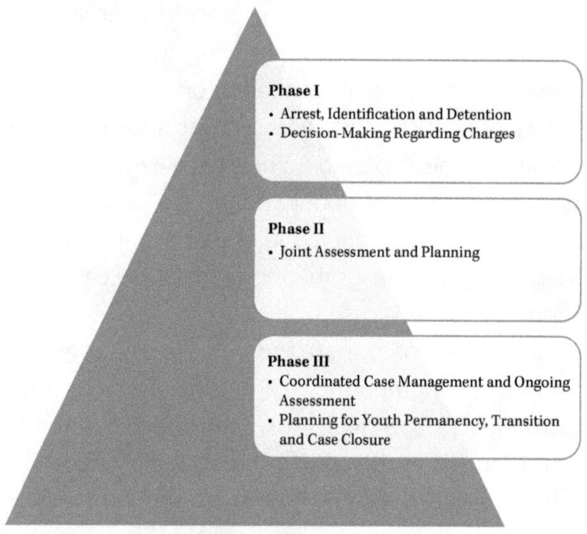

FIGURE 16.4. CYPM Phases

Studies on the CYPM (Haight, Bidwell, Choi, & Cho, 2016; Haight, Bidwell, Marshall, & Khatiwoda, 2014; Herz & Fontaine, 2012; Huang & Rhoden, 2017) reported positive impacts of the model on system change and crossover youth outcomes. Studying crossover youth in King County, Washington, Herz and Fontaine (2012) evaluated the impacts of the CYPM by comparing two randomly selected groups: the control group (N=20) entered the juvenile justice system prior to the implementation of the CYPM; the intervention group (N=20) entered the juvenile justice system after the implementation of the CYPM, and reported that the CYPM group had high rates of services use and school attendance and had much lower recidivism rates than the control group (39% versus 70%).

Haight and colleagues (2016) conducted a quantitative study using data from a Midwestern state. The authors compared the recidivism outcomes between crossover youth who received CYPM in the experimental county in 2011–2013 and three control groups of crossover youth who did not receive CYPM: 1) youth in the same county in 2008–2010; 2) youth from neighboring counties in 2008–2010; and 3) youth from neighboring counties in 2011–2013. Using propensity score matching, the authors matched the four groups (n=57 for each group) on demographics and delinquency history. The authors reported that youth receiving CYPM services were less likely to recidivate than matched youth receiving "services as usual," even when controlling for location (Haight et al., 2016).

Huang and Rhoden (2017) evaluated CYPM using a quasi-experimental design with group assignment at the county level. Miami-Dade County (MDC) was selected as the experimental county and Palm Beach County (PBC) as the control county. This study used a mixed-method approach, and both qualitative and quantitative data were collected in both counties. The qualitative data showed that in MDC, CYPM has been mainly implemented through the multidisciplinary team (MDT) meetings, in which crossover youth, their invited family members, and professionals from the child welfare, juvenile justice, and juvenile court systems participate. Although the PBC administration never adopted CYPM, in 2012 all parties involved in serving crossover youth worked together to develop their own procedure manual. Crossover hearings are similar to MDT meetings in MDC. For the quantitative part, the results show that crossover youth from MDC have a lower risk of reoffending within a year than their peers from PBC, after controlling the confounding variables of demographics and prior offenses. This difference was mediated by receiving dental and medical services referred by the child welfare agencies.

FIGURE 16.5. Multidisciplinary Team Meeting

In summary, studies of local jurisdictions from three states (Washington, Minnesota, and Florida) indicated that CYPM can help to reduce recidivism among crossover youth. These studies also suggested that the positive impacts of CYPM might be attributable to its emphasis on system collaboration, which facilitates timely access to services.

Policies Related to Crossover Youth

Policies on Identifying Crossover Youth

Image 16.3

Early identification of crossover youth can lead to better understanding of experiences and timely identification of case managers, which can allow treatment plans to involve the right stakeholders. To identify crossover youth, the most reliable approach is through administrative data sharing between the child welfare and juvenile justice systems. Such data sharing will allow intake workers on both sides to search new clients in the database of the other system and identify youth who cross over from the other system. As mentioned in the section on systems approaches, the jurisdictions that adopted CYPM or other collaborative programs usually include cross-system administrative data sharing agreements as part of their programs. Legislatively, the 2002 reauthorization of the Juvenile Justice and Delinquency Prevention Act (JJDPA, P.L. 107-273) requires states to promote the sharing of child welfare information with the juvenile court on delinquency matters (Wiig, Tuell, & Heldman, 2013). Specifically, JJDPA now contains requirements to states that promote the interaction and coordination of these systems, stipulating the following:

1. Juvenile courts have available to them the public child welfare records (including from child protective services) from that jurisdiction for juveniles before the court;
2. Policies and systems are established to incorporate relevant CPS records into juvenile justice records for purposes of establishing and implementing treatment plans;
3. Providing assurances that juvenile offenders whose placements are funded by Title IV-E Foster Care receive the specified protections, including a case plan and a case plan review.

Policies on Serving Crossover Youth During Their Involvement with Juvenile Justice

In terms of federal policy, since its 2003 amendment, the Child Abuse Prevention and Treatment Act (CAPTA, P.L. 111-320) supports states' efforts to collaborate on behalf of children who are involved in both systems (Wiig, Tuell, & Heldman, 2013). First, CAPTA allows state grants to fund the collaborative services. Specifically, Section 106(a) of CAPTA [42 U.S.C. 5106a(a)(12)] adds to the list of purposes for state grants: "Supporting and enhancing interagency collaboration between the child protection system and the juvenile justice system for improved delivery of services and treatment, including methods for continuity of treatment plan and services as children transition between systems." Second, CAPTA requires states to include in their annual state data reports the number of children under the care of the state child protection system who are transferred into the custody of the state juvenile justice system [42 U.S.C. 5106a(d)(14)].

States handle crossover youth in three different ways: concurrent jurisdiction, on-hold jurisdiction, and separate jurisdiction (Herz, Ryan, & Bilchik, 2010). Concurrent jurisdiction means allowing crossover youth to be under the jurisdiction of both the dependency[2] and the delinquency systems simultaneously, typically with one system taking lead responsibility for the child's care. The most significant advantage of concurrent jurisdiction is to allow crossover youth to retain their dependency system involvement after their involvement in juvenile justice.

In practice, on-hold jurisdiction is similar to concurrent jurisdiction, with only a slight difference (Herz et al., 2010). On-hold jurisdiction means allowing for dependency services to be interrupted until delinquency jurisdiction is terminated. When a youth is no longer in need of supervision by the delinquency court and the court finds family reunification detrimental to the youth, the county probation department either returns the case to the dependency system or conducts a joint assessment with the child welfare agencies to assess whether to reinstate the dependency status. If the results from the joint assessment suggest reinstatement, the dependency court has authority to reopen the case. On-hold jurisdiction will skip the step of filing a new dependency petition, which allows for a smoother transition back to dependency to continue receiving services (Herz et al., 2010).

Since both concurrent and on-hold jurisdictions have the advantage of retaining the youth's involvement with the dependency system after their involvement with the delinquency system, both models were widely received. Until 2006, 38 states and the District of Columbia (DC) used concurrent jurisdiction; two states used on-hold jurisdiction; and an additional nine states used a hybrid of the two approaches (Dunlap, 2006).

California was the last state using separate jurisdiction (Herz et al., 2010). Separate jurisdiction does not allow a youth to be under the jurisdiction of both the dependency and delinquency systems simultaneously. That is, once a youth in the dependency system

2 The dependency system refers to the division of juvenile court that intervenes on behalf of children exposed to maltreatment.

is under the delinquency jurisdiction, he/she is terminated from receiving services from the dependency system, such as their social worker and attorney in the dependency court. The consequence can be detrimental, since the youth can be disconnected from their advocates (e.g., social worker, attorney) and might no longer have a stable placement to return to upon discharge. Since 2005, some counties in California have transitioned into concurrent jurisdiction. In California, Assembly Bill 129 passed in 2005 (Stats. 2005, ch. 468); it provides local jurisdictions the flexibility to develop their own dual-jurisdiction protocols allowing youth to be designated as both a dependent and a ward of the juvenile court (Thomas, 2015). Until 2017, 18 out of California's 58 counties had elected to establish dual-status protocols, representing 67% of California's population. Santa Clara and Los Angeles Counties, two of the 18 counties, tracked the outcomes of their dual-jurisdiction reform and reported positive outcomes, such as lower numbers of arrests and a decrease in the severity of offenses (Judicial Council of California, 2017).

In summary, 18 counties of California and all other states use concurrent and on-hold jurisdictions to handle crossover youth, both retaining the youth's involvement with the dependency system after their involvement with the delinquency system, thereby avoiding the step of filing a new dependency petition after crossover youth are discharged from the delinquency system. The simplified transition facilitates crossover youth's access to their previous caseworkers and services that they used before their involvement in juvenile justice.

Policies on Serving Crossover Youth After Their Discharge from Juvenile Justice

In terms of federal policy, the Fostering Connections to Success and Increasing Adoptions Act of 2008 (Fostering Connections; thereafter Public Law 110-351) focuses on extending services for older youth in the foster care system, many of whom have episodes of being crossover youth. Fostering Connections has three main provisions:

1. Fostering Connections provides states the option of extending federal assistance to foster youth beyond age 18. The federal assistance refers to foster care, adoption, or guardianship assistance payments.
2. Fostering Connections extends eligibility for Chafee Foster Care Independent Living Program services to children who are adopted or enter into a guardianship at age 16 or older. For example, independent living services and the education and training voucher (ETV) tuition assistance are both considered Chafee Foster Care Independent Living Program services.
3. Fostering Connections requires that all youth be assisted to develop a personalized transition plan during the 90 days prior to aging out of foster care at the age of 18 or up to 21 as the state may elect. The transition plan includes plans on how to obtain housing, health insurance, education, employment, and mentoring after aging out.

Fostering Connections (Public Law 110-351) also specifies the eligibility of receiving these provisions. The foster youth have to meet at least one of the following eligibility criteria. In particular, the youth should be:

1. Completing high school or participating in an equivalent program;
2. Enrolled in postsecondary or vocational school;
3. Participating in a program or activity designed to promote or remove barriers to employment;
4. Employed for at least 80 hours per month; or
5. Incapable of doing any of these activities due to a medical condition.

The eligible criteria indicate that Fostering Connections incentivizes aging-out foster youth to remain engaged in education and employment. However, it can be challenging for crossover youth to meet the criteria, especially for those involved with the delinquency system who are close to the age of majority. These youth might experience disruptions in education and have delinquency records that can interfere with their employment, making them ineligible for the education and employment requirements. Moreover, they might lose connections with their caseworker and attorney at the dependency system. These youth therefore may be unable to get assistance on drafting a transition plan and may not be connected with extended services available to other aging-out foster youth (Wylie, 2014).

States vary in their policy on serving crossover youth after their discharge from the juvenile justice system. For example, in Massachusetts, the Department of Youth Services (DYS) offers voluntary community support services to every youth discharged from DYS custody (Thomas, 2015). The community support services include housing, continued education, treatment, and job training. An administrative meeting is routinely held to discuss services to include in the voluntary agreement. The DYS administration grants approvals to the agreement. The agreement is initially valid for 3 months but can be renewed every 3 months until age 21, as long as the youth complies with the conditions of the agreement (Thomas, 2015).

In summary, at the federal level, Fostering Connections (Public Law 110-351) extends services for older youth in the foster care system, many of whom have episodes of being crossover youth. However, its eligibility criteria on education and employment can be a barrier for many crossover youth to benefit from the extended services due to their experiences with disruptions in education. At the state level, states vary in their policy on serving crossover youth after their discharge from the juvenile justice system.

In conclusion, crossover youth are the youth who were victims of child abuse and neglect at home but were also involved in the juvenile justice system due to their own behavioral problems. Crossover youth are disproportionately youth of color and female as compared with the distribution of juvenile offenders in general. Related to their experiences with child abuse and neglect, many crossover youth have mental health and substance use problems, which, in turn, increase their risk of recidivism. In response to these challenges, practitioners should consider adopting evidence-based practices developed for traumatized youth in the juvenile justice system: TARGET, TGCTA, CPT, and TA-MTFC. At the program level, models such as CYPM offer jurisdictions strategies on the integration of public systems, especially the child welfare and juvenile justice systems. At the policy level, many crossover youth might not be eligible for extended services offered through Fostering Connections (Public Law 110-351) due to their difficulty with meeting the education and employment requirements. Some states developed policies to facilitate crossover youth's access to community services after their discharge from the juvenile justice system.

Case Application

The following case vignette is from observations and review of services data on youth crossover from the child welfare system to the juvenile justice system. This case vignette provides an example showing the relationship between crossover youth's adverse childhood experiences and their delinquent behaviors.

Case Vignette

John is a 17-year-old African American male who was just released from a juvenile detention center after a 6-month stay. He was charged with substance use and with a drug-dealing offense. Prior to the most recent arrest, he had been staying in a group home for nearly 4 months, which was his third placement.

He was placed into substitute care at age 15 after his mother was incarcerated due to cocaine addiction. He was the only child of his mother, who was a high school student when she became pregnant and dropped out of high school afterward. John never met his father, who left his mother after learning about her pregnancy. John has been living with only his mother ever since he can remember and feels that his mother is the only person who loves him. He still remembers his strong anger when he was first removed from his home. He was disappointed with his mother, who was a single mother and had become addicted to cocaine after dating a cocaine addict. However, when being removed from home, he felt panic for leaving a safe space, screamed at the social workers, and tried to hit them. He was first placed in kinship care in his grandmother's apartment. However, he had never been able to get along with his grandmother because he always felt that his grandmother did not like him, and she said that he was the cause of his mother's hard life. His mother quit school after she became pregnant with John. His grandmother said her daughter's life would have been much better if she had finished her education. After a major argument with John, his grandmother called his caseworker to find him a better home.

At age 15.5, his second placement was also a kinship placement, with his maternal aunt, who is married and has three young children between the ages of 2 and 7. Both his aunt and her husband have full-time jobs in the services sector and work long hours. They had limited time to supervise John, but they still agreed to take John in, as they wanted to support him. They did not anticipate John feeling unwelcome at his new school. Only two male students, who were in his class during his sophomore year, would talk to him. John started hanging out with them after school and became their friends. John remembers that when he was first offered marijuana by the two friends, he refused to take it, since he did not want to become a drug addict like his mother. However, he eventually took their offer since he wanted to fit in. Not long after, he found himself hooked on marijuana. After his aunt found marijuana in his drawer, she and her husband had a long conversation with John and asked him to promise to not use marijuana anymore. Otherwise, they said, they would call his caseworker. John broke his promise on the second day, and his aunt found him using marijuana. His aunt called his caseworker and said that she was not able to provide the supervision that John needed.

By then, John, at age 16, was placed into a group home, which housed seven other male youth. Five inhabitants were referred by the child welfare system, while the rest were referred by the juvenile justice system. He soon found that several of his housemates used marijuana. Some of them also used other drugs. They occasionally shared "experiences" on using and dealing drugs. They frequently engaged in arguments and fights for various reasons, such as the high volume of a person's speaker. John was arrested after a shift worker at his group home learned that John was dealing drugs at the street corner.

After the arrest, John was soon placed into the detention center, since the judge believed that the child welfare system had no other placement options for John. No foster homes wanted to work with a delinquent youth, and his parents were unavailable. The judge also thought that John needed intensive supervision. During his 6 months in the detention center, John talked to his caseworker only once, following his arrival. He saw his caseworker at most hearings but did not get to talk to her. When he was in the detention center, he often wondered where he would be placed next. He is not sure whether he can return to the group home. He knows that his grandmother and his aunt are not likely to take him in, especially due to his delinquency charges. He feels hopeless. He is afraid that he will be like his mother, spending years of her life being incarcerated.

DISCUSSION QUESTIONS

1. What were the risk factors for John to get involved in delinquent behaviors?
2. What theories help explain delinquency in this case? How can such theories help inform treatment options?
3. Which evidence-based practice can be implemented in the juvenile detention center to help John reduce his hopelessness and increase his confidence?
4. Which systems approaches can be implemented to coordinate the services for John?
5. Which policy contains provisions on providing aftercare services for crossover youth?

References

Abrams, L. S., & Moio, J. A. (2009). Critical race theory and the cultural competence dilemma in social work education. *Journal of Social Work Education, 45*(2), 245–261.

Ahrens, J., & Rexford, L. (2002). Cognitive processing therapy for incarcerated adolescents with PTSD. *Journal of Aggression, Maltreatment & Trauma, 6*(1), 201–216.

Baglivio, M. T., Epps, N., Swartz, K., Huq, M. S., Sheer, A., & Hardt, N. S. (2014). The prevalence of adverse childhood experiences (ACE) in the lives of juvenile offenders. *Journal of Juvenile Justice, 3*(2), 1.

Bender, K. (2010). Why do some maltreated youth become juvenile offenders?: A call for further investigation and adaptation of youth services. *Children and Youth Services Review, 32*(3), 466–473. doi: 10.1016/j.childyouth.2009.10.022

Center for Juvenile Justice Reform. (2018a). Multi-system integration. http://cjjr.georgetown.edu/multi-system-integration/

Center for Juvenile Justice Reform. (2018b). Connection to the crossover youth practice model. http://cjjr.georgetown.edu/multi-system-integration/connection-to-practice-model/

Center for Juvenile Justice Reform. (2018c). Crossover youth practice model. http://cjjr.georgetown.edu/our-work/crossover-youth-practice-model/

Centers for Disease Control and Prevention (2019a). *Preventing adverse childhood experiences: Leveraging the best available evidence.* Atlanta, GA: National Center for Injury Prevention and Control, Centers for Disease Control and Prevention.

Centers for Disease Control and Prevention. (2019b). *About Adverse Childhood Experiences.* https://www.cdc.gov/violenceprevention/childabuseandneglect/acestudy/aboutace.html

Centers for Disease Control and Prevention. (2019c). *ACEs Definitions. About the CDC-Kaiser ACE Study.* https://www.cdc.gov/violenceprevention/childabuseandneglect/acestudy/about.html

Chamberlain, P., & Reid, J. B. (1987). Parent observation and report of child symptoms. *Behavioral Assessment, 9,* 97–109.

Child Welfare Committee, National Child Traumatic Stress Network. (2013). *Child welfare trauma training toolkit: Comprehensive guide* (3rd ed.). Los Angeles, CA & Durham, NC: National Center for Child Traumatic Stress.

Chuang, E., & Wells, R. (2010). The role of interagency collaboration in facilitating receipt of behavioral health services for youth involved with child welfare and juvenile justice. *Children and Youth Services Review, 32*(12), 1814–1822.

Cohen, J. A., & Mannarino, A. P. (2008). Trauma-focused cognitive behavioural therapy for children and parents. *Child and Adolescent Mental Health, 13(4),* 158–162.

Colman, A. (2015). Milieu therapy. In *A Dictionary of Psychology*, Oxford University Press. Retrieved August 8, 2019, from https://www.oxfordreference.com/view/10.1093/acref/9780199657681.001.0001/acref-9780199657681-e-5085

Conger, D., & Ross, T. (2001). *Reducing the foster care bias in juvenile detention decisions: The impact of project confirm.* New York: Vera Institute of Justice.

Dierkhising, C. B., & Branson, C. E. (2016). Looking forward: A research and policy agenda for creating trauma-informed juvenile justice systems. *OJJDP Journal of Juvenile Justice, 5*(1), 14–24.

Dierkhising, C.B., Ko, S., & Halladay Goldman, J. (2013). *Trauma-Informed Juvenile Justice Roundtable: Current Issues and Directions in Creating Trauma- Informed Juvenile Justice Systems.* Los Angeles, CA & Durham, NC: National Center for Child Traumatic Stress.

Doyle Jr., J. J. (2007). Child protection and child outcomes: Measuring the effects of foster care. *American Economic Review, 97*(5), 1583–1610.

Dunlap, B. (2006). Dependents who become delinquents: Implementing dual jurisdiction in California under Assembly Bill 129. *Whittier Journal of Child and Family Advocacy, 5,* 507–546.

English, D. J., Widom, C. S., & Brandford, C. (2002). *Childhood victimization and delinquency, adult criminality, and violent criminal behavior: A replication and extension.* No. 192291.b National Criminal Justice Reference Services. https://www.ncjrs.gov/pdffiles1/nij/grants/192291.pdf

Fang, X., & Corso, P. S. (2007). Child maltreatment, youth violence, and intimate partner violence: Developmental relationships. *American Journal of Preventive Medicine, 33*(4), 281–290.

Ford, J. D., & Hawke, J. (2012). Trauma affect regulation psychoeducation group and milieu intervention outcomes in juvenile detention facilities. *Journal of Aggression, Maltreatment & Trauma, 21*(4), 365–384.

Ford, J. D., Kerig, P. K., Desai, N., & Feierman, J. (2016). Psychosocial interventions for traumatized youth in the juvenile justice system: Research, evidence base, and clinical/legal challenges. *Journal of Juvenile Justice, 5*(1), 31.

Ford, J. D., Steinberg, K. L., Hawke, J., Levine, J., & Zhang, W. (2012). Randomized trial comparison of emotion regulation and relational psychotherapies for PTSD with girls involved in delinquency. *Journal of Clinical Child & Adolescent Psychology, 41*(1), 27–37.

The Fostering Connections to Success and Increasing Adoptions Act, Pub. L. No. 110-351, 122 Stat. 3,958 (2008).

Fromknecht, A. (2014). Systems integration: Child welfare and juvenile justice. National Center for Juvenile Justice.

Garfinkel, L. (2010). Improving family involvement for juvenile offenders with emotional/behavioral disorders and related disabilities. *Behavioral Disorders, 36*(1), 52–60.

Grassetti, S. N., Herres, J., Williamson, A. A., Yarger, H. A., Layne, C. M., & Kobak, R. (2015). Narrative focus predicts symptom change trajectories in group treatment for traumatized and bereaved adolescents. *Journal of Clinical Child & Adolescent Psychology, 44*(6), 933–941.

Guerra, N. G., & Williams, K. R. (2006). Ethnicity, youth violence, and the ecology of development. In N. G. Guerra & E. P. Smith (Eds.), *Preventing Youth Violence in a Multicultural Society* (pp. 17–45). Washington, DC: American Psychological Association.

Haight, W., Bidwell, L., Choi, W. S., & Cho, M. (2016). An evaluation of the crossover youth practice model (CYPM): Recidivism outcomes for maltreated youth involved in the juvenile justice system. *Children and Youth Services Review, 65,* 78–85.

Haight, W., Bidwell, L. N., Marshall, J. M., & Khatiwoda, P. (2014). Implementing the crossover youth practice model in diverse contexts: Child welfare and juvenile justice professionals' experiences of multisystem collaborations. *Children and Youth Services Review, 39,* 91–100.

Halemba, G., & Lord, R. (2005). Effectively intervening with dual jurisdiction youth in Ohio. *Children, Families, and the Courts, Ohio Bulletin, 2,* 1–28.

Halemba, G., Siegel, G., Lord, R. D., & Zawacki, S. (2004). *Arizona dual jurisdiction study: Final report.* National Center for Juvenile Justice.

Healy, W. (1915). *The individual delinquent: A Text-Book of Diagnosis and Prognosis for all Concerned in Understanding Offenders.* New York: Little, Brown.

Herz, D. (2010). *Crossover Youth Practice Model Research Summary.* https://cjjr.georgetown.edu/wp-content/uploads/2015/07/CYPM-The-Research-Summary.pdf

Herz, D. C., & Fontaine, A. M. (2012). *Final data report for the crossover youth practice model in King County, Washington: 2010/2011 Cases:* Washington, DC: Center for Juvenile Justice Reform–Georgetown University. http://www.modelsforchange.net/publications/466/Final_Data_Report_for_the_Crossover_Youth_Practice_Model_in_King_County_Washington__20102011_Cases.pdf

Herz, D. C., Lee, P., Lutz, L., Stewart, M., Tuell, J., & Wiig, J. (2012). *Addressing the needs of multi-system youth: Strengthening the connection between child welfare and juvenile justice.* Washington, DC: Center for Juvenile Justice Reform, Georgetown University. https://cjjr.georgetown.edu/wp-content/uploads/2015/03/MultiSystemYouth_March2012.pdf

Herz, D. C., & Ryan, J. P. (2008). Building multisystem approaches in child welfare and juvenile justice. *Bridging Two Worlds: Youth Involved in the Child Welfare and Juvenile Justice Systems: A Policy Guide for Improving Outcomes,* 27–113.

Herz, D. C., Ryan, J. P., & Bilchik, S. (2010). Challenges facing crossover youth: An examination of juvenile-justice decision making and recidivism. *Family Court Review, 48*(2), 305–321.

Huang, H., & Rhoden, M. A. (2017). *The effectiveness of service integration: Studying the crossover youth practice model.* Tallahassee, FL: Florida Institute for Child Welfare. http://ficw.fsu.edu/sites/g/files/upcbnu1106/files/pdf-files/FR%20The%20Effectiveness%20of%20Service%20Integration-062717.pdf

Hussey, J. M., Chang, J. J., & Kotch, J. B. (2006). Child maltreatment in the United States: Prevalence, risk factors, and adolescent health consequences. *Pediatrics, 118*(3), 933–942.

Jonson-Reid, M. (2002). Exploring the relationship between child welfare intervention and juvenile corrections involvement. *American Journal of Orthopsychiatry, 72*(4), 559.

Jonson-Reid, M., & Barth, R. P. (2003). Probation foster care as an outcome for children exiting child welfare foster care. *Social Work, 48*(3), 348–361.

Jonson-Reid, M., & Barth, R. P. (2000a). From maltreatment report to juvenile incarceration: The role of child welfare services. *Child Abuse & Neglect, 24*(4), 505–520.

Jonson-Reid, M., & Barth, R. P. (2000b). From placement to prison: The path to adolescent incarceration from child welfare supervised foster or group care. *Children and Youth Services Review, 22*(7), 493–516.

Judicial Council of California (2017). *Dual-Status Youth Data Standards (AB 1911): 2017 Report to the Legislature.* http://www.courts.ca.gov/documents/lr-2017-JC-dual-status-youth-data-ab1911-standards-2017.pdf

Layne, C. M., Saltzman, W. R., Poppleton, L., Burlingame, G. M., Pasalic, A., Durakovic, E., ... Pynoos, R. S. (2008). Effectiveness of a school-based group psychotherapy program for war-exposed adolescents: A randomized controlled trial. *Journal of the American Academy of Child and Adolescent Psychiatry, 47*(9), 1048–1062. doi: 10.1097/CHI.0b013e31817eecae [doi]

Listenbee, Jr., R., Torre, J., Boyle, G., Cooper, S. W., Deer, S., Durfee, D. T., James, T., Lieberman, A., Macy, R., Marans, S., McDonnell, J., Mendoza, G., Taguba, A. (2012). *Report to the attorney general's national task force on children exposed to violence.* Washington, DC: Office of Juvenile Justice and Delinquency Prevention, Office of Justice Programs, U.S. Department of Justice.

Lundblad, K. S. (1995). Jane Addams and social reform: A role model for the 1990s. *Social Work,* 40 (5), 661–669.

Lutz, L., Stewart, M., Legters, L., & Herz, D. (2015). *Crossover youth practice model (CYPM): An abbreviated guide.* Washington, DC: Center for Juvenile Justice Reform, McCourt School of Public Policy, Georgetown University. https://cjjr.georgetown.edu/wp-content/uploads/2015/09/CYPM-Abbreviated-Guide.pdf

Marrow, M., Benamati, J., Decker, K., Griffin, D., & Lott, D. A. (2012). *Think trauma: A training for staff in juvenile justice residential settings.* Los Angeles, CA, and Durham, NC: National Center for Child Traumatic Stress.

Marrow, M. T., Knudsen, K. J., Olafson, E., & Bucher, S. E. (2012). The value of implementing TARGET within a trauma-informed juvenile justice setting. *Journal of Child & Adolescent Trauma, 5*(3), 257–270.

Maschi, T., Morgen, K., Bradley, C., & Hatcher, S. (2008). Exploring gender differences on internalizing and externalizing behavior among maltreated youth: Implications for social work action. *Child & Adolescent Social Work Journal, 25*(6), 531–547. doi: 10.1007/s10560-008-0139-8

Matulis, S., Resick, P. A., Rosner, R., & Steil, R. (2014). Developmentally adapted cognitive processing therapy for adolescents suffering from posttraumatic stress disorder after childhood sexual or physical abuse: A pilot study. *Clinical Child and Family Psychology Review, 17*(2), 173–190.

Morris, L., & Freundlich, M. (2004). *Youth Involvement in the Child Welfare and Juvenile Justice Systems: "A Case of Double Jeopardy"?* Washington, DC: CWLA Press.

National Center for Juvenile Justice. (2018). System Integration. *Juvenile Justice, Geography, Policy, Practice & Statistics.* http://www.jjgps.org/systems-integration

Office of Juvenile Justice and Delinquency Prevention. (2012). Department of Justice, MacArthur Foundation provide $2 million to support juvenile justice reform. https://www.ojjdp.gov/enews/12juvjust/120126.html

Olafson, E., Boat, B. W., Putnam, K. T., Thieken, L., Marrow, M. T., & Putnam, F. W. (2016). Implementing trauma and grief component therapy for adolescents and think trauma for traumatized youth in secure juvenile justice settings. *Journal of Interpersonal Violence*, 0886260516628287.

Ortega, R. M., & Coulborn, K. (2011). Training child welfare workers from an intersectional cultural humility perspective: A paradigm shift. *Child welfare, 90*(5).

Robert F. Kennedy National Resource Center for Juvenile Justice. (2014). *From conversation to collaboration: How Child Welfare and Juvenile Justice Agencies Can Work Together to Improve Outcomes for Dual Status Youth.* Boston, MA: Robert F. Kennedy Children's Action Corps.

RTI International. (2014). *The National Survey on Child and Adolescent Well-being II (NSCAW II) General Release, Waves 1–3* [Dataset]. National Data Archive on Child Abuse and Neglect. https://doi.org/10.34681/EBFD-GS84

Runyan, D. K., & Gould, C. L. (1985). Foster care for child maltreatment: Impact on delinquent behavior. *Pediatrics, 75*(3), 562–568.

Ryan, J., Chiu, Y. L., & Williams, A. (2011). Is there a link between child welfare and disproportionate minority contact in juvenile justice? *MacArthur's Foundation's Models for Change Research Initiative.* http://www.modelsforchange.net/publications/317

Ryan, J. P., Herz, D., Hernandez, P. M., & Marshall, J. M. (2007). Maltreatment and delinquency: Investigating child welfare bias in juvenile justice processing. *Children and Youth Services Review, 29*(8), 1035–1050. doi: 10.1016/j.childyouth.2007.04.002

Ryan, J. P., Hong, J. S., Herz, D., & Hernandez, P. M. (2010). Kinship foster care and the risk of juvenile delinquency. *Children and Youth Services Review, 32*(12), 1823–1830. doi: http://dx.doi.org/10.1016/j.childyouth.2010.08.003

Ryan, J. P., Marshall, J. M., Herz, D., & Hernandez, P. M. (2008). Juvenile delinquency in child welfare: Investigating group home effects. *Children and Youth Services Review, 30*(9), 1088–1099.

Ryan, J. P., & Testa, M. F. (2005). Child maltreatment and juvenile delinquency: Investigating the role of placement and placement instability. *Children and Youth Services Review, 27*(3), 227–249.

Ryan, J. P., Williams, A. B., & Courtney, M. E. (2013). Adolescent neglect, juvenile delinquency and the risk of recidivism. *Journal of Youth and Adolescence, 42*(3), 454–465.

Saltzman, W. R., Pynoos, R. S., Layne, C. M., Steinberg, A. M., & Aisenberg, E. (2001). Trauma-and grief-focused intervention for adolescents exposed to community violence: Results of a school-based screening and group treatment protocol. *Group Dynamics: Theory, Research, and Practice, 5*(4), 291.

Sampson, R. J., & Wilson, W. J. (1995). Toward a theory of race, crime, and urban inequality. *Race, Crime, and Justice: A Reader*, 177–190.

Scheuer, J. (1985). *Legacy of light: University Settlement's first century*. New York: University Settlement Society of New York. Retrieved February 29, 2020, from http://socialwelfare.library.vcu.edu/settlement-houses/origins-of-the-settlement-house-movement/

Shoenberg, D. (2012). Innovation Brief: Reducing Racial and Ethnic Disparities in Pennsylvania. *MacArthur Foundation's Models for Change Research Initiative*. http://www.modelsforchange.net/publications/351

Siegel, G., & Lord, R. (2005). When systems collide: Improving court practices and programs in dual jurisdiction cases. *Juvenile and Family Court Journal, 56* (2), 39–59.

Smith, C., & Thornberry, T. P. (1995). The relationship between childhood maltreatment and adolescent involvement in delinquency. *Criminology, 33*(4), 451–481.

Smith, D. K., Chamberlain, P., & Deblinger, E. (2012). Adapting multidimensional treatment foster care for the treatment of co-occurring trauma and delinquency in adolescent girls. *Journal of Child & Adolescent Trauma, 5*(3), 224–238.

Taylor, S., Fedoroff, I. C., Koch, W. J., Thordarson, D. S., Fecteau, G., & Nicki, R. M. (2001). Posttraumatic stress disorder arising after road traffic collisions: Patterns of response to cognitive–behavior therapy. *Journal of Consulting and Clinical Psychology, 69*(3), 541.

Thomas, D. (Ed.). (2015). *When Systems Collaborate: How Three Jurisdictions Improved Their Handling of Dual-Status Cases*. Pittsburgh: National Center for Juvenile Justice.

Tuell, J. A., Heldman, J. K., & Wiig, J. K. (2013). *Dual Status Youth Technical Assistance Workbook*. Boston: Robert F. Kennedy Children's Action Corps.

Widom, C. S. (1991). The role of placement experiences in mediating the criminal consequences of early childhood victimization. *American Journal of Orthopsychiatry, 61*(2), 195–209.

Widom, C. S. (1989). The cycle of violence. *Science, 244*(4901), 160–166.

Wiig, J. K., Tuell, J. A., & Heldman, J. K. (2013). *Guidebook for Juvenile Justice and Child Welfare System Coordination and Integration: A Framework for Improved Outcomes*, 3rd ed. Boston: Robert F. Kennedy Children's Action Corps.

Wylie, L. (2014). Closing the crossover gap: Amending Fostering Connections to provide independent living services for foster youth who crossover to the justice system. *Family Court Review, 52(2)*, 298–315.

Zingraff, M. T., Leiter, J., Myers, K. A., & Johnsen, M. C. (1993). Child maltreatment and youthful problem behavior. *Criminology, 31*(2), 173–202.

Figure Credits

Fig. 16.2: Source: https://philadelphiaencyclopedia.org/archive/settlement-houses/.
Fig. 16.3: Source: https://youtu.be/oODK0BfcUek.
Img. 16.1: Copyright © 2018 Depositphotos/ArturVerkhovetskiy.
Img. 16.2: Copyright © 2018 Depositphotos/photographee.eu.
Fig. 16.5: Source: https://youtu.be/oODK0BfcUek.
Img. 16.3: Copyright © 2018 Depositphotos/VitalkiRadio.

Appendix: Additional Resources

AdoptUSKids
https://adoptuskids.org/

Adverse Childhood Experiences (ACEs)
https://www.cdc.gov/violenceprevention/childabuseandneglect/acestudy/index.html

AFCARS Data
https://www.acf.hhs.gov/cb/research-data-technology/statistics-research/afcars

Arnold Ventures
https://www.arnoldventures.org/

California Evidence-Based Clearinghouse for Child Welfare
www.cebc4cw.org

Child Welfare Information Gateway
https://www.childwelfare.gov/

Children's Bureau
https://www.acf.hhs.gov/cb

ChildTrauma Academy (CTA)
https://childtrauma.org/

Con Mi Madre: Mothers and Daughters Raising Expectations
http://www.conmimadre.org/

Dual Status Youth Reform
https://rfknrcjj.org/our-work/dual-status-youth-reform/

Dual Status Youth/Multi-System Collaboration Publications
http://www.modelsforchange.net/publications/listing.html?tags=Dual+status+youth%2fmulti-system+collaboration

Evidence-Based Program Directories—Youth.gov
https://youth.gov/evidence-innovation/evidence-based-program-directories

Healthy Children—Coming Out: Information for Parents of LGBT Teens
https://www.healthychildren.org/English/ages-stages/teen/dating-sex/Pages/Four-Stages-of-Coming-Out.aspx

HRC All Children, All Families
https://www.hrc.org/resources/all-children-all-families-about-the-initiative

Institute of Education Science What Works Clearinghouse
https://ies.ed.gov/ncee/wwc/

Lambda Legal
https://www.lambdalegal.org/know-your-rights/article/youth-info-for-families

National Center for Child Traumatic Stress (NCCTS)
https://www.nctsn.org

National Child Traumatic Stress Network
https://www.nctsn.org/

National Registry of Evidence-Based Programs and Practices
https://www.federalregister.gov/documents/2015/07/07/2015-16573/national-registry-of-evidence-based-programs-and-practices

Office of Juvenile Justice and Delinquency Prevention—Model Programs Guide
www.ojjdp.gov/mpg/mpg

Parents and Friends of Lesbian and Gays
https://pflag.org/

Promising Practices Network on Children, Families, and Communities
www.promisingpractices.net

System Integration
http://www.jjgps.org/systems-integration

The Office of Justice Programs—CrimeSolutions.gov
https://www.crimesolutions.gov/about_OJP.aspx

Trauma-Focused Cognitive Behavior Therapy (TF-CBT)
https://tfcbt.org/
https://medicine.musc.edu/departments/psychiatry/divisions-and-programs/divisions/ncvc-/programs/project-best/tf-cbt

Glossary

Active efforts Efforts that are used when removing a child from the family. Caseworkers must actively explore resources within the child and family's tribe, and extended family. Caseworkers tailor interventions to be consistent with the cultural values of the child, family, and tribe (Edwards, 2015).

Adjudication A formal judgement or decision of the court. In child welfare, a key judicial decision is whether there is sufficient evidence as to whether or not child maltreatment occurred. This decision is often referred to as the "adjudication" and most often leads to a child being placed in the custody of the child welfare agency or foster care.

Adoption and Foster Care Analysis and Reporting System (AFCARS) The Adoption and Foster Care Analysis and Reporting System (AFCARS) collects case-level information from state and tribal Title IV-E agencies. This is information on all children in foster care and those who have been adopted with Title IV-E agency involvement. Title IV-E agencies are required to submit AFCARS data twice a year.

Adoption and Legal Guardianship Incentive Payment Program A federal program that provides incentives for states to increase adoptions and awards incentives for the first time for guardianship placements.

Adverse Childhood Experiences (ACEs) Childhood experiences that include all types of abuse, neglect, and other adversities that occur to people under the age of 18 years. They may or may not be traumatic, but they can have direct or compounding impact on a range of long-term outcomes.

Another Planned Permanent Living Agreement (APPLA) A permanency plan provided by the court for youth for whom reunification, adoption, guardianship, or other means of permanency are not viable. These youth are planned to age out of foster care.

Bisexual Refers to an attraction toward people of both genders. Someone who identifies as bisexual is attracted to and may form sexual and affectionate relationships with both men and women, though not necessarily at the same time. Bisexuality may also be used as a transitional term for those coming to understand their sexual orientation—a mediating position between homosexual and heterosexual. However, the idea that bisexuality is always a transitional identity is pejorative and should be avoided.

Case plan This is a federally required written document that is developed with parents or guardians of children in care. It describes the child's current placement, services to be offered to the child and family, as well as the permanency plan. It includes actions and tasks to be completed by all parties to accomplish the case plan goal.

Child abuse Child abuse is typically a family-related event, occurring when a parent or caregiver physically injures, emotionally abuses, or sexually abuses his or her child. Child abuse can also include exposing a child to domestic and other types of violence.

Child maltreatment Child maltreatment is commonly used as a generic term for child abuse and neglect.

Child welfare Services designed to promote the well-being of children by ensuring safety, achieving permanency, and strengthening families to care for their children successfully.

Child Welfare Demonstration Waivers Grants funded by the Children's Bureau that permit states to test innovative approaches to child welfare service delivery and financing (CWIG, 2018a).

Cisgender Refers to a gender identity that society considers to "match" the biological sex assigned at birth. The prefix *cis* means "on this side of" or "not across from." It is a term used to call attention to the privilege of people who are not transgender.

Clearinghouse An online repository of interventions that have been systematically evaluated according to detailed criteria. Interventions are rated in terms of the research supporting the effectiveness of the intervention. Clearinghouses are particularly useful in selecting interventions for specific outcomes and in identifying the current research base for specific interventions.

Complex trauma A term used to define the often multitude of traumas a child may experience when involved within the child welfare system. This phrase captures the harm repeated and prolonged trauma can have on a child's healthy development, specifically related to interference with the ability to form a secure attachment with a caregiver and develop a sense of safety.

Concurrent planning An approach to permanency that seeks to eliminate delays in attaining permanent families for children and youth in foster care required by the Adoption and Safe Families Act of 1997. These are efforts toward a permanent placement through adoption or guardianship and are to be made in conjunction (*concurrently*) with reasonable efforts to preserve and reunify the family.

Court-appointed special advocate (CASA) A trained volunteer from the community, appointed by the court, who advocates for the best interest of a child in a case involving child abuse or neglect.

Critical race theory Critical race theory is a theoretical framework that asserts that racism is based on a social construct of race and that racism is a common experience for people of color. The theory seeks to challenge the status quo, critiques liberalism, and the legal structure as to how to define and conceptualize race and racism.

Cross-cultural practice Occurs when practitioners and clients differ with respect to cultural values, lifestyle, and background. Cross-cultural practice considers and is responsive to these differences within the professional relationship.

Crossover youth Crossover youth, also referred to as dually involved youth, refers to youth who experienced maltreatment and also engaged in delinquency but did not necessarily receive services from the child welfare and the juvenile justice systems (Huang & Ryan, in progress).

Cultural and linguistic responsiveness A complex and evolving collection of engagement practices that acknowledge and address the diverse cultures of families, including linguistic differences, served by child welfare.

Cultural humility An approach to engagement that connects oneself to others through the practice of self-awareness, openness, and transcendence.

Culture "Includes, but is not limited to, history, traditions, values, family systems, and artistic expressions of client groups served in the different cultures related to race and ethnicity, immigration and refugee status, tribal status, religion and spirituality, sexual orientation, gender identity and expression, social class, and abilities" (NASW, 2015, p. 12).

Data-driven decision-making A process for deciding on a course of action (decision-making) based on data.

Deferred Action for Childhood Arrivals (DACA) An immigration policy established by President Barack Obama which offered temporary protection against deportation and work authorization to many undocumented college students.

Developmental perspective A perspective based on principles of brain development and recognizing what children need in order to develop to their genetic potential. It explains how developmental adversity can alter the normal developmental trajectory. This perspective recognizes that the child's chronological age is an insufficient marker of the child's developmental functioning, especially if the child's developmental pathway has been subject to chronic or chaotic adversity (Gaskill & Perry, 2014).

Differential response An alternative response to child abuse and neglect that is a strengths-based and family-centered approach with families where the risks of safety for the child(ren) are minimal.

Disparity Refers to a state of being unequal and is typically used to describe unequal outcomes experienced by one racial or ethnic group when compared to another racial or ethnic group. May also be used to describe unequal outcomes experienced by any group in comparison to the outcomes experienced by the dominant group.

Displacement (also known as post-adoption placement) A type of post-permanency discontinuity that occurs when a child is temporarily placed in foster care to get services and later returns to her or his adoptive parent or legal guardian once treatment is complete.

Disproportionality Refers to the state of being out of proportion and describes a condition that exists when the proportion of people of a certain race or ethnicity (or other group) in a target population differs from the proportion of people of the same group in a reference population. It is when higher or lower proportions of children of certain racial or ethnic groups exist in a system (e.g., child welfare) than the proportion of children of that racial or ethnic group in the general population.

Dissolution A type of post-permanency discontinuity that occurs when a child reenters foster care and the adoptive parental rights or the legal guardianship is terminated.

Dually involved youth Youth who receive services from both the child welfare and the juvenile justice systems.

Dually adjudicated youth Youth who are concurrently adjudicated by both the child welfare and the juvenile justice systems.

Emancipation The legal term used when a youth ages out of foster care by reaching the legal age of majority in their state. An emancipated youth is now considered an adult and no longer needs a legal guardian.

Empirically supported interventions (ESIs) Interventions that have been rigorously evaluated in research studies and have been shown to effectively impact desired outcomes.

Evidence-based practices Practices or interventions that are supported by empirical research. They include evaluating the best intervention for a client system, given prior research and the client's own preferences.

Evidence-based process A five-step process that guides social workers through deciding which intervention to use with a client and evaluating the impact that the intervention had on the client.

Extended care services Programs and services that are available to youth after they age out of foster care. They are designed to aid and assist youth with navigating early adulthood. These services are not governed by the child welfare system and occur on a strictly volunteer basis.

Extended foster care Programs and services that meet the needs of youth who are older than 18 years of age and have voluntarily signed themselves back into the jurisdiction of the child welfare system.

External validity The extent to which results of a study can be generalized beyond the sample used in the study. In child welfare, the population that an intervention is tested with is a key concern of external validity.

Externalizing behavioral problems A group of negative, uncontrolled behavior problems exhibited in a child's outside (external) versus internal world (Liu, 2004).

Family Group Decision Making (FGDM) A decision-making process to which members of the family group are invited and joined by members of their informal network, community groups. The child welfare agency that has become involved in the family's life is also involved for the purposes of service planning, transition planning, and permanency planning.

Family-inclusive practice The practice for child welfare workers to fully engage families in their many diverse forms and work with all family members who have parenting responsibilities for children in each family.

Federally Recognized Tribe A federally recognized American Indian or Alaska Native tribal entity that is recognized as having a government-to-government relationship with the United States and, therefore, as possessing certain inherent rights of self-government. Federally recognized tribes are entitled to receive certain federal benefits, services, and protections because of their special relationship with the United States. https://www.bia.gov/frequently-asked-questions

Fictive kin Refers to persons who are not a relative of the child or family, but rather a close family friend considered part of their kinship circle. Often serve as caregivers for a child in foster care.

Foster care drift A term used to describe the phenomenon when children remain in foster care for long periods of time with no clear plan of reunification or other plans for permanency.

Foster parent adoptions Adoptions in which the child is initially placed in a nonrelative foster home through a foster parent agreement, contract, or license. The foster parent(s) may or may not have intended to adopt at the time of the initial placement. The official decision to adopt the child is made at some point after the child was placed in the home when the child's permanency plan changes from reunification to adoption.

Gay The preferred term that refers to a person sexually attracted to the same sex. This term is the preferred term, as opposed to *homosexual*.

Gender identity expression The manner in which a person identifies and/or expresses their gender, including self-image, appearance, and embodiment of gender roles. One's *sex* (e.g., male, female, intersex) is usually assigned at birth based on one's physical biology. One's *gender* (e.g., male, female, genderqueer) is one's internal sense of self and identity. One's *gender expression* (e.g., masculine, feminine, androgynous) is how one embodies gender attributes, presentations, roles, and more.

Guardian ad litem (GAL) A person appointed by the court to investigate which solutions would be in the best interest of a child/youth, who is usually in the public child welfare system.

Homebuilders model A practice model for families with a child up to 18 years old "at imminent risk of placement into, or needing intensive services to return from, foster care, group or residential treatment, psychiatric hospitals, or juvenile justice facilities" (California Evidence-Based Clearinghouse for Child Welfare website).

Hotline A reporting system, often a toll-free phone number, to which any person can make a confidential report of suspected or known child maltreatment to the child welfare agency.

ICWA-Compliant Kinship/Foster Home An ICWA compliant kinship or foster home is one that follows and conforms with the ICWA placement preferences of: (1) a member of the child's extended family; (2) a foster home licensed, approved, or specified by the Indian child's tribe; (3) an Indian foster home licensed or approved by an authorized non-Indian agency; and (4) an institution for children approved by an Indian tribe or operated by an Indian organization that has a program suitable to meet the child's needs. An Indian foster home is one in which at least one of the foster parents is a member of a federally recognized tribe.

Implementation science An area of study focused on strategies to increase the use and accuracy of evidence-based interventions in a specific setting.

Independent Living A set of programs and services that prepare foster youth for successful adulthood. These programs and services are provided to youth prior to their aging out of care and seek to increase life skills.

Independent Living Plan This is a case plan for youth that outlines the goals and objectives that are necessary for that youth to enter into adulthood as self-sufficiently as possible.

Indian child There are legal, familial and community, and cultural definitions of who is considered an Indian child. The ICWA uses a specific legal definition of an Indian child for purposes of determining those children covered under the Act: "any unmarried person who is under age eighteen and is either (1) a member of an Indian tribe or (2) is eligible for membership in an Indian tribe and is the biological child of a member of an Indian tribe" (25 U.S.C. § 1903). Native children who are not enrolled or eligible for enrollment, and thus are not covered by the ICWA, may still be identified by their family and community, or identify themselves, as culturally Indian.

Legal permanence Legal options that describe the long-term permanent placement of children who exit the child welfare system, including reunification, adoption, and guardianship.

Lesbian A term that primarily refers to a woman who is sexually attracted to another woman. The word *lesbian* is also used for women in relation to their sexual identity or sexual behavior regardless of sexual orientation, or as an adjective to characterize or associate nouns with same-sex attraction.

Minority Professional Leadership Development (MPLD) The Minority Professional Leadership Development program is designed for emerging leaders working in child welfare. The structured program includes hands-on experience, exposure to national experts, and mentorship opportunities.

Mixed-status family A family where some family members have legal status and documentation (e.g., U.S. birth certificate, work permit) and other family members do not have similar documentation.

Multidimensional engagement Refers to the caseworker's efforts designed to build a collaborative relationship with families in child welfare. The characteristics are family inclusive, culturally and linguistically responsive, considers the continuum of child welfare services, is developmentally appropriate, and is multidisciplinary in nature.

Multigenerational parenting Parenting in which two or more adult generations are sharing the responsibility for the care of one or more children.

Neglect A form of child maltreatment when the child does not receive care for his or her developmental and other needs. Neglect is considered omission and abuse is considered commission, and they often co-occur.

Nonbinary Nonbinary, also known as genderqueer, is a spectrum of gender identities that are not exclusively masculine or feminine—identities that are outside the gender binary.

Nonbinary people may identify as having two or more genders (being bigender, trigender, or pangender); having no gender (being agender, nongendered, genderless, genderfree or neutrois); moving between genders or having a fluctuating gender identity (genderfluid); or being third gender or other-gendered, a category that includes those who do not place a name to their gender.

Nonrelative adoptions Adoption by those who do not fit any of other categories. In the majority of these cases, the first time the child and family meet is when the child is placed in the home for adoptive purposes (Electronic Code of Federal Regulations [e-CFR], 2020).

Other relative adoptions Adoptions in which the child is adopted by someone related to them through their birth parents by blood or marriage (kinship).

Peer-reviewed journal A journal that only publishes articles that have been reviewed, critiqued, and deemed acceptable by a group of expert researchers. Articles must meet certain standards to be published in peer-reviewed journals and thus are considered more rigorous and of higher quality than publications that have not been peer-reviewed.

Permanence A noun that describes the legal state of adoption or guardianship, and permanency is an adjective used to describe whether something is characterized by permanence (e.g., a permanency goal).

Permanency The stabilizing of children's living situations and preserving family relationships and lifelong connections.

Permanency planning The systematic process of carrying out, within a brief time-limited period, a set of goal-directed activities designed to help children live in families that offer continuity of relationships with nurturing parents or caretakers and the opportunity to establish lifetime relationships (Pike et al., 1997). A model of practice in which child welfare workers assess the long-term placement plan for a child in foster care on an ongoing basis, based on a child's best interests. Practice includes planning for alternative long-term permanent plans, such as adoption or guardianship, in cases where reunification is not feasible.

Permanency services A variety of services aimed at facilitating the child(ren)'s exit from care, supporting the transition out of care to reunification, adoption, or independent living.

Post-permanency discontinuity (PPD) A broad term used to describe a condition where a child or youth who has left foster care through an adoption or placement with a legal guardian, but who no longer lives with that adoptive parent or legal guardian. PPD can take several forms; the most common types of PPD are dissolution and displacement (also known as post-adoption placement).

Post-traumatic Stress Disorder (PTSD) PTSD is one of five distinct disorders in the new DSM-5 category "Trauma- and Stressor-related Disorders." Historically, this is the primary DSM label applied for individuals suffering from significant emotional and behavioral problems that appear to be related to a documented traumatic event.

Preservice training Training to prepare prospective foster and adoptive parents prior to placement of a child in their care, including development of knowledge, attitudes, and skills necessary to cope with the demands of their new role.

Prevention services Programs delivered to families and communities who are not currently served by the child welfare system that are designed to prevent child maltreatment.

Privatization The transfer of responsibility from public child welfare organizations to private agencies for designated services or functions. There are different privatization models, such as performance-based contracting, outsourcing, and public-private partnerships.

Psychotropic/psychopharmacological medication Prescription medication that targets mental health disorders.

RCNO An initialism for race, color, or national origin referred to in the Multiethnic Placement Act as amended by the Interethnic Provisions (MEPA-IEP).

Reasonable efforts Refers to activities of state social services agencies that aim to provide the assistance and services needed to preserve and reunify families.

Relational permanence Defined as a "mutually committed, life-long, family connection to an adult–parental figure" (Cushing et al., 2014, p. 74). This idea keeps the focus of a permanent relationship on the youth's perspective. It is the youth, rather than legal documents, who defines which relationships are important, whom they feel connected to, and who provides them with support (Pérez, 2017; Samuels, 2008; Sanchez, 2004).

Safety The paramount concern for the child protective services that guides the interventions and services designed to prevent, protect, and respond to the maltreatment of children.

Screening The process through which reports or referrals of possible child maltreatment are reviewed and determined to be accepted for investigation or assessment.

Sexual orientation Commonly accepted term for the direction of a person's sexual attraction, emotional or physical attraction, and its expression. Examples of sexual orientation are heterosexuality, homosexuality, and bisexuality. In a sense, sexual orientation is a social construct, and a relatively new one, most likely determined by a combination of continually interacting sociocultural influences and biological tendencies.

Stepparent adoption Adoption by the spouse of the child's birth mother or birth father (Electronic Code of Federal Regulations [e-CFR], 2020).

Termination of parental rights (TPR) The process by which a court legally terminates the rights of parents and ends the legal relationship between a child and one or both of the child's parents.

Title IV-E foster care A federal program that provides maintenance payments to financially support the daily care and supervision of eligible children in foster care. It also includes administrative costs, staff and foster parent training, adoptive parent recruitment, and state information systems.

Transgender Transgender people have a gender identity or gender expression that differs from their assigned sex. *Transgender* is often shortened as *trans*; it is also an umbrella term: in addition to including people whose gender identity is the opposite of their assigned sex (trans men and trans women), it may include people who do not identify as exclusively masculine or feminine (people who are nonbinary or genderqueer, including bigender, pangender, genderfluid, or agender). Other definitions of *transgender* also include people who belong to a third gender, or else conceptualize transgender people *as* a third gender.

Being transgender is independent of sexual orientation: transgender people may identify as heterosexual, gay or lesbian, bisexual, asexual, or may decline to label their sexual orientation.

The opposite of *transgender* is *cisgender*, which describes persons whose gender identity or expression matches their assigned sex.

Transition plan This is a plan that outlines steps necessary to ensure that the transition to adulthood will be as seamless as possible and that the youth have had time to prepare for their exit from the system.

Trauma "Individual trauma results from an event, series of events, or set of circumstances that is experienced by an individual as physically or emotionally harmful or life threatening and that has lasting adverse effects on the individual's functioning and mental, physical, social, emotional or spiritual well-being" (SAMHSA, 2014, p. 6).

Trauma-informed "A program, organization, or system that is trauma-informed realizes the widespread impact of trauma and understands potential paths for recovery; recognizes the signs and symptoms of trauma in clients, families, staff, and others involved with the system; and responds by fully integrating knowledge about trauma into policies, procedures, and practices, and seeks to actively resist re-traumatization" (SAMHSA, 2014, p. 8).

Trauma-informed approach A type of service delivery that includes provider training; routine screenings for exposure to trauma; collecting a comprehensive history of trauma;

and reliance upon evidence-based practices, consistency across the treatment team, and evaluation.

Tribal Child Welfare Agency Tribal agencies that function as the foundation of the tribal child protection system that collaborate with tribal law enforcement and tribal courts on child welfare matters. Tribal child welfare agencies provide a range of services intended to protect children who have been abused or neglected, or are at risk of abuse and neglect, and to strengthen and improve the well-being of families. Tribal child welfare agencies are much smaller in size than state agencies, and it is not unusual to find programs with two to five workers who are tasked with performing the full range of child welfare processes.

Tribal Court The Indian Child Welfare Act defines a tribal court as a court with jurisdiction over child custody proceedings and which is either a Court of Indian Offenses, a court established and operated under the code or custom of an Indian tribe, or any other administrative body of a tribe which is vested with authority over child custody proceedings.

Tribal membership Tribal membership or enrollment have criteria that are set forth in tribal constitutions, articles of incorporation, or ordinances. The criterion varies from tribe to tribe, so there are no uniform membership requirements. Two common requirements for membership are lineal descent from someone named on the tribe's base roll (the original list of members as designated in a tribal constitution or other document specifying enrollment criteria) or blood quantum (a specified degree of tribal bloodline; e.g., one-half or one-eighth). https://www.doi.gov/tribes/enrollment

Tribal sovereignty Tribal sovereignty refers to the inherent right of tribes to govern themselves and to exercise authority over matters within the borders of the tribal nation. This authority is not delegated to tribes by the United States government, but instead, tribes possess it as a consequence of their historic status as independent nations. Examples of common ways in which tribes exercise sovereignty is in forming tribal governments, determining membership criteria, maintaining law and order, and creating programs to increase the well-being of members.

Unregulated custody transfer (also known as rehoming) This occurs when the physical custody of a child is transferred by a parent to a person who is not the child's parent, stepparent, grandparent, or other adult relative; an adult friend of the family with whom the child is familiar; or a member of the child's tribe with the intent of permanently avoiding responsibility for the child's care and without taking reasonable steps to ensure the safety of the child or the permanency of the placement (CWIG, 2017). In these situations, the child welfare authorities are not consulted about, or informed of, the change in living arrangement.

Visitation Visits with family members designed for children placed in out of home care to facilitate continuity of relationships, positive parenting, and/or reunification efforts.

Well-being This condition enhances the families' capacity to meet their children's physical, mental health, and educational needs.

Index

U

V

W

Y

About the Editors

MICHELE D. HANNA, MSW, Ph.D. is an associate professor at the University of Denver Graduate School of Social Work. Dr. Hanna serves as the coordinator of the child welfare concentration at GSSW and has taught both child welfare practice and policy courses. She serves as the faculty liaison for the Child Welfare Title IV-E Stipend Program with the Butler Institute for Families. Dr. Hanna teaches master's level classes that focus on diversity, equity, and inclusion including Power, Privilege, and Oppression; Disproportionality and Disparities across Systems; Critical Race Theory Praxis; and Social Work, as well as the doctoral qualitative research sequence. Prior to pursuing her Ph.D. at the University of Texas at Austin, her professional experience included working as an adoption birthparent counselor, child protective service worker, child welfare adoption specialist, child welfare supervisor, and program field representative for a statewide adoption program. Dr. Hanna has served as a national consultant with the U.S. Children's Bureau, a research team member with the AdoptUSKids project at UT-Austin, and the evaluator for Denver's Village, a diligent recruitment grant; both of the latter projects were funded by the U.S. Children's Bureau.

ROWENA FONG, MSW, Ed.D. is the Ruby Lee Piester Centennial Professor in Services to Children and Families in the Steve Hicks School of Social Work at the University of Texas at Austin. She has conducted research in the child welfare areas of transracial and international adoptions, racial disproportionality, and victims of human trafficking. In collaboration with other universities and a private child welfare agency, she has completed a multi-site, federally funded grant whose purpose was to focus on adoption and guardianship to promote permanency stability by implementing evidence-based interventions in public child welfare systems. She has authored 11 books in areas related to neglect, transracial and intercountry adoptions, racial disproportionality, immigrant and refugee child and families, culturally competent practice, and Grand Challenges for Social Work. She is a former president of the Society for Social Work and Research and a member of the American Academy of Social Work and Social Welfare.

NANCY ROLOCK, AM, Ph.D. is the Henry L. Zucker Associate Professor of Social Work Practice and Associate Dean of Research and Training at the Jack, Joseph and Morton Mandel School of Applied Social Sciences, Case Western Reserve University. She has conducted child welfare research since 1996. Her research illuminates racial and ethnic disparities in the child welfare system and examines barriers to stability for children with child welfare experiences. Dr. Rolock is committed to using intervention research and implementation science to build evidence-informed services and supports for children and families involved in the child welfare system. Dr. Rolock has directed national research studies examining the long-term outcomes for children who have exited foster care through adoption or guardianship. Understanding the risk and protective factors associated with the long-term stability of children, and their families, is of utmost importance to the understanding of child and family well-being. Dr. Rolock seeks to illuminate these issues through her research.

RUTH MCROY, MSW, Ph.D. is a research professor and the Ruby Lee Piester Centennial Professor Emerita at the University of Texas at Austin. From 2009-2018, she held the Donahue and DiFelice Endowed Professorship at Boston College School of Social Work. Dr. McRoy has been involved in child welfare practice, teaching, and research for many years. At both the University of Texas at Austin and at the Boston College School of Social Work, she developed and taught a variety of policy and practice courses, including Contemporary Issues in Adoption and Foster Care. Throughout her career, she has conducted research and evaluation projects and published numerous articles on such topics as openness in adoptions; transracial adoptions; kinship care; recruiting and retaining adoptive families; African American adoptions in rural communities; special needs adoptions; and adoptive family dynamics. From 2002-2007, she and her research/evaluation team at the University of Texas at Austin were collaborating partners on the AdoptUSKids project, which is funded by the U.S. Children's Bureau. The team completed two nationwide studies (2002-2007) on barriers to adoption and factors associated with successful special needs adoptions. Since 2007, she has served as an AdoptUSKids collaborative partner and has continued to contribute to the literature on adoption issues and outcomes.

About the Contributors

DR. ADELINE WYMAN BATTALEN, PhD, LICSW is a therapist in the Counseling and Mental Health Services department at Harvard University and lecturer at the Boston College School of Social Work. Dr. Wyman Battalen holds a PhD from the Boston College School of Social Work, an MS in Social Work from Columbia University, and a BA in Human Development and Social Relations from Earlham College. Her practice, teaching, and research interests focus on developing and adapting clinical interventions designed to improve the mental health and well-being of children and families, especially among diverse populations, including sexual and gender minority (SGM)-identified parents and youth and families within the adoptive kinship network.

DR. JENNIFER BELLAMY is the Associate Dean for Research and Faculty Development and professor at the Graduate School of Social Work (GSSW) at the University of Denver. At GSSW she teaches research and theory courses at the master's and doctoral levels. She received her master of science degree in social work from the University of Texas at Austin in 2000. Before earning her PhD, she worked as a crisis counselor and a project coordinator for a multisite demonstration project serving young, unmarried, low-income fathers. She completed her PhD at the Columbia University School of Social Work in 2006 and postdoctoral training at the George Warren Brown School of Social Work at Washington University in Saint Louis in 2008. Her current research focuses on the engagement of fathers in child and family services, child welfare, and evidence-based practice. She is currently engaged in the development and testing of strategies and interventions to better serve fathers in child welfare, home visiting, and father support programs.

DR. JOAN M. BLAKEY is the Associate Dean of Academic Affairs at Tulane School of Social Work. She attended the University of Minnesota–Twin Cities, where she received both her bachelor of science degree in African American Studies, Sociology, and Youth Studies and master of social work degree. As an IV-E scholar, Joan Blakey worked as a child protection worker with Hennepin County and policy specialist with the State of Minnesota. She received her doctorate from the University of Chicago. While completing her doctorate, she received several prestigious dissertation fellowships. The most notable was the Minority Fellowship Program supported through the Substance Abuse and Mental Health Services Administration. Dr. Joan M. Blakey's primary research interests focus on trauma and substance abuse among women who are involved with the child protection and criminal justice systems. Her ultimate goal is to understand the healing and recovery process for women with histories of complex trauma and assist with the development of trauma-informed organizations and systems of care.

DR. ALAN J. DETTLAFF is Dean of the Graduate College of Social Work at the University of Houston and the inaugural Maconda Brown O'Connor Endowed Dean's Chair. Prior to joining the University of Houston, Dean Dettlaff served on the faculty of the Jane Addams College of Social Work at the University of Illinois at Chicago. He received his bachelor's degree in social work from TCU and a master's in social work and PhD from the University of Texas at Arlington. Dean Dettlaff's research focuses on improving outcomes for children and youth in the child welfare system by examining and addressing issues of structural and institutional racism that contribute to the disproportionate overrepresentation of children of color in this system.

DR. RONI DIAMANT-WILSON is committed to improving the lives of vulnerable populations by integrating practice and research to help meet the needs of marginalized children, families, and communities. She received her PhD from the University of Illinois at Chicago's Jane Addams College of Social Work and MSW from the University of California–Berkeley. Dr. Diamant-Wilson worked for many years as a nurse practitioner with adolescents and transitional age youth and found that a number of the youth she provided care to were also in foster care. Because of her interactions with these young people, Dr. Diamant-Wilson returned to school to study social work. Through qualitative and quantitate methods, she seeks to advance the field of social work and create a more just world.

DR. MEGAN FEELY is an Assistant Professor at the University of Connecticut School of Social Work and a Cohort Three Doris Duke Fellow for the Promotion of Child Well-Being. She holds a master's degree and PhD in Social Work from Washington University in St. Louis and a master of science in Clinical Investigation from the Washington University School of Medicine. Dr. Feely's work focuses on the prevention of child maltreatment, implementation science, and the role of the child welfare system in promoting child well-being. Her work is informed by her experience working in the nonprofit sector with children in foster care.

DR. HUI HUANG, PhD, MSW, MS, MA, is an assistant professor in the School of Social Work at Florida International University. Her social work training and areas of expertise are in child welfare, with most of her achievements related to evaluating macro-level interventions for children and families dually involved in child welfare and other public sectors. Her three primary areas of interest include adolescents involved with the child welfare and juvenile justice systems (i.e., crossover youth), former foster youth trying to navigate postsecondary education, and substance-using parents in the child welfare system.

ANNETTE JACKSON has been a social worker working with children and families at risk for over 35 years. Over the past decade, Annette has worked with Berry Street, one of the largest child and family welfare not-for-profit organizations in Australia. Berry Street provides foster care, residential care, case management, family support, community-based programs, family violence programs, and therapeutic services. Annette is a fellow of the US ChildTrauma Academy and a mentor in the Neurosequential Model. Annette is a PhD candidate with La Trobe University on helping children recover from the impacts of neglect.

ALAN KUNZ LOMELIN is a licensed social worker with master's degrees in Social Work and Criminology from the University of Texas at Arlington as well as an undergraduate degree in psychology from the University of Dallas. Alan has worked in a variety of research projects including, but not limited to, kinship care, child welfare, mental health disparities, and criminal rehabilitation. Alan is currently working as a behavioral health provider at a community clinic for Baylor Scott and White Health, working toward attaining his license as a clinical social worker. Alan is also a published author with a publication in the *Journal of Offender Rehabilitation.* Alan will begin pursuing his PhD in social work from the University of Texas at Arlington beginning fall 2020.

DR. CATHERINE LABRENZ is an assistant professor at the University of Texas at Arlington School of Social Work. As a child welfare researcher, she has explored family-centered interventions to reduce occurrences and recurrences of child maltreatment. Prior to academia, Dr. LaBrenz worked as a practitioner with families involved in child welfare in Latin America. Her work has focused on child welfare across the globe, and she has conducted research in Latin America, Europe, and the United States to identify best practices with families at-risk for child maltreatment.

DR. NANCY M. LUCERO, PhD, LCSW, is a Research Associate Professor at the University of Denver, Graduate School of Social Work, and an American Indian scholar and social work professional. Dr. Lucero is currently the Principal Investigator for the Child Welfare Capacity Building Center for Tribes, a U.S. Children's Bureau project that provides capacity building technical assistance to child welfare programs operated by American Indian and Alaska Native Nations. Dr. Lucero has experience designing and implementing practice models for tribal and urban Indian Child Welfare services, and recently completed an in-depth evaluation of the Denver (Colorado) Indian Family Resource Center's trauma-informed and culturally responsive Urban Indian Child Welfare service delivery model. Her past social work practice includes training of non-Indian professionals on culturally responsive social work practice with American Indians and providing mental health services to American Indians.

DR. GERALD P. MALLON, DSW, is the Julia Lathrop Professor of Child Welfare and the Associate Dean of Scholarship and Research at the Silberman School of Social Work at Hunter College in New York City. For more than 44 years, Dr. Mallon has been a child welfare practitioner, advocate, educator, and researcher. Dr. Mallon was the first child welfare professional in the United States to research, write about, and develop programs for LGBTQ+ youth in child welfare settings. He has also written extensively about LGBTQ+ foster and adoptive parenting. Dr. Mallon is the Senior Editor of the professional journal *Child Welfare* and the author or editor of more than 26 books. His most recent publications are *Social Work Practice with Lesbian, Gay, Bisexual, and Transgender People* (3rd edition), published by Routledge Press and *Child Welfare for the Twenty-First Century: A Handbook of Practices, Policies, and Programs* (2nd edition), co-edited with Peg Hess, published by Columbia University Press.

DR. NATHANAEL J. OKPYCH is an Assistant Professor at the University of Connecticut's School of Social Work. He studies the transition to adulthood for youth in foster care, and his research focuses on postsecondary education access and attainment, mental health, and social support. He earned a PhD from the School of Social Service Administration at the University of Chicago and holds master's degrees in Biostatistics and Epidemiology (Chicago), Social Work (Rutgers), and Clinical Psychology (Duquesne). Nathanael's professional experience includes providing mental health services to youth in residential, school, and community settings, as well as working for several years in college residence life.

DR. ALFRED G. PÉREZ, PhD, is an Assistant Professor of Social Work at Seattle University. His fields of interest include child welfare practice and policy, the adult functioning of former foster youth, formal and informal helping systems among vulnerable populations, and positive youth development. His current research examines how young adults with foster care histories experience policy decisions and the extent to which these policies attain their objectives while yielding unintended consequences. His professional experiences before academia span state government, direct child welfare practice, social welfare policy, and the federal government. Most notably, Dr. Pérez's tenure with former Arizona governor Janet Napolitano's administration included reform of the child protection services program, and former president Bill Clinton invited Dr. Pérez to deliver remarks at the White House bill signing ceremony of the Foster Care Independence Act.

DR. BRUCE D. PERRY, MD, PhD, is the Principal of the Neurosequential Network and Professor (Adjunct) in the Departments of Psychiatry and Behavioral Sciences at the Feinberg School of Medicine at Northwestern University in Chicago and the School of Allied Health, College of Science, Health and Engineering, La Trobe University, Melbourne, Victoria Australia. Dr. Perry is the author, with Maia Szalavitz, of *The Boy Who*

Was Raised As A Dog, a bestselling book based on his work with maltreated children and *Born For Love: Why Empathy is Essential and Endangered.* Over the last 30 years, Dr. Perry has been an active teacher, clinician, and researcher in children's mental health and the neurosciences, holding a variety of academic positions. Dr. Perry is the author of over 500 journal articles, book chapters, and scientific proceedings and is the recipient of numerous professional awards and honors

GEORGINA PETRONELLA is a licensed social worker (LMSW) with experience working with children, adolescents, adults, and families. She received a master's of Social Work degree from the University of Texas in Austin and a bachelor's degree in English Literature from Georgetown University in Washington, DC. She currently works as a school-based therapist with Vida Clinic in Austin, Texas. In this position, she counsels children, adolescents, and adults and implements trauma-informed and evidence-based approaches to help clients reach their goals. Before graduation, she completed her clinical internships at the Center for Child Protection and the Council on At-Risk Youth. Her professional interest areas include trauma-informed care, child welfare, and grief and loss.

DR. JON PHILLIPS, PhD, currently holds the position of Assistant Professor at the University of Connecticut School of Social Work. He has extensive practice and research experience related to the child welfare system. He has conducted quantitative, qualitative, and mixed-methods research projects focused on improving the well-being of, and service delivery to, child welfare–involved children and families. Dr. Phillips has also collaborated with scholars from the National Child Welfare Workforce Institute to identify strategies for addressing burnout among child welfare workers. His primary research interest is increasing the frequency and quality of interprofessional collaboration in the child welfare system as a means of improving child and family well-being.

DR. MEGAN HAYES PIEL, PhD, MSW, is an Assistant Professor in the Department of Social Work at the University of Texas at San Antonio. Her research focuses on improving outcomes for foster youth transitioning to adulthood, promoting foster family resilience and retention, and improving relationships and cross-system collaboration in child welfare. Her previous social work experience includes direct practice and administrative roles in foster care and behavioral health group homes and schools.

DR. JOE RYAN'S research and teaching build upon his direct practice experiences with child welfare and juvenile justice populations. Dr. Ryan is a Professor and Director of the Child and Adolescent Data Lab at the University of Michigan. He is primarily focused on linking data across systems to understand how state agencies can best collaborate to improve outcomes for children and families.

DR. MARIA SCANNAPIECO, PhD, MSW, Distinguished University Professor at the School of Social Work, University of Texas at Arlington, has conducted extensive research in the area of child welfare. Dr. Scannapieco has over 150 publications and presentations in the areas of the impact of child maltreatment, kinship care, out of home placement, youth aging out of foster care, and the mental health needs of youth in child welfare. Dr. Scannapieco has three books published with Oxford University Press: *Kinship Foster Care: Practice, Policy, & Research* (1999), *Understanding Child Maltreatment: An Ecological and Developmental Perspective* (2005), and *Understanding Mental Health Problems of Children and Adolescents: A Guide for Social Workers*, New York, Oxford University Press (2015; 2020).

DR. CHRISTINA M. SELLERS is an Assistant Professor at Simmons University in the School of Social Work. Dr. Sellers earned her MSW and PhD at the Boston College School of Social Work. She is a licensed clinical social worker with practice experience, including delivering brief motivational enhancement interventions for suicidal adolescents with co-occurring substance use. Dr. Sellers has expertise in clinical interventions with at-risk youth and training in intervention research and implementation science. Her research is at the intersection of substance use, suicide, and the child welfare system. The goal of her program of research is to develop and test interventions for substance use and suicide among adolescents in a variety of different settings.

DR. AAKANKSHA SINHA is an Assistant Professor in the Department of Social Work at Seattle University. She received her MSW and PhD from Boston College. Prior to moving to the United States, she worked as a child rights consultant for the International Labor Organization in Delhi, India. Dr. Sinha's areas of interest include global food justice, child welfare, program evaluation, and social innovation. Dr. Sinha identifies as a community-based researcher that utilized mixed-methods research to explore and understand how social identity and deep-rooted cultural norms impact community well-being in the United States and internationally. Dr. Sinha currently works with several nonprofits in the Seattle area to assist in the analysis and implementation of programs that impact children and youth of color with regard to academic success, food access, and emotional and mental well-being.

RACHEL SPEER is a licensed clinical social worker (LCSW) and is currently completing her PhD from the University of Denver Graduate School of Social Work. Her research focuses on parent-child relationships, parenting, structural inequities, discrimination, health, gender identity, sexual identity, and intersectionality.

DR. KRISTA THOMAS is a Policy Fellow at Chapin Hall. Dr. Thomas leads blended teams of policy, practice, and research experts in efforts to build the capacity of state and local human service systems across the country to execute large-scale reform initiatives and improve outcomes for vulnerable children and families. Leveraging opportunities like the Family First Prevention Services Act, Dr. Thomas partners with human service leaders to identify a set of priority outcomes, articulate a set of strategies to improve performance, execute their implementation, and monitor their effectiveness. Her areas of expertise include federal child welfare policy, programs, and monitoring; large-scale child welfare performance improvement at the state and local levels; strategic planning; evidence use in decision-making; implementation; continuous quality improvement; and differential response in child welfare.

DR. MEGAN FINNO-VELASQUEZ, PhD, MSW, is an Assistant Professor and Director of the Center on Immigration and Child Welfare in the School of Social Work at New Mexico State University in Albuquerque, New Mexico. Dr. Finno-Velasquez has spent the past 14 years working at the intersection of child welfare and immigration issues, as a child welfare practitioner, administrator, and researcher. Her research centers around the impact of immigration policy on child welfare system experiences, culturally competent maltreatment prevention strategies, and improving child welfare service system response to the needs of immigrant families. In 2019, Dr. Finno-Velasquez was appointed Director of Immigration Affairs for the New Mexico Children, Youth and Families Department in a position split with her professorship at NMSU, where she is working to build an immigration unit to improve policies and practices to support immigrant and refugee children along the Mexico border and throughout the state. Dr. Finno-Velasquez received her PhD from the University of Southern California's School of Social Work in 2015 and completed postdoctoral work with the Children's Data Network. She was a recipient of the Doris Duke Fellowships for the Promotion of Child Well-Being during her doctoral work. She completed her MSW from New Mexico Highlands University in 2007 and has a BS in Psychology and Spanish from the University of Illinois–Urbana-Champaign.

DR. KEVIN WHITE is an Assistant Professor in the School of Social Work at East Carolina University. He has over 9 years of research experience focused on understanding and improving permanency and well-being for at-risk youth and their families. His research interests developed out of 13 years of practice as a child welfare caseworker and a school social worker.

DR. JESSICA YANG is an Assistant Professor in the Social Work Department at Winthrop University. Dr. Yang is a passionate social worker, teacher, and researcher who has devoted her career to improving outcomes for marginalized youth, with a specific passion for those served by the foster care system. Currently, she is working on projects examining disproportionate discipline practices affecting students of color and the impact of foster care on individuals throughout their life span. Additionally, Dr. Yang engages in research regarding systemic racism and oppression in larger systems such as schools or child welfare and the impacts of these experiences on individuals of color. Prior to entering into academia, Dr. Yang worked in public child welfare, where she investigated allegations of child maltreatment, provided in-home services to families in need, and facilitated foster care and adoptive placements when necessary.

CPSIA information can be obtained
at www.ICGtesting.com
Printed in the USA
LVHW061136180723
752713LV00008B/16